HISTORY, POLITICS, LAW

Historians of political thought and international lawyers have both expanded their interest in the formation of the present global order. *History, Politics, Law* is the first express encounter between the two disciplines, juxtaposing their perspectives on questions of method and substance. The essays throw light on their approaches to the role of politics and the political in the history of the world beyond the single polity. They discuss the contrast between practice and theory as well as the role of conceptual and contextual analyses in both fields. Specific themes raised for both disciplines include statehood, empires and the role of international institutions, as well as the roles of economics, innovation and gender. The result is a vibrant cross-section of contrasts and parallels between the methods and practices of the two disciplines, demonstrating the many ways in which both can learn from each other.

Annabel Brett is a leading historian of late medieval and early modern political thought, with a particular interest in natural law and the law of nations. She is the author of *Liberty, Right and Nature: Individual Rights in Later Scholastic Thought* (1997) and *Changes of State: Nature and the Limits of the City in Early Modern Natural Law* (2011).

Megan Donaldson has published on nineteenth and twentieth-century shifts in treaty-making, statehood and international organisations. Her forthcoming monograph traces the evolution of secrecy in the international legal order.

Martti Koskenniemi is a leading critical scholar of the theory and history of international law. His works are studied by lawyers, historians and international relations scholars across the world. He has held visiting professorships at many of world's leading universities, is Corresponding Fellow of the British Academy, and a Member of the American Academy of Arts and Sciences.

History, Politics, Law

THINKING THROUGH THE INTERNATIONAL

Edited by
ANNABEL BRETT
University of Cambridge

MEGAN DONALDSON
University College London

MARTTI KOSKENNIEMI
University of Helsinki

CAMBRIDGE
UNIVERSITY PRESS

Shaftesbury Road, Cambridge CB2 8EA, United Kingdom

One Liberty Plaza, 20th Floor, New York, NY 10006, USA

477 Williamstown Road, Port Melbourne, VIC 3207, Australia

314–321, 3rd Floor, Plot 3, Splendor Forum, Jasola District Centre, New Delhi – 110025, India

103 Penang Road, #05–06/07, Visioncrest Commercial, Singapore 238467

Cambridge University Press is part of Cambridge University Press & Assessment, a department of the University of Cambridge.

We share the University's mission to contribute to society through the pursuit of education, learning and research at the highest international levels of excellence.

www.cambridge.org
Information on this title: www.cambridge.org/9781108829069

DOI: 10.1017/9781108903516

© Cambridge University Press & Assessment 2021

This publication is in copyright. Subject to statutory exception and to the provisions of relevant collective licensing agreements, no reproduction of any part may take place without the written permission of Cambridge University Press & Assessment.

First published 2021
First paperback edition 2023

A catalogue record for this publication is available from the British Library

Library of Congress Cataloging-in-Publication data
NAMES: Brett, Annabel S., editor, author. | Donaldson, Megan, 1981– editor, author. | Koskenniemi, Martti, editor, author.
TITLE: History, politics, law : thinking through the international / edited by Annabel Brett, University of Cambridge; Megan Donaldson, University College London; Martti Koskenniemi, University of Helsinki.
DESCRIPTION: Cambridge, United Kingdom ; New York, NY : Cambridge University Press, 2021. | Includes index.
IDENTIFIERS: LCCN 2020054748 (print) | LCCN 2020054749 (ebook) | ISBN 9781108842464 (hardback) | ISBN 9781108829069 (paperback) | ISBN 9781108903516 (epub)
SUBJECTS: LCSH: International law–Philosophy. | International law–History.
classification: LCC KZ3410 .H57 2021 (print) | LCC KZ3410 (ebook) | DDC 341.01–dc23
LC record available at https://lccn.loc.gov/2020054748
LC ebook record available at https://lccn.loc.gov/2020054749s

ISBN 978-1-108-84246-4   Hardback
ISBN 978-1-108-82906-9   Paperback

Cambridge University Press & Assessment has no responsibility for the persistence or accuracy of URLs for external or third-party internet websites referred to in this publication and does not guarantee that any content on such websites is, or will remain, accurate or appropriate.

Contents

Acknowledgments	*page* vii	
Notes on Contributors	ix	

Introduction: History, Politics, Law: Thinking through the International   1
Annabel Brett, Megan Donaldson and Martti Koskenniemi

PART I: METHODS, APPROACHES AND ENCOUNTERS   17

1   Between History, Politics and Law: History of Political Thought and History of International Law   19
Annabel Brett

2   The Past according to International Law: A Practice of History and Histories of a Practice   49
Martti Koskenniemi

3   The Context for Context: International Legal History in Struggle   69
David Kennedy

4   After Method: International Law and the Problems of History   96
Gerry Simpson

PART II: THINKING THROUGH THE INTERNATIONAL   127

LAW AND CONSTRUCTIONS OF THE POLITICAL   129

5   Carl Schmitt's International Thought and the State   131
Armin von Bogdandy and Adeel Hussain

6	Carl Schmitt on the Theory and Practice of Occupation and Dictatorship	160
	Joshua Smeltzer and Duncan Kelly	

EMPIRES, STATES AND NATIONS — 189

7	Law of Nations, World of Empires: The Politics of Law's Conceptual Frames	191
	Jennifer Pitts	
8	The History of Political Thought in the African Political Present	208
	Emma Hunter	

INSTITUTIONS AND PERSONS — 229

9	The [In]hospitable World	231
	Julia McClure	
10	Ventriloquism in Geneva: The League of Nations as International Organisation	253
	Megan Donaldson	

ECONOMICS AND INNOVATION — 283

11	Sea Change	285
	Surabhi Ranganathan	
12	The Political Economy of Context: Theories of Economic Development and the Study of Conceptual Change	309
	Joel Isaac	

GENDER — 339

13	Gender in the State of Nature	341
	Anna Becker	
14	Gender and the Lost Private Side of International Law	357
	Karen Knop	

Index — 381

Acknowledgments

This volume had its beginnings in a conference of the same title at Clare College, Cambridge on 16–17 May 2016, made possible by the generous support of the Cambridge Centre for Political Thought; the Erik Castrén Institute of International Law and Human Rights, University of Helsinki; the Trevelyan Fund of the Faculty of History, University of Cambridge; and the Lauterpacht Centre for International Law. Christina Rozeik, Anna Stürgkh, Eloise Davies, Alicia Mavor, and Daniel Allemann all gave valuable assistance with preparation of the event and orchestration of proceedings. The idea for the volume was prompted by the liveliness and diversity of exchanges at the conference, and we wish to thank those speakers who originally contributed to making the event a success and whose presence is still felt within these pages: Lauren Benton, Nathaniel Berman, Shruti Kapila, Duncan Kennedy, Anne Orford, David Runciman and Gareth Stedman-Jones.

We are immensely grateful to the present chapter authors for their commitment and engagement in making this a collection that perpetuates the vitality of that exchange in a new frame. Lawyers and historians have so much to talk to each other about, but they do not always think the same way, and our contributors have shown themselves open to a sometimes complicated dialogue in a way that we have found enormously inspiring. We would also like to thank Cambridge University Press for its part in bringing the collection into being, especially Finola O'Sullivan for her consistent intellectual encouragement and Marianne Nield for her meticulous attention to practical matters. We are grateful to the anonymous reviewers whose comments helped improve our sense of the volume and its final shape. Finally, we would like to thank our copy-editor, Heather Palomino, and our indexer, Shelley Lockwood, for their precise and painstaking work on the letter of the text.

Notes on Contributors

Anna Becker is Professor in History of Ideas, Aarhus University. She is the author of *Gendering the Renaissance Commonwealth* (2020). Her current project aims to turn upside down the focus of history of political thought by examining the rich thinking on the material foundations of a healthy body politic in the early modern world.

Armin von Bogdandy is director of the Max Planck Institute for Comparative Public Law and International Law in Heidelberg, and Professor of Public Law at Johann Wolfgang Goethe University, Frankfurt am Main. He has published widely on public international law, comparative public law, legal theory, and European law.

Annabel Brett is Professor of Political Thought and History, University of Cambridge. Her works include *Liberty, Right and Nature: Individual Rights in Later Scholastic Thought* (1997), a translation of Marsilius of Padua's *Defender of the Peace* (2005), and *Changes of State: Nature and the Limits of the City in Early Modern Natural Law* (2011).

Megan Donaldson is Lecturer in Public International Law, University College London. Her publications include 'The Survival of the Secret Treaty: Publicity, Secrecy and Legality in the International Order', *American Journal of International Law* 111 (2017); and 'The League of Nations, Ethiopia and the Making of States', *Humanity* 11 (2020).

Emma Hunter is Professor of Global and African History, University of Edinburgh. Her works include *Political Thought and the Public Sphere in Tanzania: Freedom, Democracy and Citizenship in the Era of Decolonization* (2015) and the edited collection *Citizenship, Belonging and Political Community in Africa: Dialogues between Past and Present* (2016).

Adeel Hussain is Assistant Professor of Legal and Political Theory, Leiden University, and a Senior Research Affiliate at the Max Planck Institute for

Comparative Public Law and International Law in Heidelberg. His research focuses on the political legitimacy of European legal orders, the history of international law, and Muslim political thought in India.

Joel Isaac is Associate Professor of Social Thought, University of Chicago. He is the author of *Working Knowledge: Making the Human Sciences from Parsons to Kuhn* (2012). His current work concerns how modern economics has shaped – whether by attraction or repulsion – the development of social theory and political thought.

Duncan Kelly is Professor of Political Thought and Intellectual History, University of Cambridge. He is the author of *The Propriety of Liberty: Persons, Passions and Judgement in Modern Political Thought* (2011) and *Politics and the Anthropocene* (2019). His current work is focused on the intellectual history of the First World War.

David Kennedy is Manley O. Hudson Professor of Law, Harvard Law School, and Faculty Director of the Institute for Global Law and Policy. His works include *The Dark Sides of Virtue* (2004), *Of Law and War* (2006), *The Rights of Spring. A Memoir of Innocence Abroad* (2009), and *A World of Struggle: How Power, Law and Expertise Shape Global Political Economy* (2016).

Karen Knop is Professor of Law, University of Toronto. Her works include *Diversity and Self-Determination in International Law* (2002) and the edited collection *Gender and Human Rights* (2004). She has published widely on questions of diversity, interpretation and participation as perspectives from which to re-theorise core concepts of international law, and the relationship between international and domestic law.

Martti Koskenniemi is Professor of International Law, University of Helsinki. He is the author of *From Apology to Utopia: The Structure of International Legal Argument* (1989), *The Gentle Civilizer of Nations: The Rise and Fall of International Law 1870–1960* (2002), and *'To the Uttermost Parts of the Earth': Legal Imagination and International Power 1300–1870* (2020).

Julia McClure is Lecturer in Late Medieval and Early Modern Global History, University of Glasgow. She is the author of *The Franciscan Invention of the New World* (2017). Her current book project, provisionally entitled *Empire of Poverty: The Moral Economy of the Spanish Empire*, explores how concepts and institutions of poverty were central to the legitimation, governance and business of empire.

Jennifer Pitts is Professor of Political Science, University of Chicago. Her works include *A Turn to Empire: The Rise of Imperial Liberalism in Britain and France* (2005) and *Boundaries of the International: Law and Empire* (2018). She is also co-editor of *The Law of Nations in Global History* (2017), and editor and translator of *Alexis de Tocqueville: Writings on Empire and Slavery* (2001).

Surabhi Ranganathan is University Senior Lecturer in International Law, University of Cambridge. Her publications include *Strategically Created Treaty Conflicts and the Politics of International Law* (2014); 'Ocean Floor Grab: International Law and the Making of an Extractive Imaginary', *European Journal of International Law* 30 (2019); and 'Decolonization and International Law: Putting the Ocean on the Map', *Journal of the History of International Law* (2020).

Gerry Simpson is Professor of Public International Law, London School of Economics and Political Science. His works include *Great Powers and Outlaw States* (2004), *Law, War and Crime: War Crimes Trials and the Reinvention of International Law* (2007), and the edited collection (with Kevin Jon Heller), *The Hidden Histories of War Crimes Trials* (2014).

Joshua Smeltzer recently completed his doctorate in the history of political thought at the University of Cambridge. His publications include 'Hans Wehberg and the *jus belli ac pacis* in interwar international law', *Global Intellectual History* (2018); and 'Technology, Law, and Annihilation: Carl Schmitt's Critique of Utopianism', *Journal of the History of Ideas* 81 (2020).

Introduction

History, Politics, Law
Thinking through the International

ANNABEL BRETT, MEGAN DONALDSON AND MARTTI KOSKENNIEMI

It would be difficult to find a major figure in the history of European political thought who would not have attempted to say something about how authority emerges, or is justified and critiqued, in the world beyond the single polity. Quite frequently, that effort would have involved some idea about a legal order, or at least a set of rules or regularities applicable in that world. Thomas Hobbes was neither the first nor the last major thinker who believed that the 'international' realm was characterised by the independence of states existing 'in the state and posture of gladiators', thus apparently denying that legal rules or practices or legal thinking could have much relevance therein. Yet others believed, as Immanuel Kant did, that without a constitutional vocabulary not much that was meaningful could be said about the human pursuit of freedom, and that silence about the latter would not only constitute a moral failure but an intellectual and perhaps political mistake. For a long time, the idiom of natural law claimed to offer a universally valid frame for thinking about the nature of the political, as well as providing authority for lawyers' speculations about the rules and principles governing the conduct of individuals and corporate bodies wherever they might move. The name of the relevant discipline at German universities from the late seventeenth century onwards – *ius naturae et gentium*, the law of nature and of nations – revealed the full scope of its ambition. That discipline may have died away (although that is a debatable proposition) but any political thinking worth its salt will today (perhaps especially in the twenty-first century) aim to say something about how authority emerges, is maintained or critiqued not only within but also outside the single state. The world of 'nations' or even 'humanity' is established as an important theme of political and legal speculation.

Of course, the image of 'law' among political thinkers and historians has varied as greatly as has the view of 'politics' or the 'political' among lawyers and legal historians. Perhaps typically in an academic context, until recently, specialists have not been overly keen to speak with each other about such matters. Nevertheless, not only Hobbes and Kant but many other European intellectuals have found their way into textbooks and specialist treatments by both historians of political thought and legal historians, even if the discussion of such figures has varied quite significantly. In more recent times, interest in the *international* dimension of history of political thought has converged with a *historical* turn among international lawyers. Both groups have found themselves perusing the same archive and asking intersecting questions.

But historians of international law and political thought have not met each other only or even predominantly when contemplating the large figures of European political philosophy such as Hobbes or Kant. Indeed, few of them would think that either law or politics derives from their kind of abstract thinking, or can be captured only or even predominantly by examining it. They would also likely agree that their shared efforts to understand and describe a *global* history of international law or political thought would make concentration on such European figures quite problematic. As the methodological chapters in this volume discuss, and the substantive chapters suggest, points of contact exist in moving the gaze from such figures to the development of international rules or institutions; or to the legal and governmental practices of diplomats, merchants and colonial officers; or to the position of women, the family and household. Both lawyers and historians of political thought have been interested in the genealogies of concepts such as 'state', 'empire', 'company', the development and usefulness of divisions between the 'public' and the 'private', as well as the construction of networks of global contacts across cultural divides.

This is not to say that historians of political thought and of international law necessarily see eye to eye on those topics, share similar interests and knowledge – or that their encounters have always been unproblematic. Each has paradigms and topics of especial interest that the other may sometimes find hard to understand. While lawyers may sometimes have difficulty in understanding the subtleties that distinguish the interpretations that historians produce from their materials, historians may often find alien the normative urge frequently driving the writings of international lawyers. One source of these differences lies in the way the theory–practice distinction operates in the two fields: the relationship of history of political thought to present-day 'politics' is not identical to the way international legal historians view their relationship to present-day law. But there are differences within the two fields as well as between them. In particular, Anne Orford and others have contested the terms of the 'turn to history' in international law, arguing that a commitment to contextualist intellectual history necessarily stifles engagement with the modalities of law itself, and thus the potential of critical histories to intervene effectively in the present. Similar debates over history and the present equally characterise history of political thought and intellectual history more broadly.

Our motivation for producing this collection has been to enable authors in both law and history to think about what it is that unites and differentiates their respective pursuits. There is no point in seeking to reduce either perspective to the other. But there may be reason to have a clearer view of what the other seeks to accomplish, bearing in mind that neither discipline is a homogeneous totality but each a cluster of varying approaches, policies and points of substantive interest (and that conceptual frames and expectations of good craftsmanship within each discipline are themselves historical categories, subjected to critical analysis within those disciplines). Accordingly, the volume opens with a series of chapters which reflect on how historians and lawyers approach the past. The title of this Part I, 'Methods, Approaches and Encounters', reflects the fact that debates to which these chapters contribute have sometimes been characterised as disputes over the 'method' proper to a particular endeavour – such as writing the history of international law. However, it is not clear that 'method' captures the range and complexity of the issues at stake, nor that participants in these debates are in fact engaged in the same endeavour. What connects these chapters is a register of argument: an explicitness in addressing, if not 'method', then strategy or style, or politics, of scholarship. The chapters offer accounts of what it is we try to do, as historians or lawyers – the subject-position being sometimes itself a mode of argument – and how we go about it.

Brett (Chapter 1) takes up the focus on context which has been central to debates between historians of political thought and international law – both within and beyond this collection – and among historians. However, she positions the methodology of 'meaning in context' within a broader conception of historiography as story-making, and uses that conception to argue against the reduction of history of political thought to the bare principle of contextualism, while at the same time defending its capacity as history to engage the present through the creative deployment of that same principle. Within the conceptual architecture of speech acts, and the distinctive tension between speaker and language that it involves, she illuminates the methodological and simultaneously political choices that historians must make to the extent that they study political as opposed to any other kind of thought. She goes on to sketch two alternative pathways of development within the history of political thought, which might be abbreviated as 'realism' and 'discourse', within which an encounter with historians of international law might fruitfully take place, expanding the relationship between history and politics into a triadic co-construction of history, politics and law. Finally, pointing to what she calls the 'classic' history of political thought of the later twentieth century, she makes the case for the existing historiographical creativity of the encounter with law, and suggests its promise for future history of political thought in an international and a global frame.

Where Brett looks across from history of political thought to international law, Koskenniemi (Chapter 2) examines the ubiquitous encounter between international law and history from the inside of international law itself. He opens by considering how law has always used history, both in its practical operations and in reflecting on itself, repositioning the question of 'context' within a complex and self-generative back and forth that resists schematic (or indeed polemical) generalisation. His contribution focuses on the variability of law's uses of history and the difficulty of inserting them in any closely crafted set of methodological principles. Sometimes history acts as a conservative force, he suggests, and sometimes, especially in some recent texts, as an instrument of critique. He shows the varying ways in which history is invoked in the practice of international tribunals, and then moves on to discuss some of the ways in which international lawyers have used history to define the contours of the discipline itself, including through narratives of origin. By refining the self-understanding and self-constitution of international law, through different periodisations and by focusing attention on alternatively public and private forms of authority, history of international law may contribute to the role that international law itself plays in the world.

In his contribution, Kennedy (Chapter 3) notes the affinities between critical international lawyers such as Orford, and earlier 'law in society' and 'law in context' scholarship, viewing present debates about the interaction between law and history of political thought as merely one iteration of arguments about the political implications of interdisciplinary approaches to law. However, he focuses almost entirely on the enterprise of history from within a critical international legal tradition, referring to a range of scholars who have mobilised history to critique and in the process critiqued history itself. Working himself within that tradition, Kennedy's use of 'context' dissolves any distinction between the 'context' of a past debate/text and the 'context' of present authorship. As he puts it, 'context-making is performative: it works when it generates a "context effect", changing what is known in ways that alter who can do what'. In a world of 'rule by articulation', Kennedy emphasises authorship as action – the writing or narration or speaking of what we believe to be true, rather than the recovery of something which we may not yet master. This is a task which cannot be guided by discipline-specific conventions, but only by an explicitness of strategy that allows one to assess whether one has 'hit the target', and to take responsibility for the consequences of one's intellectual interventions.

Simpson's chapter, by contrast, is oriented to a moment 'after method'. In one sense this is an effort to imagine a moment in which insights from explicit methodological debates would be absorbed and perhaps transcended (Chapter 4). In this sense, he assesses the effects of these insights, and what they might still offer. Simpson detects in the new attention to method a disruption of established chronologies, 'centurised' segmentations, and teleological visions of legal change. Like Kennedy, he sees an interrogation of anachronism and context in the writing of international legal history, and relatedly a calling into question of the notion of 'greatness': great men, great powers and their place in the unfolding and writing of history. This scrutiny of greatness needs to be extended, he suggests, beyond the obvious 'realist' targets. Many accounts of international law, of varying political inflections, characterise its history as one of accretion, but such accounts may implicitly entrench a view of international law as merely a *response* to 'the instincts of Great Powers or the pathologies of Great Men'. For all this, however, Simpson also calls into question the adequacy of 'method' to capture the breadth of current debates. There might be, he suggests, other matters at stake, although these are difficult to define – 'writerly ethics', 'style', a 'literary' rather than a 'technical' sensibility which might recover 'history in all its strangeness'.

Reading these chapters, and the debates they chart, one has the impression that a moment 'after method' is not quite here yet. The chapters acknowledge that there are questions of intellectual procedure which are, at least partially, constitutive of scholarly identity and integrity, and on which disagreements accordingly remain sharp and consequential. The question of 'context' is one such. 'Context', 'contextualism' and its variants have become not only markers of particular positions, but contested ground. Prima facie, it would seem that it is precisely in the most disputed aspects of this encounter that there are the greatest prospects for sustained conversation: 'context' invites exactly the close attention to particular characteristics of legal argument and legal *habitus* that is advocated, albeit in different ways, by both critical international lawyers and historians. But the difficulty is that contextualisation appears to offer a secure basis for critique only at the cost of consigning meaning to the past, in a kind of museum function that domesticates or controls its objects in a way that is challenged by activists the world over (don't just put a contextualising notice by a statue: take it down, change the space itself). In response, Brett argues that history is a form of narrative art that necessarily engages the present, and that history of political thought, specifically, inevitably doubles up past and present political meaning. In this she shares with the other chapters in Part I, and especially Kennedy, an emphasis on the politics of history – not only in the sense that historical choices involve political commitments, although they do, but also in the sense that authorship itself is a form of political action.

Kennedy goes beyond Brett in the way that he implicates the context of the past in the present. But both see the inevitable reflexivity of historical authorship not as a confusion or impasse that needs to be straightened out by methodology, but as a form of historical intervention or insertion of the author into the action. Context, then, does not cease to be important, but as an issue it becomes less about methodology and more about historiography, about the choices that historians either of political thought or of international law make when they use writing to draw the line between past and present, as Brett puts it. Simpson's chapter calls attention to the poetics of history as a site of 'contestation and reimagination', using the work of Hayden White as a prompt to explore the complex interface between historical and legal poetics. Here, an essentially postmodernist commitment to the liberational possibilities of writing again displaces the question of method, and, as with Kennedy, this is connected to an emphasis on the question of authorial comportment, not merely scholarly discipline. A less definable sensibility of style responds more adequately to the estrangement which is both an ethical and a cognitive self-relation to the past.

Brett, Kennedy and Simpson all address history as a form of writing, a 'writerly' engagement with the past. Yet Koskenniemi, in his opening snippets of remembered conversation, calls attention from the outset to the orality of history in the context of law, and it is again implicit in his subsequent treatment of courts as a primary site of both history and law. There are some commonalities here with Brett's sense of narrative, of the way in which the stories we tell ourselves about the past become the past, and, in Koskenniemi's contribution, become law. And yet orality complicates the emphasis on writing as the medium in which the line between past and present is drawn. Koskenniemi begins *in medias res*, in history as time that is passing, fast, as we speak (no time for novels). In parallel, 'history' as it figures in his account of practice tracks normal spoken usage in shifting between what happened, what we remember, what we self-consciously or formally choose to recall (perhaps in a particular persona, such as a judge), and only finally something that we write. The complicated mutual dynamic that Koskenniemi identifies between history in the making and law in the making both invokes and puts into question all these senses simultaneously.

Nevertheless, his emphasis on practice, defying methodological strictures, aligns his account with the other chapters in Part I. All of them privilege history as something that we are *in* above something that we write *about*. It is through this lens that they address a theme that will run throughout the volume, that of 'realism' as a paradigm both of politics and of international relations and international law. Realism (in its different forms) offers one very clear way of joining up history, politics and law in the kind of 'triadic co-construction' identified by Brett. The way in which it constructs agency and power supplies an apparently compelling picture both of politics, as political actors seek strategically to increase their power, and of law, as either an instrument in the pursuit of power or the restrainer of it (in the heroic vision of international law that Simpson identifies as perpetuating the realist optic). The historiographical consequence is to position history as a form of critical reportage, as Brett suggests in her treatment of history of political thought. Implicitly, the historian is not herself one of the 'Great Powers' or the 'Great Men', but she *sees* what they are up to on the chessboard of the world, in a photographic rather than writerly encounter with the past. As Koskenniemi notes, twentieth-century histories of international law have often associated it with the emergence, expansion and effects of modern statehood and state policy, taking wars, diplomacy and peace-making as central threads. This approach, reflecting the realist vision of politics, is to take a particular view of what international law is, where it comes from, and how it can be known, which, despite its contentiousness, is rarely made express.

Earlier and contrasting narratives had situated international law in broad trajectories of progress and enlightenment, often with a strong commitment to cosmopolitan progress, and depicted sovereignty as an obstacle to the attainment of international peace and solidarity. Although the visual metaphor of enlightenment may seem the naive counterpart to the critical trope of exposure, these histories did respond to the intuition that law is not just an effect of state power – a position more recently associated with constructivist views about the power of law as discourse, and of language as structuring the international world. In broad terms, this contrast within international law responds to the way in which Brett diagnoses the diverging possibilities inherent in the 'conceptual architecture' of speech act theory deployed as a method for history of political thought. In her handling, the move from the pole of the actor towards the pole of language demands a different historiographical voice and potentially a different historiographical form, one in which the historian is not positioned as an external reporter on language games but is herself, partially but not entirely, within the game. That sense of split-level positioning is paralleled in Simpson's appeal to meta-history, while Kennedy moves to position the historical voice more fully within the game and thus to concentrate on the performative nature of the critical legal historian's speech act.

That negotiation between inside and outside discourse, inside and outside the history that one writes, is paralleled in the history of international law and in international law itself. Studies 'internal' to law have a tendency to collapse into something other than legal history – into normative or jurisprudential analyses, bound up with the particular ways in which law incorporates and narrates history. Studies of law that are 'external' in the sense of pulling to the fore law as an instrument of powerful actors tend likewise to make the specifically legal content of the analysis disappear by emphasising the strategic and political aspects of past recourse to law. It is hard to be both inside and outside at the same time, to take the legal frame as given and to be critical of the frame itself. The chapters in Part I suggest that it is here that the real struggle over 'context' lies. As Koskenniemi suggests, however, the legal historian's stance vis-à-vis the law of the present is further complicated by the sociology of the field. As international law has expanded, the formerly tight relation between academia and the profession has loosened. Lawyers tend to be acutely conscious of law as responding to something outside law, to political, economic or technological change. But precisely because the professor of international law is no longer expected to belong to the same elite from which foreign office professionals are chosen, their simultaneously authorial and legal self-positioning is more of a choice. Necessarily familiar with the 'internal' face of law, they may choose to write from an external position – taking roughly the stance of some other social scientist – or to maintain at least a foothold within, with a claim that their account of the law's past can still sound directly in the law of today. The stakes and potential of each strategy are contingent, to be negotiated.

Behind all the chapters in Part I is a powerful sense of change – changing time and changing space – with which both history and law must grapple, and in the process confront the politics of how they do so. To capture this sense of movement, Part II of this collection is called 'Thinking through the International', with the accent on *through*. The chapters, which offer a cross-section of current work by historians and lawyers (and others who might not position themselves so clearly as either), do not speak directly to the same historical phenomena, nor necessarily to any shared conception of the international. They span diverse areas, from the twenty-first-century legal ordering of the oceans to early-modern understandings of gender in the formation of the state. Authors are not necessarily engaged in the same project or asking the same questions. But the juxtaposition of chapters illustrates the extent to which authors of different disciplinary orientations are grappling with some of the same themes, concepts or boundaries. Engaging with such a rich cross-section of work has the effect of unsettling referents and rendering disciplinary footings less sure. This disorientation will not drive us all to the *same* ground, or the same view from a given point – but might render our disparate grounds and viewpoints more contingent, and create new possibilities for interdisciplinary conversation. In this spirit, 'the international' of our title is not a fixed reference, but represents a space of conceptual movement, simultaneously in history, politics and law.

Bearing in mind the complex dynamics of that three-way relationship, and the way in which boundaries on all levels are called into question in the process, the chapters are arranged under themes of potential dialogue ('Law and Constructions of the Political'; 'Empires, States and Nations'; 'Institutions and Persons'; 'Economics and Innovation'; and 'Gender') rather than formal areas of study. Both the thematic arrangement and the distribution of 'historians' and 'lawyers' in relation to the themes have shifted since the genesis of this volume. The chapters might equally have been arranged otherwise, to privilege different interactions and affinities, and we anticipate that readers will in turn see possible new interconnections of their own. In an attempt to provoke this – but not prescribe any particular reading – we offer below a brief outline of each chapter.

The first pair of chapters tackles a central concern of the whole volume, 'Law and Constructions of the Political' (Chapters 5 and 6), through the work of Carl Schmitt. Schmitt has been the subject of extensive commentary in part because of his idiosyncrasy, so he does not here appear as a representative figure. However, his work has a canonical importance for the law–politics relation, and for the tradition of 'realist' political thought. This means that it is revealing not only as a resource in its own right, but as a foil against which others articulate disciplinary or political positions: a dual significance probed in these chapters. Von Bogdandy and Hussain (Chapter 5) note the importance of Schmitt's legal training in sharpening his systematic rigour and polemic; and in attracting his attention to the (legal) decision, and by extension the exception (concepts which would be crucial to much of his thought). They trace the grand lines of Schmitt's theorisation of the political, the state and the international, and its contribution to law. Smeltzer and Kelly in Chapter 6 probe one manifestation of Schmitt's broader commitments, namely his theorisation of the Rhineland occupation, and thus offer a fine-grained sense of the tenor of debates between Schmitt and his contemporaries. Both chapters deal with Schmitt's own treatment of law and the political, but also the stakes for Schmitt, and us, of positioning him as jurist or politician.

Rivalrous claims to genuinely juridical thought were an important part of the confrontation between Schmitt and interwar liberals, as each struggled for authority and their own vision of the law in it. Schmitt engaged in a disingenuous (re)positioning of his own after the Second World War, casting his own work as mere academic adventurism, hijacked by the practitioners of *real* politics, and thus insusceptible to criminal prosecution. The implications of the law–politics divide still resonate today, in the reception of Schmitt's thought. For von Bogdandy and Hussain, it is the particular intellectual context of the German legal academy which helped produce Schmitt as a thinker. Law and the legal academy proved highly generative of a strand of political thought which was, in turn, corrosive to law as a container for, or bulwark against, the political. For Smeltzer and Kelly (Chapter 6), too, it matters that we understand Schmitt as a jurist – but for different reasons. We must, they suggest, see him as a 'jurist [who] wanted to win his cases, and ... curated the law and its interpretation in political contexts'. This, coupled with Schmitt's own argument for the contingency of the historical situation, ought to inoculate us against reading Schmitt in the wrong way, transposing his work to timeless models of agonistic pluralism or spatial politics.

The next thematic pairing, 'Empires, States and Nations', expands reflection on the importance of the state as a conceptual frame, in and through the law of nations, for our understanding of past, present and future political order. Pitts (Chapter 7) works within the 'law of nations' as a broad language of political and moral reflection, particularly prior to the professionalisation of international law in the late nineteenth century. She highlights the role of canonical authors, particularly Vattel, in popularising a conception of nations, or states (he used the terms interchangeably) as moral communities of equal status. Although some revisionist historians of international law have understood this as accommodating pluralism, Pitts asks whether Vattel's contribution – understood not as aspiration but description – actually concealed from view the persistence of empire. Hunter, too (Chapter 8), is concerned with the historical and political implications of our (mis)understanding of the state form, particularly as it manifests itself in Africa. Like Pitts, she objects to the way in which a focus on states, and the road to their creation, 'obscures a much messier historical reality in which the jurisdiction of states has always coexisted with other sorts of authority'. She takes aim in particular at dominant popular and scholarly narratives in which the state form was imposed on a decolonising African continent from outside. Characterisations of this kind are, she notes, made in the service of a critical project, namely a search for alternative visions which failed to flourish at independence. But they reify a particular normative model of statehood, and occlude the range and intensity of local debates about future political ordering.

Hunter emphasises that the post-colonial construction of the state unfolded in relation to other sites of politics. The prospect of regional federation and greater movement and exchange across borders accommodated tensions between the new statist order and existing modes of life, and the emergence of individual rights as a matter of international concern, together with international organisations as forums for individual complaint, offered recourse for post-colonial citizens seeking to counter repressive governments. Where Pitts sees dark dimensions in the juxtaposition of informal empire (through wealth, military might or the bureaucracy of international governance) and formal sovereign equality, Hunter highlights the plasticity and potential in aspects of this duality. The post-colonial state was made, not imposed, in a world in which the state was only one of a number of sites of politics, and in which this multiplicity of sites offers some hope for emancipation.

In these early chapters, the state features as the international 'person' par excellence – but is not alone, jostling with empires, federations, corporations and international institutions of various kinds, even individuals. The thematic pairing of 'Institutions and Persons' tries to capture this sense of a variegated and crowded international (or interpolitical, per Lauren Benton) domain, and build on what has already been suggested about the way in which the theorisation of institutions and persons helps *constitute* the international or interpolitical. The chapters do not begin from any fixed definition of 'institution' or 'person'; indeed they reveal the duality of 'institution' as both intellectual configuration and concrete organisation, and examine efforts to grapple with the very notion of personhood.

McClure (Chapter 9) engages with intersecting institutions, in the sense of both configurations or complexes of ideas and practices (hospitality, poverty), and concrete, physically implanted organisations as sites of social control (hospitals, monasteries). She emphasises the 'complexity of conceptions of hospitality as a mixture of moral norms, religious obligations, and intersecting rights to travel and to access resources'; but also the instability of power relations bound up with hospitality. On one hand, it is clear that the articulation of a *ius hospitii* as part of the *ius gentium* played a crucial role in the legitimation of Spanish conquest, but it 'did not resolve the ancient tensions within the concept of hospitality as an arbitration between the power of the host/guest or giver/receiver'.

Donaldson (Chapter 10) examines the efforts of contemporaries to understand the League of Nations – the first quasi-universal, general-purpose international institution – as a person. The task of pinning down what the League *was* presented a variation on puzzles familiar to political thought, about artificial personality and collective agency. The League still 'fell somewhere between an "it", a unitary agent, and a "they", a collective of organs or members'. If it was the latter, it was not clear how the 'collective' became one – though an implicitly cosmopolitan 'public opinion' or 'popular will' often served as the *deus ex machina*. Questions about the personhood and agency of the League were particularly acute for those working within the Secretariat, and became intimately linked, in the inner life of the institution, with questions about speech. Whether and how the League might speak for the international depended on which individuals might speak for the League, and on what terms. This knitting together of abstract and concrete challenges the limits of legal and political thought, and challenges the disciplinary perspectives which shape approaches to institutions today.

These chapters illustrate, in radically different sites, the intermingling of self-consciously juridical vocabularies and traditions with other discourses. Whereas Schmittian debates posit a sharp divide between law and the political, these chapters (and others in the volume) show the porousness of this boundary. Metaphors and categories are at once juridical and open to other discourses; and juridical vocabularies and texts are invoked and interpreted by individuals who are themselves only marginally 'legal' agents. These accounts suggest the rapidity and contingency of theorisation from a profusion of possible vocabularies, each of which might yield a somewhat different repertoire of arguments. The chapters also illustrate ways in which theorisation is bounded not only by material and physical circumstances, but by notions of role or office (host, guest, international civil servant). Legal thought is shaped not only by the professional role of lawyers crafting positions for clients and sovereigns but by a wider range of roles or loyalties, imposed or chosen.

The section on 'Economics and Innovation' focuses closely on two themes already present, if only implicitly, in much of the rest of the volume. 'Economics' or 'commerce' is arguably both a discourse in its own right and a terrain over and in which law and politics are constructed. The articulation of a *ius negotiandi* and *ius hospitii* were as significant for the facilitation of appropriation and extraction as they were for setting the political relations between peoples of the 'Old' and 'New' Worlds (McClure). The imperative of forcing China open to trade revealed tensions within the law of nations about the right of a state to set its own commercial policy, and commerce as a norm of sociability between equal states (Pitts). Commentators on the League reached for analogies to private law structures of joint ownership, or the shareholder corporation (Donaldson) – more or less the transposition of financial methods onto political and state life which Schmitt decried in the putative split between sovereignty and territorial jurisdiction (Smeltzer and Kelly). As Kennedy writes, our present boundaries between economics and politics, like the boundaries between private and public, are 'of recent vintage, marked and managed in legal terms: they could be otherwise'.

'Innovation', too, has been glimpsed throughout the collection. Brett notes the 'distinctive historiographical tension' involved in the original Skinnerian handling of conceptual change in terms of linguistic innovation, poised between individual agency and structuring discourse. The particular innovation bound up with 'the state' in its distinctive modern form is foundational to both political thought and to positivist law. Pitts and Hunter have charted the way in which the state has been reconceived and articulated in different moments in the construction of an international, or interpolitical, domain; and Donaldson highlights the troubled and arguably still incomplete process of inventing the international organisation. In some of these chapters, one glimpses a notion of innovation at some remove from that central to much intellectual history: one that is gradual enough to render it difficult to identify particular moments of evolution, and in which the work of innovation might not occur exclusively or even primarily in language, but run through bureaucratic categorisations and quotidian practices, the sum and implications of which exceed deliberate design, or even awareness, of particular individuals.

Understanding 'innovation' broadly as *change*, it may seem intuitive to couple 'economics and innovation' together. One of the most influential accounts of historical change, informed generally by Marxist theory, is precisely economic in nature. The two chapters in this section, however, seek to complicate this relation. Ranganathan (Chapter 11) explores the role of law in consolidating 'an imaginary of the sea as an assemblage of jurisdictionally discrete sites of economic activity'. She traces the protean invocation of 'freedom of the seas' through time as a spur and foil to this process, and the increasingly intricate ways in which law engages with the biological complexity of the ocean world. Her chapter emphasises both the salience of a Marxist analysis *and* the somewhat autonomous operation of the law within this. The crafting of legal regimes unfolds through particular legal technique, and lawyers are driven not only by (often remote) perceptions of commercial or national interest, but by considerations of what approach would best uphold *the law itself* as a mode of governing resource allocation, bringing interest into relation with an array of more complex ideological, and political, constructions.

Whereas Ranganathan gives us a view from inside a process of innovation – the twentieth-century reimagination of the oceans – Isaac (Chapter 12) critiques the way in which intellectual historians theorise processes of conceptual change. Isaac traces affinities between a model of conceptual change common to Skinner, Kuhn and Hacking, particularly its emphasis on innovation, and Schumpeter's account of entrepreneurial action, which emphasises the entrepreneur as the source of creative response, and growth, *within* an economic system, achieving 'new combinations' of materials and forces of production. This relation between theories of conceptual change and economic thought is, Isaac concedes, 'mediated [and] indirect', much like that between *raison d'état* and historicism; but it may have significant implications. Oddly enough, a model of conceptual change which foregrounds the figure of the entrepreneur leaves questions of agency rather underdeveloped. Although 'the theory of enterprise *looks* like the description of a type of agent, … in practice there is no such … discrete social type'. Moreover, an account of innovation inflected by economic theory may also be drawn into treating innovation as 'market-led' and 'non-intentional'. Thus a theory which appears to privilege agency may foster a kind of 'fatalism' about our own capacities for political innovation. Together, these chapters invite renewed attention to questions implicit elsewhere in this collection, and in the history of international law, about how we understand change and its theorisation.

It may seem perverse to close the volume with two chapters in a section entitled 'Gender'. Foundational accounts of the political, and indeed of law as a social phenomenon, assume a progression from the individual or familial, to the communal, to the political and then the interpolitical. Gender, one might think, ought to come first. Yet these chapters insist that origins (bodily, conceptual, temporal) cannot be held in place, and show how attention to gender works against familiar narratives of foundation and development. Becker (Chapter 13) observes that, although gendered familial relations lie at the heart of the 'natural' state from, or against, which the political was defined, theorisations of the state have tended to focus on the relationships between male citizens, sequestering male–female relations from the political story. In fact, Becker argues, early modern thought represents a stark challenge to enduring fusions of the biological with a patriarchal politics. While commentaries on Roman law and on Aristotle narrated 'the Roman systematic division of private law into natural law, *ius gentium*, and civil law' as 'intricately interwoven with the development of humankind itself', gender troubled the relations between these trajectories. As Becker insists, the equality of man and woman, natural and civil marriages, childbirth and breast-feeding were tightly enmeshed with the emergence and maintenance of the 'public' and 'political' in the first place. What emerges from these writings is that women's subordination was a 'historical, but not a logical, let alone a natural, outcome'. It was an outcome, one might add, in which law played a complex role. Law entrenched subordination in some spheres, while the plurality of bodies of law in play resisted any comprehensive legitimation of this subordination.

Knop (Chapter 14) takes up this pluralism through what might be seen as a modern iteration of *matrimonium* in the *ius gentium*: the way in which marital and familial relations cut against a strict demarcation of national legal orders from each other, and of 'private' from 'public' international law. Recovering 'the lost private side' of international law helps us see the layering and interpenetration of international and national law, foreign and domestic law, as politically generative. To nationality, understood as a political bond, private international law offered a rival criterion of domicile, entailing a more holistic sense of 'homeness' (quoting Lorimer). To obligation, private international law offered a counterpart notion of 'comity', hovering somewhere between absolute obligation (then being coded as manly honour) and mere courtesy (then being coded as feminine). Knop argues that comity might be recovered, and connected with notions of 'friendship' between nations, to open up a richer tapestry of interstate relations. These two chapters together show how attention to gender and family offers a constant challenge to the imagination of the state as self-contained. Gender retains a capacity to destabilise relations between the 'natural' and the 'political', stressing the bodily and the relational alongside, and against, the political. It opens up a different temporality – a 'transnational everyday life', in Knop's words, of births, marriages, deaths and transmission of property – rather than the episodic crises on which much (public) international law scholarship is focused. And it offers, potentially, a different sense of what it means to live within a state (and under its law), and of how states might live with each other.

Gender thus has a powerful capacity to complicate the past and to renew analysis of the legal and political present, as it works across and between political entities and legal orders, forcing a sort of porousness to the other. In this it exemplifies 'the international' in the sense we intend it here, not as a fixed order between states but as a space of multiple and intersecting legal and political relationships, the history of which must raise the question of what *is* the legal and what *is* the political in the story that it tells. It is too neat to see attention to gender as the inverse of a challenge that crosses many of these chapters, that of loosening the anchoring of history of political thought and history of international law in a European paradigm; and yet there are parallels none the less. Gender, placed at the end of the thematic chapters, reflects back upon the start, with Carl Schmitt's theorisation of the political, the state and the international. Against his construction of an existential division between the space and law of Europe and what lies beyond, most of the chapters show the distinction being made in more intricate, variegated ways: through the operation of a protean *ius hospitii* across radically different cultures (McClure), or the late integration of the post-colonial state into a fabric of customary norms pre-dating these states' own creation (Ranganathan).

To be sure, there is resistance: nationalist leaders in the colonised world seek to recast states and federations as vehicles for political transformation (Hunter), and post-colonial states grasp the legal tools available to try to fashion a New International Economic Order (Ranganathan). Nevertheless, to the extent that the chapters in this volume aim at shaping intellectual trajectories for the future – and many do – the impetus is often towards a re-narration of the historical unfolding of European empire, using its intellectual resources against it. For Pitts, aspects of the old law of nations may yet offer substance for a critique of empire; Koskenniemi points out that the scope of new histories of international law is paradoxically moving back towards the old *ius gentium*, whose all-embracing nature allows us 'a fuller view of the role legal concepts and practices have had in making the world what it is'. For Knop, a recovery of gender and private international law – a body of law open to the social but reproducing distinctions between Christian, civilised polities and others – might inform relational feminist approaches to current international law. McClure sees in the ethics of hospitality, and the recognition of contradictions within hospitality at a given moment, a means of analysing how 'transcultural interactions have been managed and how unequal distributions have ... become normative'; similarly, Kennedy insists that only examination of 'the machinery allocating power and wealth within what we remember as a more coherent and virtuous order' can get us to new political horizons.

For all these contributors, new histories of political thought and of international law alike bring critical resources to politics and law in the present, and therefore an opening to a different future from the one implicitly foretold in existing narratives of the past. But a changed history is not merely an added resource for politics and law to pick up and use in the course of doing what they always did. Rather, it changes – or at least challenges – how we conceive of politics and law in the first place. History, politics and law are all mutually imbricated, and to think through the international inevitably raises the question about what it means to be 'inside' our own disciplines and conceptual resources. The challenge is how to acknowledge this enclosure while also staying open to conceptualisations of the world and its trajectory which emerge from other disciplines, traditions and ways of thinking.

PART I

Methods, Approaches and Encounters

1

Between History, Politics and Law
History of Political Thought and History of International Law

ANNABEL BRETT*

1.1 INTRODUCTION

History of this, history of that: it's easy to assume that 'history' is the same thing in each case, only with a different object. As every historian knows, however, that is not so. History is not a universal lens that can be trained indifferently on any random thing suspended in that turbid fluid called 'the past'. Rather, there is a mutually constitutive relationship between the different kinds of things historians study and the different kinds of history they write. The framing tropes of political history differ from those of cultural history, for example, and spin their objects distinctively in each case. If historians take such different approaches, however, what makes them all historians nonetheless? Is there a point at which they are not, in fact, doing history at all, but something else – law, for instance? And what is at stake in asserting such a point? The premise of this volume is that this is a conversation worth having following the 'international turn' in history of political thought and the 'historical turn' in international law. This gives practitioners of both apparently the same objects – the works of Hugo Grotius, for example, or at least the particular work of his

---

* I would like to thank my co-editors, Megan Donaldson and Martti Koskenniemi, for their infinitely rich and infinitely patient response to this chapter in the making. My thanks also to John Robertson for comments on the draft, and for the conference on 'Time and the History of Political Thought', which helped pull some things together in my mind. Finally, I would like to thank my father, Michael Brett, who studied history of political thought with Walter Ullmann in Cambridge in the 1950s, and whose insights into writing the history of Ismāʿīlism are somewhere in the background here. He sent me the article by John Wansbrough (n. 2) while I was myself studying history of political thought in Cambridge in the 1980s, introduced me to Braudel, and much else besides.

called, in English translation, *The Law of War and Peace* (or, *The Rights of War and Peace* – whose title is it anyway?). If history of political thought and history of international law are different kinds of history, however, they will spin these texts each in their own way, so that through the eyes of one they are works of political thought, through the eyes of the other works of law. But what is it for a work to be political thought rather than law?

Before we begin to explore that distinction, it is worth considering what these two approaches might have in common in the way in which they engage the present. In some sense, of course, all history engages the present. The past does not exist independently and on its own terms: what is past is so only in relation to the present, and therefore inextricably bound up with it. But the past is also something distinct from the present, something that is *not* present. History is the Janus-faced art that creates the past in the sense of a relationship with the present while simultaneously representing the past as something distinct from the present. The distinctive voice of the historian, the *histor*, depends on the ability to stabilise that distance by referring 'out' from the story to the traces of the past – the letter in the archive, the stones in the desert, 'the sword which was a sword once, in another grasp' – and to other stories read not as stories but as traces.[1] The poetry reminds us how even the most material traces are already storied in some way in the Western historical imagination. Even so, however, the past is not such traces, nor is history the facts that are constructed from them through shared conventions of reference and inference. History is the story we tell ourselves about what really happened outside the story, and those two things can never be entirely separated nor ever entirely fused unless we stop writing history altogether and content ourselves with archaeology and novels. (Sacred scripture, which fuses the inside and the outside, the story as story and the story as trace, is then a very complex and historically challenging third case.[2]) It is in the writing that this double face of history comes into relief, a graphic medium that draws lines around some things and effaces others, which just is to write the line between past and

---

[1] For the *histor*, and history as story more generally, see Paul Ricœur, 'The Narrative Function', in his *Hermeneutics and the human sciences*, ed. and tr. John B. Thompson (Cambridge: Cambridge University Press, 1981), 274–96. For the sword, 'la espada que fue espada/en otra mano', Jorge Luis Borges, 'Tankas', in *The Gold of the Tigers*, tr. Alastair Reid (Harmondsworth: Penguin Books/Allen Lane 1979), at 102–3.
[2] See John Wansbrough, '"Res ipsa loquitur": History and Mimesis'. The Albert Einstein Memorial Lecture (Israel Academy of Sciences and Humanities, 1987).

present. As Paul Ricœur put it, 'if one says that emplotment, say, concerns only the writing, one forgets that history *is* writing'.[3]

The question, therefore, is not about past and present in history generally, but whether history of political thought and history of international law have a kind of presentism built in that other kinds of history do not have – perhaps even to the extent that they elide the space for the distinctive duality of history and are therefore, in fact, not history at all. The argument would be that the peculiar temporality both of thought and of law draws the history of each inexorably into the present, collapsing the history of political thought into political thought and the history of international law into international law. This argument has a long history within the history of political thought, the very name of which seems to tug it both ways, towards an intellectual history that is part of history and a history of philosophy that is part of philosophy.[4] It has generated a long-standing methodological debate that waxes and wanes but never entirely dies – partly because methodological statements, however sophisticated, can never be more than crude reflections of the complex thinking involved in even the simplest questions of actual practice (how do I paraphrase this passage of Grotius, for example).[5] There are those who want to pull the history of political thought firmly in one direction or the other. But many of its practitioners resist that attempt. Both in their methodological statements and, far more importantly, in their substantive histories, they have in different ways negotiated the space of, and for, history in relation to philosophy. 'Far more importantly', not only because of the inevitable crudity of methodological statements, but more fundamentally because, as in all history, the past–present relationship is not propositional. It cannot be stated; it can only be written. What is distinctive to the history of political thought as a form of history is that the way in which it writes the borderline between past and present, as all history must, involves a second borderline, between history and philosophy. The Janus face of history of political thought, specifically, is that the representation of a past way of thinking is at the same time an act of political thinking in the present.

History in general is currently undergoing a new wave of self-examination as it engages with the question of the global, simultaneously with a new critical

---

[3] Ricœur, 'The Narrative Function', at 291. Ricœur mentions Paul Veyne, who did not call his book 'What is history', but 'How to write history' (see n. 31).
[4] See the Introduction in Richard Rorty, J.B. Schneewind and Quentin Skinner (eds.), *History and Philosophy: Essays on the Historiography of Philosophy* (Cambridge: Cambridge University Press, 1984).
[5] See Gerry Simpson's contribution (Chapter 4 in this volume), for a multi-faceted exploration of the limits of method in history.

awareness of the relationship between timing and spacing concepts both at a macro and at a micro level (the 'spatial turn'). The same is true of intellectual history and of history of political thought, as it grapples with the timing and spacing of the global in relation to the temporality of thought that has always been its concern. This endeavour is throwing up some of the old conundrums and some new ones, in which one might expect to find a good deal of common ground with the more recent historical turn within international law. The initial dialogue, however, has seen a series of sharp exchanges in which the relationship between history of political thought and history of international law has been pushed into a question of the relationship between history and law per se, marked by a polemical drive to establish an antagonism between the two. Somewhat to the surprise of historians of political thought, who are used to being accused by their colleagues in history of not really doing history at all, 'history of political thought' has become a stand-in for 'history' itself. Or at least, a stand-in for a pre-global form of history inadequate to the new dimensions of time and space, unlike certain other forms of intellectual history which have the capacity to rise to the challenge and on which international law can therefore happily draw. And it has been used in exactly the same way from the other side, to denounce those new dimensions as merely the latest inflated iteration in a long and tired tradition of metaphysical pseudo-history. As a result, the question of the relationship between political thought and international law as objects of history has been pushed into the background or even foreclosed altogether.

In what follows I want to consider the temporality of history of political thought in more depth by exploring two different directions in which it can be taken. With both, I consider the consequences of those different directions for thinking about law, aiming thereby to reopen the dialogue between political thought and international law from a different angle. But one final point about history in general needs to be made before I start. Historians, when they feel under pressure, have an unfortunate tendency to define themselves in terms only of one face of history, the study of the past as distinct from the present. They speak as if the historian's distinctive voice were constituted purely by stabilising the reference 'out' from the story, and they underline this emphasis by talking in terms of documents as sources, facts as independent historical truths and history as the *re*construction of what really happened on the basis of them. It is true that no historian can practise their craft without an alignment with this distinctive way of seeing ('objectivity') and the scholarly ethos it involves. At the same time, however, historians know full well that history is not sources or facts, but a story in which the reconstruction of what really happened cannot be separated from the construction of their own narrative of what really happened. It is both together that make an account historical as opposed to either factual, fictional or scriptural. To focus purely on the former, either in defending themselves or attacking others, both devalues the stories they tell and, importantly for the present contribution, flattens the distinction between different kinds of history. But this is not a point about history of political thought in particular, which, as suggested earlier, has an interface with philosophy that is not shared with all types of history. As we shall see, that interface is further complicated by the element of 'political' in its object, which brings another party to the table: politics.

1.2 HISTORY OF POLITICAL THOUGHT AND POLITICS

History of political thought tends to be identified, somewhat to its practitioners' unease, with something now generally known as 'the Cambridge School'. The Cambridge School is in turn identified with the three figures understood to have initiated this scholarly movement between the late 1950s and the early 1970s, John Dunn, John Pocock and Quentin Skinner. Reducing still further, the manifesto of this 'school' is widely taken to be the latter's 1969 article, 'Meaning and Understanding in the History of Ideas'.[6] In it, and in a series of subsequent articles, Skinner put forward a method for studying the history of ideas that turned on reading texts in historical context, defined as the context of their production. Drawing on the linguistic pragmatics of Wittgenstein, Austin and Searle, Skinner argued that texts should be seen not as expressions of timeless ideas, but as speech acts. To understand the meaning of a text as a speech act is to understand its 'illocutionary force', its peculiar point or intentionality, the character of which can only be understood against the background of contemporary linguistic conventions. The meaning of any specific utterance is inescapably public in this way. Accordingly, the historian of political thought will need to begin by reconstructing the historical discursive context. This, in turn, will be related to the social, political, institutional and cultural contexts of that discourse, according to Wittgenstein's concept of a 'language game' as not merely a shared system of signs but also 'the actions

---

[6] Q.R.D. Skinner, 'Meaning and Understanding in the History of Ideas', *History and Theory* 8(1) (1969), 3–53, repr. along with several other programmatic articles in James Tully (ed.), *Meaning and Context: Quentin Skinner and His Critics* (Princeton: Princeton University Press, 1988). It is not my purpose here to endorse these reductions, since the field of history of political thought is both variegated and changing, as I suggest in conclusion. What I say in the following about '*contextual* history of political thought' is not intended, therefore, necessarily to apply to all history of political thought. However, since the line between this approach and others within the field is not clear-cut, I have not always used the qualifier 'contextual'.

into which [that system] is woven'.⁷ From there the historian can proceed to thinking about the meaning of the individual text (or texts) as a move within that historical language game.

This proposition, now dubbed 'contextualism', has sometimes been taken to constitute a self-sufficient methodology in itself. In fact, however, it leaves open as many questions as it answers, questions that Skinner and other historians have worked on intensively in the intervening years.⁸ For present purposes, the question is over the sense of politics involved and how that inflects the issue of temporality and therefore the writing of history. What, then, makes a given language game a *political* language game as opposed to any other kind? Partly because it involves a language – a shared system of signs – for talking *about* politics as opposed to anything else (it contains words like 'king', rather than 'slab' or 'beam'). But it is also because that shared system of signs is woven into a shared activity of politics, such that to talk about politics is also political in the sense of being *part of* politics. To refer to someone as 'King', for example, even if this were entirely casual and completely uncontroversial at a given time and place, is a political act in the sense that it not only refers to but implicitly *recognises* that person's political position. This double sense of 'political' is something on which I think all historians of political thought would agree. It is what prevents the collapse of history of political thought into any other branch of intellectual history. Where they might disagree, though, is over how to construe it, and that involves their understanding of politics itself.

Developing his methodological approach in the early 1970s, Skinner made speech act and political act coincide within a Weberian understanding of legitimation.⁹ He broadly accepted Weber's view of the state as holding a monopoly of legitimate violence within a given territorial area. Skinner was not particularly interested in the violence, however. Rather, it was the demand for and the production of legitimacy which on his understanding was the defining characteristic of politics as a form of shared activity. Unlike the use of

---

⁷ Ludwig Wittgenstein, *Philosophical Investigations*, tr. G.E.M. Anscombe (Oxford: Clarendon Press, 1968), §7.

⁸ Compare, for example, 'Meaning and Understanding' with Q.R.D. Skinner, *Liberty before Liberalism* (Cambridge: Cambridge University Press, 1998), ch. 3: 'Freedom and the Historian'. For my own earlier reflection on the subject, see Annabel Brett, 'What Is Intellectual History Now?', in D. Cannadine (ed.), *What is History Now?* (London: Palgrave Macmillan, 2001).

⁹ See Kari Palonen, *Quentin Skinner: History, Politics, Rhetoric* (Cambridge: Polity, 2003), at 47–60, 78–81; Mark Goldie, 'The Context of *The Foundations*', in Annabel Brett and James Tully, with Holly Hamilton-Bleakley (eds.), *Rethinking the Foundations of Modern Political Thought* (Cambridge: Cambridge University Press, 2006), 3–19.

force, legitimation can never be a unilateral action. Rather, it is co-produced between a political speaker and a political public within vocabularies that are widely recognised and accepted as having normative force within their shared community. The agency of the former is both enabled and constrained by the normative language that both parties to the linguistic negotiation inhabit, making the speaker an actor *in* language rather than an instrumental user of it. Legitimation thus presupposes some sort of public domain, however restricted it may be, with at least some degree of political agency on the part of the relevant public. Where there is no room at all for legitimation, there is no politics and there is no *political* power, though there might be power of other kinds, for example, that of a master over a chattel slave, or military power as in an occupation.

This picture furnishes a view of political languages as not simply those that contain the vocabulary necessary to refer to the agents, bodies and institutions that characterise a political system ('king', 'parliament', 'the Home Office' rather than 'slab' or 'beam'). Rather, a political language is a *legitimating* language, one in which the normative dimension is explicitly articulated in value-laden terms having persuasive force in respect of a given public. Skinner called such a language an 'ideology' and its use 'ideological', but not in the usual pejorative sense of indoctrination, or as somehow involving false consciousness. Ideologies understood in this sense present a cut-and-dried political world view, fashioned by political–intellectual masters to be swallowed and reproduced whole, thus suppressing the political agency of their consumers. Legitimating languages in Skinner's sense, however, and in the work of J.G.A. Pocock and others, are looser associative clusters of vocabulary that rely on the agency of a political public to fill in the gaps.[10] As such they typically appeal beyond the strictly political to moral, legal, aesthetic, religious, logical and even natural scientific principles, and to other kinds of social, cultural and intellectual authority. This continuity between political and other forms of discourse has the effect of widening the relevant public beyond national boundaries, since these forms are very rarely contained within one place even though they may have a strong local inflection.[11] In turn, the looser spatial contours of such exchange alter and extend the temporal contours.

---

[10] See, for example, J.G.A. Pocock, 'The Concept of a Language and the métier d'historien', in A.R.D. Pagden ed., *The Languages of Political Theory in Early Modern Europe* (Cambridge: Cambridge University Press, 1985).

[11] See David Armitage, 'The International Turn in Intellectual History', in Darrin M. McMahon and Samuel Moyn (eds.), *Rethinking Modern European Intellectual History* (Oxford: Oxford University Press, 2014), 232–52.

Ideology in Skinner's original sense, then, is not a corruption but constitutive of politics on his understanding, and any political speaker articulating a position in normative terms will use elements of existing ideology to make their case. That use could be a straightforward rearticulation ('the king is the father of the people'); it could be a kind of ironic subversion (a satirical print, captioned 'The Father of the People', depicting the king surrounded by dozens of illegitimate children); or it could be a more thoroughgoing innovation within language which, if successful, could change the terms of political discourse as a whole (linguistically repositioning the association between 'king' and 'father' as a marker of despotism, for example). In all these cases, the ideological use of language is 'political' in a stronger sense than the everyday and unselfconscious use of common political terms of reference, wherein the ideological inflection is so weak as to reduce its political valence nearly, though not quite, to simple description. Not quite, for on this analysis both kinds of usage are involved in the constitutive role of political language in politics as a form of life. This connects the different levels and registers of political discourse, and it also connects that discourse to non-discursive features such as the layout of a parliamentary debating chamber or a princely palace. As we have already seen, all these elements of politics are further connected with broader discursive forms and institutions of social, cultural and intellectual life.

What does this approach mean for actually writing the history of political thought? The answer is that, while its distinctive way of joining up the publicity of language with the politics of legitimation precludes certain narrative choices, it leaves open a wide range of others. As in so many cases, it is flexibility and workability that have been key to its professional diffusion. Its twin poles, of political languages and those who use them, allow historians to weight them and to construct the interplay between them differently, depending on the distinctive features of the area they are looking at. They offer a choice of spatial parameters, as we have seen, and also a choice of temporal parameters. Certainly, you are not going to get the point of the satirical print if you don't know that the king as the father of the people is a standard motif of royalist ideology at a certain time and place. In that sense, the spatial and temporal parameters that the historian establishes for the speech act are indeed governed by the time and place of its production, or the 'context'. But I say 'governed', rather than 'given', advisedly: the spatial and temporal diffusion of political language means that context can never be closed, or unique, and the endless circulation of copy complicates and sometimes defies the search for an originating moment.[12] Texts

---

[12] See Jacques Derrida's simultaneous appreciation and critique of speech act theory, 'Signature Event Context', *in Margins of Philosophy*, tr. Alan Bass (Brighton: Harvester Press, 1982),

can also shift context, for example if Hobbes's *Leviathan* were to be republished two hundred years after its original publication on the other side of the world. Such movement tends to take place within longer-term patterns of social and cultural practice and circulation – texts don't (most of the time) just wash up on the beach like a message in a bottle – and tracking contextual shift within these kinds of broader patterning is one of the things that history of political thought classically does.

Nevertheless, it remains true that the republished work constitutes a new speech act in a new context. Texts have no continuous identity *as acts*, even though Hobbes's *Leviathan* may have a more or less continuous identity *as a text*. More or less, because it is not, in fact, the same text in Chinese translation, say, or even in another European language; with a new editorial foreword, with or without footnotes or an index. It is partly precisely the understanding of the new edition as a new act that helps us to see that.[13] For any specific act, however, if the contextual parameters are drawn too broadly, they will have no explanatory traction: not on the words, not on the text, but on the *point* of the words, that is, on their nature as an act. It is this feature of 'meaning in context' that led to controversy with political philosophers from the outset and continues to raise objections, as it seems to pin meaning down in time and space ('provincialism', 'containment').[14] In terms of the potential exchange between history of political thought and history of international law in which the present volume is interested, it has been seen as an insuperable barrier. International law, it is argued, should avoid 'contextualism' at all costs, because, whatever the broader continuities to which it might appeal, the discontinuity or punctuality of act-in-context denies

---

307–30; Warren Boutcher, 'Unoriginal Authors: How to Do Things with Text in the Renaissance', in Brett and Tully (eds.), *Rethinking the Foundations*, 73–92. I make the case that history of political thought can use deconstructive techniques of reading in 'What Is Intellectual History Now?', at 123.

[13] See Gérard Genette, *Paratexts: Thresholds of Interpretation*, tr. Jane E. Lewin (Cambridge: Cambridge University Press, 1997), who talks of the paratext as 'a zone not only of transition but also of *transaction*: a privileged place of a pragmatics and a strategy, of an influence on the public' ('Introduction', p. 2, emphasis in the original).

[14] See Peter Gordon, 'Contextualism and Criticism in the History of Ideas', in McMahon and Moyn (eds.), *Rethinking Modern European Intellectual History*, 32–55; critical response in Matthew Specter, 'Deprovincialising the Study of European Ideas: A Critique', *History and Theory* 55 (2016), 110–28. Gordon allows a continuing role for context in the practice of intellectual history, but argues that it cannot be exhaustive of a historical approach. On this I agree (in fact, I think many 'Cambridge school' historians would agree, since, as Gordon acknowledges, they do not have a shared methodological approach). But, by the same token, the polemical language of 'provincialism' and 'containment' seems to me to be misplaced, or at least to target a straw man.

the movement of meaning with which international law is necessarily concerned.[15]

Two points might be made in response. The first is to reiterate that historians of political thought in this vein are not looking for any kind of meaning, but for political meaning; not for sense of the words, but for the politics of their utterance. It is for this reason that they are interested in texts as acts in a very specific sense. If a historian, including an intellectual historian or a historian of law, is not interested in text-as-act in this sense, then the spatiotemporal parameters involved in the contextual approach are not a limitation in some way; they are simply irrelevant. The question, then, is whether history of international law has anything to gain from seeing texts as acts in this way. I am not qualified to answer that question, only to open an invitation to dialogue, as I shall do in conclusion. For the moment I make only the general point that, while the framing tropes and rhetoric associated with the global turn in all disciplines tend to paint any kind of 'limit' (conceptual or otherwise) pejoratively, contextual parameters do allow a historian to capture a peculiar feature of certain discursive situations that would otherwise be elusive – the politics of republishing *Leviathan* in Chinese two centuries later, say. It might certainly be possible to say that international law has no interest in this kind of politics or this kind of meaning at all. But that appears to involve a thesis, not only about contextualism, or about the relationship between history and law, but about the relationship between law and politics. It is all three terms, then, history, law and politics that need to be put in question simultaneously.

Now it might be objected here that what I have just said is disingenuous. For, the objection runs, history of political thought in this vein is *not* looking only for political meaning; 'contextualism' claims that if you don't look for that kind of meaning, 'meaning in context', you are not doing history at all. It is certainly true that Skinner's original thesis in 'Meaning and Understanding' was intended to cover not only history of political thought but the entirety of 'history of ideas' or intellectual history. One reply to this objection, then, is simply to say that whatever Skinner's ambitions in that essay, its methodology in practice works much better for history of political thought than for other kinds of intellectual history, precisely because of the politics involved.[16] And,

---

[15] The argument against contextualism in history of international law is made by Anne Orford, 'On International Legal Method', *London Review of International Law* 1(1) (2013), 111–97; critical response in Lauren Benton, 'Beyond Anachronism: Histories of International Law and Global Legal Politics', *Journal of the History of International Law* 21(1) (2019), 7–40.

[16] Tully's introductory chapter *Meaning in Context* (n. 6) is entitled 'The Pen Is a Mighty Sword: Quentin Skinner's Analysis of Politics', for that reason.

when Skinner came to develop it into a working methodology for history of political thought in the early 1970s, he made those politics explicit, as we have seen. It is perhaps for this reason that contextual historians of political thought are less invested in 'Meaning and Understanding', specifically, than are their critics. Another reply might be to point out that this objection, insofar as it is an objection relative to history of international law, implicitly assumes that such history is a kind of intellectual history; but that is precisely one of the things in question.[17] Finally, and this leads to the second point of my response, it may be true that some intellectual historians do indeed see the contextual principle as per se definitive of a historical approach to meaning. Nevertheless, the collapse of 'historical' into 'contextual' is not a necessary consequence of this way of thinking and not all historians of political thought either must, or do, endorse it.

Here it is necessary to be quite precise about the work that contextual parameters are doing in this kind of history. They provide, as I have suggested, explanatory traction on a very specific phenomenon, and it is this traction that allows 'context' to be weaponised against other kinds of meaning and other kinds of history. Contextual explanation, or making *plain*, however, is not the same thing as contextual interpretation, or making *sense*. Context might make plain the character of an act, but it is not enough to make sense of it, historically speaking. To do so requires a further element of interpretation, a creative act of making sense which necessarily breaks the bounds of time and place as it involves a different kind of meaning: meaning as in historical sense, or significance within a story. What the contextual historian of political thought is aiming for is to bridge over between these two kinds of meaning. Crucially, however, this second kind of meaning is not simply layered on top of the first like icing on a cake. The two are mutually involved, and it is in the different ways of handling that relationship that the differing interpretative possibilities of contextual history of political thought lie. I explore those possibilities more fully in the next two sections. For the moment, the important point is that in whatever way a contextual historian constructs the relationship between the two kinds of meaning, the materials for that construction do not come from the contextual principle alone.

To understand why, we need to see that the speech act, so central to this methodology and to the definition of 'context', in fact lies in an ambivalent position at the intersection of the twin historiographical poles of speaker and language. It points in both directions simultaneously without being fully

---

[17] Benton, 'Beyond Anachronism', at 24.

joined up either way. Making sense of the act involves closing the gap with one or other of the poles in ways that are not dictated by the approach but must be independently supplied by the historian. Consider on the one hand the gap between the speech act and the speaker, or the difference between writing 'the politics of republishing *Leviathan*', as I just did, and 'the politics of the republished *Leviathan*'.[18] You might be able to establish that a certain phrase had a certain meaning x, in the sense of illocutionary force or speech act, in a certain discursive context (by looking at contemporary dictionaries, for example, coupled with other contemporary accounts). You might even be able to say it was a fact. But you could never say it was a fact that, in saying that phrase in such a context, a certain person meant x. Meaning in this sense is never a simple precipitate of discursive context but always an interpretative move on the part of the historian. It involves contextual meaning, insofar as that can be established by *re*constructing the discursive context, but also a range of other features of the historical situation that the historian has picked out as salient. And that kind of salience is governed not by the context, but by the story she seeks to tell, which in turn is governed by her broader historical and political commitments. The same is true, *mutatis mutandis*, with closing the gap between the speech act and the other pole of the method, that of language. To fold a contingent speech act into a larger-scale history of political discourse requires structuring motifs (such as evolution, revolution, teleology, coincidence) that again import the historian's broader historical and political commitments. In either case, historical meaning escapes the tight parameters of contextual explanation, as the shape of the story pulls the speech act into its own shape.

In what follows I try to put these two main points, about political meaning and about historical meaning, together, by sketching two interpretative directions in which contextual history of political thought can be taken. It is not my intention here to construct another polarity, to try to force historians into one corner or another. My own commitments will inevitably emerge (that is of the essence of what I am saying), but there is a spectrum of available interpretative choices, and most historians of political thought would position themselves coherently somewhere between the extremes. Nevertheless, this rough and necessarily oversimplifying contrast may serve to bring out the further commitments involved in writing the history of political thought that are not contained in the bare principle of 'meaning in context'. These are to do with the nature of politics, in the first instance, but behind them lie deeper

---

[18] The gap is identified in Tully, 'The Pen Is a Mighty Sword', at 12.

commitments on the nature of power, of agency, indeed of reality itself. Accordingly, they bring back into play the relationship between history and philosophy with which we originally began, and which has since been rather lost in the mêlée. With each of them, I consider the place of law within their differing co-constructions of history and politics, and therefore their implications for the relationship – and for renewed dialogue – between history of political thought and history of international law.

1.3 HISTORY OF POLITICAL THOUGHT AND THE POLITICS OF POWER

One way into the difference I have in mind is by thinking about how different historians of political thought cast the relationship between the discursive and the non-discursive. In the historiographical terms that I introduced at the start of this chapter, the immediate 'outside' of history of political thought – what it immediately refers to – is historical language or discourse. That, however, involves a further 'outside', that of the non-discursive worlds in which these languages, and the speech acts within them, have their home. (They don't just float around in undifferentiated space and time.) We have to do, therefore, with a dual construction of an 'outside' – the outside of discourse in the past and the outside of the historian's story in the present. This is the co-construction of the historical and the political with which we are concerned.

To go back, then, to the picture of political languages we were sketching in the previous section, we saw that in the background to the discursive world lie a plethora of non-discursive phenomena. There are institutional sites of political discourse such as palaces and parliaments, and beyond them further sites of socioculturally authoritative discourse such as universities or other institutions of scholarship, places of worship and courts of law. There is also an endless variety of other social and cultural forms in which people produce and consume political meaning, newspapers, letters, cafés, public squares, etc. The explanatory and interpretative salience which these non-discursive aspects are given in particular cases differs from historian to historian along broadly the same lines as in all intellectual history. But history of political thought differs from other kinds of intellectual history, as we have seen, because it must take a decision on what counts as political. One way of taking that decision, associated with the position known as 'political realism', is to hold that politics is essentially about power. In other words, the original dual sense of 'political', on which all historians of political thought might agree, should be construed specifically as speech that is both about power and involved in its operation. It is power that constitutes the crucial reality of politics, the 'outside' of political discourse. Political thought that is not about power is simply not political, nor is its history properly the history of political thought.

The bare assertion that politics is about power begs the question, of course, of what exactly is power, and how does it operate. It is the element of extra-discursive, therefore, that specifies the understanding of power we are talking about here: violence, or the use of force. This does not mean that political power, on this construction, reduces to violence or force. It is possible to distinguish power and violence, conceptually speaking, in any context. Political power, especially, must establish its authority, or the power to command voluntary compliance, and that involves legitimacy and legitimation (in the Weberian sense). Nevertheless, such authority must be enforceable, or it is not authority in the relevant, political sense. In the final analysis, then, it is the threat of force or violence (and the credible command of such force) that is the central characteristic of political power as opposed to any other kind of power.[19] Behind the definitional primacy of the threat of force to politics lies an avowedly Hobbesian picture of the realities of human psychology, human action and human conflict, and likewise a broadly Hobbesian view of the state as a solution to that conflict by constituting a 'common power, to keep us all in awe', in Hobbes's phrase. It follows that the primary arena of politics is the state, on a distinctively modern understanding of it. International politics is a conceptually secondary form, however important, historically speaking, that arena may become, and however much it may impact back upon domestic politics such that the two become effectively inseparable.

As a solution to a real problem, the state is both a timebound and a local, or in other words a historical, phenomenon. In this way, political realism co-opts history to politics, and here is where it appeals to contextual history of political thought as an approach to political discourse. If we compare the realist vision with Skinner's original Weberian impulse as described above, we can see that there are clear continuities. But there are differences, too. Realism represents a more agent-centred model of politics. Politics is the field of action, and power is pulled into agency, be it of individuals or political institutions or

---

[19] See, classically, the account of 'real politics' in Raymond Geuss, *Philosophy and Real Politics* (Princeton: Princeton University Press, 2008), and before that *History and Illusion in Politics* (Cambridge: Cambridge University Press, 2001), esp. 26–8 and 21–8 respectively on the subject of power. For an excellent discussion of the political realist position, see Michael Goodhart, *Injustice: Political Theory for the Real World* (Oxford: Oxford University Press, 2018), esp. chs. 1 and 3. I am grateful to Duncan Bell for his pointer to this work.

other bodies such as corporations.[20] Skinner was interested in political action, of course; his appeal to the concept of a speech act makes no sense otherwise. But he was also interested in legitimating language as a phenomenon that constrains as much as enables agency within a shared normative horizon. Realism can, somewhat uneasily, accommodate a broader, social sense of legitimation through an appeal to a collective psychology of belief. But it also wants to keep a narrower understanding of ideology which is closer to the standard twentieth-century use of the term. Ideology is a kind of political illusion, 'a set of beliefs, attitudes, preferences that are distorted as a result of the operation of specific relations of power', distorted (characteristically) in the sense of presenting such beliefs as connected with universal interests when in fact they serve particular interests. Political philosophy can then either critically reveal that distortion, by exposing its relation to power ('critical realism'), or itself be ideological in the same sense.[21]

Political realism stands at one extreme of the interpretative possibilities offered by the basic conceptual architecture of speech acts, and it has a series of consequences for historiography. Not all historians of political thought sympathetic to this understanding of politics would endorse all the premises of the philosophical position. In particular, most would retain a much stronger role for a political public and for the reception of political discourse. Nevertheless, an appeal to politics in a broadly realist vein supplies one possible mode of writing the history of political thought, one that is likewise strongly agent-centred in its approach. It has a very firm historical voice – a strong 'outside' in the concrete and documented phenomena of political speech and political action, to which it can stably refer – giving it continuity with the classic techniques of historical writing in all fields of history. It offers a clear way of joining up the speech act with the actor in the pursuit of power, but is equally sensitive to the multiple linguistic and political failures of such attempts. It can, moreover, go beyond the specific speech act to analyse an entire political language, because its 'outside' in political action as an exercise of power allows it to conceive both in essentially the same way. Such an exercise of power could be very tightly defined in spatiotemporal terms – a specific political act like suppressing a riot or devaluing the coinage – but it could also be defined much more loosely, such as British empire in Africa, say. Likewise, the agent can be scaled up from an individual or a group of individuals to a state or a group of states ('the colonial powers', for example).

[20] For the field of action, see Geuss, *Philosophy and Real Politics*, 11, 25 ('To think politically is to think about agency, power and interests').
[21] Ibid., 34–6 for legitimation; 50–5 for ideology, quotation at 52.

Like all history of political thought, this interpretative approach has no room for the universal (in the sense of extra-historical and extra-political) truth of the expressions it studies. But political realism does have a distinctive attitude of 'seeing through' such truth claims, especially moral and religious universals. While such ideals can be pulled into real politics through an appeal to psychological motivation, taken at 'face value' they are yet further illusions that cloud a correct perception of reality.[22] Turning from philosophy to history, this in turn supplies an effective historiographical trope, that of exposure – a bringing to light, an unmasking, of the ideological slant of works that may or may not, on the face of it, look 'political' in content. The corollary of constructing the 'outside' of language in this way is to position the historian, in the present, precisely as an outsider, a critical observer or reporter. The literary form of the exposé is itself a political form, linking the exposé of past and present. The historian does not herself engage in moral condemnation, condemning the colonial powers, say, according to some universal standard of justice – or, if she does, she betrays the principles of the approach. Rather, the historian's exposé must stand for itself as a political speech act in the present. In this way, a realist history of political thought must be irreducibly political, not just in its object, but as history. The politics of both are mutually implicated.

What are the consequences of this specific co-construction of history and politics for law? A broadly realist construction of politics sees law as an act of sovereign power and the primary instrument of political government. The central case of law is therefore the domestic law of the sovereign state, just as it is the focal arena of politics. Judicial interpretation of statute is also law, if that capacity is sanctioned by the constitution as an order of sovereignty; likewise, international treaties or other forms of international law. Law in its formal aspect as an act of sovereign power is not political in the sense of ideological, and to that extent a distinction between law and politics exists. Nevertheless, legislation is inescapably political in content by the very fact that it is the primary instrument of policy, sanctioned by the state but made by those in government, and the historian of political thought will accordingly seek to connect specific pieces of legislation with the ideology of the governing party or regime. As for works of jurisprudence and legal scholarship, including legal history, any such legal discourse that is not formally law is open to being read for ideology, that is, not as law but for what it is politically trying to legitimate. For all this, however, realism cannot entirely instrumentalise law in relation to

---

[22] Ibid., 10–11.

politics, and needs to supplement the concept of politics with that of the political.[23] Law presumes legitimate authority, but it is also one of the conditions of such legitimacy, because it is part of what makes public power different from the exercise of violence in a private capacity. Any state must establish that difference, and it does so, in part, by law. In other words, political power uses law as an instrument, but in that very use is simultaneously captured by law as something that cannot be reduced to just another exercise of political power. Nevertheless, this way of thinking must hold that the terms of that capture are themselves political. There is nothing outside the political that will independently ground the distinction between law and politics.

This conception of the autonomy of the political has a long history, and there is an equally long history of opposition from those who believe that law does not reduce to the political in this way. This includes not only lawyers and legal theorists, working from within law, but moral and religious philosophers who base the legitimacy of law on transcendental grounds, for example the law of God or natural law. But history of political thought in this vein, as we have seen, is strenuously opposed to any idea that universal and transtemporal religious or moral norms or principles govern the legitimacy of politics. It follows that any historical (and indeed contemporary) articulation of or appeal to religious law or moral law *in the context of politics* is purely ideological. This has nothing to do with sincerity of belief, which is outside the political arena. People may perfectly well be sincere in their belief when they say, for example, that something belongs to natural law. But in the political arena, to say that something is natural is irreducibly political. The same will equally be true of appeals to moral norms or secular ideals, for example the idea of inalienable human rights.

To sum up so far, then, a broadly realist style of history of political thought can provide a powerful analysis of the politics of discourse. It is perhaps most at home in tightly-defined modern domestic political contexts, but it can also extend to both international and imperial contexts – at least as seen from the centre out, or to the extent that empire is politically challenged from the colonies and former colonies in the same sense of 'political'. Indeed, the modern history of empire is in some ways a perfect space for the analysis of how discursive legitimation in this form operates. Its potential to unmask the ideological bent of imperial legislation gives it a powerful critical edge, in potential synergy with the aims of critical legal scholarship within the global frame of imperial politics. No one can deny, surely, that law is at least to some

---

[23] I am indebted to Martin Loughlin, *Political Jurisprudence* (Oxford: Oxford University Press, 2017), 'Introduction', for the distinction between politics and the political as key to handling law within a strongly realist, state-centric construction of politics.

degree an instrument of policy, and that unmasking its political instrumentality is a very effective way of undercutting law's implicit claim to be beyond politics. Moreover, for a long period of its history the main form of international law was natural jurisprudence in one form or another, natural law being, as we have seen, a prime candidate for ideological exposure. But if history of international law adopts the same 'outside' of power, does that collapse critical history of international law into history of political thought? Can a strictly legal analysis capture ideological slant?

That question can be posed from the text end, too, as we did at the start. Does a piece of early modern natural jurisprudence, analysed as an ideological justification of European imperial practices, lose its nature as *law* under that analysis? A historian of political thought with an uncompromisingly realist viewpoint might be tempted to say yes. Grotius's *The Law of War and Peace*, for example, may *call* itself law, may use legal language and appeal to legal principles, but it's not *really* law. It just positions itself as such for its own political purposes. Such a response, however, is guaranteed to make historians of international law bridle. Who is the historian of political thought to say what is law and what is not? In what follows, then, I outline an alternative approach which is potentially more accommodating to a legal perspective on the texts that it studies.

1.4 HISTORY OF POLITICAL THOUGHT AND THE HISTORY OF THE POLITICAL

For all its critical drive, the extreme realist inflection of Skinnerian contextualism comes at some cost, both in terms of history and in terms of philosophy. It is invested in a Hobbesian (or 'Hobbesian', since its construction of Hobbes and of politics imply each other) vision of politics as, in some sense, *true* rather than ideological; and, for all its appeal to history, it cannot historically support that distinction. It excludes from political thought all types of thought that deny its premises, relegating them instead to a soft kind of philosophical moralism inadequate to cope with the hard realities of power. But by pushing all universal normative statements into illusion of some kind, whether ideological distortion or moral idealism, it backs both political thought and history into a corner. It leaves no room for the possibility that the moral *is* political, is 'real', and has a history as such.[24] Instead, history of

---

[24] For these concerns from the point of view of political theory, see Goodhart, *Injustice*, ch. 3, and Bonnie Honig and Marc Stears, 'The New Realism: From Modus Vivendi to Justice', in Jonathan Floyd and Marc Stears (eds.), *Political Philosophy versus History? Contextualism and*

political thought must accept the realist premises not merely on pain of ceasing to be political, but of ceasing to be history at all.

The enlistment of contextual history of political thought to drive a wedge between history and politics on the one hand, and a certain kind of philosophy on the other, is interestingly paralleled elsewhere in intellectual history, and extended to address the history of international law.[25] In both cases, however, it involves importing premises which are not contained in the bare principle of 'meaning in context' and which not all historians of political thought share. When it comes to political realism, they may quite well agree that certain kinds of contemporary political philosophy represent a form of moral pseudo-legislation to be avoided. But some of them think that to accept the realist premises is to lose rather than to gain critical purchase: at worst, simply to buy into the ideology of the modern state; at best, to write a form of history inadequate to handle pre-modern, non-Western and non-state-centric forms of political life and discourse. The strong 'outside' of both history and politics, on this model, disenfranchises from both history and politics those for whom the 'inside' is as real as the outside, particularly those whose forms of politics have their legitimacy inside sacred narrative or poetry.[26] A history of political thought that is genuinely global, therefore, needs to drop its conceptual investment in political modernity.

Accordingly, another approach to the history of political thought starts from the same basic conceptual architecture. Unlike the first, however, it takes no *prior* decision on the adjective 'political' that qualifies this 'thought' as an object of history, except that it will very broadly concern the way that human

---

Real Politics in Contemporary Political Thought (Cambridge: Cambridge University Press, 2011), 177–205.

[25] Ian Hunter's contrast between the political and the historical on the one hand, and the metaphysical on the other, goes back to *Rival Enlightenments: Civil and Metaphysical Philosophy in Early Modern Germany* (Cambridge: Cambridge University Press, 2001) and is deployed with reference to contextualism in his 'The Contest over Context in Intellectual History', *History and Theory* 58(2) (2019). Relevant to the history of international law, see for example Ian Hunter, 'Global Justice and Regional Metaphysics', in Shaunnagh Dorsett and Ian Hunter (eds.), *Law and Politics in British Colonial Thought* (London: Palgrave, 2010). Hunter is not a political realist, but the way in which he links philosophical productions to an intellectual and professional *habitus* constitutes a distinctive interpretative lens with its own consequences for reading universals.

[26] See, for example, Michael Brett on Fatimid eschatology in *The Rise of the Fatimids* (Leiden: Brill, 2001), e.g. at 127 ('the token value of the names ... was more important than the existence of such persons in the flesh. The letter of the Mahdi to the Yemen marks the beginning of the attempt to reduce the one to the other'), or Sheldon Pollock's thoughts on Sanskrit kāvya in 'Cosmopolitanism, Vernacularism and Premodernity', in Samuel Moyn and Andrew Sartori (eds.), *Global Intellectual History* (New York: Columbia University Press, 2013), 59–80.

beings live and the norms that govern that life. This very loose and open-ended field cannot be further characterised from the outside, because none of its elements is a transhistorical constant, down to the very conception of a human being – indeed of reality itself – and a fortiori of politics. This kind of history of political thought, therefore, needs to move away from politics towards the political, just as we saw the realist position must do when approaching the phenomenon of law. By contrast, however, the 'outside' of political discourse on this second approach is not power but a form of life, which folds the political within it. In consequence, the historian needs to take what we might call an 'inside out' approach to its intellectual construction, and to open a dialogue with other forms of history, social and cultural, as well as cognate fields such as literature, anthropology and religion, none of which can acquiesce in the historical 'reality' proposed by political realism. That does not mean abandoning all historical distance or critical purchase. To adopt a perspective internal to an intellectual construction is not to buy into a truth-claim which depends precisely on the premise that it is *not* an intellectual construction, but really and truly the law of nature, or the word of God, or whatever.

To think about the history of the political in this way means, broadly speaking, shifting the emphasis from the political speaker or actor towards the other historiographical pole of language.[27] The potential for that move is already contained within the original Skinnerian model of legitimation, in which the terms of shared normative language both enable and constrain linguistic agency. Hence arises Skinner's characteristic portrayal of the strong speech actor as an innovator, not a revolutionary, and the picture of contingent but ultimately far-reaching conceptual change that results from successive acts of innovation.[28] It remains true, however, that it appeals to a sharp sense of conflictual politics as what drives linguistic innovation, which is why it can be pushed towards political realism. But its distinctive historiographical tension can be relaxed in the other direction, too, towards a history of political languages or ways of talking. These provide a different kind of legitimation, or simultaneous normative enablement and constraint, at the level of broader culture and society. Different, because the shift of scale means that a political

---

[27] See Sudipta Kaviraj, 'On the Historicity of "the Political": *Rajaniti* and Politics in Modern Indian Thought', in Michael Freeden and Andrew Vincent (eds.), *Comparative Political Thought: Theorizing Practices* (London: Routledge, 2012), 24–39, for the engagement with the concept of a language in understanding the distinctive shifts and contours of the Indian 'political'.

[28] For a completely new reading of innovation in this sense, see Joel Isaac's contribution to this volume (Chapter 12).

language cannot be the straight analogue of the speech act. A political language does not 'have' a context, a clearly distinct historical 'outside' in that sense; rather it is implicated in its own context, part of its own outside. It is both situated within a historical world and simultaneously involved in creating that world, thus creating, in part, its own historical parameters or its own time.[29] It is worth remarking here that the time of a political language is typically – at least in a modern European or more broadly Western context – neither the *courte* nor the *longue durée*, but that most elusive third element of Braudel's tableau, the *moyenne durée*. One way of thinking about the history of such languages is as a way of understanding the rhythm or tempo of the historical *moyenne durée*.

There are affinities here with Michel Foucault's understanding of discursive power, the way in which discourse constructs its own subjects and objects.[30] Foucault's analysis helps us to see that in moving towards the pole of language we have not stopped talking about power, but it is power in a different sense: not the violence of putting someone in a straitjacket, or the authority to enforce it, but the power that constructs a madman who needs to be put in a straitjacket and the violence as therapy. Ultimately, it is the power of discourse to create its own reality, and consequently its own truth. It is of the essence of Foucault's position that that construction has a history, but it is not one that can be written with the techniques of classical historiography. It is not that there is no 'out there' for the historian at all – as Paul Veyne pointed out in his classic essay on the subject, this form of analysis is in a way ultrapositivist in its approach to discursive data.[31] But it is an 'out there', not an outside of a story, because the words are opaque. They are not the trace of a past reality, the story of which can be told in the present; they are not storied in any way, not a 'clue', not 'evidence', not anything that points beyond themselves. They have no historical meaning in that sense. To give them this sort of meaning involves supplying subjects and objects from outside the discourse – in Veyne's self-critique of his study of power in imperial Rome, 'governors' and

---

[29] The history of concepts, *Begriffsgeschichte*, belongs broadly within this kind of approach, and shares (on some understandings) a similar sense of modulation between inside and outside and the consequent impact on temporality.

[30] The author who has done most work on the interface between Foucault and history of political thought is James Tully; see, for example, his Foucauldian reading of Locke in *An Approach to Political Philosophy: Locke in Contexts* (Cambridge: Cambridge University Press, 1993), 179–241, and *Public Philosophy in a New Key*, 2 vols. (Cambridge: Cambridge University Press, 2008), Vol. 1, pt. I.

[31] See Paul Veyne, 'Foucault revolutionne l'histoire', in Veyne, *Comment on écrit l'histoire?* (Paris: Seuil, 1979), 347–85, here at 355–8.

'governed' – and using them to interpret talk of bread and circuses or anything else. But the transhistorical reality of governor and governed is precisely what is being denied. Rather, we have to focus on the discourse as itself, the irreducible specificity of the way in which a certain discourse at a certain time constructs the king as a shepherd and the people as his flock, for example. The result is a form of Nietzschean genealogy, which stands in some sense at the opposite end of the spectrum from critical realism, but which loops back upon it in its critical enterprise. It is likewise a kind of unmasking, and likewise an essentially political form of writing.

The late Foucault characterised his genealogical approach as 'having something to do with philosophy' in the sense of 'a politics of truth' (*une politique de la verité*), 'since', he said, 'I see no other definition of philosophy, if not this'.[32] As we saw at the beginning, the dialogue between history and philosophy has been key to the evolution of history of political thought as a discipline, and the shift towards the pole of language does indeed make space for mutual exchange between the two, resulting in a more philosophical style of history of political thought and a more historical style of philosophy. But, just as we saw earlier with the opposite end of the spectrum, most historians of political thought sympathetic to this way of thinking – and I am one, as will by now be obvious – do not, in the end, write Foucauldian genealogy or Foucauldian philosophy. They may want to preserve the insight that the construction of the political is a construction of power, that there is some violence, somewhere, that it normalises; likewise, that this construction implicates the historian in her own analysis of it, putting her in a relationship with power, be that one of resistance or complicity or (almost inevitably) both. But the governing trope of exposure, whether in a critical realist or a Foucauldian vein, is historically limiting however powerful it may be as critique. There needs to be some space for history (and for philosophy) as poietic, creative of new meaning – new stories, new worlds – and that kind of newness is created within, against, and through, old meaning or meaning in the past.[33]

History of political thought in this vein, therefore, holds on to 'meaning in context' as an essential precondition for its historical enterprise. Although it is in general a less agent-centred approach, it may involve drawing contextual parameters for a specific speech act and using independent information about

---

[32] Michel Foucault, *Sécurité, territoire, population* (Paris: Seuil/Gallimard, 2004), 4.
[33] I make this point about *poiesis* and *making* sense in 'What Is Intellectual History Now?', 123. But for 'newness' here I am indebted to Homi Bhabha, 'How Newness Enters the World: Postmodern Space, Postcolonial Times and the Trials of Cultural Translation', in his *The Location of Culture* (London: Routledge, 1994), 303–37, himself indebted to Salman Rushdie in *The Satanic Verses*.

a specific actor in order to make historical sense of it. On this understanding, however, the time and place of the text – the context, the 'outside' that gives it historical meaning – is itself inside the time and place of language, which does not have a context or an outside in the same sense. It is not that there is no outside at all: political languages are embedded in social and cultural worlds that are made in multiple ways, not just with words, and they are inflected by these worlds just as they inflect them in turn. Nevertheless, the modulation between the inside and outside of language in the past destabilises the outside of the historian's story in the present, who cannot get independent historical distance on either the one or the other, but has to work between the two, in some sense from the inside out. The result is a voice not entirely discontinuous with the voice of the classical *histor*, but not entirely continuous either, as it inserts itself into the time of its own history. From the perspective of traditional historiography, it may simply look historically unstable. But is also possible to see the history of political language as a space for new experiments in historical writing, creating new kinds of historical voice or historiographical form. One might think here of the later work of John Pocock, a history written from inside the frame of Gibbon's *Decline and Fall* like a hermit crab inside a shell.[34]

Finally, and in relation to creative possibilities for philosophy, the shift towards the pole of language impacts in turn upon the position of the speech act. Just as the instrumental model pulls the act towards the actor and the language towards the act, so to pull the approach in the opposite direction has the effect of freeing up the speech act from the actor. It is not pulled out of history altogether and then jammed back in, as in some older histories of philosophy. It remains politically ac*ti*ve. But it can exist within language as an element of a historical construction of the political without being related to the immediate politics of action, even if what we know of the actor can be folded effectively into a broader story about language. In this way, the time of language provides the space for an intrinsically historical philosophy as well as a more philosophical history of political thought. 'Our language', wrote Wittgenstein, 'can be seen as an ancient city: a maze of little streets and squares, of old and new houses, and of houses with additions from various periods'.[35] To explore the streets and squares of past political language is to reinhabit the city of language in the present, to create a new way of living in it.

---

[34] J.G.A. Pocock, *Barbarism and Religion*, 6 vols. (Cambridge: Cambridge University Press, 1999–2015).
[35] Wittgenstein, *Philosophical Investigations*, § 18.

On one definition, that just is to do philosophy.³⁶ But whatever the newness that the philosopher or historian brings into the world, its creation is and must be political, just as in all history of political thought. To translate meaning from the past into the city of the present cannot be anything else.

How does all this affect the way history of political thought views law? First, as we have seen, this iteration does not see the state as the privileged instance of the political, and international politics a secondary form shaped around the space of the state. Rather, the political is equally but differently under construction in all times and places, and equally within and between different groups of people and different geographical areas. Law belongs within the political in this broad sense, or within the city as I can now call it, in my own historical translation of early modern political language.³⁷ But there is no prior commitment to any specific relationship between law and politics, nor to any particular kind of law as the privileged instance of law, nor to any particular field of its operation. At a more fundamental level, the way in which it frees up the speech act gives more space for law to be law. As we saw, political realism does not, in fact, collapse law into politics, giving it space to breathe within the political. But because that space is structured by sovereign power, that is, the space of the state, it is both predetermined and limited. Political languages, however, exist both conceptually and historically in a broader social and cultural world, in which law also operates and which it too serves to create. For the historian of political thought, tracking the contours of law, a discourse that penetrates every aspect of society, is one way of showing how the construction of the political implicates and is implicated in broader patterns of social, cultural and economic life.³⁸ In principle, therefore, this kind of approach to history of political thought is more open to the ways in which lawyers themselves think about law, as a very broad field involving multiple forms of discursive production. This is perhaps even more true of international law with its even greater multiplicity of different forms, registers and sources. This approach is also sympathetic to the ways in which international lawyers reach out to other disciplines, such as anthropology, to understand how that kind of law is constituted. From the point of view of a history of political

---

[36] See Richard Rorty, *Contingency, Irony and Solidarity* (Cambridge: Cambridge University Press, 1989). Compare Bhabha's reference to Rorty in 'How Newness Enters the World', at 336.
[37] See Annabel Brett, *Changes of State: Nature and the Limits of the City in Early Modern Natural Law* (Princeton: Princeton University Press, 2011).
[38] See the role of law in Anna Becker's recent study of gender and the construction of the political, *Gendering the Renaissance Commonwealth* (Cambridge: Cambridge University Press, 2020), and her contribution to this volume (Chapter 13).

thought written from the inside out, law is not only a central part of that inside, but presents itself intriguingly as another kind of 'inside' in itself.

If we look back from this perspective to histories of political thought written in the second half of the twentieth century, what impresses in practice is the enormous amount of attention devoted to law. In the European and North Atlantic world that was both home to this history in professional terms and its principal object of study, developments in legal discourse play a crucial role in the story of political conceptual change. The classic shape of that story is, in one way or another, the advent of political modernity, a story that begins in the European middle ages and ends at some point later in European or more broadly Western time, depending on how the historian has constructed the modern. Whatever the construction, modernity includes the modern state. But, while the shape of the story pulls the analysis of political discourse in that direction, two key features of this kind of history of political thought act as a brake. One is the commitment to historical contingency that marks the liberal historiographical voice. The metaphor of 'foundations' is used simultaneously to tie medieval and renaissance political discourse into a forward-looking story and at the same time to set it free. It is there in Quentin Skinner's *The Foundations of Modern Political Thought* – Skinner was subsequently rather ambivalent about its teleological overtones – but also in Donald Kelley's *Foundations of Modern Historical Scholarship* and Brian Tierney's *Foundations of the Conciliar Theory*, all classics of the genre.[39] Just as with all historiographical choices, the metaphor is reflexive on the historian herself (mostly himself at this time, it must be said). To set the discourse free from the story simultaneously frees the historian in the same way, creating the historical distance key to the voice of the classical *histor*, holding the line between the inside and the outside of the story.

If we study these works carefully, and the traditions of scholarship that lie behind them, we see that a second countervailing pull on the narrative of modernity and the modern state is precisely law, and it is directly related to the first. Law *has* to be set free from the story, because it cannot be reduced to the political. The law of the European world in question, the law that plays such a key role in creating this European *moyenne durée*, is not primarily the law of

---

[39] Quentin Skinner, *The Foundations of Modern Political Thought*, 2 vols. (Cambridge: Cambridge University Press, 1978); Donald Kelley, *Foundations of Modern Historical Scholarship: Language, Law and History in the French Renaissance* (New York: Columbia University Press, 1970); Brian Tierney, *Foundations of the Conciliar Theory: The Contribution of the Canonists from Gratian to the Great Schism* (New York: Cambridge University Press, 1955, 2nd ed., Leiden: Brill, 1998). This latter is a history of the church and its law, but on this understanding it is no less history of political thought for that.

kings or commonwealths; it is an intricate web of civil law, common law, feudal law and canon law, local law and custom. In the historiography with which we are concerned, these are understood equally as fields of legal scholarship and as potential arsenals of ideological weaponry. Both the historic pluralism of European law in this period, and the non-reductive handling of it (as both law and politics, equally), contribute to a history of political thought that is undoubtedly orientated towards Western modernity, but not conceptually invested in the modern state as the focal meaning of politics. It is, in good part, the attention to law which means that this historiography takes medieval political thought seriously, and sees medieval forms of government, including the church, as political on their own terms, without the Schmittian appeal to political theology that has become so popular as the way to integrate medieval political thought into the story of modernity. Rather, political discourse borrows from legal discourse and the same is true in reverse, as both lawyers and political philosophers struggle to create the normative language within which to legitimate both specific visions of law and politics and, simultaneously, the very fields of law and politics themselves.

Part of that struggle is the way in which law constructs its own history, which is also a classic theme of the historiography in question.[40] But there is a complexity involved because law, at least in the specific historical *moyenne durée* with which we are concerned here, does not always create its past in the same way. It does so in one way through its system of internal reference, the way in which it refers to the past of law in order to make law in the present. In so doing, it pulls things that were once outside law – the political and legal institutions of ancient Rome, in the case of civil law – inside law. Detached from its original reference, the city of Rome runs up and down the ladder of Roman legal time that stretches from the Roman past to the European present.[41] In creating its own time, law creates its own world, and its history

---

[40] It is part of the 'history of history' approach associated particularly with John Pocock. See his first book, J.G.A. Pocock, *The Ancient Constitution and the Feudal Law* (Cambridge: Cambridge University Press, 1957), and Kelley, *Foundations of Modern Historical Scholarship*, as for n. 39.

[41] I am indebted here to Magnus Ryan's work on the way in which late medieval and Renaissance Roman legal scholarship gradually prised the language of 'city' away from 'the city of Rome', such that it was ultimately not Rome but the city – the *civitas*, what would become the state – that could run up and down the ladders of historical time as a transtemporal legal category. See Magnus Ryan, 'Roman Law in Medieval Political Thought', in David Johnston (ed.), *The Oxford Companion to Roman Law* (Oxford: Oxford University Press 2014), 423–51; Magnus Ryan, 'Historicity and Universality in the Political Thought of the Medieval Roman Lawyers', in John Robertson (ed.), *Political Thought, Time and History* (Cambridge: Cambridge University Press, forthcoming).

is inside that world. For the historian of political thought, that history is nevertheless political, because law's past is not the only past; there is a world outside law which gives political meaning to law's construction of its own history. But that meaning cannot be properly understood if the historian insists on trying to establish the ideological valence in a tight political context of every single legal reference to Rome, for example. In many, indeed in most cases, there will be no such valence. That is not what the law is doing; it's the wrong kind of meaning. Rather, the historian of political thought needs to take legal meaning seriously and work towards political meaning from the inside out.

As well as this, however, historians of political thought are also interested in those cases where law deliberately constructs a past for itself in order to position itself politically in the present. In this same European *moyenne durée*, the most spectacular example of this is probably the political mobilisation of legal antiquarianism in the late sixteenth and early seventeenth centuries. Legal scholars across Europe used the humanist techniques of historical philology deliberately to stop legal meaning running freely up and down the ladder of time. For François Hotman the internal time of Roman law is the ladder up which the tyranny of Rome crawls from the past to the present. It needs to be broken, as an act of both legal and political resistance, by freezing meaning at a certain time and place in the past. That means giving law an outside, a past that is not internal to law, in which legal terms have their true meaning. Political resistance, however, involves constructing that past as not merely historical but normative, in the ancient kingdom of Francogallia. In other words, Hotman's 'contextual' history of law is irreducibly political, just as we have already seen with contemporary contextual history of political thought.[42]

With *Francogallia* we have arrived back much where we left off at the end of the second section, with a work of early modern political jurisprudence. What we can see now, however, is that the either/or between law and politics with which we confronted *The Law of War and Peace* is too crude. Law is also a storymaker, also creates the past, and so the relationship between law and politics must always, in fact, be a three-way relationship between history, politics, and law. As works of legal antiquarianism and natural jurisprudence respectively, *Francogallia* and *The Law of War and Peace* might look like different kinds of legal scholarship, but both equally construct an 'outside' of

---

[42] Hunter, 'The Contest over Context', draws a similar parallel between seventeenth-century constitutional scholarship and modern contextual historiography, but to my mind downplays the politics involved in making an argument about history.

legal meaning, the one in the ancient land of Francogallia and the other in nature. Each of these, equally, provides external interpretative traction on historical legal meaning, although in very different ways. In both cases, the choice and construction of law's outside is irreducibly political, but it is not just a matter of politics. It is a historical, a legal and a political intervention all at the same time, and any historical appreciation of it needs to be able to move around between the inside and outside of all three fields.

1.5 CONCLUSION

The classic twentieth-century historiography of political thought represents a field of complex and non-reductive dialogue between history of political thought and history of law in its multiple forms. But it takes place largely on the ground of one specific European *moyenne durée*, and its governing historiographical metaphors hold the liberal line on historical contingency, and the related historical distance of the historian, in a very delicate balance. In the twenty-first century, that historiographical position has become harder to inhabit comfortably, even with the help of irony, just as has its professional home in Europe and North America. The challenge to Eurocentrism has gathered force, as we saw at the outset, resulting in a new demand for global history, including a global intellectual history. And the related collapse of the liberal consensus has equally challenged the liberal historiographical voice, pressing the question of political investment that it could hold at arm's length. Within history of political thought, the weight of the discipline has simultaneously moved forward in time, away from the medieval, and indeed the early modern, towards the nineteenth and especially the twentieth centuries. All these factors have changed it significantly, giving its international and global turn a distinctly modern temporality and a more marked political edge. Although it is still true that most historians of political thought are somewhere in the middle, there is a detectable tendency for the discipline either to move towards politics or to take a genealogical turn in some form.[43] There is a certain loss of confidence in history as an art which of itself puts the past in relation to the present, generating an apologetics about traditional historical techniques and practices and an enthusiasm for genealogy as apparently the

---

[43] It is worth saying here that genealogy is often quite fluidly understood, not always in a strictly Foucauldian or Nietzschean sense. See, for example, Melissa Lane, 'Doing Our Own Thinking for Ourselves: On Quentin Skinner's Genealogical Turn', *Journal of the History of Ideas* 73(1) (2012), 71–82.

only way of saving the Janus face of history of political thought as a form of political thinking in the present.

If we consider the possibilities for dialogue between history of political thought and history of international law in this new world of the twenty-first century, we have already seen that some of these developments mesh effectively with the concerns of historians of international law. One iteration of the international, and of the global, is indeed modern, a function of the modern state and its imperial reach, modern capital and modern technology. These are major themes both of history of political thought and of critical history of international law alike. The turn to the global has, however, brought with it a renewed interest in the Braudelian *longue durée*, a scale of time whose relationship to modernity is one of the key questions for global history, and a fortiori for global intellectual history.[44] On the one hand it seems to offer the chance to break the back of modernity entirely and write a completely different kind of history, one that is 'postmodern' in an entirely new sense. But on the other, it has no end point but the present, with the risk that its history either begs the question of modernity or becomes a genealogy of the modern in one form or another.

Similar challenges, and similar opportunities, face a *longue durée* history of political thought in a global frame.[45] The historiographical creativity of the dialogue with law in twentieth-century history of political thought suggests, however, an alternative and more oblique way in. Instead of hitting the *longue durée* head on, we might think first about how to conceive the *moyenne durée* in a global frame, which could begin and end in any place or time. Here, the 'inside out' approach of history of political thought to medieval and early modern Europe, with its attention to non-state forms of law as an essential constituent of the political, might be well and truly set free of its ties to Western modernity and in the process transformed. Such a transformation would nevertheless be open, as I have already implied, to intellectual traditions such as scripture or poetry, which tend to be more *longue durée* precisely because of the way in which they pull the outside inside narrative.[46] Either way, there lies the possibility for new experiments in global

---

[44] See Samuel Moyn and Andrew Sartori, 'Approaches to Global Intellectual History', in Moyn and Sartori (eds.), *Global Intellectual History*, 3–30, and the concluding reflections in the same volume by Frederick Cooper ('How Global Do We Want Our Intellectual History to Be?', ibid., 283–94) and Sudipta Kaviraj ('Global Intellectual History: Meanings and Methods', ibid., 295–319).

[45] See David Armitage, *Civil Wars: A History in Ideas* (New Haven: Yale University Press, 2017), introduction, and commentary in *Global Intellectual History* 4(3) (2019), Special Review issue.

[46] See above, nn. 26 and 27, and see Julia McClure's contribution in this volume (Chapter 9).

historiography, both in political thought and in international law. One might think here of Lauren Benton and Lisa Ford's construction of imperial interpolity, situated simultaneously in a global *moyenne durée* and in the 'middle' of empire.[47] We have to be prepared for such experiments to challenge our existing conceptions equally of politics, of law, and of history itself.

Established disciplines such as these tend to construct their outsides in ways that are both binary and ideological. But for an individual historian working within either political thought or international law, managing the inside and the outside of her story is a complex negotiation that cannot be reduced to one thing versus another. As we have seen, the binaries between law and politics, between history and philosophy, and between history and law, are not, in fact binaries, but triadic co-constructions of history, politics and law. And within each of these elements, there are different possible constructions available – different concepts of politics and the political, different kinds of history, different kinds of law. There is no one way in which either a historian of international law, or a historian of political thought, either may or should approach a text like *The Law of War and Peace*. It is the choice of the historian how best to create interpretative synergy between what her text is doing and what she is doing, to make a story that is resonant with meaning, be it legal or political. That does not mean that history of political thought and history of international law, in any form, will simply collapse into each other. The former's interest in political meaning inevitably pulls law out of law and into a story that is not purely of law's own making, however much it may acknowledge that law is also a story maker and a partner in creating the 'outside' of that same story. The conversation between history of political thought and history of international law will continue to have some sharp edges. But the recognition of the mutual implication of history, politics and law gives individual historians room to breathe, and room for the broader conversation to continue.

---

[47] Lauren Benton and Lisa Ford, *Rage for Order: The British Empire and the Origins of International Law, 1800–1850* (Cambridge, MA: Harvard University Press, 2016).

2

The Past according to International Law
A Practice of History and Histories of a Practice

MARTTI KOSKENNIEMI

2.1 INTRODUCTION

Law is an intensely historical practice. From Bodin to Savigny, from the veneration they have felt for the 'ancient constitution' at home to the energy with which they have embraced modernity and progress, lawyers have enlisted history to assist the power of what they have wanted to say. Law is, it sometimes feels (and is often said), precisely about the authority of the past over the present. This is true of international law as well. Working as a diplomat-lawyer, it often seemed to me that the professional service I was expected to render was to operate as the foreign ministry's historical archive. Political decision-makers tended to feel that the situations they were faced with were new and unprecedented. The lawyers were to assist them by showing what 'we' did in analogous cases five, fifteen or fifty years ago. The decision then frequently came about as *'Well, let's do now what we did then'*. There is a definite conservative wisdom in such practice. People have expectations about behaviour, based on the past, and it is often a good idea not to fail them. Indeed, much of (international) legal practice is about trying to figure out what those expectations are. In preparing a case in the International Court of Justice, counsel of the parties spend an inordinate amount of time in the archives so as to find out what agreements, understandings or patterns of behaviour may have emerged. Past facts and texts are collected into some narrative that pretends to authority, at least better authority than the story of the adversary.

All this is obvious and frequently noted. One need not be a card-carrying member of any historical school of jurisprudence to understand why it is useful to examine the past so as to determine what would be the right thing to do *now*. Law is a 'social phenomenon', we like to say, and indicate thereby that it did not suddenly fall from the sky. It is the result of accumulating experience of life in common, a condensation of what we have learned in the course of time. Even in democratic societies (and perhaps especially in them) we do not think that we have to decide our priorities every day anew. We follow rules. To follow (legal) rules, again, is to have internalised a sense that doing what people have generally done is right and that no further explanation – at least no *initial* explanation – is called for. 'I *acted in accordance with the rule*' is sufficient. We do of course often disagree about what the rule is, or how it should be understood. But we rarely question the importance of rules in social life.

To be able to say something about binding legal rules is the heart of the competence of the (international) lawyer. But history is neither the only nor necessarily the predominant way to argue about rules. They may also be debated on deontological or utilitarian grounds, and they may claim to reflect technical or scientific knowledge. The choice of the justifying vocabulary depends on the expectations of the audience. Among international lawyers, as with foreign policy experts and diplomats, historical arguments have traditionally carried much weight. A discourse that speaks about war and peace-making, sovereigns and state power, is almost automatically geared towards historical illustrations even when its point relates to the present.[1] It is a simplistic though not incorrect generalisation that historical arguments have greater pertinence in European legal contexts than in the United States – though again, US lawyers are trained to pay especial regard to what the founding fathers may once have believed. In international law, legal realism, functional jurisprudence and the policy-oriented approach used to propose setting aside rules as mere accumulations of past practice, not to be taken as decisive for determining future behaviour.[2] But the proposed turn from legal to policy conceptualism and its unabashed espousal of US foreign policy goals prevented it from entering mainstream international law. It found instead, a more accommodating audience among international relations scholars. Basic international law has continued to pursue its historical mannerisms in a way

---

[1] For a good example, see Gerry Simpson, *Great Powers and Outlaw States. Unequal Sovereigns in the International Legal Order* (Cambridge: Cambridge University Press, 2004).

[2] The classic is Myres S. McDougal, 'International Law, Power and Policy: A Contemporary Conception', *Recueil des cours* 82 (1953), 133–259. For the argument about Yale School (and policy-orientation generally) as another form of conceptualism, see Hengameh Saberi, 'Yale's Policy Science and International Law: Between Legal Formalism and Policy Conceptualism', in Anne Orford and Florian Hoffmann (eds.), *The Oxford Handbook of the Theory of International Law* (Oxford: Oxford University Press, 2016), 427–51; and for the philosophical origins of the school's pseudo-scientism, see Rián Derrig, *Educating American Modernists. The Origins of the New Haven School* (PhD, EUI Florence 2019).

that has given it a somewhat conservative and Eurocentric orientation, encouraging recent post-colonial critics to choose history as a principal platform to challenge it.[3]

Nevertheless, one need not be a Marxist to feel that '[t]he tradition of all dead generations weighs like a nightmare on the brains of the living'.[4] There have always been international lawyers who have insisted on the need to figure out new ways of thinking and acting so as to 'respond' to the political, economic and technical needs or 'challenges' in the international world.[5] This is part of the cosmopolitan progressivism of the international law profession, present in the field since its inception in the late nineteenth century. In a path-breaking book from 1964, Wolfgang Friedmann drew attention to the great changes that had occurred in international society since the early part of the century that 'must lead to a far-reaching reorientation of our conceptions of the science and study of contemporary international law'.[6] Such progressivism also inspires article 13, paragraph (1)(a), of the UN Charter, that calls for the General Assembly 'to encourage the progressive development of international law and its codification'. If the word 'modernism' has any meaningful scope, it clearly applies to that aspect of the international law profession that is intensely engaged in the reform of international law and institutions as a key aspect of its commitment to international peace and justice. Reform is the life of international institutions, and the rhetoric of constant adjustment of the law in view of the 'needs' or 'requirements' of 'development' or 'globalisation' is everywhere in international law.[7]

New critical studies have often wished to put into question the limitations and direction of reformism, the suggestion that the path to progress is obvious

---

[3] See especially Antony Anghie, *Imperialism, Sovereignty and the Making of International Law* (Cambridge: Cambridge University Press, 2005), and more recently, Rose Parfitt, *The Process of International Legal Reproduction. Inequality, Historiography, Resistance* (Cambridge: Cambridge University Press, 2019).

[4] Karl Marx, *The 18th Brumaire of Louis Bonaparte* (New York: International Publishers, 1963 [1852]), 15.

[5] One thinks often of the Chilean legal activist Alejandro Álvarez (1868–1960) who preached progressive transformation through the first part of the twentieth century. See, e.g., his *Le droit international nouveau dans ses rapports avec la vie actuelle des peuples* (Paris: Pedone, 1959). The still useful analysis of functionalist progressivism in the context of US law, and an overview of its critiques, is Robert Gordon, 'Critical Legal Histories', *Stanford Law Review* 36 (1984), republished in Robert Gordon, *Taming the Past. Essays on Law in History and History in Law* (Cambridge: Cambridge University Press 2017), 220–81.

[6] Wolfgang Friedmann, *The Changing Structure of International Law* (New York: Columbia University Press, 1964), 64.

[7] See further David Kennedy, 'When Renewal Repeats: Thinking against the Box', *New York University Journal of International Law and Politics* 32 (1999–2000), 335–500.

and inevitable, dictated by the natural laws of history itself. For the new histories, the future is not laid out in advance; present law is an outcome of struggle and compromise where alternative paths that once were open were closed as a result of some actors winning, others losing. To examine the origins of a rule or practice is often to demonstrate its contingency, and thereby – perhaps – to loosen its hold on present imagination. History may be used as a way to bring ideas and projects that were once set aside to bear on present law and politics.[8] Recent works on the non-aligned movement, the Bandung conference (1955) and the rise and fall of the New International Economic Order have quite consciously aimed to bring to present memory efforts from two or three generations past that were swept aside by the end of the Cold War and the rise of neoliberalism.[9] The moment for such histories may be especially opportune now that reformist progressivism has entered into political trouble. Consciousness of the blinding and unjust effects of economically drawn globalisation had led to questions and attacks from all sides of the political spectrum, including among many former reformists. At such a moment, turning to history may be helpful in trying to understand what went wrong and what might be worth remembering from pathways that were never followed.

International law is both a reflection of (international) society and something independent of it, a product of past behaviour and a set of normative demands about how we *ought to* behave. I have elsewhere discussed this duality in terms of the tension between 'apology' and 'utopia', the persistent need to think of international law as a concretely verifiable product of the way we have lived in the past but also a normative set of requirements about how we should live in the future.[10] It is neither history nor political morality and its truths cannot be reduced to verities produced within those other fields (though such verities may sometimes be helpful for law, too). To understand law's specificity (including that of international law), it is useful to remember that its intellectual and academic side is deeply connected to its practice, the

---

[8] For a discussion of the tropes and limitations of critical legal histories, see Christopher Tomlins, 'After Critical Legal History: Scope, Scale, Structure', *Annual Review of Law and Social Science* 8 (2012), 31–68.

[9] See Luis Eslava, Michael Fakhri and Vasuki Nesiah (eds.), *Bandung, Global History, and International Law: Critical Pasts and Pending Futures* (Cambridge: Cambridge University Press, 2017); Jochen von Bernstorff and Philipp Dann (eds.), *The Battle for International Law: South–North Perspectives on the Decolonization Era* (Oxford: Oxford University Press 2019); Sundhya Pahuja, *Decolonising International Law: Development, Economic Growth and the Politics of Universality* (Cambridge: Cambridge University Press, 2011).

[10] Martti Koskenniemi, *From Apology to Utopia: The Structure of International Legal Argument* (Reissue with a new Epilogue) (Cambridge: Cambridge University Press, 2005).

professional work undertaken in what Karl Llewellyn once called 'law-jobs'.[11] These are jobs offered by institutions that invite lawyers to produce professionally competent arguments in situations of controversy where people usually have something important at stake. The professional competence that underlies the practical side of law is above all a rhetorical skill that is tested by the persuasiveness of the arguments produced in such institutional contexts. The courtroom is the paradigm case, but professional competence in *international* law is sought after in all kinds of institutions, public administrations, non-governmental organisations, and so on.[12]

There is some useful writing on law as an 'institutional practice' showing that the types of legal argument, including historical argument, vary in accordance with changing institutional biases.[13] An international court dealing with a territorial dispute and a human rights tribunal speak differently. In the former, parties typically argue about demographic, economic and political developments. Old treaties are interpreted and their relevance pondered at length.[14] Human rights discourse is less expressly historical – but there, too, research is conducted on institutional practices and patterns of treaty interpretation. One might assume legislative institutions to be intensely interested in the foreseeable effects of their proposed rules. But when the UN's International Law Commission embarks on a codification project, it will first produce a report on the 'past practice', including the practice of legal theorising about the relevant substance; and rarely, if at all, conducts any studies on the effects of what is being proposed.[15] That is an aspect of the conservatism of that institution that puts it somewhat at odds with the modernist functionalism

---

[11] K.N. Llewellyn, 'The Normative, the Legal and the Law-Jobs: The Problem of Juristic Method', *Yale Law Journal* 49 (1940), 1355–400.

[12] Legal advisers of foreign ministries and international institutions frequently reflect publicly on their careers and practices. A recent example is Andraž Zidar and Jean-Pierre Gauci (eds.), *The Role of Legal Advisers in International Law* (Leiden: Brill, 2017).

[13] See, e.g., Neil MacCormick and Ota Weinberger, *An Institutional Theory of Law: New Approaches to Legal Positivism* (Dordrecht: Springer, 1986).

[14] This may sometimes be done also as part of an expressly post-colonial project. See the impressive Mamadou Hébié, *Souveraineté territoriale par traité. Une étude des accords entre puissances coloniales et entités politiques locales* (Paris: PUF, 2015). The work's argument – that European powers accepted the character of indigenous entities as legal subjects as they encountered them, and that it is the *period's* law and practice that must be held determinative in reading them – is problematic nevertheless. Although it grants these entities the status that Europeans later denied them (thus violating their early commitments), the question is whether what Europeans may have thought or how they had acted should be held as decisive in the first place.

[15] This reflects in part its conservative bias, in part the lack of resources to conduct studies on the foreseeable effects. In any case, the relevant causal links between UN treaties and the social world are very hard to demonstrate.

of UN diplomacy in general. Matters are quite different in such fields as trade, investment or environmental law, intensely focused on the *outcomes* and effects of their treaty processes in which respect they operate in some tension with the world of public international law.[16] But the recent appearance of historical studies also on functionally oriented rule-regimes suggests that they have lost some of their originally revisionist spirit and have become gradually integrated into the ideological world of standard multilateral diplomacy.[17]

Recent histories have sometimes told the story of the discipline of international law itself in a new way. Individual jurists have been situated in their political, academic, professional or national backgrounds. Studies have focused on international law in a particular continent or linguistic area with especial attention to non-European areas and actors.[18] It is easy to understand the attraction of such studies. They avoid dubious and Eurocentric generalisations about international law's historical role as a force for peace and progress, reminding us that international lawyers did not always have similar preferences but wrote sometimes as supporters, sometimes as critics of empire. It is hard to say what effect these histories will have on present law or the world it seeks to regulate. Maybe they do not always even seek such effects. Now that history has become an expanding and widely appreciated part of academic international law the danger exists that it loses its critical edge by limiting its

---

[16] As suggested by the anxious debates in the first decade of the 2000s over the 'fragmentation of international law'. See Gunter Teubner and Andreas Fischer-Lescano, *Regime-Kollisionen. Zur Fragmentierung des globalen Rechts* (Frankfurt: Suhrkamp, 2006); Anne-Charlotte Martineau, *Le débat sur la fragmentation du droit international. Une analyse critique* (Brussels: Bruylant, 2015); and Report by the International Law Commission, 'Fragmentation of International Law: Difficulties Arising from the Diversification and Expansion of International Law', finalised by Martti Koskenniemi, UN Doc. A/CN.4/L.682 (13 April 2006).

[17] Much recent interest has been directed to the history of human rights. See, e.g., Pamela Slotte and Miia Halme-Tuomisaari (eds.), *Revisiting the Origins of Human Rights* (Cambridge: Cambridge University Press, 2015). The origins of international trade law are interestingly discussed in Anne Orford, 'Theorizing Free Trade', in Orford and Hoffmann (eds.), *Oxford Handbook of the Theory of International Law*, 701–37. See also Guy Fiti Sinclair, *To Reform the World. International Organizations and the Making of Modern States* (Oxford: Oxford University Press, 2017).

[18] See, e.g., Arnulf Becker Lorca, *Mestizo International Law: A Global Intellectual History 1845–1933* (Cambridge: Cambridge University Press, 2014); Juan Pablo Scarfi, *The Hidden History of International Law in the Americas. Empire and Legal Networks* (Oxford: Oxford University Press, 2017); Ignacio de la Rasilla del Moral, *In the Shadow of Vitoria: International Law in Spain (1770–1953)* (Leiden: Brill, 2018). See also Martti Koskenniemi, *The Gentle Civilizer of Nations: The Rise and Fall of International Law, 1870–1960* (Cambridge: Cambridge University Press, 2001); Benjamin Coates, *Legalist Empire: International Law and American Foreign Relations in the Early Twentieth Century* (Oxford: Oxford University Press, 2016).

focus to the field's internal divisions and transformations without the ambition to expose law's complicity in the world's injustices.[19] But even if the activist aspect remained, it is not obvious what its effect will be on legal practice or the world. Because definite causalities are so difficult to establish, critical works tend to grapple with the instrumental question through such fuzzy notions as legal 'culture', 'consciousness', 'sensibility' or even 'professional competence'. They acknowledge the co-dependent relationship between legal thinking and practice on the one hand, and the world in which they operate on the other. But they remain, as Tomlins puts it, 'descriptively evocative rather than statements of theory or testable hypotheses'.[20]

One last preliminary point. Through most of international law's professional period (i.e. from the late nineteenth century onwards) textbooks used to convey an image of international legal history as part of the world-history of wars, peace-making and diplomacy, associated with the ways in which European theologians, jurists and philosophers had written on them. The teleological orientation of these histories made them part of the professional consciousness that united international lawyers in the academy with those in practice – Oscar Schachter's famous 'invisible college'.[21] This homogeneity or sense of a joint project no longer exists. The 'international' no longer stands for an obvious set of commitments and the ideological leanings of different rule-regimes are no longer necessarily in harmony. Also the academy has changed. The professor is no longer expected to belong to the same elite from which foreign office professionals are chosen. Possibilities have become available for choosing critical or avant-garde approaches that no longer presume automatic commitment to the priorities of the field.

To make these points more concrete, I will now first turn to examining some situations where international law appears to operate as a 'practice of

---

[19] For critical comments on the conservatism of purely contextual studies, see Anne Orford, 'International Law and the Limits of History', in Wouter Werner, Marieke de Hoon and Alexis Galán (eds.), *The Law of International Lawyers: Reading Martti Koskenniemi* (Cambridge: Cambridge University Press, 2017), 297–320, at 306–13. That danger appears in the most ambitious project of international law publishing, begun at the Max Planck Institute for Legal History under which to this date thirty-eight volumes have been published on various persons, events and processes especially in, though not limited to, the first half of the twentieth century. Consisting mostly of PhD works, the series provides a kaleidoscopic view of the field often from a specifically German point of view: *Studien zur Geschichte des Völkerrechts. Nomos-Verlagsgesellschaft*; list available at www.nomos-shop.de/trefferListe.aspx?action=reihe&reihe=254&rtoc=0.
[20] Tomlins, 'After Critical Legal History', 35.
[21] Oscar Schachter, 'The Invisible College of International Lawyers', *Northwestern University Law Review* 72 (1977–78), 217–26.

history'. Here, history enters competent international legal speech in a variety of reasonably well-known and accepted ways. I will then turn to the history of that practice. There is a kind of double historicism involved where the role of history within a legal culture or consciousness appears itself an aspect of the history of that culture or consciousness. The final section will examine the debates regarding the politics of writing histories of international law today.

2.2 HISTORY WITHIN INTERNATIONAL LAW

It is common to think about the nature of law and legal practice by focusing on cases and courts. This may not capture the centre of every lawyer's professional life, of course, but the properties of law and legal argument may be usefully illuminated by what courts say and do. And as they engage with history, they do this in ways that cannot be framed within the strictures of historiography. Take, for instance, the *Island of Palmas* case (1928) where the sole arbitrator Max Huber declared that 'a juridical fact must be appreciated in the light of the law contemporary with it, and not of the law in force at the time when a dispute in regard to it arises or falls to be settled'.[22] The issue arose in the context of a dispute between the United States and the Netherlands concerning sovereignty on the island of Palmas (Miangas) in the Philippine archipelago that the United States claimed had been part of the Spanish cession to the United States in the Treaty of Paris of 1898. According to the Dutch, the Dutch East India Company had exercised continuous and peaceful authority on the island from at least 1677, possibly even from the Peace of Westphalia. The Spanish were not entitled to dispose of the island. The United States based its claim on Spanish 'discovery' in the sixteenth century.

According to the sole arbitrator the matter was to be decided in light of the law 'contemporary with' the 'juridical fact' of sovereignty. What is that law? In the dictum cited above, the arbitrator excluded the date of the award, the date of signature of the Arbitration Treaty (1925), as well as the moment when the dispute 'arose' (1906) as the first US officer set foot on the island. This left three moments of potential relevance: (1) the acquisition of Spanish sovereignty in the sixteenth century; (2) US succession to Spanish rights in 1898; and (3) the moment of the award, 1928. According to Huber, whatever may have been the legal status of discovery in the sixteenth century, the 'critical date' for the case was the Treaty of Paris (1898), the moment when the United States had purportedly received its right. By that time, discovery was no longer

---

[22] *Island of Palmas case* (4 April 1928), 2 UNRIAA 829 (2006), at 845.

a valid basis for title but had been replaced by the rule of 'effective occupation'. As Huber explained, when there are two successive periods with different legal principles, both prima facie relevant for a case, then:

> a distinction must be made between the creation of rights and the existence of rights. The same principle which subjects the act creative of a right to the law in force at the time the right arises, demands that the existence of the right, in other words its continued manifestation, shall follow the conditions required by the evolution of law.[23]

The so-called intertemporal law is continuously invoked in international practice.[24] It expresses the intense relationship that international law practice has with history from what could be called a 'contextual' view, but, one that makes that context move across time.[25] The first thing it does is to relativise the normative power of the historical origin, the intention of the 'founding fathers'. Whatever the understanding of the Spaniards, the Dutch or the indigenous inhabitants in the sixteenth century, it no longer bound us today. A legal relationship must keep up to date with the changes in the world, even when they (as is almost always the case in international law) do not emerge from legislative enactment but through the elusive process that international lawyers call 'custom'. A sixteenth-century understanding (whatever it was) had lost its force by the late nineteenth century. We can only speculate why Huber did not choose the time of the award (1928) as the critical date. Perhaps he believed that the law in 1928 was the same as it had been thirty years before. Perhaps he actually did not construct his rule historically at all, but believed effective occupation to be the better rule for other reasons. And indeed, alongside the historical point, Huber added what could perhaps be called a functional explanation. 'Effective occupation' was the governing rule because it expressed the idea of *sovereignty as protection*. In a famous and influential statement, he summarised:

> Territorial sovereignty ... involves the exclusive right to display the activities of a State. This right has as corollary a duty: the obligation to protect within the territory the rights of other States, in particular their right to integrity and inviolability in peace and in war, together with the rights which each State may claim for its nationals in foreign territory.[26]

---

[23] Ibid.
[24] In a Resolution of 1975 the Institut de droit international subscribed to the Huber formulation: *Annuaire de l'Institut de droit international* 56 (1975), 536–40.
[25] The move of context across time is discussed in Anne Orford, 'On International Legal Method', *London Review of International Law* 1 (2013), 166–97.
[26] 2 UNRIAA (2006), at 839.

Huber's use of the protection concept framed the dispute in utterly Eurocentric terms.[27] The objects of protection were nationals of other colonial powers that had business on the island. Nothing was said about indigenous inhabitants, though no doubt, had Huber been asked, he would have extended the benefits of 'continuous and peaceful exercise of effective authority' to them as well. But neither they nor the inhabitants of what later became the Philippines played any role in his argument.

Huber's choice of 1898 as the critical date led him to extrapolate from the developments of old customary law and freed him from looking around in 1928. By that time, of course, the League of Nations had been set up, and the first legal recognition of colonised peoples was included in article 22 of the Covenant, which set up the mandates system and described the 'well-being and development' of former colonial territories of Germany and Turkey as a 'sacred trust of civilisation'.[28] This was a novelty, of course, and it was limited to the colonial territories of the defeated powers. But the idea was out, and it would have been possible (though perhaps unrealistic) to expect some recognition of that fact had the critical date chosen been 1928. Because it was not, the nineteenth-century principle of 'effective occupation' that had been introduced in the 1885 Berlin Final Act became the applicable law.[29]

A different reading emerged famously in 1971, at the end of the long line of cases on South Africa's administration of South West Africa. The International Court of Justice, in an advisory ruling concerning the legal status of that territory, formerly a League of Nations mandate, refused to interpret that mandate in view of the ideas prevailing at the time it was concluded (1922). Whatever agreements may have been reached when the mandates system was created had been overtaken by subsequent developments that included provision for non-self-governing territories in the UN Charter as well as the stream of resolutions and UN actions on decolonisation. The Court noted that it was 'mindful' of the 'primary necessity' of interpreting an instrument in view of the intentions of its drafters. Nevertheless, when it came to the characterisation of the mandates as a 'sacred trust of civilisation', it could not remain unaffected

---

[27] 'Protection' was a much-used justification of nineteenth-century imperial law: see, e.g., Lauren Benton, Adam Clulow and Bain Attwood (eds.), *Protection and Empire. A Global History* (Cambridge: Cambridge University Press, 2018) and the still relevant W.R. Johnston, *Sovereignty and Protection, A Study of British Jurisdictional Imperialism in the late Nineteenth Century* (Durham, NC: Duke University Press, 1973).

[28] See Anghie, *Imperialism, Sovereignty and the Making of International Law*, 115–95, and extensively Susan Pedersen, *The Guardians: The League of Nations and the Crisis of Empire* (Oxford: Oxford University Press, 2015).

[29] On effective occupation in the Berlin Final Act, see Koskenniemi, *Gentle Civilizer*, 121–7.

by later developments: 'an international instrument has to be interpreted and applied within the framework of the entire legal system prevailing at the time of the interpretation'.[30]

Here now the critical date was that of the Advisory Opinion itself. Whatever the drafters of the mandate or the Covenant had meant was irrelevant for the present. Instead, the context in which the concept of 'sacred trust' was to be understood was now decolonisation. To the immense relief of the great majority of UN members, the court chose to interpret the relations of South Africa and South West Africa (Namibia) from the perspective of the ideological sensitivities of the present. The decision underwrote the law's effort to respond to social and political change, notwithstanding rules of interpretation designed to uphold legal stability. But the present is no less complex than the past, its normative message no less pointing in varying directions. In a 1986 case concerning a boundary dispute between Burkina Faso and Mali, the proposal had been made that the existing frontier had been drawn by colonial powers in a way that had distorted demographic and economic patterns in the territory. It was suggested in the pleadings that the court might now apply equity (*infra legem*) to correct the injustices created by the colonial border.[31] But the Court refused to do this. Instead, it applied the so-called *uti possidetis* principle that consecrated the principle of 'intangibility of frontiers', explaining that:

> It is a general principle, which is logically connected with the phenomenon of the obtaining of independence, wherever it occurs. Its obvious purpose is to prevent the independence and stability of new States being endangered by fratricidal struggles provoked by the challenging of frontiers following the withdrawal of the administering power.[32]

Here now the Court expressly refused to look beyond the frontiers drawn by the colonial powers. Whatever the historical injustices, there was no reason to speculate about them. The principal task of the law was to prevent 'fratricidal struggles'.[33]

---

[30] *Legal Consequences of the Continued Presence of South Africa in Namibia, Advisory Opinion* [1971] ICJ Rep 16, para. 53.

[31] See Memorial of Mali (3 October 1985), 45 [87–8], and discussion in Emmanuel Decaux, 'L'arrêt de la Chambre de la CIJ dans l'affaire du différend frontalier (Burkina Faso/République du Mali)', *Annuaire français de droit international* 32 (1986), 215–38, at 228–30.

[32] *Case concerning the Frontier Dispute (Burkina Faso/Mali)*, Judgment [1986] ICJ Rep 554, para. 20.

[33] Of course, *uti possidetis* had a long history and it had been many times consecrated by post-colonial African leaders as well, realising the great difficulty of even attempting to restore anything like a pre-colonial status quo. Here, it seems, law turned expressly against history, or at least a certain understanding of it. A good overview is Märta Johanson, *Self-Determination and*

The point of these three cases (and others could be cited) is both to show the ubiquitous presence and variable use of arguments from history in the practice of international law as well as to stress the specificity of 'history' as it appears in international law. The demands of any method are subordinate to the pragmatics of the legal intervention operating in the context of institutional authority and decision-making. The profession itself addresses these variations in terms of the demands of 'stability' and 'change' but behind these words are much more fundamental (political) choices about the values, interests or actors that the appropriate institution wishes to prefer at any moment.[34] As Anne Orford has often stressed, maintaining a critical standpoint within international law requires that the demands of practice, history and theory are dealt with together so that none of them is expected to dictate the conditions of what good legal work is to others.[35]

2.3 HISTORIES OF INTERNATIONAL LAW

In addition to law as a practice of history, lawyers have also compiled histories of this practice. I have elsewhere discussed the general theme of the history of international law histories, including the different ways in which these histories have conceived their object.[36] Legal texts in the nineteenth century often imagined that object as inextricable from the history of European diplomacy and warfare, deriving its rules and practices as well as the related thinking and writing from the period of the wars of religion, especially the Thirty Years' war and the Peace of Westphalia. Later expositions have sometimes gone back to much earlier times, the relations that ancient Romans had with aliens, or, even further, into the treaties and diplomacy of the ancient Near East.[37]

Borders: The Obligation to Show Consideration for the Interests of Others (Åbo Akademi Universitet, 2005), 70–115.

[34] A matter I have dealt with in extenso in my *From Apology to Utopia*.

[35] See, e.g., Anne Orford and Florian Hoffmann, 'Theorizing International Law', in Orford and Hoffmann (eds.), *Oxford Handbook of the Theory of International Law*, 1–17, at 7–9.

[36] Martti Koskenniemi, 'A History of International Law Histories', in Bardo Fassbender and Anne Peters (eds.), *The Oxford Handbook of the History of International Law* (Oxford: Oxford University Press, 2012), 943–71.

[37] For the latter, see Amnon Altman, *Tracing the Earliest Recorded Conceptions of International Law: The Ancient Near East (2500–330 BCE)* (Leiden: Brill, 2012). Altman defends the appropriateness of applying the notion of 'international law' to the entities of his study by quoting the expansive definition of Grewe that focuses on a 'plurality of relatively independent (although not necessarily equal-ranking) bodies politic which are linked to each other in political, economic and cultural relationships': xxiv. This begs the question whether ideas about 'bodies politic' or notions such as 'political', 'economic' or 'cultural' can so easily be captured in such histories.

Though most histories briefly reference such ancient times, the consensus today seems to be that the proper object is the law applicable in reasonably stable relations between 'political communities' reasonably akin to states.[38] Recent histories with their focus on intercultural or colonial aspects of the law have sought the origins of the discipline in the encounter between Europeans and the inhabitants of the New World in the late fifteenth and early sixteenth centuries and the practices of colonial administration in the nineteenth century.[39] My own work that concentrated on the professionalisation of the field situated the beginning of the field in the last third of the nineteenth century.[40]

Different origin narratives produce different accounts of international law itself. They are, as Matthew Craven has put it, intervention rather than discovery.[41] Such intervention may sometimes emerge from a deliberate effort to tweak the priorities of the field. When the Belgian Ernest Nys and the US lawyer James Brown Scott in the late nineteenth and early twentieth centuries challenged the place of the Dutch Protestant Hugo Grotius as 'father' of the discipline, and singled out the writings of Spanish Catholic theologians, they were not only expanding the field but also reimagining its ideological substance.[42] When Arthur Nussbaum in 1951 replaced the writings of philosophers and natural lawyers by the treaty-making and diplomatic practices of states, he was consciously re-orienting the field towards his 'realist'

---

[38] Harald Kleinschmidt, *Geschichte des Völkerrechts in Krieg und Frieden* (Tübingen: Francke, 2013), 8. Though Grewe, for example, acknowledges the presence of legal relations between the 'autonomous communities' in Antiquity and the non-European world, he found it best to begin with the rise of the 'modern state system' operating on the balance of power in late-fifteenth-century northern Italy: Wilhelm G. Grewe, *The Epochs of International Law*, trans. Michael Byers (Berlin: De Gruyter, 2000), 13–23.

[39] Anghie, *Imperialism, Sovereignty and the Making of International Law*; Lauren Benton and Lisa Ford, *Rage for Order. The British Empire and the Origins of International Law 1800–1850* (Cambridge, MA: Harvard University Press, 2016).

[40] Koskenniemi, *Gentle Civilizer*. See also David Kennedy, 'International Law and the Nineteenth Century: History of an Illusion' *Quinnipiac Law Review* 17 (1997–8), 99–138.

[41] Matthew Craven, 'Theorizing the Turn to History in International Law', in Orford and Hoffmann (eds.), *Oxford Handbook of the Theory of International Law*, 21–37, at 34. See also Oliver Diggelmann, 'The Periodization of the History of International Law', in Fassbender and Peters (eds.), *Oxford Handbook of the History of International Law*, 997–1011.

[42] James Brown Scott, *The Spanish Origin of International Law: Francisco de Vitoria and His Law of Nations* (Oxford: Clarendon, 1934) and, out of the burgeoning 'tertiary' literature, see Paolo Amorosa, *Rewriting the History of the Law of Nations. How James Brown Scott Made Francisco de Vitoria the Founder of International Law* (Oxford: Oxford University Press, 2019); Ignacio de la Rasilla del Moral, *In the Shadow of Vitoria: International Law in Spain 1770–1953* (Leiden: Brill, 2018).

methodological and political priorities.⁴³ Another kind of international legal history opened up in Carl Schmitt's *Nomos der Erde*, although it took decades (and an English translation) for the argument about the *ius publicum Europaeum* as a violence-hedging device to access the discipline's internal conversations.⁴⁴ This direction was followed by Wilhelm Grewe and Karl-Heinz Ziegler, both of whom wrote histories of international law in terms of successive epochs of international dominance, seeking to offer a 'realistic' image of the law as a product of the interests of each moment's leading power.⁴⁵ Anghie and other post-colonial scholars, too, understood European imperial history as the central aspect of international law's past – but the message they drew from that history of course differed from that of the German lawyers. The many scholars following China Miéville to reimagine international legal history as part of the history of capitalism have likewise sought to rethink international law by including new types of materials in its scope.⁴⁶

Such realisms have produced welcome counterpoints to the narrative of international law as part of universal history with a cosmopolitan purpose. Some of them fall into the category of modernist functionalism and are amenable to criticisms often targeted at their mainstream variants.⁴⁷ The rules are too indeterminate, the causal chains too complex and the moment's – any moment's – law too fragmentary and contested to allow the kinds of determination suggested by realism. Surely law is not just a *product* of power but also a challenge to it – which is why its politics sometimes shifts from right to left, from admiration of (European) power to its anti-imperialist critique. An 'epoch' is never just one impenetrable black box but instead contains many actors and ideas that collide and struggle.⁴⁸ Much of the world that realism merely claims to describe – the 'state' itself, and the idea of 'state sovereignty' – is already

---

⁴³ Arthur Nussbaum, *A Concise History of International Law* (rev. ed.) (New York: Macmillan, 1954).

⁴⁴ Carl Schmitt, *Der Nomos der Erde im Völkerrecht des Jus Publicum Europaeum* (Berlin: Duncker & Humblot, 1950).

⁴⁵ Grewe, *Epochs of International Law*; Karl-Heinz Ziegler, *Völkerrechtsgeschichte* (2nd ed.) (Munich: Beck, 2007).

⁴⁶ China Miéville, *Between Equal Rights: A Marxist Theory of International Law* (Leiden: Brill 2005). For one such reading, see Grietje Baars, *The Corporation, Law and Capitalism. A Radical Perspective on the Role of Law in the Global Political Economy* (Leiden: Brill, 2019).

⁴⁷ See, e.g., Hans J. Morgenthau, 'Positivism, Functionalism, and International Law', *American Journal of International Law* 34 (1940), 260–84; and Nussbaum, *Concise History of International Law*.

⁴⁸ See, e.g., Martti Koskenniemi, 'Histories of International Law: Significance and Problems for a Critical View', *Temple International and Comparative Law Journal* 27 (2013), 215–40.

embedded in legal concepts, practices and categories that do not describe the real world but constitute what can been seen there. An 'alliance' or a 'treaty' are not features of the material world but often contested legal interpretations that point towards some way of acting in it. The balance of power was certainly a key concept of eighteenth-century international law. But this does not mean that the jurists would have agreed on its meaning, applicability or wisdom.[49]

But in moving closer to the historical context, does that mean loss of contemporary relevance and political power? A key question for new histories is how to give room to the many roles that law, lawyers and legal arguments play at any single moment while still seeking to keep their eye on the *longue durée* of structural causality that will help the past to speak to the present. No doubt, some new studies will go the way of functionalism while others will loosen the causal links by employing mediating notions such as 'ideology' or 'legal consciousness'.[50] At the same time, the proliferation of narrative standpoints may itself bring new materials into the field, thereby sustaining continuously critical attention to the limits of the discipline itself.

Until very recently, colonisation was virtually excluded from the history of international law.[51] This accorded with the preferences of the colonial powers themselves: for example, the most important summary of British colonial law from 1834 makes no mention at all of international law and John Westlake used to insist that Britain's relations with the Indian principalities was not a matter of international but British (imperial) law.[52] But recent studies of the history of international law focus precisely on the rules and practices governing the work of colonial administrators, even suggesting that they might lie at the 'origins of international law'.[53] But the move from wars and diplomacy to commerce and colonisation suggests that more work ought to be directed to the legal practices of contracting, shipping and banking that

---

[49] For one incisive criticism, see e.g. J.H.G. Justi, *Die Chimäre des Gleichgewichts der Europa* (Altona: Iversen, 1758).

[50] Susan Marks, *The Riddle of All Constitutions: International Law, Democracy, and the Critique of Ideology* (Oxford: Oxford University Press, 2000); Duncan Kennedy, 'Towards an Historical Understanding of Legal Consciousness. The Case of Classical Legal Thought in America 1850–1940', *Research in Law and Sociology* 3 (1980), 3–24.

[51] Jörg Fisch, *Die europäische Expansion und das Völkerrecht* (Stuttgart: Steiner, 1984), 28, and the review of literature at 28–34.

[52] Charles Clark, *A Summary of Colonial Law* (London: Sweet & Maxwell, 1834). Most work for this publication was done by Sir James Stephen, who reigned over the Colonial Office for more than twenty years. The work is a meticulous 'summary' of all laws that are applied in the different colonies and not one word is said about international law or the law of nations therein. That this would be the view of a high colonial administrator is much more understandable than why other observers happily went along.

[53] Benton and Ford, *Rage for Order*.

made long-distance trade and colonisation possible. New studies focus on the large overseas trading companies as mercantile operators but also as colonists, sovereigns and belligerent powers.[54] Further work in this vein is needed to include examinations of their internal structures and expand into the law and practice of foreign investment that undergirded the companies but also more widely accounted for the legal structures of Western global domination.[55] All this puts into question the conventional boundaries of history of international law itself.

It is perfectly natural to think that the field consists of what prior historians have included in it. Still, the present delimitation is strikingly novel – no older certainly than late nineteenth century. It is a recent offshoot of the conflict of the faculties that underlay European academic life for centuries and now appears to us as the fragmenting culture of global expertise. The conflict had its local variants. The struggle between 'civilians' and common lawyers in early seventeenth-century England was waged partly over the question of authority to speak on international contracts or the powers of colonial companies but also had much to do with the political direction of England itself.[56] In Enlightenment France, *Droit public de l'Europe* was not taught at law schools but was an idiom developed and used by diplomats, political thinkers and activist *littérateurs* and articulated as a science of negotiations, in which every participant needed to know their real interests and how best to advance them.[57] The question of what makes some substance 'belong' to (the history of) international, constitutional, commercial, or say banking law is not just about turf wars between professionals but also about the political direction of institutional and governmental practices. I have elsewhere sketched some of the struggles waged at European universities where questions about the 'ought' of international behaviour migrated between theology, politics, law and economics.[58] One could also add the more recent efforts by 'international relations' to re-conceive the field of international normativity through the canons of empirical political science so as to attain authority on matters where

---

[54] Doreen Lustig, *Veiled Power: International Law and the Private Corporation, 1886–1981* (Oxford: Oxford University Press, 2020).
[55] Kate Miles, *Origins of International Investment Law: Empire, Environment, and the Safeguarding of Capital* (Cambridge: Cambridge University Press, 2013) is a beginning.
[56] See, e.g., Daniel R. Coquillette, *The Civilian Writers of Doctors' Commons, London: Three Centuries of Innovation in Comparative, Commercial and International Law* (Berlin: Duncker & Humblot, 1988).
[57] See Gabriel Bonnot de Mably, *Principes de négociations pour servir d'introduction au droit public de l'Europe*, ed. Marc Bélissa (Paris: Kimé, 2001).
[58] Martti Koskenniemi, 'Law of Nations and the Conflict of the Faculties', *History of the Present. A Journal of Critical History* 8 (2018), 4–28.

it was previously held by lawyers. The curriculum of the law school has never been stable and the content of university courses operates in dialectical relationship with the perceived needs of legal practices.

2.4 WHAT IS INCLUDED? THE ROLE OF POWER AND POLITICS

Part of international legal history has always focused on *ideas* about the international legal order. Textbooks, journals and specialised monographs have engaged with the big names of history of political thought – Aquinas, Vitoria, Grotius, Hobbes, Rousseau, Kant ... Here, too, boundaries have been drawn mostly in a tacit way. Which theologians, philosophers, or political thinkers to include, which not? Attention to the Spanish theologians of the sixteenth century is nowadays *de rigueur*, less so Jesuits or Protestant churchmen. Do papal encyclicals belong to the history of international law? What about texts of other religions, and the practice of interpreting them? Early modernity also produced a massive literature on government and *raison d'état* that was largely (though not uniformly) hostile to law, especially in foreign relations.[59] Would not such 'opponents' be likewise part of the history of international law? Some of these texts dealt with expressly legal themes, inspiring, for example, a whole line of German eighteenth-century natural lawyers, men who in counselling German princes developed the kind of governmentality that Foucault introduced into the historical mainstream and of which Emer de Vattel remains only one example. Should they not also be part of the history of international law?[60]

'Natural law' and 'positivism' have been large items organising the *Literaturgeschichte* of the field. Individual themes have dealt with the possibility and conditions of peace among nations, self-determination, the just war, legitimacy, humanitarian intervention and human rights. Robert Redslob's 1923 *Les grands principes de droit international* traced the fate of four leading principles – peace, solidarity, state freedom and *pacta sunt servanda* – through the centuries. A more recent work by Georg Cavallar asked whether standard texts represented 'cosmopolitanism' and ended in a nuanced assessment – well, 'yes' and 'no'.[61] Studies in the liberal history of ideas mode have engaged these thinkers in normative conversations through vocabularies of law and

---

[59] Out of a wealth of recent literature, see the summary treatment in Laurie Catteeuw, *Censures et raisons d'État. Une histoire de la modernité politique (XVIe-XVIIe siècle)* (Paris: Albin Michel, 2013).
[60] See my 'Transformations of Natural Law: Germany 1648–1815', in Orford and Hoffmann (eds.), *Oxford Handbook of the Theory of International Law*, 59–81.
[61] Georg Cavallar, *Imperfect Cosmopolis: Studies in the History of International Legal Theory and Cosmopolitan Ideas* (Cardiff: University of Wales Press, 2011).

justice they themselves employ.[62] While many recent studies have aspired to read past jurists in their 'contexts', it has also seemed important to imagine those contexts as parts of *longue durée* patterns that allow measuring their contemporary significance. For the latter type of studies, it matters little whether Vitoria actually felt sympathy towards the Indians; more important is the effect of his teaching on the justification of colonialism.[63] As international lawyers work to keep the requirements of legal history and present practice together, it might be useful to bear two considerations in mind.

The first relates to the stakes in legal practice. Law is struggle. Lawyers always disagree; they disagree because they have different clients and agendas, because the institutions where they work require of them different kinds of service and the institutions matter because they affect the distribution of materials and spiritual values. At each moment in any meaningful legal context, it may be possible to identify a main position (or a structural bias) and subsidiary position that seeks to challenge it and the scheme of distribution that it stands for. There is a systemic or constructive aspect of law, too, that is especially visible in the legal academy. Here the underlying struggle is often hidden in an effort to explain the legal system as coherent and by and large rational. Historians of international law have perhaps paid too much attention to those constructions, at the cost of seeking to find out the terms of the struggle and how they are transformed at successive moments. To link legal practices to the stakes they organise and distribute might require leaving the constructivist comfort-zone into historical sociology or the history of political economy. That has been the direction of many recent critical histories. The trick here is not to believe that law's problems have already been resolved elsewhere (in history or philosophy, say) so that it would suffice to apply insights from those other fields, but to learn from them about the role that law and legal institutions have played in the lives of actual human beings. In the end, it remains for lawyers to draw the conclusions regarding how that past experience should inform today's practice.

Second, it is useful to remember that law is a linguistic phenomenon. It is about the polemical use of authoritative concepts in specialised institutional contexts with the view of supporting, defending, consolidating or attacking particular claims that usually concern distributing resources. This makes it

---

[62] Samantha Besson and John Tasioulas (eds.), *The Philosophy of International Law* (Oxford: Oxford University Press, 2010).

[63] In this respect the criticism by Cavallar in *Imperfect Cosmopolis*, 20–24, rather misses the point. See further Anne Orford, 'The Past as Law or History?', in Mark Toufayan, Emmanuelle Tourme-Jouannet and Hélène Ruiz Fabri (eds.), *Droit international et nouvelles approches sur le tiers-monde* (Paris: Société de législation comparée, 2013), 97–117.

important to examine the way in which law's linguistic meanings emerge, consolidate and are challenged. How does meaning-formation operate? What have lawyers tried to *do* when investing words with particular meanings and challenging established ones? One way to take seriously law's linguistic character is to focus on conceptual *change* in the international legal world. In this way it might be possible to balance attention to the work of *individual* legal actors with the institutional and material contexts of their work.[64] Here history appears as an analysis of how successive generations of lawyers have used authoritative legal concepts to communicate their institutional projects and how these meanings have been challenged and eventually transformed. How was law's conceptual world organised around a centre of key concepts; what did this consolidation mean in terms of the stakes of institutional decision-making and how did that centre eventually dissipate and fragment as other notions and other meanings came to challenge and possibly replace it?

One part of such history might analyse the delimitations that have marked the outer limits and internal divisions of competent law. No legal distinction is more important than the one created once upon a time in Europe between 'private law' and 'public law', property and sovereignty. That dichotomy organises everything from the nature of the claims legal subjects have to resources and the administration of political communities to the organisation of law schools. The old (though actually not *that* old) understanding of international law as an aspect of sovereign behaviour, diplomacy, war and peace is today breaking down. New interest in the constitution of the international world brings trade and commerce, international investment, human rights and new technologies within law and legal analysis. Indeed, why should the writings of Hugo Grotius be part of international legal history while the writings of Charles Davenant or Adam Smith are not? Surely the monetary theories of Martin Azpilcueta or Jean Bodin are equally important aspects of legal history as the debates on perpetual peace by Saint-Pierre and Rousseau. Property relations were once a solid part of *ius gentium* and Grotius devoted

---

[64] It is striking that a large proportion of the 'political-social' concepts included in the massive seven volumes of the *Geschichtliche Grundbegriffe* by Otto Brunner and others (including the intellectual father of *Begriffsgeschichte*, Reinhart Koselleck) are also legal concepts, many of them quite central in the *international* legal world. Although this type of conceptual history has its problems (how, for instance, to measure the relationship between the 'concept' and the material world?) it is also clearly promising, because it seems to avoid problems of 'pure' realism and 'pure' idealism and respects the specificity of legal practice as work with concepts. For one recent assessment, see Jan-Werner Müller, 'On Conceptual History', in Darrin McMahon and Samuel Moyn (eds.), *Rethinking European Intellectual History* (Oxford: Oxford University Press, 2014), 74–93.

most of Book II of *De iure belli ac pacis* to rights over land, contractual rights and rights in family relations and wrote long passages on debt and insolvency. Here, too, he was organising the international world under definite legal concepts – though ones usually left outside standard commentary. And surely it is time to take seriously Book I of Emer de Vattel's *Le droit des gens* that unfolds as a detailed survey of the universal principles regarding the policies a good prince ought to put to effect so as to see to the wealth and happiness of the nation.

These are just some examples of the conceptual delimitations that have governed lawyers' understanding of their discipline and their assignments in the world of international institutions. Recent histories that have brought new items into focus have often been inspired by the sense that those limitations have been too narrow, that items important for understanding how power operates in law have been left obscure. Hence the interest in the history of colonial administrations, the work of religious and financial authorities, business corporations and generally the legal ways of private power. As the scope of the history of international law widens and moves closer to the old *ius gentium*, it will have a fuller view of the role legal concepts and practices have had in making the world what it is. Law is a language of authority and lawyers are men and women exercising authority. Surely it is not only a technical but a political imperative to bring to light as much of that authority as possible.

3

The Context for Context: International Legal History in Struggle

DAVID KENNEDY

International legal historians write with passion and their texts can bristle with rage. Although it sounds innocent enough – putting legal doctrines, personalities and ideas in historical context – the conclusion is less 'thought you'd like to know' than 'this *matters*'. Contextual histories aim volleys at the field's commanding heights to change how we imagine international law and the world around us. International law's history is not as you were taught, international law not what you thought. And the world is not the one you are accustomed to inhabiting. If we think the world is different, perhaps it will be.

Although many are coy about their political ambitions, some do wear these projects on their sleeves. Here is Antony Anghie on history's significance for appreciating the legacies of colonialism in the contemporary world:

> My argument here is that the practices of cultural subordination and economic exploitation, which are essential aspects of colonialism, are not epiphenomenal aberrations in the international system that were remedied by the project of decolonization and self-determination. Rather, they continue to play a role in contemporary international relations and generate important analytic categories that have an enduring and crucial significance to our understanding of international law as a whole.[1]

Or here on history's lessons about the nature of sovereignty and the role of international legal doctrines in global politics:

---

[1] Antony Anghie, 'Colonialism and the Birth of International Institutions: Sovereignty, Economy, and the Mandate System of the League of Nations', *New York University Journal of International Law and Politics* 34 (2001–2002), 513–633, at 518. Anghie extended this analysis from the seventeenth to twentieth centuries in Antony Anghie, *Imperialism, Sovereignty and the Making of International Law* (Cambridge: Cambridge University Press, 2005), 115–273.

> My interest lies, however, not only in the important point that positivism legitimized conquest and dispossession, but also in the reverse relationship — in identifying how notions of positivism and sovereignty were themselves shaped by the encounter. ... Colonialism cannot be accounted for as an example of the application of sovereignty; rather, sovereignty was constituted and shaped through colonialism.[2]

Arnulf Becker Lorca places the jurist Alejandro Álvarez simultaneously in his Chilean and European/global/French historical contexts to change how we understand the relationship between the global and the local, law's role in their interaction and in subject-creation:

> [My] rereading of [Alejandro] Álvarez ... reveal[s] not only international law's plurality of senses in time and space ... but also international law's heterogeneity inscribed in the selfsame person of the international lawyer. ... My central argument is that Álvarez ... evidences the constitution of the discourse of modern international law as part of the continuous configuration of the world system. This insight suggests, first, that the construction of modern international law has been a transnational project, produced and resisted from multifarious points of reference by European and non-European international lawyers alike. ... Second, this line of enquiry also acknowledges that international law is embedded in international as well as domestic power relations.[3]

B.S. Chimni describes the project of those third world international legal histories he applauds in these terms:

> A *critical* third world approach goes further and gives meaning to international law in the context of the lived experiences of the ordinary peoples of the third world in order to transform it into an international law of emancipation. It has as its primary goal the shaping of an international law that offers a life of dignity for the poor and oppressed in the third world. It is amidst this hope that I take a sweeping look at the past, present and future of international law.[4]

Anne Orford assesses the significance of international historical context work this way:

---

[2] Antony Anghie, 'Finding the Peripheries: Sovereignty and Colonialism in Nineteenth-Century International Law', *Harvard International Law Journal* 40 (1999), 1–71, at 6.

[3] Arnulf Becker Lorca, 'Alejandro Álvarez Situated: Subaltern Modernities and Modernisms that Subvert', *Leiden Journal of International Law* 19 (2006), 879–930, at 882–3. Becker continued his historical contextual study of legal intellectuals in the semi-periphery in Arnulf Becker Lorca, *Mestizo International Law* (Cambridge: Cambridge University Press, 2015).

[4] B.S. Chimni, 'The Past, Present and Future of International Law: A Critical Third World Approach', *Melbourne Journal of International Law* 8 (2007), 499–515, at 499–500.

The stakes of the debate about the legacies of the imperial past in the multinational present are high. In part this is because the authority and legitimacy of modern international law rests on its claim to have transcended its European heritage and to operate today as a universal law capable of representing humanity. The suggestion that international law may still operate in a differentiated fashion undermines that claim to universality. In addition, the idea that imperialism is of no relevance to the contemporary global order plays a significant part in justifying the status quo. ... Questioning the extent to which decolonization has ever fully taken place thus remains a critical intervention in contemporary global politics.[5]

Sundhya Pahuja describes the methodological aspiration of work re-narrating law's past:

> Critical redescription is an attempt to redefine through narrative, a world we take for granted, inviting it to be seen differently as a mode of political engagement. As a style, critical redescription offers to legal thought the potential of story-telling in trying to understand the world differently than the way we usually know it.[6]

These academics write history to change the world. Is such an ambition plausible? If so, is changing the world something a legal historian can undertake pragmatically, with a sense of responsibility, as much as passion?

It does seem plausible. Linking people, ideas, projects and institutions to a 'context' is a familiar – and often powerful – move in contemporary professional and public reason. Lots of people try to do it – there is no reason legal historians ought not as well. People invoke context to identify powers which must be respected, and the direction history is travelling. Context establishes the frame within which problems can be identified and solutions imagined. People also turn to context for authority. This is how things are, where things stand, where things came from and where they are going – and so we must ...

For lawyers, establishing the context is a routine practice. Legal work frames the spatial and historical terrain for global political, economic and cultural rulership.[7] The legal academy, moreover, is a place where rulers are trained.

---

[5] Anne Orford, 'The Past as Law or History? The Relevance of Imperialism for Modern International Law', Melbourne Legal Studies Research Paper No. 600, 1–2.

[6] Sundhya Pahuja, 'Laws of Encounter: A Jurisdictional Account of International Law', *London Review of International Law* 1 (2013), 63–98, at 65.

[7] International law is not the only – or most important – field contributing to our sense of the global normal. International economic law, for example, establishes a 'normal' boundary between the global economy and the appropriate space for national regulation. David Kennedy, 'The International Style in Postwar Law and Policy', *Utah Law Review* (1994), 7–104. Comparative law establishes a map of things which are near and far: who is in our legal family,

Trained not in the sense of brainwashed to 'believe' or accept one rather than another idea about the world – although that certainly also happens – but trained in modes of engagement, terms of debate, frames of reference within or against which they will struggle with one another as they come to rule the world. In the legal academy, they learn how to understand, remake and disrupt the background or terrain for rulership. Establishing the context, like disrupting a taken-for-granted frame, is a strategic move you can learn. Elsewhere in the academy, professional historians offer training both in their shared professional vision of history and in the tools for its strategic disruption.

Both are worth learning because they can have consequences. Doubling down on professional common sense reinforces the plausibility of institutions and projects aligned with history's destiny. A new history might resurrect workable alternatives which were defeated, opening paths for opposition to the conventions of elite governance. A history which draws attention to the incoherence and pluralism of international legal materials may unsettle the confidence of people using them. When a context is effectively established or disrupted, some people will be empowered, some interests legitimated, others disempowered or delegitimated.

So it can be done. Indeed, it is done routinely. And it can have an effect. Like other rulership practices, making a new context ought to be undertaken responsibly, with due attention to consequences. Who will gain and who will lose? Unfortunately, conventions of historical writing inhibit many authors from acknowledging their present revisionist aspirations and from attending more concretely to the effects of their interventions. International legal historians need not be so bashful: there is ample methodological space to notice the consequences of governing in the shadow of one rather than another contextual sensibility. You could write history to change the world pragmatically, strategically, responsibly. Indeed, I hope you will.

3.1 INTERNATIONAL LEGAL CONTEXT-MAKING: DOING THINGS WITH TIME

It is easy to see why scholars would focus on international law's ideas about its history: the field's general program and the authority of international lawyers are often directly linked to the helping hand of history. Historical narratives

---

shares our tradition; who is at our stage of development? Routine law reform work establishes and reinforces this context of affinity and difference among the ruling elite. When law reformers in Chile reach out for best practices to emulate, they might look 'naturally' to France – or the United States – rather than Peru or Brazil. See David Kennedy 'The Methods and the Politics', in Pierre Legrand and Roderick Munday (eds.), *Comparative Legal Studies: Traditions and Transitions* (Cambridge: Cambridge University Press, 2003), 345–433.

reinforce international law's ancient and universal provenance and present it as a first primitive step towards a more comprehensive global legal order. In the shadow of conventional histories, one might reasonably conclude that we need not rethink international law but must rather tend it carefully. With a new history might come a new appetite for rethinking.

International lawyers are adept at tracing long pedigrees for rules they favor and undermining the provenance of others. They style their pet projects as the crest of history's progressive wave and castigate their opponents for being out of time, either anachronistic or insufficiently respectful of precedent. They present their activities as permanent or transitional when doing so seems likely to enhance their acceptance. Does the machinery of transitional justice close the door on the past or prolong and repeat past injury, even render it permanent? Policy debates can turn on perceptions of continuity and rupture. Did the UN Charter – or decolonization or 1989 or 9/11 – usher in a new era for international law or reaffirm the wisdom of its long-term commitments? Placing contemporary projects in historical time can legitimate them as wise traditions prefiguring a better future or undermine them as unrealistic or stale anachronism. History may even be offered as proof for the *legality* of international law, evidencing both law's roots in power and its normative autonomy. Conceptually it is hard to square the idea of sovereigns as the origin and enforcer of law with law as the normative fabric authorizing and governing sovereigns. But it is relatively easy to do so historically by interpreting some events as law-making and others as law-following.

Every lawyer knows that legal arrangements can speed or slow time, deferring or leapfrogging next steps. For all its strategic malleability, legal time can seem like time itself. Becoming a state seems a natural historical process that takes time, just as an occupation can be understood to be 'transitional' however long it might last. People come to believe in a future prefigured by the virtues of today's institutions, just as they accept a past landmarked by the moments of wisdom embedded in contemporary norms. What seems historically settled helps to define the terrain for possible change. Globally, it seems settled that the poor must make do within the borders and political possibilities of their territorial 'nation' while *non-refoulement* for refugees and the free movement of goods and services are the sorts of thing one must struggle to achieve. The global legal immobility of the poor is a matter of historical fact: there is and can be no right to asylum.

Within this frame, people invoke different memories as they struggle over priorities, differences which may also render the field's overall historical narrative vulnerable to retelling. Where diplomats look back on wars and tell stories about the balance of power or spheres of influence, jurists remember peace treaties, great men and their books. Different legal fields trace their origins differently: for public international law, the big dates are 1648, 1918, 1945 and 1989; for international institutions, nineteenth-century precursors and then 1918 and 1945; for human rights, 1945 and 1989; for international relations, 1815, perhaps 1848 and 1871, and then 1914 rather than 1918 and 1945. Each list is an argument. What seems salient in the past underwrites authority in the present. When the international economic law field remembers the Smoot-Hawley Tariff, crediting it with the Depression, in turn singled out as a cause for World War II and thus for the Holocaust, it does so to double down on the Doha Round of trade liberalization negotiations: we know where protectionism leads. To remember 1945, by contrast, reinforces the importance of the European Union's progressive development, just as recalling the Holocaust underwrites human rights and humanitarian intervention.

Placing particular doctrines or institutions in the long sweep of international law's progressive development can shape what we expect of them. Are international organizations in their infancy, requiring our careful protection and fealty? Their adolescence, prefiguring a better global governance to come if we are mindful of their missteps and reform their annoying impulses? Or are they long past their sell-by date, sorry reminders of good ideas which failed to pan out? We may disagree about the maturity of current international organizations, but we know the direction of progress. By naming a historical period, people indicate what they feel should be done. With 'globalization' we must become more cosmopolitan; under 'finance capitalism' we must break up the big banks. The 'Anthropocene' reminds us to be careful. Changing the pace can also change the focus: if things are speeding up, we should feel pressed to act urgently. Environmental lawyers are not the only ones to forecast catastrophe or frame these as end times. The metric of 'sustainability' brings that forecast back into the present as a program of caution.

When history seems to ratify distributions of authority, wealth and privilege with which people disagree, they have a motive to change the narrative. Two strategies beckon: adjust the story to accommodate your preferred outcome, or challenge the larger narrative. Colonialism provides the most obvious example. If for centuries international lawyers had staffed and supported imperial projects, over the twentieth century they came to see empire as a historical vestige, incompatible with a modern international law of self-determination and sovereign equality. For elites in the colonial and post-colonial periphery, this was a tremendous achievement. They had 'entered history' and could pursue participation on an equal basis in the United Nations system and in the modern process for identifying or interpreting norms and resolving disputes. Insisting on decolonization as a world-historic rupture signaled their arrival on the scene and marked a crucial stage in the progressive universalization of the international legal order. That was one strategy. At the same time – and ever more insistently over the ensuing years – others preferred to challenge the broader story of progress, and the severity of the break from colonialism. By foregrounding other contemporary doctrines, drawing different historical analogies, and articulating the periodization differently, political and economic inequality can be narrated as continuous with colonialism. All the world's peoples were always in its history. If that is how it is, participation seems less promising.

3.2 MODERN LAW AS MANAGERIAL RULERSHIP

It seems plausible to change the world by re-narrating the 'context' because contemporary technocratic or managerial governance is so thoroughly rule by articulation.[8] To situate contextualization as a move of managerial rulership means placing it within this broader practice of elite articulation: making assertions about context is one way to do things with words. People engaged in struggle assess the situation, interpret its meaning, forecast the import of doing this or that. As they do, they make assertions and arguments to one another about how things are and what should be done, about what has been decided, what it means and requires. Those articulations become effective when someone does something as a result, yielding to the assertion or claim or argument. In doing so, people often imagine themselves to be somehow *outside* the context. The facts of precedent, interest or history are *behind* them while the discretion of leaders, citizens, bosses or clients to make new facts lies *ahead*. It would be more accurate to think of context-making as performative: it works when it generates a 'context effect', changing what is known in ways that alter who can do what. Right, that is how things are, how things were, who's who and what's what.

We might think of the 'knowledge' people bring to bear in their engagements as a stack of ideas: unconscious or semi-conscious material that is taken for granted, large ideological or theoretical positions used as justifications for opposing positions, technical differences of degree in the implementation of those positions and ideas about the outcomes, what will, might or ought to happen once a particular position in these layers of ideological conviction, technical know-how and common sense is accepted.

---

[8] This picture of expert rulership is developed more fully in David Kennedy, *A World of Struggle: How Power, Law, and Expertise Shape Global Political Economy* (Princeton: Princeton University Press, 2016).

Context is certainly central to the way people think about outcomes: what will happen *afterwards* if their proposals, arguments or authority are accepted. Context here is the space where effects occur and outcomes can be seen: the rock that articulative levers aim to move. But, of course, what moves is not a rock. It is a person. A person who acts or stands down, and who must interpret and accept or reject or ignore your assertion about how things 'are'. There are many ways an assertion might lead a person to yield: mysticism, charisma, coercion and confusion are as much a part of the story as persuasion and means/ends rationality. However it occurs, the context for action – down there, where the rubber meets the road, where law in the books becomes law in action – is populated by people engaged in parallel and reciprocal knowledge work in which they too are expert. What 'is' and its consequences are the social effects of this engagement: someone asserts and someone acquiesces.

Context is most clearly part of the first layer: semiconscious ideas about how things are 'out there' which frame more routine technical and ideological debates. This is the imaginary world people experience as real: the powers that do not need to be asserted and are not worth contesting, the framework of systems and institutions and actors among which distributive struggle is understood to be possible. Here, context seems to come *before* the work of articulation and decision.

And yet this frame must itself be established. To believe one lives in a 'market economy' or 'nation-state system' and to understand what that entails requires work. In places like Davos or Washington, just as in small-town coffee shops and living rooms around the television, people tell stories about what an economy is, what politics can accomplish, and the limits and potential of law. Their stories establish and reinforce what can be taken for granted, work that makes some problems visible, some actors central – and others invisible. Their stories can change: is 'the economy' a space for a bracing individualism, for social interdependence or for careful, even austere, macroeconomic management?

It would be more accurate to picture the context that matters for the exercise of power as neither before nor after the processes of expert and public reason but within them. In contemporary rulership, one cannot simply say one wants it and take it: there must be a reason. And reasons link one to facts, prior settlements, earlier decisions which must now be recognized. The dominant style is a verdictive tangle of ought and is: asserting what ought to happen as a fact or asserting a fact as a reason. This is where training comes in. To be trained for rulership today means learning the large visions shared among elites and becoming adept at linking broad ideological commitments to technical changes which might generate a favorable result within the frame of those visions. It also means inhabiting those contextual sensibilities flexibly, with vigilant skepticism about one another's assertions.[9] It means learning to inhabit elite conceptions of the world as well as the dark arts of disruption, whether these are termed 'leadership' or 'innovation' or 'entrepreneurship' – or 'resistance'.

3.3 CHANGING THE WORLD REQUIRES STRATEGY – EVEN FOR HISTORIANS

When you've been trained to struggle by assertion and change the world by articulation, you've also learned that you need strategy. How to concentrate your forces on the weakest link, how to predict who will yield to what, how to assess the distributional consequences of inhabiting one context rather than another, challenging this assumption but not that. As a legal historian hoping to change the world, you also need a strategy. And you'll also need to anticipate, as much as one can in an unpredictable world, how changing the context will, in fact, change the world: who will win and who will lose?

Putting a famous jurist in context requires choice: what context? Their nation? Their profession? The intellectual or religious tradition in which they would have situated themselves? What they had for breakfast and whom they loved? It is not at all clear *they* should be masters of their context. Nor even that their 'historical context' be contemporaneous with their actual lives. Context may well include things of which the historical actor was himself unaware. Perhaps, as Anne Orford has argued, context should also include things that came 'later' or happened 'elsewhere'? Or happened long before or which took a great deal of time to unfold or may still be unfolding. As she writes:

> Rather than, as most scholars interested in the internationalist implications of Vitoria's thought have done before and since, placing Vitoria in a 'context' that begins with fifteenth century Scholasticism and ends with the adoption of Vitoria's innovative approach to questions of possession, commerce, war and alliance by the young Hugo Grotius, Anghie places Vitoria in a context that moves from the School of Salamanca to the late nineteenth century when empire and its rationalisation is about to take a radically new form in

---

[9] In the context of American legal thought, Duncan Kennedy describes a parallel elite sensibility when encountering legal arguments as a 'hermeneutic of suspicion': Duncan Kennedy, 'The Hermeneutic of Suspicion in Contemporary American Legal Thought', *Law and Critique* 25 (2014), 91–139.

the aftermath of the Berlin conference, and then on to the mandate system, the creation of the IMF and the World Bank, and the invasion of Iraq.[10]

It is not obvious that the present is so long 'after' fifteenth-century writing that interpretation in light of present concerns must be 'anachronistic' rather than 'contextual'. Events like 'colonialism' or 'capitalism' or 'modernism' appear only in the *longue durée* – and then there's the matter of Minerva's owl bringing past things into view for the first time.

Presumably, people who write about international legal history are guided in making such choices by their strategic objective. Although critical legal historians do seem confident there is something rotten in international law made plausible by a common misuse or misunderstanding of history, reading them, it is often difficult to say just what. The sociological mechanism they have in mind can also be hard to identify: who has what bad ideas about history, whom and how does that empower? It seems to go with the contextual style to leave this a bit murky, as if the authors rely on the reader's own sophisticated disenchantment: at once knowing and not knowing that the telling of history is a site for political struggle.

The methodological convention *not* to make the strategic objective explicit and to act as if one *were* simply trying to set things right may result from a suspicion that the success of the strategic project depends on sounding innocent in the way History with a capital H, history by historians, history disciplined only by history rather than the concerns of jurists and politicians and advocates, can sound innocent. Although we know sophisticated historians today will admit to presentist concerns, particularly if you ask them directly, something in their method or style of presentation does seem to preclude saying so too overtly. The cautious non-historian would be advised to tread more lightly still if the legitimacy of historical truth is to be successfully harnessed.[11] But coyness has costs. If you don't know where someone's

---

[10] Orford, 'The Past as Law or History?', 15 (reviewing the ambivalent reception of Anghie's work among historians and arguing that TWAIL scholarship can itself only be understood in 'context'). See also Anne Orford, 'On International Legal Method', *London Review of International Law* 1 (2013), 166–97, 170–7. She identifies these choices as central for understanding the current political significance of this critical genre. But see Quentin Skinner, 'Meaning and Understanding in the History of Ideas', *History and Theory* 8 (1969), 3–53.

[11] Authors pleading for adherence to canonical Historical method include: Randall Lesaffer, 'International Law and its History: The Story of an Unrequited Love', in Matthew Craven, Malgosia Fitzmaurice and Maria Vogiatzi (eds.), *Time, History and International Law* (Leiden: Martinus Nijhoff, 2007), 27–41 at 37–8 ('[W]hatever the intentions and purposes of the scholar studying the history of international law, he should approach the past with proper respect. This means that he should make use of the basic rules of historical methodology ... before one can learn something from the past other than what one knows from the present, one first has to let

aiming it is hard to know if they hit the target, and shyness about the effect one intends can mute attention to consequences all together.

In the legal academy, people in the 'law and society' and 'law in context' traditions have wrestled with a parallel tension. Their project also sounds innocent enough – just open the aperture, see the whole picture. Wouldn't you want to know how it turns out, where law lands, whether it works? Social contextualization offers a kind of neutral promise – make law better, strengthen its functional and pragmatic capabilities – without any particular axe to grind. But people in these traditions do have axes to grind and theirs is a 'critical' interpretive practice, aiming to discredit law's broad claims to autonomous or purely internal assessment, to outcome or interest neutrality, and to practical effectiveness. No, the law and society tradition insists, you can't assess and select among competing legal rules and interpretations by internal rumination on law's principles and purposes alone. You must attend to effects, effects for which law's process and principle are not neutral. And when you look to context, you find an enormous gap between what law says and what it does. The critical voice here is a canny one, however, the critique sliding in and out of view behind a sociological curtain of 'just thought you'd want the whole story'. We're not leftists. We're sociologists.

When people in struggle try to create a 'history effect', it is not surprising they lean on the practice of History by Historians – its authority and prestige, its marks of credible narration, its framing of action in time. In sketching a global context to believe in, experts routinely lean on the prestige and practice of the knowledge disciplines. They rely on Economics with a capital E, Sociology with a capital S, Realpolitik with a capital R, Humanitarianism with a capital H, the science of military Strategy with a capital S and, of course, Law with a capital L. Looking over your shoulder at Real Knowers, it is hard to avoid feeling disciplined by their gaze. But leaning on an academic discipline is quite different from performing *within* an academic discipline.

If there are 'real' Sociologists and Geographers and Political Scientists, they may see more complexity than people with projects who invoke and imitate

---

the past be the past – at least as far as this is humanly possible.'); Georg Cavallar, 'Vitoria, Grotius, Pufendorf, Wolff and Vattel: Accomplices of European Colonialism and Exploitation or True Cosmopolitans?', *Journal of the History of International Law* 10 (2008), 181–209, at 184 ('Unlike commentators like Robert Williams, Antony Anghie or Brett Bowden, and like Paul Keal, I argue for a nuanced assessment. I emphasise the complexity of the history of international legal theory, which suggests that we cannot conveniently pigeonhole divergent authors under a heading such as "Western totalizing discourse". Very often, false continuities are constructed, for instance, between the 18th and the 19th centuries. . . . Some contemporary critics seem to have chosen the wrong authors and ignored the ambiguity of texts.').

them. People in struggle grab what is useful, what they remember, what they think will work to produce a 'context effect'. They borrow tidbits and analytics, 'findings' and consensus views, as well as the social prestige and framing conventions that go with these fields. Even the scientific uncertainty of divided disciplines rarely diminishes enthusiasm for interdisciplinary borrowing and leaning – quite the reverse. The more diverse a prestigious field's internal divisions, the more useful it can be as a validator, the wider the range of situations in which it can provide a welcome shoulder to lean on. In borrowing a historical shoulder, it makes sense to imagine that history is Fact rather than interpretation and to understate its disputed or constructed character. In this, it is not the method of the supporting field which disciplines. It is the shared method of those who struggle to create an effect by invoking them. International legal histories lean on an *image* of capital H History which they hope will be shared by those they are trying to affect. For these purposes, it doesn't matter what real Historians think – until an adversary thinks to cite them.

Method is always somewhat like this. It's the method of a field when it *works* as the method of the field – when one escapes criticism for 'method crimes'. I know that graduate students often worry about 'method' and feel there must be some secret sauce no one has yet explained. I've always thought there was really only one method – you figure out what you're interested in, who or what you're against, and then read a lot and talk to people and think hard and try to figure it out. But of course, being heard also requires submission to expectations. There are elements of skill or technique for knowing and reporting – how firm a pediment of footnotes, what kind of statistical evidence counts, how much archival work is 'enough'. There are the conventions of the discipline or field about what can be said – and what need not be said – that define the margin of maneuver for novelty. Must one have a policy proposal – must it be realistic? There may be literatures to which one must refer and others one can – or should – ignore. You need to know what is taken for granted about periods and structures and agents so you know when you're pushing against a settled line and can be sure to have your ducks in order. And you can't draw them all into question at once. Then there are intellectual traditions with which you may wish to affiliate or disaffiliate because method is also the expression and acknowledgement of influence.

As I read them, the international legal contextualists' method is a kind of imitative pastiche, written with several influences (or disciplining conventions) in mind: those of 'professional' academic Historians as they imagine them, those of the international legal histories they aim to refute, those of 'critical' historical work in law with which they may be familiar, and those methodological cautions and proposals learned from the critical social theory of the last half century, most prominently as promoted by Michel Foucault. The result is a kind of loose vulgate for making historical arguments. In my experience, among these methodological influences, there are resources enough to create an effect without hiding one's animus under a barrel, just as there are tools for an after-action assessment to pinpoint collateral damage amidst the targets hit.

3.4 INTERNATIONAL LEGAL HISTORY: A TALE OF TWO STYLES

To understand international law's contextual historians strategically, we might begin by placing them within and against the historical traditions of the field. Two or more centuries ago, European international jurists imagined their history animated by natural law – a kind of ethical unfolding, whose continuities expressed the good and true.[12] There were lots of ideas about what that meant, of course, but a loosely shared picture of what history was for. In the nineteenth century, international lawyers began to imagine a history animated by power, its continuities expressive of sovereign consent and the nature of political life among sovereign beings.[13] The contrast between eighteenth-century international law situated in the context of 'nature', and nineteenth-century international law in the context of 'power', seemed very important. Lots seemed to turn on it. What role for law in war, for example? Must wars be just – or must they be fought to vindicate agreed entitlements by means accepted among civilized powers? Is sovereignty a matter of consolidated military power prior to law, source of law's own authority – or the opposite? Although it was possible to work out ways to legally dominate other people in both vocabularies, in working out the doctrinal details, adjusting the claims of this or that authority, establishing the role for legal professionals, imagining the possibilities for international collaboration and alliance, a lot seemed to

---

[12] See Martti Koskenniemi, *The Gentle Civilizer of Nations: The Rise and Fall of International Law, 1870–1960* (Cambridge: Cambridge University Press, 2001), 20–24. Anghie links the emergence of natural law to the colonial context in Antony Anghie, 'Francisco de Vitoria and the Colonial Origins of International Law', *Social & Legal Studies* 5 (1996), 321–36, at 323 ('Vitoria . . . creates a new system of international law which essentially displaces divine law and its administrator, the Pope, and replaces it with natural law administered by a secular sovereign. Thus, the emergence of a secular natural law – the natural law which was proclaimed to be the basis of the new international law – is coeval with . . . his resolution of the problem of the legal status of the Indian, for it is this problem which initiates Vitoria's inquiry.') See also Emmanuelle Jouannet, 'Universalism and Imperialism: The True-False Paradox of International Law?', *European Journal of International Law* 18 (2007), 379, at 380–2.

[13] See Anghie, 'Finding the Peripheries'.

hinge on the difference. A world of sovereignty-as-consolidated-power gives things like 'colonialism' or 'nationalism' a different shape, feel and trajectory than they had in a world of 'sovereign rights' and law-as-natural-reason.

Over the last century, as international law has come to be understood both as the expression of humanist wisdom and as a tool for practical management, two quite different approaches to the field's history have developed.[14] The field seems both to have inherited and to have overcome each historical tradition. That international law has somehow risen above or escaped the vicissitudes of its origin to become *both* the expression of universal reason *and* the expression of consolidated power is what makes it a useful practical tool. Each tradition persists, but in a soft and indistinct way, each in the shadow of the other's potential invocation. Even the most ethically authoritative norms are thought to express universal assent, while even the most hard-boiled expressions of legitimate coercion carry a patina of virtue. Each can also serve as a limit for the other. As a pragmatic person, you are unlikely to be moved by the invocation of historical wisdom which points to an impractical result. And if what you are doing also somehow expresses the wisdom of the ages, it would be churlish to focus on this or that unfortunate consequence. As a result, in using international legal materials to make assertions about who is entitled to do what, it is possible to draw on both notions, happily switching between or combining them.

Because this vague or agnostic sense for law's roots is what makes it useful for problem-solving, thinking too much about historical origins might mess things up. Treading lightly helps both to reinforce international law's normative authority and excuse the shortcomings of its projects. If human rights norms, for example, express both universal ethics and universal consent, any attention to their historical roots in this or that culture and political initiative can only be de-legitimating. At the same time, the claim to express a universal ethics is buttressed by a historical sense for international law's progressive teleology; a weak force bending the world slowly toward justice. As a result, mainstream international law likes its history lite and people using international law for practical purposes have only a loose sense for its history. Contemporary textbooks typically begin with a 1648 rupture from a world of empire, war and religion into a two-century meditation on the nature of law among sovereigns, punctuated by a lineage of 'naturalist' and 'positivist' jurists before a turn in the twentieth century to modern institutions, courts and

---

[14] See David Kennedy, 'Tom Franck and the Manhattan School', *New York University Journal of International Law and Politics* 35 (2003), 397–435; David Kennedy, 'The Disciplines of International Law and Policy', *Leiden Journal of International Law* 12 (1999), 9–133, at 91–4.

doctrines.[15] One finds few mainstream works assessing the 'contribution' of a past jurist to international law's accumulated wisdom or rooting contemporary doctrines in political and cultural history.[16]

On the other hand, work *challenging* international law's authority and usefulness has turned ever more avidly to history, both by placing key jurists in the context of the messy local circumstances in which they wrote and by revisiting international law's links with darker historical episodes like colonialism or fascism. These efforts aim to undermine both the claim to universal wisdom and to settled and accepted power. If we can think of Grotius less as a timeless origin for eclectic wisdom than as a lawyer for the Dutch East India Company with an axe to grind,[17] by analogy we might come to see everyone who uses international law as a person with a project. If international law is made and applied in ruthless struggle, we would not be surprised to find that its rules and institutions expressed the interest of winners, from sixteenth-century imperialists to modern hegemons.[18] And that it differed in place and time as people harnessed it more or less successfully for different ends. Taken together, these moves aim to destabilize the taken-for-granted

---

[15] See, e.g., Lori Damrosch and Sean Murphy, *International Law: Cases and Materials* (6th ed.) (St Paul: West, 2014), xvii–xxix.

[16] For two classic examples, both focusing on Grotius, see Hersch Lauterpacht, 'The "Grotian Tradition" in International Law', *British Yearbook of International Law* 23 (1946), 1–53; Hedley Bull, Benedict Kingsbury and Adam Roberts (eds.), *Hugo Grotius and International Relations* (Oxford: Oxford University Press, 1992). For a recent example, see Philippe Sands, *East West Street: On the Origins of Genocide and Crimes against Humanity* (New York: Knopf, 2016) (tracing the origin of the contemporary focus on individual rather than collective rights to the influence of Lauterpacht during the immediate post-war period at the expense of Lemkin's contemporaneous alternative ideas).

[17] See, e.g., Ileana Porras, 'Constructing International Law in the East Indian Seas: Property, Sovereignty, Commerce and War in Hugo Grotius' De Iure Praedae – The Law of Prize and Booty, or "On How to Distinguish Merchants from Pirates"', *Brooklyn Journal of International Law* 31 (2006), 741–804, at 744–8; David Kennedy, 'Primitive Legal Scholarship', *Harvard International Law Journal* 27 (1986), 1–98, at 1–13, 76–95; Peter Borschberg, 'Hugo Grotius, East India Trade and the King of Johor', *Journal of Southeast Asian Studies* 30 (1999), 225–48, at 230–41 (arguing that the Dutch East India Company's 'negotiations with the King of Johor were crucial in stimulating Grotius to formulate his ideas on the issues of sovereignty, trade, just war and alliance-making').

[18] See, e.g., Anghie, *Imperialism, Sovereignty and the Making of International Law*, particularly at 190–4 (suggesting that the technologies devised in the mandate system to manage relations between the colonizer and colonized can be traced in the contemporary management practices of successors like the Bretton Woods institutions); Frédéric Mégret, 'From "Savages" to "Unlawful Combatants": A Postcolonial Look at International Humanitarian Law's "Other"', in Anne Orford (ed.), *International Law and Its Others* (Cambridge: Cambridge University Press, 2006), 265–317, at 299–303 (describing the use of arguments which once excluded 'savages' from the protections of the law of war in the contemporary 'war against terrorism').

notion that international law expresses a normative continuity from an origin in reason and political settlement through an imperfect but pre-figurative present toward a redemptive future in which wisdom and power will lie down comfortably with one another.

The imbalance between express and implied historical styles can make contextual histories seem preoccupied with the dark sides. Vitoria may have been a universal humanist, but he turned those ideas to justify the occupation and murder of America's indigenous peoples. The League was not only a failed experiment in collective security, but the continuation of colonialism by other means, inventing practices of statistical oversight to facilitate the transition from colonial to post-colonial control. The International Criminal Court is not only the culmination of historic efforts to render individuals responsible, and the precursor for a global system of criminal justice, but a novel way to continue the interventions of the North Atlantic in the affairs of Africa.[19] Antony Anghie, the most well-known of recent contextual historians, traces a dark continuity across three hundred years: in each period, using completely different intellectual, institutional and doctrinal resources, Europeans managed to consolidate relations of inequality with the peoples of the South.[20]

In this spirit, people have turned to history for large-scale course corrections in the field's contemporary self-image. If you think international law is global or cosmopolitan or universal, think again: it's European.[21] As Martti Koskenniemi has put it:

> One can do international law better or worse, but the criteria of excellence have been set by Europeans: Cicero and Roman law, Catholic intellectuals, Vitoria in the sixteenth or Louis le Fur in the twentieth century, protestant activists, Hugo de Groot in the seventeenth, or Johann Caspar Bluntschli in

---

[19] B.S. Chimni, 'International Institutions Today: An Imperial Global State in the Making', *European Journal of International Law* 15 (2004), 1–37, at 13 ('The establishment of international criminal tribunals (ICT) form[s] *a crucial element* of the nascent global state. While welcome in themselves, powerful states are unlikely to be the subject of their attention. A North-South divide characterizes the punishment of international criminal conduct. It is extremely unlikely that the leaders and armed personnel of Northern states would ever be dragged before the ICC. In any case, the US is extremely hostile to the ICC and is busy signing bilateral agreements with states to ensure that no American soldier is ever tried before it.').

[20] For the now classic demonstration of this proposition, see Antony Anghie, *Imperialism, Sovereignty and the Making of International Law*.

[21] See, e.g., Jouannet, 'Universalism and Imperialism', 380 ('That classical international law was the product of European legal culture is an incontestable fact that no-one now questions. International law was born with the modern European period. The first rationalist, humanist and liberal version of international law in effect came into being between the 16th and the 18th centuries, within the natural law school in Europe, and was then imposed in imperialistic manner throughout the whole world during the 19th and the first half of the 20th centuries.').

the nineteenth century ... None of these men thought of Europe in merely local terms, but generalized it into a representative of the universal. The principle of generalization may have changed: Roman civilization (and law), Christianity, the 'humanity' of the Enlightenment, science and capitalism in the nineteenth, modernity in the twentieth and globalization in the twenty-first century. It is hard to tell these ideas apart. They all claim the status of an Esperanto, transcending the time and place in which they are spoken.[22]

Where the conventional view had left defenders of international norms – particularly human rights norms – to unearth parallel normative developments in other cultures, revisionist historians have castigated the field for participating in the universalization of so particular a vision and insisted that other voices pursuing other agendas were available, sometimes playing a role, more often being ignored or rejected.[23]

---

[22] Martti Koskenniemi, 'International Law in Europe: Between Traditional and Renewal', *European Journal of International Law* 16 (2015), 113–24, at 114. Discussing his earlier work, he notes: 'In the *Gentle Civilizer*, I tried to give close "anthropological" attention to the contexts in which international law emerged as a cultural sensibility among a class of late-19th century European liberal and Protestant professionals. Instead of depicting it as part of some universal metaphysic I described international law as a platform or a vocabulary for the political project of a small group of activist lawyers, hoping to make it appear as a narrow – indeed "exotic" – aspect of fin de siècle European culture. Such genealogies may operate to pinpoint the "particular" that is hidden by the discipline's universal voice': Martti Koskenniemi, 'Histories of International Law: Dealing with Eurocentrism', *Rechtsgeschichte* 19 (2011), 152–77, at 174; see also Matthew Craven, *The Decolonization of International Law: State Succession and the Law of Treaties* (Oxford: Oxford University Press, 2009), 22 (aiming to provincialize (or, exoticize and make less-than-universal) the influence of Europe in international law).

For a seminal attempt at 'provincializing' Europe from its status as the singular and unavoidable context for historical knowledge, see Dipesh Chakrabarty, *Provincializing Europe: Postcolonial Thought and Historical Difference* (Princeton: Princeton University Press, 2000), 16. The attempt to provincialize the European narrative in international law has been used for emancipatory claims from the South: see, e.g., B.S. Chimni, 'Asian Civilizations and International Law: Some Reflections', *Asian Journal of International Law* 1 (2011), 39–42 (recognizing the distinct contribution of Asian states to the evolution and growth of international law doctrines and practices); Arnulf Becker Lorca, 'Alejandro Álvarez Situated', 883 (arguing that Álvarez, a Latin American lawyer and intellectual, was central to the global history of international law, having participated in developing the discipline's modern constellation of concepts, institutions, and practices while remaining embedded in the intellectual and political struggles of his native Chile and of Latin American states within the international system). For an anthology of anti-Eurocentric historical work, see Bardo Fassbender and Anne Peters (eds.), *The Oxford Handbook of the History of International Law* (Oxford: Oxford University Press, 2012). For a critical review, see Anne-Charlotte Martineau, 'Overcoming Eurocentrism? Global History and the Oxford Handbook of the History of International Law', *European Journal of International Law* 25 (2014), 329–36.

[23] See, e.g., Chimni, 'Asian Civilizations and International Law', 41–2 ('For instance, R.P. Anand has pointed out that in formulating his thesis on the freedom of the seas, Grotius was "aware of

Moreover, if you think international law manages or governs relations among equal sovereign states ..., nope, it's about reinforcing unequal relations among regions, nations and cultures.²⁴ Nor is international law best understood as 'public', innocent of economics or above national cultural and family traditions. The laws of families, of markets and of sovereigns developed in parallel, everywhere entangled with one another.²⁵ If you

---

the long tradition of freedom of navigation in the Indian Ocean" and got a "helpful cue from the Asian state practice of freedom of commerce and trade between various countries and peoples without any let or hindrance". Indeed, according to Anand, freedom of the seas "is one principle which Europe acquired from Asia through Grotius."' Chimni concludes: 'The areas in which Asian states have historically made a substantial contribution to the development of international law include the law of the sea, international humanitarian law, and international environmental law. These have been amply recorded in the writings of both Asian and Western scholars.').

[24] See, e.g., Obiora Chinedu Okafor, 'Newness, Imperialism, and International Legal Reform in Our Time: A TWAIL Perspective', *Osgoode Hall Law Journal* 43 (2005), 171–91, at 176–7 (arguing that TWAIL (Third World Approaches to International Law) scholars 'are solidly united by a *shared ethical commitment* to the intellectual and practical struggle to expose, reform, or even retrench those features of the intellectual legal system that help create or maintain the generally unequal, unfair, or unjust global order'); Anghie, 'Colonialism and the Birth of International Institutions' (arguing that international law created two models of sovereignty for Europeans and non-Europeans, placing them in an unavoidable hierarchy, and that post-war international institutions reproduce these inequalities); Chimni, 'The Past, Present and Future of International Law', 511–12 (arguing that coming to terms with 'the dark past of international law' will mean that '[i]nternational law's role in legitimising and sustaining colonialism and non-territorial imperialism will come to be recognised. The story of resistance to colonial and neo-colonial international law will become an integral part of the story of international law. ... The project of emancipation will then find a home in the *new* history of global law.'); and Chimni, 'International Institutions Today', 6–24 (arguing that 'imperial' relations of inequality continue to characterize contemporary intergovernmental organizations, causing a loss of autonomy and the displacement of sovereign economic decision-making authority for third world states while promoting transnational capital). The argument crediting international law with colonial violence has its opponents. See, e.g., Ian Hunter, 'The Figure of Man and the Territorialisation of Justice in "Enlightenment" Natural Law: Pufendorf and Vattel' (2013) 23 *Intellectual History Review* 289–307.

[25] See Martti Koskenniemi, 'Empire and International Law: The Real Spanish Contribution', *University of Toronto Law Journal* 61 (2011) 1–36, at 11–12 ('I would like to suggest that the principal Spanish contribution is not in those express arguments but in the development of a whole vocabulary that has since come to delineate the imperial dimensions of international law. At the heart of this vocabulary stand three notions already familiar from Roman law and medieval Christianity – *dominium, ius gentium,* and the *bellum iustum* ... the most important Spanish contribution to the practice of empire lies in the recovery of those three notions and in giving them a meaning through which it was possible to react not only to the *duda Indiana* – the concerns of conscience raised by the Spanish activities in the Indies – but to three further transformations that took place in the period: the formation of centralized political communities – states – that demanded absolute loyalty from their citizens; the emergence of a global economic system based on private ownership and the search for profit; and continuous warfare, not only against the infidel, but among Christian rulers themselves.'); Matthew

thought economic and gender justice were someone else's problems, you were wrong. And it's not secular either: its roots lie and continue to grow from Christian religious political projects.[26] Religion did not go away with the turn to positivism; protestant theology informed European cosmopolitanism, missionary work accompanied the legal imagination of the colonial encounter, and religious ideas and actors were central to the twentieth-century origins of 'human rights'.[27] The claim that 1648 inaugurated a secular settlement among sovereigns should itself be placed in the context of its most emphatic assertion: the post-1945 Cold War insistence that international law can be outside and above 'ideology'.[28]

Revisionist histories like these would seem to open the door for careful assessment of the distributive consequences of ideas about context. What real world difference does it make for these people to know this rather than assume that? And yet, it is surprising how little attention has been devoted to assessing the pathways by which a new context becomes power. All too often, we are left with broad historical analogies and generalizations.[29] When tendentious work

---

Craven, 'Colonialism and Domination', in Fassbender and Peters (eds.), *Oxford Handbook of the History of International Law*, 862–89, at 864–5 (providing 'an outline sketch of this putative "relationship" between international law and colonial practice across the 16th–19th centuries in a way that ... avoids the indulgence of believing that the law of nations was somehow abstracted from the material processes of colonial rule', and drawing attention to 'the parallel transition from a post-feudal mercantile economy to one centered (in Europe at least) upon industrial production and finance capital.'). On the complex historical relationship between the laws of families, markets and sovereigns, see Duncan Kennedy, 'Three Globalizations of Law and Legal Thought: 1850–2000', in David Trubek and Alvaro Santos (eds.), *The New Law and Economic Development: A Critical Appraisal* (Cambridge: Cambridge University Press, 2006), 19–73, at 32–4; Duncan Kennedy, 'Savigny's Family/Patrimony Distinction and Its Place in the Global Genealogy of Classical Legal Thought', *American Journal of Comparative Law* 58 (2010), 811–41; Janet Halley, 'What is Family Law? A Genealogy', *Yale Journal of Law and the Humanities* 23 (2011), 1–109 (Part I), 189–293 (Part II); see also Hilary Charlesworth, Christine Chinkin and Shelley Wright, 'Feminist Approaches to International Law', *American Journal of International Law* 85 (1991) 613–45, at 638–43 (discussing the public/private distinction in international law).

[26] John D. Haskell, 'The Scandal of Disenchantment: Blind Spots in Contemporary Anglo-American Approaches to the History and Politics of International Law', *Memphis Law Review* 44 (2013), 37–94, at 66. See also Hunter, 'The Figure of Man' (criticizing 'post-colonial' focus on the colonial encounter as a crucible for early modern ideas about natural law rather than the influence of Protestant theology on intra-European territorial disputes).

[27] Samuel Moyn, *Christian Human Rights* (Philadelphia: University of Pennsylvania Press, 2015), 11–12.

[28] See, e.g., Leo Gross, 'The Peace of Westphalia, 1648–1948', *American Journal of International Law* 42 (1948), 20–41.

[29] See, e.g., James Thuo Gathii, 'Neoliberalism, Colonialism and International Governance: Decentering the International Law of Governmental Legitimacy', *Michigan Law Review* 98 (2000), 1996–2055, at 2024 ('Although it may be too simplistic to draw analogies between the

seeks innocent passage as historical correction, it can dim the appetite for investigation of the machinery of impact and the consequences of knowledge work. But it is not only the coy methodological habits of the historians themselves which get in the way. The consequences of historical contextualization are difficult to predict.

That international law was entangled with religion or trade or colonial power: good or bad for whom? It could be that international law's – altogether false – claims to be secular, universal, progressive and fair-dealing made – and still make – the world a better place. Or that the armature held up by such claims supported lots of other things one might regret toppling. I suspect not, but one would have to show that. If people knew norms were forged in the colonial encounter, they might find them less compelling. But tainted origins would not be the end of the story. Today, we might applaud the distributive effects of norms forged in the colonial encounter. We'd have to figure that out.[30]

It is hard to say what would happen were people to accept international law's roots in Christian or European culture, or come to see it as an expression of pan-European aspirations and the Orientalizing imagination of European civilization about its various others. People who resist the authority of human rights norms may be comforted to learn their origin is a foreign religious victory rebranded as a universal consensus. People who promote human rights norms may be chastened, more open to alternative ethical visions and cultural authorities – or they may double down and shore up human rights' universalist credentials by comparative study. On the other side, linking international law with universal reason might raise the status of the discipline, but it might also mark the profession as effete, elite, unfit to exercise state power.

Placing a nominally 'public' international law in the context of its many engagements with 'private' and 'commercial' affairs would foreground the

---

contemporary fad of collapsed states (which justifies foreign intervention for democracy, human rights, and economic restructuring) and nineteenth-century international law scholarship on ideas such as *terra nullius* and civilization (defined as Western) that justified colonization, there is nonetheless a continuity of ideas here. There is an undeniable genealogy in the sense that the idea of collapsed states replicates nineteenth-century colonial international legal discourse. In fact, as recently as 1995, a leading international lawyer, Inis Claude, suggested that a solution to the phenomenon of collapsed states was a return to the trusteeship system which failed by allowing too many states to become independent before they were prepared for the responsibilities of statehood.').

[30] For thoughts on how one might trace the distributional impact of legal arrangements and ideas, see Kennedy, *A World of Struggle*, 171–217.

continuities between 'sovereignty' and 'property'.³¹ But which would get stronger as a result: sovereignty or property? If people understood the historical novelty of imagining 'international law' to be removed from economics, would 'free trade' be more or less persuasive? Might European social democracy seem more reasonable, neoliberalism less so? Perhaps Europeans would be more confident in the historical pedigree of their position in trade wars, the Americans more entrenched in the need to depart from history. It is hard to predict whose hand would be strengthened. Or say people can be convinced that what happened to the family – its localization, its relegation to a space neither market nor state, its association with 'culture' – is part of what made the 'international' what it has become: cosmopolitan, global, 'above' the complexities of cultural or national difference. Would human rights more readily defend the veil or its prohibition?

If international law was forged in the colonial encounter, developed as a tool and expression of colonial domination, and continues to ratify inequality, it can be discredited without identifying the mid-level machinery through which it distributes power, wealth or prestige in the world. As analogues to colonial practice, United Nations disaster relief, development or international criminal law need not be unpacked or assessed in detail to be weakened. But would it be easier to think globally about poverty once we saw international law as colonialism? Antony Anghie's historical analysis leads him to suggest that post-war international institutions – especially the World Bank and International Monetary Fund – reproduce the inequalities of states in a way that makes it more difficult to think about poverty globally.³² But it is difficult to generalize about the consequences of historical reinterpretation. Although some post-colonial elites might assert their authority more effectively, experience their victimhood more profoundly, the result for populations who live under their rule would remain obscure. And some national actors might more readily defend their inaction as powerlessness.

---

[31] See Craven, 'Colonialism and Domination', 882, 888 ('Political economy seemed to demand a separation between sovereign authority and private ownership to which end a differentiation between *imperium* (sovereignty or jurisdiction) and *dominium* (property) was important ... The key theme that I have sought to sketch out, is the shift from a conception of colonial rule framed in terms of *dominium*, to one structured around the idea of *imperium* ... Colonialism was not just about acquiring things as property, but about turning things into property.').

[32] Anghie, 'Colonialism and the Birth of International Institutions'. On the contemporary political valence of third world historical revisionism, see also Obiora Chinedu Okafor, 'Critical Third World Approaches to International Law (TWAIL): Theory, Methodology, or Both?', *International Community Law Review* 10 (2008), 371–8; Makau Mutua, 'What Is TWAIL?', *Proceedings of the American Society of International Law* 94 (2000), 31–8.

Beyond these distributional effects, intensifying the historical complexity of international law should make it easier to appreciate its multiplicity. It has been – and still is – different things to people in different times and places. It should be easier to remember that international lawyering is a different job in France and in New York, in Chile and in China, in a university or a foreign ministry or corporate firm once we grasp that being an international jurist today is an altogether different job from the one Vitoria or Grotius – or Vattel or Lorimer or Elihu Root – had. Different conceptual universe, different geography, different historical time.[33] Today, international law is not 'universal' even within the North. It is different in Europe and the United States, each home to a variety of traditions and approaches in struggle with one another. International law in the semi-periphery and periphery has been something else again, in each society inflected as much by local political or intellectual struggles as by engagement with the European or American 'centre'.[34]

This sensitivity to pluralism might qualify the conventional sense that international law has had a consistent project for hundreds of years: it is about peace, not conflict; it settles war and constrains its violence; it comes after empire and stands above religious or ideological conflict. An orientation to universality and coherence has made it difficult for international law to grapple with the hodge-podge of legalities that crisscross the globe: formal and informal, national and local and so-called international, corporate and public and private and criminal. Repositioning jurists in their time and place should help the discipline embrace international law's pluralism, fragmentation and inconsistency.

Rather than foregrounding pluralism, however, contextual histories are often tempted to replace one coherence with another. So we find that international law was 'really' about something like finding a universal solution to the problem of cultural difference or managing unequal relations in the key of equality. Yet if international law is really religious and commercial and private and European and colonial and rooted once and always in conflict, is there still 'an' international law? Pulling the pieces together in large-scale narratives, contextual work can make it yet more difficult to identify the

---

[33] Even Suárez, Vitoria and Grotius inhabited different worlds. See Kennedy, 'Primitive Legal Scholarship', 1–13; Hunter, 'The Figure of Man'.

[34] See, e.g., Fleur Johns, Thomas Skouteris and Wouter Werner (eds.), special issues in 'The Periphery Series': 'The League of Nations and the Construction of the Periphery', *Leiden Journal of International Law* 24 (2011), 797; 'India and International Law', *Leiden Journal of International Law* 23 (2010), 1; 'Taslim Olawale Elias', *Leiden Journal of International Law* 23 (2010), 289; and Arnulf Becker Lorca, 'Alejandro Álvarez Situated'.

impact on specific struggles. Mainstream histories wrap things in a gauze of cosmopolitan virtue which makes wins and losses for specific interests less important than keeping history's progressive march on track. When revisionist histories place international law in the context of large historical forces like 'colonialism', 'capitalism' and 'patriarchy' it can have a somewhat similar effect.

Contextual histories are most effective as criticisms of the contemporary use of international legal materials when they avoid the temptations to reaffirm the field's coherence or shy away from assessing its distributional impact.[35] People today use international legal materials with a sense both for their virtuous promise *and* for their strategic usefulness. Although they don't 'believe' in the virtuous self-image which forms the backdrop for their strategic pragmatism, the weak link remains the *relationship* between their strategic pragmatism and this strikingly undogmatic faith. Together these make it seem plausible to operate strategically for one's interest in a language of universal virtue. International lawyers have a similar attitude toward the field's theoretical weaknesses and contradictions. Perhaps there is no way to square sovereign authority with international legality: one must simply *choose* law, choose to see the world ordered and constituted by law as a kind of professional ethics, a virtue chosen in the shadow of a dark political history. This leaves the common sense of global legal managers somehow gnomic, contradictory and ad hoc.

Although one can use history to criticize such a practice for its unswerving immoral and unjust consequences, it might be better to think of international legal materials and authors as archaeological fragments that happened to survive – pottery shards from Pompeii – rather than as constitutive ideas for the transhistorical errors of the discipline. This might help to reframe

---

[35] Martti Koskenniemi has critiqued this tendency to avoid attention to distributional outcomes in both historical and contemporary international law scholarship, arguing that the tendency to prioritize the 'order' or the constitutional dimension in international law places winners and losers in the background. See, e.g., Martti Koskenniemi, 'The Fate of Public International Law: Between Techniques and Politics', Modern Law Review 70 (2007), 1–30, at 18–19 ('Law has integrity as a system, either in the Anglo-American image, through the constructive operations by which lawyers decide cases, or in the continental perspective, through the systematizing efforts of legal science. But the system only says that everything should be decided according to it – which is to say no more than that, whatever the decision, it should be made by *legal* institutions, in particular institutions populated by public international lawyers. But if that is all the law says, it only underwrites the structural bias of its institutions. This may seem fine if one is a member of those institutions oneself. But if one does not share their bias, but rather thinks of them as part of the problem, then constitutionalism has no compelling force. Surely what matters is whether it is a *good* constitution, whether it empowers the *right* people, whether it allocates resources in accordance with the *right* bias.').

international law as a discontinuous grab-bag of things people try as they struggle with one another. We would then want to figure out the work these textual shards did in the world, their distributive impact, their sociological usefulness in battle.[36] This might help detach contemporary legal materials from their place in an imagined 'system' to reveal the mechanisms by which they bring about unwanted consequences in particular places. If we see international law implicated in contemporary injustice despite its optimistic and reformist mien, the trick, it would seem to me, would be to foreground the incoherence, multiplicity and pluralism of the legal field, opening the door for sustained attention to the mid-level sociological mechanisms by which international legal ideas and institutions contribute to the routine distribution of power, wealth, status, honor or shame. The antidotes to undesirable international legal rulership, in short, are attention to its incoherent pluralism and distributional impact.

3.5 A POST-WAR INTERNATIONAL ORDER UNDER SIEGE: LESSONS FROM CRITICAL HISTORIES

When contextual historians chastise the international legal profession for supporting an unjust order in the name of cosmopolitan virtue, the analogy with criticism of elite commitments to liberal internationalism can be uncomfortable. It threatens to cast the international legal historian with the forces of populism, nationalism, mercantilism and authoritarianism. It is easy to think, wait, that's not what we had in mind. One understandable reaction is retreat: doubling down on the post-war liberal order. Legal intellectuals are not alone in this. After the Trump election in the United States, many progressives suddenly felt the liberal international order didn't look so bad. People who had shown little sympathy for America's hegemonic role in global affairs

---

[36] For examples which push in this direction, see Fleur Johns, Richard Joyce, and Sundhya Pahuja (eds.), *Events: The Force of International Law* (Oxford: Routledge, 2011); Pahuja, 'Laws of Encounter'; Luis Eslava and Sundhya Pahuja, 'Between Resistance and Reform: TWAIL and the Universality of International Law', *Trade, Law and Development* 3 (2011), 103–30, at 129 ('What our methodological turn offers ... is an avenue ... to start locating the international in those places that usually escape our attention and yet regulate our lives, especially the lives of the billions who are subject to developmental interventions.'); Luis Eslava, *Local Space, Global Life: The Everyday Operation of International Law and Development* (Cambridge: Cambridge University Press, 2015), 264–87 (highlighting the 'increasing localization of international obligations and responsibilities' (at 264) and the 'ways in which local jurisdictions and residents are being constructed as the new carriers of international aspirations towards sustainability and progress' (at 302), while also describing 'multiple forms of resistance' against such processes (at 271)).

found themselves strangely disturbed by the prospect that it might be rolled back, commitments to allied defence unwound, humanitarian interventions curtailed, free trade repurposed for national economic growth. Nor was it so tempting to criticize the vocabularies of elite rule, the gentle norms and dulcet tones of conventional diplomacy and statecraft, once people with real authority in the North Atlantic began to deviate from them.

But contextual histories also suggest a more productive way to understand what's going on, reminding us that imagining a liberal/cosmopolitan world requires a lot of forgetting. It has hardly been humanitarian or liberal for everyone. Nor has it been orderly. Contemporary arrangements echo colonial arrangements we readily identify as unjust. Closer examination of our flat world of global markets and liberal commitments would excavate an equally chaotic struggle for advantage. Contextual histories are particularly useful for this purpose when they examine the machinery allocating power and wealth within what we remember as a more coherent and virtuous order. When they do, they may suggest ways to understand the contemporary situation without casting populist outsiders as the only alternative to an insider elite consensus.

Foregrounding the distributional consequences of mid-level legal and institutional arrangements in a disordered – or multiply ordered – world would also give us a different picture of the losers. They have not been left out: they have been defeated. In this, the post-war liberal order is not unlike mercantilism or empire. The machinery is different – the roles of public and private law, of local government and global financiers have all been reshuffled. Economic activities have always been linked to political power. Corporations and investors have always relied on powerful states to protect their influence and every hegemonic power has developed an infrastructure congenial to its interests. The point of 'free trade' is not only to generate global gains, but to do all in one's power to get and keep those gains for oneself, our city, our country. And people today are just as ruthless about this as ever. Following Nixon's decision to decouple the dollar from gold, US Treasury Secretary John Connally is reported to have said: 'my view is that the foreigners are out to screw us, and therefore, it's our job to screw them first.'[37] It is not only Americans who talk this way.

A history of law's role in domination and distribution would clarify the ways in which such sentiments are given expression in regimes which seem impartial, even benevolent. The legal institutions of European Union and London financial hegemony, for example, are not only avatars of peace and prosperity.

---

[37] Quoted in Hobart Rowen, '"Big John," The Comeback Kid', *Washington Post*, 17 June 1993.

They establish hierarchies of haves and have nots when monetary union becomes a recipe for debt bondage, or free movement for the periphery and social protection at the center becomes an engine for relative wealth and stagnation.

Although the global order may not have been benevolent, however, neither was it ever an iron cage. Then, as now, elites struggled to hold it together. As they worked to manage things for advantage, they always confronted alternative voices, even – or especially – among themselves. That's why it was a struggle. Historians have unearthed a range of voices from the semi-periphery within international law. Although one could imagine them simply to have 'participated' in universalizing European ideas, historians like Arnulf Becker tell a different story. They were engaged in their own local political projects, saw and established a different international law with a different intellectual canon, different focal points and meanings. He calls it 'mestizo international law', cohabiting with the global order of its day.[38] The analogy is suggestive: perhaps today's alternatives – and the political space to pursue them – have also been there all along.

We might read contextual histories of international law as critiques of the idea that politics is outside expert rule. They argue that international law did not evolve as the distillation of political action into universal wisdom. Nor is the 'legality' of international law a function of its separation from political discretion, its scientific objectivity and interpretation by mandarin jurists. If international law was made in the back and forth of political and economic conflict, rather than a law rising out of and above or coming after politics, it would be better to think of politics having been there all along.

And all along there were choices. One need not choose between the modest reformism on offer from the mavens of elite management and outsider agitation. Where money, credit, labor and capital – like political power and right – are legally constructed, they could be and have been put together in lots of ways. The legal boundaries between economics and politics, like those private and public actors, are of recent vintage, marked and managed in legal terms: they could be otherwise. There may be more possibilities within the framework of the nominally liberal global order, just as there have been in other eras. Historical work is particularly helpful when it revives heterodox analyses and experiences which have been forgotten as the particular institutions we ended up with were canonized as order, equilibrium, even justice.

---

[38] Becker Lorca, *Mestizo International Law*.

By tracing the impact of legal arrangements on political and economic trajectories, historians could illuminate how economies put together differently would operate differently and how they might be changed by altering the direction for the routine work of managing the 'system', adjusting the entitlements and expectations that link people in relationships of relative privilege and vulnerability. To rearrange them would require struggle on the terrain where inequality is established and maintained. But this is not a matter of outsider populism or detached academic reflection. It is a matter, in Max Weber's words, of the strong slow drilling through hard boards in the institutional arrangements and vocabularies of modern expert rule. Historians can help us get started.

4

After Method: International Law and the Problems of History

GERRY SIMPSON*

'Ah ... yes ...' Lord Kessler's faint smile and tucked-in chin suggested an easily mastered disappointment. 'And what is your chosen field?'
'Mm. I want to have a look at *style*,' Nick said. ...
Lord Kessler appeared uncertain.[1]

You're gone; I am learning to live in history.
What is history? What you cannot touch.[2]

In the spirit of 'thinking through the international' and reflecting on the ways of (historical and juridical) seeing that might enliven (or temper) such thinking, I want to ask a question and make a small plea.

The question concerns what international legal history might look like 'after method'. I am happy to wear, for these purposes, the too-seamless itinerary assumed by the question; it's not as if, after all, many of the international lawyers who wrote history in the past did not think about method. What *has* happened, though, is that there is now a new, probably more systematic, certainly more self-conscious, discipline-wide orientation towards thinking about historical method – and in the aftermath of this change, it has become at least less likely that international legal histories will be written with blitheness about, or resistance to, or disregard for, method. Part of this orientation has required an encounter with, and a taking seriously of, techniques of studying the past found

---

* Andrea Bianchi, Matthew Craven, Ayça Çubuçku, Justin Desautels-Stein, Emily Kidd White and Tom Poole read and commented on this paper. Megan Donaldson read and edited with great care, intelligence and attention to detail. I thank them. Thanks also to Annabel Brett, Martti Koskenniemi and the participants in the workshop at Clare College, Cambridge, *Thinking through the International: History, Politics, Law*, 16–17 May 2016.
[1] Alan Hollinghurst, *The Line of Beauty* (London: Picador, 2005), 54.
[2] Robert Lowell, 'Mexico', in *For Lizzie and Harriet* (London: Faber & Faber, 1973), 30–34, at 31.

in other fields ('History' would seem to be a good place to begin), but another part of it has provoked a series of thoughts about what it might mean either to have a historical method that is distinctively legal (one that perhaps learns from the protocols found in other fields but at the same time breaches some of the apparent prohibitions stipulated in those same fields) or to study a context that is somehow linguistic or structural or is, itself, 'a legal context'.[3]

But while much of the chapter describes international law's encounter with method and how the field might look after that encounter, I want to issue a plea concerning the limits of method. Maybe this plea is just another array of questions: Is there method that is not method? Or is method all method? Or, what lies beyond method (or 'after method') that makes a particular piece of history or legal scholarship attractive to us? The simplest way to put this is to say that when I read international law or fiction, or watch a film, I quite often have a sense – sometimes within minutes – that I am in good or bad hands. And a consideration of this sense cannot be exhausted by an attention to method (or 'method' does not seem quite the right word to capture our intuitions about these things, or, if you like, our intuitions about intuition).[4] I am not certain how I would describe this quality – I have settled on literary virtue (absent the strong moral implication) but sometimes it appears as a species of writerly ethics, sometimes as a 'way of seeing' and, no doubt, sometimes it really does map quite neatly onto a set of methodological prescriptions.[5] Warning: for those who don't share this experience (or think the explanations for it are banal), the last part of the chapter will have been in vain.

---

[3] On 'legal' contexts, see Justin Desautels-Stein, 'International Legal Structuralism: A Primer', *International Theory* 8 (2016), 201–35. For a defence of the idea of a distinctive legal method, see recent work by Anne Orford ('On International Legal Method', *London Review of International Law* 1 (2013), 166–97; 'The Past as Law or History? The Relevance of Imperialism for Modern International Law', in Mark Toufayan, Emmanuelle Tourme-Jouannet and Hélène Ruiz Fabri (eds.), *Droit international et nouvelles approches sur le tiers-monde: entre repetition et renouveau* (Paris: Société de législation comparée, 2013), 97–117).

[4] On substituting style for method while at the same time articulating a resistance to the idea of adjudicating among international legal 'methods', see Martti Koskenniemi, 'Letter to the Editors of the Symposium', *American Journal of International Law* 93 (1999), 351–61.

[5] Style might be a promising contender but it has over-inclusive and under-inclusive associations. For an example of the former, see David Kennedy's 'The International Style in Postwar Law and Policy: John Jackson and the Field of International Economic Law', *American University International Law Review* 10 (1995), 671–716(where 'style' refers to a whole doctrinal-theoretical approach to the field). In the latter vein we have the idea that 'style' might refer to a prose style, narrowly understood: e.g. a tendency to write in regimented subject-verb-object sentences, a liking for judiciously selected adverbs, a passion for sparkling adjectives. For a discussion of style as persuasion, see Andrea Bianchi, *International Law Theories: An Inquiry into Different Ways of Thinking* (Oxford: Oxford University Press, 2017), 299–301.

4.1 HISTORICAL PRECINCTS

I spent time in Brisbane some years ago (at a conference on the history of international society) and noticed that it had a cultural precinct.[6] There were signs everywhere announcing the position of the visitor or resident in relation to culture (e.g., 'you are three kilometres from the cultural centre', or 'veer left for the cultural precinct'). It was not clear to me what was being said about the rest of the city. Perhaps this was an intimation that other parts of Brisbane were an acultural sphere of capitalist expansion (a free fire zone of unplanned skyscrapers and anonymous shopping malls). On the other hand, it was apparent that more organic and unofficial cultural centres had appeared all over the city in the interstices of the de-cultured city (in lanes, along railway lines, in disused building sites).

This all reminded me of Rem Koolhaas's generic city, a contemporary city (no longer situated in history) that re-creates its own historical district (Vancouver's 'Gastown', say); Koolhaas calls this place 'Lipservice'.[7] For a long time, international law, too, had its historical district: the place — most often the chapter of a book – a reader went to do, or acquire, some history, a chapter often, usefully, titled 'History of International Law'. Doctoral students, in imitation of this, would wonder if their dissertations ought to have 'a history chapter'. This chapter might then act as an overture to the main body of the thesis. Except, very often, it wasn't an overture because the motifs did not reappear. What followed, instead, was an ostensibly historyless present. At various points in its history, then, international law has occupied this historyless present, a moment where either there is no discernible encounter with history (not even 'a memory of a memory' (Koolhaas, again)) or where the history recounted is so attenuated as to constitute a form of historylessness or where the historical periods referred to are stripped of 'everything that makes them different; so that they all look more or less like our own'.[8]

In recent years, though, the history of international law has come in from the cold and become a vibrant field of multidisciplinary scholarship.[9] This (re)

---

[6] The conference led to Tim Dunne and Christian Reus-Smit (eds.), *The Globalization of International Society* (Oxford: Oxford University Press, 2017).
[7] Rem Koolhaas, *Generic City* (Sassenheim: Sikkens Foundation, 1995). See, too, François Hartog, *Regimes of Historicity*, trans. Saskia Brown (New York: Columbia University Press, 2015).
[8] Bertolt Brecht, *Brecht on Theatre*, # 36 (3rd ed.) (London: Bloomsbury Methuen Drama, 1964).
[9] E.g. Chenxi Tang, *Imagining World Order: Literature and International Law in Early Modern Europe, 1500–1800* (Ithaca: Cornell University Press, 2018).

turn to history has been hotly pursued by a serious sensitivity to method or a newish historiographical self-awareness. Now, every sub-field has its history and then its counter-history, and then its anxiety that perhaps all these previous histories were methodologically suspect or even inept – a mere writing down of some things that happened and then some other things that happened but weren't noticed the first time round.[10] We seem now to be in a third stage where even unusually sophisticated accounts of international legal episodes or developments are the subject of criticism on the grounds of flawed or unconvincing or insufficiently contextualised historical method. And this attention – mostly sympathetic, robust, friendly – has come both from within the discipline (e.g. Peevers) and from outside it (e.g. Hunter, Keene).[11]

Whatever happens now must happen in the wake of this period of methodological restlessness. Why *this* material in *this* way from *this* position with *this* attitude and *this* method? Why *this* writer? Of course, there is no guarantee that some international legal histories won't trundle on in blissful ignorance or innocence in the same way that popular history seems immune from the methodological preoccupations of academic historians or historians of political thought. History as 'one damned thing after another' will continue to be written just as international law as 'one damned rule after another' will continue to be practised.[12]

In this chapter, I want to argue that this moment of self-consciousness (an extended moment dating back to the early work of some people featured in this collection) offers an opportunity for international lawyers to maintain or consolidate a sensibility about the world that I want to think of as literary

---

[10] In the history of international criminal law, which I will turn to later in the chapter, we had in the first mode M. Cherif Bassiouni, *Crimes against Humanity: Historical Evolution and Contemporary Application* (Cambridge: Cambridge University Press, 2011) and Geoffrey Robertson, *Crimes against Humanity: The Struggle for Global Justice* (London: Penguin, 1999); in the second Gerry Simpson and Kevin Heller, *The Hidden Histories of War Crimes Trials* (Oxford: Oxford University Press, 2013); and in the third Immi Tallgren and Thomas Skouteris (eds.), *The New Histories of International Criminal Law: Retrials* (Oxford: Oxford University Press, 2019). See generally Matthew Craven, 'Theorising the Turn to History in International Law', in Anne Orford and Florian Hoffmann (eds.), *The Oxford Handbook of the Theory of International Law* (Oxford: Oxford University Press, 2016), 21–37.

[11] See, e.g., Charlotte Peevers, 'Conducting International Authority: Hammarskjöld, the Great Powers and the Suez Crisis', *London Review of International Law* 1 (2013), 131–40; Ian Hunter, 'Global Justice and Regional Metaphysics: On the Critical History of the Law of Nature and Nations', in Shaunnagh Dorsett and Ian Hunter (eds.), *Law and Politics in British Colonial Thought: Transpositions of Empire* (New York: Palgrave Macmillan, 2010), 11–29.

[12] A phrase variously attributed to Toynbee and Henry Ford but found in a fruitier version in Alan Bennett's play *The History Boys* (London: Faber & Faber, 2008).

rather than technical.[13] And this split between the literary and the technical partly reflects the experience of reading the literature on intellectual international history or international intellectual history (the diction is David Armitage's)[14] or historical method. Here one encounters at the same time an array of techniques for doing better history (richer contexts, a watchfulness around anachronism, a vigilance about the relationship between polemic and description) but also (and this is more true of some traditions than others) – and alongside this – a sense that the most compelling or resonant histories possess literary virtues or writerly sensibilities that might be hard to domesticate as a form of 'method'. Of course, there is a whole tradition (White, Ankersmit, Jenkins) that wants to think of history as having fictive power (as having *only* fictive power).[15] I am not incurious about this debate but this chapter is mostly about a gnawing sense that when it comes to method something other than 'method' is at stake.

To put this more concretely, when we are acquainting ourselves with a prospective new friend, we would not ask 'What form of the novel do you prefer?' but instead the more common (and less pretentious): 'What novels do you read?'. So that asking which methods produce the most invigorating or politically radical or truthful histories of international law might be like asking someone what forms of the novel she admires instead of noticing the book she carries in her handbag.[16] I would not want to push this too far. Clearly, we all have powerful aesthetic preference for certain methods of novel writing. No one can prefer Camus, Joyce and Woolf, or Roberto Bolano and Tom McCarthy without admitting that plot and character might be peripheral to what is necessary to the success of a novel.

---

[13] For a defence (or advocacy) of these literary pursuits, see my *The Sentimental Life of International Law* (forthcoming); 'The Sentimental Life of International Law', *London Review of International Law* 3 (2015), 3–31. For examples of syntheses of the literary and legal, see Tang, *Imagining World Order*; Ed Morgan, *The Aesthetics of International Law* (Toronto: University of Toronto Press, 2007). See, too, for a more general philosophical treatment, Martha Nussbaum, *Love's Knowledge: Essays on Philosophy and Literature* (New York: Oxford University Press, 1990) and *Poetic Justice: The Literary Imagination and Public Life* (Boston: Beacon Press, 1996).

[14] David Armitage, *Foundations of Modern International Thought* (Cambridge: Cambridge University Press, 2012).

[15] See, e.g., Hayden White, *The Content of the Form: Narrative Discourse and Historical Representation* (Baltimore: Johns Hopkins University Press, 1987); Frank Ankersmit, 'Historiography and Postmodernism', *History and Theory* 28 (1989), 137–53; Keith Jenkins, *Rethinking History* (London: Routledge, 1991).

[16] For a (contentious) reading of Nietzsche's understanding of 'truthfulness', see Bernard Williams, *Truth and Truthfulness* (Princeton: Princeton University Press, 2002), 12–19.

My hunch is that we might understand the relationship between historians of international political thought (I am just going to call them 'historians' from now on) and international lawyers in terms of both method and writerly ethic; and that what unites some of us might be a shared aesthetic around international law in history, whatever might be the specifics of the methodologies that divide us.

I will devote part of the chapter to a discussion of some of the special problems (related to time, context and 'greatness') lawyers face when they face history (and here, taking my cue from Jennifer Pitts's idea of conceptual frames, I want to think about the sorts of historical worlds international lawyers inhabit and reproduce as a result of their predispositions).[17] All of this will lead to a plea for a post-method in which these worlds can be opened up to acts of contestation and reimagination.

4.2 INTERNATIONAL LAW/INTERNATIONAL HISTORY: SPECIFIC PROBLEMS, CONCEPTUAL FRAMES, INHABITED WORLDS

'We can know everything except ourselves' (Stendhal).[18]

Some dialogue across fields produces stasis. At interdisciplinary conferences and meetings it is not uncommon to experience a kind of need coming off the other discipline. Among international lawyers, one becomes a type of international lawyer (an institutional engineer, a woman with fancy ideas about Hannah Arendt, a dyed-in-the-wool textualist, a post-positivist, a man in exile from the Department of English Literature). Among strangers, one becomes merely an international lawyer: the Ambassador for Customary International Law. There is a rabbi in Philip Roth's *Plot against America* who knows everything but doesn't know anything else. And sometimes I have felt like that rabbi at, say, international relations conferences. I am expected to know everything about international law but nothing about anything else. My method is legal (I read cases and am obsessed with textual detail), theirs is political (they know what's going on in the world). So, as David Kennedy pointed out years ago, what is produced is an emaciated account of both fields, a co-dependency.[19] This is obviously not a good thing.

---

[17] Pitts, this volume.
[18] Quoted in Carlo Ginzburg, *Threads and Traces: True, False, Fictive*, trans. Anne C. Tedeschi and John Tedeschi (Berkeley: University of California Press, 2012), 149.
[19] David Kennedy, 'The Disciplines of International Law and Policy', *Leiden Journal of International Law* 12 (1999), 9–133.

There is another interdisciplinary story to be told though. From the intellectual history and international relations side has come a serious engagement with international legal history that leaves behind, indeed seeks to disturb, some of the commonplaces of the interdisciplinary space to produce defamiliarising and unorthodox depictions of the field. Amidst all this promising work, the encounter with international history and with 'method' has exposed again at least three special problems for international law: one related to the arrangement of time (or what Scott thinks of as the relations between temporality and history), a second concerning the relationship between anachronism and context in international legal history, and a third involving the idea of 'greatness' (or, more specifically, ideas about individual greatness, great powers and great crises).[20]

Arrangements of Time

Marc Bloch once remarked on the way in which historical periods always arrive neatly as 'centuries'[21] before he went on to condemn the tendency of synchronic histories to narrate 'pell mell events whose only connection was that they happened around the same time'.[22] International law has been prone to centurise its history. One-hundred-year slices of human existence are presented as hermetic moments in time, sheared off from their immediate predecessors and precursors. Whole centuries go missing (the eighteenth century, for a while, seemed lost: a Vattelian stop-gap between a Westphalian seventeenth century and a 'scientific' or 'positivistic' nineteenth century). The nineteenth century, itself, has been a victim of this general inclination to press different events or circumstances into the service of the one hundred year histories. The Congress of Vienna is collapsed into the Berlin Conference or the men of 1873, with insufficient regard for the way in which developments in the century cut against one another, or seem discontinuous.

This centurising reflex has tended to accompany, too, a historical method through which history is endowed with a purpose. From the perspective of contemporary international lawyers, the (centurised) nineteenth century has played a constitutive role in these sequential histories. It is the century that came before: before the modern, before the transformation, before institutions. In the standard narrative, it is embryonic; here are the inchoate, half-

---

[20] David Scott, *Omens of Adversity* (Durham, NC: Duke University Press, 2014).
[21] Marc Bloch, *The Historian's Craft*, trans. Peter Putnam (New York: Knopf, 1954 [1941]), 183.
[22] Ibid., 23.

baked beginnings of everything we are now familiar with: tiny fragments of arbitration (*Alabama Claims*), the hesitant opening moves towards an international *humanitarian* law (Brussels, St Petersburg), early signs of an institutionalist spirit (the Universal Postal Union).

A post-method sensibility, then, requires us to remember that we *are* remembering the nineteenth century and, sometimes, bringing into being the idea of it *as a* century. So, recent history has reminded us that though the nineteenth century is remembered as an era of 'sovereignty' it was, in the first quarter of the century alone, a period in which sovereignty was revived as a reaction to Napoleonic expansion but then seriously compromised by an interventionist ethic arising out of the Holy Alliance's preoccupation with revolutionary constitutionalism. After method, the nineteenth century has become many centuries: a 'long' nineteenth century beginning with the French revolution and ending with the Treaty of Versailles, or a 'short' nineteenth century framed by 1815 and the emergence of a public law of Europe and the Franco-Prussian war, or a nineteenth century of plural colonialisms, or a 'last five minutes' (Kennedy) of the Hague Peace Conferences or the professionalisation of international law, or the humanisation of war project.[23] Or the nineteenth century is imagined *as* the imagined nineteenth century: the illusion of sovereignty, positivism, philosophy, unmoored jurisprudence, the international legal order before pragmatism and so on.[24]

Meanwhile, smoothly linear chronicles of history – perhaps even the relationship between time and history itself – have been disrupted and disarticulated in recent accounts.[25] To take the nineteenth century again, it has been posited in anti-linear readings as a moment of discontinuity rather than the incomplete prelude to the modernisation and renovation of international law in the early twentieth century. The centrality of the colonial encounter in the nineteenth century has, of course, been emphasised by contemporary international lawyers (Tony Anghie, Liliana Obrégon).[26] Their scepticism

---

[23] On professionalisation, see Casper Sylvest, 'International Law in Nineteenth-Century Britain', *British Yearbook of International Law* 75 (2004), 9–70. On international law as professional activity, see Jean d'Aspremont, Tarcisio Gazzini, André Nollkaemper and Wouter Werner (eds.), *International Law as a Profession* (Cambridge: Cambridge University Press, 2017).

[24] In this regard the 'after method' period stretches back at least as far as David Kennedy's 'International Law and the Nineteenth Century: History of an Illusion', *Nordic Journal of International Law* 65 (1996), 385–420.

[25] Scott, *Omens of Adversity*, 1–20.

[26] E.g. Liliana Obrégon Tarazona, 'The Civilized and the Uncivilized', in Bardo Fassbender and Anne Peters (eds.), *The Oxford Handbook of the History of International Law* (Oxford: Oxford University Press), 917–39.

about international law's roots in a sovereignty-founding moment at Westphalia (or Utrecht) or in a slow rise to civilisation through law, is as pronounced as that of Carl Schmitt or Wilhelm Grewe, and the dark implications of nineteenth-century colonialism are present in Anghie and in Schmitt (though the darkness has to be read into the latter).[27]

But the nineteenth century is an outlier, too, in the work of someone like Charles Alexandrowicz who, *partly*, refuses this line of progressive development in favour of what he calls a 'historicized international law'[28] in which the colonial period is an exception or gap in the universalisation of international law.[29] Alexandrowicz's method is not dissimilar to that of Grewe and Schmitt, in one sense at least. He emphasises the way in which the European powers re-write the history of international law itself (in Alexandrowicz's case by forgetting the prior existence of non-European civilisations and states in order that these occluded peoples might be 'admitted' to a newly assembled family of nations).[30] His response is to produce an archive partly cleansed of what he thinks of as international law's Eurocentrism. This choice of archive can be seen as an embrace of a shared predicament (his appreciation of the continuities between Polish self-assertion and wider anti-colonial struggle) and an accident (on being appointed to a chair in India, he found himself with access to Indian records) as well as a political gesture (Alexandrowicz was committed to the idea of international law as a global, egalitarian, universal family of nations, a project in relation to which the nineteenth century, far from being constitutive, was an aberrant period of European exceptionalism). The idea, then, was to fashion a new temporality, one that would, in turn, close the gap

---

[27] Schmitt's nostalgia for empire is clear from the language he uses when referring to it as 'heroic' or 'great'. The problem of nineteenth-century empire, for Schmitt, was not that it was a form of land appropriation but that it marked a decline from, or 'epilogue' to, the 'great' imperial enterprises of the sixteenth and seventeenth centuries: Carl Schmitt, The Nomos of the Earth in the International Law of the Jus Publicum Europaeum, trans. G.L. Ulmen (New York: Telos Press, 2006), 226. For Anghie, the problem of international law in this period lies not in its failures but its successes.

[28] David Armitage and Jennifer Pitts, '"This Modern Grotius": An introduction to the life and thought of C.H. Alexandrowicz', in David Armitage and Jennifer Pitts (eds.), C.H. Alexandrowicz, The Law of Nations in Global History (Oxford: Oxford University Press, 2017), 1–31, at 15.

[29] For Alexandrowicz history *was* method. For him, precisely, studying the contemporary alone was a guarantee of irrelevance. Part of international law's problem in 1963, say, was that it was refusing to take its own history seriously in favour of 'a lifeless repetition of historical slogans'. See his 'Some Problems in the History of the Law of Nations in Asia', in Law of Nations in Global History, 76–82, at 76.

[30] Though Alexandrowicz states that this nineteenth-century development was a political initiative whose 'juridical significance was negligible': ibid., 81.

between 1815 and 1945.³¹ The sacred cows (Westphalia was unimportant compared to, say, a treaty signed by the Ottomans and France in 1535; Vienna, a wrong turn) were slain.³²

It would be wrong, though, to think of Alexandrowicz's method as entirely anti-progressive. For him, the commercial spirit (via Kant and Cobden) would, after all, inevitably prevail over systems of cultural superiority and sovereign exclusion. The method, then, is a form of positivism (he relies heavily on the voluntary compacts of legal persons) but the theory is anti-positivistic and teleological (these legal persons are not all sovereigns, positivism's nineteenth-century exclusions are repudiated and there is a strong commitment to the idea that 'the principle of universality of nations was and is inherent in a law derived from reason and not based on human will alone').³³ In a sense, then, and more generally, Alexandrowicz's elision of the nineteenth century might serve as a model for denaturalising or re-historicising the periodisations we have come to live and write amidst.

Anachronism

Alongside this desire for *telos*, a certain variety of international law has been conducted in an unselfconsciously anachronistic mode. The idea is to find antecedents and map them onto contemporary circumstance or to take ideas and reify them across centuries. Alongside this is a 'mania' to find the origins of something or other.³⁴ In this way, Pufendorf's 'state system', reduced to a mere precursor, is read directly and seamlessly onto the UN Charter inter-sovereign order or nineteenth-century 'society'.³⁵ This is a compulsion in an area I work in – international war crimes law – where the field of history is configured as a galaxy of free-floating precedents. 'The past is a foreign country and, look, they do things the same way there', whether it be banning poison tip arrows (rather like chemical weapons) or offering immunity to visiting diplomats (cue reference to *The Iliad* or Shakespeare) or deploring bad behaviour (surely an early incarnation of 'crimes against humanity'). This hyper-anachronism is especially prevalent in judicial doctrine – law's histories as opposed to histories of law – where it becomes a search for 'historical

---

[31] Armitage and Pitts, 'This Modern Grotius', 20–21.
[32] Ibid., 19.
[33] Alexandrowicz, 'Some Problems of History', 79.
[34] The word is Marc Bloch's.
[35] For Pufendorf's discussion of states-systems, see Samuel von Pufendorf, *Of the Law of Nature and Nations* (Oxford: Clarendon Press, 1934 [1672]), 1043–51.

validation'.³⁶ So, a post-war court at Nuremberg was happy to announce that 'aggression' had been a crime since 'time immemorial' (in the *Ministries* trial) while the District Court of Jerusalem, in 1961, styled Adolf Eichmann as a 'latter-day pirate', as if he had merely plundered some merchant vessels on the high seas.³⁷

In international criminal law, as we shall see later, the search for origins, or 'usable history', is part of an effort to establish the authority of a new and insecure legal project. In this way, categories like 'aggression' or 'piracy' move through time in an uncomplicated, acontextual manner that is surely red meat to a certain sort of historian of political thought on the lookout for facile homologies. Of course, international lawyers are not alone in adopting this approach to history. Similar commitments to anachronism are found in the work of structural realists in political theory for whom international history is marked by the repetition and recurrence of timeless dilemmas (to appease or not to appease, that is always the question) or is imagined as a timeless zone of the tragic.³⁸

More recently, however, after method, international legal history has been obliged to defend (often robustly) its commitments to anachronism.³⁹ And with this development has come an understanding that the debate over anachronism is partly a political struggle over the meaning of history and the requirements of the present, and perhaps not so much a 'choice of method'. Thus, the typical response to the problem of anachronism – a turn to context – should itself be understood as a political choice or a series of Russian-doll political choices (which context?) embedded in the larger decision to make 'context' (with its pre-existing methodological biases, its scholarly tradition) important so that contextualism becomes both political decision and indeterminate method.⁴⁰

Meanwhile, the deployment of deliberately acontextual reasoning can also have a political potency, whether it involves taking the 'war on terror', and its accompanying ensemble of governing practices, and assimilating them to, say, nineteenth-century imperialism,⁴¹ or showing how the Anglo-American

---

³⁶ Armitage, *Foundations of Modern International Thought*, 10.
³⁷ As Hannah Arendt put it when she heard the court invoke piracy as a precedent: 'the world's press had not gathered in Jerusalem to find Bluebeard in the dock': Hannah Arendt, *Eichmann in Jerusalem* (New York: Penguin, 1994 [1963]), 263–5, 276.
³⁸ Reinhold Niebuhr, *Moral Man and Immoral Society: A Study in Ethics and Politics* (New York: Scribner's Sons, 1948 [1932]).
³⁹ See works by Orford, cited above at n. 3.
⁴⁰ See Kennedy, this volume.
⁴¹ Antony Anghie, *Imperialism, Sovereignty and the Making of International Law* (Cambridge: Cambridge University Press, 2005).

defection from the UN collective security system resembled the clash between papal authority and secular natural law, or pointing to resemblances across time between mandate and international administration, or noticing some parallels between the Moscow Show Trials and the work of the international tribunals. Though these comparisons might be methodologically suspect, the claim will be made that they do important heuristic or political work, which a fully contextualised (whatever *that* might entail) reading of the historical circumstance would blur or undercut.

Indeed, an influential form of international legal history thinks of apparently innocuous contemporary practices and doctrines as being implicated in imperial, or more overtly violent, logics and tendencies in the past. Thus, does every apparently progressive or neutral legal norm of the present have its avatar in some more facially political or exploitative norm in the past. A certain sort of history, then, is designed to offer a 'paleo-ontological' (Baxi) examination of these norms. Concepts are wrenched from the past as part of a provocative political project.[42] In the end it may be that, as Josef Engel puts it: 'every historical judgement is an analogical judgement'.[43] To be a lawyer is to spend one's day making analogical judgements. What historians might think of as 'a lack of context' (the absence of culture, event, social surroundings), might simply be a different sort of context: a linguistic context, a textual context, a legal context.[44]

Greatness

A context that international law has struggled with, and against, is the context of 'greatness', whether manifest as a focus on individuals or on the concrete or material conditions of international diplomatic life. At least one methodological imperative inherited from other fields is a suspicion of history as a history of Great Men and their activities (Terry Eagleton calls this sort of work 'philistine') or as a sequence of crises or as a mere effect of Great Power politics.

---

[42] There is, at the same time, a need for a certain amount of wariness around the insistence that this or that engagement with Baldus or Lorimer is important because it might tell us something about the porousness of borders today or about the origins of self-defence. Here, history might feel too instrumentalised.
[43] As quoted in Alberto Toscano, 'The Spectre of Analogy', *New Left Review* 66 (2010), 152–60, at 153.
[44] See Kennedy, this volume. The idea of legal context is discussed in Desautels-Stein, 'International Legal Structuralism'.

The 'Second Epilogue' to *War and Peace* is an essay denouncing the historical method of the novel itself. At one point, Tolstoy remarks:

> The theory of the transference of the collective will of the people to historical persons may perhaps explain much in the domain of jurisprudence and be essential for its purposes, but in its application to history, as soon as revolutions, conquests or civil wars occur – that is, as soon as history begins – that theory explains nothing.[45]

The novel, of course, plays the chamber politics of Russian aristocratic life against the deeds and misdeeds of historically significant figures as well as fictional heroes and anti-heroes. One interpretation of *War and Peace*, then, is that the novel struggles against its author's theory of history. The centrality of great historical persons, for Tolstoy, is essential to the success of a piece of literature (the structural novel was to come later) and essential in 'the domain of jurisprudence' but as history it explained nothing.

The discipline of international law has conducted a similar internal struggle with the concept of 'greatness', as expressed through an attention to the 'real' underlying forces of history, in its accounts of history and its chosen methods. There is a method of international legal history, for example, that will continually refer back to a set of lightly interrogated facts or realities as the authentic or ultimate ground of international law or historical development.[46] And this history is sometimes written in a dismissive tone: a jeremiad against the blindness or idiocy of those who would base their historical accounts on something other than the realities of history. There are contemporary manifestations of this but the modern masters of this form of hegemonic determinism are two otherwise quite distinct (and distinctive), German scholars, Carl Schmitt and Wilhelm Grewe.[47]

Grewe's method is macro-historical, periodising, pseudo-scientific and 'realist' but at the same time concerned with the styles (of governorship, of scholarship) that gave each of his epochs their own spirit.[48] Like almost everyone who has ever written histories of international law he seeks to bring theory and practice together (though it is clear here that practice will tend to

---

[45] Leo Tolstoy, *War and Peace* (Penguin, 1999 [1869]), 1282.
[46] On the relationship between 'reality' and 'fact', see, e.g., Richard Rorty, *Contingency, Irony, and Solidarity* (Cambridge: Cambridge University Press, 1989), 7–8; Hayden White, *Metahistory: The Historical Imagination in Nineteenth-Century Europe* (Baltimore: Johns Hopkins University Press, 2014 [1973]), 41–53.
[47] J.S. Watson, 'A Realistic Jurisprudence of International Law', *Year Book of World Affairs* 30 (1980), 265–85.
[48] Wilhelm G. Grewe, *The Epochs of International Law*, trans. Michael Byers (Berlin: De Gruyter, 2000), xii, 6.

4 After Method

dictate the kinds of styles available to be deployed within different moments of international legal history). So, for Grewe, international legal history was, famously, catalogued as Spanish, French, British and US–Soviet epochs, in which the international law of the period was an expression of the dominant power's style of global leadership.[49] Throughout *Epochs* there is an elevation of theory (the style of scholarship predominating at any one time) but also a preference for 'facts' (the idea of a European sovereign state system or the balance of power or the institution of permanent diplomacy) over 'theories' (of late-mediaeval universalism or papal authority).[50] Accordingly, concrete political systems conditioned by the style of the dominant power were to be preferred over the ahistorical, autonomous, legalisms of contemporaries like Hans Kelsen (a section of *Epochs* is entitled 'Legal orders corresponding to changes in the state system').

Grewe's sweeping macro-history at least permits (or doesn't prevent) Grewe from asking the sorts of questions that became the basis for a later historical turn.[51] Indeed, there are commonalities between Grewe and later legal historians who want to think of international law as having been shaped or constituted in its encounter with colonialism or Great Power preference. And, of course, Grewe is an important figure for the purposes of this chapter because his history is attentive to styles (of hegemony). Grewe's 'style' is both broader and narrower than the style I discuss here: it encompasses the politics, method and constitutional presuppositions of the dominant imperial powers, but not the deeper methodological questions about how histories get to be written, far less whether method exhausts the sorts of questions that could be asked about such historical writing. However, Grewe's emphasis on style nevertheless demands an attention to the ways in which international law is written (its presiding languages, national forms and so on) that is not always present in international legal history.

The centrality of the concrete, the imperial, and 'the real' mark out Grewe and Carl Schmitt as contemporaries and co-sympathisers. Certainly, the

---

[49] Though this did not mean international legal scholarship was 'nationalised'. The Spanish Age produced Grotius, the French Age failed to give rise to a single great French international lawyer. On the idea of international law as a native or foreign language in the contemporary scene, see Anna Dolidze, 'How well does Russia speak the language of international law?' *Open Democracy* (2015), available at www.opendemocracy.net/od-russia/anna-dolidze/how-well-does-russia-speak-language-of-international-law.

[50] And especially facts that are then converted into, or acknowledged as, legal forms. See Grewe's discussion of the Treaty of Utrecht and the balance of power: *Epochs*, 282.

[51] In particular, asking whether a particular international legal order operates as a Christian order, an occidental order, a civilised order or a universal system of law.

Schmitt of *Der Nomos*, at least, is more gnostic than Grewe with his discussion of, say, the 'katechon' (or the etymologies of the 'nomos' itself).[52] But alongside all of this is the obsessive quest for the 'concrete' grounds of political order.[53] Here, again, as with Grewe, and the post-war American political realists, it is assumed that there exists an underlying order or set of relations or real social circumstance obscured by something less real (the legal order, or liberalism or parliamentary democracy or some aesthetic or ethical superstructure).[54]

But what are we to make of this longing for 'concreteness'? It appears repeatedly in Grewe's work and Schmitt's and, in the field in general, it represents a kind of methodological *telos* – one often detached from any preoccupation with greatness – in its various sociological (New Haven), statist (positivism) and naturalist (the quest for a secure, secular basis ('conscience of mankind')) variants. In Schmitt's case, the concrete is everywhere. The 'exception' produces a moment of revelation in which 'the power of real life breaks through the crust of a mechanism that has become torpid by repetition', the friend–enemy distinction clears away the normative or supervening or spiritual in order to fully illuminate and make plain the political and the real (little wonder that a de-theologised – maybe even de-politicised – version of Schmitt's thinking became the basis of American Cold War realism).[55] Meanwhile, *The Nomos of the Earth* is, itself, a story of physical appropriations of land, sea and air.[56] This craving for the tangible, or the underlying, is of course a feature of the social sciences in general but for Schmitt and Grewe it is a style encrusted into method. The concrete relations are always

---

[52] Though this is a minority position, I suspect. For Rob Howse, the international legal writing has been much less influential than the two founding texts of Schmittianism (*Concept of the Political* and *Political Theology*), each of them free of most of this mysticism.

[53] On etymology, see Schmitt, *The Nomos of the Earth*, 336–42. On the *Katechon*, see 59–62. For a fresh reading of the *Katechon*, see Richard Joyce, 'International Law and the Cold War', in Matthew Craven, Sundhya Pahuja and Gerry Simpson (eds.), *International Law and the Cold War* (Cambridge: Cambridge University Press, 2019).

[54] This sort of thinking is all over a certain kind of American realism: see, e.g., Hans J. Morgenthau, 'Positivism, Functionalism, and International Law', *American Journal of International Law* 34 (1940), 260–84.

[55] Carl Schmitt, *Political Theology*, trans. George Schwab (Chicago: University of Chicago Press, 2005), 15.

[56] In his Author's Foreword, Schmitt quotes Goethe: 'All petty things have trickled away, [/] Only sea and land count here'. In fact, Schmitt's gloss on this betrays an anxiety about his method. As he puts it, these references to sea and land and concreteness should not indicate that he is taking an 'elemental-mythological approach'. He goes on: 'this would not do justice to the essentially jurisprudential foundations of the book, which I have taken much pains to construct': at 37.

somewhere (often out of reach) underpinning everything and to be juxtaposed to the abstractions of certain kinds of legalism, but their restatement as a series of synonyms sometimes feels more like theological yearning than social science.[57]

These gestures to political reality are suspect, of course. For all the reasons given by White and Ankersmit, but also because, in the case of Grewe, the author himself, it seemed, could only bear so much reality.[58] As others have pointed out, *Epochs* manages to offer a millennium-long political history of international law without saying very much at all about the war it was written in the midst of. So, while Grewe can sound like Ian Hunter or Quentin Skinner when he demands that we 'acknowledge the concrete intellectual historical position of a Vitoria, a Gentili or a Grotius',[59] he manages to avoid this sort of positioning when he celebrates the work of Schmitt.[60] In both Schmitt and Grewe, there is a concrete context that remains enigmatically out of sight, and this is also the shadow of a predicament hanging over the chosen method. Grewe, for example, retained his chair in international law throughout Hitler's reign. This leads to some peculiar historical ellipses beginning with Frowein's biographical account of Grewe, which reads as if Grewe began his academic career in 1945.[61]

---

[57] In the sense, and perhaps *only* in this sense, the work comes to resemble concrete poetry: the concreteness of form producing an eventual abstraction of thought. See, e.g., Emmett Williams, *An Anthology of Concrete Poetry* (New York: Something Else Press, 1967).

[58] The allusion is to Eliot. Grewe could not quite consistently stick with his method, in any case. See his reliance on the judgements of international courts or academic literature in establishing the continued existence of a universal international order, at 648.

[59] *Epochs*, 2, 70 *passim*.

[60] This contrasts with, say, Rob Howse, who insists that Schmitt himself believed arguments have to be read as 'polemical or situational' (see Robert Howse, 'Schmitt, Schmitteanism and Contemporary International Legal Theory', in Anne Orford and Florian Hoffmann (eds.), *Oxford Handbook of the Theory of International Law* (Oxford: Oxford University Press, 2016), 212–30, at 213; see also Smeltzer and Kelly, this volume). Irony and bathos seem to be the presiding tropes when Grewe speaks about Nazi Germany. About the Third Reich he has this to say: 'The more these dictatorships deviated from the standard of civilisation, the more it was important to avoid breaking diplomatic links with them and to conserve the ties which bound them to the rules of international law' (585). The Second World War is described in passive, sanitised terms: 'With the outbreak of war in 1939 … in land warfare the execution of hostages played a sad role as a reprisal against the activities of partisans' (626). (Compare this to the views expressed by German émigré Georg Schwarzenberger, in *International Law and Totalitarian Lawlessness* (London: Jonathan Cape, 1943).) If euphemism is the dominant style when it comes to the Second World War, hyperbole is the preferred mode in other instances; the occupation by Iranian revolutionary students of the US Embassy in Tehran is later described as a 'terrorist action' (at 641).

[61] In frontmatter to Grewe, *Epochs*. For a delicate appraisal of this period of German international law with some insights into the relationship between Grewe and Schmitt, see

This chapter is partly an exercise in understanding history as a matter of taste or aesthetics, and I have written elsewhere about the way in which the acknowledgements in a work of scholarship might work against the ideas being expounded in the text itself.[62] In Grewe's case we have a lapse of taste that makes him think it is important to register that the publication and writing of *Epochs* were each impeded by 'air raids' or that it might be a matter of self-satisfaction that he had resisted the efforts of the authorities in the post-war era to modify his work.[63]

Grewe and Schmitt had an ambiguous (perhaps not so ambiguous in Schmitt's case) relationship to Hitler and his policies. In a great many popular accounts of the past, of course, such men *make* history and are, themselves, consequently made by a particular historical method (as Marx alleged Victor Hugo does to Bonaparte in *Napoleon le Petit*).[64] But a typical disciplinary training in international law will tend to lack many references to leading statespersons (these characters are perpetually offstage, lending their names to the occasional doctrine (Truman, Brezhnev, Monroe) or providing the odd moment of context (Stalin, Nehru et al.)). On the other hand, in 1919, when a committee was established at the Versailles Peace Conference to consider the question of war crimes trials for the defeated German elite (including the Kaiser), the then-revolutionary idea was to make greatness the very subject of international criminal adjudication.

Labouring under a curious but revealing title, 'The Commission on the Responsibilities of the Authors of the War', the Commission's deliberations turned out to be stormier than anyone had anticipated. In effect, the Commission enacted a series of debates around opposing views of history, wrestling from the outset with the title it had been given (and the first of its tasks) and the whole idea of 'authorship'. In what sense is history or war authored? And who authors it? Or is 'authorship' the wrong metaphor?

The Commission eventually held that wars were not authored by Great Men (at least not in a way that would give rise to individual criminal

---

Bardo Fassbender, 'Stories of War and Peace. On Writing the History of International Law in the "Third Reich" and After', *European Journal of International Law* 13 (2002), 479–512, esp. 503–6.

[62] Simpson, 'The Sentimental Life of International Law'.

[63] In the preface to the second edition (1984), Grewe says of post-war censorship: 'it was stipulated that a publication was now only possible under certain conditions which I was not prepared to accept. It had already been a remarkable accomplishment to avoid *any alteration* to the text by the censor during the Third Reich.': Grewe, *Epochs*, xi (emphasis added).

[64] Karl Marx, *The 18th Brumaire of Louis Bonaparte* (New York: International Publishers, 1969 [1852]), 8.

responsibility). And this accords with an international law that will emphasise, as the motors of international diplomacy, the slow accretion of norms, or the intensification of a certain form of practice or the steady construction of institutions rather than the inclinations of statespersons. Since the field understands itself to be a practice of taming the instincts of Great Powers or the pathologies of Great Men, it makes sense to underplay these figures in its own history.

But international law can be understood also as the enactment of a Tolstoyan struggle between the institutional and diplomatic structure of international political life and the agency of great men. This latter tendency is reflected, first, in an intellectual history, or 'the study of past thoughts' (in Skinner's elegant formula), of an international law consisting in what great men *thought* at different times.[65] This is the history of international law from Gentili to Wolff and Vattel and then on to Oppenheim or Kelsen and beyond.[66] This tendency, in turn, has been buttressed and complicated by the increasing attention given to the biographies of international legal practitioners as part of a general biographical turn in the field.[67] Alongside all of this, we would have to register the histories written and authorised by international tribunals, which think of war and atrocity as an emanation from the evil minds of elite state and military leaders possessing 'individual responsibility' and 'criminal intent': international legal history via Milošević, Pinochet and Goering.[68]

Meanwhile, war crimes tribunals also write the history of international law as a line of great, defining crises from Nuremberg to the former Yugoslavia and the Rwandan genocide. This could be understood as both a departure

---

[65] See Stefan Collini, 'What Is Intellectual History?', *History Today* 35(10) (1985), 46–8.

[66] On recurring criticisms that history focused on a small aristocratic elite and their intellectual contribution constitutes a form of 'classism', see Armitage, *Foundations of Modern International Thought*, 31–2.

[67] See Andrew Lang and Susan Marks, 'People with Projects: Writing the Lives of International Lawyers', *Temple International and Comparative Law Journal* 27 (2013), 437–53; Armitage and Pitts, 'This Modern Grotius', 21–3, 28–31. One thought, suggested by Carlo Ginzburg, is that we could usefully turn our attention to the *readers* of history. So, what is interesting in Keene's account is not so much that a number of treaties were created in a particular period but that they were read in different periods by different audiences in order to establish a certain way of doing international law ('one cannot just read the books; one must also understand the readers': Edward Keene, 'The Age of Grotius', in David Armstrong (ed.), *Routledge Handbook of International Law* (Abingdon: Routledge, 2009), 126–40, at 127). See for thoughts along these lines, Ginzburg, *Threads and Traces*.

[68] See, for a fuller discussion, Gerry Simpson, 'Linear Law: The History of International Criminal Law', in Christine E.J. Schwöbel (ed.), *Critical Approaches to International Criminal Law: An Introduction* (Abingdon: Routledge, 2014), 159–79.

from, and a confirmation of, existing tendencies in international law's historical methodologies. On one hand, international lawyers go to the past in search of regularity, pattern and uniformity (a sequence of treaties, a practice 'consistent and universal'). But another way of writing international legal history will precisely think of it as a response to crisis ('Kosovo', 'Rwanda', 'Libya') or a history of post-war settlements (1648, 1713, 1815, 1919, 1945). And indeed, whole legal methods have been built round this sort of thing.[69] Hilary Charlesworth and others have criticised this over-attention to crises and the deforming effects this has had on international legal culture, and that seems right. On the other hand, a certain sort of revolutionary moment – whether blueprint or singularity – might be understood as having transformed the ground on which judgement itself is made.[70]

In this section, then, and to recapitulate before coming to a conclusion, I have tried to re-describe international law's preoccupations with time, *telos* and greatness as a way of suggesting that the historical field could be disrupted and its dominant tendencies denaturalised. What, then, might come after method?

4.3 AFTER METHOD

These special problems I have identified suggest that, in the end, individual methodological pre- and proscriptions can sometimes cut both ways. Grewe's attention to 'context' might be viewed as under-whelming, selective, and reductive or it might act as a bold, sweeping antidote to Kelsenian legalism; Schmitt's anti-Weimar manoeuvrings will either seem deliciously prophetic or dismally authoritarian (or both); Alexandrowicz's pluriverse could be

---

[69] W. Michael Reisman and Andrew R. Willard, *International Incidents: The Law that Counts in World Politics* (Princeton: Princeton University Press, 1988); Burns H. Weston, Richard A. Falk and Hilary Charlesworth, *International Law and World Order: A Problem-Oriented Coursebook* (St Paul: West Group, 1997). See, too, Grewe, *Epochs*, and its dependence on the demarcation of epochs and the fixing of major turning points, e.g. at 28.

[70] The language is from Toscano's review of Canfora ('Spectre of Analogy'), the theorising is Badiou's (*Polemics*, trans. Steve Corcoran (London: Verso, 2012)), the application to international law is found in Fleur Johns, Richard Joyce and Sundhya Pahuja (eds.), *Events: The Force of International Law* (Abingdon: Routledge, 2010). A relatively recent reference to the need to be attentive to 'Events' one might be living through is found in Martti Koskenniemi, 'Histories of International Law: Significance and Problems for a Critical View', *Temple International and Comparative Law Journal* 27 (2013), 215–40. For the idea of a crisis as a juridical moment of decision, see Reinhart Koselleck, trans. Michaela W. Richter, 'Crisis', *Journal of the History of Ideas* 67 (2006), 357–400, at 359–60. On the revolutionary moment as a vantage point from which to observe history at its most 'vivid', see Scott, *Omens of Adversity*, 3.

celebrated as a form of perspicacious anti-imperialism or dismissed as the product of a method borne out of serendipity rather than intellectual decision. Choice of method does not always (or, for some readers, very often) determine what we take to be convincing work. 'Fully' contextualised account is read as depoliticised antiquarianism. Anachronistic faux pas becomes playfully defiant, cross-historical gesture. Biographical retrieval is great man fetish. Finger-on-the-pulse contemporariness is 'discipline of crisis'.

So, *after method*, we might experience simply a greater awareness of the choices open to us along with an awareness that these are choices, and a sense that these choices are both methodological and political: decisions we make rather than decisions that are made for us (by context, by choice of field, by disciplinary tradition). 'Interest ... precedes method', as Catherine MacKinnon put it almost forty years ago.[71] So, the decision to write about the experience of the ordinary soldier in Tolstoy, or the working classes in E.P. Thompson or the pirate society in Marcus Rediker is a matter of method and politics.[72] In international legal history, such choices are constantly having to be made, whether they involve thinking from below (Rajagopal), writing history from a particular place (the Russian history of international law or the Ottoman experiences of legality), conjuring forms of micro-history (Eslava's Bogotá or Istanbul) or simply attending to a different archive (Alexandrowicz).

After method, too, we might approach the idea of crisis differently: as opportunity and danger. Just as concepts might be viewed as abstractions travelling freely across time *and* as situated sites of argument about the world, so, too, events are no longer just happenings that arrive on our desks to be periodised or interred (Grewe, Schmitt, Wheaton) but are to be treated with wariness (Charlesworth) or as moments of possibility, and political (Badiou) or theoretical (Johns, Joyce and Pahuja) renewal.[73]

There might be, in turn, a more acute awareness that we *write* history. The master-theorist of history in this mode (though he denied that he wrote 'philosophy of history') is, of course, Hayden White. For White, style and

---

[71] Catharine A. MacKinnon, 'Feminism, Marxism, Method, and the State: Toward Feminist Jurisprudence', *Signs* 8 (1983), 635–58, at 636–7.

[72] And position, of course. As Alexandrowicz notes, a certain distance from power or fashion has a habit of widening perspective and perspicacity. See his 'Doctrinal Aspects of the Universality of the Law of Nations', in *Law of Nations in Global History*, 168–79.

[73] There is a hint of arbitrariness in the choice of some events: 'The peace of Westphalia, 1648, may be chosen as the epoch from which to deduce the history of the modern science of international law.': Henry Wheaton, *History of the Law of Nations in Europe and America*, (New York: Gould, Banks & Co, 1845), 69.

method merge, and the method of discerning or describing history becomes the style of writing it. Style, no longer quite after method, is always and perpetually with it. Or, better still, is the origin of it. Thinkers as diverse as Althusser and Alain have identified the metaphorical thought that provokes or initiates the philosophical endeavour. But it is White who makes of this a virtuoso performance in identifying what we might, clumsily, call the stylishness of history. According to White, the poetic act – less elegantly, part of a 'prefigurative' cognitive structure – is anterior to the particular analysis of field and object, indeed establishes the object and 'the modality of the conceptual strategies he will use to explain it'.[74] When it comes to these modalities, White identifies a number of different emplotments (I will discuss these a little more when I return to the history of international criminal law). Suffice to say here, White regards this not as a choice of method (to be applied to an object of study in order to produce the greatest correspondence between the past and the history of that past) but as a deep moral and aesthetic decision that pre-dates archive and method.[75] No wonder, then, that in White's work there is a commitment to bringing out the writerly, literary, sentimental (or personal) aspects and dimensions of history-writing (it may be the case also, according to one writer, that histories written under such conditions – and with their 'sensitivity to narrative, literary form, and poetic technique' – mark a return to the better aspects of the idioms of seventeenth-century humanism).[76]

After method, or after the inter-disciplinary methodological encounter, we might see, too, that it is very probable that what we have here are shared predispositions and virtues (maybe even tonalities) rather than shared methods. Sometimes these virtues might involve something as simple as the ability or inclination to read the small print alongside the larger structural changes. Marc Bloch wrote in 1941 that the best history features a sort of zooming and stretching, a moving back and forth between attention to minute detail and awareness of large-scale transformation. This may simply be a fidelity (or is it a form of infidelity?) to text and context. What did Grotius actually say here? And did he say it over here too? And did he fail to say it there? So, for example, in nuanced accounts across the three fields of international law, international history and international political theory, we end up with a picture of Grotius as a person concerned with private rights and private war (permitted where there was no existing public authority (say the

---

[74] See, e.g., *Metahistory*, 30.
[75] Ibid.
[76] Christopher N. Warren, 'John Milton and the Epochs of International Law', *European Journal of International Law* 24 (2013), 557–81, at 559.

Dutch East Indies)) or concerned to describe highly variegated forms of authority, or a Grotius in possession of a coherent historical consciousness as he amasses his eclectic material rather than the cartoon figure of the disciplinary imagination who manages to invent sovereignty *de novo* and reconcile naturalism and positivism while losing control of his hodgepodge of historical sources.[77] In a way, then, to be *for* Grotius (or to retrieve the anomalies in Grotius) is to be against Grotianism. To approach Grotius is to be aware that one is approaching from a particular place – Whitean cognitive structure already *in* place – and to remember that this poetic, pre-analytic moment already screens out a number of Grotiuses (how many international lawyers think Grotius's extensive poetry is part of his international law or that Milton's work on marriage or circumcision might constitute a form of international law?).[78]

We might learn, too, from best work in other fields that international law has power as an organising idea of international political life. Recent historical work has thickened and complicated international law's own critical project about this power by demonstrating that international legal ideas mattered hugely in determining how certain worlds were constructed, how certain practices were named and renamed, how certain possibilities were closed, perhaps forever.[79] The easy clichés of an international law somehow always on the outside of a politics or a social practice seem less present in such work. I remember saying to my college professor back in 1986 that I wanted to write my honours dissertation on the law of war crimes. In the afterwash of his disapproval, one phrase stuck out. He said there was little point in this sort of study since it was 'purely historical'. I pressed on with it, perhaps drawn to a subject that promised both 'purity' and 'history'. Later he warned me that 'nothing had happened since the Second World War and the Nuremberg Trials'. What did it mean for nothing to have happened? What was the nature of this absence? Wouldn't it be interesting to discover why something *hadn't* happened?

There has been a tendency among lawyers to believe that at different points of history nothing happened. Isabel Hull's recent book was, after all, an argument against the long-standing canard that during the Great War

---

[77] Edward Keene, *Beyond the Anarchical Society: Grotius, Colonialism and Order in World Politics* (Cambridge: Cambridge University Press, 2002), 38 (describing how Grotius is 'squeeze[d] ... into a small box' in order to accommodate the demands of an early nineteenth century adoption of unified sovereignty and to resist future Napoleonic ambitions).
[78] On Milton, see Warren, 'John Milton and the Epochs of International Law'.
[79] See, e.g., Isabel Hull, *A Scrap of Paper: Breaking and Making International Law during the Great War* (Ithaca: Cornell University Press, 2014).

international law simply hadn't happened.[80] But we have also been given, or given ourselves, at various moments, the impression that nothing happened before 1603, or nothing in the first half of the nineteenth century or nothing during the Cold War.[81]

And after method, we might find the struggle over context and anachronism means that international legal work is productively reread. When I teach Tony Anghie's book on international law and empire, students say: 'Yes, we know this'. Well, the reason they know whatever it is they know, is because of the book and the intellectual activity it provoked. It is striking to consider how outré Anghie's book was when it was first published (indeed, considered for publication). Now part of a new orthodoxy on the relationship between colonialism and international law, it was treated at the time as a methodologically suspect polemical intervention. Before the recent turn to method, though, it had acquired a kind of encrusted presence in the discipline. After method, we might find ourselves reading Anghie differently: first, paradigm shift, then monument (outside TWAILish circles *Imperialism* ossified and came to stand for a few desultory propositions about 'empire' or 'colonialism' or 'positivism') and now site of interdisciplinary contention. Did the book underplay the variousness of colonial encounters, the immediate political circumstances of Vitoria or the sheer physicality of the extra-European world into which Europe ventured? Does it overstate the continuities between war on terror and nineteenth-century empire? Who knows? Methodological cross-hatching has reactivated the book – no longer a monument to be gingerly circumnavigated but part of a conversation about history and method.

Similarly, after method, we might see how whole sub-disciplines understand themselves through the forms of writing and methods that are required in order for a set of ideas to join a conversation or be deemed competent. I have already spoken about international criminal law's historical method but it is worth considering in a little more detail how limited in ideological and stylistic range the field's *loci classici* were. A selection of the founding texts of the field would have to include Cherif Bassiouni's monumental works on crimes against humanity, Theodor Meron's essays calling for the humanisation of the laws of war, Antonio Cassese's bootstrapping articles on war crimes

---

[80] Ibid.
[81] On the latter, see Matthew Craven, Sundhya Pahuja and Gerry Simpson, *Cold War International Law* (forthcoming). On absence, see Fleur Johns, *Non-Legality in International Law: Unruly Law* (Cambridge: Cambridge University Press, 2013).

and Geoffrey Robertson's panoramic celebrations of the origins of international criminal law. What sort of histories do these efforts depend upon?

The first thing to note is that this is a very distinctive, early, project with its own presiding methods, and it generated a mass of mimetic work as the field began to establish itself. Hayden White's dictum that every field is constituted by what it forbids its practitioners to do seems apposite here.[82] And it is White, of course, who organises the writing of realist history into four genres: romance, comedy, tragedy and satire. The point in deploying White, here, is to think of these founding histories as acts of creation or ideological gestures, and to try to work out how such acts are produced and how they aim to persuade, and what a set of 'criteria of plausibility' might do to the range of thought available to us.[83]

In Whitean terms, then, to write as an international criminal lawyer is to write in the 'romantic' style – redemptive, eschatological, transcendent.[84] White's description of Jules Michelet's romantic style will be familiar to contemporary observers of international criminal law with its perpetual 'striving to become':

> the historian must write his histories in such a way as to promote the realization of the unity that everything is striving to become. And ... everything appearing in history must be assessed finally in terms of the contribution it makes to the realization of the goal or the extent to which it impedes its realization.[85]

In the field of international criminal law histories were initially written in precisely this style. Three methodological tendencies seem very obviously present in the histories of this discipline: a commitment to a pre-history of absence (compare this to the search for origins engaged in by international tribunals); an appeal to an instinctive internationalism (whereas the past is a place where normative projects are dissolved in the politics of the domestic); and an incipient naturalism.

So, all precursors were simply a 'striving to become' an institutional system dedicated to ending impunity, preferably—and certainly at least in the shadow of—international courts. Everything local (the German post-WWI trials in Leipzig), merciful (any decisions to free or rehabilitate), experimental

---

[82] Hayden White, *Tropics of Discourse* (Baltimore: Johns Hopkins University Press, 1978), 126–7 (invoking Nietzsche).
[83] Michael S. Roth, 'Foreword: "All You've Got Is History"', in *Metahistory*, xvii.
[84] *Metahistory*, 8–9.
[85] Ibid., 150.

(Napoleon's exile on Elba and, then, St Helena) or diplomatically subtle (the various decisions to accord immunity to high-ranking officials) was cast as ineffectual or insufficiently punitive, or simply formed part of a primitive pre-history of 'failure'.

This standard story begins with the disappointing non-hanging of Wilhelm II after Versailles, followed by the turning point (or 'promise') of Nuremberg, then a regrettable fifty-year gap in which international criminal law goes into abeyance, prior to the re-emergence of international tribunality in the Balkans and in Rwanda and the consummation of the project at Rome with the establishment of the ICC.[86] The normative commitments aimed at ending impunity. The institutional preferences were strongly in the direction of permanent international criminal jurisdiction. The politics was a thin neo-naturalist anti-sovereignist and anti-hegemonic humanitarianism. The 'method' was a combination of an episodic, selective and anachronistic 'magpie' history, with an exceedingly rigid periodisation, topped off with a kind of inevitabilism. The style was largely, as I have said, 'romantic',[87] and the tone unvaryingly solemn, sometimes turgid; a seriousness of moral purpose weighing heavily on the prose. This method meant that historical counter-examples or anomalies or comic juxtapositions had to be set aside as possible blasphemies. In the most influential of these accounts, Geoffrey Robertson's *Crimes against Humanity*, history is a storehouse of missed opportunities and mistakes. The Moscow Show Trials are read as a vulgar politicisation – to be contrasted with the rise of human rights or the establishment of an international criminal law – rather than symptomatic precedent for the Nuremberg and Tokyo War Crimes Trials.[88]

There were maverick accounts, of course: the journalism of Rebecca West, the *New Yorker* essays of Hannah Arendt, the political theory of Judith Shklar

---

[86] For the 'turning point' idea (no longer would war criminals be 'protected' by state sovereignty), see Antonio Cassese, *International Criminal Law* (2nd ed.) (Oxford: Oxford University Press, 2008), 27–31; for the sense in which international criminal law (this 'great business') might have its own momentum, somehow detached from history, see Geoffrey Robertson, *Crimes against Humanity* (3rd ed.) (London: Penguin, 2006). The early historical accounts of the development of international criminal law that fail to stick with this script have been more or less, themselves, written out of history (see, e.g., Maurice Hankey, *Politics, Trials and Errors* (Oxford: Pen-In-Hand, 1950); see also F.J.P. Veale, *Advance to Barbarism* (Appleton: Nelson, 1953); Montgomery Belgion, *Victors' Justice* (Hinsdale: Henry Regnery, 1949); and Freda Utley, *The High Cost of Vengeance* (London: Allen & Unwin, 1949)).

[87] I have written elsewhere on bathos as a style of international criminal law history: Simpson, 'Unprecedents', in Tallgren and Skouteris (eds.), *New Histories of International Criminal Law*, 12–29.

[88] Robertson, *Crimes against Humanity*, 23–5.

and the dissenting judgement of Justice Pal in post-war Tokyo. But it is striking that these writings adopted a much more sardonic mode in their style and tone. For a long time, this jarred with the existing conventions of solemnity. Pal's history, for example (one that, in recounting the story of international criminal law and empire, applied irony and tragedy rather than romance), was not published by the IMTFE following the trial. It was too early for such things. Arendt encountered a different set of problems with her *New Yorker* essays on Eichmann. The tone was occasionally flip and the method was loose and journalistic (this was, decidedly, not *The Origins of Totalitarianism*), leaving Arendt open to accusations that she had failed to understand the predicament of the Jewish leadership or had been cavalier with legal principle or had adopted an ironic sensibility when nothing but moral propriety was acceptable.

Wherever one stands on such matters, Arendt at least opens up the possibility of speaking about crimes against humanity in a style that rejects the hubris and moral self-satisfaction of the dominant conventions of international criminal law (from Robert Jackson 'staying the hand of vengeance' (a few weeks after Hiroshima and Nagasaki) to Richard Goldstone entitling his autobiography, 'For Humanity'). Indeed, one of the reasons I keep coming back to Rebecca West and her description of the Nuremberg Trial as a 'citadel of boredom' is because of the way in which she decentres the Nuremberg Trial in the vernacular of irony while applying the journalistic equivalent of a micro-historical method.

> Often people said, 'You must have seen some very interesting sights when you went to the Nuremberg Trial'. Yes, indeed. There had been a man with one leg and a child of twelve, growing enormous cyclamens in a greenhouse.[89]

In the citadel, mankind was busy inventing itself or setting down some juridical markers ('crimes against humanity', 'the conscience of mankind' and so on). Outside, there is the everyday business – a kind of declension – of growing flowers and getting around on one leg amidst the rubble left after the recent and second Allied bombing raid on an already-bombed-out city. The tone is humorous but the method is deadly serious.[90]

West, Arendt and a handful of others were the exception to prevailing accounts. Now, however, we find ourselves in an 'after method' moment in

---

[89] Rebecca West, *A Train of Powder* (New York: Viking Press, 1955), 3, 127.
[90] This passage is drawn from my 'Sentimental Life of International Law'.

the field (or at least a moment when its methods have become more varied and irresolute, and its histories more iconoclastic).[91] Mostly, this involves the retrieval of alternative sites of criminalisation (forgotten local, hybrid, internationalised trials), new origins (the Moscow Show Trials, the nineteenth century's anti-slavery agitations) or an 'international criminal law' that is not retributive at all. It is possible, also, to hear a tonal difference in some of the new work in the field (it needs to be said that this new scholarship remains a minority enterprise). Histories of international criminal law now come in a variety of styles: pastoral, tragic, satirical, zen.[92]

4.4 AT TATE BRITAIN

'After method', in this chapter, has had two different meanings. In developing the first meaning, I have described an encounter between the historical disciplines and international law that seems full of promise. The methodological inheritance I have sketched can clearly offer international lawyers a fresh way into their own histories. The dilemmas of presentism or context seem much more alive to us now and we might want to understand 'method', less as a tranche of prohibitions or list of dispensations, and more as an invitation to think about, defend and elaborate a distinctive method of one's own. But I have insisted, too, that method does not fully capture what we find appealing or resonant about the work we read and respond to. So, in the second case, 'after method' refers to the extra-methodic virtues of compelling and resonant history.

I will finish this chapter by offering a brief epilogue (perhaps more of a prolegomenon) on what I want to call literary virtue after method. And the reason we might want to think of this as literary is because it resembles the best fiction. What is it to be Shostakovich in the 1930s? One answer is found in Julian Barnes's novel, *The Noise of Time*, which I happened to be reading as

---

[91] Earlier work in this vein includes Ed Morgan, 'Retributory Theater', *American University Journal of International Law and Policy* 3 (1988), 1–64; Shoshana Felman, 'Theaters of Justice: Arendt in Jerusalem, the Eichmann Trial, and the Redefinition of Legal Meaning in the Wake of the Holocaust', *Theoretical Inquiries in Law* 1 (2000), 465–507; Immi Tallgren, 'The Sensibility and Sense of International Criminal Law', *European Journal of International Law* 13 (2002), 561–95.

[92] See, e.g., pastoral: Gerry Simpson, 'Human Rights with a Vengeance: One Hundred Years of Retributive Humanitarianism', *Australian Yearbook of International Law* 33 (2015), 1–14; tragic: Tor Krever, 'Dispensing Global Justice', *New Left Review* 85 (2014), 67–97; satirical: Immi Tallgren, 'Who Are "We" in International Criminal Law?', in Christine E.J. Schwöbel (ed.), *Critical Approaches to International Criminal Law: An Introduction* (Abingdon: Routledge, 2014), 71–95; zen: Barry Hill, *Peacemongers* (St Lucia: University of Queensland Press, 2014).

I wrote this. The quality that emerges from the exchange between writer (Barnes) and writee (Shostakovich) is sympathetic engagement with predicament.[93] Similarly, and this hews close to some familiar and proximate methodological credos, a tonally convincing history might at least start with the predicament of a treatise writer in 1884 or a publicist in 1589 or an institution-builder in 1919 or, indeed, the predicament of those who had been in the habit of receiving international law rather than making it. When we feel the predicament of writer and subject as we do in literature, this history produced seems both indirect and more plausible. In theories of laughter, there is a Bergsonian comedy of correction, which doesn't sound very funny. And here I suppose I am concerned about corrective histories, or histories that are merely corrective or hubristically corrective. Bloch, again, calls this 'the mania for making judgments'.[94] Some of the wisest historiographers seem highly attuned to this. Indeed, in the case of someone like David Scott, it becomes the subject-matter itself: a mood of tranquillity and regret, or rumination that some historians have demanded as a substitute for strident revision.[95] There is a history that consists in a tirade against the past or, at least, the people who lived there and the terrible mistakes they made. Then, there is the historiographical equivalent, which most of us are susceptible to, of condemning all previous historians who failed to properly understand or describe that past. There is little point in writing history unless one thinks one can amend it in some way. But, attention to predicament requires a certain amount of sensitivity to the past.

An associated literary virtue requires a sensitivity to the present and future as well. A lot of conventional history in these fields holds the present in a certain position as it moves into the past. So, the present is understood to be, say, self-evidently, the era of globalisation or technique or market or, to go back to earlier 'presents', the clash of universalist ideologies or the culmination of this or that progress or anti-progress narrative. This is not quite a methodology – though certain methodologies will enact it – but more of predisposition or what Hartog calls, 'a regime'.[96] In Hartog's case it is not so much that only the present exists but that the present exists only as a present.[97] Thus we have the idea of 'a history of the present' – one that unnerves and reveals the conditions of possibility that define the present is familiar enough now from work on

---

[93] Julian Barnes, *The Noise of Time* (London: Jonathan Cape, 2016).
[94] Bloch, *Historian's Craft*, 23.
[95] David Scott, *Conscripts of Modernity: The Tragedy of Colonial Enlightenment* (Durham, NC: Duke University Press, 2004).
[96] Hartog, *Regimes of Historicity*.
[97] As he argues *passim* capitalism has neither a past nor a future.

genealogy.[98] Or, to put it less abstractly, historians are enjoined to vigilantly watch over the present (Charles Péguy).[99]

The question that might dog us (or inspire us) here is the question of what we want from history or what history demands from us. What conceptions of the present force us into a certain way of thinking about the past?[100] What attitude to the present or demand made by an imagined present threatens to obliterate those strange or alien aspects of the past histories and past thinkers that might be suggestive of a different politics? If every political arrangement is understood as 'sovereignty' or even anti-sovereignty then we might deny ourselves the resources to think about alternative political futures. I am not even sure if this is a literary style or an aesthetic or a matter of craft.[101] It may be more and less than 'method'.[102] Sometimes it might even be 'a mood'. Lukács wrote his *Theory of the Novel* in a mood of 'permanent despair over the state of the world'.[103] It is likely that such a mood will inform if not determine certain methodological predispositions.

* * *

The Tate Britain recently curated an exhibition called *Artist and Empire*. Apart from giving the impression that Empire had been a series of glorious defeats or, at least, 'Last Stands' (Gordon, Wolfe), there was a surprisingly large number of paintings depicting treaty-making and negotiation. So, one story offered (though I am mutilating the exhibition here) as one moved from Room 2 to Room 3 of the Gallery was of imperial expansion as a period of treaty-formation followed by a catalogue of British military disasters: as if the British had somehow been hoodwinked by international law into a bunch of unequal treaties. Of course, things tended to work the other way. But the paintings themselves are actually quite ambiguous. This was not really just international law being brought to some extra-European world. There was a degree of mutuality (though one wouldn't want to overstate this). The most

---

[98] See, e.g., Akbar Rasulov, 'New Approaches to International Law: Images of a Genealogy', in José Maria Beneyto and David Kennedy (eds.), *New Approaches to International Law: The European and the American Experiences* (The Hague: TMC Asser-Springer, 2012), 151–91.
[99] As quoted in Hartog, *Regimes of Historicity*, xvii.
[100] Upendra Baxi, 'New Approaches to the History of International Law', *Leiden Journal of International Law* 19 (2007) 555–66. Baxi invokes Benjamin's 'redemptive history': one filled by 'the presence of the now'.
[101] Christopher N. Warren, *Literature and the Law of Nations, 1580–1680* (Oxford: Oxford University Press, 2015).
[102] See Bloch's defence of the poetic: *Historian's Craft*, 8.
[103] Georg Lukács, *The Theory of the Novel*, trans. Anna Bostock (Cambridge, MA: MIT Press, 1971 [1920]), 12.

striking thing about one of the paintings (dating from 1773), Agostino Brunias's *Sir William Young Conducting a Treaty with the Black Caribs on the Island of St Vincent*, is the representation of the Black Carib chief, Chatoyer, who assesses his interlocutors with a look of wry appraisal: as if the historical context of empire had stepped out of the painting to comment directly upon it. Suddenly, this subaltern gaze at the treaty-makers suggests treaties as instruments of anachronism: not quite fit for purpose or out of step with the times, or fictions to be treated with amusement or disdain.

'After method', then, we might look at history anew. Yes, with sympathy for the choices and milieux of our protagonists and a greater sensitivity to the detail of their social, cultural, and political lives and their worlds of struggle (Scott), yes, with a refusal of the easy traditions of linearity and expansion and unity (history as a history of 'dead effects' (Benjamin)) in favour of a setting down of complexity in its fullness. But most of all with the intuition that after method, we might be able to see history in all its strangeness.

For us, as lawyers, history, for sure, is an itinerary (and generator) of norms or precedents – sometimes wrenched from their context – but it is also a place where we might go to feel estranged from the current world so that we revisit it as strangers *and* habituées, and experience both its abject familiarity and closeness as well as, and at the same time, its sheer unlikeliness and mutability.

PART II

Thinking through the International

Law and Constructions of the Political

5

Carl Schmitt's International Thought and the State

ARMIN VON BOGDANDY AND ADEEL HUSSAIN*

5.1 INTRODUCTION

On 21 April 1947, in a Nuremberg interrogation cell, two seasoned German lawyers assessed the merits of political thought for international law. At stake was a death sentence. On one side was Robert Kempner, a former chief legal adviser to the Prussian police, whose botched attempt to outlaw the Nazi party had brought him minor prominence in the early 1930s.[1] After losing his position and citizenship to Nazi racial laws, Kempner, like many Jewish civil servants, had fled Germany's increasingly hostile conditions. After four years in Italy, Kempner reached the United States in 1939, and there found employment at the Justice Department, before being dispatched back to Germany in the aftermath of the Second World War. Sitting opposite Kempner was Carl

---

* We would like to warmly thank Jean d'Aspremont, Jochen von Bernstorff, Kanad Bagchi, Thomas Clausen, Henrik Enroth, Rainer Forst, Matthias Goldmann, Jürgen Habermas, Stefan Kadelbach, Shruti Kapila, Siraj Khan, Martti Koskenniemi, Heike Krieger, Adam Lebovitz, Alastair McClure, Chris Moffat, Reinhard Mehring, Silvia Steininger, Leonie Vierck, Benedict Vischer and Samuel Garrett Zeitlin for their valuable help. We also thank Annika Müller and Megan Donaldson for their thoughtful editing. Unless otherwise noted, all translations were made by the authors.

[1] In 1930, Kempner submitted a police report mapping NSDAP violations of Weimar's criminal code to the *Oberreichsanwalt* (General Attorney). No criminal proceedings were initiated. The reason for ignoring the NSDAP's misconduct was, as Heinrich Brüning, the then chancellor, later bemoaned from exile in the United States, a gross misreading of Adolf Hitler's political prowess and ambition. Robert M.W. Kempner, *Der verpaßte Nazi-Stopp: Die NSDAP als staats- und republikfeindliche, hochverräterische Verbindung; Preußische Denkschrift von 1930* (Frankfurt am Main: Ullstein, 1983), 7–14.

Schmitt, a public law professor[2] who had once been lampooned as the 'notorious weather vane on the roof of the Third Reich'.[3] Others saw in Schmitt 'Hitler's key man', the 'leading international lawyer in Germany', 'the Nazi expert on constitutional law',[4] and, in a characterisation betraying at least some convulsion of phobic attachment, 'perhaps the greatest authority on the Nazi theory of the state'.[5] Still others, like the Schutzstaffel's weekly magazine *Das Schwarze Korps*, wrathfully condemned Schmitt for 'falsifying history' and cheering for a slinking Catholicism that threatened to corrode the foundations of the Third Reich.[6] The US Chief Counsel for War Crimes had tasked Kempner with evaluating whether Schmitt's academic texts, particularly his theorisation of space and his combative understanding of politics, warranted a full-blown charge before the Nuremberg Military Tribunal – a special court set up for German war criminals, who, while part of the wider National Socialist project, missed the cut to be brought before the International Military Tribunal's great chamber.[7]

In the course of these interrogations, Schmitt claimed that his influence on Nazi Germany's political leadership had been limited. His *Großraum* theory and concept of the political, on which much of Kempner's case rested, were mere scholarly 'adventures' poking into the prevalent political landscape, hardly prescriptive roadmaps for political leaders to implement. 'According to my intentions, the method used, and the form', Schmitt insisted, the scholarly work was 'just a pure diagnosis ... which I am still inclined to defend in front of any academic faculty in the world'.[8]

---

[2] For biographical details, see Reinhard Mehring, *Carl Schmitt: A Biography* (Cambridge: Polity Press, 2014); Joseph J. Bendersky, *Carl Schmitt: Theorist for the Reich* (Princeton: Princeton University Press, 2014); Jan-Werner Müller, *A Dangerous Mind: Carl Schmitt in Post-War European Thought* (New Haven: Yale University Press, 2003).

[3] Fritz Morstein Marx, 'Totalitarian Politics', *Proceedings of the American Philosophical Society* 82 (1940), 1–38, at 4.

[4] These quotes are taken from the *Daily Mail* and *Times* articles on 4 April 1936, as cited in Carl Schmitt, *Antworten in Nürnberg*, ed. Helmut Quaritsch (Berlin: Duncker & Humblot, 2000), 118.

[5] V.J. McGill, 'Notes on Philosophy in Nazi Germany', *Science & Society* 4 (1940), 12–28, 23.

[6] 'Geschichte – richtig gesehen!', *Das Schwarze Korps*, 10 December 1936. There is a marked anti-Catholic shift in *Das Schwarze Korps* from mid-1936, with a firework of cartoons lampooning 'prudish' Catholic morality.

[7] In the first interrogation, Kempner told Schmitt that the potential charge was (intellectual) 'preparation of a war of aggression'. Whether or not this constituted a criminal act under Control Council Law No. 10 – the legal foundation for the prosecution of German war criminals – is discussed at length, and ultimately rejected, by Helmut Quaritsch in Schmitt, *Antworten in Nürnberg*, 16–27. An English translation of these interrogations can be found in: 'Interrogation of Carl Schmitt by Robert Kempner' (I–III), *Telos* 72 (Summer 1987), 97–129.

[8] Schmitt, *Antworten in Nürnberg*, 54f.

In his written statements to Kempner, Schmitt lamented that academic inquiries into constitutional law, international law and political theory were always at risk of being manhandled 'without much thought and context' to advance crude Machiavellian 'interests and other instrumental causes'.[9] While during periods of relative political calm such scholarly gestures enjoyed 'generous freedom of thought', in times of war, the same concepts could swiftly be hijacked and 'propagandistically employed' as nihilism-inducing bombs.[10] A scholar was powerless to prevent his popular reception being besmirched by party-political taint. In Schmitt's reading, any wise man's attempt to ideologically nurture the leader of a totalitarian state was in any case ludicrous, or, as Alexandre Kojève held in a debate with Leo Strauss, 'wholly ineffectual'.[11]

Schmitt also had a deeper conceptual issue with the Nuremberg trials. Throughout his academic career, Schmitt combated liberalism, with its universalist aspirations and cosmopolitan pretensions.[12] In Schmitt's telling, liberalism was romanticism's deformed offspring, a political theology[13] which, intoxicated through modern shamanic practices like rationality, technological development and secularism, had deluded itself into the belief that it was progressing towards global peace.[14] Reality looked much bleaker. Schmitt even placed a sharp conceptual wedge between democracy and liberalism. In the former, Schmitt proclaimed, a homogeneous group of people legitimised a muscular decider; whereas the latter unsatisfactorily answered the critical questions of legitimacy by recourse to fickle parliamentary representation.[15]

---

[9] Ibid., 88.
[10] Ibid.
[11] The Strauss–Kojève dialogue famously revolved around the question of whether philosophers should abstain from mingling in politics. Leo Strauss, *On Tyranny: Corrected and Expanded Edition, Including the Strauss-Kojève Correspondence*, ed. Victor Gourevitch and Michael S. Roth (Chicago: University of Chicago Press, 2000), 206.
[12] John P. McCormick, *Carl Schmitt's Critique of Liberalism: Against Politics as Technology* (Cambridge: Cambridge University Press, 1997).
[13] There has been substantial debate on whether Schmitt ultimately moulded a political theology himself, given that he remained deeply steeped in Catholicism and freely dropped biblical concepts to feed his political philosophy. This seems implausible. When Schmitt accuses liberalism of crypto-theological thinking, he is primarily concerned with its borderless concept of enmity. Just like theological thinking, where the enemy challenges the very foundation of one's belief and therefore needs to be eradicated to confirm faith, liberalism possesses similar missionary tendencies. This forces liberalism to produce a notion of absolute enmity, close to the theological meaning of the term. Schmitt's idea, as outlined later in the chapter, is different. On liberalism as political theology, see Carl Schmitt, *Politische Theologie* (Berlin: Duncker & Humblot, 1934), 49–66.
[14] Carl Schmitt, *Politische Romantik* (München: Duncker & Humblot, 1919).
[15] Carl Schmitt, *The Crisis of Parliamentary Democracy*, trans. Ellen Kennedy (Cambridge, MA: MIT Press, 2000), 22–33.

With this criticism in tow, Schmitt can be read as the repressed subconscious to dreamy Weimar as well as to the new liberal world order, that, to him, could not live up to the fading European international order, the *jus publicum Europaeum*. This European public law, as Schmitt persuasively demonstrated in his major post-war work *The Nomos of the Earth*, derived its normative muscle from a mildly secularised form of Christianity. For Schmitt, the *jus publicum Europaeum* had successfully stabilised relationships between European states for roughly two hundred years, until, in 1939, it was crushed by the might of an Anglo-American commercial and maritime empire.[16] Schmitt framed this transition in his 1942 book *Land and Sea: A World-Historical Meditation* as the victory of sea powers over land powers.[17] But while these novel Anglo-American hegemonic forces had successfully supplanted the old concrete order of European monarchies, states and nations, as Schmitt grieved, they had failed to substitute for it a similarly effective international order, stuffing international law with a quixotic mix of conflicting norms instead.[18]

Who had the authority to bring him in front of a war tribunal to begin with, asked Schmitt, if there was no meaningful international order in sight? And in the absence of any immediately binding international norms, Schmitt raged, what else was this judicial spectacle in Nuremberg but a bunch of victors and Jewish expatriates affirming their power in taking brutal revenge?[19] While Schmitt was soon released from detention, and retired to his childhood home in Plettenberg, where he would spend the rest of his life in relative quiet, the interrogation process highlighted international law's anxieties when confronted with conflicting imagined political futures, weaknesses that still plague it today.

The chapter looks at Schmitt's international thought and in particular combs through his works on international law and the state. It suggests that Schmitt's political ideas are better understood within his legal thought. By way

---

[16] Carl Schmitt, *The Nomos of the Earth in the International Law of the Jus Publicum Europaeum*, trans. G.L. Ulmen (New York: Telos Press, 2006), pt. III.
[17] Schmitt's blatant anti-Semitism makes this a difficult read. Carl Schmitt, *Land and Sea: A World-Historical Meditation*, trans. Samuel Garrett Zeitlin (New York: Telos Press Publishing, 2015).
[18] Schmitt, *Nomos*, pt. IV.
[19] The alleged 'self-righteousness' of German-Jewish émigrés is a major recurring theme in Schmitt's diary. On 14 March 1948, he writes: 'The military, techno-industrial, and economic giants, that want to subjugate us and keep us on the ground – without any attempts to getting to know us. They are just throwing us like fodder in front of the émigrés.' Carl Schmitt, *Glossarium: Aufzeichnungen der Jahre 1947–1951*, ed. Eberhard Freiherr von Medem (Berlin: Duncker & Humblot, 1991), 115.

of examining Schmitt's *The Concept of the Political*, this chapter further elucidates the ways in which early-twentieth-century critics of liberalism wrestled with, and sought to counteract, liberalism's alleged alienating potential; its expansionist economics; its sacred individualism; its universalist inclinations, and the spatial ordering in international law it fuelled. In so doing, this chapter speaks directly to the relevance of political thought for international law. It also engages with contemporary debates on sovereignty and the legitimate use of violence in international conflicts. Schmitt's thinking about the international, with his flagging of abstract political ideas, offers a ground on which to read the history of international law in conjunction with the history of political thought, and to think the state through the international.

5.2 INTELLECTUAL FORMATION: WHAT'S ON THE LAWYER'S MIND

In the 1993 article *Carl Schmitt in the Intellectual History of the Federal Republic*, published eight years after Schmitt's death, Jürgen Habermas distilled Schmitt's entire intellectual development into a single sentence, which is worth quoting in full:

> A critical attitude towards modernity because of an upbringing in a Catholic milieu; a marriage which led to a distancing from the church; a defiant provincialism; a certain uneasiness with all things urban; the generational event of the First World War and the complex of Versailles; additionally an existential pioneering spirit to venture 'from Goethe to Hölderlin'; a turn against humanism more generally; a Latin-Catholic and Greek-Neopagan critique of the enlightenment tradition, channelled through Donoso Cortes or Nietzsche; an intellectual elitist stance snubbing the party state, democracy, public sphere (*Öffentlichkeit*), and discussion; deep contempt towards all things egalitarian; and then, of course, the Führer, who ultimately sealed their common fates.[20]

According to Habermas, all of the above applies to Martin Heidegger's intellectual formation as well; hence the plural. But what Habermas omits in his evenly exhaustive and insightful enumeration, is that throughout his life Schmitt's thought remained steeped in German legal debates.[21]

---

[20] Jürgen Habermas, 'Unser aller Avancierriese: Carl Schmitt in der politischen Geistesgeschichte der Bundesrepublik', *Die Zeit*, 3 December 1993.

[21] Günter Maschke, 'Carl Schmitt in den Händen der Nicht-Juristen: Zur neuen Literatur', *Der Staat* 34 (1995), 104–29.

Carl Schmitt was a German jurist.[22] For Schmitt this meant nine years of thorough legal training at the universities of Berlin, Munich, and Strasbourg, followed by a lengthy practical stint at the Higher Regional Court in Düsseldorf, a second state examination, a doctorate, and an extensive *Habilitation*. The skill of sharply demarcating concepts and subsuming empirically discernible social facts under them, sometimes denigrated as *Begriffsmagie* (magic of concepts), are but the most visible cues that link Schmitt's writing back to the legal training and practice he underwent.[23]

In the early decades of the twentieth century, at the very beginning of his scholarly endeavours, Schmitt groaned at the perfunctory theoretical models German jurists employed to capture the complexities of modern statehood, and at their narrow thinking with respect to the relation between law and politics. There were a number of cases that excited Schmitt. In 1860, to pick out only one of many instances, roughly three decades before Schmitt's birth, Wilhelm I commanded the reconstruction of the Prussian Army, in what is now known as the *Heeresreform*.[24] This incident rapidly snowballed into a severe constitutional conflict between the increasingly self-confident parliament and the king.[25]

The German liberal legal scholar Gerhard Anschütz, editor of Georg Meyer's standard public law textbook *Lehrbuch des Deutschen Staatsrechts*, set out to disentangle the constitutional tussle some fifty years later. But after some cursory attempts to shed light on the situation with his legal toolbox, Anschütz settled for a capitulation instead. Cases where parliament wrangled with the king, wrote Anschütz, were moments in which the reach of conventional 'public law had come to an end'.[26] Constitutional provisions could not help jurists to grasp such intricate institutional matters with their legal methods.

---

[22] On 23 September 1947, Schmitt noted in his diary that above all he 'had always written and spoken as a jurist only to and for other jurists. It was my misfortune that the jurists of my time had turned to legal positivism and become mere technicians of applying the law, deeply ignorant and uneducated … Therefore, harking non-jurists could jump on each of my words and formulations and rip me apart as a cunning desert fox.' Schmitt, *Glossarium: Aufzeichnungen der Jahre 1947–1951*, 17.

[23] Volker Neumann, *Carl Schmitt als Jurist* (Tübingen: Mohr Siebeck, 2015).

[24] For an excellent contemporary historical account of the *Heeresreform* of 1860, see Heinrich von Sybel, *Vorträge und Abhandlungen*, ed. Conrad Varrentrapp (München: R. Oldenbourg, 1897), 262–90.

[25] Christopher M. Clark, *Iron Kingdom: The Rise and Downfall of Prussia 1600–1947* (Cambridge, MA: Harvard University Press, 2006), 516f.

[26] Gerhard Anschütz and Georg Meyer, *Lehrbuch des Deutschen Staatsrechts* (München: Duncker & Humblot, 1919), 906.

Schmitt was not recommending that jurists should have fought more rounds against politics before throwing in the towel. They should not have stepped into the ring to begin with. The very structure, function, and historical role of legal scholarship, argued Schmitt, prevented it from waltzing as an opposition-science (*Oppositionswissenschaft*).[27] Anschütz, for one, had stumbled because his scholarly gaze had remained fixed on squeezing out answers to politically charged questions from positive laws alone, as Schmitt would later critique.[28] The strait-jacketing of law to correspond squarely to written norms and formal procedure, thundered Schmitt, had been the collective failure of a whole generation of liberal jurists.[29] Schmitt wanted no membership in their club. Instead, he meticulously tailored legal garb to fit exceptional political conditions: specifically, for extreme cases in which public order had vanished and liberal *Allgemeine Staatslehre* came to its limits.[30]

Sharpening a focus on the state of exception, or, to use the rumbling German compound word *Ausnahmezustand*, in Schmitt's eyes, revealed that while law may well have receded from public life, order in a 'juristic sense' almost always prevailed. What liberal jurists were quick to label 'disturbance', 'collapse', 'end of law', or altogether 'anarchy', on closer inspection commonly constituted the very exception which sustained the handy legal rules of their 'day-to-day' work.[31] For liberal jurists to refuse serious engagement with the *Ausnahmezustand*, Schmitt teased, was comparable to a theologian rationally ruling out the occurrence of miracles on which his own faith was based. You cannot have one without the other. Schmitt concluded that in a juristic sense, the state of exception, while 'suspending the prevailing legal order', was

---

[27] Schmitt blames legal positivism for having created this false dichotomy: 'Legal positivism puts the law normatively into an opposition against the political leadership and if necessary against the legislator itself; it is typical for legal positivism to claim that the law is wiser than the legislator.' Carl Schmitt, 'Die geschichtliche Lage der deutschen Rechtswissenschaft', *Deutsche Juristen-Zeitung* 41 (1936), 15–21, 16.

[28] Schmitt, *Politische Theologie*, 21.

[29] Carl Schmitt, 'Die geschichtliche Lage der deutschen Rechtswissenschaft', 17.

[30] In a 1926 review of Meinecke's *Idee der Staatsräson*, Schmitt has the following to say about the distinction of normal and abnormal situations: 'Whoever presumes that an abnormal situation exists—whether because he sees a radical abnormality in the world, or because he only regards a particular situation as abnormal—will resolve the problem of politics, ethics and the law differently from someone who is convinced that in principle a normal condition prevails, even if this condition of normality is slightly marred.' (this translation is Keith Tribe's): Carl Schmitt, 'Zu Friedrich Meineckes "Idee der Staatsräson"', *Archiv für Sozialwissenschaft und Sozialpolitik* 56 (1926), 226–36.

[31] Carl Schmitt, *Political Theology*, trans. George Schwab (Cambridge, MA: MIT Press, 1985), 12.

essentially the only way to 'establish a new order'.³² The *Ausnahmezustand* had been made juristically palpable.

'A philosophy of concrete life', Schmitt argued against Anschütz, 'cannot withdraw from the exception and from the extreme case; rather, it has to show [the] keenest interest in the exception'.³³ Schmitt's determination to overcome such embarrassing legal capitulations is already visible in his earliest writings. In the untranslated 1912 book *Gesetz und Urteil: Eine Untersuchung zum Problem der Rechtspraxis* a young Schmitt sheepishly asks a basic question: 'When is a judge's decision correct?'³⁴ Most jurists would diligently answer, a decision is correct if the law has been interpreted and applied correctly to the individual case. Schmitt rejects this definition. He remonstrates that little is won by relating the juristic validity of a judge's ruling to the written legal code. Irrespective of how sophisticated the hermeneutic approach of hammering meaning out of legal norms is – in German legal scholarship a predictably complex method called *Methodenlehre*³⁵ – at a certain point, one always finds oneself at a hermeneutic loss for meaning.³⁶ Legal relationships in modern societies are far too knotty to be folded neatly into positive legal codes, or 'resolved' wholesomely through *Methodenlehre*.

A glance at the ways in which judges perform their juridical duties, Schmitt argues, makes it plain that they are not merely reconstructing laws mechanically, like robots.³⁷ Through their rulings, judges are instead engaged in the practice of making law. Schmitt reasons that, practically speaking, a judge's train of thought when writing an *Urteil* is essentially the following: will my ruling withstand appeals in front of another chamber, or will my ruling be overturned? With a wink to the categorical imperative, Schmitt concludes with the following crisp and potent definition: a judge's decision can be validated theoretically if 'it can be assumed that another judge would have ruled in the same way'.³⁸

---

[32] Schmitt, *Politische Theologie*, 18ff.
[33] Ibid., 21.
[34] Carl Schmitt, *Gesetz und Urteil: Eine Untersuchung zum Problem der Rechtspraxis* (Berlin: Otto Liebmann, 1912), 4.
[35] For a succinct introduction to *Methodenlehre*, see Karl Larenz and Claus Wilhelm Canaris, *Methodenlehre der Rechtswissenschaft* (Berlin und Heidelberg: Springer, 1995).
[36] An excellent overview can be found in Robert Alexy, *Theorie der juristischen Argumentation: Die Theorie des rationalen Diskurses als Theorie der juristischen Begründung* (Frankfurt am Main: Suhrkamp, 1991), 17–43.
[37] For nineteenth-century precedents to these debates, see Regina Ogorek, *Richterkönig oder Subsumtionsautomat? Zur Justiztheorie im 19. Jahrhundert* (Frankfurt am Main: Klostermann, 2008).
[38] Schmitt, *Gesetz und Urteil*, 74.

In his first extensive academic work, Schmitt dissociated legal decision-making from positive legal norms and formal validity. Schmitt would repeat this trick in his theorisations of the state and the international. In the same way in which a ruling's validity rested outside written laws, whether in the legal convictions of fellow judges or the moral convictions of a population at large, the state, too, could not be confined to mechanically following a written script of constitutional norms. Consequentially, Schmitt's famous juristic definition of sovereignty presses liberal constitutionalism against the idea that the state of exception ushers in the fundamental possibility of 'unlimited' jurisdictional competence, in which '[s]overeign is he who decides on the exception'.[39] Decisions make the law and not the other way around. This legal decisionism undergirds his political thought and not least his concept of the political.

5.3 THE CONCEPT OF THE POLITICAL

In March 1927, Carl Schmitt penned *The Concept of the Political* in a stream of consciousness, finishing it in just under four weeks. Schmitt noted his relief when his wife Duška Todorovic, after an early reading, expressed 'enthusiastic endorsement'.[40] The short tract, first published in the prized journal *Archiv für Sozialwissenschaften und Sozialpolitik*, was a response to a number of pressing issues in the political landscape of Weimar Germany. Schmitt's scathing polemic against universal humanitarianism, Weimar's parliamentary democracy and the Versailles Treaty, his urge for a strong leader to legitimise the domestic legal order, and his fear of an aroused cosmopolitan elite succeeding in outlawing war itself, all crystallised in this 33-page article.[41]

From the outset, in this work, Schmitt's political thought on the state is concerned with the international in two distinct, yet interrelated ways. On one hand, Schmitt's political theory engages directly with the essence of modern global politics and its capacity for transnational orders. On the other, Schmitt constructs the state as just one historically contingent political form in which 'the political', the relation of man to a potential public enemy, can nestle. Any state's external public enmity requires another political unity against which to direct its antagonism. As long as 'there will be a state on earth', writes Schmitt, 'there will be a multiplicity of states'. The political world is 'a pluriverse, not a

---

[39] Schmitt, *Political Theology*, 5, 7.
[40] Mehring, *Carl Schmitt: A Biography*, 188.
[41] Carl Schmitt, 'Der Begriff des Politischen', *Archiv für Sozialwissenschaft und Sozialpolitik* 58 (1927), 1–33.

universe'.[42] In Schmitt's telling, any viable international order ultimately ought to stabilise the eternal antagonism inherent in the political within spatially contingent zones of influence.

After reading Schmitt's theories on international order, one of Hans Kelsen's more prominent students, Josef L. Kunz, credited Schmitt with possessing 'talent and brains'. Kunz also found Schmitt's colourful writing style 'a pleasure'. However, he characterised Schmitt as someone who 'has, of course, never been a jurist, but a politician'.[43] Schmitt's later work *Völkerrechtliche Großraumordnung*, into which he wove some preliminary thoughts on how to recalibrate the spatial order in international law was, for Kunz, 'not a study in international law, but a political thing'.[44] Hans Wehberg, the publisher of a pacifist journal with the declared purpose of 'foster[ing] international understanding' and 'promot[ing] international organisations', broadly shared Kunz's views.[45] But Wehberg responded to Schmitt's writing with a political counterproposal. All lawyers should stop critiquing the current global order and instead work productively towards building stronger international alliances: the 'greatest task of our generation'.[46]

If internationalists like Wehberg and Kunz advocated international cooperation, they based their proposals on the conviction that humans share universal values (however thin they may be) on which collective institutions can be erected. Schmitt's *raison d'état* fought hard against such assumptions and the political projects they produced, and it was this, more than his direct involvement in the Nazi party, which caused internationalists to impute political ambitions to Schmitt. Schmitt became a card-carrying member of the NSDAP only in May 1933, months after Hitler had become chancellor. Public law, Schmitt's bread-and-butter discipline, was, however, not important enough to be given a representative place in the higher echelons of Nazi bureaucracy. And even if it had been, Schmitt was probably an unlikely candidate. His resolutely statist convictions were at odds with the totalitarian state modelled by the Nazis; and Schmitt's insistence well after Hitler decided to invade the Soviet Union on the legal validity of the Molotov–Ribbentrop Pact, in which

---

[42] Carl Schmitt, *Der Begriff des Politischen* (München: Duncker & Humblot, 1932), 54.
[43] Josef L. Kunz, [review of *Völkerrechtliche Grossraumordnung*], *American Journal of International Law* 34 (1940), 175–6, at 176.
[44] Ibid.
[45] Hans Wehberg, 'Carl Schmitt, Völkerrechtliche Grossraumordnung mit Interventionsverbot für Raumfremde Mächte: Ein Beitrag zum Reichsbegriff im Völkerrecht', *Die Friedens-Warte* 40 (1940), 134–5.
[46] Hans Wehberg, 'Universales oder Europäisches Völkerrecht? Eine Auseinandersetzung mit Carl Schmitt', *Die Friedens-Warte* 41 (1941), 157–66, at 166.

Nazi Germany and the Soviet Union had agreed a spatial division of Eastern Europe, would not win Schmitt favours with party members, either.[47] However, some of Schmitt's writing, his anti-Semitism in particular, gelled with the right wing sabre-rattling against Weimar's liberal democracy and its burdensome international obligations, the so-called *Versailler Diktat*.

In Paul Kahn's reading, which perhaps comes closest to Schmitt's, *liberalism* constitutes a sophisticated pre-political abstraction that ultimately derives the validity of laws from reason alone. Kahn posits this reason-based abstraction against what in philosophical terms may be called a phenomenological one – one that is based, for instance, on most things spatially and temporally grounded that can be experienced. In this way, then, as Schmitt and Kahn would agree, the birth defect of liberal theories of law lies in their desiring generalities to systematise, compare, and structure the world without having experienced it.[48] For Schmitt, sovereignty is not an abstract category but something to be experienced, for instance, during the theatrical explosion of violence in a civil war. This sits uneasily with liberal theories that privilege reason.

For Schmitt, everything that did not measure up to these high standards of neutrality looked political or at least suspicious. In early 1936, Schmitt alleged in a short article under the confident title *The Historic Situation of German Jurisprudence* for the *Deutsche Juristen-Zeitung*, Germany's leading law review, that liberal state-theory masqueraded its own universalist aspirations as 'abstract generality'.[49] Any critique of their hidden agenda was immediately disqualified as irrational or political. Liberals believed, continued Schmitt, that only they could truthfully lay claim to humanity's absolute values (*Menschheitswerte*) and to rationality. Schmitt elaborated this point further in a slightly more accusatory tone:

> They posited themselves as purely juridical, purely scientific and ultimately as solely 'pure'. In so doing they disqualified as unscientific and 'impure' every non-liberal, particularly every national jurisprudence.[50]

What if the last obstacle towards the achievement of what liberal jurists claimed as universal *Menschheitswerte* was man himself, noted Schmitt

---

[47] An exploration of this theme can be found in Samuel Garrett Zeitlin's insightful introduction 'Propaganda and Critique', in Schmitt, *Land and Sea: A World-Historical Meditation*, xxxi–lxix, at xxxviii.
[48] Paul W. Kahn, *Putting Liberalism in Its Place* (Princeton: Princeton University Press, 2005), ch. 1.
[49] Schmitt, 'Die geschichtliche Lage der deutschen Rechtswissenschaft', 21.
[50] Ibid.

smugly. Were liberal jurists willing to wipe out humanity as a whole, after smearing all but an enlightened few as being political?[51]

Schmitt looked at the international through antagonistic relationships. This stemmed from his anthropological understanding of the nature of man. The most dominant property of man, contended Schmitt, lies in his aggressiveness. Public law, which regulates the relationship of a citizen with the state, has to be seen solely in this light. This view is totally at odds with contemporary approaches like global constitutionalism, global administrative law, and international public law. Yet, even proponents of such, arguably more progressive, approaches do not overlook the role conflict plays in societies. Historically speaking, one could even claim that the emergence of the individual as a state subject and a bearer of natural rights took hints from *raison d'état* theorists. Statists had long argued that the principle of absolute sovereignty was hospitable for the emergence of contractual relations between states – a state of nature par excellence. Bringing this international principle back to the level of the individual within a singular state prompted much of the natural law thinking amongst legists in post-Renaissance Europe.

What truly distinguished all these thinkers and approaches from Schmitt was that, for the latter, antagonism was central. It was not a footnote to social life, or a side effect that could be treated using robust mechanisms of peaceful resolution or arbitration. Schmitt went so far as to say that the state's ability to wage war against another state constituted the most important point for thinking about international order. If in his work Schmitt considered other mundane human concerns like friendship, cooperation, or for that matter even understanding, it was mainly in order to increase a state's fighting capacity. In the following, we survey some of these ideas from Schmitt's work, making an excursus into some of the most potent twentieth-century concepts of political action – both on an individual and on state level – as well as tapping into a long-standing tradition in the history of political thought.

Schmitt's *Concept of the Political* attracted considerable controversy. Just a few years after its first publication in 1927, it had been debated in a wide range of domestic and international academic journals, from political science and public law, to history, religion, philosophy, and even theoretical economy. It is thus not surprising that Schmitt's thought influenced law-makers in Germany and public policy thinking abroad, both at the time and since. The friend–enemy distinction Schmitt lionised has gone mainstream. In an editorial published shortly after the September 11 attacks, in the *Frankfurter Allgemeine Zeitung*, for example, the political theorist Georgio Agamben

---

[51] Ibid., 22.

swiftly linked George W. Bush's reaction ('you are either with us or against us') to a wider Schmittian undercurrent in US politics.[52]

For Schmitt, a single dualism explains the essence of politics. He famously writes: 'The specific political distinction to which political actions and motives can be reduced is that between friend and enemy.'[53] Schmitt derived this dualism from a number of straightforward anthropological assumptions. Humans have always organised themselves in collectivities. In these collectivities they need a space to validate and affirm their existence. Ultimately, they can only do so when facing the actual possibility of killing and dying for their collectivities. Schmitt is not inclined to justify these assumptions any further.[54] In Schmitt's understanding, they are 'self-evident' social facts deeply rooted in human nature. Hans Morgenthau agreed with Schmitt on this point, and ventured to develop this thought further, most prominently in his work *On the Derivation of Politics from the Essence of Man*, which in time turned into a surprisingly durable chipboard in international relations theory.[55]

However, Herbert Marcuse, among others, was not convinced. In 1934, Marcuse elaborated his qualms at length in an essay for Max Horkheimer's *Zeitschrift für Sozialforschung*, by then being printed from exile in Paris. Marcuse looked closely at the concrete discursive strategies which totalitarian *Weltanschauungen* utilised to combat liberalism, and contested Schmitt's theorisation of the political. Why would perfectly reasonable citizens of a polity want to take up arms and fight a state-defined public enemy, Marcuse asked.[56] Not for any rational reasons, declared Schmitt. Human life was too valuable and could thus not be weighed against any rational justifications, be they economic, cultural, or moral in nature.[57]

---

[52] Giorgio Agamben, 'Heimliche Komplizen: Über Sicherheit und Terror', *Frankfurter Allgemeine Zeitung*, 20 September 2001. The argument outlined in this chapter, which states that Schmitt remained rooted in German legal scholarship, presses against Agamben's larger point that Schmitt's *Concept of the Political* was a direct response to Walter Benjamin's essay *Zur Kritik der Gewalt* (On Violence).

[53] Carl Schmitt, *The Concept of the Political*, trans. George Schwab (Chicago: University of Chicago Press, 2007), 26.

[54] Heinrich Meier, *Die Lehre Carl Schmitts: Vier Kapitel zur Unterscheidung Politischer Theologie und Politischer Philosophie* (Stuttgart: Metzler, 2012), ch. 3. Sam Zeitlin pointed out this reference.

[55] Morgenthau's realism regards the will to power as the most persuasive and continuous quality man possesses: Hans Morgenthau, 'Über die Herkunft des Politischen aus dem Wesen des Menschen' (1930), as cited in Oliver Jütersonke, *Morgenthau, Law and Realism* (Cambridge: Cambridge University Press, 2010), 60.

[56] Herbert Marcuse, 'Der Kampf gegen den Liberalismus in der Totalitären Staatsauffassung', *Zeitschrift für Sozialforschung* III, no. 2 (1934), 161–94, at 184.

[57] 'There is no rational reason, no norm however valid, no exemplary plan, no social ideal however great, no legitimacy or legality, which can justify that humans kill each other for it.' Schmitt, *Der Begriff des Politischen*, 1932, 37.

Rather, antagonism and violence, as Schmitt elaborated, were *seinsgemäße* (existential) facts.[58] But if this was the case, Marcuse reasoned, philosophical existentialism, in its new political avatar, had just jumped into the conceptual justification-gap to legitimise and validate violence.[59] Similarly, Hannah Arendt, when first encountering Schmitt's existential explanation for killing and dying, intuitively put a big question mark next to Schmitt's remarks.[60] Schmitt trumpeted that his definition of the political was 'neither war-endorsing nor militaristic, neither imperialistic nor pacifistic'.[61] 'It is barbaric', Arendt scribbled into her copy.[62] But Arendt and Marcuse's bewilderment about Schmitt's thesis would hardly have triggered a response. In Schmitt's view, he did not bear the burden of proof for describing reality. If anyone wanted to alter it by striving towards a political ideal, the burden of proof was on them.

In any case, Schmitt claimed that, in a utilitarian sense, his antagonistic concept of enmity was far more humane than mainstream 'ethical-moral' calls to arms which, when challenged, necessarily conjured up the image of an absolute enemy to be 'destroyed and eradicated'.[63] His was not a philosophy of indiscriminate slaughter and dehumanising enmity. Internationalists were just misguided, Schmitt claimed, when they thought that war could be outlawed through international law. Foremost amongst such activist historians was the director of the Carnegie Endowment for International Peace, a pacifist with the unfortunate name James T. Shotwell. On 1 March 1927, during the inaugural speech for the Carnegie chair at Berlin's recently established Hochschule für Politik, Shotwell showcased the results of a major research project on the consequences of the First World War and feverishly anticipated what he called a 'turning point in the history of the world'.[64]

Working together with a number of prominent historians, Shotwell had reached the conclusion that the social and economic effects of the First World War had cut far deeper than anything previously known to mankind. From time immemorial up until roughly the age of enlightenment, people's lives

---

[58] Ibid., 9.
[59] Marcuse, 'Der Kampf gegen den Liberalismus in der Totalitären Staatsauffassung', 185.
[60] Arendt was working with the 1933 edition of Schmitt's *Der Begriff des Politischen* (Hamburg: Hanseatische Verlagsanstalt, 1933); the question mark can be found on p. 31. Bard Library, Arendt Collection, JX1315.S3 1933.
[61] Schmitt, *Der Begriff des Politischen*, 1932, 21.
[62] Bard Library, Arendt Collection, JX1315.S3 1933, 16.
[63] Schmitt, *Glossarium: Aufzeichnungen der Jahre 1947–1951*, 8.
[64] James T. Shotwell, 'Are We at a Turning Point in the History of the World?', in *Carnegie Endowment for International Peace: Yearbook 1927* (Washington DC: Carnegie Endowment, 1927), 103–12, at 103.

had chiefly been ordered by repetition in accordance with the 'routine of nature', for instance the imperative to 'sow and reap'. Then industrialisation hit with its 'conquest' of time and space.[65] The routine of nature suddenly decreased in importance. Mankind moved from a static-repetitive world to one of change and dynamism, which ushered in 'speedy shipment of ... products', lessened travel times, and promoted science – in short, the 'Industrial Revolution' turned the world upside down.[66]

For Shotwell, this mighty transformation required new political forms, and a new 'law of the world community'.[67] This involved rethinking the concept of war. In pre-modern times, European states had waged wars within fixed limits. Wars were 'controllable' and 'a legitimate exercise of sovereignty, the final argument, the *ultima ratio* of governments', with a well-defined place in political theory.[68] But in the modern age war had lost its *raison d'être*. The world had moved so closely together in economic, social, and cultural terms that the 'losses inflicted upon an enemy' quite frequently 'turned out to be one's own'. Through technological advances in war machinery, Shotwell proclaimed, the '[v]ictor and victim may suffer a common disaster'. For these reasons any aggressive war fought for the sake of national policy should be criminalised.[69]

Rather unexpectedly, such ideas crystallised in the Kellogg–Briand Pact of 1928, popularly known as the Pact of Paris. Article I of the Pact provided that all signatories 'condemn recourse to war for the solution of international controversies' and 'renounce it as an instrument of national policy in their relations with one another'.[70] Schmitt was furious that Germany had joined the Pact, which, to him, was to Germany's political disadvantage. In a lecture given a couple of years later, on the same premises of the Hochschule für Politik, Schmitt complained that 'with this kind of jurisprudence, it has become impossible to know what war is'.[71]

Schmitt argued that, while the outlawing of war was the declared aim of the Kellogg–Briand Pact, the participating states had accomplished precisely the opposite. Violence in retaliation against a pact-breaking country had just been

---

[65] Ibid., 105.
[66] Ibid., 106.
[67] Ibid.
[68] Ibid., 107.
[69] Ibid., 109.
[70] David Hunter Miller, *The Peace Pact of Paris: A Study of the Briand–Kellogg Treaty* (New York and London: G.P. Putnam's Sons, 1928), 251.
[71] Carl Schmitt, *Nationalsozialismus und Völkerrecht* (Berlin: Junker und Dünnhaupt, 1934), 8f.

legitimised as police action for the infringement of a transnational contract.[72] And this situation, Schmitt worried, might quickly descend into an endless war, in which liberal powers would portray lawbreaking countries (almost in theological terms) as absolute enemies of humanity that had to be eradicated from the face of the earth.[73]

Even decades later, Schmitt noted in his diary how 'fatal' Shotwell's lecture had been for Germany's destiny.[74] If one were to look for a precedent, according to Schmitt, the lecture was as devastating as Schelling's Berlin seminar of 1841 (in which an old Schelling had attempted to root out the zealous urge to action that Hegel had sparked in the hearts of some of his student followers).[75] By endorsing the abolition of wars of aggression, Shotwell was, for Schmitt, trying to set in stone Germany's territorial disadvantage after the First World War. The whole outlawry movement, sniffed Schmitt, was a power-political move of the victors to preserve the status quo and stifle the legitimate territorial ambitions of up-and-coming nations, Germany in particular. For Schmitt, the real question that internationalists like Shotwell failed to answer was the following: 'Just because war has ceased to be calculable, has it ceased to be?'[76]

A 'Realpolitik of peace', as Shotwell envisaged it, Schmitt wrote disdainfully, with its holy trinity of Locarno, the League of Nations, and the Permanent Court of International Justice, was but a sleight of hand to distract from the central place of enmity in politics.[77] Even more critically, Shotwell had confused technological progress in the 'dynamic age' with some form of collective moral advancement. As Schmitt remarked, a man who replaces his postilion with an imported motorcycle does not necessarily turn into a flag-swinging pacifist.[78] Technological progress had nothing to do with either moral outlook or ethical behaviour.

As mentioned earlier, Schmitt takes the readiness of a polity to engage in an armed conflict against another polity as the starting point for public law. Both domestic public law and international law collapse and remain trapped in

---

[72] Ibid., 10.
[73] Schmitt, *Glossarium: Aufzeichnungen der Jahre 1947–1951*, 6f.
[74] Ibid., 7.
[75] Amongst the seminar crowd was a twenty-one-year-old Friedrich Engels, who later raged against Schelling's endeavour to domesticate the mighty 'dragon of Hegelianism': Friedrich Engels, *Schelling und die Offenbarung: Kritik des Neuesten Reaktionsversuchs gegen die Freie Philosophie* (Leipzig: Robert Binder, 1842), 6.
[76] Schmitt, *Glossarium: Aufzeichnungen der Jahre 1947–1951*, 7.
[77] Ibid.
[78] Carl Schmitt, *Der Begriff des Politischen*, 1933, 58.

Schmitt's core thesis. They can only be understood, interpreted and practised in the dim light of the possibility of armed conflict. If Schmitt's concept of the political were to be pitted against the state, Schmitt's money is on the former.[79] In Schmitt's reading, the state, understood in its conventional form as a political unity of a people, provides one convenient shell in which the political can house itself but, if need be, the institutional shell can always be swapped with another organisational form that fares better at institutionalising enmity. Schmitt thus flipped the conventional relationship between the state and politics upside down, and challenged much of the inherited knowledge of state theorists; a truly Copernican stroke.

The most seminal move of the *Concept of the Political* remains its definition of the political as the most intense human relationship. In slightly more technical language, Schmitt views the political as modal or phenomenal. The intensity of that relationship results from the fact that a potential combative encounter allows for legitimate killing. Recent scholarship has highlighted Schmitt's intellectual debt to Morgenthau, who, in his doctoral dissertation *Die Internationale Rechtspflege: Ihr Wesen und ihre Grenzen*, criticised the clear conceptual boundaries that Schmitt had drawn in the first edition of *Der Begriff des Politischen* between the economic, moral, and political *Lebenswelten*. Morgenthau argued that the division into detached fields did not serve Schmitt's argument well, and was unnecessary. Therefore, according to Morgenthau, it made much more sense to brand any conflict as 'political' if and when the two former opponents or competitors were willing to slip out of their corporate uniforms to engage in the act of killing. Any conflict could thus transform into a political one. Politics was a question of intensity, not a wholly different sphere. Schmitt quietly adopted these insights in his 1932 edition.[80]

Schmitt further emphasises that the friend and the enemy concept 'are to be understood in their concrete and existential sense, not as metaphors'.[81] From a constructivist point of view, the enemy is more important to Schmitt than the friend.[82] This is evident from the extensive space Schmitt devotes to the enemy in his writings. Friendship plays a marginal role and Schmitt's understanding of it remains limited. When he does evoke the concept, it is usually in the context of a group's homogeneity, or some other form of close-knit

---

[79] Schmitt, *Concept of the Political*, 19.
[80] William Hooker, *Carl Schmitt's International Thought: Order and Orientation* (Cambridge: Cambridge University Press, 2009), 38f.
[81] Schmitt, *Concept of the Political*, 27.
[82] Jacques Derrida, *The Politics of Friendship*, trans. George Collins (London: Verso, 2005).

association and togetherness, for instance a *Volk* (a people).[83] The concept of the enemy is defined far more exhaustively. The enemy is not necessarily an outsider. In a state of civil war, the enemy could also come to be another faction, a 'domestic' or 'internal' enemy, or just any group rebelling against the polity.[84]

One might ask, why exactly does the concept of the state depend on the concept of the political? According to Schmitt, the friend–enemy distinction is an ontic dictum, whereas the state is only one among several possible institutional forms of an eternal friend–enemy relationship. This does not downgrade the role of the state. On the contrary, Schmitt celebrates the state as a huge civilisational achievement. In the modern age, he argues, the state can lay claim to two important functions: as a polity, on the inside it overcomes deadly conflict and shields its people from it, on the outside, it civilises this conflict.[85] In essence, the state succeeds in resolving a political crisis by producing political unity and exercising effective leadership over a homogeneous people. The true political, however, is confined to the state's relationship with other states. In this international arena, the state may not be able to directly overcome conflicts in the same way as through the production of internal cohesion, but it can channel antagonism into a civil *Gestalt*.

According to Schmitt, the state constitutes post-enlightenment man's most mature political form for the exercise of violence. Even against the background of Germany's distinctive statist tradition, Schmitt's emphasis on the state is noteworthy. The state may even have been the single most important reason for the Nazi party's scepticism of Schmitt. Their emphasis on the people's movement (*Volksbewegung*) did not correspond well with Schmitt's more statist approach. After a number of heavy attacks in *Das Schwarze Korps*, the Sicherheitsdienst der Schutzstaffel (secret police) sourced expert opinions to curtail Schmitt's influence on Hitler's cabinet through Hans Frank, a minister. On 17 December 1936, in a secret evaluation of Schmitt's continued political suitability as Preußischer Staatsrat, once a powerful position but under Nazi rule a ceremonial post, a prominent public law professor, Felix Genzmer, denounced Schmitt as an opportunist whose state theory was too Catholic, too statist, and, to convince even the last spook in the Sicherheitsdienst der Schutzstaffel, considerably tainted by Jewish thinkers.

---

[83] Schmitt, *Concept of the Political*, 27.
[84] Ibid., 121.
[85] These are well-known tropes in German jurisprudence: see, e.g., Georg Wilhelm Friedrich Hegel, *Vorlesungen über Rechtsphilosophie 1818–1831*, ed. Karl-Heinz Ilting (Stuttgart-Bad Cannstatt: Friedrich Frommann, 1972), 324–53.

5 Schmitt's International Thought and the State 149

It was, Genzmer concluded his scorching report, 'astounding to the whole academic community' how a man of dubious reputation like Carl Schmitt had 'acquired party membership' and even the 'respected title of Preußischer Staatsrat'.[86] About a week later, Hermann Göring, the then Minister President of Prussia, had to personally intervene to silence the attacks.[87]

Schmitt's concept of the state is narrow. It is not exactly what Max Weber would have called an 'ideal type'. As a classificatory category, Schmitt's concept of the state operates chiefly as a polemical concept. For Schmitt polemic does not equal bad writing. It is not an aesthetic category. Rather, polemic constitutes the only meaningful way of adopting any stance at all. In stuffing the state concept with his belligerent understandings of the political, Schmitt attacked the mainstream state theories that were circulating at the time. When states started collapsing in the latter part of the twentieth century, Schmitt was quick to add to the preface of his 1963 edition that the 'era of statehood had come to an end'. But Schmitt never elaborated this thought. Ernst Forsthoff, a loyal disciple of Schmitt and a legal theorist in his own right, developed it further. In 1971, he trumpeted, somewhat surprisingly, that the Federal Republic of Germany was not a true state. For Forsthoff Germany constituted little more than a by-product of the Cold War, constantly in danger of being extinguished by a whiff of history.[88]

With his assumption of the fundamental aggressiveness of man, Schmitt positioned himself in a long tradition in European political thought. He repeatedly traced his intellectual genealogy to Thomas Hobbes and Jean Bodin. Historically speaking, as Schmitt substantiated his negative anthropology, all communities that had shunned the doctrine of original sin – which for Schmitt equals men's innate aggressiveness – had ended in disaster.[89] Aggressiveness is so important to Schmitt that he notes in the *Glossarium*: 'With every child a new world is born. For God's sake, then every new-born child is an aggressor!'[90]

---

[86] Carl Schmitt Akte, Sicherheitsdienst des RFSS SD Hauptamt 1936, Aktenzeichen 4062/68, FA 503(1), 241f, Institut für Zeitgeschichte, Munich.
[87] In a two-page letter to *Das Schwarze Korps*, Göring lambasted: 'it is simply unacceptable that your newspaper publicly denounces a person that I have given my confidence to and even promoted to such a high public office. If in the future you will ever want to accuse a Preußischen Staatsrat of any misgivings again, you will come to me first. If I see fit, I will provide for all further arrangements ... You will stop your press campaign against Staatsrat Professor Dr. Carl Schmitt at once.' Hermann Göring to Redaktion Das Schwarze Korps, 21 December 1936, in ibid, 237.
[88] Ernst Forsthoff, *Der Staat der Industriegesellschaft. Dargestellt am Beispiel der Bundesrepublik Deutschland* (München: C.H. Beck, 1984 [1971]), 158.
[89] Schmitt, *Concept of the Political*, 64f.
[90] Schmitt, *Glossarium: Aufzeichnungen der Jahre 1947–1951*, 320.

For Schmitt, aggressiveness is not just important for its ontic premise but also for the dynamic element it provides. While Schmitt expresses objections to bellicose or militaristic readings elsewhere, stressing that '[w]ar is neither the aim nor the purpose nor even the very content of politics', war always remains an 'ever present possibility'; it is always 'the leading presupposition'.[91] Schmitt's anthropological assumptions offer plenty of grounds for disagreement. A less bleak reading of human nature could highlight mankind's extraordinary potential for cooperation, an assumption that is supported by many sociologists, psychologists, and anthropologists.[92]

Like Schmitt's anthropological premise, more optimistic theories foregrounding man's cooperative behaviour have blind spots, too. But today the institutional advancement of an international common good is hardly based on such romantic visions of man. Conflict theories, too, can acknowledge the value and possibility of continuous cooperation. Immanuel Kant, most prominently, employed a sceptical anthropology as the very foundation of his universalistic proposals for perpetual peace. Pleading for international institutionalised cooperation does not equate to promoting pacifism in any straightforward sense. Similarly, acknowledging the creative dynamic of conflict does not imply adopting enmity as the essential human relation to understand human behaviour, domestic public law, or public international law. Much of the advancement and cooperative developments in the European legal space in the aftermath of the Second World War would have been simply impossible in Schmitt's thinking.[93] But it seems that Schmitt would be content to counter that his was not a debate on the nature of humans. Instead, it was an attempt to provide a juristic and epistemic framework for the state of exception.

Schmitt holds that true insight requires thinking from an exception. While the fight for life and death is not omnipresent, to Schmitt, it is a probable scenario which, because of its seriousness, needs to be taken as the decisive starting point for conceiving everything else. 'That the extreme case appears to be an exception does not negate its decisive character but confirms it all the

---

[91] Schmitt, *Concept of the Political*, 34.
[92] Leo Strauss made this point early on in Leo Strauss, 'Anmerkungen Zu Carl Schmitt, Der Begriff Des Politischen', *Archiv für Sozialwissenschaft und Sozialpolitik* 67 (1932), 733. For extensive research in the field of psychology, see Nathan C. DeWall, Craig A. Anderson, and Brad J. Bushman, 'The General Aggression Model: Theoretical Extensions to Violence', *Psychology of Violence* 1 (2011), 245–58.
[93] See the illuminating article by Marco Dani, 'Rehabilitating Social Conflicts in European Public Law', *European Law Journal* 18 (2012), 621–43, at 621–5.

more.'[94] With these premises, the decisive human relationship to ground politics is enmity. As with Hobbes, it is omnipresent as long as there is no common legal order backed up by a muscular institution. True order in this sense is by necessity concrete order. For Schmitt, the institutional structures underpinning international law were too thin, and lacked any means of coercion. Cognitive, semantic, reputational, or symbolic means of international institutions could not make up for international public authority.[95] In Schmitt's world, the protector has to be obeyed. Schmitt elevates the Hobbesian link between protection and obedience to constitute the necessary, one might say even 'eternal', basis for order: *protego ergo obligo*.[96] In this light, international law and in particular international institutions appear insurmountably weak. At best, conceptions of an international public law and international authority are romantic pipedreams.

For Schmitt, the very possibility of statehood is predicated on conflictual relationships between these states. According to the logic of protection and obedience, order would vanish as soon as protection became superfluous. Following this logic, the plurality of states causes an external threat, thus providing for social integration and hence for the viability of states. The state 'presupposes the real existence of an enemy and therefore coexistence with another political entity'.[97] This encourages states to channel their aggressive potential and to employ it creatively to stimulate the dynamism of history.

In addition, the plurality of states has normative value in so far as it is the precondition of different ways of life, allowing as it does for diversity or identity in today's parlance. This is another kernel of realist thought, and it is an important reason for war. 'Each participant is in a position to judge whether the adversary intends to negate his opponent's way of life and therefore must be repulsed or fought in order to preserve one's own form of existence'.[98] Schmitt's interpretation of otherness is bellicose in nature; 'stranger' can almost always simply be replaced with 'enemy'. He writes, 'The political enemy ... is ... the other, the stranger; and it is sufficient for his nature that he is, in a specially intense way, existentially something different and alien.'[99] Accordingly, theorems of transitional, let alone cosmopolitan citizenship, are lacking any foundation.[100]

---

[94] Schmitt, *Concept of the Political*, 35.
[95] Ibid., 38.
[96] Ibid., 52.
[97] Ibid., 53.
[98] Ibid., 27.
[99] Ibid.
[100] Ibid., 40.

Schmitt's ideas of international order could hardly be more at odds with these theorems. On 1 April 1939, two weeks after Nazi troops had marched into Czechoslovakia, Schmitt lectured at the Institut für Politik und Internationales Recht in Kiel on how to reorganise the spatial order in international law. The prevalent models of liberal jurists, mourned Schmitt, were all 'inauthentic and outdated'.[101] The Covenant of the League of Nations was itself deeply flawed in his opinion. On the one hand, it celebrated the principle of sovereignty and the integrity of state borders, yet, on the other, 'regional understandings' like the Monroe doctrine remained anchored in article 21 of the Covenant, if only as measures to 'secur[e] the maintenance of peace'.[102]

In Schmitt's telling, the Monroe doctrine was functionally operating to keep 'spatially alien powers' out of the US's wider sphere of influence in the Americas. This formed the nucleus of Schmitt's thinking about the Großraum (great space). Schmitt's Großraum stood in sharp contrast to British imperialism, as the latter rested, at least in theory, on the 'universalistic-humanitarian concerns' stemming from 'individualistic-liberal' premises. According to Schmitt, if states were horizontally equal in an international arena, the vertical universalistic and missionary overgrowth had to be entirely shaved off for international relations to function properly.

What made the Großraum intuitively intelligible, Schmitt reasoned, was a state's duty to protect its own people dwelling outside its borders in relative geographic proximity. The significant German minority in Middle and Eastern Europe therefore drastically extended the German Reich's zone of influence and responsibility over these smaller states. 'Spatially alien' states, just like the Monroe doctrine had long established, were prohibited from intervening in the Großraum. The Großraum's borders could thus be drawn much wider than those of the Reich. In flowery language Schmitt styled the Großraum as a concrete geographical space 'in which the sun of the Reich may rise'. Schmitt presented his theory as a kind of salvation for the insurmountable problems of current international law, which had become, for Schmitt, allergic to the very principle of statehood, labouring instead to secretly abolish the state concept through the 'universalistic-imperial' register of a singular world law. In Schmitt's eyes, the Großraum did justice to more

---

[101] Carl Schmitt, *Völkerrechtliche Großraumordnung mit Interventionsverbot für raumfremde Mächte: Ein Beitrag zum Reichsbegriff im Völkerrecht* (Berlin: Deutscher Rechtsverlag, 1939), 12.
[102] 'Treaty of Peace with Germany', in *United States Treaties and International Agreements* 2 [1918–1930] (1969), 43–240, art. 21; available at www.loc.gov/law/help/us-treaties/bevans/m-ust000002-0043.pdf.

practical 'planetary demands' of spatially dividing up the world. It spoke to the hegemonic realities of international relations. And now that Germany had emerged as a 'powerful Reich', it was ready to 'design, support and carry' this spatialised international law.[103]

5.4 IMPLICATIONS FOR DOMESTIC PUBLIC LAW AND INTERNATIONAL LAW

Conceiving the polity through the international, and perceiving the state through war, is highly consequential for understanding domestic public law as well as international law. With respect to domestic public law, *The Concept of the Political* targeted the understanding, interpretation, and implementation of Weimar constitutional law, in order to pave the way for a more authoritarian form of government. If the state's ability to wage war is critical for its survival, one needs a strong state, which in Schmitt's view necessitates effective leadership over a homogeneous people. Advocating such a form of political unity seems to be Schmitt's most important motive.[104] Domestic political conflict is only acceptable as long as it does not weaken the state's ability to mobilise for war. Thus, the conservative argument for the primacy of foreign policy is further radicalised. Apparently, Schmitt's ideal is a political unity whose domestic politics consists in merely administering things and persons.[105]

This primacy of the international is also highly consequential for a state's internal organisation and liberal parliamentary democracy.[106] Mutilating parliamentarism by clipping its discursive elements is one of the key suggestions of *The Concept of the Political*. The book also advocates a strictly anti-individualistic interpretation of the law. According to Schmitt, fundamental or human rights should not stand at the core of public law, given that one essential point of political community and public law is the very power to order an individual into a fight for life and death, to demand the readiness to

---

[103] Carl Schmitt, *Völkerrechtliche Großraumordnung mit Interventionsverbot für raumfremde Mächte*, 88.
[104] For a detailed reconstruction, see Thomas Vesting, 'Erosionen Staatlicher Herrschaft: Zum Begriff des Politischen bei Carl Schmitt', *Archiv des Öffentlichen Rechts* 117 (1992), 4–45, at 4–6.
[105] Ernst-Wolfgang Böckenförde, 'Der Begriff des Politischen als Schlüssel zum staatsrechtlichen Werk Carl Schmitts', in *Complexio Oppositorum: Über Carl Schmitt*, ed. Helmut Quaritsch (Berlin: Duncker & Humblot, 1988), 283–99, at 285.
[106] On the context of these debates, see Christoph Gusy (ed.), *Demokratisches Denken in der Weimarer Republik* (Baden-Baden: Nomos, 2000); Ulrich K. Preuß, 'Carl Schmitt and the Weimar Constitution', in Jens Meierhenrich and Oliver Simons (eds.), *The Oxford Handbook of Carl Schmitt* (Oxford: Oxford University Press, 2016), 471–89.

kill and die.[107] According to *The Concept of the Political*, true statehood requires a strong executive with potentially dictatorial powers and the ability to impose emergency rule, including the ability to abrogate the entire legal order:

> The endeavor of a normal state consists above all in assuring total peace within the state and its territory. To create tranquillity, security, and order and thereby establish the normal situation is the prerequisite for legal norms to be valid. Every norm presupposes a normal situation, and no norm can be valid in an entirely abnormal situation.[108]

This implies the power to declare someone an 'internal enemy', a person no longer protected by the law. The possibility of defining its enemies is constitutive of the concept of the people, it is the 'essence of its political existence'.[109]

In this view, pluralism belongs to the international sphere, not to domestic politics. Within a state, pluralism, be it political or social in nature, threatens the state's very existence.[110] Even though *The Concept of the Political* remains vague on what kind of homogeneity is required and how to deal with people that do not fit in, it seems clear that Schmitt's theory not only allows, but encourages state policy against troublemakers and potential non-troublemakers.

The Concept of the Political is just as consequential for international law as it is for domestic public law. It presents almost all elements of today's conventional understanding as deficient or even misleading. In the light of Schmitt's text, the idea of an international public law with international institutions which, endowed with their own instruments of power, inclusively advance a common transnational good seems virtually fanciful. The very concept of *international law* is questioned, and thus the discipline's identity as it prevails today. Schmitt considers the term *international law* misleading as it suggests a certain independence from states. Since such independence is impossible in Schmitt's view, organisations such as the League of Nations appear as foreign policy instruments of powerful states, not as truly *international*, that is, independent, organisations.[111] What the conventional understanding depicts as *international law* appears rather as external relations law when seen through Schmitt's eyes.

---

[107] Schmitt, *Concept of the Political*, 46.
[108] Ibid.
[109] Ibid., 49.
[110] Ibid., 37f.
[111] Ibid., 55–6. On the concept-constituting aspect, see Henry G. Schermers and Niels M. Blokker, *International Institutional Law: Unity within Diversity* (5th rev. ed.) (Leiden: Martinus Nijhoff, 2011), §44.

Schmitt holds the conventional focus of international law to be too narrow for understanding the order between states, disputing Heinrich Triepel's key contribution. Triepel, perhaps the most important of Weimar's conservative public law scholars,[112] had introduced a seminal as well as categorical distinction between *Landesrecht* (domestic law) and *Völkerrecht* (international law).[113] To Schmitt, this is a mere façade. He advocates a broader field, which he first terms *jus gentium* and later *jus publicum Europaeum*. This field embraces not only *public international law* in its conventional understanding, but also common constitutional standards and a common regime of property protection, roughly something like a *transnational economic law*. Schmitt's later book on the *jus publicum Europaeum* devotes much attention to such common European constitutional standards as well as to a common economic constitution before the First World War. Accordingly, to Schmitt, the narrow field of *international law* simply misses the core point of what is necessary to fully appreciate the order between states. Similar to Schmitt's other key statements, there is a certain plausibility to this assertion, as is shown by current attempts to take a broader view on the history of international law[114] or on the concept of European law.[115]

Schmitt also challenges the conventional understanding of progress in international law, in particular with respect to the innovations introduced after the Second World War. Schmitt presents the 1914 *jus gentium* as a peak of civilisation, claiming that it had civilised war. *The Concept of the Political* mocks what contemporary international law hails as epochal progress. For Schmitt, the *jus ad bellum* stands at the core of international law.[116] Along these lines, accepting the authority of an institution such as the UN Security

---

[112] On Triepel, see Ulrich M. Gassner, *Heinrich Triepel: Leben und Werk* (Berlin: Duncker & Humblot, 1999); Armin von Bogdandy and Reinhard Mehring (eds.), *Heinrich Triepel – Parteienstaat und Staatsgerichtshof Gesammelte verfassungspolitische Schriften zur Weimarer Republik* (Baden Baden: Nomos, 2021).
[113] Heinrich Triepel, *Völkerrecht und Landesrecht* (Leipzig: C.L. Hirschfeld, 1899).
[114] Martti Koskenniemi, 'What Should International Legal History Become?', in Stefan Kadelbach, Thomas Kleinlein and David Roth-Isigkeit (eds.), *System, Order, and International Law: The Early History of International Legal Thought from Machiavelli to Hegel* (Oxford: Oxford University Press, 2017), 381–97.
[115] Armin von Bogdandy, 'Was ist Europarecht?', *JuristenZeitung* 72 (2017), 589–97; Armin von Bogdandy, 'The Idea of European Public Law Today', in Sabino Cassese, Armin von Bogdandy and Peter Huber (eds.), *The Max Planck Handbooks in European Public Law. Volume 1: The Administrative State* (Oxford: Oxford University Press, 2017), 1–29.
[116] Schmitt, *Concept of the Political*, 45; Carl Schmitt, *Ex Captivitate Salus: Erfahrungen der Zeit 1945/47* (Köln: Greven, 1950), 71; Carl Schmitt, *Der Nomos der Erde: Im Völkerrecht des Jus Publicum Europaeum* (Berlin: Duncker & Humblot, 1988), 19, 62, 112f., 115, 120, 165, 180, 189, 194f., 213, 222, 232f., 247, 255, 258, 264f., 273f., 284f.

Council threatens statehood, the prohibition of the use of force expressed in article 2(4) of the UN Charter appears fanciful to true states, and weak states have no right to exist.[117] '[U]nder specific circumstances', international institutions may offer 'a very useful meeting place', but nothing more than that.[118]

Were one to accept Schmitt's reading, this would have important implications for how to understand public international law today. Following Schmitt, much of the field's core terminology then would appear confusing, misleading, or as ideological 'baggage'. This is not limited to the concept of the international, but also applies to many other core concepts such as humanity, universalism, and the idea of progress. Schmitt considers much of this terminology as a smokescreen for US hegemony, and posits 'demasking' it as a central task of legal thought. To borrow one of Schmitt's famous assertions: 'Whoever invokes humanity wants to cheat'.[119]

Yet, to be sure, Schmitt does not provide an answer to the question of how to establish social order under these premises. At least since the Second World War, Schmitt considered the 'Westphalian' state-centred order obsolete, particularly because, given the prerequisite of being able to wage war independently, only few polities still formed true states. This is how to understand Schmitt's dark assertions in the book's 1963 edition that 'the era of statehood' has ended; it does not mean that all states have ceased to exist, or that using the term *state* has become pointless. One should only remember that some of Schmitt's master students founded the journal *Der Staat* in 1962, a project Schmitt remained close to throughout the 1960s. However, for Schmitt, the interstate order based on states' military autonomy had come to an end. At the time of the Cold War, with two blocs antagonistically facing each other, each led by a superpower, this hypothesis seemed anything but fanciful, though it problematically reduced matters even then.

5.5 SCHMITT'S *BEGRIFFSMAGIE*

Schmitt offers no theory that falsifies opposing approaches – such as a cooperation-oriented public international law in general, and reconstructions of the law of international institutions by legal scholarship in view of international public authority, a transnational common good and an inclusive shaping of politics in particular – nor tells us why such approaches are unfounded. Schmitt's argumentation, however, does not deprive his books of their relevance. On the contrary, the indisputable success alone confirms

---

[117] Schmitt, *Concept of the Political*, 49–53.
[118] Ibid., 56.
[119] Schmitt, *Der Begriff des Politischen*, 1932, 42.

the general pattern that works built on weak premises can be successful and can even advance scholarship.[120]

One of Schmitt's major achievements is that he brilliantly coins concepts which potently rearticulate the ancient world-view of particularism. Ernst Jünger considered these coinages as Schmitt's actual genius – to borrow Jünger's vivid metaphor, Schmitt's concepts are like a 'mine that explodes silently'.[121] This achievement is easier to understand when one thinks about what constitutes a *Begriff*. As Schmitt states, minting concepts requires more than just describing the discursive usage of a word; a concept needs to be filled with genuine insight.[122] That is why Schmitt denies the conventional definition of the state as 'the political status of an organized people in an enclosed territorial unit' any conceptual character.[123] In Schwab's translation, *The Concept of the Political* holds that a concept 'can speak clearly for itself'.[124] The German original makes an epistemologically stronger claim: a concept is 'ohne weiteres einleuchtend', that is, self-evident.[125] However, the friend–enemy distinction is by no means self-evident, as is shown by the existence of many different concepts of the political.[126]

More recent research, for instance the works of the historian Reinhart Koselleck, fares better at explaining what Schmitt actually achieved by coining his concepts. Words express a concept when they identify or distinguish something, combining various phenomena, experiences, theories, or data so as to provide insights that transcend the mere designation of situations or issues.[127] Assessed against this standard, Schmitt indeed coins strong concepts.

---

[120] The naïve Hegelianism expressed in the foundational works of German administrative law can be seen in Otto Mayer, *Deutsches Verwaltungsrecht* (Berlin: Duncker & Humblot, 1895). For more detail, see Reimund Schmidt-De Caluwe, *Der Verwaltungsakt in der Lehre Otto Mayers: Staatstheoretische Grundlagen, dogmatische Ausgestaltung und deren verfassungsbedingte Vergänglichkeit* (Tübingen: Mohr Siebeck, 1999), 206f.

[121] Ernst Jünger, 'eine Mine, die lautlos explodiert', as quoted in Reinhard Mehring, *Carl Schmitt. Aufstieg und Fall: Eine Biographie* (München: C.H. Beck, 2009), 424.

[122] Much of this is lost in Georg Schwab's otherwise fine translation. Schmitt, *Concept of the Political*, 19.

[123] Ibid.

[124] Ibid., 26.

[125] Schmitt, *Der Begriff des Politischen*, 1932, 26.

[126] For a critique, Hans Morgenthau, *La notion du "politique" et la théorie des différends internationaux* (Paris: F. Boisseau, 1933), 48–58.

[127] Reinhart Koselleck, 'Einleitung', in Otto Brunner, Werner Conze, and Reinhart Koselleck (eds.), *Geschichtliche Grundbegriffe: Historisches Lexikon zur politisch-sozialen Sprache in Deutschland* (Stuttgart: Klett-Cotta, 1972), xiii–xxiii; Reinhart Koselleck, *Vergangene Zukunft: zur Semantik geschichtlicher Zeiten* (Frankfurt am Main: Suhrkamp, 1995), 119. This understanding has a Schmittian background itself: see David Egner, 'Begriffsgeschichte und Begriffssoziologie', in Andreas Busen and Alexander Weiß (eds.), *Ansätze und Methoden zur Erforschung politischen Denkens* (Baden-Baden: Nomos, 2013), 81–102, at 81f.

Schmitt's texts succeed in coalescing experiences, modalities of understandings, and theories in a succinct formula (the friend–enemy distinction) that renews the relevance of a certain realist tradition in European political thought in an era epitomised by incipient mass democracy and international interdependence.

In this way, Schmitt renews, reformulates, and focuses *raison d'état* assumptions from two thousand years of political thought for his era: the primacy of foreign policy, the precariousness of a law-based international order, the omnipresence of life-threatening forces, the need for leadership and a high degree of social integration as preconditions of domestic order, but also the appeal of heroism, of the readiness to sacrifice, of heartfelt community, centred in a political leader, and not least the unease vis-à-vis a commodified and technologised society craving for continuous progress.

Furthermore, Schmitt provides a highly illuminating reconstruction of the history of international law, a history of rise and decline rather than of linear progress. Very few have succeeded in crafting a similarly gripping history of international law. Milestones such as Wilhelm Grewe's *The Epochs of International Law* or Martti Koskenniemi's *Gentle Civilizer of Nations* are hard to imagine without Schmitt's writings.[128]

5.6 CONCLUSION

In the summer of 1981, in Plettenberg, the journalist Eberhard Straub enquired of a 93-year-old Schmitt what role the vocation as a jurist had played in his life. Schmitt pondered over the question at length; then raised his voice slowly to respond with the words of Hugo Ball, the founder of the Dada movement. 'Carl Schmitt is a man', Ball had once uttered at a soirée in Berlin, 'who is entirely immersed in the of his vocation's conceptual tools; and this is the only way in which he can make sense of his era.' 'For me', Schmitt added, 'there was only one vocation and that was the law.'[129]

---

[128] Wilhelm G. Grewe, *The Epochs of International Law*, trans. Michael Byers (Berlin: Gruyter, 2000); Martti Koskenniemi, *The Gentle Civilizer of Nations: The Rise and Fall of International Law, 1870–1960* (Cambridge: Cambridge University Press, 2001).

[129] The original quote: 'Carl Schmitt ist ein Mann, der in der Gewissensform seiner Begabung seine Zeit erlebt.' In the next sentence Schmitt makes clear that he understands *Begabung* as his juristic vocation and that for him *Gewissensform* (a word difficult to render into English) equates to the juristic vocation's conceptual tools through which one can make sense of empirical reality. To our knowledge the interview remains unpublished, but the original audio clip can be streamed from the webpage of the Carl Schmitt Gesellschaft e.V.

Retrospective statements such as this one, condensing the entirety of a life into a single sentence, are prone to conceal as much as they reveal. But this chapter has shown that Schmitt's self-understanding seems less contorted. There is an astounding continuity in the ways in which Schmitt tackled the major theoretical questions of his scholarly life. The interpretation that Schmitt cloaked himself in the garb of a legal academic to repel prosecution attempts after the Second World War may well have its merits. However, Schmitt may also have simply continued to act according to his deep-rooted desire to firmly anchor politics within *Allgemeine Staatslehre*.

Schmitt remains an influential source of inspiration for the necessary critique or 'deconstruction' of contemporary international law. With powerful eloquence, Schmitt proclaims that 'the most horrible war is fought but in the name of peace, the most horrible oppression is enforced but in the name of freedom and the most horrible inhumanity is committed but in the name of humanity'.[130] This is an important sting, not only for liberal constitutional thought.

---

[130] Schmitt, *Der Begriff des Politischen*, 1932, 94.

6

Carl Schmitt on the Theory and Practice of Occupation and Dictatorship

JOSHUA SMELTZER AND DUNCAN KELLY

6.1 INTRODUCTION

'It is painful to speak of the Rhineland as an object of international politics.' So began one of Carl Schmitt's earliest published forays in the field of *Völkerrecht*, 'The Rhineland as an Object of International Politics'.[1] Originally a speech delivered on April 14, 1925 to commemorate the thousandth anniversary of the Rhineland, Schmitt's admission of pain echoes the sentiments of humiliation and contempt experienced by German lawyers across the ideological spectrum during the post-war period of occupation.

This chapter situates Schmitt's writing on the Rhineland within the political and discursive context of contemporary debates about mixed occupation and the relationship between forms of occupation and state sovereignty in order to draw out the originality and polemical cast of Schmitt's own contribution. Schmitt dramatically rejected the idea of a 'mixed' or 'hermaphroditic' structure within which the French occupation of the Rhineland could be rendered legally compatible with the idea that Germany as a nation-state retained its political sovereignty. His focus on what he would elsewhere defend as a resolutely historicist form of 'concrete order thinking' about both politics and law grounded this critique of the idea of mixed sovereignty. It did so by tying it to his wider sense that Germany had become merely an 'object' of international politics, which in turn signaled something about the decline of a traditional and shared European space of public international law within which the laws of war had been established. That shared tradition of global partitioning, which justified colonialism in the name of civilization, had now boomeranged onto a defeated Germany in a strategic move by the victorious

---

[1] Carl Schmitt, 'Die Rheinlande als Objekt internationaler Politik', in *Positionen und Begriffe* (4th ed.) (Berlin: Duncker & Humblot, 2014), 30–8.

Allied powers. Or so he claimed. Using Schmitt's post-war history of the law of nations, *Der Nomos der Erde*, as a historical pivot, we show how Schmitt came to link his understanding of occupation and his rejection of the legal fiction of divided, mixed or suspended sovereignty, to his similar concerns with states of siege, dictatorship and exception from his earliest writings. Relocating Schmitt's writings on the law of nations within the domestic and international crises provoked by the occupation of the Rhineland thus offers a determinate historical perspective from which to see the original contours of his later and better-known approaches to the study of law and politics.

6.2 THE OCCUPATION OF THE RUHR

When Schmitt arrived at the University of Bonn in 1923, having received his first permanent position after a brief exile in 'limbo' at Greifswald, he returned to the Rhineland in the very moment of acute political crisis that shaped his writings on the law of nations for the decade to come.[2] This crisis had its roots in the allied occupation of the Rhineland, which began as a result of the Armistice of November 11, 1918. The Armistice stipulated the complete evacuation of German military forces from the left bank of the Rhine.[3] German administrative districts falling on the western side of the river were declared to 'be administered by the local authorities under the control of the allied and United States armies of occupation'.[4] At the same time, the Armistice called for the establishment of a 'neutral zone' on the eastern side of the Rhine that created a fifty-kilometer buffer. The extent of this initial occupation – excluding the extension into the Ruhr in 1923 – encompassed roughly 12,000 square miles and seven million inhabitants, close to 11 percent of Germany's population at the time.[5] Thus, the occupation following the Armistice was initially a military occupation of German territory born out of the context of the possibility of a continued war.

The Treaty of Versailles put a formal end to the war, but it continued the allied occupation of the Rhineland. Indeed, the economic blockade continued for several months following the Treaty, and has prompted a vigorous debate ever since about the relationship between military tactics and political

---

[2] Reinhard Mehring, *Carl Schmitt. Aufstieg und Fall* (Munich: C.H. Beck, 2009), 130, 140.
[3] 'Terms of Armistice with Germany, November 11, 1918', in *United States Treaties and International Agreements* 2 [1918–1930] (1969), 9–19, art. V; www.loc.gov/law/help/us-treaties/bevans/m-ust000002-0009.pdf.
[4] Ibid.
[5] Ernst Fraenkel, *Military Occupation and the Rule of Law* (London: Oxford University Press, 1944), 6.

ethics.[6] But more pointedly still, Germany was to remain sovereign over the territory only in exchange for US and British assurances of defense against possible German aggression.[7] Furthermore, the territory of the Rhineland was to remain occupied for up to fifteen years as a quasi-buffer-zone, with the gradual removal of occupying forces at five-year intervals.[8] The costs of the occupation were to be paid by the German government, though these costs were not credited against the reparations debt.[9] In addition, the occupation was envisioned as a form of bargaining for the fulfillment of Germany's end of the Versailles treaty obligations, and article 430 made clear that the Allied powers retained a punitive power over Germany:

> In case either during the occupation or after the expiration of the fifteen years referred to above the Reparation Commission finds that Germany refuses to observe the whole or part of her obligations under the present Treaty with regard to reparation, *the whole or part of the areas specified in Article 429 will be re-occupied immediately by the Allied and Associated forces*.[10]

The fate of the Rhineland thus became intimately linked to the international legal order established by the Treaty of Versailles. A domestic feeling of dishonor amid defeat was thereby amplified by the perceived manipulations of international law into the justification of *Realpolitik* by the Allies.

John Maynard Keynes had signaled his awareness of the instability of the settlement, and even if his financial accounting has been challenged, his assessment of the political implications of an enforced peace remains prescient.[11] More broadly, however, lawyers and politicians amplified the colonial

---

[6] On the nature of the blockade, its 'rationality' in terms of a logic of attritional warfare and the evolving response of the Allies to German submarine warfare, see the classic discussion by Avner Offer, *The First World War: An Agrarian Interpretation* (Oxford: Oxford University Press, 1991), esp. pts. III–IV. Cf. David Stevenson, *Cataclysm: The First World War as Political Tragedy* (New York: Basic Books, 2004), ch. 10; L.E. Davis and S.L. Engerman, 'International Law and Naval Blockades during WW1', in *Naval Blockades in Peace and War: An Economic History since 1750* (Cambridge: Cambridge University Press, 2006), 159–237, at 160ff; Mary Elisabeth Cox, 'Hunger Games: Or How the Allied Blockade in the First World War Deprived German Children of Nutrition, and Allied Food Aid Subsequently Saved Them', *Economic History Review* 68 (2015), 600–31.

[7] Conan Fischer, *The Ruhr Crisis 1923–1924* (Oxford: Oxford University Press, 2003), 11.

[8] 'Treaty of Peace with Germany', in *United States Treaties and International Agreements* 2 [1918–1930] (1969), 43–240, art. 429; https://www.loc.gov/law/help/us-treaties/bevans/m-ust000002-0043.pdf.

[9] Gordon A. Craig, *Germany, 1866–1945* (Oxford: Clarendon Press, 1978), 437.

[10] 'Treaty of Peace with Germany', art. 430 (emphasis added).

[11] John Maynard Keynes, *The Economic Consequences of the Peace* (London: Macmillan & Co., 1919); Marc Trachtenberg, *Reparations in World Politics: France and European Economic Diplomacy, 1916–1923* (New York: Columbia University Press, 1980).

and highly gendered dimensions of this occupation for their own ends. Propagandists like E.D. Morel stoked fears of a 'black horror' on the Rhine in the form of French colonial troops occupying the territory, allegedly raping and pillaging as they went, thus allowing the 'shame' of peace by *Diktat* to mirror the manufactured 'shame' of a European power subdued by soldiers who, at least in the eyes of international law and its norms, had typically been seen as 'barbarians' and should not have been fighting in a 'white' and 'European' war in the first place.[12]

Within the broader context of this perceived national dishonor in the wake of Versailles, the Rhineland occupation also became an integral part of German efforts to undercut the legitimacy of the '*Diktatfrieden*'. Turning the principles laid out in the opening articles of the Treaty against the actual implementation of the treaty in the Rhineland, for example, was a popular strategy. Where Wilson had championed the right to self-determination, the High Commission proclaimed a right to 'veto the appointment of any German official designated to serve in the occupied territories if in the opinion of the High Commission such action is necessary for the maintenance, safety, and requirements of the Allied and Associated forces'.[13] This direct reference to article 3 of the *Rheinlandabkommen* was upheld in order to claim that the Allied forces were violating a sacred principle of German legal thought, the *Rechtsstaat*.[14] Indeed, such interplay between domestic political and rhetorical positioning alongside wider international legal argument structured much of German strategy during the 1920s. As Susan Pedersen has shown, by the time Gustav Stresemann was able to negotiate entry into the League of Nations, German capacity to align its contemporary domestic politics with the broader anti-colonial nationalism that had emerged in response to the imperialist internationalism of the post-war settlement rendered Germany a clever player of the 'mandates game'.[15]

For Schmitt, however, all of this paled in comparison to the events of the crisis that began on January 11, 1923, when columns of French and Belgian soldiers marched into the *Ruhrgebiet* to ensure that Germany would fulfill its

---

[12] There is a vast literature on this topic. Most recently in the context of the history of international law and its blindness or amnesia about the racial dynamics of this particular episode, see Rotem Giladi, 'The Phoenix of Colonial War: Race, the Laws of War, and the "Horror on the Rhine"', *Leiden Journal of International Law* 30 (2017), 1–29, esp. 8ff., 13f., 17f., 20, 24ff. (on Schmitt particularly).
[13] Fraenkel, *Military Occupation*, 122.
[14] Ibid., 129.
[15] Susan Pedersen, *The Guardians: The League of Nations and the Crisis of Empire* (Oxford: Oxford University Press, 2015).

reparation obligations. In turn, the German government called for passive resistance against the occupation, the only form of resistance left to a demilitarized country, which included efforts 'to impede the transport of merchandise and raw materials'.[16] However, strikes by workers triggered an economic crisis in the region, as the national government no longer received tax revenue from the region in the same moment that it issued replacement wages for striking workers. As a result, the occupation created a crisis in the assertion of state territorial sovereignty, as well as instigated a more diffuse economic pressure that made passive resistance ultimately ineffective.[17]

Consequently, on September 26, 1923, Stresemann called for an end to the program of passive resistance, driven by the realization that it was draining state coffers and crippling the economy of the Ruhr.[18] However, economic crisis had laid the conditions for a separatist movement in the Rhineland, which briefly succeeded in October 1923 in proclaiming a *Rhenische Republik* and plunging the region into further chaos. Although the movement eventually collapsed, its legal recognition by Paul Tirard, the high commissioner of the Inter-Allied High Commission, only fueled suspicions of a wider international attempt to separate the Rhineland from the German Reich. Amid this confusion and political upheaval, leading German lawyers moved to reappropriate the language of occupation to try and reconcile the facts on the ground with the artifice of legalistic conceptual construction, in order to defend the idea that Germany, while nevertheless occupied, retained the formal marks of sovereignty.

6.3 THEORIES OF MIXED OCCUPATION

The primary figures elucidating a theory of mixed occupation were Carl Heyland and Karl Strupp. Strupp was a full professor at University of Frankfurt, editor of the *Zeitschrift für Völkerrecht*, as well as the prestigious *Wörterbuch des Völkerrechts*. Heyland, a younger contemporary working at the University of Gießen, became a central authority on the law of occupation, particularly the occupation of the Rhineland, after the publication of his *Die Rechtsstellung der besetzten Rheinlande* in 1923, in the Stier-Somlo *Handbuch des Völkerrechts*. Their articles constitute the most authoritative contributions

---

[16] Hans Mommsen, *The Rise and Fall of Weimar Democracy*, trans. Elborg Foster and Larry Eugene Jones (Chapel Hill: University of North Carolina Press, 1996), 129, 132.
[17] Fischer, *Ruhr Crisis*, 80.
[18] Mommsen, *Weimar Democracy*, 139.

6 Theory and Practice of Occupation and Dictatorship 165

to the theory of occupation as it relates to the situation in the Rhineland, and manufactured the dominant response of German international lawyers to the occupation. Both advocated a theory of *Mischbesetzung*, or mixed occupation, to describe the unique status of the Rhineland occupation. But it was Strupp's conceptual contention that had the most eye-catching claim:

> the occupation of German territory ... as a result of the Armistice legally presents a hermaphroditic [*Zwittergebilde*] structure. On the one hand, it is important to note that the Armistice is an end to military operations and not the end of the state of war; on the other hand, the occupation exists on the basis of a contract and not on the basis of military events.[19]

This hermaphroditic structure was new and anomalous, combining a view of the post-Armistice occupation as both a continuation of the state of war *and* a contractual, legal arrangement. It was therefore neither an *occupatio bellica*, nor an *occupatio pacifica*. As a result, the authors held that, although the German state had transferred its territorial jurisdiction to the occupying powers, sovereignty was still retained by the German state, for it had merely signed a contractual agreement in regard to the administration of its territory for a set time period. This theory soon became a dominant interpretive framework, as the theory of mixed occupation was embraced by the *Reichsgericht* [Imperial Court of Justice] as its official characterization.[20]

As Heyland's post-war analyses made clear, prior to 1919, most German jurists had distinguished between two broad cases of occupation. First, there was the 'occupation of a stateless territory, i.e. the establishment of the territorial jurisdiction of the occupier in a territory previously stateless', a case which was taken to apply primarily in the context of colonial expansion.[21] Occupation of the Rhineland was not a form of colonial rule based on the

---

[19] Karl Strupp, 'Das Waffenstillstandsabkommen zwischen Deutschland und der Entente vom 11. November 1918 im Lichte des Völkerrechts', *Zeitschrift für Völkerrecht* 11 (1920), 252–81, at 265: 'Die Besetzung deutscher Gebiete ... auf Grund des Waffenstillstandsvertrages stellt juristisch ein Zwittergebilde dar. Einerseits ist daran zu denken, dass der Waffenstillstand ein Ende zwar der Kriegsunternehmungen, nicht aber des Kriegszustandes ist, andererseits liegt hier eine auf Vertrag, nicht auf die Tatsache kriegerischer Ereignisse gegründete Besetzung vor.'

[20] By the end of World War II, it was possible to characterize the Occupation of the Rhineland as an example of *occupatio pacifica*. See Max Rheinstein, 'The Legal Status of Occupied Germany', *Michigan Law Review* 47 (1948), 23–40, at 24. Similarly, see Judge Advocate General's School, *Law of Belligerent Occupation* (United States Army, 1945), 14.

[21] Carl Heyland, 'Occupatio Bellica', in *Wörterbuch des Völkerrechts Band 2*, ed. Karl Strupp (Berlin und Leipzig: Walter de Gruyter & Co., 1925), 154–70, at 155: 'Die Okkupation staatslosen Gebietes, d.h. die Begründung der Gebietshoheit des Okkupanten innerhalb eines bisher staatslosen Gebietes'.

principle of *territorium nullis*,²² so the first category was rejected out of hand. By contrast, Heyland reserved a different category for the occupation of foreign *state* territories – or more accurately, where a state was recognized by European powers – which could take three forms, namely 'a) as a military occupation, b) as a peaceful occupation' or, emerging separately after 1919, 'c) as an occupation by virtue of an armistice'.²³ Each of these subcategories had a distinct implication for the sovereignty of the occupied territory and the issuing of ordinances.

Beginning with the classical form of *occupatio bellica*, Heyland explained that the state of occupation could only be brought about as a result of a proclamation by the leader of the occupying forces, and their military force.²⁴ Here, he drew explicitly on the text of article 42 of the Hague Convention of 1907, which stated that 'a territory is considered occupied when it is actually placed under the authority of the hostile army. The occupation extends only to the territory where such authority has been established and can be exercised'.²⁵ This meant that the 'authority of the occupier in a militarily occupied territory is a purely factual process [*tatsächlicher Vorgang*]'.²⁶ Since *occupatio bellica* is based on the military exercise of power, its validity can only be measured by the extent to which the occupation itself is enforceable militarily. In other words, as another contemporary suggested, 'occupation in time of war is based on only the actual condition, and therefore requires no independent legal theory'.²⁷

Since the state of war was of a 'temporary nature', the occupation must arrive at some sort of a quasi-permanent legal foundation at its end.²⁸ Here, there were also two possibilities. Either the occupier loses the area militarily and is forced to retreat, or the occupier retreats voluntarily, both cases leading to a reversion to the previous legal order or the *status quo ante*.²⁹

---

²² Richard Tuck, *The Rights of War and Peace* (Oxford: Oxford University Press, 1999), 121, has argued that this distinction only came into existence in the late seventeenth century and turned on the source of law in the occupied territories.
²³ Heyland, 'Occupatio Bellica' (1925), 155.
²⁴ Carl Heyland, 'Occupatio Bellica im Weltkrieg', in *Wörterbuch des Völkerrechts Band 3*, ed. Karl Strupp (Berlin und Leipzig: Walter de Gruyter & Co., 1929), 474–5, at 474.
²⁵ Heyland, 'Occupatio Bellica' (1925), 155: 'Ein Gebiet gilt als besetzt, wenn es tatsächlich in der Gewalt des feindlichen Heeres steht. Die Besetzung erstreckt sich nur auf Gebiete, wo diese Gewalt hergestellt ist und ausgeübt werden kann.'
²⁶ Ibid.: 'Die Herrschaft des Okkupanten im kriegerisch besetzten Gebiet ist rein tatsächlichen Vorgang.'
²⁷ R. Erich, 'Einige völkerrechtliche Kriegs- und Friedensfragen', *Zeitschrift für Völkerrecht* (1919), 45–56, at 50.
²⁸ Ibid., 50–1.
²⁹ Heyland, 'Occupatio Bellica' (1925), 170.

6 Theory and Practice of Occupation and Dictatorship 167

Or, secondarily, Heyland pointed to the historical precedent of occupation leading to *debellatio*, or 'the complete defeat and annihilation of the independent existence of the occupied state', following which the territory would be incorporated into the victor's state.[30] Neither claim, however, explained who held sovereignty during occupation.

To do that, Heyland turned to positive law, and particularly article 43 of the Hague Convention. Article 43 emphasized that occupation begins the moment there is 'an actual transition of legal authority into the hands of the occupier', which by necessity assumes the suspension of the territorial jurisdiction [*Gebietshoheit*] of the occupied state.[31] This does not suggest that the sovereign has changed, but rather that 'the hostile [meaning the occupied] sovereign stays the ruler of the territory'. Nevertheless, 'he is for the duration of the occupation merely limited in the actual exercise of his territorial sovereignty'.[32] The temporary nature of occupation is legally reframed as a suspension of territorial jurisdiction by the sovereign power, not the permanent loss of political or legal sovereignty during such time as occupation lasts.

Heyland's argument turns on this finessing of the conceptual relationship between the sovereign of a territory and the exercise of territorial jurisdiction [*Gebietshoheit*], the former expressing the traditional legal claim to sovereignty, but the latter capturing real, concrete jurisdiction over the land in the present tense. Thus, belligerent occupation could be understood as 'the forcible suspension of the hostile sovereign from the exercise of territorial jurisdiction [*Gebietshoheit*] in the occupied territory'.[33] This means that even while the territory is under the complete physical control of the occupying military, the existing sovereign formally retains their legal claim until they have been removed through a peace treaty, or the sovereign has been vanquished in the sense of *debellatio*, or the occupation has come to its agreed-upon end. However, this remained conceptually ambiguous, though Heyland tried to ground this ambiguity in his account of what happened in Belgium during the war. Then, the sovereign had fled outside its own territory to Le Havre, but 'with the end of the occupation, the native sovereign – so long as he has not lost the territory as a result of annexation or concession through a

---

[30] Ibid., 155: 'Völliger Niederwerfung und Vernichtung der selbstständigen Existenz des okkupierten Staates dem Okkupanten angegliedert wird.'
[31] Ibid., 156: 'der tatsächliche Übergang der gesetzmäßigen Gewalt in die Hände des Besetzenden.'
[32] Ibid.: 'Der feindliche Souverän bleibt der Gebietsherr. Er ist für die Dauer der Besetzung nur an der Ausübung seiner Gebietshoheit tatsächlich verhindert.'
[33] Ibid.: 'Die gewaltsame Suspension des feindlichen Souveräns von der Ausübung der Gebietshoheit im besetzten Gebiet.'

peace agreement – obtains once more the full exercise of territorial jurisdiction in the occupied territory'.[34]

One seemingly paradoxical result of this understanding of military occupation in relation to sovereignty, according to Heyland, is that 'the territorial jurisdiction exercised by the occupant in the occupied territory is that of the occupied state, whose position the occupier effectively stepped into as a result of the occupation'.[35] Since it is the sovereign's territorial jurisdiction which has been transferred to the occupying forces, the occupier is acting through the sovereign's original claim. However, the occupier is not bound by the same limitations on the exercise of state authority as the sovereign; rather, 'he acts much more without being limited by the constitutional limitations, which were implemented for the hostile sovereign', and is instead only bound by the 'interest of his own warfare as well as the protection of the population in that territory'.[36] This had formed part of the German legal defense against the suggestion that its earlier occupation of Belgium had been illegal. In response, Germany had stressed the 'consensual' aspects of its occupation.[37] This was in part because it had been undertaken according to principles outlined in article 43 of the Hague Regulations, and in part because Germany had been crucial to the drafting of those regulations. Occupation was therefore presented as being in line with the norms underpinning the laws of occupation, particularly as they pertained to economic superintendence, taxation, security and welfare.[38] Now, though, under occupation by Allied troops pending reparation payments, the same German lawyers were forced to revert to a narrower and more technical discussion of the laws of occupation in order to try to retain national sovereignty amid military occupation. Simultaneously, lawyers for the victors shifted their language from a previously narrow defense of occupation in order to attack German infractions upon the laws of war, so

---

[34] Ibid., 170: 'Mit dem Ende der Besetzung erlang der einheimische Souverän, sofern ihm das besetzte Gebiet nicht infolge von Annexion oder Abtretung im Friedensvertrag verloren geht, wieder die volle Ausübung der Gebietshoheit im besetzten Gebiet.'

[35] Ibid., 157: 'Die Gebietshoheit, die der Okkupant im besetzten Gebiet ausübt, ist die des okkupierten Staates, an dessen Stelle der Okkupant infolge der Besetzung tatsächlich getreten ist.'

[36] Ibid.: 'Er handelt vielmehr ungebunden an die verfassungsmäßigen Schranken, die dem feindlichen Souverän gesetzt waren, allein ... im Interesse seiner eigenen Kriegsführung, sowie zum Schutze der im besetzten Gebiet befindlichen Bevölkerung.'

[37] Eyal Benvenisti, *The International Law of Occupation* (Princeton: Princeton University Press, 1993), ch. 12.

[38] On this, see Benvenisti, *Law of Occupation*, esp. 7ff., 33f., 46; Isabel V. Hull, *A Scrap of Paper* (Ithaca: Cornell University Press, 2015), 41, 44ff., 51ff., 317.

that they could now themselves justify a more expansive rendering of what was valid in the Rhineland.[39]

Heyland briefly mentioned two opposing arguments raised by contemporary jurists as to the relation between occupation and *Gebietshoheit*. On the one hand, but without giving a source for the view, Heyland described a position according to which the authority exercised by the occupier is not derived from any state, but rather from the norms of international law itself. He rejected the strong version of this view, because the assumption of 'a highest authority in international law ... means a contradiction in itself, because international law only has relations between nations as its subject'.[40] Nevertheless, for Heyland, international law is the only limitation on the exercise of the territorial jurisdiction of the occupying state. For while the Hague Convention (1907) established that occupation was not an unlawful action [*Deliktshandlung*], it could be 'only through the norm of the international laws of war' that any 'limit' to 'the exercise of territory sovereignty inside the territory of a hostile state' might occur.[41] As a result, the conditions for the exercise of state authority in occupied territories is for Heyland contained entirely in the following proposition: '*Actions of the occupier inside the occupied territory are lawful insofar as no demonstrable provision of the law of war stands in opposition.*'[42] Thus, if one wanted to oppose particular ordinances or actions undertaken by the occupying force, the only legal recourse would have to be found in existing international law.

On the other hand, Heyland also rejected another common position in contemporary law, that the 'occupier exercises its own territorial sovereignty in occupied areas', which is interpreted as *extending* onto the occupied territory.[43] Here, Heyland replied by arguing that the language of article 43 explicitly stipulated a 'transfer' [*Übergang*] of *Staatsgewalt*, not an extension [*Ausdehnung*] of it. This meant that it could not be the case that state power was derived from the occupier. Simply put, to 'transfer' something implies that it is 'given' and not extended from one source to another.

---

[39] Benvenisti, *Law of Occupation*, esp. 49–52.
[40] Heyland, 'Occupatio Bellica' (1925), 157: 'Eine völkerrechtliche höchste Gewalt gibt es nicht. Sie bedeutet einen Widerspruch in sich selbst. Denn das Völkerrecht betrifft nur zwischenstaatliche Verhältnisse.'
[41] Ibid., 155: 'durch Kriegsgewalt begründete und nur durch Normen des Kriegsvölkerrechts begrenzte Ausübung von Gebietshoheit innerhalb des Gebietes eines feindlichen Staates.'
[42] Ibid., 157: '*Maßnahmen des Okkupanten im besetzten Gebiet sind insoweit rechtmäßig, als nicht ein nachweisbarer Satz des Kriegsvölkerrechtes einschraenkend entgegensteht.*'
[43] Ibid.

At the same time, an antithetical version of occupation originating in times of peace (*occupatio pacifica*) could be found in the law of nations. This version necessitated the explicit *contractual consent* of the occupied state and could not originate in force. Rather, being based on contract the terms and conditions of occupation are explicitly stipulated in the text of the agreement. This pointed in theory to the existence of a higher (sovereign) power that could determine in advance the jurisdiction of any occupying forces. However, this concept remained drastically under-theorized in German-language texts of the period. The *Handbuch* contains two pages of discussion on peaceful occupation, while giving over twenty pages to the theory of belligerent occupation. That suggests its use more as an analytical concept than a developed theory in German international law.

An occupation following an armistice, however, implied something different from either a purely belligerent or a purely peaceful occupation, and this required a theory of '*Mischbesetzung*', or mixed occupation.[44] Heyland had imported his understanding of occupation following armistice directly from Strupp's earlier article on the *Zwittergebilde*. For example, he wrote that 'cases of occupation of foreign territory are to be subsumed under the concept of an occupation following an armistice, in which a state occupies a territory of another, hostile state, which the occupying state had not already occupied militarily'.[45] In other words, although following a period of war, the occupied territories were not themselves captured during the conflict. Furthermore, this sort of occupation usually starts during a time of war, but when the actual operations of war had ceased.[46] As a result, the occupation cannot be seen to be an extension of *occupatio bellica*, but rather must be based on a different principle. This principle, and here Heyland refers directly to Strupp, is grounded upon the prevention of future conflict. It underpins an 'occupation oriented towards security of an eminently peaceful nature'.[47]

Heyland claimed that occupation beginning from an armistice was necessarily closer to the pacific type, as it 'does not take place – like belligerent occupation – against the will of the occupied state through an act of military

---

[44] Strupp, 'Das Waffenstillstandsabkommen', 265.
[45] Carl Heyland, 'Waffenstillstandsbesetzung', in *Wörterbuch des Völkerrechts Band 3*, ed. Karl Strupp (Berlin und Leipzig: Walter de Gruyter & Co., 1929), 315–22, at 315: 'Unter den Begriff der Waffenstillstandsbesetzung sind diejenigen Fälle einer Besetzung fremden Staatsgebietes zu subsumieren, in denen ein Staat auf Grund eines Waffenstillstandsvertrages Gebiet eines anderen, mit ihm im Kriege befindlichen Staates besetzt, das er nicht schon kriegerisch ... besetzt hat.'
[46] Ibid.
[47] Ibid., 316: 'Sicherungsbesetzung eminent pazifistischer Natur.'

occupation, but rather as in the cases of peaceful occupation with the consent of the occupied state, on a contractual basis'.[48] This had two further consequences. First, because the occupation requires the consent of the occupied state at the outset, the occupied state is still sovereign, as it has freely given up its sovereignty through a contract.[49] This points to the dominant legal positivism of the period, that international law is created through treaties entered into by sovereign states, which can generate stable claims through shared recognition.[50] By 1919, in contrast to 1871, however, many international lawyers had come to see international organizations and norms as functionally equivalent to the actions of domestic states, at the same time as they generalized the sphere of the international to encompass humanity itself, in order to reject traditional and domestic models of sovereignty.[51] Second, the site of justification had changed. Instead of military force as the impetus for the creation and judgment of legal norms, German lawyers focused 'in the first instance [on] the provisions of the armistice' that could serve as the basis for the 'legal situation created by an occupation following an armistice'.[52]

Distinguishing between a military occupation and an occupation based on an armistice, Heyland argued that the Hague Convention no longer directly applied to the governance of occupied territory, as it was only designed to apply in instances where the territory was initially captured as a result of 'military success'. Those norms were derived from the condition of an occupation based on power, not contract. Moreover, because such territories were not taken through military force alone, the rights given to an occupying force could not surpass those given to it during times of war. Thus, even though the Hague Convention could not be taken to apply directly to instances of mixed occupation, it formed the maximal boundary for those powers an occupier might wield.

---

[48] Ibid., 315: 'Sie erfolgt nicht – wie die kriegerische Besetzung – gegen den Willen des okkupierten Staates durch einen Akt kriegerischer Gewalt, sondern wie in den Fällen friedlicher Besetzung kraft Vertrages mit Einwilligung des okkupierten Staates, auf vertraglicher Grundlage.'

[49] Ibid., 317.

[50] Guillaume Sacriste, 'The Force of International Law', *Law and Social Inquiry* 32 (2009), 83–107; more broadly, Martti Koskenniemi, *The Gentle Civilizer of Nations: The Rise and Fall of International Law, 1870–1960* (Cambridge: Cambridge University Press, 2001).

[51] Cf. Martti Koskenniemi, 'Nationalism, Universalism, Empire: International Law in 1871 and 1919', paper delivered as part of the 'Whose International Community? Universalism and the Legacies of Empire' lecture series, Columbia University Department of History, April 2005.

[52] Heyland, 'Waffenstillstandsbesetzung', 316: 'Für die Beurteilung der durch die Waffenstillstandsbesetzung geschaffenen Rechtslage sind in erster Linie etwaige Bestimmungen des Waffenstillstandsvertrages massgebend.'

In a subsequent piece, Heyland went on to argue that the legal situation in the Rhineland could no longer be classified as an occupation based on an armistice. Following Versailles, it had become a 'peaceful occupation based on a treaty for the purpose of security'.[53] Therefore, Germany's territorial jurisdiction was 'only restricted insofar as the jurisdictional powers granted to the occupying powers as a result of the Peace Treaty, the *Rheinlandabkommen*, or norms of customary law extends'.[54] As a result, anything not explicitly mentioned in a treaty or agreement was within the power of the German state, while those areas mentioned in the treaty were only contractually extended to another sovereign power. The state limited itself, on its own terms, to this sort of temporary occupation, in a conceptual construction that is analogous to the sort of self-binding account of state sovereignty as juristically fictive but historically and practically real, previously outlined by writers like Georg Jellinek.

These constructions of mixed occupation structured the interpretations embraced by the *Reichsgericht* [Imperial Court of Justice] in their official characterization of the occupation. Although on two occasions in 1920 the court had relied on a theory of belligerent occupation in its ruling, it switched its official interpretation in 1922, declaring it 'no longer upholds the theory that the occupation of the Rhineland under the armistice agreement was a belligerent occupation, as it originally held'. Now it maintained that the essential source of the occupiers' power was in 'the wording ... of the armistice agreement'.[55] These discourses of the *Mischbesetzung* became so successful in part because they allowed Germany to retain the distinction between an Allied occupation of the Rhineland, and the earlier German occupation of Belgium.[56] But they also had critical implications for dealing with the legality of ordinances issued by the Inter-Allied High Commission to govern the territory. The Commission made extensive use of such instruments, issuing roughly eighty by the end of 1922.[57] Their content ranged from bans on publications, performances, and concerts perceived as critical of the

---

[53] Carl Heyland, 'Rheinland-Abkommen (nach dem Stande vom 1. Januar 1923)', in *Wörterbuch des Völkerrechts Band 2*, ed. Karl Strupp (Berlin und Leipzig: Walter de Gruyter & Co., 1929), 359–96, at 359: 'Vertrag beruhenden friedlichen Besetzung zu Sicherungszwecken.'
[54] Heyland, 'Rheinland-Abkommen', 360: '[ihre Gebietshoheit] ist nur insoweit eingeschränkt, als die den Besetzungsmächten auf Grund des FV.s des Rheinlandabkommens oder völkergewohnheitsrechtlicher Normen eingeräumten Hoheitsbefugnisse reichen.'
[55] Fraenkel, *Military Occupation*, 186.
[56] Ibid., 186–7.
[57] Carl Heyland, 'Zur Lehre vom Verordnungsrecht der interalliierten Rheinlandkommission', *Zeitschrift für Völkerrecht* (1922), 44–64.

Commission, including a special ban on materials debating the *Kriegsschuldfrage*,[58] to authorizing the confiscation of furniture.[59] These ordinances were used to authorize the arrest of members of the public who refused to greet the occupying forces.

However, it was the debate over the lifting of immunity for elected representatives that tested the extent of the High Commission's jurisdiction. After several instances of elected officials being imprisoned under the authority of a French military court, the *Reichskommissar* von Starck wrote on 30 May, 1921, reminding the Commission of the immunity granted to representatives by article 37 of the Weimar Constitution. The High Commission's response to the letter stated 'the [C]ommission is of the view, that no provision of the Peace Treaty nor of the *Rheinlandabkommen* provides this immunity, and that the *Rheinlandabkommen* much rather contains in Article 3 a general provision on the competency of the military courts in the occupied territory'.[60] The response articulated a view that would continue to haunt Weimar legal theory, namely that the source of law in the occupied territories was not the Weimar Constitution, but rather the Versailles Treaty. And furthermore, that it was the interpretation of these terms put forward by the Commission, and not that offered by the Weimar government, which would have practical force.

Heyland, however, immediately picked up on the text of article 3 to argue that the ordinances themselves lacked legal force, as the authority granted by the article was extremely limited.[61] Article 3 stated that 'The high commission has the authority to issue ordinances, so far as it is necessary for the assurance of the maintenance, security, and the needs of the military forces of the allied and associated powers ... these ordinances have legal force.'[62] That would seem to make ordinances on the monopoly of sherry, for example, irrelevant to

---

[58] *Die politischen Ordonnanzen der interalliierten Rheinlandkommission und ihre Anwendung in den Jahren 1920–1924* (Berlin: Heymann Verlag, 1925), 5.

[59] Heyland, 'Verordnungsrecht', 52.

[60] Ibid.: 'Sie ist der Ansicht, dass keine Bestimmung des Friedensvertrags oder des Rheinlandabkommens diese Immunität vorsieht, dass vielmehr das Rheinlandabkommen in seinem Artikel 3 Bestimmungen von ganz genereller Art über die Zuständigkeit der Militärgerichte im besetzen Gebiet enthält.'

[61] This argument was pursued by others in identical ways, though without any scholarly reference to Heyland. See J.M. Bumiller, 'Die Rechtsstellung der besetzten Rheinlande', *Zeitschrift für ausländisches öffentliches Recht und Völkerrecht* 1 (1929), 328–45.

[62] Heyland, 'Verordnungsrecht', 45–7: art. 3(a) text from *Die Verträge über Besetzung und Räumung des Rheinlandes und die Ordonnanzen der interalliierten Rheinlandoberkommission in Coblenz* (Berlin: Heymann Verlag 1925), 45: 'Der Hohe Ausschuß ist befugt, Verordnungen zu erlassen, soweit dies für die Gewährleistung des Unterhalts, der Sicherheit und der Bedürfnisse der Streitkräfte der alliierten und assoziierten Mächte nötig ist ... Diese Verordnungen haben Gesetzeskraft.'

their considerations.[63] Equally, if the basis of all the ordinances was to be purely military, then it seemed that the Commission was nothing more than an 'appendage of military administration'.[64] As one commentator noted, 'a complete military dictatorship rules in the occupied territory; the will of the hostile military commanders, who exercise unlimited power, is authoritative for everything'.[65] Thus, even while German lawyers advanced a theory of mixed occupation, the reality of the occupation seemed to point in an altogether different direction. These were precisely the sorts of contradictions and tensions which would be explicitly rejected by Schmitt, whose analyses of sovereignty, international law and occupation built on his earlier reflections on the state of siege and military dictatorship.

6.4 CARL SCHMITT ON THE THEORY AND PRACTICE OF OCCUPATION

While both Strupp and Heyland maintained a distinction between formal claims to sovereignty and actual territorial jurisdiction, Carl Schmitt denied the very possibility of this distinction. His argument is that a controlling power will freely agree to 'leave the uninteresting leftovers (of power) to the occupied people under labels such as sovereignty and freedom'.[66] However, these words have 'lost their former meaning' precisely because a right of intervention in the last instance abrogates any power of the supposedly sovereign state. Rather, 'as a result of the vagueness of these concepts, [the occupying power] has unlimited power'[67] over the occupied territory.

Indeed, it was precisely within the context of the crises of 1923 that Schmitt, now the director of an 'Institute for International Law and Politics' at the University of Bonn,[68] first wrote to his publisher with the idea of writing a textbook on the law of nations as he began to think about the status of the Rhineland.[69] Although that project never came to fruition, his shorter texts on the law of nations show an underappreciated engagement that has

---

[63] Heyland, 'Verordnungsrecht', 45.
[64] H.C., 'Die Besatzungsheere in Deutschland. Ihr Menschenbedarf und ihre Kosten', *Weltwirtschaftliches Archiv* 18 (1922), 75–93, at 79: 'Anhängsel der Militärverwaltung.'
[65] H.C., 'Besatzungsheere in Deutschland', 76: 'In dem besetzten Gebiet herrscht vollkommene Militärdiktatur; massgebend für alles ist der Wille der feindlichen Truppenbefehlshaber, welche eine schrankenlose Gewalt ausüben.'
[66] Schmitt, 'Rheinlande', 31: 'den ihn nicht interessierenden Rest überläßt er gerne dem beherrschten Volk unter Namen wie Souveränität und Freiheit'.
[67] Ibid.: 'Und infolge ihrer Unbesimmtheit hat er eine grenzlose Macht.'
[68] Mehring, *Carl Schmitt*, 141.
[69] Ibid.

implications for how we should think about Schmitt's relationship to the theory and practice of international law, and what he saw as its anti-political claims to justification at the bar of humanity.[70]

Schmitt located the origin of what he took to be a novel form of occupation in prior colonial forms of occupation, newly applied to forms of governance on European soil. For it was 'in the era of imperialism [that] a different form of domination was developed, which avoided a public political subjugation'.[71] As a result, the state was allowed to continue to exist, but only in a superficial form, because although there was the appearance of 'freedom and sovereignty', the population itself was degraded [*Herabwürdigung*] and stripped of those very attributes that were proclaimed. Importantly, Schmitt claimed that the notion of a protectorate had also been supplanted by more sophisticated methods of control. Although under a protectorate the subjected state would be proclaimed to be free and sovereign, the imperial power retained a right of guardianship [*Vormundschaft*] that enabled it to represent the protectorate at the international level. As was the case of English rule over Egypt and the mandates system of the League, just as much as US authority over Cuba, Haiti, San Domingo, and Panama, a legal right of intervention allowed the imperial state to assert its sovereignty in moments of exception without relying on a legally recognized protectorate. In Schmitt's summary, 'with all these rights of intervention, it is always to be observed that as a result of the vagueness of such concepts [such as protection against foreign interests, protection of independence, public order and security], the ruling power decides according to its own discretion, and thereby holds the political existence of the controlled state in its hand'.[72] Thus, the sovereignty left to subjected states was only the appearance of control, which could be arbitrarily annulled by the controlling power. For Schmitt, this condition signaled a transformation in the hitherto extant *jus publicum Europaeum*.

Previously, the law of nations had made a distinction between Christian (civilized) and non-Christian (un-civilized) nations, and it was still possible to speak of 'Christian international law and the law of Christian nations'.[73] The

---

[70] William Rasch, 'Anger Management: Carl Schmitt in 1925 and the Occupation of the Rhineland', *The New Centennial Review* 8 (2008), 57–79, esp. 58ff., 64ff., 67f., 70f.

[71] Schmitt, 'Rheinlande', 28: 'Im Zeitalter des Imperialismus haben sich andere Formen der Beherrschung herausgebildet, die gerade eine offene politische Unterwerfung vermeiden.'

[72] Ibid., 29: 'Bei allen diesen Interventionsrechten ist immer zu beachten, dass infolge der Unbestimmtheit solcher Begriffe die herrschende Macht nach ihrem Ermessen entscheidet und dadurch die politische Existenz des kontrollierten Staates in der Hand behält.'

[73] Ibid., 32: 'vom christlichen Völkerrecht und vom Recht der christlichen Nationen'. This argument is developed in Schmitt's post-war history of the Law of Nations as constituting the

slippage in terms of how colonial power-politics trumped the political sovereignty of those who were colonized through mere force, and which was now applied to a European nation-state, was what motivated Schmitt's ferocious attacks on international law as a sop for cynical *Realpolitik*.[74] However, Schmitt further claimed that Versailles had changed this relationship through the vagueness of the terms of the treaty, which permitted a permanent intervention into the political existence of the Rhineland, and of Germany as a whole. The distinction between colonial rule and rule over European territories had therefore become ambiguous, and the treaty left open only four possibilities for the future of the Rhineland. First, to transform it into a separate and legally distinct state from the rest of Germany; second, to use an international commission to de facto eliminate German sovereignty over the area; third, to turn the Rhineland into a quasi-extension of the Saarland; or, fourth, to transform it into an *État-tampon* against German aggression. In each of these cases, Schmitt saw the Rhineland becoming a mere object of international politics, the equivalent of Cuba under United States control.

Furthermore, each of these plans displayed anew the methods by which a territory could be made into merely technical object. For example, while the battle over Schmitt's beloved *Elsaß-Lothringen* was fought over the possibility of annexing the territory, annexation had disappeared from the options open for the future of the Rhineland. Schmitt attributed this shift to Wilson's right of self-determination [*Selbstbestimmungsrecht*] of a nation, which he took to mean that 'every nation as subject can decide its own political and state existence'.[75] However, the treaty that Wilson helped to design had instead created the conditions under which the Rhineland was unable to decide its own fate. Further, French reluctance to annex the Rhineland was not a sign of their kind-heartedness; rather, their hesitancy showed that there were more advantages to not annexing the territory directly, but following one of those four alternative paths.[76] In line with the general security policy of the French

---

fundamental dividing line of the *Respublica Christiana*. See Carl Schmitt, *Der Nomos der Erde im Völkerrecht des Jus Publicum Europaeum* (5th ed.) (Berlin: Duncker & Humblot, 2011), 25–35, 69–75; cf. Joshua Smeltzer, 'On the Use and Abuse of Francisco de Vitoria: James Brown Scott and Carl Schmitt', *Journal of the History of International Law* 20 (2018), 345–72.

[74] Benno Gerhard Teschke, 'Fatal Attraction: A Critique of Carl Schmitt's International Political and Legal Theory', *International Theory* 3 (2011), 179–227.

[75] Schmitt, 'Rheinlande', 27: 'Selbstbestimmung heißt doch wohl, dass ein Volk als Subjekt seine eigene politische und staatliche Existenz bestimmt.'

[76] There was some effort at the time to distinguish between what could be called the 'French Public Opinion' versus the government position. See Charles Seignobos, 'Die öffentliche Meinung Frankreichs und der Vertrag von Versailles', *Zeitschrift für Politik* 12 (1923), 80–94, at 86.

state during the war, this tied back to the Franco-German antagonism that had structured Clemenceau's willingness to see reparations as delayed recompense for the Franco-Prussian war half a century before.[77] In fact, that longer-run backdrop also formed the intellectual-historical context out of which Schmitt's thinking developed. For instance, Edgar Löning, the one-time editor of Johann Kaspar Bluntschli's *Staatslehre*, and populariser of Francis Lieber's thinking on occupation and the laws of war, published contemporary accounts of governmental administration in Alsace during the 1870–1 war, which Schmitt would use in his discussions of siege and military occupation.[78] French writers in the wake of 1871, for their own part, routinely looked back to 1848–9 to counter contemporary discussions of occupation and its legitimacy on the part of Germany, moving towards the idea of a 'real' versus a 'fictive' state of siege.[79] That sort of division between a real military state of siege, and a fictive political one, would underscore French writing about occupation in the immediate aftermath of the Great War too, providing ideas Schmitt would also embellish.[80]

For Schmitt, the next step was to understand what interest the 'ruling powers' had in not annexing a territory. This, he claimed, was entirely transparent. It was about avoiding the need to grant citizenship to the populations of occupied territories.[81] In turn, this underscored a dramatic shift in the understanding of population for *raison d'état*. During the period of *Kabinettspolitik*, population growth was still seen as functionally necessary for the extension of political power. However, in this new understanding, it was possible to benefit economically from exploiting a population while also refusing it citizenship, and thereby minimizing the distribution of economic benefits. In short, this was another update of colonial power. Furthermore,

---

[77] On French 'security' policy, see Peter Jackson, *Beyond the Balance of Power* (Cambridge: Cambridge University Press, 2013), 132, 136. More broadly, Christian Baechler, 'L'Alsace Lorraine dans les relations franco-allemandes de 1918 à 1933', in Jean-Marie Valentin, Jacques Bariety and Alfred Guth (eds.), *La France et l'Allemagne entre des deux guerres mondiales* (Nancy: Presses Universitaires de Nancy, 1987), 69–97.

[78] Edgar Löning, 'L'Administration du Gouvernement-Général de l'Alsace durant la Guerre de 1870–1871', *Revue du droit international et de legislation comparée* 4 (1872), 622–50; 5 (1873), 69–136; on Bluntschli and Lieber, see Duncan Kelly, 'Nationalism and Cosmopolitan Humanity in Mid-Nineteenth-Century American Political Science', in Joel Isaac, James T. Kloppenberg, Michael O'Brien, and J. Ratner-Rosenhagen (eds.), *Worlds of American Intellectual History* (New York: Oxford University Press, 2017), 115–32.

[79] Théodore Reinach, *De l'état de siège: Étude historique et juridique* (Paris: F. Pichon, 1885).

[80] Paul Romain, *L'État de siège politique (Histoire, Déclaration, Effets, Levée)* (Albi: Imprimerie des Orphelins apprentis, 1918), 24f. See too Doris Appel Graber, *The Development of the Law of Belligerent Occupation 1863–1914* (New York: Columbia University Press, 1949), 264f.

[81] Schmitt, 'Rheinlande', 30.

Schmitt argued that there were clear reasons why, under international law, it was wise for states to avoid annexation: they could avoid being bound by the demands of state succession, under which they would be required to extend citizenship to the population of the annexed territory and to fulfill treaty obligations and debts created by the predecessor.[82] By designing a system of intervention rights enshrined in treaties, states could avoid the legal obligations of annexation while simultaneously gaining de facto control over a territory, and German lawyers were quick to see that this is precisely what the mandates system of the League offered the great powers.[83]

Schmitt's contribution to the discussion of the legal occupation of the Rhineland was therefore quite different to the leading accounts of mixed occupation offered by Heyland and Strupp. Yet although he offered no citations in the text of his speech, he still pointed to the same problematique as they had done, namely that the occupation blurred the distinction between peace and war due to its mixed form, and could not police the political boundary positions adequately or effectively. Schmitt wrote that 'through such indeterminacies the border between war and peace is itself left vague, and elementary concepts, such as war and peace – without whose clear differentiation the cohabitation of peoples is absolutely impossible – lose their straightforward meaning and dissolve into a torturous indeterminate state'.[84] However, what for others appeared as a conceptually beneficial means of differentiating the current German situation from its previous occupation of Belgium, Schmitt took as an indication of a deeply unsettling shift in the meaning of occupation and its implications for the Rhineland. This renders his position in debates about international law around World War I quite unusual, cutting against both the standard presentation of his work in histories of international law, while emphasizing the rapidity of his turn toward a political critique of American-inspired international law that presented itself as literally abolishing war as a legitimate political option for states.[85]

Equally, if Schmitt was keen to develop the idea that the colonial forms of international law that had structured the *jus publicum Europeaeum* were now,

---

[82] Ibid.
[83] Heinrich Schnee, 'Die Kolonialmandate', *Zeitschrift für Politik* 12 (1923), 161–71, at 163.
[84] Schmitt, 'Rheinlande', 33: 'Durch solche Unbestimmtheiten aber wird die Grenze zwischen Krieg und Frieden selbst unbestimmt gelassen, und elementare Begriffe, wie Krieg und Frieden, ohne deren klare Unterscheidung ein Zusammenleben der Völker überhaupt unmöglich ist, verlieren ihren einfachen Sinn und lösen sich auf sie einen quälenden Zwischenzustand.'
[85] Cf. Hull, *Scrap of Paper*, 318 (on 'war positivism' in Germany); Oona Hathaway and Scott Shapiro, *The Internationalists* (London: Penguin, 2017), 116, 121, 218ff.

inappropriately, being applied to the occupation of a European state, then this would also show the claim to occupational neutrality on the part of the allies to be little more than a 'power decision', or an act of imperial politics. This would illustrate the mythology of a 'shared' set of interests and cultures among the people of Europe, and prompt the famous thought that the sphere of the political is really a gauge for measuring the level of intensity between friends and enemies, particularly in this case between Germany and France.

Once again, Schmitt was returning to some of his earliest published work on the state of siege and dictatorship. His first thoughts on those subjects, developed from a sample lecture given to colleagues at Strasbourg in the context of World War I, assessed the state of war and its effects on military command and procedure. He concluded that there was no legal 'right' to command that could be derived from the state under military occupation, such that it would legally grant the military commander his authority. Rather, such authority was simply practical and dependent upon his control and assessment of the military situation. The separation of military occupation and the 'political' or 'fictive' state of siege outlined there, would readily be redeployed in the language of a 'real' and political *jus publicum Europaeum* that was newly dethroned by the 'fictive' legality of Allied occupation and blockade.[86] In effect, Schmitt turned the language of legal artifice against those who had theorized the artifice of a mixed occupation, in order to dramatize the political content and context of a transformation in international law.

In a state of siege, traditional justifications for the separation between legislation and implementation were sidelined, with power and authority centralized in the singular body of the executive. Under a dictatorship, although the conceptual distinctions between legislation and implementation remained, their separation was in practice eliminated because *either* the legislative *or* the executive completely took over.[87] Therefore, although the political consequences may seem similar, from a legal point of view one needs to differentiate between a military state of siege and its possible use as a political tool on the one hand, and on the other to notice whether the legislative power has superseded the executive, or vice versa, to understand the realities of dictatorship. Schmitt's political theory of dictatorship, which built on his analysis of siege conditions from long-term European history as

---

[86] Carl Schmitt, *Die Militärzeit 1915–1919: Tagebuch Februar bis Dezember 1915*, ed. Ernst Hüsmert and Gerd Giesler (Berlin: Akademie Verlag, 2005), 429; Mehring, *Carl Schmitt*, 90.

[87] Carl Schmitt, 'Diktatur und Belagerungszustand', in Carl Schmitt, *Staat, Großraum, Nomos: Arbeiten aus den Jahren 1916–1969*, ed. Günter Maschke (Berlin: Duncker & Humblot, 1995), 16.

well as the immediate context of World War I, deployed the history of modern political theory to present an opposition between liberal claims about how constitutionalism could create new forms of politics (sovereign dictatorship), and liberal amnesia about the technique of (commissarial) dictatorship as conventional, if prudential, crisis management.[88]

Schmitt used the occupation of the Rhineland as an opportunity to praise the function of authority in establishing the basis of political community, even claiming that 'no human coexistence is possible without an open and clear authority'.[89] Schmitt's argument, however, was that the structure of international governing commissions – the High Commission in the case of the Rhineland – lacks precisely the open and clear character essential to authority. This is because the structure of the commission functions to conceal the 'foreign' and 'invisible' powers ruling through the 'governmental apparatus'.[90] Indeed, with reference to the public nature of state authority Schmitt argued that the modern condition is fundamentally distinct from that of the early-modern period. While theologians and jurists of those earlier periods discussed the limits of obedience and the right of revolution, 'they all presuppose that the authority [Obrigkeit] will publicly position itself with the entire force of its political will'. Even the despicable tyrant, Schmitt argued, was held to be acting publicly, arguing that while 'the tyrant abuses his power ... he demands obedience and loyalty, justly or unjustly, but at least in complete candour'.[91] By contrast, 'modern methods lead to concealing the actual power and to transforming the publicity and representation of state life into an empty façade', even if they do so in the name of forms of publicity and transparency through political representation.[92]

There seem to be three distinct issues raised by this analysis in Schmitt's account. First, he maintained that modern forms of political control originate in the evolutionary dominance of the economic sphere. 'We are experiencing

---

[88] Duncan Kelly, 'Carl Schmitt's Political Theory of Dictatorship', in Jens Meierhenrich and Oliver Simons (eds.), *The Oxford Handbook of Carl Schmitt* (Oxford: Oxford University Press, 2017), 217–44.

[89] Schmitt, 'Rheinlande', 33: 'Kein menschliches Zusammenleben ist möglich, ohne eine offene und klare Autorität.'

[90] Ibid.: 'Regierungsapparat'.

[91] Ibid., 34: 'Der Tyrann mißbraucht seine Macht ... Er verlangt Gehorsam und Treue, mit Recht oder Unrecht, aber jedenfalls für sich in voller Offenheit.'

[92] Ibid.: 'Die modernen Methoden gehen aber dahin, die wirkliche Macht zu verheimlichen und Öffentlichkeit und Repräsentation des staatlichen Lebens zu einer leeren Fassade zu machen.' For a recent discussion of the vexed politics of transparency, see Stefanos Geroulanos, *Transparency in Postwar France: A Critical History of the Present* (Stanford: Stanford University Press, 2017).

today', he wrote, 'the first, extremely dangerous attempts to transfer the methods of modern industrial and financial practice onto political and state life, and to hide the real relations of power in a system of interrelated companies [Schachtelgesellschaften] and the fictitious founding of companies [Scheingründungen].'[93] More than merely an aside, Schmitt believed these forms of control originated as economic instruments. They were to be castigated the moment they encroach upon the separate sphere of the political, even though the imbrication between merchant companies that acted like states, and states that cultivated forms of representation that made them look like companies, had been a long-standing concern of historians of early-modern state formation and imperialism. For Schmitt, the very success of this mutually constitutive model in modern Europe, however, had been the eventual prioritizing of forms of depoliticized thinking. 'The contemporary leading type of economic-technical thought', he argued, 'may no longer even perceive a political idea'.[94]

Second, Schmitt claimed that the forms of control at stake in the Rhineland occupation now had a quasi-permanent character given their economic, rather than political or military, justifications. This rendered the Rhineland something new, in comparison to classical theories of belligerent and peaceful occupation, that 'could only be something transitional, a provisional measure of relatively short length'.[95] The ultimate consequence of this view is that 'the above described moral duties, as they arise against the rightful state authority, do not apply for the occupying power and, as a result, do not apply for the occupying bureaucratic authorities [Besatzungsbehörden]'.[96]

Third, Schmitt articulated a distinction between the forms of governance suitable to Europeans – referred to elsewhere in the essay as belonging to 'civilized nations' – and non-Europeans. While he thought international commissions could be used for such issues as rendering the Danube River navigable for ships, using it as a form of government violated the particular dignity of European peoples. Here, he argued that 'every European people

---

[93] Schmitt, 'Rheinlande', 34: 'Wir erleben heute die ersten, höchst gefährlichen Versuche, Methoden moderner industrieller und finanzieller Praxis auf das politische und staatliche Leben zu übertragen und in ein System von Schachtelgesellschaften und Scheingründungen die wirklichen Machtverhältnisse zu verstecken und im Unsichtbaren zu lassen.'
[94] Schmitt, Politische Theologie, 68: 'die heute herrschende Art ökonomischisch-technischen Denkens vermag eine politische Idee gar nicht mehr perzipieren.'
[95] Schmitt, 'Rheinlande,' 35: 'dass es sich bei solchen Besetzungen nur um etwas Vorübergehendes handeln kann, um ein Provisorium von verhältnismäßig kurzer Dauer'.
[96] Ibid.: 'Die oben erwähnten moralischen Pflichten, wie sie gegenüber der rechtmäßigen Staatsgewalt bestehen, gelten nicht für die Besatzungsmacht und infolgedessen auch nicht für die Besatzungsbehörden'.

with its own national consciousness is appalled at the thought of being governed and controlled by foreigners', for it violates the sense of natural community [*Gemeinschaft*] established by the state and nation.[97] Worse than being ruled by one foreign power, an international commission compounds the problem, for the territory is ruled neither by the best interests of the inhabitants, nor the interests of a single foreign power, but is conditioned by political and economic disputes between multiple powers. It is in this sense that the Rhineland had become an object, for its future was conditional on the outcome of decisions among foreign powers. By highlighting the political dimensions of economic decisions, and the ways in which the norms of international law were subject to political calculation, Schmitt offered a highly polemical counterpoint to contemporary theories of occupation and sovereignty. And one way to see quite how foundational this moment was for his later work, is to consider the way in which it all came together in another searing polemic, *The Nomos of the Earth* (1950).

6.5 OCCUPATION AND *THE NOMOS OF THE EARTH*

Schmitt's history of the law of nations focused on the ways in which, 'precisely here – in the economy', Schmitt wrote, 'the old spatial order of the earth lost its structure'. This began with the actions of a sea-faring British Empire, was entrenched in the globally integrated but avowedly 'free' economy of the early nineteenth century, and out of which globalization, regional hegemony, or the model of a closed commercial state, remained the leading options for modern politics.[98] Occupation, siege, and dictatorship threatened the viability of these options, and hence the stability of politics in modern Europe.

Indeed, when Schmitt returned to the theory of occupation in this work, he explicitly made the link between the institutions of occupation and the state of siege. He claimed there was a 'remarkable existential relation' joining 'the legal institute of militarily occupied territories in the law of nations and the state of siege or of emergency [*Belagerungs- oder Ausnahmezustand*] within a constitutional state [*konstitutionellen Verfassungsstaates*]'.[99] Both theories cut to the core of state sovereignty as refracted in its international and domestic contexts.

---

[97] Ibid.: 'Jedes europäische Volk von einigem nationalen Bewußtsein empört sich bei dem Gedanken, von Fremden regiert und beherrscht zu warden.'
[98] Carl Schmitt, *The Nomos of the Earth in the International Law of the* Jus Publicum Europaeum, trans. G.L. Ulmen (New York: Telos Press Publishing, 2006 [1950]), 237, 234f.
[99] Schmitt, *Nomos der Erde*, 182.

6 Theory and Practice of Occupation and Dictatorship 183

But in turning to the concept of occupation, Schmitt's first move was to trace the institution of occupation within the context of seventeenth- and eighteenth-century understandings of the *jus publicum Europaeum* to argue that there was in fact no separate legal institution of military occupation; all occupied territory belonged to the occupier. This conception was a direct result of the accompanying concept of 'state sovereignty, to which the effective, state organized power in a defined area belongs, extends from itself onto the area of its effective state power'.[100] Thus, the moment a territory came under the effective control of a foreign military, the territory experienced an '*immediate change in sovereignty*'.[101] In other words, a separate conception of military occupation distinct from the extension of state sovereignty could not have existed at the beginning of the *jus publicum Europaeum* because of the equivalence of sovereignty with effective territorial jurisdiction.

However, Schmitt claims that this understanding of occupation in the eighteenth century was also tied together with a particular understanding of the constitution [*Verfassung*] of the territory. In the first instance, 'occupiers of the eighteenth century allowed the present law, particularly private law, to remain in force: private property and acquired rights, hence the entire social structure, remained untouched to a large degree'.[102] Thus, the relevant conception of constitution was purely legal – 'the person of the ruler and his surroundings as well as state administration and justice' – but excluded the social and economic sense of 'the constitution' of a nation.[103] Although this conception was challenged by the Napoleonic Wars, it was restored through the Vienna Congress and, for Schmitt, embodied in the thought of Talleyrand, who promoted what Schmitt called the 'purely state character of war' in contrast to the English maritime (total) warfare.[104] However, in insisting on the purely inter-state character of war, Talleyrand established a concept of occupation once again limiting the ability of the occupying force to change the social and economic structure of the occupied territory. As a consequence of this military rendering of occupation, 'the holder of occupation powers is required to be – despite the remaining mistrust of the military – a military commander [*Militärbefehlshaber*], not a civilian commissar'.[105]

---

[100] Ibid., 173.
[101] Ibid. (emphasis in original).
[102] Ibid.
[103] Ibid., 174.
[104] Ibid., 176. See also Carl Schmitt, *Land and Sea: A World-Historical Meditation*, trans. Samuel Garrett Zeitlin (Candor: Telos, 2015).
[105] Schmitt, *Nomos der Erde*, 176.

Schmitt saw the Napoleonic Wars as a key moment in the shifting meaning of the state and its sovereignty, as 'jurists of the individual German states [*Einzelstaaten*]' posited a conceptual distinction between the 'state itself and the particular holder [*Inhaber*] of state power' as a means to insist on the continuity of the state as a legal institution.[106] Furthermore, this allowed for a distinction between the state and the legitimacy of any particular ruler's claim over it. Thus, 'in opposition to the particular, legitimate or non-legitimate, legal or illegal holder [*Inhaber*] of state sovereignty, in opposition to changing regimes, now emerges the legal subject of the state – characterized through territory, subjects, and organized domination [*Herrschaft*] – also at the domestic level with complete juridical clarity'.[107]

It was precisely this conceptual distinction, opened by the jurists of *Kurhessen*, which Schmitt claimed had allowed for the emergence of the modern understanding of *occupatio bellica*. By distinguishing between the state and the holder of state power, military occupation could emerge as the practice of changing state power while simultaneously leaving the state in place. On this reading, 'occupation was no longer a land appropriation and did not result in territorial changes, but rather resulted in a merely provisional and merely de facto possession [*Inbesitznahme*] of the land and the things found on it, as well as an equally provisional and de facto subjugation of the men, their administration and their justice to be found on the occupied territory'.[108] Thus, for Schmitt, the concept of a military occupation only came into focus through the nineteenth century as a response to the Napoleonic Wars and their consequences for the territorial division of German states.

The resulting description of the theory of occupation mirrors his earlier description of commissarial dictatorship in historical terms. In his prior studies of dictatorship, Schmitt proposed Bodin as the originator of a view of the commissarial dictatorship of the public person and Rousseau as the progenitor of an idea of sovereign dictatorship. Bodin offered Schmitt the distinction between a commissar and an official, and thus between the techniques available to the magistrate and the commissar. On his terms, a dictator under such an account would be like the 'absolutist action commissar', or a 'conceptually necessary commissar, whose activity is legally observed', strictly delimited and presupposed by the distinction between law and ordinance.[109]

---

[106] Ibid.
[107] Ibid., 177.
[108] Ibid., 178.
[109] Carl Schmitt, *Die Diktatur* (Berlin: Duncker & Humblot, 2006 [1921]), 33–35, 38f.

6 Theory and Practice of Occupation and Dictatorship

In the move toward the unified modern nation-state, Bodin's limiting framework of commissarial action for dealing with the emergency situation also helped lay the conceptual foundations for a modern distinction between sovereignty and government.[110] Having spent time elaborating the consequences in the history of political thought, however, by the time he returns to the question of military occupation, Schmitt now claims that the provisional understanding of military occupation cuts to the core of the shared *jus publicum Europaeum*, and highlights a fundamental contradiction in its own logic:

> how is it possible to construct a state authority, exercised through a state power on foreign state territory against the will of a foreign sovereign, without a change in sovereignty? ... State sovereign power is, however, above all effective power. The occupying state extends his effective power onto the territory of his opponent; the opponent no longer has effective power; nevertheless, the effective expansion of power is supposed to bring with it no change in sovereignty, no change in regime, and no change in constitution. How is that possible, both theoretically and in reality? Referencing the sovereign will of the occupier, who voluntarily refrains from changing sovereignty, would be a mere fiction and theoretically an entirely empty, practically very precarious justification.[111]

Schmitt argued that the true character of this occupation was overlooked by jurists precisely because they maintained a dualistic approach to the law of nations, one that had mistakenly limited their understanding of the prior foundational concepts of siege and dictatorship. In other words, if it is assumed that all law is either exclusively domestic or exclusively international, then it is not possible to notice that military occupation in fact operates on both levels, and therefore is a crucial issue across the terrains of both domestic and international politics. Schmitt diagnosed this as the habitual problem of positivist jurisprudence, which extreme or exceptional moments highlighted with the utmost clarity. This is precisely what links the two concepts of military occupation and the state of exception for Schmitt. He wrote that 'in both cases, a condition – which requires extraordinary measures and therefore breaks through [*durchbricht*] the constitution – should indeed be bound to the continued validity of the same constitution'.[112] Conventional theories of

---

[110] Richard Tuck, *The Sleeping Sovereign* (Cambridge: Cambridge University Press, 2017).
[111] Schmitt, *Nomos der Erde*, 179.
[112] Ibid., 182. *Verfassungsdurchbrechung* is a concept Schmitt developed in Schmitt, *Verfassungslehre* (Berlin: Duncker & Humblot, 2017 [1928]), 99, 106.

military occupation and the state of exception attempt to ignore this fundamental challenge, which is to say, they attempt to depoliticize a highly political situation by transposing it into the realm of jurisprudence.

6.6 CONCLUSIONS

As the German émigré and former student of Carl Schmitt, Ernst Fraenkel, noted in 1944, 'a future historian ... can find in the Rhineland of the early 1920s the microcosm of most of those forces which during the 1930s were to break through as eruptive powers and ultimately bring about the collapse of the Versailles system'.[113] Fraenkel's own ethnography of Nazi law, which attacked Schmitt's move to defend something akin to the prerogative state, knew the importance of seeing local context in wider conceptual perspective. His discussions of the lived experience of dictatorship and siege in practice hold up a progressive mirror to Schmitt's stylized oppositions.[114] But it is certainly true that Schmitt's own engagement with the occupation of the Rhineland contains the microcosm of his future work on the law of nations. For Schmitt, the occupation of the Rhineland was inseparable from the legal order established by the Treaty of Versailles, and it motivated his early and emphatic rejection of both. Schmitt unmasked the politics behind those concepts used to justify the economic and strategic goals of the victorious great powers. By approaching the occupation of the Rhineland in this way, he could argue that, despite all claims to the contrary, the purported sovereignty of the German Reich had been abrogated in all but name. Furthermore, Schmitt's approach here also points to a central feature of his work as it would continue to develop, namely the necessity of situating legal concepts within their own historical-intellectual horizons, or as he called it, a form of 'concrete orders thinking', grounded in the basic thought that 'an historical truth is only true once'.[115]

Given that, the idea that one might reasonably expect to find a singular 'key' to Schmitt's international legal and political thought simply at the level of his texts, particularly about the concept of the political itself, without attention to the concrete legal and political circumstances of their production is surely a category mistake. Legalistic or purely theoretical interpretations of Schmitt's

---

[113] Fraenkel, *Military Occupation*, 3.
[114] Jens Meierhenrich, *The Remnants of the Rechtsstaat: An Ethnography of Nazi Law* (Oxford: Oxford University Press, 2018).
[115] Carl Schmitt, *Dialogues on Power and Space*, trans. Samuel Garrett Zeitlin (Cambridge: Polity, 2015).

international legal writings will not get us very far in trying to learn the practical lessons that Schmitt can still teach international lawyers and historians, namely that as a jurist, he wanted to win his cases, and he curated the law and its interpretation in political contexts to the best of his ability in order to do so. But those curatorial exercises took place in determinate historical contexts, and without recourse to them, we will simply be left taking Schmitt purely at his own word. Given his claim about historical truths being true only once, that might well be a rather awkward place to be. Some contemporary left-wing Schmittian scholars – who transpose his belligerent conceptual work into a form of 'agonistic pluralism' and support the idea of a spatial, liberal politics based on *Großräume* and *Reich* – would do well to remember that.[116]

---

[116] Cf. Chantal Mouffe, *The Return of the Political* (London: Verso, 2005); Matthew Specter, 'What's Left in Schmitt: From Aversion to Appropriation in Contemporary Political Theory', in Meierhenrich and Simons (eds.), *Oxford Handbook of Carl Schmitt*, 426–54.

Empires, States and Nations

7

Law of Nations, World of Empires: The Politics of Law's Conceptual Frames

JENNIFER PITTS[*]

From the perspective of political theory, the history of international law may be seen as a significant and underexplored aspect of a broader phenomenon: the involvement of moral universalism, and especially liberalism, in forms of domination in spite of and indeed partly because of universalist moral commitments, commitments that remain compelling and perhaps unavoidable even given their complicity with domination. Law seems a version of this dilemma that demands particular attention for a number of reasons: among others, because the structure of legal argument demands treating like cases alike, and because legal arguments made in the past have not just a conceptual hold on the present but also more concretely institutionalized forms of influence than is often the case for the normative arguments treated in the history of political thought.[1] The history of legal argument warrants more attention, I think, than it has received from political theorists, but I share the doubt recently expressed by Martti Koskenniemi about whether international lawyers and historians of political thought who study the history of international law are really working as differently as some have claimed.[2]

---

[*] I am grateful to participants at the conference 'History, Politics, Law: Thinking through the International' (University of Cambridge, 16–17 May 2016), especially Annabel Brett and Martti Koskenniemi, and to Adom Getachew and Lisa Wedeen, for discussion of an earlier draft. I thank SAGE Publications and Harvard University Press, respectively, for permission to reprint some passages that first appeared in my 'International Relations and the Critical History of International Law', *International Relations* 31 (2017), 282–98; and *Boundaries of the International. Law and Empire* (Cambridge, MA: Harvard University Press, 2018).

[1] See Anne Orford, 'The past as law or history?', in Mark Toufayan, Emmanuelle Tourme-Jouannet and Hélène Ruiz Fabri (eds.), *Droit international et nouvelles approches sur le tiers-monde* (Paris: Société de législation comparée, 2013), 97–117, at 107–9.

[2] Compare Ian Hunter's critique of Anghie in 'Global Justice and Regional Metaphysics: On the Critical History of the Law of Nature and Nations', in Shaunnagh Dorsett and Ian Hunter

Koskenniemi has spoken critically of interdisciplinary conversations that entrench static self-conceptions on the part of the participating disciplines, and he speaks enthusiastically of the attitude 'let's see what's going on there, and whether we can use what they use for our purposes'.[3] Although it is tempting, then, to consider what international law can bring to history and political theory, and vice versa, perhaps the more important task, which has in fact been taken up across these disciplinary divides, is to think outside the liberal episteme. This has meant a repudiation of the once standard mode of writing the history of international law, which, in keeping with liberal self-understandings, tended to be teleological and triumphalist, and to overlook the role of power in the ascendancy of certain legal norms or institutions. The belief or desire that law could furnish some perspective outside or above politics, that it provides a merely technical, and essentially apolitical, vocabulary and set of institutions for adjudicating conflict or mitigating suffering, remains powerful among some who write histories of international law, and histories are still being written that are insufficiently attentive to international law's politics and imperial entanglements. Liberal political theory has been prey to a similar aspiration to serve as a neutral arbiter between competing systems of value or conceptions of the good, and has been likewise slow to reckon with the imperial nature of modern liberal states and the often intense involvement by liberal thinkers in the practice and justification of imperial domination.[4]

For historians of political thought, the law of nations is a vital if neglected discourse for this reckoning given its importance as a language and framework for political argument used broadly in public debates and by political thinkers, especially prior to the consolidation of international law as an academic discipline in the second half of the nineteenth century.[5] The presence of

---

(eds.), *Law and Politics in British Colonial Thought: Transpositions of Empire* (New York: Palgrave Macmillan, 2010), 11–29, and Anne Orford's defense of different approaches in history versus law: Orford, 'The past as law or history?'; but also see Martti Koskenniemi, 'Vitoria and Us: Thoughts on Critical Histories of International Law', *Rechtsgeschichte* 22 (2014), 119–35, criticizing contextual history as insufficiently critical.

[3] Alexandra Kemmerer, '"We do not need to always look to Westphalia…": A Conversation with Martti Koskenniemi and Anne Orford', *Journal of the History of International Law* 17 (2015), 1–14, at 5.

[4] For elaborations of these last two points, see Jennifer Pitts, 'The Critical History of International Law', *Political Theory* 43 (2015), 541–52; and 'Political Theory of Empire and Imperialism', *Annual Review of Political Science* 13 (2010), 211–35.

[5] Christopher Warren, *Literature and the Law of Nations 1580–1680* (Oxford: Oxford University Press, 2015), argues that the significant presence of the law of nations in early-modern literature waned in the eighteenth century as the law of nations began to take on more concrete

the *droit des gens* or law of nations in works for general audiences suggests the degree to which this was once a language of moral and political thought rather than a narrowly legal and academic doctrine.[6]

Of particular interest for political theory, I want to suggest here, are the images or figurations that legal theories create to make the world conceptually tractable, and to make normative claims about global interactions. In addition to serving as a powerful political discourse both in supplying justifications for the actions of imperial states and their agents and in furnishing resources for the criticism of abuses of power by imperial states – international law's 'imperial' and 'counter-imperial' dimensions[7] – the law of nations and international law have long done a third sort of work with respect to empire, which has been to efface the imperial aspect of European states and the hierarchical nature of the modern global order. As James Tully has argued, 'the world legal and political order is best characterised as an imperial order of some kind', yet 'our dominant languages of disclosure and research conceal and overlook the imperialism of the present'.[8] As accounts of the law of nations came to be structured by a conception of nations as moral communities equal in status with, and independent of, one another, they had the effect of denying theoretical space for the consideration of European imperial actions. It is that third sort of work, what Tully calls disclosure and I have here called the politics of law's conceptual frames, that this chapter will explore through a reading of Vattel's *Droit des gens* (1758) and its reception in early-nineteenth-century British debates. This argument is less about the explicit justificatory work legal arguments were made to do, and more about the questions law of nations discourse made intelligible, and the phenomena it drew attention to or obscured. How did it come to be, I want to ask, that even as the major European states were becoming global empires, leading theorists of international law and politics were conceiving of the international realm as a community of free and equal nations, and of Europe in particular as a political society distinctively free of the outdated and atavistic politics of imperial

---

institutional and disciplinary forms such as specialized curricula, and as literature came to be more narrowly linked with imaginative writing (at 19–22).

[6] In this less doctrinally precise usage, questions of the grounds, or legal nature, of the law of nations tend not to be addressed.

[7] See Sundhya Pahuja, *Decolonising International Law* (Cambridge: Cambridge University Press, 2011), 1; Emmanuelle Jouannet similarly describes international law as 'intrinsically ambivalent', 'simultaneously an instrument of domination and an instrument of emancipation': *A Short Introduction to International Law* (Cambridge: Cambridge University Press, 2014), 1.

[8] Tully, 'On Law, Democracy and Imperialism', in *Public Philosophy in a New Key* (Cambridge: Cambridge University Press, 2008), vol. 2, 127–65, at 127–8.

domination? And what were the implications of this disjuncture for their ability to theorize and evaluate global political relations and events?

Vattel influentially conceptualized the international sphere as a space inhabited by free and equal states conceived as national communities, a depiction that for Vattel represented both a normative ambition and a rough description of the world around him.[9] As an aspiration, this image encapsulated a commitment to the political autonomy of diverse communities that has been a central pillar of modern international political discourse, in the form of the principle of self-determination. Combined with Vattel's universalism – the belief that the law of nations applied to all of humanity – and his commitment to universal human concern despite the fragmentation of humanity into different political communities, the aspiration had considerable critical force in the face of abuses of imperial power. As description, however, it was deceptive, in that it gave little conceptual purchase on the features of hierarchy and imperial extension that characterized the world system in Vattel's day, and continue to do so.

The emancipatory promise of Vattel's theory was captured by the historian of international law who, perhaps more than any other, anticipated the current scholarship in the critical history of international law, the Polish-British lawyer and historian C.H. Alexandrowicz (1902–75). Alexandrowicz, working at the University of Madras in the early years of Indian independence (1951–61), sought in the pre-nineteenth-century history of the law of nations a precedent and a model for the egalitarian and inclusive international legal order he, along with many jurists of the so-called New States, was working to instantiate.[10] Alexandrowicz meant to set the historical record straight, from what he saw as its unfortunate Victorian detour, to show that international law both in theory and in practice had been far more inclusive than it was to become in the nineteenth century. At the center of Alexandrowicz's powerfully argued historical work lay the claim that there had been a radical shift in the history of the law of nations at the turn of the nineteenth century, from an earlier naturalist universalism – which took the law of nations to be based on the law of nature and therefore to apply universally – to a Eurocentric positivism that radically restricted the scope of the law of nations. His normative commitments to the equality of post-colonial states and to a non-

---

[9] As David Armitage has noted, Vattel may have been the moral and political writer with the greatest global influence in the early nineteenth century: Armitage, *Foundations of Modern International Thought* (Cambridge: Cambridge University Press, 2013), 222.

[10] See David Armitage and Jennifer Pitts (eds.), C.H. Alexandrowicz, *The Law of Nations in Global History* (Oxford: Oxford University Press, 2017).

hierarchical global order based on mutual respect among states and societies drove his historical research. He was explicit and passionate about these commitments, and at the same time a historian who sought to understand his subjects in their own terms. He was also, until a few articles in the mid-1970s, at the very end of his life, someone who assiduously avoided thinking of his subject in terms of politics. That is, despite all he did to dispute the conventional narratives of international law, and to castigate them in moral terms, Alexandrowicz refrained from challenging them on political grounds. Instead, he wrote about positions he opposed as simply bad history or bad law, or bad law because it rested on bad history.[11]

Alexandrowicz saw his historical argument as a purely legal one that avoided the 'political point of view'.[12] This omission on Alexandrowicz's part compromised his ability to discuss the complicity of international law with imperial power. His purpose was to show that colonial-era agreements should not be considered legally binding on post-colonial states and thereby to restore to international law its emancipatory role. But in arguing in this way, he drew an untenable distinction between the legal and the political. In contrast, as Martti Koskenniemi argues, 'There is no space in international law that would ... not involve a "choice" – that would not be, in this sense, a *politics of international law*.'[13] It is that insistence of the more recent legal scholars writing the history of international law that law is always political that I think marks the most profound advance with respect to the otherwise compelling historiographical example that Alexandrowicz represents. I examine Vattel in this chapter in part because of his importance for Alexandrowicz's historical argument. I ask what role his theory of the law of nations, as arguably the most important authority during precisely the period that Alexandrowicz himself saw as marking the turn toward 'Eurocentric egotism' in international law, might have played in that turn, despite Alexandrowicz's own reading of Vattel's law of nations as emancipatory and egalitarian in relation to extra-European states.

---

[11] This was his position on the International Court of Justice judgment in the *South West Africa* cases [1966] ICJ Reports 6. For discussion, see Armitage and Pitts, '"This Modern Grotius": An Introduction to the Life and Thought of C.H. Alexandrowicz', in *Law of Nations in Global History*, 1–31, at 21–3, 28–31.

[12] Alexandrowicz, 'The Juridical Expression of the Sacred Trust of Civilization' (1971), in *Law of Nations in Global History*, 336–46, at 346.

[13] Koskenniemi, 'Epilogue', in *From Apology to Utopia* (Cambridge: Cambridge University Press, 2005), 562–617, at 596.

7.1 VATTEL: LAW'S CONCEPTUAL FRAMES

With respect to the history of empire, Vattel has been discussed primarily for his agriculturalist account of property, used to defend settler colonialism in the nineteenth century.[14] This emphasis in the scholarship reflects the fact that Vattel's *Droit des gens* has relatively little to say about empires. His own seeming indifference to the global and imperial dimensions of the interstate politics of his day may be due in part to biography: he was a Swiss subject of the Prussian king Frederick the Great and a diplomat most concerned with continental politics in the German states.[15] The global imperial concerns of France and Britain that were such a dominant part of those states' experience of the Seven Years' War and subsequent decades through the fall of Napoleon – and thus for French and British thinkers such as Diderot or Bentham or Adam Smith – were muted for Vattel in a way that shaped his influential framing of the ostensibly 'universal' law of nations, as much in his occlusions and omissions as in his overt arguments.[16] The unselfconscious universality of Vattel's text, that is, may stem from his distance from the truly global politics of the major imperial states, France and Britain. Whatever the cause, the repercussions were significant, for his model was to serve an important ideological function in the context of European imperial expansion.

Among the reasons for Vattel's global influence was that he proved compelling and useful for a wide variety of figures in the British Empire, at that time the global hegemon, and a crucial space in the making of international law.[17]

---

[14] See Antony Anghie, 'Vattel and Colonialism: Some Preliminary Observations', in Peter Haggenmacher and Vincent Chetail (eds.), *Vattel's International Law in a XXIst Century Perspective* (Boston: Martinus Nijhoff, 2011), 237–53. Vattel was routinely cited in support of Britain's right to settle New Zealand in mid-nineteenth-century debates: see, e.g., the House of Commons debates of June 17, July 7, and July 23, 1845 in Hansard, 3rd Ser., vol. 82, cols. 970–1025.

[15] See André Bandelier, 'De Berlin à Neuchâtel: La Genèse du Droit des Gens d'Emer de Vattel', in Martin Fontius and Helmut Holzhey (eds.), *Schweizer im Berlin des 18. Jahrhunderts* (Berlin: Akademie Verlag, 1996), 45–56; and Tetsuya Toyoda, *Theory and Politics of the Law of Nations: Political Bias in International Law Discourse of Seven German Court Councilors in the Seventeenth and Eighteenth Centuries* (Leiden: Martinus Nijhoff, 2011).

[16] Note the inconclusive evidence of the series of volumes attributed to Vattel as a co-editor, called the *Mémoires pour servir à l'histoire de notre tems*, par l'Observateur hollandois, rédigez et augmentez par M.D.V. (Frankfurt and Leipzig: Aux Dépens de la Compagnie, 1757–58); these address both the American and the Asian theaters of the war in a way that might suggest greater attention to the war's extra-European facets than the *Droit des gens* implies.

[17] On the early-nineteenth-century British Empire as a major site for the creation of international law, see Lauren Benton and Lisa Ford, *Rage for Order: The British Empire and the Origins of International Law, 1800–1850* (Cambridge, MA: Harvard University Press, 2016).

Vattel's universalist and aspirational law of nations had considerable critical potential with regard to European states' conduct beyond Europe that was discarded in the nineteenth century, as Vattel himself was ultimately dispensed with as a superannuated authority. At the same time, his nineteenth-century readers held on to the Vattelian conception of European states as nations, not empires, in ways that obscured the operations of European imperial power.

Vattel inherited from the tradition of Pufendorf and Wolff the conception of states, or nations, as moral persons. It is significant that he used the terms nation and state interchangeably: states appear, in his account, as communities in which all the individual members are morally bound to work together on their individual and collective self-perfection.[18] He depicted a world of such nations dealing with each other as legal equals no matter their size or their relative power – in his famous analogy, 'a dwarf is as much a man as a giant; a small republic is as much a sovereign state as the most powerful kingdom'. This vision of diverse communities granted legal equality and the autonomy to work out their collective lives together free from the interference of outsiders is in many ways a powerfully attractive one. As grounds for treating diverse peoples equitably, it was drawn upon from the time of Vattel's earliest readers, such as Edmund Burke, who cited Vattel when charging that Britain had violated the law of nations in relation to Indian polities and in expropriating Jewish merchants in the West Indies during the American Revolutionary War.[19] British critics of the first Opium War likewise used Vattel to argue for China's equal rights under the law of nations, as I note below. And, as mentioned, for Alexandrowicz, arguing in the 1950s for the legal equality of newly decolonized states, Vattel represented a principled legal universalism

---

[18] 'Les Nations, ou Etats sont des Corps Politiques, des Sociétés d'hommes unis ensemble pour procurer leur salut & leur avantage, à forces réünies': Vattel, *Droit des gens* (Leiden: Aux depens de la Compagnie, 1758), vol. 1, 1; see Béla Kapossy and Richard Whatmore (eds.), *The Law of Nations* (Indianapolis: Liberty Fund, 2008), ix–xx. Unless otherwise noted, I cite from this edition, which uses an anonymous eighteenth-century translation (London, 1797); also see Ben Holland, *The Moral Person of the State: Pufendorf, Sovereignty and Composite Polities* (Cambridge: Cambridge University Press, 2017); and, for discussion of the emergence of an elision between nation and state in late-eighteenth-century French thought (though without reference to Vattel), Istvan Hont, 'The Permanent Crisis of a Divided Mankind', in *Jealousy of Trade: International Competition and the Nation-State in Historical Perspective* (Cambridge, MA: Harvard University Press, 2005), 447–528.

[19] Edmund Burke, 'Speech in Reply' [Warren Hastings impeachment proceedings], May 30, 1794, in P.J. Marshall (ed.), *Writings and Speeches of Edmund Burke* (Oxford: Oxford University Press, 2000), vol. 7, 281–334, at 290–2; 'Motion for an inquiry into the seizure, etc., of private property in St. Eustatius, 14 May 1781', in *The Speeches of the Rt. Hon. Edmund Burke* (London: Longman, Hurst, Rees, Orme, and Brown, 1816), vol. 2, 244–68, at 256–7.

that predated nineteenth-century Eurocentric positivism.[20] But Vattel presented an international community of equal sovereign nations not simply as an aspiration or normative standard but rather, or also, as a plausible description of the world around him: one that rendered opaque the fact that Europe's most important powers were highly differentiated, hierarchical global empires with European metropoles rather than national (and implicitly territorially bounded) communities.[21]

Vattel quickly became the major authority on the law of nations, especially in Britain, so that his implicitly republican doctrine was put to work by an avowedly imperial state.[22] Joseph Chitty, the editor of the 1834 English edition of Vattel's text, supplemented the text with British colonial and admiralty law and added interpretive notes to make Vattel more clearly useful for British imperial dilemmas.[23] Chitty's heavily amended text is typical of nineteenth-century editions of Vattel published in Europe and Latin America, such as Andrés Bello's *Princípios de Derecho de Jentes [Gentes]* (Santiago de Chile, 1832), or the Portuguese philosopher and diplomat Silvestre Pinheiro Ferreira's *Droit des gens, revue et corrigée avec quelques remarques de l'editeur* (Paris, 1838), whose title, like that of the 1863 French edition by Paul Pradier-Fodéré ('Vattel ... augmentée [et...] mise au courant des progrès du droit public moderne'), announces the editor's extensive interventions.[24] Like

---

[20] C.H. Alexandrowicz, 'The New States and International Law' (1974) 3 Millennium 226; and *Law of Nations in Global History*.

[21] Vattel largely disregarded the violence of European commercial and imperial expansion and instead more consistently singled out various Muslim rulers who, though he did not exclude them from the domain of the law of nations, he frequently depicted as knowingly violating its provisions; see, e.g., *Law of Nations*, 413–14 (II.xvii.§273).

[22] See C.G. Fenwick, 'The Authority of Vattel [Part I]', American Political Science Review 7 (1913), 395–410; Emmanuelle Jouannet, *Emer de Vattel et l'émergence doctrinale du droit international classique* (Paris: Pedone, 1998), 14–15; F.S. Ruddy, 'The Acceptance of Vattel', in C.H. Alexandrowicz (ed.), *Grotian Society Papers 1972* (The Hague: Martinus Nijhoff, 1972), 177–96; Ian Hunter, '"A Jus gentium for America." The Rules of War and the Rule of Law in the Revolutionary United States', Journal of the History of International Law 14 (2012), 173–206; Mark Hickford, '"Decidedly the most interesting savages on the globe": An approach to the intellectual history of Māori property rights, 1837–53', History of Political Thought 7 (2006), 122–67, at 123–33.

[23] Chitty, for instance, took Vattel's key principle that a nation is charged with its own self-perfection, so other states may not interfere in its affairs, to mean that states may not recognize another state's rebelling colonies, because that would constitute undue interference in a state's internal affairs, straining that principle to the breaking point. Vattel, *Law of Nations*, ed. Joseph Chitty (London: S. Sweet, 1834), 141–2. In another significant departure from Vattel, Chitty asserted that when there was doubt about a legal principle, 'Christianity ... should be equally appealed to and observed by all as an unfailing rule of construction' (liv–lv).

[24] See Elisabetta Fiocchi Malaspina, 'La ricezione e la circolazione di "Le Droit des Gens" di Emer de Vattel nel XIX siecolo', *Materiali per una storia della cultura giuridica* 43 (2013),

Chitty, Pinheiro Ferreira and Pradier-Fodéré larded their editions with extensive commentary, drawing heavily on Martens, Klüber, and Wheaton to bring Vattel 'up to date'. Pradier-Fodéré's revision included a lengthy discussion of the membership of the international community (in comments on book I, chapter 1 that dwarf the original text), a rebuttal of Vattel's defense of China's right to restrict commerce, and a celebration of the expansion of the French empire: 'In less than fifty years, France has recovered the rank that the carelessness of governments or the misfortune of the times had taken from her.'[25] In these editions, Vattel's text sometimes seems to serve as little more than scaffolding for nineteenth-century commentary that departs considerably from his arguments.

Chitty's edition was well timed to contribute to British debates leading up to the first Opium War, in which Vattel's text was a ubiquitous point of reference. For those who supported the use of military force to compel China to allow the opium trade, Vattel's arguments about commerce were inconvenient, because he categorically supported every state's right to regulate commerce in whatever way it deemed in the best interests of its people. A few pro-war authors tried, not very convincingly, to use Vattel to support the claim that China was obliged to accept the opium trade, but others, recognizing that Vattel's account of commerce undercut their position, bit the bullet and argued for excluding China from the community protected by the law of nations.

I want to suggest that the pressure brought to bear on the pro-war position by a universalist application of Vattel's principles can be seen as a contributing factor in the movement toward the exclusion of China from the 'family of nations' altogether as well as in the displacement of Vattel as a legal authority. Such a move can be seen not only in the British but also the American response to the war, for instance in an essay by John Quincy Adams that was celebrated by the pro-war side and printed in the *Chinese Repository*, the major English-language publication in Canton.

Adams, like so many participants in this debate, felt the need to reckon with Vattel's categorical defense of a nation's right to order its commercial policy as it sees fit. He first (and not very convincingly) rejected Vattel as self-contradictory. Having dispensed with the inconvenient authority of Vattel

---

303–19; and Malaspina and Nina Keller-Kemmerer, 'International Law and Translation in the 19th century', *Rechtsgeschichte* 22 (2014), 214–27.

[25] Pradier-Fodéré (ed.), *Le droit des gens ... par Vattel* (Paris: Gillaumin, 1863), vol. 1, 498. On the 'glory' that France and Britain achieved by forcing an end to China's and Japan's commercial restrictions, see vol. 1, 275–6, n. 1.

on the subject of commercial independence, though, Adams still embraced Vattel's picture of a world of equal states. But Adams also drew on a discourse of oriental despotism in which Vattel had really not participated, and which, since Montesquieu, had depicted European states as uniquely capable of engaging other states with mutuality, while Asian states were constitutively imperial. Adams combined this picture with a Vattelian account of the international community as one of nations to maintain that China had stubbornly excluded itself from that community. The Chinese, he argued, followed a 'churlish and unsocial system' that contravened the principle of equality among nations that was the cornerstone of the European law of nations.[26] The crux of Adams's argument was that China

> admits no obligation to hold commercial intercourse with others. It utterly denies the equality of other nations with itself, and even their independence. It holds ... all other nations with whom it has any relations, political or commercial, as outside tributary barbarians reverently submissive to the will of its despotic chief.[27]

He cast the war as an encounter between a British 'nation' that wanted only to vindicate the values of equality and reciprocity, and a Chinese 'empire' that, in rejecting the norms of the international community, had excluded itself from that community.

Critics of the war were on firmer ground with Vattel, and the Chinese authorities also drew on him for support. One of Commissioner Lin Zexu's early requests when he arrived in Canton to stamp out the opium trade was for the translation of several passages from Vattel, and the opium contraband he declared was entirely in keeping with Vattel's principle that states have perfect liberty to set and change at will their commercial policy.[28] The translated

---

[26] Adams, 'Lecture on the War with China, delivered before the Massachusetts Historical Society, December, 1841', in *The Chinese Repository* XI (1842), 274–89, at 277.

[27] Ibid., 281.

[28] See Chang Hsi-T'ung, 'The Earliest Phase of the Introduction of Western Political Science into China', *Yenching Journal of Social Studies* 5 (1950), 1–30, at 10–15; Immanuel C.Y. Hsü, *China's Entrance into the Family of Nations* (Cambridge, MA: Harvard University Press, 1960), 123–5; and Lydia Liu, *The Clash of Empires: The Invention of China in Modern World Making* (Cambridge, MA: Harvard University Press, 2004), 118. Liu argues that 'Lin's use of international law in these transactions was strategic', on the grounds that he had selectively translated passages 'strictly confined to the issues of how nations go to war and impose embargoes, blockades, and other hostile measures' rather than taking the text as a whole: Liu, 'Legislating the Universal: The Circulation of International Law in the Nineteenth Century', in Liu (ed.), *Tokens of Exchange: The Problem of Translation in Global Circulations* (Durham, NC: Duke University Press, 1999), 127–64, at 141. But this is to mark too stark a boundary between opportunism and simple willingness to engage sources the British themselves

passages were then published by Chinese state officials in a collection of European thought.²⁹ But although the Chinese turn to Vattel made perfect sense – he had been the dominant legal authority for decades and he unambiguously supported their position – he was precisely at this moment, and arguably for the very reason that he did so clearly support their position, being declared obsolete in the West. When the American missionary William Martin set out to translate a text of international law into Chinese in the early 1860s, he considered translating Vattel but then decided Vattel was outdated and instead chose the American Henry Wheaton's *Elements of International Law*, first published in 1836, which he saw as more timely, arguably precisely because of Wheaton's insistence that the law of nations was not universal. This was an argument that Wheaton made ever more insistently in the editions of his text published after the first Opium War, in which he argued that international law 'has always been, and still is, limited to the civilized and Christian people of Europe or to those of European origin'.³⁰ The 'Mohammedan and Pagan nations of Asia and Africa', he now wrote, had recently shown an inclination:

> to renounce their peculiar international usages and adopt those of Christendom. ... The same remark may be applied to the recent diplomatic transactions between the Chinese Empire and the Christian nations of Europe and America, in which the former has been compelled to abandon its inveterate anti-commercial and anti-social principles, and to acknowledge the independence and equality of other nations in the mutual intercourse of war and peace.³¹

Note that here again China appears as an empire and Britain as a nation.

The Opium War, then, marks an important turning point, when the implications of Vattelian universalism sat so uncomfortably with a dominant political position in a European imperial state that Vattel had to be dismissed as an authority and China expelled from the community of states to whom the

---

considered authoritative, on a subject on which Lin considered himself in the right and on which Vattel unambiguously supported his position.

²⁹ Wei Yuan, *Hai Guo Tu Zhi* [*Illustrated Records of the Oversea Countries*] ([Shaoyang]: Gu wei tang, Qing Xianfeng 2 [1852]); see the tendentious translation of the work's preface in John F. Davis, *China during the War and since the Peace* (London: Longman, Brown, Green, and Longman's, 1852); and see Chang Hsi-T'ung, 'The Earliest Phase'.
³⁰ Wheaton, *Elements of International Law* (6th ed.) (Boston: Little Brown, 1855), 16.
³¹ Ibid., 20, 22. Compare Wheaton, *Elements of International Law: With a Sketch of the History of the Science* (London: B. Fellowes, 1836 [1st ed.]), vol. 1, iii–v, 51–3, where he describes the mutual influence of the public law of Europe and that of the 'Mohammedans' in 'Turkey and the Barbary states'.

law of nations applied and, with other non-European states, rendered candidates for entry into a European order rather than, as they had been for Vattel and Burke, presumptive members of a universal legal community. And yet Vattel's legacy remained profound in the framing of that European order as one of equal and independent nation-states, not global empires.

As international law came in the latter half of the nineteenth century to be increasingly a self-conscious discipline, its major practitioners came to argue that international law had to be understood as a historically particular system that had arisen under the distinctive circumstances of early-modern Europe and was constantly adjusting to the 'growing wants of a progressive civilisation'.[32] They were, consequently, preoccupied in a way that Vattel had not been with delineating the scope of the international community, expounding the criteria for admission into that community, managing its gradual expansion to encompass some excluded states, and specifying the legal status of various societies they deemed inadmissible. Vattel thus left a mixed legacy to twentieth-century international thought: the critical purchase of his normative account of sovereign equality was lost in the nineteenth-century rejection of his universalism, while his model lived on as a misleading descriptive schema.

7.2 BENTHAM: AN IMPERIAL GLOBAL STRUCTURE

An intriguing but ultimately failed alternative can be found in the evolution of Bentham's thought on international law and international relations. Bentham was perhaps the only political thinker to rival Vattel's influence on a global scale in the early nineteenth century, with readers and correspondents from Latin America and Haiti to India and the Middle East. Writing in the wake of the Seven Years' War and the American Revolutionary War, Bentham argued in the 1780s that the most fundamental precondition for global peace was that all states must emancipate their colonies. At this point, Bentham, unlike Vattel, conceived of the international realm as a space of empires and saw imperial ambitions and imperial violence as the greatest threats to international peace. (As I noted above, many of his French and British contemporaries shared this imperial frame, as is evident from the centrality of European imperial expansion to some of the most influential works of the 1770s and

---

[32] Travers Twiss, *The Law of Nations Considered as Independent Political Communities* (Oxford: Clarendon Press, 1884), 'Preface to the Second Edition', v. On the professionalization of the discipline, see Martti Koskenniemi, *The Gentle Civilizer of Nations: The Rise and Fall of International Law, 1870–1960* (Cambridge: Cambridge University Press, 2001); and Casper Sylvest, 'International Law in Nineteenth-Century Britain', *British Yearbook of International Law* 75 (2005), 9–70.

1780s, such as Adam Smith's *Wealth of Nations*, or Raynal and Diderot's *Histoire des Deux Indes*, though Bentham was writing in a more overtly legal idiom.) Bentham's early writings on international law depict the international politics of his era as dominated by the effects of colonial expansion. Colonization was, in Bentham's words, the 'race of vulgar ambition' and a 'war against mankind'.[33] Above all, he saw colonies as the chief cause of war in the modern world. He cited as recent examples the war against Spain in the 1740s (the War of Jenkins' Ear), and the Seven Years' War, whose violence, he said, stretched from 'North America to the East Indies', and which, in the needless destruction it caused Britain, demonstrated 'the extreme folly, the madness of war'. Bentham saw a global system dominated by empires as structurally doomed to incessant violence. Colonies provoked wars not only by multiplying the possible sources of conflict but also because in their newness, and distance from Europe, they were fraught with uncertainty, which Bentham saw as a key source of instability and aggression. His project for the codification of international law was driven by the aim of quelling conflict by reducing uncertainty. A code would do so, he thought, in part by minimizing the many offenses against international peace that were committed by sovereigns unsure of, or in good-faith disagreement about, what constituted their obligations toward one another. But the greater danger to peaceful commerce and cooperation was empire. Bentham's attention to the imperial nature of the world's major powers allowed him to see, and to make explicit, what remains possibly implicit, but certainly obscure, in Vattel: that a legal system premised on the reciprocity and equality of independent states should require first of all that they give up their empires and become, in fact, the territorially compact political communities that Vattel had hypothesized.

When Bentham returned to the project of codifying international law in the late 1820s, his vision of the international realm had in important respects moved closer to Vattel's (if perhaps unwittingly, given his disdain for Vattel's theory as 'old-womanish and tautological').[34] In the notes on international law that he sent to the barrister and former colonial judge Jabez Henry, in the hope that Henry would develop them into a treatise or code, Bentham accepted a number of the essential features of Vattel's picture of the international realm: states must recognize each other as equals; each pledges to respect the regime, religion, and customs of all the others; and each is oriented not only toward keeping peace with the others, but also toward 'mutual good

---

[33] 'Emancipate your colonies!' (1793), in John Bowring (ed.), *The Works of Jeremy Bentham* (Edinburgh: W. Tait, 1838–43), vol. 4, 407–18, at 408, 416.
[34] Bowring (ed.), *The Works of Jeremy Bentham*, vol. 10, 584.

will' and 'mutual good offices'. But Bentham now limited the community of states under international law to 'all civilized nations[,] which at present is as much as to say, all nations professing the Christian Religion'.[35] This was a radical departure from both Vattel's and his own earlier presumptive universalism. Bentham was now also far more modest in his aspirations for the code than he had been. Above all, he gave up the hope of taming imperial ambitions. In describing the 'Utility of a body of International law', he first noted the 'Good which it is not capable of effecting – preventing a Sovereign who has purposes for conquest from endeavouring to carry them into effect'.[36] Rather, the code's main function would be to reduce uncertainty about states' respective rights and duties, so that inflated ideas of 'rights violated' might be kept from 'stir[ring] up angry passions and anti-social affections'. Along with this greater modesty went a complete abdication of Bentham's original prescription for international peace, the emancipation of all colonies. Instead, the principle of universal equality now required (just as Chitty did) that states not interfere in one another's colonies, or as Bentham put it:

> Fundamental principles to be agreed upon by all the States: (1) universal equality. No State to pretend to any authority over any other State (a) on sea, (b) on land in the territory of a barbarous nation not being a member of the Congress. (2) All States to be upon a par in Congress, whatsoever the form of government.[37]

Bentham, then, made a complete about-face on international law and empire. He gave up on the key prescription for global peace that he had made as a young man, he accepted the restriction of the international legal community to Christian Europe, and he accepted that the system's major powers would be vast global empires with utter legal impunity – at least with respect to international law – in their conduct in their colonies. For help in turning this sketch into a code of international law, he turned to a man whose reputation was built on his work as a colonial official. Bentham's motivations can be obscure, and it is hard to account for what may have happened within his own mind from the 1780s to the 1820s to bring about this change. (It may have been partly to do with the shift of the center of gravity of imperial domains from the settler colonies of the Americas – which had mostly established their independence by the late 1820s – to India and other non-white populations.

---

[35] Jeremy Bentham, 'International Law', June 11, 1827, British Library, Add MSS 30151, ff. 13 and 15b.
[36] Ibid., f. 15b.
[37] Ibid., f. 17.

But it is worth stressing that in the earlier period Bentham insisted on the emancipation of all colonies, India specifically included, and not just colonies whose loudest voices were white settlers.)

Whatever his own reasons, there is no question that the change in Bentham's thinking tracks a more general development in European thinking in this period, one that we also see in the shift from Vattel's original text to the Chitty edition of the 1830s. We begin with a universalist account of an international community that is not limited to Europe, that is made up of states understood as moral communities protected by political autonomy to work out their collective life. We end with a vision of an international community of equal states limited for the time being to Europe; states understood in a dual way as legal equals vis-à-vis each other but also as global empires controlling vast territories and populations as they see fit. International law speaks, in this model, only to the interactions between European states; it is not equipped to analyze those states as empires, to hold them to legal account, or to recognize the global order as one that is structured hierarchically.

7.3 CONCLUSION

We inhabit a world that is still in an important respect like Vattel's: in which the dominant image of the international sphere as a legally egalitarian world of nation-states, one we inherited from him, exists alongside imperial structures of power and law that are hard to acknowledge and come to grips with in the terms provided by that image. As in Vattel's thought, aspirational models continue to obscure abuses by the powerful, Rawls's *Law of Peoples* being an influential recent example. Rawls acknowledged that no existing states (especially not the global 'liberal' hegemon, the United States) satisfy the criteria for liberal peoples in his account. But the structure of his theory includes no conceptual space for injustices perpetrated by so-called liberal states and the global economic and political order they dominate, for liberal polities are considered under the rubric of ideal theory, and non-ideal theory considers only injustices by 'outlaw' states and in 'burdened societies' implicitly located outside the community of liberal industrialized states.[38] Beyond Rawls, international law's identity as an emancipatory project with an

---

[38] John Rawls, *The Law of Peoples: With "The Idea of Public Reason Revisited"* (Cambridge, MA: Harvard University Press, 1999); on historical patterns of such hierarchy, see Gerry Simpson, *Great Powers and Outlaw States: Unequal Sovereigns in the International Legal Order* (Cambridge: Cambridge University Press, 2004).

essentially European genealogy continues to shape the liberal frameworks dominant in the global justice literature, theories of humanitarian intervention, and the liberal strand of international relations scholarship. Such perspectives overlook or elide the deep substantive inequalities that are inscribed in formally equal legal principles, as well as the profound legal asymmetries imposed on post-colonial states during decolonization and that continue to structure the global order. The literatures on contemporary cosmopolitanism and humanitarian intervention have tended to ask how liberal states and societies should respond to the pathologies they encounter *out there*, and how they might intervene to relieve poverty and promote democracy, rather than understanding the prosperous and relatively stable societies of the global north and the impoverished and too often authoritarian states of the global south as products of the same long history of asymmetrical interaction, mutual constitution, and exploitation for profit. While supporters of the Responsibility to Protect, commonly known as R2P, acknowledge, as older debates around humanitarian intervention often did not, the conditions of global hierarchy that contribute to humanitarian crises, the universalistic conceptual frame of the R2P principle – that all sovereignty is conditional on a state's ability to protect its population – obscures the fact that the principle is only ever invoked in cases in the global south.[39] As the President of the UN General Assembly, the Nicaraguan diplomat Miguel D'Escoto Brockmann, argued in a 2009 debate on the responsibility to protect, the history of abuse of humanitarian arguments for the use of force by colonial powers and powerful states in the post-colonial period has led to profound distrust of R2P as simply the latest iteration of that history. Given the 'lack of trust in developing countries when it comes to the use of force for humanitarian reasons', he argued, we 'first need to create a more just and equal world order, including in the economic and social sense, as well as a Security Council that does not create a differential system of international law geared towards the strong protecting, or not protecting, whomever they wish'.[40]

The legacies of imperial history – of phenomena ranging from the global slave trade and the appropriation of vast agricultural land in the western hemisphere, to wars of decolonization, and the myriad proxy and covert wars of the post–World War II period – include both acute ongoing consequences

---

[39] See Cristina Lafont, 'Human Rights, Sovereignty and the Responsibility to Protect', *Constellations* 22 (2015), 68–78. For a powerful critique of even the most subtle defenses of the construal of sovereignty as responsibility, see Adom Getachew, 'The Limits of Sovereignty as Responsibility', *Constellations* 26 (2019), 225–40.

[40] United Nations General Assembly, July 29, 2009, A/63/PV.97, p. 3.

for formerly colonized societies and the more often overlooked but likewise transformative effects on metropolitan states, their economies, their militaries, and their politics.[41] Since the nineteenth century, these have been consistently racialized patterns, since, as Anghie has written, 'Race, transmuted into the more comprehensive notion of "civilization," is central to the very definition of international law.'[42] Unequal international standing has routinely been the fate of non-white states, from the 'burdened' membership of states such as Ethiopia and Liberia in the League of Nations to the constraints on sovereign prerogatives imposed on post-colonial states.[43]

Conventional narratives of a progressive international law saw it emerging among Western European nation-states and gradually expanding outward to encompass the globe, both spreading sovereignty and taming state violence as it went. The recognition by critical histories of international law that the aspirations for universal justice it articulated have been repeatedly intertwined with hierarchy and domination make possible the chastened hope that international law may yet be mobilized in more emancipatory ways. Perhaps, as Burke, Alexandrowicz, and the British critics of the Opium War believed in relation to the forms of imperial domination they faced, Vattel's twin commitments to the autonomy of political communities and the duty of universal concern remain valuable critical resources for our own dilemmas.

---

[41] Tarak Barkawi stresses the ramifications of colonial or 'small wars' for domestic politics and civil–military relations, particularly such conflicts as the Vietnam War for the United States and the Algerian War for France in 'Political Military Legacies of Empire in World Politics', in Sandra Halperin and Ronen Palan (eds.), *Legacies of Empire: Imperial Roots of the Contemporary Global Order* (Cambridge: Cambridge University Press, 2015), 27–45. On the contribution of New World conquest to European economic growth and military and industrial dominance, see Kenneth Pomeranz, *The Great Divergence: China, Europe, and the Making of the Modern World Economy* (Princeton: Princeton University Press, 2000).

[42] Anghie, 'Decolonizing the Concept of "Good Governance"', in Branwen Gruffydd Jones (ed.), *Decolonizing International Relations* (Lanham: Rowman & Littlefield, 2006), 109–30, at 110.

[43] See Adom Getachew, *Worldmaking after Empire: The Rise and Fall of Self-Determination* (Princeton: Princeton University Press, 2019); Siba N'Zatioula Grovogui, *Sovereigns, Quasi Sovereigns, and Africans: Race and Self-Determination in International Law* (Minneapolis: University of Minnesota Press, 1996); Anghie, *Imperialism, Sovereignty and the Making of International Law* (Cambridge: Cambridge University Press, 2005).

8

The History of Political Thought in the African Political Present

EMMA HUNTER

This is a book about history: the 'historical turn' in international law on the one hand, and the 'international turn' in the history of political thought on the other. Yet the arguments explored here matter not just because they change the way we understand the past, but because our readings of the past are fundamental to all critical perspectives on the present and the future. In this chapter, I focus on Africa, and what thinking about the history of political thought in mid-twentieth-century Africa means for our understanding of political ordering.

According to a dominant narrative, both popular and scholarly, the states which were established in mid-twentieth-century Africa were imposed from outside. Basil Davidson's description of the state in Africa in his book *The Black Man's Burden* as an 'alien' imposition which has never fully taken root has struck a powerful chord.[1] Decolonization and independence, for Davidson, did not constitute 'a restoration to Africa of Africa's own history, but the onset of a new period of indirect subjection to the history of Europe'.[2] In this perspective, decolonization was characterized by continuity as much as change, as '[t]he fifty or so states of the colonial partition, each formed and governed as though their peoples possessed no history of their own, became fifty or so nation-states formed and governed on European models, chiefly the models of Britain and France'.[3]

Recent histories of international law adopt a similar framework in which the independence of most African countries in the mid-twentieth century appears

---

[1] Basil Davidson, *The Black Man's Burden: Africa and the Curse of the Nation-State* (London: James Currey, 1992), 12.
[2] Ibid., 12.
[3] Ibid., 10. On the continued resonance of this perception of the state in Africa, see Paul Nugent, 'States and Social Contracts', *New Left Review* 63 (2010), 35–68, at 38.

as a powerful illustration of a pattern in which, far from marking the dramatic transformation for which nationalist leaders had hoped, independence from colonial rule in the 1960s saw the imposition of Western forms of political organization on non-Western societies, and made little difference to the global political order established under imperialism. Siba N'Zatioula Grovogui, echoing older arguments about the limits of mere 'flag' independence, understands decolonization to have been a missed opportunity to 'fully restore African sovereignty and self-determination'.[4] Instead power was simply transferred from departing colonial elites to their chosen successors who 'appropriated Western political and juridical idioms, which they attempted to adapt to their own struggle'.[5]

For Grovogui, this is not simply a state of affairs to be accepted. Rather, exposing the 'shortcomings of decolonization in Africa' provides the foundations for a critical project in the present. Grovogui argues that alternative visions of political order which failed to prosper at independence should now be picked up by a new generation prepared to take seriously radical pan-African critiques of existing models of the state and of international society, and if necessary to isolate Africa from an international system which has rarely served it well.[6]

This is a powerful call to arms. It rests, however, on a particular historical view of independence: as something that was done to Africa from outside, and in which international society acts upon Africa as an external force. It sets up a normative model of statehood which African states are seen as having failed to attain.[7] As such, while it speaks to a broad truth about the continuation of

---

[4] Siba N'Zatioula Grovogui, *Sovereigns, Quasi Sovereigns and Africans: Race and Self-Determination in International Law* (Minneapolis: University of Minnesota Press, 1996), 196. For an example of the argument that formal independence failed to constitute a complete decolonization in relation to Tanzania, see Haroub Othman, 'The State in Tanzania: Who Controls It and Whose Interests Does It Serve' in Haroub Othman (ed.), *The State in Tanzania: Who Controls It and Whose Interests Does It Serve* (Dar es Salaam: Dar es Salaam University Press, 1980), 1–18.

[5] Grovogui, *Sovereigns, Quasi Sovereigns and Africans*, 196.

[6] Ibid, 206–7.

[7] The political scientist Robert Jackson has coined the term 'quasi-states' to describe those 'territorial jurisdictions which were formed under colonial rule and emerged into the light of day by an international legal transaction – decolonization – whereby sovereignty was transferred from European states to indigenous governments', but which are sustained 'from above by international law and material aid': Robert Jackson, *Quasi-States: Sovereignty, International Relations and the Third World* (Cambridge: Cambridge University Press, 1991), 2, 5. Citing Jackson, Grovogui refers to a consensus among scholars that 'most former colonies do not possess the requisite attributes of statehood': Grovogui, *Sovereigns, Quasi Sovereigns and Africans*, 182.

colonial boundaries after independence, it somewhat jars with our developing understanding of the political thought of decolonization from the perspective of the African intellectuals and politicians who sought to create new political societies in the mid-twentieth century, and of the place of the international in their political thinking. As this chapter will show, the building of new states went hand in hand with new formulations of international society.

The growing body of work on the political thought of decolonization takes as its starting point the need to decentre the nation-state, both in our assumptions about the possibilities open to contemporary actors and in our own analysis. Doing so first means situating the arguments for independent statehood in context, but there are different ways in which this has been done. In this chapter, I shall first briefly set out the problems with a view of independence as characterized simply by the export of a modular form of statehood, and argue that by starting from local spatial and temporal contexts we can better see the ways in which a homology of language masked locally specific arguments over what sort of state should be created. This reminds us that the political thought of the era of decolonization, in Africa and beyond, was a creative process, and one rooted in African realities, even as the borders inherited from the colonial period were, in some cases reluctantly, maintained.

I shall then turn to consider the place of the international in this story. The history of international political thought can be understood as the history of how people in the past increasingly came, in David Armitage's words, 'to imagine that we inhabit a world of states'.[8] But the focus on states as the building blocks of international society has often obscured the fact that people have never imagined that they live only in a world of states. In the past as in the present, people have considered themselves not only to be citizens of a state, but also members of wider communities that transcend the boundaries of states. In the twentieth century, such wider communities included religious, regional or pan-African communities, as well as membership of a universal human community. An alternative way of approaching the history of international political thought is therefore to focus on the relationship between these coexisting conceptions. I do so here by combining a history of how individuals might conceive of themselves as citizens or subjects of individual states, subject to the positive law of those states, with one of how they might simultaneously think of themselves as members of a universal

---

[8] David Armitage, *Foundations of Modern International Thought* (Cambridge: Cambridge University Press, 2012), 13.

human community, subject to natural law or, in the twentieth century, to the positive law of new international institutions.[9]

Although the mid-twentieth century marked a new phase in the history of states, this new phase emerged in the context of a new phase in the history of conceptions of a universal human society, as the Universal Declaration of Human Rights seemed to establish in 1948 'the universalistic inclusion of all humanity in the set of morally relevant subjects of political concern and action'.[10] Recent work by Samuel Moyn and others has sought to downplay the significance of this moment, arguing that the 1940s was characterized as much by the resurgence of the nation state as by the dawn of an era of human rights.[11] Yet the novelty of articulating the right to elect one's own government as a universal right owing to all by virtue of their humanity should not be overlooked. In this sense, the new African nation-states of the mid-twentieth century did indeed have international origins. This is particularly true in states such as Tanzania, the focus of much of my discussion here, which was a United Nations Trust Territory.

After independence, a conception of rights which transcended individual states continued to serve as an intellectual and political resource for political thinkers and actors. Annabel Brett has argued that, viewed from the perspective of early modern Europe, the 'sharp break between "inside" and "outside" upon which the modern state in theory rests' was a product of 'tense negotiation' rather than a 'settled conception'.[12] We might helpfully think about the mid-twentieth century as constituting a new phase in this 'tense negotiation' over the limits of the state and its jurisdiction. This helps us both to understand the contingency of the states established in the past, in Africa as elsewhere, and to identify from where change has come before and from where, potentially, it may come again.

8.1 MAKING POLITICAL SOCIETY IN AN INTERNATIONAL AGE

For a long time, the assumption that the nation-state was the natural basis of the international political order dominated approaches to writing the history

---

[9] Annabel S. Brett, *Changes of State: Nature and the Limits of the City in Early Modern Natural Law* (Princeton: Princeton University Press, 2011), 13.
[10] Samuel Moyn, 'The Universal Declaration of Human Rights in the History of Cosmopolitanism', *Critical Inquiry* 40 (2014), 365–84, at 367.
[11] Ibid., *passim*.
[12] Brett, *Changes of State*, 3, 5.

of twentieth-century decolonization.[13] Since the nation-state was understood as the inevitable end point, the central question to be asked was how colonies came to arrive at the position of being independent nation-states. Until very recently, much writing about African independence and the post-colonial state in Africa followed this pattern. As for other parts of the post-colonial world, the history which tended to be written was either one in which decolonization was constituted by a simple transfer of power from colonial authority to post-colonial elite, or one in which the rise of nationalist movements and euphoria of independence was swiftly followed by disappointment, as post-colonial states proved unable to deliver the promises which had been made to their citizens or to assert themselves internationally. As Jeffrey Ahlman has recently written, '[t]he narrative that arose in these world regions was therefore one centered on not only the foundation of the twentieth-century postcolonial nation-state, but, just as importantly, its political, economic, and civic demise'.[14] Held up against a model of the Westphalian state, African states were found wanting, and writing about post-colonial states has tended to focus on explaining their perceived weakness. For the authors of a recent handbook of African politics, for example, the central element of the post-colonial state in Africa which warranted explanation was precisely this weakness, evident both in states' inability to project their power internally and in their unequal position in the international system.[15]

As we have seen, the critical lesson that has often been drawn, both by scholars and in popular writing, was that the states which had been formed at independence were somehow unsuited to African realities. Yet by the late twentieth century, it no longer seemed so obvious that the global triumph of the nation-state was permanent. The nation-state everywhere seemed to be under pressure from what was labelled 'globalization', a catch-all term for a range of economic, political, legal and material challenges to the ability of nation-states to assert exclusive control over their territories. In this context, historians increasingly revisited their earlier assumptions about the naturalness of the nation-state and took up the question of why it was that, by the

---

[13] Karuna Mantena, 'Popular Sovereignty and Anti-Colonialism' in Quentin Skinner and Richard Bourke (eds.), *Popular Sovereignty in Historical Perspective* (Cambridge: Cambridge University Press, 2016), 297–319.
[14] Jeffrey Ahlman, *Living with Nkrumahism: Nation, State, and Pan-Africanism in Ghana* (Athens: Ohio University Press, 2017), 3.
[15] David M. Anderson and Nic Cheeseman, 'An Introduction to African Politics', in David Anderson, Nic Cheeseman and Andrea Scheibler (eds.), *Routledge Handbook of African Politics* (New York: Routledge, 2013), 19–38.

mid-twentieth century, it had come to be taken for granted as the core building block of international society.

One answer was to suggest that the globalization of the nation-state was a product of a history whereby ideas first developed by European jurists in the eighteenth century which envisaged an international order made up of free and equal independent states gradually attained global reach. The foundational text here is often taken to be Emer de Vattel's 1758 *The Law of Nations*, which redefined 'independence' as a positive good.[16] The text travelled the world in the later eighteenth and nineteenth centuries.[17] For David Armitage, while it would be 'anachronistic to see the origins of a world defined by states as early as 1648 and the Peace of Westphalia which is often held to have inaugurated a "Westphalian order" of mutually acknowledged independent states', he argues that 'it is not inappropriate to see events of the late eighteenth-century and early nineteenth-century Atlantic world as an anticipation of what would come to much of the rest of the globe 200 years later'.[18]

The relative uniformity of political languages about states and sovereignty over a long period and across a wide geographical range is certainly superficially striking. As David Armitage has shown, the very words which had been used to claim independence in eighteenth-century America were translated and redeployed to similar ends by anti-colonial nationalists across the world in the twentieth century. Yet the words of the American Declaration of Independence meant very different things in 1940s Indonesia or 1950s Tanganyika to what they had meant in 1770s America, as did understandings of the nature of the international order which those advocating independence sought to join. We should therefore resist the temptation to see the world that emerged in the mid-twentieth century as nothing but the final realization of a process which had begun much earlier, and should think more carefully about the specific context in which mid-twentieth-century arguments for independence were made.

At the same time, focusing only on how we came to live in a world of states obscures a much messier historical reality in which the jurisdiction of states has always coexisted with other sorts of authority. Modern colonial states sought to confine their subjects within individual territories and within empires. Empires were ruled in a way which differentiated between different categories of colonial subjects and, crucially, imperial governors insisted on

---

[16] Armitage, *Foundations of Modern International Thought*, 224.
[17] Lauren Benton and Lisa Ford, *Rage for Order: The British Empire and the Origins of International Law 1800–1850* (Cambridge, MA: Harvard University Press, 2016), 20.
[18] Armitage, *Foundations of Modern International Thought*, 191–2.

their right to determine who could possess which rights within their jurisdiction.[19] This they claimed on the basis of a model of statehood which defined statehood in terms of the ability to reject external interference in internal affairs.

Yet the insistence of colonial powers on the rejection of external interference was always a rhetorical claim more than settled fact. As Lauren Benton and Lisa Ford have emphasized, the ability of colonial states to maintain exclusive jurisdiction over those living within their borders was constantly challenged in practice by the movement of peoples across the world, and by the multiple allegiances held both by peoples on the move and those who might not move physically but were nevertheless part of religious, ethnic, national or racial communities which transcended the borders of states and empires.[20] In the nineteenth century, the porousness of the internal and the external often served to extend the reach of empires. In the twentieth century, it also served as a means of challenging them.

8.2 THE UNITED NATIONS, THE UNIVERSAL DECLARATION OF HUMAN RIGHTS AND SOVEREIGNTY

One of the consequences of the Second World War was the demise of the League of Nations and the foundation of the United Nations in 1945. There was of course a great deal of continuity between the two institutions. Many of the same people who had staffed the League of Nations went to work for the United Nations. Both institutions were, on some level, founded on an understanding that the international order was, or would become, one based on nation-states. While the United Nations came to encompass many more states than the League of Nations had done, it was dominated by a small group of powerful countries just as the League had been. Nevertheless, the early 1940s marked the birth of a new way of thinking about the world.[21]

When it was founded in 1920, the League of Nations marked a new phase in the history of international organization and offered a new way for colonized

---

[19] Benton and Ford, *Rage for Order*, 116; Sukanya Banerjee, *Becoming Imperial Citizens: Indians in the Late-Victorian Empire* (Durham, NC: Duke University Press, 2010); Jane Burbank and Frederick Cooper, *Empires in World History: Power and the Politics of Difference* (Princeton: Princeton University Press, 2010).

[20] Benton and Ford, *Rage for Order*, 115; Lauren Benton and Adam Clulow, *Protection and Empire: A Global History* (Cambridge: Cambridge University Press, 2018).

[21] This section draws on arguments made at greater length in Emma Hunter, *Political Thought and the Public Sphere in Tanzania: Freedom, Democracy and Citizenship in the Era of Decolonization* (Cambridge: Cambridge University Press, 2015), ch. 2.

peoples to attempt to circumvent colonial legal structures and reach outside colonial empires to an international body. But at the same time, the League rested on and promoted a particular conception of the international order. In this conception, self-government, and thus full membership of international society, depended on having achieved a standard of civilization which was defined in terms of the culture and institutions of the modern West.

This conception travelled far beyond the League's debating chambers. For instance, in the pages of *Mambo Leo*, a periodical published by the Education Department in Tanganyika which played a key role in explaining Tanganyika's new status as a League of Nations Mandate, the League was tellingly described in 1923 as an association of 'civilized nations'.[22] Since full membership of international society depended on achieving 'civilization', then much discussion in the public spheres of the colonial world focused on what 'civilization' meant and how to achieve it. Across the colonial world, a strikingly similar set of ideas about what progress entailed reappear, focusing on hard work, self-improvement and associational culture, though these ideas coexisted with arguments over whether civilization necessarily meant westernization.[23]

Yet alongside a discourse which divided the world into those parts which were deemed to be 'civilized' and those which were in progress towards 'civilization', a division often by the late nineteenth century understood in racial terms, there was a powerful trend of thought which argued for an international order based on equality. Cemil Aydin has shown how pan-Asian and pan-Islamic thought provided ways of claiming an equal place in the world. In the first half of the twentieth century, pan-Africanist thought increasingly played a similar role in Africa and the Atlantic world.[24] The 1940s marked a key transitional moment in the history of this counter-narrative of thinking and activism demanding equal rights for all, linking this demand to a language of freedom, self-determination and democracy. This shift was embedded in the 1948 Universal Declaration of Human Rights (UDHR). This declaration affirmed the principle that all human beings were 'born free and equal in dignity and rights'. These rights were owing to all and by virtue of their humanity, not as members of a particular state.

---

[22] The term used was 'mataifa yenye ustaarabu'. 'Habari za dunia' ('World news'), *Mambo Leo*, December 1923, 3.
[23] Emma Hunter, '"Our Common Humanity": Print, Power, and the Colonial Press in Interwar Tanganyika and French Cameroun', *Journal of Global History* 7 (2012), 279–301; Kai Kresse, *Guidance (Uwongozi) by Sheikh al-Amin Mazrui: Selections from the First Swahili Islamic Newspaper* (Leiden: Brill, 2017).
[24] Hunter, *Political Thought and the Public Sphere in Tanzania*, 68.

Although the Declaration increasingly came in the second half of the twentieth century to be seen as overly dependent on a Western tradition of individual rights, at the time it was understood to be a new attempt to articulate a set of principles which could be common to all. In 1947, the recently established UNESCO brought together thinkers from across the world to feed into the process. The explicitly global foundations and reach of the UDHR marked a change from anything which had come before.

An understanding of a right to elect one's own government as being a universal right, not, as under the League, restricted to those who had achieved a standard of 'civilization', was embodied in the foundation of the United Nations Trusteeship Council in 1947 that provided international oversight of those territories which had formerly been League of Nations Mandates.[25] Whereas the mandate system envisaged a long and slow path to self-government, particularly for those territories classed as 'B' or 'C' mandates, the United Nations had a much shorter time frame in mind. Opening the Trusteeship Council in March 1947, the United Nations Secretary-General articulated this vision of the Council's role clearly, saying that '[f]ull success ... will automatically put this organ out of existence, since your ultimate goal is to give the Trust Territories full statehood'.[26]

One part of the history of the 1940s and 1950s was therefore the new articulation of a domain at the international level to which individuals and groups in colonized societies could appeal, circumventing the efforts of colonial states to contain their populations within their borders. For those parts of Africa that had been German colonies and became League of Nations mandates, the League had offered a new site of politics, particularly through the petitioning system. The circumstances in which petitions could be sent to the League of Nations were tightly controlled, and petitions had to come through the mandatory power, if they were sent from the mandate itself. The right to petition the League was employed far more enthusiastically in some mandate territories than others – indeed, very few petitions were received from Tanganyika. Nevertheless, the right to petition opened up a new space. As Susan Pedersen has written, '[p]etitioning [the League] mattered not because it offered petitioners redress but because it allowed them to enter and speak in a multi-vocal, international arena. It was one of the key mechanisms (publicity

---

[25] Mark Mazower, 'The End of Civilization and the Rise of Human Rights: The Mid-Twentieth-Century Disjuncture', in Stefan-Ludwig Hoffmann (ed.), *Human Rights in the Twentieth Century* (Cambridge: Cambridge University Press, 2011), 29–44, at 30.

[26] United Nations Trusteeship Council (UNTC), First session, 26 March 1947, *Official Records*, 5.

being another) through which a previously binary relationship – colonizer, colonized – was triangulated.'[27]

The United Nations in turn offered still more possibilities for addressing an international audience. Trusteeship territories were visited every three years by a Visiting Mission, and these Visiting Missions travelled around Trusteeship territories, meeting groups and individuals and receiving petitions. But the international and the local did not only intersect in Africa, they also met in New York, where petitioners could appear before the Trusteeship Council to state their case. Admittedly only a tiny fraction of the colonial world came under the Trusteeship regime; but we should not underestimate its significance. Writing about the relationship between human rights and decolonization in Africa, the historian Meredith Terretta suggests that 'scholars might consider UN Trust Territories as central, rather than exceptional or peripheral'.[28] In the case which Terretta explores, the appearance of Um Nyobe, leader of Cameroon's nationalist party, in front of the Trusteeship Council in New York in 1953 was a spur to the party adopting petitioning as a key weapon in their struggle. The impact was dramatic – the number of Cameroonian petitions processed by the Trusteeship Council rose from 16 in 1951 to 505 in 1955.[29] But more than this, Terretta argues that 'the principles outlined in the UN Charter and the UDHR' increasingly shaped the Cameroonian political imaginary.[30]

In Tanganyika too, the status of being a United Nations Trusteeship Territory shaped the way Tanganyikan intellectuals and activists thought about their place in the world. When the Trusteeship Agreement was reached in 1946, it was translated into Swahili by the Government's Information Officer and copies were distributed throughout the Territory.[31] Tanganyikans took seriously the idea that the British did not have unlimited sovereignty over Tanganyika, but that the governance of Tanganyika was under international supervision. According to government reports, at the meeting in 1954 which led to the establishment of Tanganyika's nationalist party, TANU, '[t]here was much play with the notion that the territory is

---

[27] Susan Pedersen, *The Guardians: The League of Nations and the Crisis of Empire* (Oxford: Oxford University Press, 2015), 94.
[28] Meredith Terretta, '"We Had Been Fooled into Thinking the UN Watches Over the Entire World": Human Rights, UN Trusteeship Territories and Africa's Decolonization', *Human Rights Quarterly* 34 (2012), 329–60, at 358.
[29] Ibid., 339.
[30] Ibid., 342.
[31] Ulrich Lohrmann, *Voices from Tanganyika: Great Britain, the United Nations and the Decolonization of a Trust Territory, 1946–1961* (Berlin: Lit. Verlag, 2007), 47.

governed by the United Nations with Britain acting in a clerical capacity and that the Queen is not the Queen of Tanganyika and should not be referred to as "Our Sovereign"'.[32]

In turn, TANU sought to make the wider population aware of Tanganyika's status, publishing and distributing a Swahili-language document about the Trusteeship Council.[33] They also made productive use of the Universal Declaration of Human Rights. When in 1955 TANU translated the document into Swahili, they sold 3,815 copies in six weeks.[34] When rural disturbances developed in the province of Handeni a year later, the colonial government reported that the Declaration was being used as a basis from which to criticize colonial government policies and to demand that rights be respected.[35] At the same time, individuals and groups took advantage of the Visiting Missions which travelled through Tanganyika and the opportunity to appear before the Trusteeship Council in New York.

The ability to transcend colonial borders and to appeal to the United Nations on the basis of rights owing to all by virtue of their humanity was an important part of the international history of decolonization. But as recent research has emphasized, there is another aspect to the place of the Universal Declaration of Human Rights in the international thought of decolonization. Many of those who responded to UNESCO focused not on the rights of individuals but on the importance of society and the relationships between individuals within societies. The drafting committee itself included people such as Eleanor Roosevelt, whose thinking was firmly situated within an Anglo-American tradition, but also figures such as Charles Malik, Carlos Romulo and René Cassin, whose focus was much more on individuals within society, and on these individuals' duties as well as their rights. The result, as Samuel Moyn has emphasized, was that the UDHR was 'a profoundly communitarian document – precisely a moral repudiation of dangerous individualism, albeit one equally intended to steer equally clear of communism'.[36]

For the philosopher Jacques Maritain, who played a key role in linking the natural law tradition and a language of human rights in the early 1940s and

---

[32] 'Summary of the Territorial Conference of the Tanganyika African Association held at Dar es Salaam on the 6th–10th July, 1954', National Archives UK, CO 822/859, 1.
[33] Lohrmann, *Voices from Tanganyika*, 63.
[34] Ibid.
[35] Hunter, *Political Thought and the Public Sphere in Tanzania*, 153.
[36] Samuel Moyn, 'Personalism, Community and the Origins of Human Rights', in Stefan-Ludwig Hoffmann (ed.), *Human Rights in the Twentieth Century* (Cambridge: Cambridge University Press, 2011), 85–106, at 105.

went on to play an important role in the creation of the UDHR, man was by nature a 'political animal', inclined to form political society. For Maritain '[t]he aim of political society, as of all human society, implies a certain work to be done in common'. And this aim was 'the good human life of the multitude, the betterment of the conditions of human life itself, the internal improvement and the progress – material, of course, but also and principally moral and spiritual – thanks to which man's attributes are to be realized and made manifest in history'.[37]

The right to participate in government, and the injunction in the Declaration that the 'will of the people shall be the basis of the authority of government', was developed in this context. Creating new states was not an end in itself but an essential step in order to enable human flourishing. Considering this element of mid-twentieth-century thinking reminds us of the positive case for sovereignty, not simply as the removal of illegitimate colonial power but as an argument that only by acquiring the right to choose their own government would it be possible for people to embark on building a better future. It was this transformative potential which made sovereignty so attractive, and which explains why so many people at the time were so invested in it.

This point may seem obvious, but it bears repeating in the light of the disappointments that followed independence in Africa, and the sense that this independence was compromised in practice by the persistent ability of more powerful states, international institutions and corporations to exert their will on weaker states. Despite these later disappointments, independence at the time was not considered as simply the result of a juridical transaction which saw Western forms of political order imposed on non-Western societies. Sovereignty was imagined not simply as a transfer of power from one set of elites to another, but as constituting an exciting moment of possibility, one in which the citizens as well as the leaders of new states were invested.

When we explore the political language of the time in new African states, we are reminded of the nexus of positive terms associated with independent statehood – independence, self-government, sovereignty.[38] For the Kenyan nationalist Tom Mboya, it was the patriarchal metaphor of independence as being able to shut the door on one's own house which resonated. For others, it was the potential which independence offered to make choices and to build a

---

[37] Jacques Maritain, *The Rights of Man and Natural Law* (London: The Centenary Press, 1944), 26.
[38] Martti Koskenniemi, 'Conclusion: Vocabularies of Sovereignty – Powers of a Paradox', in Hent Kalmo and Quentin Skinner (eds.), *Sovereignty in Fragments: The Past, Present and Future of a Contested Concept* (Cambridge: Cambridge University Press, 2010), 222–42, at 236.

new society. As Martti Koskenniemi has written, this is the realm of the 'bright side to sovereignty that describes the character of collective life as a *project* – a set of institutions or practices in which the forms of collective life are constantly imagined, debated, criticized and reformed, over and again'.[39]

Independence was thus not an end in itself; it meant the ability to create a new and better society. For the Ghanaian nationalist leader Kwame Nkrumah, writing in 1947, '[t]he peoples of the colonies know precisely what they want. They wish to be free and independent, to be able to feel themselves on an equal footing with all other peoples and to work out their own destiny without outside interference and to be unrestricted to attain an advancement that will put them on a par with other technically advanced nations of the world'.[40]

Independence mattered to contemporaries because it represented a chance to do something different. For R. Kaminyoge Mwanjisi, Publicity Secretary of Tanganyika's nationalist party TANU, in a speech delivered on a visit to Kilwa in southern Tanganyika in 1958, '[t]he freedom which we demand is not simply that of escaping the shame of being ruled'. Independence meant the ability to do practical things which would make life better for the citizens of the new state. 'The task of getting water in Tanganyika is not the task of the British Government, they are not hurt by it', he said. To solve this problem required an independent Government which 'will take steps to put the problems of the citizens first'. The reason that it would take these steps was that it would be held accountable by its citizens in a way that a colonial government would not, for, he continued, '[t]he people will say to their government: "we have paid our taxes, you must remove our problems"'.[41]

8.3 SOVEREIGNTY AND THE POST-COLONIAL STATE

If the leaders of new African states understood independence as the basis from which to undertake new collective projects, their challenge after independence was to carry their citizens with them. This is the domain in which we find early post-colonial nation-builders arguing back against those who understood independent statehood in negative terms, as meaning the absence not only of the colonial state but of any state power at all. We hear these arguments at one remove in an article published in the journal *Africa* in

---

[39] Koskenniemi, 'Conclusion', 241.
[40] Ahlman, *Living with Nkrumahism*, 49.
[41] Letter from R. Kaminyoge Mwanjisi, 'Shida ya Maji Kilwa', *Mwafrika*, 19 December 1959, 3.

1965, which reproduced a letter sent to a colonial official in 1961 by Gicha Mbee, a resident of Mbugwe in rural northeastern Tanzania.[42]

In this letter, Mbee describes the discussions which had followed independence in Mbugwe. The older men, he recounts, imagined independence to mean an end to what they saw as the constraints on their lives which colonial rule imposed. At public meetings, they questioned why those who had held power in pre-colonial times had not been restored to their positions, why licences were still needed to hunt game, and why the end of colonial rule had not meant an end to taxation. The problem, Mbee wrote, was that 'everyone understands Freedom to mean that we shall rule ourselves – this has been thoroughly explained – but the elders and the youths interpret self-rule in different ways, and this has caused misunderstanding and quarrelling'.[43] The response of the younger men was 'to explain the meaning of Freedom under modern conditions', that is, freedom within the political society.[44]

In Ghana, where the nationalist leader and first President Kwame Nkrumah had long argued that self-government would only ever be a first step in a more far-reaching project of transformation, Jeffrey Ahlman has recently argued that independence in 1957 provided an opportunity for an argument 'over the social contract of self-rule'. Nkrumah's party, the Convention People's Party, demanded that citizens commit 'both to the collective struggle against colonialism and to the Nkrumahist nation-building project' and in return would 'come to enjoy the social and material benefits national reconstruction had to offer', benefits ranging from education to full employment.[45]

In many cases, it was in arguments over taxation and the raising of revenue that social contracts were renegotiated. The expectation of an end to taxes after independence was heard across much of the continent. In response, governing parties and local governments had to make a positive case for taxation and frame the payment of taxes as a duty of citizenship, rather than an illegitimate demand made by the state.[46]

The rhetoric by which post-colonial state-builders sought to meet these challenges seemed to embrace a vision of the state on the Westphalian model, in which sovereignty entailed the right to reject external interference. They were now able to close the door on their own house and were assertive of their right to do so. New parliaments quickly turned to debating who could and

---

[42] Gicha Mbee, 'Letter from Mbugwe, Tanganyika', *Africa* 35 (1965), 198–208, at 199.
[43] Ibid.
[44] Ibid.
[45] Ahlman, *Living with Nkrumahism*, 88–9.
[46] Nugent, 'States and Social Contracts'; Hunter, *Political Thought and the Public Sphere in Tanzania*, ch. 7.

could not be a citizen of the newly independent states, often setting requirements that went beyond simple place of birth to encompass more far-reaching commitments to newly independent states.[47] While the leaders of the 1950s had criticized the artificiality and unworkability of the states which had emerged from the colonial partition of Africa and called for new kinds of federations, post-colonial states were in practice often reluctant to relinquish aspects of their newly won sovereignty to supranational bodies. When the international human rights organizations that had been allies before independence moved to criticize new laws which endangered the human rights of the citizens of post-colonial states, they were swiftly told that democratically elected governments had the right to introduce preventive detention and similar measures if they judged it essential for the security of their states.[48]

Yet if we look more closely, we can see that the reason that post-colonial African states were so anxious to advocate this conception of sovereignty was precisely because they knew that the picture was more complicated than a map of sovereign states would suggest. In their speeches at the United Nations, for example, we can see that they were able to believe simultaneously in the right of states to reject external interference and in the existence of rights owed to all by nature of their humanity and membership of a universal human society which gave them the right to criticize other states' actions within their own borders. The United Nations, and the solidarity provided by the Afro-Asian bloc of newly independent states, provided a forum in which the leaders of new states actively sought to defend the rights of those living, for example, under Portuguese rule in Africa or in Apartheid South Africa.[49]

If we are to understand where critical potential lay in the post-colonial state, one way of doing so is considering the ways in which appealing to a moral and political order beyond the state could provide a resource to the citizens of post-colonial states, just as it had to the subjects of colonial states. To explore this theme in more detail, I look first at the ways in which international languages of rights which had been so powerful for anti-colonial activists, particularly in those parts of Africa which had been Trusteeship Territories of the United Nations, could be redeployed by those who sought to challenge repressive rule in the post-colony. Second, I consider the ways in which correspondents to the Swahili-language newspaper *Baraza*, published in Nairobi but read across

---

[47] Ronald Aminzade, *Race, Nation, and Citizenship in Postcolonial Africa: The Case of Tanzania* (Cambridge: Cambridge University Press, 2013).
[48] Meredith Terretta, 'From Below and to the Left? Human Rights and Liberation Politics in Africa's Postcolonial Age', *Journal of World History* 24 (2013), 389–416.
[49] Ibid.

East Africa, appealed both to older regional forms of governance and to individual connections across the region against independent governments whose concern with building nation-states challenged older flows of people and goods.

8.4 NATION-STATES AND UNIVERSAL RIGHTS AFTER INDEPENDENCE

After independence, new post-colonial states in Africa sought to claim for themselves the ability to determine what rights their citizens could have. As Meredith Terretta has recently shown, when, in 1965, Roger Baldwin of the International League of the Rights of Man tried to persuade the Tanzanian government to rethink its use of preventive detention laws, the Tanzanian response was to insist that while such laws had clearly been illegitimate when enacted by a colonial government, they were of a different nature when enacted by a post-colonial government which was itself an expression of the will of the people.[50]

But although post-colonial states sought to contain their citizens within their borders, those individuals continued to reach outside the state, often using a language of rights. In Cameroon, the opposition activist Dr Marcel Bebey-Eyidi continued from prison his long-standing correspondence with Roger Baldwin. He lamented the fact that, because Cameroon was now no longer a Trusteeship Territory but an independent state, it was impossible for the United Nations to act 'due to the principle of "non-interference"', even as '[t]he rights of man are completely violated in our country'.[51] And in Tanzania, where opposition became increasingly difficult in the course of the 1960s and 1970s, some of those who found themselves in detention appealed to new bodies like Amnesty International which increasingly sought to support individuals against their governments. The result was growing criticism of Julius Nyerere's use of preventive detention in Amnesty International reports over the course of the 1970s.[52]

Anti-colonial activists had challenged colonial rule by reaching beyond the barriers which colonial governments sought to erect and appealing to a set of rights including, but not limited to, the right to choose one's own government,

---

[50] Ibid., 402.
[51] Ibid., 414.
[52] James Brennan, 'Julius Rex: Nyerere through the Eyes of His Critics, 1953–2013', *Journal of Eastern African Studies* 8 (2014), 459–77, at 476 n. 89.

owed to all by virtue of their humanity. The same imaginative potential was open to citizens of post-colonial states too, and in this way the international continued to shape political imaginaries after independence. While African post-colonial states often closed down potential avenues for opposition, reaching outside the state could provide one way of attempting to challenge the actions of those states. But it also provided a way of challenging the claim that sovereignty meant that powers should lie exclusively at the level of the nation-state, and it is to this question that we now turn.

8.5 NATION-STATES AND REGIONAL ORDERS

Comparing maps of late colonial and post-colonial Africa suggests a picture marked by continuity of colonial borders. But what these maps do not show are layers of governance and imagined governance which cut across those borders. Both the French and the British empires in Africa had often in practice been governed regionally rather than straightforwardly as territorial states, so that in addition to imperial legal and political structures, there were also regional structures of government and law. In the case of East Africa, although British attempts in the 1920s to create an East African Federation had failed, more modest efforts to centralize the delivery of key services were more successful. By the time of independence, significant parts of government activity were administered at the East African, rather than the territorial, level, through the East African High Commission which was established in 1948. It is striking how many areas of life came under the High Commission's auspices, ranging from the economic dimensions of currency and tariffs to transport through East African Railways and Airways to cultural institutions such as the East African Literature Bureau.

As Tanganyika's independence approached in 1961, the High Commission became the East African Common Services Organization, establishing the principle that services would continue to be developed at the regional level after independence. But nationalist leaders in East Africa were open to the possibility of something more far-reaching. While colonial projects for an East African federation had been bitterly opposed by African politicians, in the early 1960s East African leaders followed post-colonial leaders elsewhere in the world in espousing a willingness to sacrifice their newly won sovereignty in the cause of unity. In Tanganyika, Julius Nyerere even offered to postpone Tanganyika's independence so that it would coincide with independence for Kenya and Uganda, allowing them immediately to federate. This he would do, he said in a speech, 'rather than take the risk of perpetuating the balkanisation of East Africa'.⁵³ In June 1963, the leaders of Tanganyika, Kenya and Uganda committed themselves to federation. But the optimism of June 1963 quickly faded and political federation proved impossible to achieve.⁵⁴ The East African Community which was finally established in 1967 has generally been seen as a project of limited scope and without great public support, lamented by few when it finally collapsed in 1977.⁵⁵ Projects of regional federation therefore seem to have had little traction in national contexts.

But if we look beyond the high politics of federation, a different story can begin to be told. A long-standing history of movement around the region and the existence of English and Swahili as lingua francas meant that newspapers like the Swahili-language *Baraza*, published in Nairobi from 1939 but read across East Africa and with contributions to its letters pages from across the region, constituted a space for reflection and comment on the downsides as well as the advantages of nation-state building projects and regional integration. The voices we hear in *Baraza* are those of a cosmopolitan elite, committed to greater unity. Their arguments for closer integration were often pragmatic. Those doing business across borders, for example, complained about the difficulties caused by having different currencies. Yet there were also more positive arguments for regional unity. The editorials in *Baraza* consistently argued for the East African Community to be a first step towards a closer political union. This argument was, for example, made in the editorial in December 1967 which marked the establishment of the East African Community, and it was sustained through a difficult period in 1971 and 1972 when Idi Amin's seizure of power in Uganda, opposed by Julius Nyerere of Tanzania, saw the Community effectively cease to function.⁵⁶

As tensions eased in 1972, a powerful *Baraza* editorial called for greater regional unity as an essential final step in completing the process of decolonization. The editorial repeated calls on East Africa's leaders to go beyond economic unity and establish a full political union. While the East African Community has often been seen, both at the time and since, as a technocratic project, distant from popular concerns, *Baraza* claimed to be

---

⁵³ Ali A. Mazrui, 'Tanzania versus East Africa', *Journal of Commonwealth Political Studies* 3 (1965), 209–25, at 210.
⁵⁴ Chris Vaughan, 'The Politics of Regionalism and Federation in East Africa, 1958–1964', *Historical Journal* 62 (2019), 519–40.
⁵⁵ Arthur Hazlewood, *Economic Integration: The East African Experience* (London: Heinemann, 1975); Christian P. Potholm and Richard A. Fredland, *Integration and Disintegration in East Africa* (Washington DC: University Press of America, 1980).
⁵⁶ Editorial, 'Uzazi wa Ujamaa Mpya', *Baraza*, 30 November 1967, 4.

speaking for ordinary people who, the newspaper argued, were the ones who suffered from the artificial barriers placed in their way by national borders, separate currencies and restrictions on moving to work or do business in neighbouring countries.[57]

Political leaders, *Baraza* argued, had once rejected national borders as artificial creations, imposed by colonial states without consulting the people. Now these same leaders were themselves imposing barriers between peoples. Echoing didactic texts used in schools in the region, *Baraza* recalled a historical past in which there was no distinction between Kenyans, Tanzanians and Ugandans.[58] The people of East Africa had mixed freely, on a basis of equality, and would do so again once the barriers put in their way by political leaders had been removed. For the editor of *Baraza*, it was only through creating a united East Africa that full independence would be achieved.

8.6 CONCLUSION

This chapter is about the history of political thought in the African present. In what way, then, might situating the mid-twentieth-century history of state-making in an international context contain critical potential for the present and the future? What can the history of political thought offer to our contemporary dilemmas?

For much of the last fifty years, a dominant popular and scholarly view of African independence has understood it as something conferred from outside, by legal transfer of power. In a reading where decolonization is understood simply as an imposition from outside, it is not only hard to see where change came from in the past, it is also hard to see where change might come from in the future. Yet a view of the post-colonial state in Africa as an imported form, imposed from outside, risks setting up a dichotomy between two extremes.

On the one hand, there is the tendency which we see in much political science writing about contemporary Africa, to focus on explaining and understanding the 'weakness' of states, within a discourse that sets up a normative ideal of what a state should be and finds African states wanting. This lends itself to a reading of the past fifty years in which the future course of Africa's new states was set at independence, taking little account of the change that has happened since independence, and in which future change is hard to envisage. At the other extreme, this same reading of the past can lend itself to an

---

[57] Editorial, 'Twadai shirikisho leo!', *Baraza*, 1 June 1972, 4.
[58] See, e.g., W.J. Bentley, *Civics for Uganda* (Kampala: Longmans of Uganda, 1966), 61.

analysis in which change, if it is to come, must come from a radical break from the state forms that were established at independence and the creation of something completely new, though quite what this might look like is seldom spelled out.

In contrast, I have argued here that the state was not simply imposed from outside in mid-twentieth-century Africa. It was reflected on and argued about by people (and not only political leaders) who were consciously making their own history in local and indeed regional contexts. For many contemporaries, the establishment of independent states was not simply an external imposition, it was also an active appropriation. The international was part of the process of state-making; it was in dialogue with conceptions of international society that the state was created. This helps explain the contingent nature of the state and the form it often took in mid-twentieth-century Africa.

In this way, the history of the political thought of decolonization offers an important perspective on the foundation of the modern state in Africa in which the international is an intrinsic part of the story rather than separate from it. We have seen that in the early post-colonial period, the positive argument for creating new political communities not as an end in itself but as an essential precondition for human flourishing was the basis for ambitious projects undertaken by new states to improve the lives of their citizens. Nearly sixty years on from independence, there is now a long history of states seeking to negotiate an effective social contract with their citizens, characterized by moments of success as well as moments of failure.[59]

But by taking seriously the way in which membership of a state coexisted with membership of an international society in the colonial and well as the post-colonial period, our attention is also drawn to an important intellectual resource for citizens trying to create change from below after independence. If we see the history of decolonization as in part a product of individuals reaching out beyond the boundaries within which colonial states sought to enclose them, to claim rights owing to them by virtue of their humanity, we can better see where change has come from in the past, and where it might come from again.

The rights that people were understood to have by virtue of their humanity, rights which states could not simply take away, continued to serve as a potential means of challenging the power of new post-colonial states, as they had served as a resource to challenge colonial states. In this way, where the ability to effect change in their capacity as citizens of post-colonial states was

---

[59] Nugent, 'States and Social Contracts'.

limited, then appealing beyond the state could be invoked as a strategy. At the same time, a sense of being part of a human community which transcended nation-states provided the basis for an argument to alter political structures to make connections across nation-states possible. While a great deal of work has focused on the failure of federations as political projects in Africa (as elsewhere), visions of political communities which transcended the nation-state continued to play an important role in the political imaginary. Cosmopolitan conceptions of a common humanity provided a language in which to challenge the attempts of nation-states to insist on hard borders and instead seek to re-weight the balance between individual states and supranational communities, as for example in arguing for more powers at the East African level rather than the level of the nation-state.

By putting the African state and international society into the same analytical frame in the period around independence, we can therefore see the state as a contingent form, subject to change over time through human thought and action. And if we understand states to have been made in dialogue, we can better understand how they have changed in the past, and how they might change again.

Institutions and Persons

9

The [In]Hospitable World

JULIA MCCLURE

9.1 INTRODUCTION

From Late Antiquity the customs and institutions of hospitality facilitated the development of global connectivity. The institutional landscape of premodern Eurasia coalesced around customs of hospitality. Wayfarers could expect to receive food and lodgings in the monasteries, hospitals, and *fondacos* that laced the pilgrimage and trade routes that criss-crossed Eurasia and interwove different world religions.[1] These institutions of hospitality provided sustenance for strangers in need. These strangers could be foreign travellers, merchants or pilgrims, or they could be the poor, who had become strangers in their own society through their poverty and were forced to look for support beyond family networks. However, while nominally providing simply for those in need, hospitality in fact provides a framework for the mediation of a variety of exchanges and, most importantly, facilitates the construction and legitimation of power asymmetries. As Derrida observed, hospitality is always conditional,[2] and, as this chapter will show, this conditionality can be manipulated to institutionalise power asymmetries. Hospitality is a framework for movement *between*: between different places, between having the basic necessities or not, and between orders of power. As such it facilitated global movement across Eurasia from Late Antiquity, and played an important role in the expansion and transformation of global interactions that took place from the sixteenth century with the opening of the transatlantic, and later transpacific, worlds. Performances of hospitality formed part of early encounter

---

[1] Olivia Constable, *Housing the Stranger in the Mediterranean World: Lodging, Trade, and Travel in Late Antiquity and the Middle Ages* (Cambridge: Cambridge University Press, 2009).
[2] Jacques Derrida and Anne Dufourmantelle, *Of Hospitality*, trans. Rachel Bowlby (Stanford: Stanford University Press, 2000), 55. Derrida explains that hospitality is exercised through 'filtering, choosing, and thus by excluding and doing violence'.

narratives, from Columbus's meeting with the Taíno Americas to Captain Cook's encounter with the Polynesians in the Pacific. These stories of hospitality oiling the cogs of pre-modern connectivity are haunted by the parallel stories of betrayal and the making of the colonial world, the lingering indigestion of this convivial sociality.

In the Western tradition the concept of hospitality (*hospitium*) is derived from *hospes* (host, guest or stranger), which comes from the Latin root *hostis* (stranger or enemy). Within the exchange of hospitality mastery and communication clash, and it is not always clear which party will benefit and which will be wounded. The act of hospitality seemingly generously provides for the stranger, but that stranger may be both guest and enemy. The act of hospitality may be ethical, but it is also political. Practices of hospitality facilitate the construction of power asymmetries not only through the negotiation of the stranger as both guest and enemy, but through the manipulation of the ontological limitations of the stranger, the question of who 'the stranger' can be.

Hospitality, welcoming and providing for the stranger, is part of the deep history of international relations, and it also helps explain why so many international relations are asymmetrical. Hospitality is a not only a framework for movement between places and needs but between power formations. Like the discourse of protection recently studied by Lauren Benton and Adam Clulow, hospitality 'represented a basic currency of interpolity relations', whose 'legal status is difficult to pin down'.[3] Derrida explained that the 'collusion between the violence of power or the force of law (*Gewalt*) on the one side, and hospitality on the other, seems to depend, in an absolutely radical way, on hospitality being inscribed in the form of a right',[4] yet the power of hospitality is derived from its multidimensionality, its ability to bridge the gaps between cultural practices and intersecting rights of varying legal status. This fluidity is open to manipulation. As Derrida observed, the conditionality of hospitality means that the guest is always hostage, but the host can also become hostage, such that the laws of hospitality 'make everyone into everyone else's hostage'.[5] Both guests and hosts, then, can be hostages; but hospitality as a power praxis goes beyond this. Hospitality provides a starting point for the transformation of the coordinates of 'host' and 'guest', as well as between guest and enemy. When European colonialists travelled to distant shores they arrived as guests operating within the normative framework of

---

[3] Lauren Benton and Adam Clulow, 'Empires and Protection: Making Interpolity Law in the Early Modern World', *Journal of Global History* 12 (2017), 74–92, at 74–5.
[4] Derrida, *Of Hospitality*, 55.
[5] Ibid., 125.

hospitality, but they transformed the landscape of hospitality such that they became hosts. As colonialism developed, the institutions of hospitality (from hospitals to monasteries) were transplanted to the Americas where the Amerindians were received as guests (strangers/enemies) much like the poor in Europe.

The early conquistadores conceptualised themselves as guests in the New World, but as colonialism unfolded the poles of the host–guest relationship switched and Amerindians became, not rich hosts inviting the conquistadores to the banquet table of the Americas, but a people struck by poverty and in need of hospitality. Bartolomé de Las Casas and other so-called defenders of the Indians often referred to the Amerindians as 'poor and wretched', making the comparison between the Amerindians and the poor in Europe. Referring to the Amerindians as *'personas miserables'* was not simply a rhetorical description of unfortunate people but had been developed in Canon Law during the Middle Ages, as *personae miserabilis*, to denote a juridical condition whereby the poor could legally claim certain protection, a protection which was in place of self-governance. This construction of the Amerindians as poor and needing care began to take shape legally. In 1539 Francisco de Vitoria suggested that the Amerindians might need special legal protection as they were unable to govern themselves, and Las Casas asserted that they should have the legal protections of the *miserables* in Europe.[6] The definitive contribution to this construction of the Amerindians as poor came in the writings of Juan de Solórzano Pereira (1575–1655), who drew upon the legal category of the poor in Europe, *personae miserabilis*, to re-situate the Amerindians in colonial society. As Susan Scafidi explains:

> reasoning from time-honoured principles of medieval law, [Solórzano] discovered that legal analogy would allow him to identify Native Americans with the poor, wretched members of European society. Analogy ossified into a set of rules and expectations, and Indians – elite and otherwise – became wards to be educated and protected by guardians under the special protection of the Spanish legal system.[7]

---

[6] Woodrow Borah, *Justice by Insurance: The General Indian Court of Colonial Mexico and the Legal Aides of the Half Real* (Berkeley: University of California Press, 1983), 81. Mónica Díaz observed the lasting legacy of this, noting that the way indigenous people were differentiated in the eighteenth century in terms of *'clase'* 'reflects the way society had been built upon criteria from centuries earlier, and it survived to keep the *pueblos de indios* in a lower place in the social ladder': Mónica Díaz, 'Legal Pluralism and the "India Pura" in New Spain: The School of Guadalupe and the Convent of the Company of Mary', in Santa Arias and Raúl Marrero-Fente (eds.), *Coloniality, Religion, and the Law in the Early Iberian World* (Nashville: Vanderbilt University Press, 2014), 221–40, at 231.

[7] Susan Scafidi, 'Old Law in the New World: Solórzano and the Analogical Construction of Legal Identity', *Florida Law Review* 55 (2003), 191–204, at 204.

Legal analogy constructed Amerindians as a vulnerable, incapable, and powerless people and placed them under the protection of the church and crown. This 'protection' and 'care' was increasingly channelled through the physical institutional sites of hospitality that had been developed to care for/govern the poor in Europe. The institutional sites of hospitality became deposits for Amerindian subjects and played a role in shaping the colonial society of the Spanish Empire.[8]

The sixteenth century was a threshold in the construction of inequality, both within Europe and globally. New visions of social order combined with hardening attitudes towards the poor led to the transformation of cultures and institutions of hospitality. Around the world Europeans began to build empires, establishing and institutionalising asymmetrical and appropriative relations with the peoples whom they encountered. Within Europe the poor were no longer honoured guests, but were increasingly seen as enemies. Policies and programmes of assistance were increasingly embedded in paternalistic discourses, social assistance was increasingly institutionalised, and these sites of social assistance increasingly became sites of control. In the Americas, the impact of the colonial invasion intensified across the sixteenth century and shook the socio-economic fabric of Amerindian society, increasing multiple forms of poverty as well as disrupting indigenous networks of social assistance. Amerindians were reconstructed as poor through socio-economic degradation and legal analogy. Those constructed as poor, in the Old World or the New, were to become strangers everywhere while the rich would be strangers nowhere.

Theories of hospitality have been integral to conceptions of ideal societies in the Western tradition.[9] The Ancient Greeks developed the concept and customs of hospitality, believing that providing for and not fearing the stranger constituted a civilised society and distinguished them from the barbarians.[10] This idea was continued by the Romans, and references to hospitality can be found across classical texts. Within the classical framework hospitality was not just a custom but also part of the Western legal tradition and the right to

---

[8] For more on the role of hospitals in Spanish imperialism, see Gabriela Ramos, 'Indian Hospitals and Government in the Colonial Andes', *Medical History* 57 (2013), 186–205.

[9] Hospitality is not a static universal but has been interpreted and deployed in different ways by different societies. Further, exchanges are always contextually contingent and often have multiple codings. See also Francesca Trivellato, Leor Halevi and Cátia Antunes (eds.), *Religion and Trade, Cross-Cultural Exchanges in World History 1000–1900* (Oxford: Oxford University Press, 2014).

[10] See Ladislaus J. Bolchazy, *Hospitality in Antiquity: Livy's Concept of Its Humanising Force* (Chicago: Ares Publishers, 1995). Bolchazy identifies seven categories of hospitality in the Roman world: avoidance or mistreatment of strangers, Apotropaic hospitality, Medea category of hospitality, Theoxenic hospitality, *ius hospitii* or *ius dei*, contractual hospitality, and altruistic hospitality.

hospitality, *ius hospitii*, became part of Roman law. During the Renaissance, humanists revived the idea of hospitality. This was not to be the universalist basis of an equal society, however, but rather a strategy of inequality. As Sanjay Subrahmanyam observes, we need to 'examine how notions of universalism and humanism emerge in various vocabularies, and yet how these terms do not in fact unite the early modern world, but instead lead to new or intensified forms of hierarchy, domination and separation'.[11] Hospitality proved a malleable material for the legitimation of power asymmetries. Not only did it mediate movements between enemies and guests, and guests and hosts, but as a cultural practice that was both legally and morally normative it both hardened into the physical spaces of institutions and provided the fluid medium for the movement between different worlds.

The history of hospitality in the sixteenth century is the history of the opening of worlds for some, and the closing of worlds for others. This chapter begins with an exploration of how the normative cultural practice of hospitality provided a framework for the Spanish encounter with the Tlaxcalans. It then surveys the divergence of the application of hospitality as a body of legal and moral norms. It highlights how the Spanish tried to justify their appropriation of resources in the New World by drawing upon hospitality as a legal resource, at the same time that elites restricted systems of hospitality for the poor in the Old World and eroded the legal and moral foundations of the poor as recipients of hospitality. It concludes with a reflection of how the Spanish transformed the coordinates of hospitality in the New World to become hosts extending institutions of hospitality to Amerindian guests, transposing the infrastructure of hospitality as a system of control as it had been developed in sixteenth-century Europe. The sixteenth century witnessed an inhospitable divergence, as Europeans extended claims to hospitality in the New World which were simultaneously being denied to those in need in the Old. It simultaneously experienced a convergence of power in the institutional sites of hospitality, namely hospitals, which were designed to assist and control those guests who were also enemies.

9.2 ENCOUNTERING THE INHOSPITABLE WORLD

When the Spanish conquistador Hernán Cortés arrived in the capital he described how the Aztec ruler Moctezuma greeted him with great ceremony.[12]

---

[11] Sanjay Subrahmanyam, 'Connected Histories: Notes towards a Reconfiguration of Early Modern Eurasia', *Modern Asian Studies* 31 (1997), 735–62, at 739.

[12] Cortés, Second Letter, in *Hernan Cortes: Letters from Mexico*, ed. and trans. Anthony Pagden (New Haven: Yale University Press, 1986), 47–159, at 84.

Moctezuma gave Cortés 'various treasures of gold and silver and featherwork, and as many as five or six thousand cotton garments, all very rich and woven and embroidered in various ways'.[13] According to Cortés, Moctezuma also gave him the gift of power to rule, bidding him to take his position upon 'a very rich throne'.[14] Moctezuma then assured Cortés that 'here you will be provided with all that you and your people require, and you shall receive no hurt, for you are in your own land and your own house'.[15] Not long after this Cortés's troops captured Moctezuma, executed an Amerindian who had reportedly killed some Spanish soldiers, and demanded to be shown where the gold mines were.[16] The available descriptions of the conquest of Mexico depict a scene of betrayed hospitality, with the imprisoned Moctezuma the archetypical wronged host. Gideon Baker uses the case of Cortés and Moctezuma to demonstrate that hosts are also vulnerable to conditions of unconditional hospitality, as in the case of Moctezuma 'no host has come closer to offering unconditional hospitality and never have the results of hospitality been more terrible, indeed genocidal, for a host community'.[17]

Cortés's account of the conquest of Mexico portrays a host betrayed, but in the events leading up to this he narrates a story of the conquistadores as guests betrayed. In his 'First Letter' Cortés reports that as he arrived with his troops on the shores of the Yucatan Peninsula 'certain Indians came to us in a canoe bringing some chickens and a little maize, which was barely enough for a single meal, and told us to take it and leave their land'.[18] Cortés subsequently engaged in battle and captured the city.[19] Cortés then reported that the chieftains brought gold ornaments 'which were thin and of little value'. He informed them that they would not leave and that the Indians 'must hold as their lords the greatest monarchs on earth and must serve them as their vassals'. He continued: 'having arranged this friendship, the captain informed them that the Spaniards who were with him had nothing to eat nor had they

---

[13] Ibid., 85.
[14] Cortés, Second Letter, in *Letters from Mexico*, 85. Anthony Pagden explained that for Las Casas, 'Moctezuma's "donation" to Cortés constituted a legitimate political charter': Anthony Pagden, *Spanish Imperialism and the Political Imagination: Studies in European and Spanish-American Social and Political Theory 1513–1830* (New Haven: Yale University Press, 1990), 32.
[15] Cortés, Second Letter, in *Letters from Mexico*, at 86.
[16] Ibid., 92–5. The Florentine Codex recounts a similar story: *Florentine Codex, Book 12, The Conquest of Mexico*, ed. Arthur J.O. Anderson and Charles E. Dibble (Santa Fe: School of American Research, 1975), 5, 44.
[17] Gideon Baker, 'The Spectre of Montezuma: Hospitality and Haunting', *Millennium: Journal of International Studies* 39 (2010), 23–42, at 25.
[18] Cortés, First Letter, in *Letters from Mexico*, 3–46, at 19.
[19] Ibid., 20.

brought any food from the ships and begged them therefore to bring us provisions for as long as we might remain in their land'.[20] Cortés continued to report his attacks on the Amerindians in relation to their poor hospitality or obstruction to the Spanish taking food. As J.H. Elliott explained, this first letter was a political document designed to persuade Charles to retrospectively sanction Cortés's actions.[21] Cortés was making the case for the legitimacy of the conquest as he described the violence. In addition to the Amerindians not responding to the *Requerimiento*, they were defying norms of hospitality by denying the Spanish enough food or the ability to land and find food.

Cortés wrote his second letter while preparing for the siege and re-conquest of Tenochtitlán in 1520. This letter was also a narration of events and a plea for authorisation. He continued to describe how the contours of hospitality defined his journey to the Aztec capital. As he arrived in the kingdom of Cempoal he wrote that he was 'very well received and accommodated by all the natives' who 'provided the provisions I needed for the journey'.[22] But as he moved on he crossed an 'uninhabitable' desert, where his 'people suffered from thirst and hunger'.[23] He reports the limited hospitality, writing that in Tascalteca they were received with fanfare and received food 'though not sufficient'.[24] Cortés framed the events leading up to their next battle with the Amerindians in terms of wronged hospitality again: 'during the three days I remained in that city they fed us worse each day, and the lords and principal persons of the city came only rarely to see and speak with me'.[25] For Cortés, this decline in hospitality was an indicator of deteriorating relations and a warning of conflict. Their Yucatan interpreter, Geronimo de Aguilar, advised that the Indians were going to kill them, and they instead took the Amerindians by surprise, imprisoning their leaders and setting buildings on fire.[26] This Spanish attack could have been interpreted as an ambush, but Cortés used the declining hospitality as contextualisation.

Cortés's account of the final events of the conquest of Moctezuma's Aztec empire may seem like a case of host betrayed but Cortés's narration of events contains more nuance than this. According to Cortés, when Moctezuma handed him the goods, and power (symbolised by the throne) of the Aztec empire he also reorientated the landscape of host and guest. Moctezuma

[20] Ibid.
[21] J.H. Elliott, 'Cortés, Valázquez and Charles V', in *Letters from Mexico*, xi–xxxvii, at xxii.
[22] Cortés, Second Letter, in *Letters from Mexico*, 55.
[23] Ibid.
[24] Ibid., 72.
[25] Ibid., 73.
[26] Ibid.

admits that they are guests like the Spanish: 'for a long time we have known from the writings of our ancestors that neither I, nor any of us who dwell in this land, are natives of it, but foreigners, who came from distant parts; and likewise we know that a chieftain, of whom we are all vassals, brought our people to this region'. Cortes's account of Moctezuma's admission that the Amerindians knew themselves to be guests narrates the start of the reorientation of the guest–host coordinates.

Within three years Cortés, approximately three hundred Castilians (most of whom had never engaged in warfare before), and 'a few thousand untrained and unpredictable allies' had taken over a population estimated to contain at least 50,000 adults and an empire estimated to have been about 125,000 square miles.[27] This extraordinary occurrence was, in part, facilitated by manipulations of hospitality, the norms of which also helped fashion the veneer of legitimacy.

In the years after the conquest of the Caribbean and Mexico, the Spanish developed an extractive regime of resources and labour, organised through the *encomienda* and *mita* systems. Many of the New World's natural resources were appropriated into the stream of commerce flowing across the Atlantic. Cortés's raid on Moctezuma's treasure chest paled in comparison. In the case of silver, it is estimated that between 1503 and 1660 some 250,000 tons of New World silver poured into the Andalusian city of Seville,[28] where the *Casa de Contratación* was established to manage this unprecedented extraction of resources. As Europeans told themselves a story of how this was legitimate, they once again tapped the benevolent resource of hospitality.

9.3 A LEGAL AND MORAL DIVERGENCE

Ordering the New World

Around sixteen years after Cortés conquered and plundered the Aztec capital, and as commodities and precious metals flowed through Spain, the Dominican scholar and so-called founder of international law Francisco de Vitoria set about theorising the legitimacy of this appropriation in his lecture *De Indis*, delivered in 1539. Here, Vitoria drew upon classical understandings of hospitality as a moral norm and created the right to hospitality

---

[27] See Hugh Thomas, *Conquest: Montezuma, Cortés, and the Fall of Old Mexico* (New York: Simon & Schuster, 1993).
[28] Patrick O'Flanagan, *Port Cities of Atlantic Iberia, c. 1500–1900* (Oxford: Routledge, 2008), 52.

(*ius hospitii*) to justify the colonial appropriation of the Spanish empire.[29] Vitoria made an important contribution to the Western legal tradition, and his work contributed to the way hospitality was theorised within the natural law tradition, a position which persisted until the Enlightenment.[30] As Anthony Pagden has also observed, he transformed hospitality from an ancient Greek custom to a right under the law of nations (*ius gentium*).[31] Vitoria's deployment of the right to hospitality came under the title of 'natural partnership and communication' (*ius communicandi*) and included the right to travel and dwell in the Americas, the right to common property (such as 'running water and the open sea, rivers, and ports', and other natural resources such as gold or pearls), and the right to become citizens.[32] Vitoria explained that these rights, and especially the rights of trading and rest, were available to everyone according to *ius gentium*, the law of nations.[33]

Vitoria opened the Americas to claims of hospitality which went beyond the things of necessity, arguing that resources that were available before the division of private property (*divisio rerum*) could be claimed in the Americas according to the *ius gentium*. Vitoria developed this right to hospitality (*ius hospitii*), and also the right to trade (*ius negotiandi*), as 'soft' rights which facilitated colonial appropriation without reference to a right of possession. This contributed to the framework of legitimation for the opening of the veins of Latin America.[34] Martti Koskenniemi has assessed Vitoria's use of *ius negotiandi*, arguing that this 'begins to reveal an international system of commerce, based upon the free use of their dominium by private merchants and bankers, which princes were not entitled to impede'.[35] Similarly, Porras observed that Vitoria's deployment of *ius negotiandi* and *ius hospitii* (underpinned by his conception of *ius gentium*) facilitated the transformation of the natural environment into natural resources, into commodities, that could be appropriated and placed into the stream of commerce. For Porras this explains 'the structural link between international law's long standing commitment to

---

[29] See Vitoria, 'On the American Indians', q. 3 art. 1, in *Vitoria: Political Writings*, ed. Anthony Pagden and Jeremy Lawrance (Cambridge: Cambridge University Press, 1991), 278–84.
[30] See Gideon Baker, 'Right of Entry or Right of Refusal', in Gideon Baker (ed.), *Hospitality in World Politics* (Basingstoke: Palgrave, 2013), 41–68, at 42.
[31] Anthony Pagden, 'Human Rights, Natural Rights, and Europe's Imperial Legacy', *Political Theory* 31 (2003), 171–99.
[32] See Vitoria, 'On the American Indians', 278–84.
[33] Ibid., 281.
[34] The story of this appropriation is laid out in Eduardo Galeano, *Las Venas Abiertas de América Latina* (Montevideo: Siglo, 1971).
[35] Martti Koskenniemi, 'Empire and International Law: The Real Spanish Contribution', *University of Toronto Law Journal* 61 (2011), 1–36, at 26–7.

commerce and its inability to act decisively on behalf of the environment'.³⁶ Vitoria's use of *ius negotiandi* and *ius hospitii* as legitimations for the appropriation of natural resources helped pave the way for the environmental exploitations which still structure inequalities in Latin America today.

Vitoria drew upon the classical world to model projections of the ideal global order. To explain why it was that the Amerindians had to welcome the Spanish according to the customs of hospitality, Vitoria cited Virgil's verses:

> What men, what monsters, what inhuman race,
> What laws, what barbarous customs of the place,
> Shut up a desert shore to drowning men,
> And drive us to the cruel seas again!
> (Aeneid I. 539–40, Dryden's translation)³⁷

Vitoria also drew upon the Christocentric principle of hospitality. He reminded his audience that 'it is a law of nature to welcome strangers, this judgement is to be decreed amongst all men', and cited the gospel of Matthew where Christ warned 'I was a stranger and ye took me not in' (Matt. 25:43).³⁸ This use of the figure of the stranger to whom hospitality must be granted is strategic. Vitoria had discredited both the idea that the Emperor could be master of the whole world,³⁹ and the idea that the pope is monarch of the whole world,⁴⁰ but he salvaged a universalist vision of the world built upon the projection of a human community unified by Christianity. He cited St Augustine who wrote 'when one says Love thy neighbour, it is clear that every man is your neighbour' (*De doctrina Christiana* I.30.32), explaining that 'the Spaniards are the barbarians' neighbours' and 'the barbarians are obliged to love their neighbours as themselves'.⁴¹

It is no surprise that Vitoria should draw upon the writings of St Augustine to make this rhetorical move. Vitoria was a Dominican. Western monasticism had been based upon the Rule of St Augustine (c. 400 CE), but it was adopted by the mendicant Dominican Order when it was established in 1216. The Augustinian Rule advocated a common life, where members of the community lived without individual property and held things in common. The Dominicans were one of the mendicant orders that revolutionised the institutional landscape in the thirteenth century by transcending the institutional

---

³⁶ Ileana Porras, 'Appropriating Nature', 641.
³⁷ Vitoria, 'On the American Indians', 278.
³⁸ Ibid., 279.
³⁹ Ibid., 252–8.
⁴⁰ Ibid., 258–64.
⁴¹ Ibid., 279.

site of the monastery and instead realising their institutional identity as they moved through civic spaces begging for alms, valorising a culture of need.[42] Their brothers with whom they shared things in common were not those with whom they shared a monastic space but the people they met on the street who gave them alms.

It is worth remembering that this Augustinian model of hospitality was not informed by an idealised equality but by an idealised hierarchy. The Augustinian Rule stipulated that 'food and clothing shall be distributed to each of you by your superior, not equally to all, for all do not enjoy equal health, but rather to each one's need'.[43] Here we see that in this idealised community people should have access to things of necessity but that there should be a hierarchy of distribution of resources according to needs decided by the superior. This hierarchy also distinguished between the voluntarily poor and the real poor, explaining that 'they who owned nothing should not look for those things in the monastery that they were unable to have in the world'. It advocates a limited hospitality stipulating that these poor should receive the things of necessity, but they 'should not consider themselves fortunate because they have found the kind of food and clothing that they were unable to find in the world'.[44] They should have nothing in excess of what they need. Instead it prescribed moderation and self-denial, to 'subdue the flesh'.[45] When Vitoria extended the idea of hospitality to the Americas, this was based upon the notion of a universal community, but this was not intrinsically egalitarian but highly differentiated.

Vitoria referred to the Amerindians throughout *De Indis* as 'the barbarians'. Engaging with his interlocutors who were critical of the faculties of the Amerindians, Vitoria considered their weaknesses, their lack of Christianity, their lack of rationality, and other foibles, but he concluded that they had the right to own their own property. Vitoria circumvented this unfortunate (for the Spanish Crown) conclusion by invoking the universal custom of hospitality, a way to access resources without claiming a property right. This hospitality was conceptualised as universal, but it created criterion for differentiation, for inclusion and exclusion. The Ancient Greeks had developed one of the earliest notions of hospitality, of welcoming the stranger, but they had also

---

[42] The most radical of these mendicant Orders were the Franciscans, who formed a new religious life as they formulated a new rule Regula Vitae, which demanded the renunciation of common and individual property.
[43] Rule of St Augustine, in *Explanation of the Rule of St Augustine* (Fall Creek: Revelation Insight Publishing Co., 2008), 24.
[44] Ibid.
[45] Ibid., 27.

used this as a mechanism for distinguishing themselves from primitive societies which feared strangers, a strategy which continued to define the Roman Empire.[46] As Vitoria drew upon this classical conception of hospitality, he also tapped into its ancient politics, using it as a mechanism to differentiate and exclude. Vitoria stated that 'to refuse to welcome strangers and foreigners is inherently evil'.[47] Antony Anghie has charted Vitoria's contribution to the history of international law, arguing that Vitoria was 'concerned not so much with the problem of order among sovereign states but the problem of order among societies belonging to two different cultural systems'.[48] Anghie contends that Vitoria resolved this 'by focusing on the cultural practices of each society and assessing them in terms of the universal law of *ius gentium*'.[49] We see here that it was hospitality in particular that made the point of departure for colonial differentiation permissible for Vitoria.[50]

Vitoria's discussion of hospitality also had tangible negative implications for the indigenous population of sixteenth-century Mexico: he concluded that if the Spanish were denied these rights of hospitality, they may lawfully go to war. Furthermore, the Amerindians would become 'treacherous foes against whom all rights of war can be exercised, including plunder, enslavement, deposition of their former masters, and the institution of new ones'.[51] Vitoria added that under these circumstances 'the Spanish could have seized the lands and rule of the barbarians, so long as it was done without trickery or fraud and without inventing excuses to make war on them'.[52] Historically this last caveat might suggest that the original Spanish betrayal of the Amerindians prevented the Spanish from becoming legitimate rulers in the Americas, but this was not the conclusion drawn by his audience. In Vitoria we see that Amerindian obstruction or contravention of Spanish assertion of their claims to resources according to the right of hospitality could justify the reconstitution of the conquistadores from guests claiming hospitality to hosts administering hospitality to increasingly impoverished Amerindian guests.

Ordering the Old World

As the Spanish extended their right to hospitality in the Old World, based upon their needs as travellers, these rights were restricted for the poorest

---

[46] See Bolchazy, *Hospitality in Antiquity*.
[47] Vitoria, 'On the American Indians', 281.
[48] Antony Anghie, *Imperialism, Sovereignty and the Making of International Law* (Cambridge: Cambridge University Press, 2005), 28.
[49] Ibid.
[50] Vitoria, 'On the American Indians', 278.
[51] Ibid., 283.
[52] Ibid., 283–4.

people within Europe. Within the Christian tradition, poverty had been considered to be a sacred condition in the Middle Ages and the poor might expect to receive the things they needed by wandering around and begging. In the thirteenth century the mendicant orders had valorised poverty and the socio-religious culture of need and had institutionalised this way of living as a religious life. These mendicant orders fashioned themselves on the poverty of Christ and embodied the New Testament message that God was present in strangers in need (Matt. 25:43). However, in the sixteenth century attitudes towards the poor and ideas of how they should be provided for within an ideal society diversified. As the Spanish extended their right to hospitality in the Old World, based upon their needs as travellers, these rights were restricted for the poorest people within Europe. The first town to develop a new plan for society was the town of Ypres in 1525. A report of this revolution in poor relief can be found in *Forma subventionis pauperum*, published in 1531, which was compiled by multiple authors in defence of the scheme. Like *De Indis*, *Forma subventionis pauperum* drew upon classical ideas about hospitality to develop models of ideal societies, but with contrasting results. The *Forma* was a new model for an ideal society designed for 'the plentiful increase of good social order',[53] but for the town officials of Ypres this was to be realised by restricting hospitality for the poor. The *Forma* cited Seneca who said that 'only need compels people to beg',[54] and Plato, who 'judged all manner of beggars to be put out of his Republic'.[55]

The social policies outlined in *Forma subventionis pauperum*, including the restriction of the movements of the poor and their access to hospitality, were part of broader debates about the rights and freedoms of the poor that took place in sixteenth-century Europe. Treatises such as *Forma subventionis pauperum* were used to inform new repressive policies against the poor's ability to seek hospitality. In 1531 Charles V drew upon this text as the basis for a series of poor laws and prohibited begging throughout the empire.[56] Restrictions on the freedom of the poor to travel and to seek hospitality were opposed by the mendicant orders, who had built their existence on these freedoms. The criminalisation of poverty in Spain was opposed in particular by the Dominican Domingo de Soto, who published *Deliberacion en la causa de los pobres* in 1545 (simultaneously in Latin and Spanish) in response to a

---

[53] City of Ypres, *Forma Subventionis Pauperum* (1531), in Paul Spicker (ed.), *The Origins of Modern Welfare* (Bern: Peter Lang, 2010), 101–40, at 130.
[54] Ibid., 123.
[55] Ibid., 124.
[56] F.R. Salter, *Some Early Tracts on Poor Relief* (London: Methuen, 1926), 34, and a further poor law in 1540.

1540 poor law. De Soto reminded people that the poor had natural rights,[57] not only to the things of necessity (*ius necessitatis*) but also to travel (*ius periginandi*) and to seek hospitality (*ius hospitii*). For de Soto, this *ius hospitii* was not absolute or unlimited but contextually contingent. De Soto was clear that the poor should not only have bread but all the things they needed.[58] De Soto stipulated that the poor received the things they needed through alms (*limosnas*), but this did not fully locate power with the giver (or host), since he justified his position by citing St Gregory, who had explained that everyone was obliged to give to the poor according to their ability, and that it was also important to defend the poor.[59] De Soto also looked to classical texts, and invoked the Roman law right of foreigners to beg.[60] De Soto's *Deliberacion*, which drew upon a range of classical and theological sources, highlights the continuing complexity of conceptions of hospitality as a mixture of moral norms, religious obligations, and intersecting rights to travel and to access resources. The language of rights, of *ius hospitii*, did not resolve the ancient tensions within the concept of hospitality as an arbitration between the power of the host–guest or giver–receiver.

Significantly, the debates about hospitality (from the rights of the poor to travel and to seek alms to the ways they could access resources), which broke out in Europe in the sixteenth century, need to be placed within a global context. First, as noted by Annabel Brett, de Soto's investigation of the right to travel, part of his discussion on the rights of the poor, has international considerations that have been overlooked by the earlier commentators.[61] Further, Vitoria's discussion of hospitality in the New World was part of this broader sixteenth-century debate. Placing this sixteenth-century intellectual history in a more global context highlights the divergence in accepted practices and uses of hospitality that took place between the Old World and the New at this time. While the Spanish Crown favoured the expansion of hospitality in the New World, it also favoured its restriction in the Old.

The *Forma subventionis pauperum* wrote that 'the freedom to beg in public may be restrained by civil laws'.[62] The Scheme of Ypres's opposition to extending hospitality in the city was clear; it stated:

---

[57] Developing from both Roman and Canon law.
[58] Domingo de Soto, *Deliberacion en la causa de los pobres* (Madrid: Instituto de Estudios políticos, 1965), 13.
[59] Ibid.
[60] Andreas Blank, 'Domingo de Soto On Justice to the Poor', *Intellectual History Review* 25 (2015), 133–46, at 138.
[61] Annabel S. Brett, *Changes of State: Nature and the Limits of the City in Early Modern Natural Law* (Princeton: Princeton University Press, 2011), 17.
[62] *Forma Subventionis Pauperum*, 124.

these strong and lazy beggars everywhere were living at their pleasure without any labour, in sloth and idleness, like drones. They are a nuisance to many, eating other people's food, always wandering, always unstable, without the restraint or control from anyone, shameless, unpunished, running as they pleased ... by the emperor's command, sturdy beggars should be banished from the realm.[63]

While Vitoria emphasised that hospitality should be extended to strangers in the New World, the *Forma* opposed this for the Old. Ypres prescribed how the city's poor should be looked after, not those coming from elsewhere, and it opposed the free movement of the poor to beg for alms.[64] The *Forma* explained that:

> God approved nothing better than kindness towards our neighbour for he that loves his neighbour fulfils the law. We think then that pity should be stretched to all poor people on every side, buy yet in such manner that order is maintained. We prefer our own citizens, whose persons and manners we know, to strangers with whom we have no acquaintance.[65]

It justified this by explaining that in the situation of limited resources, the city had to prioritise its poor citizens. Ypres protects further against strangers staying, 'no house shall be let to strangers without the consent of the Senate'.[66] In addition to drawing upon classical sources, the *Forma* cited St Augustine, *On True Religion*, who wrote 'a man cannot justly help everyone he loves unless he helps those that are nearest unto him'.[67]

While *De Indis* had explained that the Spanish travelling to the New World had the right to stay, the *Forma* clearly restricted the rights of strangers to stay. The *Forma* accepted that 'strangers ought in no wise to be forgotten', stipulating that 'we give therefore to every poor stranger what he needs, and we are able to provide', qualifying that this means 'meat and drink and beds'. But it was emphatic about the restrictions on this hospitality, noting that this must be restricted to hospitals and not public begging, and that this should be limited to 'two, three, four days or sometimes longer till they are strong and able to continue'.[68]

---

[63] Ibid., 120.
[64] Ibid., 119–20.
[65] Ibid., 127.
[66] Ibid., 129.
[67] Ibid., 136.
[68] Ibid., 128.

Vitoria had explained that the Spanish should have the right to become citizens in the New World, but such rights were denied by the Ypres *Forma* to travellers in the Old World. It stipulated that 'those strangers who come to live in our city and to take alms, with a great flock of children, we do not accept'.[69] Although it added the exception that sometimes necessity such as the catastrophes of war, shipwreck, fire, might cause the city to accept more people, even then it warned that 'we take no more of these people than the public purse can afford to maintain'. The *Forma* projects a model of the world with a very restricted hospitality, writing that 'there is nowhere in the world that can receive and contain all poor people. There is no common chest anywhere that could sustain them all.'[70]

As Europeans were appropriating the goods of the Amerindians in the Americas and seeing this through the contorted lens of hospitality, scholars in Europe were thinking about hospitality in a way that protected the giver rather than the receiver. These measures concerned not only improving provisions for the poor, but protecting the rich. It wrote: 'the rich men's houses are not haunted with these idle parasites'.[71] And 'the poor thank the rich for everything they have'.[72] The policies concerned moving power from the poor, and strengthening governance:

> the three griefs of this world – beggary, beggars and begging – do not rule this city as they did before. Parasitical paupers, much to the harm of the community, were abusing the generosity of good men. Now they are denied the gains they had from begging, they are being brought to a quiet and sober manner of life.[73]

The *Forma subventionis pauperum* advised that anyone opposing these recommendations, freely claiming their *ius hospitii* and *ius perigrinandi*, should be punished:

> we should say something about insolent poor people, who obstinately reject a law that forbids begging. They complain, as if a right had been taken from them, that they are not free to beg, when in times past they did what they wanted. They wandered at their pleasure, running up and down, and reckoning nothing unlawful for them. This is not, as they think, liberty, when everyone does as he pleases; rather it is wasteful licence, which as Comicus says, debases us all. True liberty is ruled by reason. Reason

---

[69] Ibid., 129.
[70] Ibid.
[71] Ibid., 132.
[72] Ibid., 134.
[73] Ibid., 132.

considers not how much one would like, or but always looks what is appropriate.[74]

The *Forma* does not deny that the poor should have access to the things of necessity, but it explicitly states that poor access these things through controlled streams of charity and not as a right.

The Valencian humanist Juan Luis Vives was living in Northern Europe and was inspired by the 1525 Ypres scheme later detailed in the *Forma*. In 1526, he wrote *De subventione pauperum*, which he addressed to the councillors and the senate of Bruges. Its opening statement indicates how he too drew upon the classical world to advocate restricted hospitality in Europe: 'Cicero says that it is a duty of travellers and visitors to avoid over-curiosity when abroad or in a foreign state'.[75] Vives advocated more restricted hospitality and increased control of those who seek it, recommending that magistrates focus on 'producing good citizens',[76] and reminding that charitable measures 'require specific conditions which appear only too rarely in our times'.[77] Vives also advocated the restriction of the free movement of the poor: 'beggars in good health who wander about with no fixed dwelling-place should submit their names, and state the reason for their mendicancy to the Senate'.[78] While Vitoria had advocated that hospitality meant that citizenship should be extended to strangers, Vives wrote that 'of the able-bodied vagrants, those who are aliens should be returned to their own country' (but they should have their journey provided for).[79] For Vives there were distinct hierarchies of hospitality – native-born coming before the foreign, disabled before the able – and he assessed various degrees of weakness relating to age, gender, health, and circumstance. Vives was not suggesting that nobody should receive charity, but he advocated strict criteria which were to be meticulously scrutinised by authorities. More precise inclusion meant more precise exclusion in the sixteenth century. As Derrida explained, 'exclusion and inclusion are inseparable in the same moment'.[80]

Nor were those receiving hospitality supposed to be considered equal to those who provided it. Hospitality was a therefore a method for establishing a hierarchy of identities. *De subventione pauperum* is framed in paternalistic

---

[74] Ibid., 138.
[75] Juan Luis Vives, *On Assistance to the Poor (De Subventione Pauperum)*, trans. Alice. Tobriner (Toronto: University of Toronto Press, 1999), 33.
[76] Ibid., 36.
[77] Ibid., 37.
[78] Ibid., 38.
[79] Ibid., 39.
[80] Derrida, *Of Hospitality*, 81.

terms and suggests awareness that there will be opposition to the competing visions of social order; Vives wrote that 'these poor, buried in squalor, filth, shame, idleness and crime, think they are being dragged into slavery if their condition is ameliorated'.[81] The idea that the guest may feel wronged is anticipated and coercion expected: 'the Senators appointed to make these examinations and perform these duties should be given authority to coerce and compel obedience, even to the point of imprisonment, so that the Senate will be aware of the recalcitrant'.[82]

As previously mentioned, Charles V used the *Forma subventionis pauperum* and the *De subventione pauperum* to inform the series of poor laws that he issued in the sixteenth century. Defenders of the rights of the poor in Europe were ultimately unsuccessful in holding back the tides of discriminatory policies. De Soto's attempt to defend the poor may even have made matters worse. De Soto argued that expelling the poor simply relocated the problem.[83] As a possible solution, and probably not the one that de Soto intended, in 1552 Charles V ordered that anyone found begging without license be considered a vagabond and subjected to four years' galley service on a first attempt, eight on a second, life on a third.[84] This brings into focus the divergence in the norms of hospitality between the Old World and the New. Those who, perhaps driven by the necessity of poverty, had attempted to claim a *ius hospitii* in Spain might have found themselves sentenced to forced maritime labour for the Spanish Empire which grounded its appropriation abroad on the same rights of hospitality it denied to the poor in Europe.

In the sixteenth century there was a battle to assert visions of ideal societies. The mendicants had built their orders around the freedom to beg, and they contested the criminalisation of these rights in Europe. Advocates of the new social order in Europe did not just oppose the freedom of movement of the poor, but also the mendicant orders that championed them. For example, the Ypres *Forma* explicitly opposed the *vita religiosa* of the mendicant orders,

---

[81] Vives, *De Subventione Pauperum*, 52.
[82] Ibid., 38.
[83] Domingo de Soto, 'Deliberación en la Causa de los Pobres, Salamanca, 30, de enero de 1545', in Félix Santolaria Sierra (ed.), *El Gran Debate Sobre Los Pobres en el Siglo XVI* (Barcelona: Ariel, 2003), 49–116. Domingo De Soto also opposed other aspects of the divergence of norms of hospitality between the Old World and the New; in *De iustitia et iure* he wrote that Europe's resources should also be open to mining by others as the Americas were.
[84] Linda Martz, *Poverty and Welfare in Habsburg Spain: The Example of Toledo* (Cambridge: Cambridge University Press, 1983), 30. This might seem draconian, but as with many aspects of poor relief, it had precedents in Italy. In the 1520s and 30s Venice began to introduce poor laws, confining beggars to hospitals, and drafting able-bodied beggars to maritime service for the Venetian fleet.

writing that it 'is better to follow the soberness and discretion of the holy poor men, in Jerusalem at the beginning of the church, after they were converted to the faith. They lived contented with the alms that were given to them, neither running nor begging anywhere. They stayed at home, and applied themselves quietly and thankfully to prayer and contemplation.'[85] However, on both sides of the Atlantic, advocates of new models of hospitality did not suggest that hospitality be distributed through monastic or ecclesiastic institutions as it typically had been in the Middle Ages, but through hospitals.

9.4 A POWER CONVERGENCE FOR THE POOR IN EUROPE AND THE AMERINDIANS IN AMERICA

In the late Middle Ages and Early Modernity, hospitals were not only concerned with caring for the sick, but also the poor. In Western Christendom they were an offshoot of the hospitable function of the monasteries. Following the recommendations of treatises such as *Forma subventionis pauperum*, *De subventione pauperum*, charity was increasingly channelled through hospitals. Hospitals were sites of control as well as care. In the sixteenth century the institutions of hospitals evolved and proliferated, and the poor were increasingly confined to hospitals that were specifically for the poor. Poor bodies were increasingly associated with malaise, and the poor person entering the hospital was seen to need curing, physically, spiritually and morally. Chapels were part of the infrastructure of early modern Spanish hospitals, and inhabitants were expected to receive confession and religious instruction during their stay. This use of hospitals as sites of indoctrination as well as care had a long precedent as Spanish monarchs had established hospitals in newly conquered cities during the *reconquista* to facilitate the conversion of Muslims.[86] As the sixteenth century unfolded, religious instruction was not enough and labour was seen to be necessary for curing the poor of their tendency towards idleness.

While religion remained central to the hospitals, during the transformations of the sixteenth century ecclesiastic authorities lost their monopoly of these institutions. Vives had advocated that the state control the poor through hospitals.[87] For Vives, the ideal society could be developed through the centralisation of control; he wrote that 'liberty is found in yielding obedience

---

[85] *Forma Subventionis Pauperum*, 123.
[86] Jon Arrizabalaga, 'Poor Relief in Counter-Reformation Castile', in Ole Peter Grell, Andrew Cunningham and Jon Arrizabalaga (eds.), *Health Care and Poor Relief in Counter-Reformation Europe* (Abingdon: Routledge, 1999), 151–75, at 153.
[87] Vives, *De Subventione Pauperum*, 37. Vives noted the classical precedent in an aside mentioning that the Greek word is *Ptochotrophia*.

to the magistrates of the community rather than in that encouragement to violence or in the opportunity for widespread license in whatever direction caprice may lead'.[88] Vives advocated reform and increased control of the hospitals: 'when all the leeches have been eliminated from the hospitals, the resources of each institution should be examined'.[89] Here we see the power dynamics of the conditionality of hospitality, identified by Derrida as the desire to distinguish between guests and parasites.[90] These sixteenth-century hospitals were also spaces where humanistic visions of ideal societies could be realised, which meant purification from cultures of greed. Vives had written that in the hospital there should be enough but 'there should be no luxury by which they might easily fall into bad practices'.[91] Hospitality would be provided, but with austere conditions. Despite the austerity of the hospital regimes, wealth was on display in the architecture and art commissioned by the founders and benefactors of the hospitals, emphasising the power and importance of the hosts. This is illustrated in the building of the hospital of *Las Cinco Llagas* in Seville which opened in 1558, a building so grand it became the seat of the Andalusian parliament.

Across the Atlantic, hospitals continued to play an important role in power formations. The ways in which the extractive labour regimes of *encomienda* and *mita* played a role in the reorganisation of the lives and resources of the Amerindians is well known, but the role played by institutions of hospitality is less well known yet equally important. On the site where Cortés first met Moctezuma, a hospital was built, the hospital of *La Purísima Concepción y Jesús Nazareno*, founded by Cortés. Hospitals were also power statements, and they helped to structure the Spanish empire.

Around 1531 one of the *oídors* (judges) of the second Audiencias of New Spain, Vasco de Quiroga, founded the hospital town of Santa Fe, in the northwest periphery of Mexico City. This experiment to create an ideal community using the institution of hospitals was inspired by Thomas More's *Utopia*, a book he had borrowed from the library of the Franciscan Juan de Zumárrraga. Quiroga's hospital town of Santa Fe is another important example of the role that the humanistic recovery of classical models of hospitality played in the construction of visions of global order in the sixteenth century. The hospital town of Santa Fe provided basic resources for the Amerindians but was aimed

---

[88] Ibid., 38.
[89] Ibid., 41.
[90] Derrida, *Of Hospitality*, 59.
[91] Vives, *De Subventione Pauperum*, 41.

at facilitating conversion.[92] Quiroga's hospital towns were concerned with saving *and* controlling the lives of the Amerindians at the same time: Amerindians living in the hospital town were subject to a comprehensive regime of religious instruction. The regulations of the lives of the Amerindians were laid on in the *Doctrina Christiana*, which even stipulated the clothes that Amerindians could wear. As with the poor hospitals being developed in sixteenth-century Spain, inhabitants were not only required to receive communion and participate in a regime of religious instruction but also to work.

Quiroga continued to emphasise the importance of hospital towns for controlling rebellious Amerindians. In 1535 he wrote *Información en Derecho* explaining the importance of creating communities of patrilinear families with indigenous and Spanish overseers. His policies were put to the test when he was sent to Michoacán following the Chichimec rebellion in 1533. He developed a new hospital town of Santa Fe de la Laguna in Michoacán, the plans of which are mapped out in his *Ordenanzas*. Quiroga wanted to use hospitals for the total reorganisation of Amerindian society and behaviour,[93] but as with other sites of mission there were also opportunities for resistance and adaptation. For example, despite Quiroga's plan for patrilinear communities, the Purhépecha social structure of *guatapera*, a form of women's community, survived in the hospital towns and formed the basis of hospitals especially for women.[94]

The colonial project to use hospitals to reorganise Amerindian society in sixteenth-century Mexico highlighted the way in which the Spanish had transformed themselves into hosts and the indigenous populations into guests. Yet the game of hospitality cannot be controlled so easily. As a system of intersecting rights and customary practices aimed at negotiating the power relationship between hosts and guests, hospitality tends towards a more fluid formation in which the ambiguity of the power relationship between guest and host can be manipulated but cannot be overcome.

9.5 CONCLUSION

We live in inhospitable times, with Europe becoming more closed than ever to 'strangers' and those in need. It therefore seems an appropriate moment to

---

[92] This hospital town is depicted on the map of Tenochtitlán produced by Alonso de Santa Cruz c. 1550, now in the Uppsala Library.

[93] Fintan B. Warren, *Vasco de Quiroga and his Pueblo-Hospitals of Santa Fe* (Washington DC: Academy of American Franciscan History, 1963), 27.

[94] Bernardino Verástique, *Michoacán and Eden: Vasco de Quiroga and the Evangelization of Western Mexico* (Austin: University of Texas Press, 2000), 135.

reflect on the deep, and often dark, history of hospitality, to expose the normative assumptions and institutional processes that generate asymmetrical relationships and to consider the ways in which multiple inclusions can generate multiple exclusions. As Gideon Baker has observed, hospitality ethics 'is a large, and largely untapped normative resource for those who want to critique the exclusions of world politics'.[95] The issues raised by histories of hospitality are central to today's debates about the politics of migration and freedom of movement, and the boundaries of legal communities. As Cavallar observed, debates regarding hospitality relate to important questions for today's world, such as 'how do we balance the right of the political community to self-preservation with the right of the individuals to free movement?'[96] The complexity of hospitality exposes the permeability and the malleability of boundaries between friends and enemies, insiders and outsiders. In this way hospitality remains important to the way in which we imagine global communities.

This chapter does not intend to offer an exhaustive overview or comprehensive genealogy of the concept of hospitality in the Western tradition, but to offer a thin slice from the sixteenth century to highlight the tensions and contradictions that have characterised the history of this concept. Hospitality is also an interesting test case for signposting future directions in global intellectual history since it is, by its definition, a dynamic concept: multidimensional, contextually contingent, and providing a framework for physical movement between places and metaphysical movement between positions of power. As such, it tests the boundaries of contextual determinism, translation, and the politics of knowledge, going beyond discourses of hybridity to bring into focus the continuous dynamics of movement and power. As globalisation discourses continue to monopolise public and academic debates, the history of hospitality offers a resource for analysing the ways in which transcultural interactions have been managed and how global communities have been imagined, and to reflect upon how unequal distributions have been legitimated and become normative.

---

[95] Gideon Baker, 'Introduction', in Baker (ed.), *Hospitality and World Politics*, 1–17, at 4.
[96] Georg Cavallar, *The Rights of Strangers: Theories of International Hospitality, the Global Community and Political Justice since Vitoria* (Aldershot: Ashgate, 2002), 393.

10

Ventriloquism in Geneva: The League of Nations as International Organisation

MEGAN DONALDSON*

10.1 LAW AND THE INTERNATIONAL ORGANISATION

For international lawyers, the League of Nations is an institution of great symbolic and doctrinal importance. With its quasi-universal membership ('universal' of course heavily qualified), open-ended mandate, and inauguration of an 'international civil service', the League broke from the more limited institutional forms of nineteenth-century interstate cooperation, and helped shift 'international organisation' from a general aspiration of ordered interaction to a more specific legal category of inter-governmental entities.[1] However, the League was an irritant in the international legal order as well as an agent of law's expansion. It posed new legal questions concerning its own status and personality; the nature of relations with states and others; and the regulation of officials working within it. The emergence of the League thus offers a revealing vantage point on the workings of early-twentieth-century international legal thought, and the modes of analysis we can bring to bear upon it.

---

* This chapter draws on Megan Donaldson, 'From Secret Diplomacy to Diplomatic Secrecy: Secrecy and Publicity in the International Legal Order c. 1919–1950' (JSD, NYU School of Law, 2016). With thanks to Surabhi Ranganathan for comments and conversation on these themes, and Moran Yahav, who sparked my thinking about our very limited juridical grasp on the inner lives of institutions. Unless otherwise signalled, translations from French are my own. I am grateful to Samuel Zeitlin for help with German.
[1] On the various meanings of 'international organisation' pre-1945, see Pitman B. Potter, 'Origin of the Term International Organization', *American Journal of International Law* 39 (1945), 803–6.

Interwar thinking about the League is often treated by doctrinal texts today in narrow terms, as a subset of questions about the legal personality of international organisations later settled by a 1949 advisory opinion of the International Court of Justice,[2] or as laying the foundations for the emergence of a distinct 'law of international organisations'.[3] Yet debates about the League were more wide-ranging, and perplexing, than these frames suggest. The League was a novel, even disturbing creature in a world of states and empires. Legal commentators found it difficult to grasp the League's relations with member states. Was the League an actor in its own right (albeit animated and constrained by the decisions of member states); or a mere shorthand for the combination of member states themselves? And how did the Secretariat – the closest the League had to human agents – relate to the League itself, and its members? These questions invoked puzzles already familiar to political and legal thought, about artificial personality and collective agency, but against the backdrop of renewed ferment over the conceptualisation of the state,[4] and the nature of (international) law.[5]

This chapter probes interwar thinking about the League, its nature and authority, as an instance of legal innovation. It focuses in particular on the way in which the League, like other institutions, presented more than a static object of inquiry. By their workings, institution and office shift the conditions and terms in which deliberation about their nature occurs. This was particularly evident in the League's Secretariat: the human nucleus of the institution. As Susan Pedersen has argued, the Secretariat became a site of political thought in its own right: an 'arena within which ... the scope, practice and

---

[2] *Reparation for Injuries Suffered in the Service of the United Nations*, Advisory Opinion [1949] ICJ Rep 174.

[3] Though some of this work does acknowledge that the League was not readily assimilated into such synthetic accounts of institutions as did exist, or their underlying 'functionalist' assumptions. See Jan Klabbers, 'The Emergence of Functionalism in International Institutional Law: Colonial Inspirations', *European Journal of International Law* 25 (2014), 645, at 649–50; Jan Klabbers, 'The Transformation of International Organizations Law', *European Journal of International Law* 26 (2015), 9–82, at 32.

[4] On the way in which thinking through the international institution prompted new questions about the state, and vice versa, Leonard V. Smith, *Sovereignty at the Paris Peace Conference of 1919* (Oxford: Oxford University Press, 2018) 7, 30–3; and, tracing this pattern over a longer time-span, Guy Fiti Sinclair, *To Reform the World: International Organizations and the Making of Modern States* (Oxford: Oxford University Press, 2017). On the diversity and creativity of interwar thinking on subjecthood as it pertained to mandates, minorities, and individuals, see Natasha Wheatley, 'Spectral Legal Personality in Interwar International Law: On New Ways of Not Being a State', *Law and History Review* 35 (2017), 753–87.

[5] Smeltzer and Kelly, this volume; Von Bogdandy and Hussain, this volume.

legitimacy of internationalism were fought out'.[6] This process shifted understandings of the 'international' as a subject and source of authority, just as the League, in offering new sites and procedures for political discourse, gave both governments and new actors ('civil society', mandatory peoples, minority populations, aspiring member states, ostensibly impartial and cosmopolitan 'experts') a means of articulating claims, albeit not on terms exactly of their own choosing; and so reshaped prevailing legal and political categories.

The chapter seeks to bring out this quality of the institution – at once abstract and concrete, artificial and material, its operation shaping the conditions of its own analysis – by tracing a theme which recurs in very disparate ways as contemporaries sought to make sense of the League: a concern with *speech*. Speech is implicated in agency, personality and the constitution of a political sphere, and the identification of he who authorises speech has been central to the theorisation of sovereignty and the state.[7] It is thus unsurprising that discussions of the nature and authority of the League circled uneasily around whether and how the League might speak for some kind of 'international' position, and who might in turn speak for the League – or make the League speak (hence the reference to 'ventriloquism' in my title). More basic questions about speech – who could say what, to whom – also proved a pressing concern for those within the Secretariat, as they felt their way into new offices. Senior Secretariat staff shrank from speaking for the League themselves. Instead they cultivated the League as a scene of speech of a certain kind (public, harmonious exchange between member state delegates, in keeping with the valorisation of liberal democracy and open diplomacy in the wake of the First World War), and tried to curb the more confronting challenges to a diplomatic order of interstate speech. This orchestration depended on a sort of underground exchange of information and opinion between Secretariat staff, government officials and non-governmental organisations (NGOs); and it necessitated, in turn, quite strict control of what Secretariat staff said to the world at large.

The chapter moves from the 'outside' to the 'inside' of the League, with a focus on the Secretariat. It begins by sketching efforts of commentators (legal and otherwise) to get to grips with the League in the 1920s (Section 10.2). It turns then to the gradual elaboration, within the Secretariat, of a *modus*

---

[6] Susan Pedersen, 'The League of Nations as a Site of Political Imagination' (Nicolai Rubinstein Lecture, Queen Mary University of London, 15 March 2017), available at https://academiccommons.columbia.edu/doi/10.7916/D80K3SK5.

[7] Quentin Skinner, 'Hobbes on Persons, Authors and Representatives', in Patricia Springborg (ed.), *The Cambridge Companion to Hobbes's Leviathan* (Cambridge: Cambridge University Press, 2007), 157–80.

operandi of institutional life, managing the public speech of delegates, balancing public circumspection on its own part with tacit flows of information (Section 10.3). This system, always precarious, broke down in the 1930s, as exemplified in an exchange between an outspoken internationalist on the Secretariat staff and his more conservative colleagues. Here, an official's speech threatened the hierarchy in the Secretariat and its conception of the League; but, for that official, it was the silence of the hierarchy – the failure to speak – which traduced a proper understanding of the institution (Section 10.4). This coupling of quite distinct sites, actors and sources is of course not a comprehensive, even representative, account of interwar thinking about the League, but the movement between formal and lived facets of the institution offers a way of re-examining the bounds of international legal thought, and of the disciplinary perspectives we bring to the international organisation today (Section 10.5).

10.2 ENCOUNTERS WITH THE LEAGUE AS A 'NEW STATE OF THINGS'

The Covenant of the League of Nations was curiously oblique in its innovation. It did not explicitly provide for the *creation* of a League, but rather 'establishe[d] the League by presuming it', referring to the existence of a new entity whose 'action … shall be effected through' various organs.[8] The Covenant identified an array of areas in which the League was expected to work: prevention of war, the advancement of disarmament, the oversight of a *sui generis* 'mandatory' administration of former German colonies and Ottoman territories; together with improvement of labour conditions; repression of the traffic in women and children and the drug trade; the development of freedom of communication and transit, and the equitable treatment of commerce. Other treaties in the peace settlement added obligations concerning the administration of certain 'internationalised' territories, as well as oversight of the treatment of 'national minorities' in the newly created states of Eastern Europe. The Covenant envisaged the League not just as a new agent, but as a locus for the organisation of international life in its ensemble. It was to take control of all existing international bureaux and commissions, and review periodically members' treaty arrangements.

---

[8] David Kennedy, 'The Move to Institutions', *Cardozo Law Review* 35 (2017), 841–988, at 950; Covenant of the League of Nations, in 'Treaty of Peace with Germany', in *United States Treaties and International Agreements* 2 [1918–1930] (1969), 43–240, Part I; available at www.loc.gov/law/help/us-treaties/bevans/m-ust000002-0043.pdf.

The Covenant text laid out only the rudiments of the institutional structure: an Assembly (of representatives of all Members), and a Council (representatives of the allies and four further states, the selection of which would be contentious throughout the interwar period), each meeting at least once a year. The Assembly and Council were to operate on the basis of unanimity, except in certain specified cases. The Covenant also created a permanent Secretariat, comprising a Secretary-General and 'such ... staff as may be required', appointed by the Secretary-General with the approval of the Council.

The League had an ambivalent relationship to contemporary understandings of the role of law in an interstate order. The creation of the League registered in some accounts as a shift from a (chaotic, conflictual) politics into a more law-governed world. But the League, with its emphasis on discussion and consultation, was at some remove from the nineteenth-century 'peace through law' programme of compulsory judicial, or at least arbitral, dispute settlement,[9] and the Covenant itself might be read as foreshadowing a movement from formalist legal text *to* politics, albeit of a newly institutionalised kind: what one of its drafters called a 'new form of international political life'.[10] However, the coupling of far-reaching responsibilities and minimalist institutional prescriptions gave little real sense of how the League would work. It was not that there had been no thought about how the League would operate, nor that Covenant provisions were drafted without deliberation (although in some instances this was the case). Rather, drafters and commentators had glimpses of something, but its full contours were expected to take shape only later, as the institution began to function.

Once in existence, the League fell to be parsed in familiar vocabularies. Jurists' discussion of 'the League' gravitated towards interlinked debates over what *kind* of a body the League was, and – relatedly – whether it could be conceived of as a legal person in its own right, distinct from the (somewhat arbitrary) list of its member states and empires.[11] Aspects of the Covenant

---

[9] Stephen Wertheim, 'The League of Nations: A Retreat from International Law?', *Journal of Global History* 7 (2012), 210–32.

[10] M.F. Larnaude, *La Société des Nations. Conférences faites à MM. les Officiers du Centre des hautes études militaires de l'École supérieure de la Guerre et de l'École supérieure de Marine* (Paris: Imprimerie nationale, 1920), 8. On the duelling understandings of the League in relation to a politics/law divide, see Kennedy, 'The Move to Institutions', 868–9.

[11] Britain having succeeded in having both the British Empire and each of Canada, Australia, New Zealand and India as founding members, with India being particularly exceptional since it arguably would not have satisfied the 'independence' threshold for new members seeking admission after the League's creation. On the ways in which the creation of the League inflected existing thinking about statehood, sovereignty and personality for peripheral polities,

gestured at independent legal status for the League at international law, conceived derivatively as akin to that of a state,[12] but the text was not decisive. German-language scholars took up these questions with particular energy. Questions about the nature of the League were seen through the lens of long-standing debates, shaped by the shifting forms of the German polity, about the legal nature of 'confederations of states' [*Staatenverbindungen*].[13] The most systematic commentary on the Covenant, by the pacifist jurists Walter Schücking and Hans Wehberg, argued that the League satisfied Georg Jellinek's influential definition of 'confederation': a permanent, agreement-based alliance of independent states for the purposes of protecting their territory as against external enemies, and keeping the peace between them.[14] However, this scholarship on confederations was connected to larger disputes over the character of international law itself. Jellinek, having grounded his account of the binding force of international law on the notion of the 'self-binding' will of states, was unable to concede to a confederation legal personality in its own right.[15] To articulate the League as having a legal existence independent of its members – at least vis-à-vis those members – Schücking and Wehberg invoked instead the private-law analogy of the 'community of joint ownership' [*Gemeinschaft zur gesamten Hand*]: a community which would, within the sphere of its competences, have a legal unity opposable to members.[16]

The jurisprudential ferment of the interwar opened up contrasting approaches, but perhaps not ones which offered any greater possibility of grasping the League's legal, political, social and bureaucratic existence in a holistic way. Kelsen and the Vienna School, liberated by their larger precepts,

---

see Megan Donaldson, 'The League of Nations, Ethiopia and the Making of States', *Humanity* 11 (2020), 6–31.

[12] Covenant, art 2; art 7(4) ('[r]epresentatives of the Members of the League and officials of the League when engaged on the business of the League' should enjoy 'diplomatic privileges and immunities', as ambassadors did).

[13] See, e.g., Kraus, *Vom Wesen des Völkerbundes* (Berlin: Deutsche Verlagsgesellschaft für Politik und Geschichte, 1920), 12–13.

[14] Walther Schücking and Hans Wehberg, *Die Satzung des Völkerbundes: Kommentiert* (2nd ed.) (Berlin: Franz Vahlen, 1924), 103. Schücking had already, and somewhat eccentrically, seen in the Hague system of a standing court of arbitration the germ of a world confederation [*Weltstaatenbund*]: *The International Union of the Hague Conferences*, trans. Charles G. Fenwick (Oxford: Clarendon Press, 1918), 86.

[15] On Jellinek's views, Jochen von Bernstorff, *The Public International Law Theory of Hans Kelsen: Believing in Universal Law* (Cambridge: Cambridge University Press, 2010), 55–7.

[16] Schücking and Wehberg, *Die Satzung des Völkerbundes*, 103–19. Bernstorff suggests that this merely recasts the difficulty of reconciling the sovereign will of states with the existence of some countervailing entity: Bernstorff, *Public International Law Theory of Hans Kelsen*, 142.

saw neither states nor the League as pre-legal persons, but rather as personations of legal orders, both of which might be integrated into an overarching universal law.[17] Schmitt, on the other hand, with his insistence on the primacy of concrete (statist) order, argued that a genuine 'league' [*Bund*] required a certain political homogeneity. For Schmitt, the League of Nations lacked this homogeneity, being rather an arbitrary league of victors. Thus, there might be in Geneva a 'political–practical purposive entity' [*politisches Zweckgebilde*] but not a League capable of asserting legal personality in its own right or constituting any legal order whatsoever.[18]

Both Anglophone and French works noted the German-language discussions, but tended not to follow them in detailed integration of the League into existing categories. The 'international legal personality' of entities other than states had been largely ignored, or brusquely denied, in Anglo-American international law prior to 1919,[19] and the treatment of group personality in early-twentieth-century pluralist thought seems not to have seeped into international legal discourse.[20] Oppenheim was typical of Anglo-American approaches to the League in proceeding by way of negatives (the League was *not* a super-state, nor a confederation, nor a mere alliance), and concluding, by a process of exhaustion, that it was of a *sui generis* kind.[21] Whereas Schücking and Wehberg, concerned to place the League within a pre-existing

---

[17] See, e.g., *Das Problem der Souveränität und die Theorie des Völkerrechts* (Tübingen: Mohr, 1920).

[18] 'Die Kernfrage des Völkerbundes' (1924); see Bernstorff, *Public International Law Theory of Hans Kelsen*, 136–45.

[19] P.E. Corbett, 'What Is the League of Nations?', *British Yearbook of International Law* 5 (1924), 119–48, at 120; David J. Bederman, 'The Souls of International Organizations: Legal Personality and the Lighthouse at Cape Spartel', *Virginia Journal of International Law* 36 (1996), 275–377, at 333–49.

[20] On the translation of Gierke into English, and the brief efflorescence of English pluralism, David Runciman, *Pluralism and the Personality of the State* (Cambridge: Cambridge University Press, 1997).

[21] See, e.g., L. Oppenheim, 'Le caractère essentiel de la Société des Nations', *Revue générale de droit international public* 26 (1919), 234–44, at 238; Alfred Eckhard Zimmern, *The League of Nations and the Rule of Law* (London: Macmillan, 1936), 283–8. Corbett, on the other hand, argued there was no harm in ranging the League within a category of 'confederation', as long as regard was paid to the specific terms of the Covenant: Corbett, 'What Is the League of Nations?', 147–8. For a relatively rare Anglo-American discussion of the League informed in detail by Jellinek's work, John William Burgess, *The Sanctity of Law, Wherein Does It Consist* (Boston: Ginn & Co, 1927), 275ff. For other treatments of the personality question, see, e.g., Manfredi Siotto-Pintor, 'Les sujets de droit international autres que les états', *Recueil des Cours de l'Académie de Droit international* 41 (1932), 245–362; John Fischer Williams, 'The Status of the League of Nations in International Law', in *Chapters on Current International Law and the League of Nations* (London: Longmans, 1929) 477, 480–2.

category of 'confederation', had seen in the Covenant various rights (of legation, of war and peace) analogous to those enjoyed by states, more literal readings of the Covenant in British scholarship emphasised that most of the stipulations in the Covenant applied to *members*, rather than to 'the League'.[22] The strongly sociological and functionalist tendencies of French scholarship also precluded a strong focus on personality,[23] emphasising instead disparate sites of intensifying social interdependence.[24] The French jurist Larnaude, who had served as one of France's representatives on the commission drafting the Covenant, likened the League to a trade union or free association: an 'instrument of co-operation ... a standing agency facilitating common action by states animated by the co-operative spirit'.[25]

Even where it was conceded, recognition of international legal personality as such did not answer definitively questions about the agency of the League. As Kelsen had earlier observed of public law theory of the state, legal thinking had a tendency to hypostatise the 'legal person': scholars moved from personhood to agency, like 'mythological thinking, which, anthropomorphically, suspects a dryad behind every tree ... Apollo behind the sun'.[26] Legal person or not, the ability of 'the League' to act in any full sense was constrained by the decision procedures of its various organs and in turn by the determinations of governments of member states. On paper, then, the League fell somewhere between an 'it', a unitary agent, and a 'they', a collective of organs or members – and, if the latter, it was not clear how the collective became a unity.[27] Whether they began from a categorisation of legal persons, or the text of the Covenant, legal accounts could only restate these puzzles in more technical language, or gesture to the possibility of future evolution of the institution through iterative interpretations of the Covenant.

---

[22] See, e.g., Corbett, 'What Is the League of Nations?', 143–4.
[23] Prominent treatises, like Fauchille's, merely noted the different positions taken by other authors: Paul Fauchille, *Traité de droit international public* (8th ed.) (Paris: Rousseau, 1922) vol. 1, 215–16.
[24] Perhaps pursued most systematically by Georges Scelle; see, e.g., his early 'Essai de systematique de droit international', *Revue générale de droit international public* 30 (1923), 116–42.
[25] Zimmern, *League of Nations and the Rule of Law*, 289 (italics omitted).
[26] Kelsen, *Das Problem der Souveränität*, 18.
[27] To borrow language from an anecdote conveyed by Brierly: 'I remember in the early days of the League meeting [an MP] who had just returned from a first visit to Geneva. He said he had discovered that the League was not "it" but "they".' In other words, 'the League' as such could do little in its own right; it must be the members that acted: J.L. Brierly, 'The Covenant and the Charter', *British Yearbook of International Law* 23 (1946), 83–94, at 85.

Anglo-American lawyers were quick to liken the League to a biological or evolutionary phenomenon (a pattern with parallels in constitutional law).[28] Political scientists and international relations theorists, together with supporters of the League in governmental office and public life, often took a markedly anti-formalist stance, rejecting efforts to parse the Covenant for answers and emphasising the League's role as a locus for practical cooperation and the gradual cultivation of internationalist sensibility.[29] The emphasis on dynamism was part of a political promise: that the League would transform itself over time, incorporating the defeated powers and correcting what even many strong League supporters conceded were iniquities in the peace settlement. But it was not clear what would *generate* the change, allowing the League or its members to achieve anything more than had been possible in previous forms of negotiation or alliance. To put the question in the organic terms often used by contemporaries, what was it that would bring the League to 'life'?

Whether lawyers or not, Anglo-American commentators tended to see the animating force of the League in 'public opinion' or 'popular will'.[30] In 1919, Viscount Bryce, a leading advocate for the League, emphasised the need to create 'not only the machinery of a League, but that moving and guiding power which dwells in the opinion of enlightened and liberty-loving men all the world over'.[31] In a similar vein, but using 'will' instead of public opinion, Alfred Zimmern, the first professor of 'international relations' as an academic discipline in Britain, proclaimed in 1935:

> By itself [the League] is nothing. Yet the peoples persistently regard it as Something. That impalpable Something is not a legend or a myth. It exists. It has even exercised authority, controlled the rulers of states and prevented war. But that Something does not reside in a tabernacle at Geneva. It is communicated to Geneva by the peoples of the Member States. It is their will and their will alone which can make the League a living reality.[32]

---

[28] On transposition of this metaphor, Fiti Sinclair, *To Reform the World*, 44.
[29] Wertheim, 'The League of Nations: A Retreat from International Law?'.
[30] Smith also notes the emphasis on transnational public opinion, but takes it as evidence for a narrower Wilsonian redefinition of states as analogous and accountable to reasoning, liberal individuals, something which might not reflect the breadth and diversity of references to 'conscience' and 'will': Smith, *Sovereignty at the Paris Peace Conference*, 30.
[31] Viscount Bryce, 'The Covenant: A Critical Commentary', *Manchester Guardian* (29 March 1919), 25. See also, e.g., 'Commentary on the League of Nations Covenant' (prepared by the FO) in Cmd 151 (1919), 12; William H. Taft and others, *The Covenanter: An American Exposition of the Covenant of the League of Nations* (Garden City: Doubleday, Page & Co., 1919) 74 (a collection of articles published by some of the League's foremost supporters in the US).
[32] Zimmern, *The League of Nations and the Rule of Law*, 284.

This invocation of 'public opinion' and the 'will of peoples' did reflect features of the League's design, particularly innovative procedures for the settlement of disputes, intended to inform (presumptively peace-loving) publics in the states concerned, and thereby slow governments' recourse to force.[33] Yet 'public opinion' also served as a helpful *deus ex machina* to resolve the larger puzzle of collective agency inherent in the League. A cosmopolitan public opinion would transcend differences between governments, bringing them together and thus sustaining the League as a unitary actor rather than a mere collective of member states. Reference to 'public opinion' could also smooth the tensions involved in claims that the League would be a site of new diplomacy, not of mere states and governments, but of peoples. The apparent inclusiveness of 'public opinion' obscured the narrow formal membership of the League. It also masked the tensions between (self-identified) 'peoples' and 'nations', and the statist and imperial order which offered them only uneven and imperfect representation.[34] Even within member states, while 'public opinion' seemed to connote broad-based democratic engagement, it could also be limited to a much narrower elite opinion, the *'conscience juridique du monde civilisé'*.[35]

Questions about whether the League was, either legally or politically, independent of member states, would persist in discussions among delegates.[36] However, the task of establishing the Secretariat presented the questions in a particularly acute way. Many British internationalists, in particular, had imagined only a small Secretariat, facilitating direct functional cooperation between national ministries and expert delegates.[37] On this conception, the League, while perhaps enjoying formal legal personality, was not really an

---

[33] For example, the mandated delay of three months from an arbitral award, judgment or Council report before a member state might make war, and requirement for publication of papers and statements at various stages of the Council resolution process: Covenant, arts 12, 15.

[34] On the effect of re-describing the world as one of nations rather than empires, see Pitts, this volume. The internal Secretariat correspondence examined in Section 10.4 below exemplifies recurrent shifts in interwar debates between nation and state, depending on the nature of the argument being made, and the extent to which interlocutors are situating themselves in formalist legal argument.

[35] Martti Koskenniemi, *The Gentle Civilizer of Nations: The Rise and Fall of International Law, 1870–1960* (Cambridge: Cambridge University Press, 2001), 15–16, 41–54, 96–97; Stephen Wertheim, 'Reading the International Mind: International Public Opinion in Early Twentieth-Century Anglo-American Thought', in Nicolas Guilhot and Daniel Bessner (eds.), *The Decisionist Imagination: Sovereignty, Social Science, and Democracy in the Twentieth Century* (New York: Berghahn, 2019).

[36] Smith, *Sovereignty at the Paris Peace Conference*, 222–8.

[37] Martin David Dubin, 'Transgovernmental Processes in the League of Nations', *International Organization* 37 (1983), 469–93.

actor in its own right, but rather a nexus for interstate cooperation. Instead, the first Secretary-General, Sir Eric Drummond, built up a cohort of officials divided into functional areas and constituting an 'international civil service'. This gave the League a presence in the world, and set of human agents, beyond the periodic gatherings of member-state delegates who remained representatives of their own governments. Of course, the Secretariat had been understood as purely administrative, *serving* the League rather than embodying it, so it was hardly, in Kelsen's terms, the 'dryad behind [the] tree' of the League's formal personality. Yet the existence of a corps of Secretariat officials, charged under internal regulations with regulating their conduct with the interests of the League alone in view, and enjoying diplomatic privileges and immunities under the Covenant, represented a marked break with the statist legal order.

The extent of this innovation is registered in foreign ministries' efforts to grasp the new situation. Foreign ministry officials could, in general terms, accept that the League was an independent institution. But they were disconcerted when they realised that they might have to accord their nationals serving on the Secretariat staff diplomatic privileges and immunities *against their own government*. In the early months of the League's existence, when the infant Secretariat was based in London rather than Geneva, it seemed absurd to the Foreign Office to accord British nationals on the Secretariat staff diplomatic privileges on their home soil, as though they were in the service of some foreign state. Cecil Hurst, the Foreign Office legal adviser, had to spell out to colleagues that a British subject in the service of the League would 'owe duties to a unit other than his own country': the League had created 'a new state of things'.[38] To explain the stakes of this new loyalty, Hurst invoked a familiar context of Anglo-French rivalry. Secretariat staff, he warned colleagues, might be privy to 'all the secrets' bearing on any acute political crisis. It was worth the British accepting the international allegiance of British nationals – and concomitant lack of British government access to the 'secrets' in their possession – to ensure that the French government was equally unable to assert jurisdiction over *its* nationals in the Secretariat when they passed through France.[39] Of course, it was difficult to envisage the British government seeking to extract such information from British nationals by formal legal process, so the example was hypothetical in the extreme. Yet Hurst was here prescient in linking the independence of the League with the knowledge and communications of the individuals working for the Secretariat, and in

---

[38] Memo Hurst, 15 April 1920, UK National Archives, FO 371/4312.
[39] Ibid.

grasping that the institution would take 'life' not only from the workings of *public* opinion, but from new circulations of secret information.

10.3 SPEECH IN THE INSTITUTIONAL LIFE OF THE LEAGUE[40]

Leaders of the Secretariat, as the bureaucratic nucleus of the League, had to animate 'the League' as an entity distinct from its members, while also glossing the Secretariat's own relation to the institution. This challenge played out most systematically in the vexed question of staffing the putatively 'international' civil service. Maintaining this 'international' quality required Drummond to resist the idea that powerful states had a right to place their nationals in the Secretariat, or that staffing ought to reflect the cross-section of League members (generally an effort by Latin American and Asian states to correct the over-representation of Western European personnel). But there was never a simple opposition between 'national' affiliations of recruits and an ideal of internationalist meritocracy.[41] The presence of nationals of key members in the Secretariat's upper echelons was not a simple acquiescence to member states' demands. It reflected also Drummond's concern that internationalism must remain anchored in national sensibilities, and his recognition of what Hurst had intuited: that the Secretariat's work to animate the League depended on channels of information and influence between Geneva and European capitals.

The Secretariat was reluctant to assert itself as a corporate body, or to speak *for* the institution. The Secretary-General resisted calls to give his annual report as a major public speech. The Information Section within the Secretariat was prohibited by Drummond from producing anything in the nature of pro-League 'propaganda', and as a result churned out primarily dry, factual documents which failed to ignite much interest. The Secretariat's chief contribution was to work, quite literally, behind the scenes. After experimentation in the early days, and negotiation with government representatives, the Secretariat became quite adept at stage-managing, for example, 'public' sessions of the League Council with enough substantive discussion to stimulate press interest, and offer a simulacrum of public diplomacy, and yet

---

[40] This section draws extensively on findings in Donaldson, 'From Secret Diplomacy to Diplomatic Secrecy'.

[41] On the dynamics of recruitment, see Klaas Dykmann, 'How International Was the Secretariat of the League of Nations?', *International History Review* 37 (2015), 721–44; Karen Gram-Skjoldager and Haakon A. Ikonomou, 'The Construction of the League of Nations Secretariat. Formative Practices of Autonomy and Legitimacy in International Organizations', *International History Review* 41 (2017), 257–79.

not so much dissension that they would reveal and risk escalating genuine conflicts. Although the Secretariat sometimes invoked 'public opinion' as a force in advance of governmental consent, recalling the more dynamic and optimistic visions of the League's future trajectory, the Secretariat tended to restrict, rather than expand, avenues for concrete expressions of opinion in the League apparatus. Circulation of petitions and other unsolicited material from NGOs was limited, particularly where it offended the governments of powerful European member states. And the Secretariat staff were deft in their use of the rhetoric of 'public opinion': as the Secretariat came under increasing scrutiny in 1930, Drummond equated the strength of the League with 'its hold on public opinion' but also 'the Governments and Administrations *through which public opinion acts*', negating any independent action of opinion – potentially oppositional to governments – on the League.[42] Drummond sometimes even denied that the League was 'an institution with an existence separate from Governments', insisting that it was 'organically nothing but the totality of States which are its Members'.[43] Even new transnational work on matters such as mandates and minorities, drugs, trafficking and anti-slavery, in which non-government organisations were actively involved, entailed an interplay between newly formalised and public deliberations, on one hand, and a close but largely informal cooperation, on the other – albeit sometimes with governments and sometimes with non-government organisations, and inspired by quite divergent agendas on the part of individual officials.[44]

Secretariat staff, reflecting on their work in 1939, commented that they had been a 'shadow *corps diplomatique*':

> it has been taken for granted that the Secretariat should make suggestions and proffer advice. ... It is expected to know the desires of the various delegations, and to play a large part in reconciling, by private negotiations, any conflicting views. In the case of the Council the silent elimination of conceivable

---

[42] Drummond, preface to League of Nations Secretariat, *Ten Years of World Co-Operation* (League of Nations, 1930), vii (emphasis added).
[43] Ibid., 401.
[44] For detailed accounts, see, e.g., Susan Pedersen, *The Guardians: The League of Nations and the Crisis of Empire* (Oxford: Oxford University Press 2015); Jane K. Cowan, 'Who's Afraid of Violent Language?: Honour, Sovereignty and Claims-Making in the League of Nations', *Anthropological Theory* 3 (2003), 271–91; Carole Fink, *Defending the Rights of Others: The Great Powers, the Jews, and International Minority Protection, 1878–1938* (Cambridge: Cambridge University Press, 2004); Suzanne Miers, *Slavery in the Twentieth Century: The Evolution of a Global Problem* (Walnut Creek, CA: AltaMira Press 2003); Amalia Ribi Forclaz, *Humanitarian Imperialism: The Politics of Anti-Slavery Activism, 1880–1940* (Oxford: Oxford University Press, 2015).

difficulties is carried so far that any unforeseen observation by a Member comes as a disagreeable surprise, and is felt as a reflection upon the Secretariat. Moreover, the Secretariat has frequently been the initiator of proposals on matters of substance.[45]

A colleague observed that

> it was the officials of the Secretariat who often indicated, in the corridors, the desired direction that the deliberations of various organs of the League should take, and it was [the officials], too, who in most cases prepared the texts of the reports of these organs as well as of proposals and draft resolutions, and sometimes even the speeches which were to be given by delegates.[46]

These reflections are more candid than some of the public efforts to distil officials' experiences which would occur during the Second World War, under the auspices of Chatham House and the Carnegie Endowment.[47] Taken at face value, they arguably imply a greater degree of control by the Secretariat over the ensemble of the League's work than in fact existed, particularly in instances of acute political controversy. And these reflections head in different directions. For some officials the Secretariat's activity was a laudable contribution. For others, particularly when considering the years after 1933, when Drummond was succeeded as Secretary-General by Joseph Avenol, this closet diplomacy was less a genuinely internationalist practice than an improper solicitousness of the positions of powerful members (a concern embraced by others, and detailed in Section 10.4 below). Yet these comments are revealing of the *modalities* of the Secretariat's work, and of the connection between conceptions of the Secretariat and the League, on one hand, and the more intimate and quotidian practices of speech which underpinned this, on the other (speech in corridors, and preparation of the speeches others would give in public).

Officials recognised that the Secretariat's acquiescence in an informal traffic in information which these practices sometimes involved was difficult to reconcile with its role as a genuinely international body in the service of all

---

[45] [Believed to be J.V. Wilson], 'The Secretariat after the War' (written c. 1939–40), League of Nations Archives [hereafter LNA] S559.

[46] [Illegible], 'Quelques idées sur l'organisation et les fonctions du Secrétariat', 5 (sent to Lester, 30 Jan 1942, apparently in response to an invitation to officials to share their thoughts), LNA S559.

[47] On the way in which the Chatham House reflections were instrumentalised by former officials, and steered by the Foreign Office, in different directions, see Benjamin Auberer, 'Digesting the League of Nations: Planning the International Secretariat of the Future, 1941–1944', *New Global Studies* 10 (2016), 393–426.

League members. In the course of early efforts to think through the terms on which the Secretariat held information gleaned from governments, an official acknowledged that '[t]he theory that officials of the Secretariat could withhold information from the Members of the League merely by treating it as private would indeed be dangerous.' On the other hand, imposing any more egalitarian principle that information held by the Secretariat must be available to all member states would choke off the flows of information on which the Secretariat relied.[48] The Director of the Political Section agreed: 'for the moment' the Secretariat must avoid working on 'principles' and instead 'seize the opportunities ... to inform ourselves more completely than [we could] through purely official avenues, by accepting the – inevitable for the present – conditions applicable to this sort of communications'.[49] The Secretariat's need for information, particularly from governments, was such that officials sought and accepted it where they could, and subject to the demands for confidence imposed by individual interlocutors. This position seems never to have been revisited; indeed it was rare to see the problem even articulated again with this clarity.

Governments, for their part, understood well the influence of the Secretariat (periodic squabbles over the share of posts going to individuals of different nationalities were about not only national prestige but also perceived possibilities for steering the Secretariat's decision-making). But the novel role of the Secretariat was only palatable to governments because Secretariat staff were largely effaced in the public presentation of the League as institution. The Secretariat's often-obscured influence was to some extent compatible with liberal internationalist understandings of the dynamism and evolutionary character of the League. Nevertheless, the role of the Secretariat as a 'shadow *corps diplomatique*', practising what might be understood as a new secret diplomacy in its inevitable reliance on uneven and confidential sources of information, would have been difficult for even the most ardent League supporter to acknowledge openly. In superficial terms, it would have confirmed long-standing accusations from Germany that the League was merely a front for Anglo-French interests (although, in fact, nationals of these countries were not uniformly serving governmental priorities).[50] This reality lay beyond the intellectual parameters of many juridical views of the institution, and was

---

[48] Memorandum by M. Colban regarding the access of Members of the League of Nations to documents in the International Secretariat, Special Circular No. 203, 15 August 1922, LNA R574 [11/5304/5304].
[49] Minute Mantoux, 13 July 1920, LNA R574 [11/5304/5304].
[50] See, in this vein, discussion of Schmitt's criticism of the League, in Smeltzer and Kelly; and Von Bogdandy and Hussain; this volume.

difficult in normative terms to reconcile even with the more practical and sociological accounts produced by political scientists and internationalists. And yet, the existence of 'the League' as an entity of some political consequence would have been impossible without this hinterland of bureaucratic activity.

The maintenance of this system required discretion on the part of Secretariat staff. Staff were prohibited by internal rules from disclosing matters of which they had knowledge by virtue of their role, and from speaking in public about current political problems. Both rules were, however, often compromised by the need to gather information, and exchange something in return. There was a sort of tacit relaxation of these rules within certain bounds: high officials tolerated or even encouraged informal 'liaison' work to build relations with governments and internationalist audiences. This craft and compromise in turn depended on a loose camaraderie among Secretariat officials: a shared commitment to a particular vision of the institution and its role. This was always fragile, but broke down completely in the 1930s. An influx of staff supportive of fascist regimes in Italy and Germany meant that Secretariat personnel were increasingly divided (manifest in the felt need, by 1932, for all staff to make a 'declaration of fidelity' to the League).[51] Staff with strong pacifist and internationalist commitments distrusted the second Secretary-General, Joseph Avenol, who manifested pronounced fascist sympathies. As the sense of common purpose frayed, control over speech broke down, and questions about the nature of the League, the intellectual preoccupations of jurists and political scientists, became urgent matters of personal conscience for Secretariat staff.

10.4 SPEAKING IN, AND FOR, THE LEAGUE IN A MOMENT OF CRISIS

Struggles within the Secretariat played out particularly starkly in the confrontation between Konni Zilliacus, an official in the Information Section of the Secretariat, and his superiors.[52] Zilliacus had worked for the Information

---

[51] With varying degrees of ceremony, officials of different grades had to undertake 'to exercise in all loyalty, discretion and conscience the functions that have been entrusted to me as an official of the Secretariat ... to discharge my functions and to regulate my conduct *with the interests of the League alone in view* and not to seek or receive instructions from any Government or other authority external to the Secretariat of the League of Nations.': see register of signatures in LNA S943 (emphasis added).

[52] Zilliacus, the cosmopolitan son of a Swedo-Finnish father and an American mother, had been born in Japan, where his father, a proponent of Finnish independence, was living in exile.

Section since 1920. His role formally involved production of the League's official documents, but he also undertook 'informal' liaison work with labour and socialist groups, tacitly accepted by his superiors. Beyond this, he also pursued further, unsanctioned 'publicity' work. In particular, Zilliacus was a prolific pseudonymous author, producing some of the more acute and candid descriptions of the new diplomatic dynamics in Geneva.[53] When League members refused to use the full possibilities of collective sanctions laid out in the Covenant to resist Japanese expansion in Manchuria, Zilliacus stepped up his clandestine publications, and leaked quantities of information about the Japan–China conflict. He was appalled by the League's failure to respond effectively to the Italian invasion of Abyssinia in 1935, and the efforts of Avenol, to head off confrontation of aggressors within League forums, and in response intensified his unofficial lobbying. This activity did not go unremarked. Annual reports written by Zilliacus's superiors – generally positive prior to 1934 – begin to note 'a certain tendency ... to be animated by personal considerations of a political character which sometimes undermine the objectivity of his work'.[54] By mid-1938, Avenol was complaining that Zilliacus had 'created much difficulty and suspicion' in trying 'to propagate [personal] convictions in the press and among the public in defiance of the decisions of the Council and the Assembly'.[55] Zilliacus's official role, coupled with strong political commitments, thus placed him at the heart of tensions over speech – both in the public animation of 'the League' as a political actor, and in the Secretariat's policing of its staff's speech.

In August 1938, Zilliacus wrote Avenol a letter of resignation, condemning the 'official doctrine or political principle' of the Secretariat and urging Avenol to speak out against violations of the Covenant.[56] As Pedersen makes clear, the arguments mobilised by Zilliacus in this correspondence were not

---

Zilliacus graduated with a BA from Yale during the First World War, and served with British military missions to Russia, where he opposed the Allies' anti-revolutionary intervention, and wrote anonymously to the London press detailing British activities which Churchill had denied in the Commons. Zilliacus was a supporter of the British Union for Democratic Control (a small but influential organisation devoted to increasing parliamentary control over foreign policy) and, along with many radical Liberals involved in the UDC, joined the Labour Party after the First World War. See Archie Potts, *Zilliacus: A Life for Peace and Socialism* (London: Merlin, 2002), 1–16.

[53] See, e.g., C. Howard-Ellis [Zilliacus], *The Origin, Structure and Working of the League of Nations* (Boston: Houghton Mifflin, 1928).
[54] A. Pelt, comments on Certificate as to Grant of Annual Increment, 26 December 1934. Unless otherwise indicated, all materials pertaining to Zilliacus here cited are in LNA S912/Zilliacus.
[55] Second meeting of the Appointments Committee, 23 May 1938, re Annual report on Mr Zilliacus.
[56] Zilliacus to Avenol, 9 August 1938.

new: he was presenting an array of positions taken since the League's inception about the institution's authority, albeit in ways reflecting his experience of Secretariat life.[57] In this moment, though, the very existence of this polemical text raised concerns about renegade speech, as Avenol feared that Zilliacus, a notorious strategic leaker with a known intention to stand for office as a Labour candidate in Britain, would publish the letter and any reply Avenol gave (indeed this fear may explain Avenol's petty initial refusal to accept Zilliacus's letter as a valid letter of resignation at all).[58] Although formal proceedings against Zilliacus seem to have been abandoned in the chaos of the Secretariat's final months, an indignant official in the Personnel department, possibly the Frenchman Henri Vilatte, annotated the letter, challenging Zilliacus's conception of the League and the Secretariat. These marginal notes in response are suffused with irritation, and possibly motivated as much by personal animus than disinterested intellectual engagement. Nevertheless, the two lines of argument, letter and marginal notes, read together, re-stage controversy over the nature of the League and Secretariat in a manner shaped by the authors' personal experience as officials.

Zilliacus's letter opened with an assertion that Secretariat officials were 'responsible to the Secretary-General alone and through him to the whole League', not to individual governments. Insofar as the Secretariat dealt with governments directly, it did so 'in their [i.e. states'] capacity as Members of the League and subject to our [i.e. officials'] loyalty to the League as a whole.' This entailed that 'The Covenant became our charter. ... we exerci[s]ed our functions of collecting data, drafting reports, giving advice and making suggestions, assuring publicity for League activities ... in such a way as to work on the basis of the Covenant.' This function 'became particularly important when Governments disagreed about what ought to be done'.[59]

This opening established 'the League' as an entity in its own right, above governments (although brought into being by them). Yet by this time 'the League' as a unitary actor was crippled; it could not take decisions in accordance with the provisions of the Covenant governing its key organs. Perhaps for this reason, Zilliacus moved quickly from 'the League' to the Secretariat, eliding distinctions between the two, and emphasising instead the centrality of the Covenant. However, the spectre of disagreement about 'what ought to

---

[57] Pedersen, 'The League of Nations as a Site of Political Imagination' (focusing on the letter itself).
[58] Avenol to Zilliacus, 25 August 1938; Zilliacus to Avenol, 30 August 1938; Avenol to Zilliacus, 1 September 1938; Avenol to Zilliacus, 2 September 1938.
[59] Zilliacus to Avenol, 9 August 1938.

be done' was difficult to dispel. A marginal annotation challenged Zilliacus's confidence, asking 'who is the best judge in last resort?' Zilliacus's letter conceded that governments were responsible for taking decisions, but insisted that the Secretariat had to 'prepare' those decisions 'on lines compatible with the obligations of the Covenant'. The marginal voice returned at this point: 'are governments and officials agreed on that?' If not, 'who can arbitrate?'

These questions – 'who is the best judge?', 'who can arbitrate?' – have for us particular echoes (Augustinian, Hobbesian, Schmittian); though their meaning for Vilatte may well have been a more local tussle for authority. And, while such questions have been, for Hobbes, part of the case for a unitary and supreme sovereign, they here amount to an assertion that *no one* could decide. If the Secretariat would not assert its own interpretation, it was left to members divided amongst themselves, and the failure of the whole project on which the Secretariat's own position was premised.

Zilliacus's letter had in fact refrained from asserting any formal interpretive authority on the part of the Secretariat, or even offering any strong account of custom or previous practice as generating new powers of the Secretariat in some legally cognisable way. Rather, in falling back on the Secretariat's 'preparation' of decisions which would then be 'taken' by governments, he was invoking a sociological reality of the institution's operation as a 'tradition'; and suggesting merely that this de facto role of the Secretariat – 'this unprecedential relationship of the Secretariat to the Governments Members of the League' – be maintained, with conflicts being managed by the craft of Secretariat officials.

Zilliacus admitted that it had grown 'more difficult' to function in this way since 1933, but insisted that, if there was some choice to be made, the only course was to 'stick to the Covenant'. The Secretary-General's argument that the Secretariat was merely an administrative body was incoherent. If the Secretariat was to function at all, it had to do so on the basis of the Covenant: 'The political duty of loyalty to the obligations of the Covenant underlies and informs all the administrative and advisory functions of the Secretariat'. This entailed, for Zilliacus, the Secretariat taking a clearer public stand against violations of the Covenant: Secretariat staff animating 'the League' more forcefully as against the governments of member states.

This course would have been in accordance with one reading of the staff undertaking to 'regulate my conduct with the interests of the League alone in view', but Zilliacus's repeated invocation of the Covenant as a placeholder for the League itself in fact undercut his position. The Covenant certainly gave the *Secretariat* no substantive role. Perhaps sensing the difficulty of an argument which elevated the Secretariat staff as spokesmen for the League and

Covenant over the states which had brought both into being, Zilliacus also offered an alternative approach. He suggested that there was, properly understood, no real conflict between serving the League and serving member states. As he put it, the League 'is not merely a congeries of governments, but also the treaty obligations of the Covenant, *by which the nations are bound that the governments temporarily represent*. ... We owe loyalty to those obligations and to the idea behind them as much as we do to the governments.'[60]

This argument echoed efforts to cast the League as a League of peoples rather than governments, and with commentators' invocations (discussed in Section 10.2) of 'public opinion' as an animating force. But this, too, was something of a dead end in the working-out of a credible theory of the League's authority, and Zilliacus's place within it. As the marginal annotation put it, 'who can ... validly represent within the League those nations & responsibly speak for them if not the G[overn]ments? Or are we a superstate?' Any dismissal of governments as legitimate representatives for the more enduring 'nations' entailed an assertion of Secretariat officials' own authority to act for these nations. Zilliacus had no real answer, other than to invoke technique; what he saw as a peculiarly Anglo-American 'mingling of idealism and realism'; an indefinable 'political responsibility to the Covenant'.

For the marginal annotator, Zilliacus's allegation that the Secretariat was failing in its duty and had 'incurred a share of the political responsibility for denying the victims of aggression – Abyssinia, Spain, China – their rights' was a brazen challenge. Zilliacus's claims to identify the proper course elicited a mocking comment: 'L'individu contre l'état! Sole arbiter'. Moreover, there was dissensus within the Secretariat, not only between the Secretariat and member states or governments. The marginal voice questioned Zilliacus's assumption that, 'there is only one way of conceiving our duty of loyalty to the principles of the Covenant', including loyalty to the Secretary-General and his professed vision of the Secretariat.

At points, Zilliacus cast officials' deference to the Covenant as a sort of ethical commitment independent of consequentialist reasoning. Favouring the standards imposed by the Covenant might lead to the Secretariat's advice being ignored; but 'the responsibility for disregarding their treaty obligations would rest squarely on [governments], in the eyes of the world including their public opinion', and 'the Secretariat would have done its duty'. However, this was not really a disavowal of instrumentalism, but an argument for the one remaining instrumental strategy which seemed open to internationalists.

---

[60] Zilliacus to Avenol, 9 August 1938 (emphasis added).

Zilliacus warned that the Secretariat was 'in danger of losing the respect and confidence *of the Governments and sections of public opinion that are still loyal to what the League stands for*' (implicitly, especially a future Labour government in Britain).[61] Zilliacus here makes the shift seen elsewhere in League practice, from an abstract 'public opinion', figured as the 'eyes of the world', which typically underpinned accounts of the League's authority, to a much narrower, more concrete and strategic notion of 'public opinion' as electorally significant views in Britain.

Throughout the letter, Zilliacus is wrestling with some of the same fundamental questions about the nature and authority of the League that had arisen from the first moment of its creation. He switches between different starting points for his analysis, from the Covenant text to the League itself, as an already-existing person to whom political duties of loyalty were owed. The texture of his arguments ranged from formalist invocation of the Covenant as a 'treaty obligation' to anti-formalist assertion that such obligations bound 'nations' in some timeless way distinct from the legal apparatus of states and governments. Zilliacus worked hard to integrate the Secretariat into the juridical identity of the League, but ultimately was forced to fall back on a 'tradition' with no formal expression, an 'unprecedential relationship' in which the Secretariat's role within the League remained on a purely de facto footing.

Even if this de facto authority, crafted from bureaucratic and diplomatic skill, could be attained, it was dependent on the Secretariat taking a unified view, and the whole exchange around the letter itself had grown out of discord *within* the Secretariat. It seemed very difficult to ground the argument that the Secretariat alone could speak for the League, and to claim that, in doing so, the Secretariat had some higher representative function. Efforts to press the Secretariat to speak for the League as an embodiment of the 'international' ultimately drove Zilliacus well beyond the universe of legal and political obligation, and abstract ideals, into a *realpolitik* alliance between the Secretariat and perceived internationalist publics in Britain.

10.5 THINKING THROUGH THE INTERNATIONAL ORGANISATION

The League, though superseded after the Second World War, has had a long afterlife. It furnished the basic model of an 'international organisation' which persists today. The United Nations differed from the League in important

---

[61] Ibid. (emphasis added).

respects, particularly the powers granted to the Security Council, but it inherited the League's model of an 'international civil service', with staff characterised as 'responsible only to the Organization', and such responsibilities having an 'exclusively international character'.[62] Aspects of the League's workings, carried over into and developed in the United Nations, have formed the kernel of a 'law of international organisations' or 'international institutional law'. I here turn attention from efforts of interwar thinkers to grapple with the League, to efforts today to think about the longer arc of international organisations and their work.

The model of a (putatively universal) international organisation, and 'international' staff, with the somewhat unstable notions of authority and affiliation this entails, has been open to distinct political projects. Whereas Zilliacus's concern was that the League (or the Secretariat *as* the League) was not doing *enough*, not speaking when it should, international officials in different circumstances have sometimes been able and willing to make far more than Drummond or Avenol had done of the possibilities inherent in 'international' authority. Anne Orford, for example, has charted the way in which Hammarskjöld's posture of a 'neutral' international figure underwrote the expansion of UN administration in post-colonial states during the Cold War,[63] and Guy Fiti Sinclair has traced the rhetorical and practical means through which international organisations of various kinds have entrenched an influence well beyond the formal powers sketched in their founding instruments.[64] Such accounts illustrate the role played by international organisations in shaping normative expectations of statehood, and setting the terms of decolonisation. Though the United Nations remains unique in the breadth of its mandate and its 'constitutional' position in the international legal order, there are now myriad international organisations, with diverse but far-reaching remits, and secretariats which may play extensive, often under-theorised, roles. International organisations have emerged as important, if unevenly influential, sites of power, operating in an ensemble of states but also corporate and varied 'civil society' actors.

---

[62] Bruno Simma et al. (eds.), *The Charter of the United Nations: A Commentary* (3rd ed.) (Oxford: Oxford University Press, 2012), vol. 2, 2024. On this continuity, see also the comments of the UN Secretary-General, Dag Hammarskjöld, 'The International Civil Servant in Law and in Fact', lecture delivered at Oxford University, 30 May 1961, available at www.daghammarskjold.se/wp-content/uploads/2019/10/ics_100_no_4_oxfordspeech.pdf.

[63] Anne Orford, *International Authority and the Responsibility to Protect* (Cambridge: Cambridge University Press, 2011).

[64] Fiti Sinclair, *To Reform the World*.

Lawyers, historians and many others have shared a conviction that there is something of importance to explore in the development of our present international institutional landscape. They have also shared an intuition that bringing this role to light might demand that we shift the conventional focus of disciplinary inquiries. Thus, to take two recent examples, Orford has argued that, to understand current theories of the state and authority, we must 'treat the archives of bureaucrats and international civil servants with the care and attention that was previously devoted to glossing the pronouncements of philosophers, judges or legal theorists'.[65] Orford also poses a frontal challenge to contemporary doctrinal reasoning in the area of use of force, peacekeeping and humanitarian intervention, arguing that the chief work of the 'responsibility to protect' programme of the 1990s lay in its retrospective legitimation of powers assumed by the United Nations Secretariat since the 1960s. Susan Pedersen has urged historians and political theorists to pay more attention to the Secretariat (and, by extension, like bodies) as 'a site for political innovation and political thought'.[66]

Proliferating studies of international organisations have in turn elicited questions about what might be gained and lost by different disciplinary perspectives and, of particular relevance here, the stakes of a legal or juridical, as opposed to historical, account of these institutions.[67] The interaction between law and (intellectual) history in the history of international law has to date been framed primarily as a debate about anachronism and contextualism.[68] The argument that law is distinctively concerned with making meaning move across time (to take Orford's vivid phrase), and that

---

[65] Anne Orford, 'On International Legal Method', *London Review of International Law* 1 (2013), 166–97, at 183–4. In a similar vein, concerning the general absence of serious study of international bureaucracies within international relations, see Jarle Trondal and others, *Unpacking International Organisations: The Dynamics of Compound Bureaucracies* (Manchester: Manchester University Press, 2010); John Mathiason, *Invisible Governance: International Secretariats in Global Politics* (Bloomfield, CT: Kumarian Press 2007).

[66] Susan Pedersen, '2017 Nicolai Rubinstein Lecture', abstract, https://projects.history.qmul.ac.uk/hpt/category/the-nicolai-rubinstein-lecture/.

[67] Orford, 'On International Legal Method'.

[68] For an articulation of the argument in these terms, see Anne Orford, 'The Past as Law or History? The Relevance of Imperialism for Modern International Law', in Mark Toufayan, Emmanuelle Tourme-Jouannet and Hélène Ruiz-Fabri (eds.), *Droit international et nouvelles approches sur le tiers-monde: entre répétition et renouveau* (Paris: Société de législation compare, 2013); Orford, 'On International Legal Method'; and for responses on these terms, see Kate Purcell, 'On the Uses and Advantages of Genealogy for International Law', *Leiden Journal of International Law* 33 (2020), 13–35; Lauren Benton, 'Beyond Anachronism: Histories of International Law and Global Legal Politics', *Journal of the History of International Law* 21 (2019), 7–40.

its history thus cannot be captured adequately by contextualist historiographical methods – at least without losing the critical potential of historical approaches in the first place – deserves a fuller treatment than I can offer here. But it does not, I think, exhaust the promise of interdisciplinary conversation.

I want here to take the institution, and the League in particular, as an alternative starting-point. The League case allows us to reflect on the role played by legal discourse in the construction of the international organisation as a category, and on the stakes of the disciplinary perspectives we bring to bear on this history. Just as the League seemed to its contemporaries a perplexing thing, resistant to any comprehensive conceptualisation, it can, I suggest, be a (helpful) irritant for us as well. Institutions, like states, are creatures in and of law, bringing facticity close to the surface of legal analysis. They testify also to the power of intellectual construction, while reminding us that this construction is never wholly intellectual; it is a social, cultural, bureaucratic and often extra-textual phenomenon. The institution as an object of inquiry allows us to see anew the diversity within law and history, and the scope for exchange between them.

The League case illustrates the diversity and instability of early 'legal' thinking about the international institution. To the extent that commentators even understood themselves as anchored definitively in law rather than, for example, political science and a then-emergent discipline of international relations, writers across these boundaries were working with similar conceptual resources (corporation, league, confederation and the like). These commentators, and individuals like Zilliacus, argued in intersecting ways – as in Zilliacus's experimentation with treaty interpretation as one technique alongside others. Even among authors most readily characterised as legal scholars, analyses took diverse starting points. They ranged from efforts to foreground the League as an entity, and classify it alongside 'confederations' and other like persons, to efforts to bracket the institution itself and focus on the interpretation of its founding treaty, or on the legal order of which it was a creation. Lawyers reached for analogies in the corporation, national legal institutions, and a universe of extra-legal metaphors, particularly the League as part of a growing organism of world organisation. This was in part a response to the way in which the legal framework of the League itself stipulated openness to contingency and innovation (as in the paucity of provisions concerning the Secretariat in the League Covenant), and it drew on metaphors with resonance in the constitutional law of the common law world, but also undermined the notion that there was any self-contained and closed legal discourse.

The fact that it is difficult to delineate a domain proper to law in contemporary accounts of the League's founding calls into question how we might today demarcate our approaches to the international organisation. Our own disciplinary orientation matters to some extent, but disciplinary identification alone is a crude measure. Historians of empire and internationalism and law and political thought might be interested in quite different things; they will see organisations in different lights. Lawyers, too, will differ in their intellectual and professional stance. Some will be seeking to craft arguments and produce knowledge within protocols internal to contemporary law which, while uneven and elastic, implicit or explicit, substantive or procedural, and changeable over time, circumscribe the significance and interpretation of past acts and texts.[69] Others who identify primarily as lawyers may probe how law and legal institutions have evolved, how they work, and what they generate, in ways deeply informed by experience internal to law, but not themselves subject to the protocols which would constrain legal argument today.[70]

This is not to say that the divide between work 'internal' to law and beyond it is simple, or closed. It is constructed over time, from both within and without, and politically salient, given law's peculiar capacity to shape institutional and governmental action. Although Orford's assertion of a 'juridical method' of critically engaging the past – as distinct from a historical method – has been framed primarily as an intervention in the terms of interdisciplinary exchange between law and history, it can also be read as addressing law itself as a discipline: a challenge to the limits of what counts as speaking *within* law, on law's terms. Although the assertion that there is a – by implication unitary – 'juridical' mode of engaging the past would seem to flatten distinctions between those writing in a manner internal to law and those less accepting of these strictures, it might also function as an invitation to work precisely at the limits. Orford's work on the United Nations can be read in this light: it presents a narrative and pattern of reasoning that is intuitively familiar to lawyers, centred on authority, jurisdiction and powers; but is recognisably *not* speaking within the protocols conventionally considered to shape law's engagement with the past; the work is illuminating precisely because it, for example, illustrates the intricate and oblique jurisgenerativity of disciplines,

---

[69] For an example of this, the constraining effect of 'sources' doctrine, see Rose Parfitt, 'The Spectre of Sources', *European Journal of International Law* 25 (2014), 297–306.

[70] Notably, e.g., Kennedy, 'The Move to Institutions'; Klabbers, 'The Transformation of International Organizations Law'; Klabbers, 'The Emergence of Functionalism in International Institutional Law: Colonial Inspirations'; Guy Fiti Sinclair, 'Towards a Postcolonial Genealogy of International Organizations Law', *Leiden Journal of International Law* 31 (2018), 841–69.

documents and practices which have no claim to legal effect on any formal account of sources. Much of the force of this reading comes not from being subsumed within an existing juridical method but from the *partial* intelligibility within law which it produces, and the pressure this places on our judgment of what counts as operating within law.

The League case illustrates the way in which writings within law and history can speak to each other. At the most basic level, accounts which read across the boundaries of law's internal understanding, whether they are styled histories or something else, help illuminate what is missed in a purely internal legal account of the institutional past, and the work that law (in all its diversity) is doing. While the consolidation of a law of international organisations has drained international organisations of the startling quality they had for interwar commentators, recovery of the earlier perplexity makes clear the extent to which current questions remain connected to foundational puzzles. Questions about the nature of international organisations' interactions with the wider legal order are related to persistent unease in the legal conceptualisation of the international organisation itself. There is, for example, an enduring oscillation between focusing on the founding treaty as an instrument of institution-creation, with the institution having no 'objective' personality as against third states in the absence of their recognition of it, and focusing on the existence of an institution, however created, as a reality opposable to all states.[71] Problems of corporate agency subsist, as evident, for example, in the challenges of integrating international organisations – particularly those drawing on national forces, personnel and resources in their operations – into a law of responsibility for international wrongs.[72]

The question of speech which recurred in so many different guises in the League, and particularly in the ambiguous relation between Secretariat and institution, remains only partially addressed by law. Although the management of flows of information from governments and non-government networks has been central to the development of complex interrelations between states and international organisations, these have never been fully registered in legal terms. Still today, they barely feature in accounts of the law of

---

[71] On the International Law Commission's evolution from a 'treaty' conception (at the forefront in the working out of the law governing treaties between international organisations, or between such organisations and states), to a qualified 'subject' conception (in connection with work on the responsibility of international organisations): Fernando Lusa Bordin, *The Analogy between States and International Organizations* (Cambridge: Cambridge University Press, 2018), 53–68.

[72] James Crawford, *State Responsibility: The General Part* (Cambridge: Cambridge University Press, 2013), 188–213.

international organisations, beyond reference to inviolability of institutional archives and rules prohibiting unauthorised disclosure of information from staff. This studied indifference to bureaucratic processes is part of the formalising and abstracting work that law does. Yet these flows of information and modes of speech cannot readily be separated from questions of responsibility and authority in and through institutions.

Relatedly, a largely statist sources doctrine[73] has obscured the complex ways in which international organisations and their organs act in the international legal order. It is evident that these organisations may catalyse multilateral treaty-making and incubate customary norms in myriad ways (for example, by eliciting official statements and producing material records from which customary law is discerned). But other aspects of organisational action are less readily assimilated. For example, secretariats, in interpreting founding charters, making decisions in matters before them, or pursuing policy work, may also adopt interpretations of law on particular points, and shape the terms in which legal questions are framed and debated.[74] This works too for the secretariats' own status. Bureaucratic craft and rhetorical self-positioning can settle into what Zilliacus called a 'tradition', an 'unprecedential relationship' which, while difficult to reconcile with founding texts, comes to shape the understanding of governments and interlocutors, and help crystallise pathways of influence over substantive points of law.

Of course, as in the interwar period, legal discourse is internally diverse. Some Anglo-American perspectives, in particular, informed by a common law sensibility, animated by a wider sense of 'governance' or 'administration', and increasingly informed by social scientific investigation of how institutions work in practice, are more likely to capture diffuse and potentially jurisgenerative practice that is not intelligible within a more orthodox emphasis on formal delegation of powers from states. These approaches eschew preoccupation with the legal forms of transnational decision-making and focus instead on its procedure. This may entail careful attention to knowledge and speech: who shapes decision-making and how. But these approaches, while arguably still part of an internal legal account (on a loosely positivist model), will nevertheless face a certain limit to what can be said in a manner internal to

---

[73] I.e., the orthodox position that law has its source in treaties (in which case it binds only the parties); custom (theoretically, binding all states other than those which systematically and deliberately object to the norm from its moment of inception); or, less frequently, 'general principle' (that is, a principle, like non-retroactivity of criminal prohibitions, which is widely shared in the domestic legal systems of the world).

[74] For a study which approaches this question, albeit taking sources doctrine as its foil, José E. Alvarez, *International Organizations as Law-Makers* (Oxford: Oxford University Press, 2006).

law. The more pressure is put on the outer reaches of this perspective, the more one finds oneself confronted with basic questions about the concept of law being invoked.[75]

Law has done much of the work to ensure that we have come, in the space of a few decades, to accept as familiar fundamentally novel structures of authority and responsibility. However contingent law's operation might be, its vocabularies and techniques offer a powerful vector through which past events can take on new significance in the present. History offers one way of seeing this work of law in a way which is not bound by law's own protocols. Of course, histories which touch on international organisations may do so quite differently – including situating international organisations in a larger matrix of states, corporate actors and social movements in a way which de-centres organisations, or emphasises the constraints on or conditions of their influence in particular moments. Nevertheless, such accounts, even when not framed in a fashion internal to law, can sound in law (for example, by unsettling accepted premises of past legal decisions, dominant interpretations of texts, and the normative horizons of legal practitioners).

This is not to say, however, that history (of one kind or another) offers a stable external viewpoint. What emerges from the League case is how profoundly the institution challenges historical as well as juridical analysis, creating shared dilemmas. The dynamic quality of institution and office – the advent of an entity which then, in its workings, changes the terms on which individuals think and act, and others judge it – is a problem for both history and law. Each confronts the interrelation of thought and action ('practice' having elements of each), and the related (but distinct) opposition between the institution's textual and extra-textual workings.

This chapter might, for example, have been framed as a conceptual history. The arguments I trace here could be seen as part of a moment of innovation: the emergence of a 'concept' of the international organisation and international civil service (the two, as presently understood still, being inextricably linked). There is a marked shift around the interwar period in the usage of 'international organisation' which would bear this out. Yet this process of innovation is arguably more iterative and multidimensional than some characterisations of conceptual change in intellectual history.[76] It involves quite

---

[75] See, e.g., the stand-off between 'international public authority' and 'global administrative law' conceptions of the increasingly complex realm of law, or law-like governance, beyond the positivist interstate framework underlying conventional public international law: Paul Craig, *UK, EU and Global Administrative Law: Foundations and Challenges* (Cambridge: Cambridge University Press, 2015), 623–35.

[76] On the politics of characterising conceptual change in particular ways, Isaac, this volume.

marked concrete reforms to the workings of governments and diplomacy, and the invention of new bureaucratic practices, which then feed into a loosely shared endeavour to grasp these new conditions. Intellectual framings work in complex ways with social and bureaucratic practices: conceptualisation may well precede changes in practice; but the latter (sometimes hesitantly deliberate, sometimes not animated by any unitary plan) also re-present the intellectual problem in new guises at different points.

This is borne out by the observations of those whose historical work has been most concerned with how the social history of the international civil service, and civil society mobilisation, meets the formal facets of the institution. To put the issue in Foucauldian terms, this is about the way in which sovereignty as practices of government relates to sovereignty in its more formal juridical (and political) sense. Something of this finds its echo in much recent work. Gram-Skjoldager and Ikonomou write of the need to probe 'the institutional landscape where the individual and ... surroundings meet – where concrete meaning is produced through institutional practice'.[77] Wheatley's study of the mandate petitioning procedure underlines the complexity of historicising a process in which the actual mobilisation and participation of non-state actors shapes the international legal category of the petitioner. She calls for a 'history of international legal personality that is always looking around the corners of the concept itself'.[78]

The account of the League in this chapter links the speech of and for an institution, and more fine-grained controls on the speech of its human staff. It forces together formal conceptions of an institution, made possible by the actions of human agents who are both looking to formal notions of authority and working in their interstices. The abstracting work of law introduces limits to how much of this picture can be juridically relevant to any internal legal argument today (though the limits are not stable or impermeable). Historical accounts offer one means of putting these limits in question, but the practice of history encounters its own challenges in the institution. Either disciplinary stance entails questions about what we ourselves would say now, and why.

---

[77] Gram-Skjoldager and Ikonomou, 'The Construction of the League of Nations Secretariat'.
[78] Natasha Wheatley, 'New Subjects in International Law and Order', in Glenda Sluga and Patricia Clavin (eds.), *Internationalisms: A Twentieth-Century History* (Cambridge: Cambridge University Press, 2017), 265–86, at 273.

Economics and Innovation

11

Sea Change

SURABHI RANGANATHAN*

In his famous 1968 essay, 'The Tragedy of the Commons', Garrett Hardin chose the sea as an illustrative example. '[T]he oceans of the world continue to suffer from the survival of the philosophy of the commons', he wrote.[1] 'Maritime nations still respond automatically to the shibboleth of the "freedom of the seas". Professing to believe in the "inexhaustible resources of the oceans," they bring species after species of fish and whales closer to extinction.'[2] Using this and other examples Hardin argued for enclosure or – as he later phrased it – *management* of the commons, under private property or taxation regimes.[3] In the absence of enclosure, 'total ruin' was inevitable.[4]

Hardin was not wrong in identifying the threat of depletion facing the ocean. But his example was misconceived. For it relied upon, at best,[5] an older imaginary of the ocean, which was even then under substantial legal reconstruction. Hardin was referring – explicitly in later work[6] – to arguments made by the young Hugo Grotius, whose legal brief for the Dutch East India Company, published in

---

* With thanks to the volume editors, and the conveners and participants of the Cambridge International Relations and History seminar for their advice and suggestions on the manuscript.
[1] Garrett Hardin, 'The Tragedy of the Commons', *Science* 162 (1968), 1243–48, at 1245.
[2] Ibid.
[3] See Garrett Hardin, 'Extensions of "The Tragedy of the Commons"', *Science* 280 (1998), 682–3, at 683. Hardin also refers to the tragedy of unmanaged commons in Garrett Hardin, 'An Ecolate View of the Human Predicament', in Clair N. McRostie (ed.), *Global Resources: Perspectives and Alternatives* (Baltimore: University Park Press, 1980), 49–71, at 50.
[4] Hardin, 'Tragedy of the Commons', 1247.
[5] Lauren Benton offers a rich account of the flourishing of early-modern European understandings of the ocean as 'variegated spaces transected by law' alongside representations of it as free of law: Lauren Benton, *A Search for Sovereignty: Law and Geography in European Empires 1400–1900* (Cambridge: Cambridge University Press, 2010), 104–61.
[6] Hardin, 'Extensions', 682.

part as *Mare Liberum* in the early seventeenth century, had described the ocean as unoccupiable, inexhaustible, indeed unalterable for better *or* worse via human activity, and as irreducible to private ownership or state sovereignty.[7]

Grotius had argued that the ocean exceeded legal disposition: 'no part of [it could] be accompted in the territory of any people'; it was originally, and would remain, a commons.[8] Sovereigns could exercise certain jurisdictions *at* sea – they could capture and punish pirates, and regulate fishing and other activities by their own nationals. They could also police the waters on behalf of other sovereigns with their agreement.[9] Relying upon instruments of scientific measurement, inter-sovereign treaties might even indicate precise areas of the seas in which the delegation would operate. But the seas themselves could not be partitioned by such treaties: 'And consequently if any treaties had been made which rested on such a distinction, I said in the *Mare Liberum* that the thing is not affected but the persons are obligated.'[10] Neither by unilateral proclamation nor by mutual agreement could sovereigns reduce the sea to territorial jurisdiction, for the sea was not like land.

These ideas were challenged by Grotius's contemporaries, especially for failing to distinguish between coastal waters, which could be enclosed, and the farther removed 'main sea'.[11] The free sea thesis was subsequently qualified – Grotius himself concurring – to exclude narrow bands of water over which control could be exercised from the coast.[12] Qualifications relating to navigation, fishing, and the laying of submarine cables also followed in the eighteenth and nineteenth centuries.[13] But while they regulated some uses of

---

[7] Hugo Grotius, 'The Free Sea', trans. Richard Hakluyt (1609), reprinted in *The Free Sea*, ed. David Armitage (Indianapolis: Liberty Fund 2004), 1–62.

[8] Ibid., 30. And further (ibid., at 31–2):
the rents which are set down for fishing upon the sea-coast are reckoned in the number of royalties, and bind not the thing, that is, the sea or fishing, but the persons. Wherefore subjects over whom the commonwealth or prince have power to make a law by consent may peradventure be compelled to these burdens and impositions, but the right of fishing everywhere ought to be free to foreigners, that servitude be not imposed on the sea, which cannot serve. For the reason of the sea and of a river is not the same ...

[9] Ibid., 31, and Hugo Grotius, 'Defense of Chapter V of the *Mare Liberum*', trans. Herbert Wright (1928), in *The Free Sea*, ed. Armitage, 75–130, at 128–30.

[10] Grotius, 'Defense of Chapter V', 112.

[11] William Welwod, 'Of the Community and Propriety of the Seas' (1613), in *The Free Sea*, ed. Armitage, 65–74, at 74.

[12] The so-called cannon-shot rule was gradually formalised into a rule permitting coastal states to exercise sovereign control over a stretch (usually 3 nautical miles) of the waters and seabed adjacent to the coast.

[13] Examples include the Convention for the Protection of Submarine Telegraph Cables (1884); International Convention for Regulating the Police of the North Sea Fisheries Outside

the sea, the treaties concluded on these matters could be represented as instantiating the Grotian idea of inter-sovereign agreements binding their subjects, not a general legal disposition of rights over the sea. Perhaps, then, they could still be described as underpinned by the idea of a free sea.

But it is fair to say that in 1968, the year of Hardin's writing, the ocean could no longer be described as exceeding territorial disposition. Starting with the Truman Proclamations of 1945,[14] states were claiming exclusive sovereign rights over larger areas of the ocean. These claims, and the arguments made by diplomats and lawyers in their support, not only substantially enclosed the ocean; they also altered how the ocean was understood and imagined, constructing a legal geography that diverged from the physical. Moreover, in the increasingly reduced areas that remained commons, the freedom of the sea was itself becoming a delimited legal institution: shorthand for agreed rights and, importantly, obligations governing access and use. If the four Geneva Conventions of 1958 represented an important stage in this process,[15] the adoption of the 1982 UN Convention on the Law of the Sea (LOSC) – the so-called constitution for the oceans – was a culmination, making it clear that the validity of conduct in areas beyond national jurisdiction derived not from a prior freedom, but from permissions confirmed through law. Later agreements have added further conditions determining rights in, and on, the sea.[16] With these instruments, the ocean has become fully incorporated into law.

This is important to emphasise. For the threat of depletion that Hardin rightly envisaged is not the result of freedom. Rather, it has been facilitated by legal regimes – already well under construction by 1968 – that govern extractive activity. Hardin himself would not acknowledge this, blaming in later work as he did in the earlier the corrupting notion of the freedom of the sea: 'Now the once unlimited resources of marine fishes have become scarce and nations are coming to limit the freedom of their fishers in the

---

Territorial Waters (1882); and countless bilateral treaties on commerce and navigation over the seas.

[14] Proclamation 2668 – Policy of the United States with respect to Coastal Fisheries in Certain Areas of the High Seas; and Proclamation 2667 – Policy of the United States with respect to the Natural Resources of the Subsoil and Sea Bed of the Continental Shelf, 28 September 1945.

[15] Convention on the Territorial Sea and the Contiguous Zone, Convention on the High Seas, Convention on Fishing and Conservation of the Resources of the Living Resources of the High Seas, and Convention on the Continental Shelf.

[16] Including: UN Fish Stocks Agreement (1995); various regional fisheries agreements; and the Agreement relating to Part XI of the UN Convention on the Law of the Sea (1994). Negotiations are also currently underway on an agreement relating to the conservation and sustainable use of marine biological diversity of areas beyond national jurisdiction.

commons. ... (And still the shibboleth, "the freedom of the seas," interferes with rational judgment.)"[17]

* * *

While Hardin's ideas about the commons are problematic, to say the least, and have attracted much and deserved critique,[18] in this chapter I would like to think with his assertion of the freedom of the sea, which sits at first sight at odds with my assertion of the ocean's substantial legal incorporation by the time of Hardin's writing. Hardin is not alone in suggesting that the sea still, somehow, remains outside the law, a space of freedom. Such a sense is also conveyed in, for instance, utopian projects for building human habitats on the ocean. In 2008, Silicon Valley venture capitalists, Patri Friedman and Peter Thiel, established The Seasteading Institute (TSI), with the announced aim of establishing novel ocean-floating cities that could provide hubs for societal innovation:

> The world needs a place where those who wish to experiment with building new societies can go to test out their ideas. All land on Earth is already claimed, making the oceans humanity's next frontier.[19]

Here TSI propagates the idea of the 'offshore' as a space of complete autonomy, beyond the writ of positive law and settled traditions, so that to leave land is to shed the burden of inherited ideas and concepts in favour of entirely new social experiments. Again, this is not actually the case. TSI rapidly descended from this elevated notion of freedom in describing its first concrete project: a now-cancelled plan for building a floating structure in the territorial waters of French Polynesia, which was to enjoy not original freedom but a delegation of some powers of autonomy, in return for monetary consideration.[20] Yet the prospect of freedom on the sea remains an important imaginative element of TSI's vision.

Why do such representations of the freedom of the seas persist? As I will discuss below, that they do is revealing of an enduring political economy of the law of the sea, which distributes rights and constraints in an uneven way,

---

[17] Hardin, 'Extensions', 682.
[18] Notably, Elinor Ostrom, *Governing the Commons: The Evolution of Institutions for Collective Action* (Cambridge: Cambridge University Press, 1990). Recent analyses contextualising Hardin's ideas include Fabien Locher, 'Cold War Pastures: Garrett Hardin and the "Tragedy of the Commons"', *Revue d'histoire moderne et contemporaine* 60 (2013), 7–36, and mine: Surabhi Ranganathan, 'Global Commons', *European Journal of International Law* 27 (2016), 693–717.
[19] www.seasteading.org/about/.
[20] www.seasteading.org/floating-city-project/.

such that some indeed enjoy an unlimited access to the ocean's resources, where others face exclusion. TSI is thus merely voicing the expectation of select individuals about the ease with which *they* will be able to use the sea; while Hardin is – probably unconsciously, but more tellingly for that – obscuring the uneven operations of international law in protecting the impunity of some corporations and states to exploit the ocean by describing their actions as the exercise of a universal freedom. The 'freedom of the sea' is a rhetorically powerful trope for talking about (or rather, not talking about) the ways in which the law shapes access to the oceans. To make these points, I will focus on the legal regimes addressing the two ocean commons: the high seas and the deep seabed.

I will then turn to the further question of what accounts for these legal regimes. One candid explanation offered in legal scholarship is that international law is simply epiphenomenal to the interests of powerful states. This explanation has several shortcomings: it does not interrogate which interests, and remains too crudely deterministic, obscuring both the workings of legal ideology, and the internalised *lawyering* techniques by which legal change is facilitated or resisted. Above all, it reduces international law solely to an emanation of underlying – but underexplored – political configurations. Against this type of explanation, I argue that the production of the particular political economy of the ocean regimes under discussion turned critically on law and legal technique, shaped by as well as reinscribing a capitalist political economy. My argument will join other voices in calling for a focus on the more subtle elements that have informed international law's contents and distributive effects: in particular, the doctrinal commitments, class locations, and social dynamics of the 'invisible college of international lawyers' who were the architects of our international legal order.[21] In the final section I suggest that such a focus is a necessary stepping-stone to self-reflection about the frames within which we engage on questions relating to nature, resources and the oceans today, a time of undeniable and rapid literal sea change.

11.1 FROM THE FREE SEA TO AN OCEAN OF LAW

Let me begin, then, with the argument that since 1945, the law has substantially incorporated the ocean. My point is not simply that there is now a lot more international law pertaining to the sea, although that is indubitably true. The LOSC, together with its implementing agreements, 'provides the

---

[21] Oscar Schachter, 'The Invisible College of International Lawyers', *Northwestern University Law Review* 72 (1977–8), 217–26.

framework within which most uses of the seas are located';[22] and even so is only one among many instruments that may be listed. Taking examples solely from two websites – the International Maritime Organization's list of instruments relating to shipping,[23] and New York University's Globalex entry on international fisheries law[24] – we might count thirty-one multilateral treaties concluded in the period between the Truman Proclamations and the adoption of the LOSC. For the same period, a standard textbook on the law of the sea lists fifty-one multilateral treaties speaking to various uses of the sea.[25] These numbers are probably not comprehensive even for multilateral treaties: they include only some regional instruments, and entirely exclude bilateral treaties, non-binding declarations, and memoranda of understanding. They also do not include instruments concluded before the mid-twentieth century, and the very large number of instruments adopted subsequent to the LOSC. Individually, none of these treaties enjoys universal application (the LOSC itself cannot count the United States and twenty-eight other states among its parties, although fourteen of these are signatories) but collectively they add up to a dense network of legal regulations. Moreover, they are embedded within customary international law, which *is* universally applicable, and part of which was codified by the LOSC. We may further take note of the array of international institutions with competence on oceans issues, the slate of regulations issued by each, and the number of maritime disputes before international courts and tribunals. All of this adds to the conclusion that, rather than exceeding the law, the ocean is an intensely juridified space.

But that alone is not my point. More crucial is the impact of all this law on how the ocean is understood and encountered. Here, I suggest that the law has consolidated an imaginary of the sea as an assemblage of jurisdictionally discrete sites of economic activity.[26] It has accomplished this via at least three conceptual divisions: into zones within and beyond national jurisdiction; into regimes of land and water; and into regimes addressing specific living and non-living *resources*.

---

[22] Robin Churchill and Vaughan Lowe, *The Law of the Sea* (3rd ed.) (Manchester: Manchester University Press, 1999), 24.
[23] www.imo.org/en/About/Conventions/ListOfConventions/Pages/Default.aspx.
[24] Abdullah Al Arif, 'An Introduction to International Fisheries Law Research', *GlobaLex* (February 2018), www.nyulawglobal.org/globalex/International_Fisheries_Law.html#_edn4.
[25] Yoshifumi Tanaka, *The International Law of the Sea* (2nd ed.) (Cambridge: Cambridge University Press, 2015).
[26] For reasons of space, my arguments here are abbreviated. For a fuller account, including a tracing of the developments that fully enclosed the ocean floor, see Surabhi Ranganathan, 'Ocean Floor Grab: International Law and the Making of an Extractive Imaginary', *European Journal of International Law* 30 (2019), 573–600.

The first division shrinks what may now be regarded as the oceanic commons: *not* internal waters, territorial seas, contiguous zones, exclusive economic zones, archipelagic waters, or the continental shelf. In the words of Arvid Pardo, who is sometimes described as the 'father of the new law of the sea'[27] (replacing the old father, Grotius), these zones add up to an enclosure of 'perhaps as much as forty percent of ocean space'.[28] Some of these zones were drawn on the assertion of 'natural' criteria they do not follow. The continental shelf, for example, was asserted on the idea that it represented a natural prolongation of coastal territory, but the legal continental shelf exceeds the geological shelf in many instances, and may encompass areas which are not in any physical sense a prolongation of coastal land, including even deep seabed. And all of these zones were drawn with reference to economic information they do not cite: thus the areas brought within national jurisdiction enclosed all known oil and gas resources, commercially exploitable minerals, and most of the world's commercial fishery resources.[29]

The second division might appear at first sight to have its basis in the idiosyncrasy of lawyers, who insisted, as though it were a matter of great discovery, on 'the distinction, obvious to the layman, between land on the one hand and water on the other hand'.[30] Thus, in justifying shelf claims in the years after the Truman Proclamations, legal commentators advanced arguments such as that an 'infinitely thin' membrane divided the subsoil of the seabed and the water column, and permitted the removal of resources which were then wholly those of the bed, not of the sea.[31] However, such claims emerged not from specious geology but economic logic: a separation of

---

[27] See, e.g., Malta Department of Information, Press Release No. 202 (19 February 2002); outside his home state (Malta), other institutions offer the more limited but still generous accolade of the 'Father of the Law of the Sea Conference': see, e.g., UN Press Release SEA/1619 (16 July 1999).

[28] Arvid Pardo, 'The Convention on the Law of the Sea: A Preliminary Appraisal', *San Diego Law Review* 20 (1982–3), 489–503, at 496–7. A year later, Pardo would assert that the area enclosed represented '[u]p to forty percent or more of ocean space': Arvid Pardo, 'Before and After', *Law and Contemporary Problems* 46(2) (1983), 95–105, at 101.

[29] See Pardo, 'The Convention on the Law of the Sea: A Preliminary Appraisal', 497.

[30] D.H.N. Johnson, 'The Legal Status of the Sea-Bed and Subsoil', *Zeitschrift für ausländisches öffentliches Recht und Völkerrecht* 16 (1956), 451–99, at 461.

[31] See ibid., 462–3. To be fair, this was not Johnson's own argument. He admitted that the land/water distinction was not coherent in all instances: 'It must be conceded, however, that phenomena such as drying shoals present awkward problems to the jurist who would seek to exaggerate even so simple [a] distinction as that between land and water. There may, after all, be a wonderful unity in nature capable of defying all distinctions which jurists or anyone else find it convenient to draw.' Ibid., 461.

the bed and water permitted occupation of the former without conceding existing rights ('freedoms') of navigation and fisheries in the latter.[32]

The second division also provided fresh impetus for the third: if land and water were indeed to be treated separately, some classification of the contents of the ocean as falling within one or the other had to be made. The LOSC consolidates the following allocations: for areas within national jurisdiction, petroleum and minerals are placed under the regime of the continental shelf, as are living organisms legally qualified as 'sedentary' – including crustaceans, which swim.[33] The rest are under the water regimes of the territorial sea and the exclusive economic zone. For areas beyond national jurisdiction, all living organisms are placed under the regime of the high seas – including, e.g., rock-embedded microbial communities[34] – administered via a patchwork of regional fisheries regimes. The thin membranes that fragment the interconnected ecosystems of the ocean are legal and conceptual, not physical.

Grotius had accepted a technologically enabled striation, based on the reach of arms from the coast, which became the three-mile rule; The twentieth century 'new' law of the sea was also of course catalysed by technological developments. However, one of its paradoxical characteristics is that ultimately its key jurisdictional zones were specified on a mathematical basis, rather than strictly by reference to physical features or the reach of particular technologies for exploitation. If we read the Grotian conception as one rejecting that mathematical striations could generate legal lines delimiting the ocean,[35] the new law of the sea is replete with such lines. The question is how these lines alter the freedom of the sea, and what to make of Hardin's suggestion that they do not. In the two following sections, my argument will be that the new law of the sea performs a paradoxical function: it constricts

---

[32] See, e.g., Humphrey Waldock, 'The Legal Basis of Claims to the Continental Shelf', *Transactions of the Grotius Society* 36 (1950), 115–48. Of course, with the subsequent enclosure of part of the water column, these freedoms would be reduced; but the juridical distinction between land and water was maintained.

[33] See Chie Kojima, 'Fisheries, Sedentary' (December 2008), in *Max Planck Encyclopaedia of Public International Law* online, Oxford University Press, para. 2.

[34] Stefan Helmreich offers a wonderful study of the liminal presence of these microbes, at the intersections of water and land, life and non-life, space and place: Stefan Helmreich, *Alien Ocean: Anthropological Voyages in Microbial Seas* (Berkeley: University of California Press, 2009).

[35] The concept of 'striated' space is from Gilles Deleuze and Felix Guattari, *A Thousand Plateaus*, trans Brian Massumi (Minneapolis: Minnesota University Press, 1988), 474; and I borrow the image of 'lines in the ocean' from Henry Jones, 'Lines in the Ocean: Thinking with the Sea about Territory and International Law', *London Review of International Law* 4 (2016), 307–43; it is also evoked in Benton's description of spaces 'transected by law': Benton, *A Search for Sovereignty*, 105.

freedom, whether understood as the pure absence of legal restrictions or as liberty from 'dependence on the goodwill of others'[36] for many, but enables a privileged few to use the sea in a relatively unconstrained way. The few who enjoy the benefits are, in a sense, the same few who also enjoyed the benefits of the old law of the sea: transnational corporations and imperial ('developed') states. As I will show, their rights to the sea were recouped from efforts to build an alternative legal order of the oceans that fostered substantive equality in the use and distribution of ocean resources. In speaking of the 'shibboleth of the "freedom of the seas"', Hardin stumbles upon this political economy of the law of the sea, although his critique was almost certainly inadvertent.

11.2 WHO HAS THE FREEDOM OF THE SEA?

At first sight the law of the sea simply introduces even-handed constraints on the freedom of the sea. It delimits what now remains as the common sea and subjects these common areas to resource regimes. Thus, fishing on the high seas is governed by licences and quotas issued by regional fisheries management organisations (RFMOs). Meanwhile, the exploration and exploitation of deep seabed minerals is licensed by the International Seabed Authority (ISA), established under the LOSC.

It is indeed possible to view these regimes as necessary to protect rights to access and use the sea, since their stated purpose is to foster sustained exploitation of the resources of these areas.[37] Thus, with respect to fisheries, the RFMOs seek to ensure that in each season stocks are fished only to a degree from which they may recover for the next season. And, with respect to seabed minerals, the ISA offers the dual promise, to contractors of legal security of tenure over specific mining sites (necessary to the nature of the activity undertaken); and to the international community as a whole of the protection of the marine environment, as well as some share in the mining profits, by way of application of the principle that the deep seabed is 'the common heritage of mankind'. Described in these terms, we might say that these regimes, while

---

[36] Quentin Skinner, *Liberty before Liberalism* (Cambridge: Cambridge University Press, 1997), 119.
[37] This view was expressly stated by the International Law Commission among others: 'Any freedom that is to be exercised in the interests of all entitled to enjoy it, must be regulated. Hence, the law of the high seas contains certain rules, most of them already recognized in positive international law, which are designed, not to limit or restrict the freedom of the high seas, but to safeguard its exercise in the interests of the entire international community.' 'Articles concerning the Law of the Sea with commentaries' (1956), in *Yearbook of the International Law Commission* (1956), vol. II, 265–301, at 278.

introducing some constraints, are what make continuing economic activity possible in the ocean.

A closer look at the detail of these regimes, however, reveals a more complicated picture. They oversee an uneven distribution of rights and constraints. Fisheries regimes, as Andrew Serdy reveals in his excellent study, although formally still informed by the principle of the freedom of the sea, have tended to be configured along an 'insider' versus 'outsider' dynamic, that benefits states with established fishing industries at the expense of those with nascent deep-water and distance fisheries.[38] Previously, in the 1950s, this was in the guise of the misleadingly termed 'abstention' doctrine, under which Japan, just emerging from occupation, was discouraged by the United States from fishing salmon in Bristol Bay for the sake of conservation of the stock; the criteria for abstention were so worded as to preserve the US fishing industry's 'access to the fishing grounds of the west coast of Central and South America and the Grand Banks of Newfoundland respectively'.[39] The United States might have succeeded in incorporating the doctrine of abstention into international fisheries law, but for 'an excessively frank remark in its favour' by a member of the International Law Commission (ILC) during the ILC's work on the 1958 Geneva Conventions: he called it the 'principle of justified exclusion of third parties'.[40]

Today RFMOs, dominated by states with established fisheries operations, promote a kind of 'neo-abstentionism'.[41] That is, they use criteria for allocating national fishing quotas that are designed to exclude new entrants. Thus, barring a few expediently co-opted ones, post-colonial ('developing') states that are new to a fishery or lack domestic fishing fleets might learn that they do not qualify to participate in that fishery, because they lack 'a real interest'[42] in it. Or, if their real interest is conceded, they might be accorded a zero allocation, or one that makes investment in that fishery untenable.[43] This is done on the argument of conservation: that there is simply no quota left over

---

[38] Andrew Serdy, *The New Entrants Problem in International Fisheries Law* (Cambridge: Cambridge University Press, 2014). I found Serdy's work all the more interesting for not taking distribution as its starting problematic; rather, Serdy is concerned about the tragedy of the commons following from the imperfect enclosure of fisheries. It is in the course of exploring efforts towards and possibilities for a more stringent regime of property rights in fisheries that his analysis very precisely reveals the political economy holding in place the current framework.

[39] Ibid., 70.

[40] Ibid., 71.

[41] See ibid., 73ff.

[42] A term used in the UN Fish Stocks Agreement (1995), art. 8(3).

[43] Serdy offers the example of the North Atlantic Fisheries Organization's allocation of only 69 tonnes of redfish to the Republic of Korea in 1997, which was too little to be profitably

after national allocations to existing users have been made – the heavily-overcapitalised fishing industries of existing quota holders strongly resisting suggestions that they might relinquish part of their usual allocation to new entrants.

Their interests hardly accommodated within the regional fisheries regimes, new entrants are also dissuaded from operating outside them. Through the growing use of a tidy form of words, their fisheries – *unregulated*, but in the absence of membership to further qualifying treaties, covered by the principle of the freedom of the seas – are assimilated to the crime of *illegal* fishing.[44] The clamour against 'illegal, underreported and unregulated' (IUU) fishing conflates rather different challenges, obscures the distribution issues that lead certain states to avoid joining regional fisheries regimes, and, further, conceals from view the ways in which the insiders in those regimes might be undermining conservation efforts by overfishing. Overfishing by insiders is also illegal fishing, but tends to attract little criticism, and almost no sanctions.[45] Moreover, such overfishing may follow already too-high fishing quotas, set at unsustainable limits due to industry pressure. Together with the further problem of illegal fishing in the under-policed exclusive economic zones of other states, such practices deserve much greater scrutiny than they receive.

Fisheries in the ocean commons are thus made an illicit activity for some fishers, while others, able to avoid all but the appearance of constraint, enjoy it as a freedom. But this freedom is not simply the legacy of the older imaginary. It is, rather, an absence of obligation that has been nurtured in the face of alternative conceptions of fisheries regulations that had circulated in the 1950s and 60s. In the early 1950s, the International Law Commission had briefly considered proposals for establishing an international authority with a general competence to regulate high seas fisheries.[46] Although it did not take this idea forward, the idea remerged in the 1960s in proposals seeking that all of the ocean beyond national jurisdiction be declared the common heritage of mankind, such that its resources could be exploited 'with due consideration for their conservation, and for the benefit of all peoples of the world'.[47]

---

fished; prior to joining the organisation Korea had fished 9,000 tonnes of redfish in the same area: Serdy, *The New Entrants Problem*, 96.

[44] See ibid., 141ff.
[45] Ibid., 145.
[46] Ibid., 11–12.
[47] From the text of the draft resolution submitted to the UN General Assembly by the Commission to Study the Organization of Peace: Draft Resolution and Working Paper, 21 August 1967, S-0858-0005-03, UN Archives, New York.

One of the most ambitious versions of this idea, a comprehensive Ocean Space Treaty drafted by Pardo, and submitted by Malta to the UN General Assembly in 1971,[48] would have removed fishing from the list of high seas freedoms altogether, turning it instead into an activity undertaken exclusively by, or under the control of, an international organisation, which had the responsibility to ensure conservation of fish stocks, foster ocean research capabilities of technologically less advanced states, and redistribute the revenue earned, giving special attention to the needs of developing states.[49] The proposed treaty also required states to transfer a percentage of the revenues derived from fisheries within their zones of national jurisdiction to the international organisation, and mandated their cooperation with this organisation vis-à-vis fisheries close to the border between national and international jurisdiction.[50]

These ideas obviously did not succeed. It was ironically Pardo himself who had provided the tools for their subordination, by way of an earlier proposal to the UN General Assembly which sought to limit the application of the common heritage principle to mineral resources of the deep seabed.[51] That earlier proposal was a key the reason why oceans issues had again grabbed the attention of international lawmakers in the late 1960s and 70s. The demand for a comprehensive renegotiation of the law of the sea crystallised into the Third UN Conference on the Law of the Sea (and therefrom the LOSC), which took up, inter alia, the challenge of creating a common heritage regime for the deep seabed. However, radical suggestions for regulating fisheries were quietly displaced by a reasserted 'freedom of the sea' that now required states to cooperate towards establishing region- or species-specific regimes, which operate in the unequal ways described above.

At the very moment that Hardin was offering the sea as an example of a tragic commons, there circulated conceptions that aimed to maximise opportunities both for redistribution and for protection of its 'ecological integrity'.[52] That an unequal freedom of fishing was nevertheless maintained did not

---

[48] 'Draft Ocean Space Treaty', Working paper submitted by Malta to the Committee on the Peaceful Uses of the Seabed and the Ocean Floor beyond the Limits of National Jurisdiction, UN Doc. A/AC.138/53, 23 August 1971.

[49] Article 5 excludes fisheries from the freedoms of the seas. Fisheries in the international oceans area are instead included within the common heritage framework set out in Part IV of the Draft Convention.

[50] See 'Draft Ocean Space Treaty', arts. 59 and 61.

[51] General Assembly, First Committee Debate, UN Doc. A/C.1/PV.1515–1516, 1 November 1967; see also Malta, Request for the inclusion of a supplementary item, UN Doc. A/6695, 18 August 1967.

[52] From language used in the Draft Ocean Space Treaty: see ch. XXV.

represent simply the carrying on of an old 'shibboleth', but the deployment of mechanisms to preserve the interests that that old shibboleth had served.

11.3 THE RETREAT OF THE COMMON HERITAGE OF MANKIND

The regime for the deep seabed is a further illustration of the same dynamic of unequal freedom, even though at first sight it may appear rather as a subversion of it (given that the law removes the deep seabed as a whole from under the umbrella of principle of the freedom of the sea). The UN General Assembly adopted Pardo's 1967 suggestion to designate the international area of the seabed and its (mineral) resources the common heritage of mankind, in view of a then-emerging industrial interest in the possibilities of mining deep seabed minerals.[53] The provisions of the LOSC clarified that the area designated as the common heritage was non-appropriable; that its resources must be exploited for the equitably shared benefit of all states; and that such exploitation should not result in serious harm either to the surrounding marine environment, or to the mineral export economies of land-based mineral producers (the worst affected of which should be compensated for loss of earnings). Part XI of the LOSC set out an extremely detailed regime specifying the rights and obligations of states and the powers and functions of the ISA.[54]

Amongst the aspects of this regime that might appear radical was the flesh that LOSC gave to the idea of common benefit: not just a redistribution of profits from seabed mining, but also arrangements enabling the participation of developing states in the mining activity. Thus, the LOSC gave the ISA its own mining arm, the 'Enterprise', which could involve developing states in the activity of seabed mining both indirectly (by mining on behalf of the international community) and directly, by engaging them in cooperative ventures. The LOSC also required developed states to provide several forms of assistance to developing states: identifying mining sites to be banked with the ISA for their use or use by the Enterprise; transferring technology on reasonable terms; providing training to personnel; and following production policies to avoid glutting the market for minerals. The ISA was also to

---

[53] Declaration of Principles Governing the Sea-Bed and the Ocean Floor, and the Subsoil Thereof, beyond the limits of National Jurisdiction, GA Res. 25/2749, 17 December 1970.
[54] In this discussion of the possibly radical elements of the LOSC regime, I draw on some previous writing, including Surabhi Ranganathan, 'The Law of the Sea and Natural Resources', in Eyal Benvenisti, Georg Nolte and Keren Yalin-Mor (eds.), *Community Interests Across International Law* (Oxford: Oxford University Press, 2018), 121–35.

reallocate funds transferred by developed states in the form of licence fees and mining royalties to developing states.

Another radical element was that developing states were ensured a say in the administration of seabed mining. The ISA was given two principal organs: an Assembly of all LOSC parties – developing states thus enjoying a numerical majority – and a Council with restricted membership. The division of powers between the two was important: while the Council was empowered to advise the Assembly on regulations and procedures, and to approve or reject mining contracts, the Assembly was designated as the supreme organ, and was to function as the legislative arm, enjoying final decision-making authority on matters of general policy and on points of detail such as the most equitable allocation of economic benefits.

The decade-long seabed negotiations had been regarded as a test case for the possibility of decolonising international law, and for the law's potential to address developing states' demands for a 'new international economic order' (NIEO), in which they would be active producers of industrial wealth and participants in establishing global economic arrangements.[55] The elements of the seabed regime that catered to these aspirations were even more meaningful than a share in the mining profits; for all that such a share represented a major potential monetary inflow received as a matter of right, and not as a matter of aid.

But, once again, it is worth focusing on the details. For they reveal a regime in retreat almost from the moment of its inception. The narrowing of the common heritage principle commenced from Pardo's very act of introducing it to the UN General Assembly. As noted above, he initially advocated it only vis-à-vis the seabed, and not the high seas as well. Pardo recollected that he did so to avoid 'the suspicion and opposition' that would follow if major powers suspected him of seeking to replace the umbrella principle of freedom of the sea with the common heritage principle. He estimated that they might not have been as concerned with a proposal limited to the deep seabed alone, for it had 'until then had aroused little interest in international lawyers and governments'.[56] Yet this initial narrowing, accompanied by Pardo's inflated representation of the mineral wealth of the deep seabed and its ease of

---

[55] In the words of a leading scholar from the developing world, the LOSC negotiations were regarded as 'a microcosm of the possibilities the future held and the inauguration of a new era in international relations': B.S. Chimni, 'International Law Scholarship in Post-colonial India: Coping with Dualism', *Leiden Journal of International Law* 23 (2010), 23–51, at 38.

[56] Arvid Pardo, 'The Origins of the 1967 Maltese Initiative', *International Insights: A Dalhousie Journal on International Affairs* 9(2) (1993), 65–9, at 66–7.

recovery,[57] set in motion dynamics that would further constrict the common heritage principle.

This was, first, by a reduction of the area of the seabed regarded as common heritage: Pardo had considered that most, if not all, of the seabed beyond the stretches of the continental shelf over which national jurisdiction had already been claimed, would come within the international seabed area. However, from the skilful deployment and disregard of the rationale of natural prolongation, very broad continental shelf claims emerged instead, which, as mentioned, enclosed all petroleum resources.

Second, within the area in which it applied, the common heritage principle was further constricted by the introduction of a market approach in the guise of the 'parallel system'. Initial proposals advocated by developing states would have permitted only mining by the Enterprise. This was not acceptable to developed states and corporations, who wanted to run their own mining operations – in fact their initial preference had been for a minimal international regime that would simply operate a registry of mining claims. In the mid-1970s, during the months between the LOSC negotiation sessions, Henry Kissinger conducted a series of bilateral discussions with influential developing states, seeking to persuade them of a compromise in the form of a parallel system permitting both the Enterprise and state-sponsored corporations to undertake mining operations. This, he asserted, would be a viable system, since there were 'more than 100 valuable sites on which operations could be conducted at present'.[58] In fact, in private meetings a small group of developed states – the United States, the United Kingdom, France, Japan and the Soviet Union – had conceded that, given the mineral concentrations on each possible mining site, the economics did not support multiple mining operations. (They also agreed that seabed mining would generate 'insignificant' revenues for distribution among developing states for the foreseeable future.)[59]

The seemingly radical LOSC provisions to facilitate developing state participation in seabed mining were thus part of the bargain for the parallel system, and lose their sheen once the calculations underlying that system are recognised. Owing to their first mover advantage, developed states expected their major mining corporations to monopolise seabed mining to the extent the activity was technologically and economically viable. And they protected this advantage in various ways: in addition to the parallel system, they also

---

[57] I discuss the significance, underlying context and substantive merits of Pardo's famous speech, in Ranganathan, 'Global Commons', 711–13.
[58] Meeting with Kenyan officials, 13 August 1976, KL/14/1, Kenya National Archives.
[59] Per records in FCO 76/733, UK National Archives.

obtained a scheme to protect their 'pioneer investor' status that amounted to 'an almost complete rewriting of the Convention's rules on the sea-bed mining in their favour'.[60]

Pardo, although continuing to laud the common heritage principle as a 'far-reaching innovation', and the establishment of the ISA as a 'precedent of incalculable importance', deplored the way in which it had been given effect in the LOSC.[61] He pointed out the parallel system rested on fallacious assumptions; and effectively ensured that no mining in the international seabed area would be able to compete with mining operations for those same minerals in areas within the national jurisdiction of states.[62] Critical voices from developing states pointed out that many of the other supposed benefits were also illusory: the production limitations that had been agreed were based on a 'nickel formula' that responded to the concerns of major developed state producers like Canada; they did not protect producers of other seabed minerals, especially cobalt; and the transfer of technology obligations were limited to first-generation technology, and that too either upon commercial terms or where the transfer would not impose a substantial cost upon the transferor.[63]

Yet, by and large, developing states and third world lawyers remained invested in the mining regime. Perhaps the continued bitter criticisms of its 'socialist' character[64] contributed to the perception that some sort of ideological victory had been won: the NIEO had stalled neoliberalism. Thus, as the US stance against the common heritage regime strengthened, the Group of 77 'assumed a role as the guardian of the integrity of the Convention'.[65] The United States, meanwhile, refusing to sign the LOSC, steered other developed states into an alternative regime, under which they would recognise each other's unilaterally issued mining licences; justifying this by invoking, yet again, the principle of the freedom of the seas, as still applicable to the deep seabed. The 'reciprocating states regime', as it was

---

[60] Churchill and Lowe, *Law of the Sea*, 230.
[61] Arvid Pardo, 'Before and After', 97–8; Pardo, 'A Preliminary Appraisal', 491.
[62] Pardo, 'A Preliminary Appraisal', 500 n. 45.
[63] See B.S. Chimni, 'Law of the Sea: Imperialism all the Way', *Economic and Political Weekly* 17 (1982) 407–12; B.S. Chimni, 'Law of the Sea: Winners Are Losers', *Economic and Political Weekly* 17 (1982), 987–92. See also Mohammed Bedjaoui, *Towards a New International Economic Order* (New York: UNESCO, 1979), 221–39.
[64] See, e.g., James Malone, 'The United States and the Law of the Sea after UNCLOS III', *Law and Contemporary Problems* 46(2) (1983), 29–36, at 31; see also Markus G. Schmidt, *Common Heritage or Common Burden* (Oxford: Clarendon Press, 1989).
[65] Martti Koskenniemi and Marja Lehto, 'The Privilege of Universality: International Law, Economic Ideology and Seabed Resources', *Nordic Journal of International Law* 65 (1996), 533–55, at 543.

called, remained in operation until the major shifts of 1989 persuaded the UN Secretary-General to attempt a renegotiation of the seabed regime. Now taking place under altered geopolitical conditions, and within exclusive settings, these new negotiations generated substantial amendments to the LOSC regime, under the Orwellian doublespeak of an 'Agreement for the Implementation of Part XI'.[66] Adopted in 1994, this new agreement dismantled much of the parallel system and altered the balance of decision-making authority between the ISA Assembly and Council. It based seabed mining squarely on commercial principles; the language of common heritage was retained, but effectively limited to a commitment to redistribute a share of the profits generated from seabed mining.

While a prominent Western scholar regarded the new regime as an 'excellent example of adapting international law to new circumstances',[67] a leading scholar from the third world described it as a 'mutilation' of the common heritage ideal.[68] The concern was that, for all that the original Part XI regime of the LOSC had also been flawed, in the 1994 agreement the term 'common heritage of mankind' had 'lost its original meaning and substance when it symbolised the interests, needs, hopes and aspirations of a large number of poor peoples ... The deep seabed will now be exploited on commercial terms, irrespective of the needs and interests of the weaker members of the international community'.[69]

Recent developments both bear out and complicate this prediction. Seabed mining, which had mostly disappeared from view for two decades after the conclusion of the 1994 Agreement, owing to economic and technological unviability, is now again a focus of industry interest. The ISA is drafting regulations for it. Thus far, the expert advice it has received on the valuation of seabed minerals reinforces the conclusion privately reached by developed states four decades ago: there will be insignificant revenues for redistribution.[70] Developing states appear increasingly resigned to this

---

[66] I trace the battle of attrition between the LOSC institutions and the states participating in the reciprocating states regime, and the negotiation of the Implementing Agreement, in Surabhi Ranganathan, *Strategically Created Treaty Conflicts and the Politics of International Law* (Cambridge: Cambridge University Press, 2014), 147ff.

[67] Louis B. Sohn, 'International Law Implications of the 1994 Agreement', *American Journal of International Law* 88 (1994), 696–705, at 704–5.

[68] Ram Prakash Anand, 'Common Heritage of Mankind: Mutilation of an Ideal', in Ram Prakash Anand, *Studies in International Law and History: An Asian Perspective* (Leiden: Martinus Nijhoff, 2004), 180–96.

[69] Ibid., 196.

[70] See, e.g., Richard Roth and Carlos Muñoz Royo, Update on Financial Payment Systems: Seabed Mining for Polymetallic Nodules, Presentation made to the Annual Meeting of the

outcome. A few – the Pacific Island states of Nauru, Tonga, Kiribati and the Cook Islands – are capitalising on the remaining benefits attached to their developing state status under the 1994 regime, such as the availability of reserved mining sites, and hope to derive direct financial revenue by acting as the sponsor states for mining corporations to receive ISA licences.[71] But their potential gains in the form of sponsorship fees are undercut by the pressure of competition from other developing states willing to play a sponsor role. In any event, for many stakeholders, the question of distribution of benefits has now taken a subordinate position to another key concern, which had been largely set aside during earlier negotiations: the protection of the marine environment from the impacts of seabed mining.

Elsewhere, I and others have further critiqued the common heritage principle for its consolidation of a primarily extractive imaginary of the international seabed, such that the common heritage is understood purely in terms of seabed mining. But even taking seabed mining as the driving interest of the common heritage regime, we might note the gradual recession of the idea of redistribution in favour of commercial considerations. As in the case of the fisheries regime, the arrangements on the one hand enclose the area: seabed mining can only take place via an ISA licence or – for minerals on the continental shelf – via licence from the coastal state. On the other hand, there is increased freedom for private corporations. The parallel system secured their ability to mine under state sponsorship; the reciprocating states regime enabled investments to be made on unilateral licences; the 1994 agreement placed mining upon a squarely commercial footing, lowering corporations' costs and enhancing their opportunities to select a suitable sponsor state.

In the present, deep-sea activism mainly – and necessarily – focuses upon obtaining regulations which will ensure that corporations make essential expenditures on scientific research and assessment of ecological impacts of mining. However, there are fears that while the language of the regulations will express environmental aims (as the LOSC regime once did redistributive ones), few actual constraints will operate.

Council of the International Seabed Authority, 16 July 2018, https://ran-s3.s3.amazonaws.com/isa.org.jm/s3fs-public/files/documents/mit-ppt.pdf. I also rely here on observations gathered while attending this meeting.

[71] These states all have current contracts for exploration of seabed minerals. For an analysis of especially Nauru's efforts to position itself as a sponsor state, see Isabel Feichtner, 'Mining For Humanity in the Deep Sea and Outer Space: The Role of Small States and International Law in the Extraterritorial Expansion of Extraction', *Leiden Journal of International Law* 32 (2019), 255–74.

11.4 THE MAKING OF THIS LAW OF THE SEA

Thus far, I have tried to uncover how the 'new' law of the sea allocates rights and constraints. But I have not squarely addressed the reasons why we have this law. Going by some theories, there may not be much to address; the answers are evident. In their economic analysis of international law, Jack Goldsmith and Eric Posner posit that international law is epiphenomenal to the interests of states, especially powerful ones. Treaties and customary law emerge from such states 'acting rationally to maximize their interests, given their perceptions of the interests of other states and the distribution of state power'.[72] The law reflects the underlying configuration of state interests, and when the interests change, so does the law. Moreover, state interests, identifiable in terms of the preferences of the state's leadership, are exogenous to international law.[73] International law does not afford precepts for state action, but rather serves as a medium for coordination, and as the expression of the agreed expectations of the moment. Before more gullible audiences, it may also serve as a kind of 'happy talk', a virtuous language of common concerns, which cloaks states' pursuit of self-interest.[74]

By Goldsmith and Posner's logic, then, there is usually very little to explain about why we have the international law we have. Any rule or treaty under study will predictably reflect the underlying configuration of state interests. It is only specific details (why a 200-mile exclusive economic zone rather than 175 or 225) or anomalies (why a regime departs from a rational choice prediction) that we might need to explain by a thicker analysis of the conjuncture in which the rule arose. Otherwise, broadly sketched context is enough. And so, for example, says Posner vis-à-vis the new law of the sea:

> The ... regime of open access to natural resources was tolerable as long as the oceans were effectively an inexhaustible resource. But population growth, technological change, and economic development have increased demand for the ocean's resources to the extent that overexploitation and congestion have become serious problems; in the meantime, advances in marine technology have made control over larger portions of the ocean possible. States have responded by extending authority over larger portions of the waters and seabed and subsoil, albeit subject to certain rights of other states; and trying to

---

[72] Jack L. Goldsmith and Eric A. Posner, *The Limits of International Law* (Oxford: Oxford University Press 2005), 3.
[73] Ibid., 6.
[74] Ibid., 180.

create international mechanisms for the regulation of areas and activities beyond the control of individual states, an effort that has made notable gains in the safety of navigation and overflight.[75]

Now, it must be said that Goldsmith and Posner's book is a refreshingly candid account of international law's function and possibilities. The evaluation they offer – 'international law does not shift power or wealth from powerful to weak states'[76] – goes against the grain of valorising narratives, and appears to correspond with the analysis of the law of the sea in this chapter.[77] But for all its frankness, the critique stops a few steps short. There are several questions that Goldsmith and Posner do not assess in a rigorous way. Let us consider these.

First, what are these interests that powerful states seek to pursue? For all that they are able to pinpoint these interests almost by guess in their examples, Goldsmith and Posner prefer to 'avoid strong assumptions about the content of state interests and assume that they can vary by context',[78] though they do note that in every state, 'elites, corporations, the military, relatives of dictators – have disproportionate influence'.[79] Why not, then, carry this further, to note the convergence between these groups within most states to pinpoint the class interests that are consolidated into the structures and institutions of the state, and espoused as state interests. Why not also, in presenting, as they do, a typology of state interactions as reflecting either coincidence of interest, coordination, cooperation, or coercion, foreground the scramble for resources and markets that shape the choice between these dynamics? In sum, why stop at analysing international law as epiphenomenal to the political interests of powerful *states*; why not reveal it as reflecting (perhaps not wholly, but substantially) the configuration of the politico-economic interests of the capitalist class within – and outside – these states?[80] Such analysis would provide further gloss on their explanatory framework. Among other things, and not discounting the particular forms and relations that have both characterised

---

[75] Eric A. Posner and Alan O. Sykes, 'Economic Foundations of the Law of the Sea', *American Journal of International Law* 104 (2010), 569–96. Posner and Sykes also demonstrate this approach in their writing, which engages with specific context only with respect to the more curious rules of the LOSC that cannot be explained on a purely economic analysis.

[76] Goldsmith and Posner, *Limits of International Law*, 11.

[77] Ibid., esp. ch. 8.

[78] Ibid., 6.

[79] Ibid.

[80] B.S. Chimni, for example, offers such an account, sketching a materialist history of international law from 1600 to the present: see B.S. Chimni, *International Law and World Order: A Critique of Contemporary Approaches* (2nd ed.) (Cambridge: Cambridge University Press, 2017), 477ff.

capitalism and law in different periods, such analysis makes transparent the linkage between the 'old' and 'new' laws of the sea; how it is that both serve similar sorts of interests; what has changed or not with respect to the qualifying members of the 'in-group' whose interests are thus served; why the extractive imaginary persists despite the voices expressing concerns about the social and ecological costs of activities like seabed mining; and, importantly, the ways in which institutions of private law (property and contract) as well as public international law interact to stabilise extractive activity.[81] It also explains why the NIEO, radical enough in its demands for redistribution and equity between states, in other respects did not offer a fundamental challenge to the ideology of capitalism.[82]

Second, the explanation of international law as epiphenomenal to state interests opens the way to a reductive account both of 'mainstream' international lawyers, that is, the majority of the (Western and Western-educated) academics and state officials who engage in the daily business of drafting, interpreting, systematising and refining the law and producing legal arguments to explain and evaluate state conduct; and of the processes of legal change. Goldsmith and Posner come close to reading mainstream lawyers either as careerists assisting states in dressing up self-interest in the language of law, or detached idealists harping on the black letter of legal rules while naively disregarding the real forces shaping international law. There are, of course, international lawyers of both descriptions. But the four decades of archival records and legal commentaries relating to the making of the 'new' law of the sea reflect more complex dynamics in the shaping of lawyers' attitudes towards new political, economic, and technological developments, and consequently in the shaping of the new law.

For those involved, outside explicitly political negotiations, asserting or changing the law was not a simple matter of dressing up state interest in legal terms, but of the methodical explication of state practice or treaty text; and contested and attritional operations of squeezing meaning out of (or into) viscous legal concepts in support of outcomes perceived as desirable. The more substantive changes that were advocated – such as enclosure of the continental shelf – were justified on arguments both of collective interest, as well as what was

---

[81] On the last point, see illustratively Martti Koskenniemi, 'Sovereignty, Property and Empire: Early Modern English Contexts', *Theoretical Inquiries in Law* 18 (2017), 355–89; Katharina Pistor, *The Code of Capital: How the Law Creates Wealth and Inequality* (Princeton: Princeton University Press, 2019).
[82] As Nils Gilman notes, the NIEO represented a call for socialism between states, but remained 'studiously agnostic about the proper form of internal organization of national economies, being quite amenable to *capitalism within states*'. Nils Gilman, 'The New International Economic Order: A Reintroduction', *Humanity* 6 (2015), 1–16, at 4.

pragmatic given reality, including the reality of vested legal rights and economic practices. Where changes were derided, this too was on the same terms.

To focus on just one set of lawyers (British), in one period (the 1950s), advocacy for or against proposed changes was at least partly also in terms of what that meant for international law itself. Thus, arguments for altering the principle of the freedom of the sea to enable enclosure of the continental shelf were made on the basis that it was necessary to demonstrate the law's flexibility towards developments that were both desirable (catering to the world's needs for petroleum) and inevitable. Lauterpacht, for example, argued that it was 'unlikely that any purely doctrinal opposition of lawyers – even if otherwise well founded – would be able to stem the hitherto uniform progress of claims and developments, which are not intrinsically unreasonable, in the matter of the "continental shelf".[83] If international lawyers adopted a flexible stance, they might succeed in 'containing [shelf-related claims and] developments within the channels of moderation and order'.[84] Reviewing a decade of international legal scholarship and practice following the Truman Proclamations, D.H.N. Johnson noted the 'remarkably constructive spirit' that international lawyers had shown; while it was no light matter to modify 'an important principle such as the freedom of the seas which has stood the test of time and has already contributed so much to human welfare', international lawyers were to be commended for modifications of it that were 'necessary in the general interest of mankind'.[85]

Equally instructive is the episode, two decades later, concerning efforts by the UN Institute for Training and Research to prepare a list of 'existing and evolving principles and norms of international law relating to the new international economic order'. For lawyers at the UK's Foreign and Commonwealth Office, the concern was 'shoddy' methodology, such that

> anything and everything which has even been mentioned as forming part of a NIEO is ipso facto fit for inclusion on the list ... without the slightest attempt to undertake the hard grind of analysing how far any particular item can be actually said to represent a rule of international law, or in which terms, subject to what qualifications, etc. etc.[86]

Of course, other concerns also operated: for the FCO's economic relations department it was more bluntly that they opposed the establishment of the NIEO. But there is something interesting about the terms of the legal response

---

[83] Hersch Lauterpacht, 'Sovereignty over Submarine Areas', *British Yearbook of International Law* 27 (1950), 376–433, at 378.
[84] Ibid.
[85] Johnson, 'Legal Status of the Sea-Bed and Subsoil', 452, 456.
[86] FCO 58/2627 (1982), UK National Archives.

here. It may be possible to dismiss this as simply dressing up state interest (in countering the NIEO) as legal rectitude (concerns about shoddy method). That would be even more compelling if one considers the new international economic law that did emerge out of NIEO contestations: a transnational law of contracts that developed states proposed via identification of general principles of law; while efforts to reform colonial property arrangements by developing states via General Assembly resolutions were discredited as legally untenable.[87] Or, to go back to the earlier example, we might see in the calls for flexibility on continental shelf claims again the dressing-up of certain state interests in more appealing terms. But it is far more interesting, and a more potent critique, to consider the structures of thought within which such responses arise and take root. What is it that shapes these lawyers' perceptions of what is a necessary application or change of the law, or an undesirable threat to it? And why do these arguments stick, such that proposed alternative regimes – in the case of the deep seabed even regimes adopted *as* law for a time – are displaced in favour of the law that we do have today?

Analyses of international law's epiphenomenality glide over international law's political economy as well as its constitutive power. It is, I think, more valuable to think of the elements of contingency and false contingency that give shape to the law;[88] and with respect to the latter, to pay closer attention to how structural necessity gets reified into doctrinal necessity such that mainstream international lawyers – insisting upon the separation of law from 'politics' – come to regard particular interests as objective ones. There is particular value to examining the processes of legal drafting, interpretation and systematisation; the sites where struggles for law play out; where actions are qualified as illegal or juris-generative; where interventions become classified as desirable or disruptive – all by international lawyers who are taught to see themselves as acting as agents of the international community, motivated by '*la conscience juridique*'.[89] Most of all, these processes reveal the enduring power of liberal capitalist ideology, which underpins the social and intellectual worlds of the international lawyers involved, and which re-inscribes the dynamics of inequality described in this chapter.

* * *

---

[87] Antony Anghie, 'Legal Aspects of the New International Economic Order', *Humanity* 6 (2015), 145–58; see also Antony Anghie, *Imperialism, Sovereignty and the Making of International Law* (Cambridge: Cambridge University Press, 2005), 196ff, esp. 226–35.

[88] On false contingency, see Susan Marks, 'False Contingency', *Current Legal Problems* 62 (2009), 1–21.

[89] Schachter, 'The Invisible College', 225–6.

The arguments that I have made in this chapter will I hope suggest both a descriptive and an ironic use of the title phrase. I have sought to show that there *has* been a sea change in how we imagine the ocean today: divided by zone, medium, and type of resource, both at the shallow ends and in the deep, and entirely legally incorporated. This was not the ocean we had prior to the mid-twentieth-century intensification of ocean law-making. On the other hand, there has been no sea change in the type of interests that both the old law and the new privileged. The new law of the sea also echoes the old in continuing to group some uses of the (common areas of the) sea, including fishing, under the label of 'freedom'. This freedom has a different meaning: it is not the natural and prior freedom asserted by Grotius, but a delimited legal institution, in which rights to access and use the sea are specifically and unevenly distributed, subject to obligations, by particular – and, effectively, generally applicable – resource management regimes. Yet both types of freedom generate similar effects in terms of facilitating the economic activity of a fortunate few. For these actors, the substantive capacity to sail and fish in the seas was supported by a formal right under the old law; the new law meanwhile accords them priority so as to leave their actions relatively unconstrained. But the lack of constraint under the new law is not simply a lingering legacy of the old law – or the old 'shibboleth', as Hardin asserted. It has emerged via moments of contestation over the ordering of the ocean, and by the retrenchment of more radical proposals for redistributing the benefits of ocean exploitation.

Recognising this is important in view of a third sense in which we might understand 'sea change' – literally. The sea *is* changing, in worrying ways. It is overheating, acidifying, overrun with plastic, depleted of fish, and rising. Major summits have been organised to publicise these issues, and law-making efforts are even currently underway to address them. What fails to be mentioned, however, is that all of this takes place within a paradigm in which a further capitalisation of the 'blue economy' remains the goal, and in which the law is seen as purely a solution to the old shibboleths that produced the tragedy of this great commons. This obviously limits what can and must be achieved: bold new frameworks that privilege ecological protection and redistribution. I have argued in this chapter that we notice that the law itself has consolidated an extractive imaginary of the ocean; and that the forces that perpetuate this imaginary are not just the crude self-interest of states, but a more deep-rooted political economy, which also shapes modes of thought and practice among lawyers as to what it means to be acting for the common benefit.

12

The Political Economy of Context: Theories of Economic Development and the Study of Conceptual Change

JOEL ISAAC

In this chapter, I shall examine some of the ideological aspects of how historians and social theorists have learned to think about conceptual change. At issue in this enquiry is what 'historicism' in the contemporary human sciences amounts to. Historicism is often seen as the product of the changing understanding of time and human action brought about by the emergence of *raison d'état* and the rise of the modern state; some also trace its roots to the interest in anthropology and the history of civilisation that emerged from early-modern natural jurisprudence.[1] Whatever the vocabularies used in earlier forms of historicism – reason of state, natural law, nationalism, the philosophy of history – today the historicist is more likely to speak in the language of economics.

To be sure, contemporary historicism does not wear these commitments on its sleeve. But we can glimpse them in its intuitive, often untheorised, understanding of historical change. A central thesis of latter-day historicism is that the turn to history in any normative field, from philosophy to political theory to international law, shows that our concepts are subject to radical, unpredictable conceptual change. For the contemporary historicist, the whole point of appealing to historical context is that the political and moral concepts we employ to describe and evaluate our world are themselves subject to change; that is why the advocates of what is sometimes called contextualism

---

[1] Friedrich Meinecke, *Machiavellism: The Doctrine of Raison d'État and Its Place in Modern History*, trans. Douglas Scott (New Brunswick, NJ: Transaction, 1998), bk. 3; idem, *Historism: The Rise of a New Historical Outlook*, trans. J.E. Anderson (London: Routledge and Kegan Paul, 1972); Michel Foucault, *Security, Territory, and Population: Lectures at the Collège de France, 1977–1978*, trans. Graham Burchell (Basingstoke: Palgrave Macmillan, 2007), 255–61; Reinhart Koselleck, *Critique and Crisis: Enlightenment and the Pathogenesis of Modern Society* (Cambridge, MA: MIT Press, 1988); Frederick C. Beiser, *The German Historicist Tradition* (Oxford: Oxford University Press, 2011).

insist that our political and moral concepts can be understood and evaluated only when we have located them in the wider system of categories from which – so the contextualist argues – they derive their meaning. The phenomenon of conceptual change is thus the keystone of the contextual approach. Yet it is seldom asked whether our models for conceptual change themselves express – consciously or otherwise – ideological commitments.

In what follows, I shall try to show that the standard model of conceptual change held by proponents of contextualism bears striking affinities to theories of entrepreneurial action. As we shall see, the key link between theories of economic development and the study of conceptual change in the human sciences is their shared appeal to the notion of 'innovation'. Innovation-talk is rife in interpretive theories of social action. Quentin Skinner's 'innovating ideologists'; Thomas Kuhn's 'essential tension' between innovation and tradition in the history of science; Ian Hacking's 'making up people'; the 'norm entrepreneurs' of contemporary international relations theory – in these and other instances, innovation is widely regarded as the template for understanding conceptual change. But innovation is a term with a distinctive history. I will argue that to conceive of conceptual change as a form of innovation is to conflate social agency with a theory of entrepreneurial action that took shape in the early years of the twentieth century, and which was to some degree universalised in much social and political theory thereafter.

Innovation has been above all a concept associated with technical advancement. Since the publication of Joseph Schumpeter's seminal *The Theory of Economic Development* (1911), the problem of technical change or innovation has been a problem for economic accounts of the enterprise form. *Enterprise* has been defined as the carrying out of innovations within an existing economic system. My central point in this chapter is that, when pressed into the service of a theory of cultural or ideological change, the idea of innovation is far from unproblematic. The search for an economics of innovation has been riven by fundamental political disagreement: some writers in Schumpeter's generation argued that free markets were themselves engines of innovation; others argued that the basic research and long-term technological investments that underpinned economic innovation were 'public goods' best provided by the state, not markets. Innovation was a political concept from the beginning – even if in some cases the argument was that innovation was best encouraged by the exclusion of political action from the economy, and the letting of markets alone by government. The very idea of conceptual change as involving ideological/conceptual innovation has not evaded these basic political implications of innovation theory. At times, the account of conceptual innovation embraced by social theorists edges advocates of contextualism towards a kind of political fatalism – towards an embrace of a 'market-led' account of conceptual change.

If our 'historicist' understandings of conceptual change are indeed based in some respects on theories of economic development, how was this connection forged? I do not claim that the social theorists and historians whom I will consider in this chapter read and directly applied the doctrines of Schumpeter. So what kind of claim am I making? My view is that, just as the connections between *raison d'état* and historicism were mediated and indirect, so too economic theories of development have a complex, mediated relation to the working theory of development that underpins contextualist accounts of conceptual change. *Raison d'état* was more than just a doctrine of statecraft; it also implied a theory of self-government that would allow the individual to survive in a hostile, even warlike, civil sphere.[2] Likewise, economic doctrines of development and growth have become, in late modernity, more than just academic theories: they also imply modes of individual comportment, such as maximising one's income, hedging against risk, taking chances for large pay-offs, and so on.[3] Among its other facets, economics is also a discourse that provides a framework for individuals to live within a modern form of temporality that cuts us off from the past and projects us – at what can seem to be ever-accelerating speed – into an unknown future.[4] From this perspective, it is not surprising at all to find that our theories of social action have been informed by economic language that has been tailor-made for the conditions of modern society and economy. We see the substitution of economic models of action for less utilitarian conceptions in its most egregious forms, for example, in the conscious projection of rational choice theory and behavioural economics into political theory and sociology.[5] But my thesis is that this happens in more subtle forms, too, such as in more obviously

---

[2] Richard Tuck, *Philosophy and Government, 1572–1651* (Cambridge: Cambridge University Press, 1993).
[3] Michel Foucault, *The Birth of Biopolitics: Lectures at the Collège de France, 1978–1979*, trans. Graham Burchell (Basingstoke: Palgrave Macmillan, 2008); Timothy Mitchell, 'Econometality: How the Future Entered Government', *Critical Inquiry* 40 (2014), 479–507; Jonathan Levy, *Freaks of Fortune: The Emerging World of Capitalism and Risk in America* (Cambridge, MA: Harvard University Press, 2012); Eli Cook, *The Pricing of Progress: Economic Indicators and the Capitalization of American Life* (Cambridge, MA: Harvard University Press, 2017); Dan Bouk, *How Our Days Became Numbered: Risk and the Rise of the Statistical Individual* (Chicago: University of Chicago Press, 2015).
[4] Reinhart Koselleck, 'Modernity and the Planes of Historicity', in *Futures Past: On the Semantics of Historical Time*, trans. Keith Tribe (Cambridge, MA: MIT Press, 1985), 3–20.
[5] S.M. Amadae, *Rationalizing Capitalist Democracy: The Cold War Origins of Rational Choice Liberalism* (Chicago: University of Chicago Press, 2003).

historicist forms of social theory. As I explain towards the end of the chapter, this economistic (in a broad sense) rendering of conceptual change fudges the question of agency in ways that lead to fatalism. I find little to celebrate in that outcome; but we should be aware that it represents a tendency in our current forms of historicism, so that we can then ask ourselves what we should do about it.

12.1 SCHUMPETER ON INNOVATION

Any attempt to link innovation to social change owes an enormous debt to Joseph Schumpeter. It was Schumpeter who, in *The Theory of Economic Development* (1911), 'traced all disrupting economic change to innovations and identified the innovator with the entrepreneur'.[6] As Schumpeter saw it, the entrepreneur was the source of the 'creative response' within an economic system. He redefined a slew of economic phenomena – profits, the credit system, interest, and business cycles – in terms of the innovations pioneered by the entrepreneur. Indeed, in the first edition of the *Theory*, Schumpeter used the innovating entrepreneur as a model for creative activity in other fields, such as art and politics. In these fields, too, there were automatic, mechanical responses within the system, and moments of creative agency that fundamentally reshaped that system.

Without innovations – the 'carrying out of new combinations' of materials and forces of production by the entrepreneur – there simply would not be any economic development or change worthy of the name. Yet Schumpeter by no means intended to discount the ordinary, day-to-day operation of the economy in a commercial state. On the contrary, the backdrop of secure private property, the division of labour, and free competition would ensure that productive resources were allocated to their highest-valued uses, as determined by consumer demand.[7] But this interdependent system of production and exchange, regulated by competitive prices, did not by itself provide conditions for substantive economic growth. Rather, it was as Walras and Böhm-Bawerk had described it: an adaptive mechanism that sought to bring the forces of production and consumer demand into equilibrium. Accordingly, certain phenomena that looked like changes in the system were,

---

[6] Mark Blaug, 'Entrepreneurship before and after Schumpeter', in Richard Swedberg (ed.), *Entrepreneurship: The Social Science View* (Oxford: Oxford University Press, 2000), 83.

[7] Schumpeter, *The Theory of Economic Development: An Inquiry into Profits, Capital, Credit, Interest, and the Business Cycle*, trans. Redvers Opie (New York: Oxford University Press, 1961), 5–9.

as Schumpeter put it, merely changes in the 'data' – the inputs and outputs of the system. Shifts in levels of demand, population growth, a rise or fall in the total social product, even spontaneous changes in consumer tastes – these were for Schumpeter not *economic* changes, but shifts in non-economic variables: they involved temporary disruptions in the 'circular flow' of the system, which the price mechanism would tend naturally to correct.[8]

Schumpeter's eventual appeal to an innovation model of economic development was rooted in a fundamental rethinking of the very phenomenon of social change. On the one hand, he made it clear that the bathetic treatment of shifts in wealth, population, and consumer tastes in neoclassical economic theory – their treatment as mere variables in a system of equations describing the conditions for a competitive equilibrium – was part of a 'rationalisation' of social processes that Weber had famously described. Still, Schumpeter's purpose was not to deny the fact of social change, but to ensure that it was properly understood. Although he insisted that neoclassical theory defanged certain kinds of change, it also had the beneficial effect of leading social analysts away from 'the metaphysical treatment of social development'. Much as historians do today, Schumpeter rejected 'every search for a "meaning" of history'. For in the typical case this rested on the assumption that 'a nation, a civilisation, or even the whole of mankind, must show some kind of uniform unilinear development'. Recent forms of 'evolutionary thought that centre in Darwin' were just the latest instance of this unfortunate mystification of social change.[9] But if economic development could not be understood as changes affecting an economic system from the 'outside' like population growth or changing consumer psychology, nor as a kind of metaphysical development, then in what did it consist?

Schumpeter had a definite answer. 'By "development", therefore, we shall understand only such changes in economic life as are not forced on it from without but arise by its own initiative, from within.'[10] Genuine change was something generated from *within* the economic system. And if it could not be triggered by changes in consumer tastes or fluctuations in other such variables, then it necessarily had to be the result of *productive* activity. In other words, it had to involve innovation: the 'carrying out of new combinations' of the materials and forces of economic production. The entrepreneur, in turn, was defined as the person or group that carried out those innovations. Here Schumpeter located 'the fundamental phenomenon of economic

---

[8] Ibid., 62–5.
[9] Ibid., 57.
[10] Ibid., 63.

development. The carrying out of new combinations we call "enterprise"; the individuals whose function it is to carry them out we call "entrepreneurs".[11] By definition, economic development was for Schumpeter a discontinuous process. It disrupted the circular flow of the price system and brought about a realignment of that system: wholly new parts of the system might emerge, new channels of distribution and exchange would be opened up, and others permanently shut down. This was not an incremental or additive process. Economic change entailed the introduction of new and unfamiliar products, new and untested methods of production, new markets where they had not previously existed, the conquest of new sources of supply, and new forms of corporate and industrial organisation.[12]

12.2 THREE PERSPECTIVES ON CONCEPTUAL CHANGE

The language of innovation, development, and enterprise, which Schumpeter captured so neatly, is pervasive in discussions of conceptual change among historians. It provides a means for making sense of how historians have reconciled their insistence that disruptive change is the heart of the discipline, with their rejection of anything that smacks of teleology, determinism, reductionism and schematism. To flesh out these claims about the place of innovation as a creative response to existing conditions, I turn now to three examples of the use of the language of enterprise in recent intellectual history. These come from the writings of Quentin Skinner, Thomas Kuhn and Ian Hacking. I use the term 'intellectual history' loosely: all three authors whom I shall discuss are as much concerned with philosophical questions as they are with the empirical reconstruction of cultural or ideological change. Nevertheless, all three work with historical sources in their attempt to grapple with philosophical questions concerning morality, cognition, and metaphysics. Moreover, each of these figures has long been cited as among the most important writers on methodological matters in their respective fields: the history of political thought, the history of science, and the history of the human sciences.

We can start with the work of Quentin Skinner. Historians of political thought have long drawn on the language of innovation when describing the phenomenon of conceptual change. For example, the contextualist counterpart to dictionaries of political and ideological 'keywords' is called *Political*

---

[11] Ibid., 74.
[12] Ibid., 66.

Innovation and Conceptual Change.[13] It seems likely that one inspiration for this title was a central figure in Skinner's earliest writings on conceptual change: the 'innovating ideologist'. Skinner has often noted that conceptual change can come in the form of waves of neologisms or transvaluations of existing normative terms, but he has focused most of his attention on the kind of conceptual change that is brought about by innovators.[14] Innovating ideologists seek to cast in a more favourable light what is, in the existing normative vocabulary of a society, a morally or politically questionable activity. One way of carrying out this task of legitimation, Skinner notes, is to fight on the ground of the existing evaluative term used to characterise the practice; this one may do by attempting to use the term in a way that reverses or neutralises the negative evaluative force it typically holds. But Skinner has typically trained his attention instead on how innovators attempt to *redescribe* the existing activity using more positive evaluative terms.[15] This is a rhetorical technique concerned with the 'colouring' of social perceptions that the classical rhetoricians termed *paradiastole*.[16]

One of Skinner's key examples of this kind of rhetorical enterprise involves the defenders of incipient 'capitalist' practices in early-modern England. When Skinner first wrote on this topic, his aim had been to rethink Weber's famous thesis about the role of the Protestant work ethic in preparing the conditions for the rise of capitalism. Although a projected book on the topic was left in abeyance, Skinner did redeploy some of his findings in his methodological writings.[17] As Weber had indicated, Elizabethan merchants and their advocates certainly had used the vocabulary of Protestant Christianity to describe commercial activities. The terms in question implied positive evaluations of the activities thus described; the purpose of using these descriptive-evaluative terms was to legitimate capitalist enterprise. The aim of these innovating ideologists was to recategorise a set of questionable social

---

[13] Terrence Ball, James Farr and Russell L. Hanson (eds.), *Political Innovation and Conceptual Change* (Cambridge: Cambridge University Press, 1989).
[14] For Skinner's treatment of the other two forms of conceptual change, see 'Retrospect: Studying Rhetoric and Conceptual Change', in *Visions of Politics*, vol. 1: *Regarding Method* (Cambridge: Cambridge University Press, 2002), 179–82.
[15] Quentin Skinner, 'Some Problems in the Analysis of Political Thought and Action', *Political Theory* 2 (1974), 292–9.
[16] Skinner, 'Retrospect', 182–5. For a helpful exposition of paradiastolic redescription as a form of political action, see David Runciman, *Political Hypocrisy: The Mask of Power, from Hobbes to Orwell and Beyond* (Princeton: Princeton University Press, 2008), 30–5.
[17] Mark Goldie, 'The Context of *The Foundations*', in Annabel Brett and James Tully, with Holly Hamilton-Bleakley (eds.), *Rethinking the Foundations of Modern Political Thought* (Cambridge: Cambridge University Press, 2006), 3–19, at 8.

practices so as to remove the moral opprobrium that hindered their pursuit. Having often described these moves of the innovating ideologist in invidious terms as a 'trick' or 'sleight of hand', which turned on the 'manipulation' of settled linguistic conventions, Skinner has come to insist upon the inherent possibility of rhetorical redescription of *any* behaviour that can be ranged under the names of the virtues and vices.[18] In either case, however, the innovating ideologist is a quasi-entrepreneur who mobilises existing linguistic and cultural resources and deploys them in unfamiliar ways. This involves a creative response from within an existing system of conventions. One of Skinner's expositors glosses the role as follows:

> The innovating ideologist is neither a utopian nor a *Realpolitiker*, but someone who deals with 'untoward' claims by using some possibilities as resources which are recognised as being available in the situation but which are not commonly used to alter the situation. To legitimate a change means thus, to persuade the audience to accept the view that it is really only a question of using some already legitimate possibilities in an unconventional manner.[19]

Skinner's innovating ideologists, like Schumpeter's entrepreneurs, work with a stock of extant 'resources' or habitual forms of categorisation. Innovation, in both cases, consists in putting these *existing* resources to *novel* uses. An ideological innovator, like a Schumpeterian entrepreneur, is not merely an 'inventor' or keenly imaginative person: they are *someone who actually acts to bring about the redeployment of existing resources* – in the innovating ideologist's case by attempting to reclassify some existing, untoward form of behaviour. The innovating ideologist, like the entrepreneur, must be trying to bring about this effect – to exercise leadership in the use of language (and, by extension, moral or political categories). We shall return presently to this comparison between Skinner and Schumpeter.

Let us turn next to Thomas Kuhn's attempt to create a genuinely *historical* philosophy of science. If historians of political thought like Skinner have studied the mechanisms of innovation in politics and moral life, historians of science have done the same for scientific innovation. Like Skinner, Thomas Kuhn explicitly invoked the concept of innovation in his methodological writings. Indeed, he began using the term at the very same time that he first introduced the concept of the paradigm into his account of the enterprise (again, Kuhn's word) of 'normal science'. These terms were

---

[18] Skinner, 'Retrospect', 182.
[19] Kari Palonen, *Quentin Skinner: History, Politics, Rhetoric* (Cambridge: Polity, 2003), 52–3.

associated in Kuhn's lexicon with the notion of 'creativity'. In two essays published immediately before the appearance of his seminal *The Structure of Scientific Revolutions* (1962), Kuhn explained how these concepts fitted together. 'Creativity' came first. During the latter half of the 1950s, American intellectuals and policymakers were fixated on the problem of how to define and nurture creativity in the pursuit of science and technology. As has been explained many times, this concern with how to foster innovation was fuelled by the post-Sputnik anxiety over apparent Soviet technological supremacy.[20] Many psychologists, economists and policymakers maintained that the creative personality, defined by its open-mindedness and flexibility, was the source of scientific and technological innovation. Creativity research became an industry in the post-war academy, and Kuhn was soon drawn into it. Yet Kuhn resisted the nostrums of the creativity industry. He crystallised his thinking on this topic – and in the process hit upon the major idea of his theory of science – in two overlapping essays: 'The Essential Tension: Tradition and Innovation in Scientific Research', which he prepared in 1959 for the third of a series of conferences on 'the identification of creative scientific talent'; and 'The Function of Dogma in Scientific Research', an expanded and (by Kuhn's own admission) somewhat distinct version of 'The Essential Tension' delivered at a conference in Oxford on the nature of scientific change.[21]

In Kuhn's theory, the 'essential tension' that beset creative work in science could be found in its dependence on what he variously described as 'traditionalism', 'dogma', or 'convergent thinking' within particular subdisciplines. The creativity theorists were making a mistake, Kuhn maintained, in supposing that 'flexibility and open-mindedness' were the 'characteristics requisite for basic research'.[22] His counter-thesis was that genuine breakthroughs in science, as opposed to incremental increases in knowledge, were

---

[20] Jamie Cohen-Cole, *The Open Mind: Cold War Politics and the Sciences of Human Nature* (Chicago: University of Chicago Press, 2014); David A. Hounshell, 'The Medium Is the Message, or How Context Matters: The RAND Corporation Builds an Economics of Innovation, 1946–1962', in Agatha C. Hughes and Thomas P. Hughes (eds.), *Systems, Experts, and Computers: The Systems Approach in Management and Engineering, World War II and After* (Cambridge, MA: MIT Press, 2000), 255–310.

[21] Kuhn, 'The Essential Tension: Tradition and Innovation in Scientific Research', in *The Essential Tension: Selected Studies in Scientific Tradition and Change* (Chicago: University of Chicago Press, 1977), 225–39; idem, 'The Function of Dogma in Scientific Research', in A.C. Crombie (ed.), *Scientific Change: Historical Studies in the Intellectual, Social and Technical Conditions for Scientific Discovery and Technical Invention, From Antiquity to the Present* (London: Heinemann, 1963), 347–69.

[22] Kuhn, 'Essential Tension', 226.

possible only because scientists within a given field or subdiscipline underwent through a process of 'relatively dogmatic initiation into a pre-established problem-solving tradition that the student is neither invited nor equipped to evaluate'.[23] The process of scientific education was thus a more-or-less authoritarian exercise in closing down, for the initiate, open-ended or ambiguous thought-patterns, and the inculcation of a dogmatic commitment to specific ways of modelling problems and determining what would count as legitimate solutions to those problems. Only with these arguments in place could Kuhn have zeroed in on the notion of the paradigm, which was precisely defined as the model problem-solutions communicated by the exercises for students in the standard textbooks of a subdiscipline.[24] Of these textbook exercises, Kuhn observed: 'Nothing could be better calculated to produce "mental sets" or *Einstellung*.'[25] Counter-intuitively, however, this 'omnipresent' reliance in the advanced sciences upon 'preconceptions and resistance to innovation' was 'symptomatic of characteristics upon which the continuing vitality of research depends'. This all-but-unyielding commitment to traditional ways of problem-solving within a scientific field provided 'the individual scientist with an immensely sensitive detector of the trouble spots from which significant innovations of fact and theory are almost inevitably educed'.[26] Scientific revolutions were thus conceived as episodes of innovation in the fullest sense – as moments in which entire categorisations of phenomena and modes of inquiry were reclassified or abandoned, and in which the scientific landscape was thereby transformed.

Kuhn further filled out these ideas concerning the nature and sources of creativity in science in short comments for a conference held in 1960 on the economics of innovation.[27] At this time, the attempt to understand the economic dimensions of research and development was reaching a peak of intensity, for the same reasons that 'creativity' had become a watchword within the American academy. What, economists were asking, was the optimal allocation of resources to invention (usually called research-and-development)? Could markets, even in theory, achieve such an optimal allocation, or must basic research be treated as a public good and (because of the market

---

[23] Kuhn, 'Function of Dogma', 351.
[24] See my remarks in *Working Knowledge: Making the Human Sciences from Parsons to Kuhn* (Cambridge, MA: Harvard University Press, 2012), 210–26.
[25] Kuhn, 'Essential Tension', 229.
[26] Kuhn, 'Function of Dogma', 349.
[27] *The Rate and Direction of Inventive Activity: Economic and Social Factors* (Princeton: Princeton University Press, 1962). Papers in the volume were presented at a conference held in the spring of 1960.

failure inherent in the production of optimal amounts of public goods) be provided, at least to some degree, by the state? In his responses to the economists, Kuhn made it clear that genuine innovation – the kind of creativity he was exploring in his work on scientific revolutions – was a feature of basic scientific work, and not of the work of engineers and 'inventors' further downstream in the flow of scientific knowledge. Kuhn drew a sharp distinction between basic research on fundamental problems, whose process of development his theory of scientific change could explain, and the work of tinkerers and inventors, who used existing knowledge in inventive ways. Scientists and technological adepts were different species. Citing his own account in 'The Essential Tension' of the wellsprings of scientific creativity, Kuhn insisted that the only genuine realignments of existing knowledge came from those basic researchers immersed in a scientific tradition: '[T]he basic scientist, unlike the inventor, requires for his work a deep immersion in a pre-existing tradition ... Without an immersion in that tradition he could scarcely operate as a scientist at all. The inventor, in contrast, requires little similar immersion.'[28]

I have stressed this additional feature of Kuhn's theory of scientific development in order to underscore the substantive content given to the concept of innovation in Kuhn's thought. Neither for Skinner nor for Kuhn is it an empty metaphor. Innovation begins with the innovator seizing on existing resources – a background of concepts or classifications – given to the scientist by their dogmatic initiation into the discipline. If innovation, as in Schumpeter, is about the reallocation of existing resources, their rearrangements in the service of new and entirely unforeseeable ends, then Kuhn's zeroing in on paradigms and the convergent thinking they promoted was itself not a simple addition to his prior theory of revolutions (which focused on consensus, not paradigms, as the source of convergent thinking) but a necessary and transformative feature of that theory. Only with that assumption in place could Kuhn claim that creativity in science – innovation, as he often called it – was made possible by dogmatic training. The realignment of conceptual categories that occurred during a revolution could only happen in fields of inquiry marked by the hegemony of a paradigm communicated through textbooks.

Ian Hacking's writings on 'human kinds' offer a further illustration of how conceptual change is theorised under the rubric of innovation and enterprise. 'Innovation', it must be said, is not one of Hacking's words, but his exploration of the dynamic change built into the function of human kinds pursues many

---

[28] Kuhn, Comment on Donald W. MacKinnon, 'Intellect and Motive in Scientific Inventors: Implications for Supply', in *Rate and Direction of Inventive Activity*, 379–84, at 383.

of the same themes as Skinner's writings on ideological innovation. Moreover, the language of enterprise is unmistakable in Hacking's work on the human sciences.

Human kinds, as Hacking describes them, have some peculiar characteristics. For a class of behaviour to qualify as a human kind, it must have four properties. It must be, or have been, a 'relevant' kind, namely a classification widely recognised and applied by the members of a society. It must be the kind of behaviour associated with people; that is, it must be behaviour explicable in terms of our concepts of persons, rather than animal behaviour that could be explained ethologically. It must be a kind of behaviour about which members of a society want to have knowledge, so as to enable intervention of some sort. Lastly, it must be a kind of behaviour that defines a particular type of person.[29] Hacking has sought to demonstrate that, once we grasp these singular features of human kinds, as opposed to natural kinds, we will understand the way in which they generate, by their very nature, a dynamic process of radical cultural change.

Human kinds can produce major ideological or cultural changes because they recategorise, and place in a new moral light, an activity that did not previously hold the associations it does in its new classification. If this sounds like the enterprise of *paradiastole*, it both is and isn't: there are no rhetorical savants in Hacking's story, although there are armies of concerned professionals who help to build the human kind into a component of a culture. Skinner has emphasised the kinship between his account of conceptual change and Hacking's treatment of human kinds. According to Skinner, Hacking's reconstruction of the history of the concept of child abuse exemplifies the process whereby 'a virtue can come to be recognised as a vice'.[30] The emergence of the human kind of 'child abuse' in the 1960s bears the hallmarks of what Skinner calls ideological innovation. What would come, by the 1980s, to be identified as child abuse appeared to earlier generations as 'wholesome discipline in the rearing of children'.[31] As Hacking observes, 'no one had any glimmering, in 1960, of what was going to count as child abuse in 1990'.[32] Once the human kind began to take shape, and appear increasingly 'relevant' within a society, then, in rapid order, there was a transvaluation of certain

---

[29] Hacking, 'The Looping Effect of Human Kinds', in Dan Sperber, David Premack and Ann James Premack (eds.), *Causal Cognition: A Multidisciplinary Debate* (New York: Oxford University Press, 1995), 357.
[30] Skinner, 'Retrospect', 185.
[31] Ibid.
[32] Hacking, 'The Making and Moulding of Child Abuse', *Critical Inquiry* 17 (1991), 253–88, at 257.

activities involved in the discipline of children. This is the moment of ideological innovation, which in the case of child abuse occurred in around 1980 or so. Actions and attitudes regarded as good practice in one generation were 'viewed as cruelty in the next. Nothing in the conduct of adults need in the intervening period have changed. What will have changed, if the new evaluation is accepted, is the sensibility of the community.'[33]

We have identified above some examples in Skinner's writings of this process of ideological innovation. What Hacking shows, in addition, is that the fashioning of these new human kinds creates entirely new forms of expertise, of authority, and new social sensibilities. Human kinds are mechanisms for the production of new kinds of people. New kinds of persons are constructed by using these new forms of knowledge and the powers or capacities – of expert intervention, or punishment, and so on – that they provide. Because persons often absorb these categories into their own conception of themselves as subjects, it follows that human kinds are not neutral descriptions of an existing social reality: they constitute, and change, the very reality they purport to describe. The changes they effect may in turn encourage people to act in novel ways, to act, say, as victims of abuse, or as sufferers of a mental illness; or they may change their behaviour in the light of the new description, whether by resisting the application of the label or by changing the evaluative force it possesses. In the wake of such changes triggered by the classifications, new classifications, appropriate to the new situation, may be needed. Hacking calls this the 'looping effect of human kinds'.

Truth, power, ethics – Hacking's analytical categories are avowedly borrowed from Foucault.[34] Although there is nothing in these forms of analysis that directly suggests the language of enterprise, Hacking has been in the forefront of those who have emphasised that regimes of power/knowledge are indeed, if only in a metaphorical sense, *productive*: as we have noted, they produce new kinds of persons. Hacking's discussion of the new possibilities for personhood opened up by new modes of power/knowledge is thick with references to the 'manufacturing' and 'invention' of new kinds of people.

---

[33] Skinner, 'Retrospect', 186.
[34] Specifically, the 'historical ontology of ourselves' sketched in Foucault's famous essay 'What is Enlightenment?', *The Foucault Reader: An Introduction to Foucault's Thought*, ed. Paul Rabinow (London, Penguin, 1991), 32–50. Foucault speaks of three axes of such a study: the 'truth through which we constitute ourselves as objects of knowledge', the 'power through which we constitute ourselves as subjects acting on others' and the 'ethics through which we constitute ourselves as moral agents'. On Hacking's use of these categories, see Hacking, 'Historical Ontology', in *Historical Ontology* (Cambridge, MA: Harvard University Press, 2002), 1–26.

Speaking of the sudden profusion of diagnosed cases of multiple personality disorder around 1875, Hacking observes that the first such case 'got the split-personality industry underway'.[35]

No doubt this might be treated as a throwaway remark, but in fact the rhetoric of the sudden expansion of a new 'industry' is a consistent feature of Hacking's work on human kinds. In the wake of innovations there emerge wholly new forms of enterprise. Hacking writes: 'Social change creates new categories of people, but the counting [of such people in social statistics] is no mere report of developments. It elaborately, often philanthropically, creates new ways for people to be.'[36] Not only do new possibilities for personhood, with no precedent in the antecedent culture, emerge at such moments. So, too, do new systems of knowledge: truths about the motives of suicides or what makes for excellence in waiting tables or the mark of the most innovative 'scientists' and so on. And so also do new institutions for the exercise of power: new professions devoted to the therapeutic treatment of the mentally ill, for example, or voluntary groups devoted to defending the interests of patients. In Hacking's writings, these new persons, truths and techniques of power emerge in a dynamic fashion, just as a new, profitable industry will attract a deluge of capital, labour and entrepreneurial activity. For example, as soon as state bureaus began to recognise the significance of the statistics they had begun collecting, there followed in rapid order an 'avalanche of printed numbers'; after the first diagnosis of a split personality, there followed a 'rush of multiples', and in their wake an expanding collection of clinicians, journals and conferences.[37] Hacking has argued that these sudden emergences of new persons and forms of power/knowledge are often transient: a new human kind emerges, spreads quickly and fades soon thereafter, on the model of an 'epidemic'.[38] These are not permanent windows, then, being opened on to eternal truths about human nature: they are 'culture-bound syndromes' or 'transient' ways of being.

12.3 CONCEPTUAL CHANGE AS INNOVATION: A MODEL

In the previous section I have tried, in a fairly loose way, to line up three accounts of conceptual change with Schumpeter's theory of innovation-led

---

[35] Hacking, 'Making Up People', in *Historical Ontology*, 99–114, at 101.
[36] Ibid., 100.
[37] Ibid., 100–2.
[38] See, esp., Hacking, 'Pathological Withdrawal of Refugee Children Seeking Asylum in Switzerland', *Studies in History and Philosophy of Biological and Biomedical Science* 41 (2010), 309–17.

development in the economy. I will now try to draw out some of the characteristic features of the innovation model of conceptual change found in the work of Skinner, Kuhn and Hacking. Four features are critical to this model: *endogeneity, uncertainty, incommensurability*, and *creativity* (although these criteria overlap in various ways, and not all are found in any one approach to conceptual change). But they do, I think, provide a useful way of formalising the innovation model implicit in recent discussions of conceptual change.

Endogeneity is a complex-sounding term word for a simple idea. In econometrics, prices are said to present an 'endogeneity problem'. This is because the value of the price variable within the economic system is determined by other values within the system that are, in reciprocal fashion, themselves determined by price: producers change their price in response to shifts in demand; consumers change the amount of the good they demand in response to price shifts. It follows that changes in price refer back to other variables in the system whose values are determined by, among other things, prices. This is something like a feedback loop. The phenomenon of innovation in Schumpeter's definition is also endogenous in that it refers back to the existing properties of a system: the set of consumer wants, technological means, and factors of production. Economic change in a substantive sense must involve the recombination of the relevant elements of these factors: the creation of new wants, new technologies and forms of organisation, the diversion of productive resources to new productive ends, and so on. Moreover, these creative responses can be understood as creative only in terms of the existing system.

If endogeneity is a key criterion of development on Schumpeter's model, the same holds for many theories of conceptual change. For a long time, Skinner imagined the innovating ideologist as working exclusively within an existing system of conventions that governed the performance of speech acts. Conceptual innovation, in Skinner's analysis, is not unbridled creativity but the intentional repurposing of descriptive-evaluative terms with the aim of hindering or enabling certain forms of social enterprise. This is the sense in which conceptual revolutionaries are usually 'obliged to march backward into battle'.[39] Even if Skinner would now resist the claim that the use of normative vocabulary is uncontroversially settled – the neighbourliness of the terms for the virtues and vices make this kind of steady state of social sensibilities unlikely – it remains the case that innovating ideologists must work with and against existing classifications of social practices. Meanwhile, Kuhn's

---

[39] Skinner, 'Some Problems', 295.

insistence that genuine innovation in science can happen only when a field of inquiry has acquired paradigms likewise assumes that change is a function of a particularly effective kind of socialisation into the unquestioning use of an existing set of classifications and professional standards. A scientific revolution, in Kuhn's theory, can never come from the outside: it has to be generated endogenously by the crisis of an existing paradigm.

The looping of human kinds, as described by Hacking, is also an endogenous process. Hacking's reasoning here is straightforward: the things it is possible to do or to be depend upon the self-descriptions or categories available to agents. To act intentionally is to act under a description, as G.E.M. Anscombe insisted long ago.[40] It follows that 'if a description is not there, then intentional actions under that description cannot be there either'.[41] Self-understandings or descriptions are thus constitutive of a practice or institution: without them, the practice could not exist.[42] It is on just this point that the internal, self-referential nature of conceptual change becomes clear. When novel theories or categorisations of human behaviour produce new human kinds, they open up new possibilities for agency. These novel theories may make explicit self-understandings that are implicit in a practice; or they may cast those self-descriptions in a different moral light altogether by making it appear a much more or much less legitimate kind of enterprise. It follows from these ways in which new descriptions emerge and interact with agents that the gap between description and object assumed in theories of the natural world cannot exist in the same way for social theories.[43] Our concepts of persons and their activities do not exist outside social practices, but are constitutive of them.

This mutual interaction between descriptions and practices is highlighted in several approaches to the phenomenon of conceptual change in addition to Hacking's. The elision of concepts and practices is the basis for Charles Taylor's discussion of social theory as practice, and it underpins the theory of the 'social imaginary' that both Taylor and French post-Marxist theorists have defended in their attempt to revise the concept of ideology.[44] Skinner, too, has stressed the compatibility of his own view of the relations between

---

[40] G.E.M. Anscombe, *Intention* (Oxford: Basil Blackwell, 1957).
[41] Hacking, 'Making Up People', 108.
[42] Charles Taylor, 'Social Theory as Practice', in *Philosophy and the Human Sciences: Philosophical Papers*, vol. 2 (Cambridge: Cambridge University Press, 1985), 91–115, at 93.
[43] Ibid., 101.
[44] A point stressed in Samuel Moyn, 'Imaginary Intellectual History', in Darrin M. McMahon and Samuel Moyn (eds.), *Rethinking Modern European Intellectual History* (New York: Oxford University Press, 2014), 112–30. See also Charles Taylor, *Modern Social Imaginaries* (Durham,

normative vocabulary and social institutions with the work of Hacking, Taylor, and Castoriadis.[45] To show how innovating ideologists manipulate evaluative terms in order to legitimate social action is 'to recognise the point at which our social vocabulary and our social fabric prop each other up'.[46] To a quite remarkable extent, then, change, when understood as innovation, is a self-referential process. Conceptual change depends on responses formed within, and only intelligible within, the system itself. And this change is discontinuous precisely because it alters the fundamental premises of the system itself.

A corollary of change of this kind is that it is highly unpredictable. *Uncertainty* is an inevitable product of a process of development driven by innovation. There is no logical relationship between the system before and after a period of innovation, for the simple reason that ordinary classifications are themselves transformed. This is what makes for uncertainty, as opposed to predictable variation or change. The creative response of the entrepreneur, for Schumpeter, 'can practically never be understood *ex ante*; that is to say, it cannot be predicted by applying the ordinary rules of inference from the pre-existing facts'.[47] Charles Taylor has made a similar point about the difficulty of predicting conceptual change in the human sciences. The 'conceptual unity' that allows for successful prediction in the natural sciences 'is vitiated in the sciences of man by the very fact of conceptual innovation which in turn alters human reality. The very terms in which the future is to be characterized if we

---

NC: Duke University Press, 2003); Cornelius Castoriadis, *The Imaginary Institution of Society*, trans. Kathleen Blamey (Cambridge, MA: MIT Press, 1987). On the internal connection between concepts or descriptions and social institutions, Castoriadis's following comment is telling:

> There is thus a *unity* of the total institution of society; and, upon further examination, we find that this unity is in the last resort the unity and internal cohesion of the immensely complex web of meanings that permeate, orient, and direct the whole life of the society considered, as well as the concrete individuals that bodily constitute society. This web of meanings is what I call the "magma" of *social imaginary significations* that are carried by and embodied in the institution of the given society and that, so to speak, animate it.

Castoriadis, 'The Imaginary: Creation in the Socio-Historical Domain', in *World in Fragments: Writings on Politics, Society, Psychoanalysis, and the Imagination*, trans. David Ames Curtis (Stanford: Stanford University Press, 1997), 3–18, at 7.

[45] Skinner, 'Motives, Intentions, and Interpretation', in *Visions of Politics*, vol. 1, 90–102, at 102; idem, 'The Idea of a Cultural Lexicon', *Visions of Politics*, vol. 1, 158–74, at 174; idem, 'Retrospect', 185–6.

[46] Skinner, 'The Idea of a Cultural Lexicon', 174.

[47] Schumpeter, 'The Creative Response in Economic History', in idem, *Essays on Entrepreneurs, Innovations, Business Cycles, and the Evolution of Capitalism*, ed. Richard V. Clemence (New Brunswick, NJ: Transaction, 1989), 221–31, at 222.

are to understand it are not all available to us at present. . . . Human science is largely *ex post* understanding.'[48]

In the economic realm, uncertainty is the result of dynamic competition in a system of free enterprise. Here we are close to Schumpeter's remarks in *Capitalism, Socialism, and Democracy* (1942) about the relentless pressure brought to bear on producers by capitalism's perennial gale of creative destruction. Capitalism was by its very nature 'a form or method of economic change and not only never is but never can be stationary'. Innovation ceaselessly brought about great leaps in production, product markets, and so on. 'The opening up of new markets, foreign or domestic, and the organizational development from the craft shop and factory to such concerns as U. S. Steel illustrate the same process of industrial mutation . . . that incessantly revolutionises the economic structure *from within*, incessantly destroying the old one, incessantly creating the new one.' Endless revolution through innovation entailed the ever-present danger of an industry or firm – however successful at a given moment in time – being rendered obsolete. Accordingly, this process of revolutionary change driven from within left business leaders in a situation of pervasive uncertainty: 'competition of the kind we now have in mind acts not only when in being but also when it is merely an ever-present threat. It disciplines before it attacks.'[49]

It must be said that Schumpeter was not a theorist of uncertainty. He preferred to focus on the creativity of entrepreneurs in carrying out new combinations – a point to which we shall presently turn. The American economist Frank Knight, Schumpeter's contemporary, drew the necessary connections between enterprise and uncertainty. As Knight saw it, the enterprise form existed because of the ineradicable presence of uncertainty in economic life. Like Schumpeter, Knight recognised that economic change was revolutionary in character, and as such it obeyed no law. Although many aspects of economic change could be given a probability value and hedged against in various ways (stock and futures markets, large-scale corporations, insurance contracts, etc.), some could not. The key point about 'new combinations' were that they were not just unpredictable, but unimaginable, or at any rate impossible to hedge against: to think otherwise was to suppose that manufacturers of carriages could have taken the odds on the possibility of the successful rise of the motorised automobile before the Model T was a glint

---

[48] Taylor, 'Interpretation and the Sciences of Man', in *Philosophy and the Human Sciences*, 15–57, at 56.
[49] Schumpeter, *Capitalism, Socialism, and Democracy* (Abingdon: Routledge Classics, 2010), 72–5.

in Henry Ford's eye. The advantage of a system of free enterprise, Knight maintained, was that it privatised the losses that came from the innovation of new products, technologies of production, and so on. If entrepreneurs collected vast profits when their speculative enterprises found ready customers, that simply lured more entrepreneurs into generating new products, even if many of them never panned out.[50]

The unpredictability of the products of conceptual innovation is widely recognised. We have already noted Hacking's remark that no one in 1960 could have imagined what would count as child abuse in 1990. In a similar fashion, suicide is for Hacking an institution in American and European societies in a way it was not before the ethos of suicide was created by social studies of the phenomenon in the nineteenth century.[51] There was no law that could have predicted the emergence of this ethos, any more than the emergence of autism or the *garçon de café* could have been predicted before the descriptions needed for understanding oneself and others in this way had been created and absorbed into social practices. Kuhn also insisted upon the uncertainty that surrounded the resolution of revolutions. Once a normal science was in crisis, there was no decision rule that determined how one should choose a successor theory. No one criterion or social condition determined progress through a revolution; in practice, a combination of factors, from generational succession to various sociological and aesthetic criteria to the natural realignment of taxonomic distinctions within a field brought a new paradigm into place.[52] This stance led many to label Kuhn a relativist. Finally, Skinner has repeatedly disavowed any 'general theory about the mechanisms of social transformation', and remains 'suspicious of those who have' such a theory.[53] Conceptual change is something we can track after the fact, but it is as unpredictable as is the course of social history itself.

The phenomenon of *incommensurability* is in a sense the obverse of the uncertainty or unpredictability of innovation. Economic change as Schumpeter describes it involves a vision of competition as rivalry between different forms of enterprise. In dynamic economic change, what destroys existing firms is not an identical firm that sells the same product for a lower price; instead, a wholly different kind of technology, product, organisational

---

[50] Frank H. Knight, *Risk Uncertainty, and Profit* (Mineola, NY: Dover Publications, 2006), 363–6.
[51] Hacking, 'Making Up People', 112–13.
[52] Kuhn, *Structure*, 152, 157–9, 181–7; idem, 'Rationality and Theory Choice', in Kuhn, *The Road Since Structure*, ed. James Conant and John Haugeland (Chicago: University of Chicago Press, 2000), 208–15.
[53] Skinner, 'Retrospect', 180.

form, or the opening of an entirely new market, renders an existing enterprise or industry obsolete. That entails, in turn, a fundamental lack of comparability between what emerges after innovation, and what could have been. 'Creative response', Schumpeter wrote in one of his last published essays, 'changes social and economic situations for good, or, to put it differently, it creates situations from which there is no bridge to those situations which might have emerged in its absence'.[54] The obvious analogue here is Kuhn's discussion of the incommensurability between pre- and post-revolutionary theories. Although the concept of motion has a place in both Aristotelian and Newtonian physics, not just the criteria but the objects or situations captured by this term are different in the two systems. So too are the other terms or classifications through which it is defined.[55] Because innovation revolutionises fundamental classifications of objects and situations, much as economic innovation generates new combinations of resources, there can be no common measure across periods of conceptual innovation. It would be odd, for example, to think that the practice of bargaining or playing chess existed before the rules or self-understandings that constitute those practices were formed: for example, arranging pieces of carved wood around a chequered board in order to create an agreeable display is not a form of proto-chess, or a practice to be measured somehow against the activity of chess playing. These two activities simply have no common measure.

A final feature of the innovation model of conceptual change is *creativity*, which we have discussed at various points above. What is most striking about the kind of creativity involved in innovation is that it involves destruction as well as creation. Or rather, creativity requires destruction of older forms or 'combinations'. The endogenous character of innovation – the fact that it works from within and with reference to existing forms – already indicates this reciprocal relation between creativity and destruction. The fact of incommensurability also underscores the radical character of the displacement of older forms. As an engine of incessant 'revolutions' in economic or cultural life, innovation must face two ways: backward towards the forms it supersedes, and forward towards the new combinations or possibilities for agency it creates. Fritz Redlich, who spent his career building upon Schumpeter's vision of entrepreneurship, described the creative destruction of economic change as 'daimonic'.[56]

---

[54] Schumpeter, 'Creative Response', 222.
[55] Kuhn, 'What Are Scientific Revolutions?', in *The Road since Structure*, 13–32.
[56] Fritz Redlich, 'The Business Leader as a "Daimonic" Figure', *American Journal of Economics and Sociology* 12 (1953), 163–78, at 163–4.

The main thrust of Kuhn's arguments about the peculiar nature of creativity in science was that genuine scientific change required the side-lining of pre-existing paradigms. For a revolution to take place, a community of scientists had first to be indoctrinated in traditional modes of puzzle-solving within their field. It was this socialisation that made possible the emergence of crises, and the revolutionary overthrow of a regime of normal science. To those who thought of creativity simply as inventiveness and open-mindedness, Kuhn replied that conceptual innovation also entailed the obsolescence of whole ways of discovering the truth. For Hacking and Skinner, too, giving a genealogy of a human kind or a term of normative vocabulary means showing how a new classification or description revolutionises existing institutions. Both have tried to chart the rise and fall of classifications that underpin entire social practices.[57] In many cases, it requires an innovating ideologist to displace one way of categorising an activity with another that casts it in a wholly different ethical light.

12.4 ENTREPRENEURSHIP AND AGENCY

Innovation seems to offer everything that a historian could want from a theory of historical development. It highlights the unpredictability and uncertainty of change. It rejects progress in favour of a discontinuous understanding of change. And it makes change the product of the agency of historically embodied persons: persons who work with, transform, and understand themselves in terms of new classifications. Yet this apparent surrogate for a theory of progress has a major difficulty responding to a basic question. Who or what actually causes innovation to take place?

At first blush, the answer is simple: the entrepreneur. One analogue of the entrepreneur for intellectual historians, as we noted above, is Skinner's innovating ideologist. But here we have to pause. Are the actions of the innovating ideologist actually responsible for bringing about conceptual change? The evidence is equivocal. In the essay that first introduced the concept of the innovating ideologist, Skinner was careful to disavow any causal claim about the role of Protestant vocabulary in the rise of capitalism. After commenting that it had 'become a commonplace amongst historians to repudiate any suggestion that the principles of Protestant Christianity played a causal role in the development of capitalist practices', Skinner went on to defend the conclusion that, even if large-scale industrial capitalism pre-dated the

---

[57] Skinner, 'Retrospect', 179–80; Hacking, 'Making Up People'.

Reformation, 'the Protestant work ethic was particularly well adjusted to *legitimating* the rise of capitalism, and in this way helped it to develop and flourish'.[58] Providing a conducive ideological environment for a social practice is of course very different from actually creating such an institution. Skinner would, I assume, agree: his insistence on the relative looseness of fit between changing social practices and normative vocabulary is one reason why he has been so eager to repudiate any 'general theory' of the relations between conceptual and social change. But where does this leave the conceptual entrepreneurs whom he studies? When defending his emphasis upon the recovery of authorial intentions as a vital part of the interpretation of any historical text, Skinner has downplayed the autonomous agency of any one author. Although, for Skinner, the author is not, as Foucault and Barthes averred, 'dead', it is 'obvious that the approach I am sketching leaves the traditional figure of the author in extremely poor health. . . . It is certainly an implication of my approach that our main attention should fall not on individual authors but on the more general discourse of their times.'[59] This puts Skinner's approach in line with Pocock's work on the history of political discourses.

Here, then, is the puzzle. Even in Skinner's account of innovation, which of all of the approaches we have considered takes very seriously the importance of the role of leadership in bringing about conceptual change, the causal responsibility of agents in bringing about cultural change is unclear. When describing the actions of the innovating ideologist, Skinner works with a deliberately thin notion of agency, which makes innovating ideologists stakeholders, so to speak, in the process of cultural change, but which also makes their actions, in many cases, 'precipitates of their contexts'.[60] Both Hacking's and Kuhn's models of conceptual innovation, meanwhile, leave even less space for instrumental action in the process of conceptual change. Kuhn scandalised the creativity theorists by arguing that creativity was not a property of personality, but of 'community structure'. The root of this difficulty with the agency problem – with who or what brings about innovation – can, I think, be traced to an ambiguity in the concept of entrepreneurship itself. In a word, the theory of enterprise *looks like* the description of a type of agent, but in practice there is no such agent or discrete social type.

---

[58] Skinner, 'Some Problems', 300.
[59] Skinner, 'Interpretation and the Understanding of Speech Acts', in *Visions of Politics*, vol. 1, 103–27, at 118.
[60] Ibid. As I understand it, this view of intentional action is close to what Mark Bevir calls 'weak intentionalism' in his *The Logic of the History of Ideas* (Cambridge: Cambridge University Press, 1999), 54.

I can begin to explain what I mean here by repeating Schumpeter's definition of the concept of entrepreneurship in *The Theory of Economic Development*. 'The carrying out of new combinations we call "enterprise"; the individuals whose function it is to carry them out we call "entrepreneurs".' This definition encourages us to think of the entrepreneur as a particular type or class of person, and of innovation as a kind of act. Infamously, the first edition of Schumpeter's *Theory* treated the entrepreneur as Dionysian figure, whose creative response to given conditions was the basis not just of economic change, but of dynamic development in the arts, politics and science.[61] While not given to the young Schumpeter's flights of fancy about world-making entrepreneurs, theorists in the Austrian tradition such as Von Mises and Kirzner have likewise treated entrepreneurial action as a paradigm of action under conditions of limited knowledge.

Despite appearances, however, entrepreneurship does not describe a stable class of persons or a particular kind of activity. Rather, it is a *function* defined by a set of *abilities*. In Schumpeter's schema, this function was of course the carrying out of new combinations. It followed that one could call an entrepreneur 'all who actually fulfil [this] function'. This was a broad definition insofar as it could include not just '"independent" businessmen', but even '"dependent" employees of a company'. The requisite abilities of such an entrepreneur included '"initiative", "authority" and "foresight"'. This sensitivity to opportunities, along with the power to create new combinations, described a form of nous and boldness that could hardly constitute an office. Innovation 'can no more be a *vocation* than the making and execution of strategic decisions, although it is this function and not his routine work that characterises the military leader'. Accordingly, the existence of entrepreneurship was often obscured by the fact that it could emerge within many roles, whether of the independent businessperson, the salaried manger, or the financier. 'But whatever the type, everyone is an entrepreneur only when he actually "carries out new combinations," and loses that character as soon as he has built up his business, when he settles down to running it as other people run their businesses.' Finally, '[b]ecause being an entrepreneur is not a profession and as a rule not a lasting condition, entrepreneurs do not form a social class in a technical sense, as, for example, landowners, or capitalists, or workmen do'.[62] An economy could allow for displays of entrepreneurial genius just as warfare might allow for the expression of military genius, but such performances were

---

[61] Richard Swedberg, 'The Social Science View of Entrepreneurship: Introductions and Practical Applications', in *Entrepreneurship: The Social Science View*, 14.
[62] Schumpeter, *Theory*, 74–5, 77–8.

necessarily *sui generis*, and could in the end be identified only by their consequences. An economy would want such abilities to be exercised, certainly, but this was so insofar as it would need to make best use of all productive factors.

Schumpeter's contemporaries took different positions on the precise nature of the entrepreneurial function and the abilities it demanded, but they shared this general view of entrepreneurship as a productive factor within an economic system. Frank Knight, as we have seen, sought to justify free enterprise as a response to the uncertainty of productive activity. A producer had to 'take the responsibility of forecasting the consumer's wants'; as an economy grew larger and more complex, 'a large part of the technological direction and control of production are still further concentrated upon a very narrow class of producers, and we meet with a new economic functionary, the entrepreneur'. The function of the entrepreneur was to bear the uncertainty of economic life, to take responsibility for decisions on production and to reap the profits or losses that resulted. In practice, then, 'the primary function or problem' of the entrepreneur was not executing a plan, but 'deciding what to do and how to do it'. The more diversified and technologically complex an economy became, the greater the uncertainty involved in this function of decision. This generated in turn a greater specialisation of the decision function in entrepreneurs, and placed a greater premium upon the abilities that Schumpeter had identified: the ability to exercise foresight and seize the initiative. Entrepreneurs were 'acting, competing on the basis of what they *think* of the *future*'. As with Schumpeter, Knight rejected the notion this ability defined a vocation: it was a position of authoritative decision-making into which a person could come from many existing occupations and social positions. The problem of entrepreneurship was thus one of determining the optimal supply of a factor, 'entrepreneurial ability'.[63]

Once entrepreneurship is made over in this way into a factor of production – albeit of a peculiar sort – the question arises of the means by which it is supplied. And it is on just this matter that political issues become visible. Can innovation be actively planned? That is to say, can it be supplied through collective action or central planning? Or can only the necessary conditions for its emergence be established, because innovation is the spontaneous result of the right kind of economic or social institutions? Theories that stress the importance of uncertainty and incommensurability in the process of innovation typically reject the idea that innovation is something that can be planned

---

[63] Knight, *Risk, Uncertainty, and Profit*, 268–9, 273, 279, 282–3.

or organised through collective action. Knight's theory of enterprise is a case in point. As I have said, for Knight the enterprise economy was an *adaptation* to the fact of uncertainty in economic life: it was the best available means of coping with the calculable risk and incalculable uncertainty that beset productive activity in any reasonably complex economic system. This process of adaptation centred on the increasing specialisation of productive activity, such that the truly uncertain aspects of production – those that required deciding what to do in the face of uncertainty – would be borne by those with the most demonstrable entrepreneurial ability. Here Knight drew a parallel with evolutionary biology: 'Centralization of this deciding and controlling function is imperative, a process of "cephalization," such as has taken place in the evolution of organic life, is inevitable, and for the same reasons as in the case of biological evolution.'[64]

The drawing forth of entrepreneurial ability thus depended upon the evolutionary pressure exerted by the fact of ineradicable uncertainty in economic life. Knight did not romanticise the realities of free enterprise: business competition in the modern world, said Knight, was marred by monopolisation and inefficiency. Nevertheless, the ever-present spectre of uncertainty, and the promise, however distant, of profit it offered, did encourage the development of a system of private owners ready to gamble their assets in search of business success. The only alternative to letting free enterprise evolve as a quasi-natural process was to substitute public for private ownership. But Knight was adamant that there were no known political mechanisms by which a society could supply to itself the benefits of innovation. The problem with centralised economic planning, for Knight, was not that it was radical but that it could not induce the kind of risk-taking that private enterprise did: 'The great danger to be feared from a political control of economic life under ordinary conditions is not a reckless dissipation of the social resources so much as the arrest of progress and the vegetation of life.' Private enterprise, in contrast, encouraged owners to play a game that, on aggregate, they seemed likely to lose; but society benefited from the innovation and welfare gains they generated, while the losses involved were borne by the private rather than the public sector. In Knight's view, then, the state should do all it could to secure private property and freedom of contract, and then allow the process of competition, however imperfect, to draw forth innovation.[65]

Trust 'natural' processes of competition; resist the conscious planning of production – this was the message of innovation theory in economics. This

[64] Ibid., 268–9.
[65] Ibid., 361–6.

observation helps us, I think, to explain the tendency of accounts of conceptual innovation to invoke naturalistic tropes, and to underplay the importance of intentional collective action in bringing about conceptual change. Models of conceptual change that employ the analytics of enterprise will often treat innovation as a property of a *system* which evolves in a non-intentional manner – hence the descriptions of conceptual change as quasi-natural moments: 'speciation', 'epidemics', volcanic 'eruptions', and so on. What looks on the face of it like a theory of conceptual change that places agency front and centre will often in practice back off from the claim that innovation is a collective, self-conscious process. Innovation is, in this sense, something we must understand, and prepare for, but which we can never catch up to or reliably control. This is perhaps its own kind of philosophy of history, albeit one that is profoundly open-ended. In fact, Reinhart Koselleck's definition of the modern idea of progress comes close to what we have in mind when we think of innovation. In the concept of progress, Koselleck writes,

> is contained the idea that following industrialization and the growth of technology, the conditions of our prior experience will never suffice to predict coming surprises and innovations. Since the eighteenth century, progress produces a necessity for planning, but its goals must be constantly redefined as a result of the steady influx of new factors. The concept of progress encompasses precisely that experience of our own modernity: again and again, it has yielded unforeseeable innovations that are incomparable when measured against anything in the past.[66]

It is worth underscoring, in conclusion, the extent to which this fatalism about the twin inevitability and uncontrollability of innovation under modern industrial capitalism rests on matters of political judgment. For Knight, only an ideal form of democracy, radically different from the reality of competitive democratic politics, stood any chance of nurturing entrepreneurial ability in a socialised economy.[67] Kuhn, too, bucked the consensus among advocates of the democratic control of basic scientific research by insisting that only a decentralised system of inquiry, guided by esoteric professional norms, could produce innovation.[68]

---

[66] Reinhart Koselleck, '"Progress" and "Decline": An Appendix to the History of Two Concepts', in *The Practice of Conceptual History: Timing History, Spacing Concepts*, trans. Todd Samuel Presner et al. (Stanford: Stanford University Press, 2002), 218–35, at 233.
[67] Knight, *Risk, Uncertainty, and Profit*, 360–1.
[68] Steve Fuller, *Thomas Kuhn: A Philosophical History of Our Times* (Chicago: University of Chicago Press, 2000).

Yet for some of its theorists, innovation did not necessarily demand a kind of neoliberal regime, in which competitive conditions, but not developmental ends, were set by political institutions. Schumpeter, for his part, began to allow himself over the years to consider the possibility that innovation might either cease under socialism, or simply become automated.[69] He came less and less to think of innovation as the act of a demiurge-entrepreneur, and more as the function of an ability that was scattered throughout a population.[70] There was no special reason why a socialist regime could not develop this productive factor, just as it was not (as Schumpeter saw it) impossible for a socialist economy to solve the calculation problems involved in allowing consumer demand to determine the allocation of resources to production.

Perhaps the most illuminating commentary on the politics of innovation came from a figure a generation younger than Schumpeter and Knight, the British economist Maurice Dobb. In *Capitalist Enterprise and Social Progress* (1925), which we can loosely call a pre-Marxist study by an author soon to embrace socialist economics more fully, Dobb made clear that the presence of uncertainty was to an important degree itself a *political* choice. A good deal of the uncertainty that Knight identified, such as uncertainty of income and uncertainty about the intentions of others, was 'relative only to individualist conditions'. If it was recognised that the entrepreneur function (which Dobb defined as the capacity for adjustment and innovation within an economic system) could be realised in at least three systems of enterprise, including a socialist one, then 'the importance of uncertainty to the problem and the burden it imposes is not so great as those who generalize uncritically from an individualist society lead one to suppose'.[71] Radical uncertainty was the product of decentralised, competitive production – it was one of the wages of capitalism.[72]

When, in the mid-1930s, Dobb made his contribution to the socialist calculation controversy, his argument turned on the issue of how free enterprise and socialist economies dealt with the challenge of rapid innovation and the increased rate of capital accumulation such periods of rapid technical change produced. In a system of private enterprise, Dobb noted, it

---

[69] Schumpeter, *Capitalism, Socialism, and Democracy*, 116–19.
[70] Swedberg, 'Social Science View', 15.
[71] Dobb, *Capitalist Enterprise and Social Progress* (London: George Routledge & Sons, 1925), 37–8. The three forms in which Dobb proposed that the entrepreneurial function could be realised were: classless individualism, communism, and capitalist undertaking.
[72] This was part of its appeal, something noted by Knight, *Risk, Uncertainty, and Profit*, 238. On the persisting appeal of uncertainty and its connections with the history of political economy in the United States, see Levy, *Freaks of Fortune*, 308–16.

would only be profitable to invest in new technical processes once interest rates had fallen in the face of a growth in capital accumulation. But that would mean that investments in these new technical processes would come at some later date, and that in the meantime capital would be invested in plant that was already on the way to obsolescence. This entailed both waste of investment in an already outmoded technology and the loss of benefits derived from the longer-term usefulness of the most innovative new technologies. In contrast, the state in a socialist economy could lower the rate of social discount on those proven new technical processes that would only be appealing for investors in a private enterprise economy perhaps ten or twenty years hence. Instead of giving over the process of innovation to the evolutionary development of the capitalist economy, the collective action of a political community through the state could actively secure the benefits of innovation as a public good. Dobb gave a vivid illustration of this difference in a discussion of the 'pursuit-curve':

> A dog is situated at right angles to the path along which his master is bicycling. The dog is running towards his master, and, influenced by a simple conditioned reflex, runs always in the direction of his master at the given moment; with the result that his path in pursuit of his master is a curve. But if the dog could have acted on forethought and calculation, he would have taken a straight line to the point along the path which his master would presently reach. A planned economy, it would seem, should take a similar line towards a technical level of the future; and the ultimate economising of capital to produce a given result (or, conversely, the more rapid rate of technical advance financed by a given rate of investment) will be the difference in length between the straight line and the curve.[73]

At the time, Dobb's intervention pleased neither his socialist interlocutors nor the critics of planning. But it was directed at issues of economic innovation and political control that waxed in importance as the calculation controversy cooled. In the post–Second World War years, questions of economic innovation and growth moved to the centre of the political stage. Debates about the optimal rate of social discount swirled around precisely the dilemmas of investment in long-term public infrastructure projects that Dobb had considered. The policy of lowering the social discount rate for projects with pay-offs for multi-generational publics (but not necessarily for consumers in the present) received a favourable hearing from a new cohort of economists with a

---

[73] Dobb, 'Economic Theory and the Problems of a Socialist Economy', *Economic Journal* 43 (1993), 588–98, at 597.

good understanding of problems in political philosophy.[74] Meanwhile, discussions of the optimal allocation of resources to research and development increasingly emphasised the shortcomings of market provision and the need to treat scientific research – that is, innovation – as a public good.[75] Dobb's conception of innovation as a political value, and his view of uncertainty as to some degree a political choice about the organisation of an economy, were thus not wholly misguided.

* * *

I record these debates not because there is any easy translation of arguments for innovation planning into discussions about conceptual change. I do so simply because the tendency to think of innovation as a kind of force of nature, defined by radical endogenous change, uncertainty, incommensurability, and daimonic creativity, itself bears the marks of ideological struggle. In its efforts to model conceptual change on the theory of innovation, the study of conceptual change is itself embroiled in a political argument about the kinds of control we can exercise over the processes of cultural and ideological development. Most often, writers on conceptual change have underplayed agency and collective action and embraced naturalistic metaphors in making sense of cultural change. Such a move concedes, in practice, the argument to those who believe that the process of discovery – the creation of novelty through research – cannot be subject to democratic control and collective decisions on the ends of inquiry. At the very least, the vigour with which this claim was contested by economists of technical change during the twentieth century suggests that we need not share this fatalism about the wellsprings of conceptual change. Here, then, is another way in which we can speak of a politics of context – or perhaps, as the foregoing suggests, a political economy of context.

---

[74] See, e.g., Stephen A. Marglin, 'The Social Rate of Discount and the Optimal Rate of Investment', *Quarterly Journal of Economics* 77 (1963), 95–111.
[75] Richard R. Nelson, 'The Simple Economics of Basic Scientific Research', *Journal of Political Economy* 67 (1959), 297–306; Kenneth J. Arrow, 'Economic Welfare and the Allocation of Resources for Invention', in *Rate and Direction of Inventive Activity*, 609–26.

Gender

13

Gender in the State of Nature

ANNA BECKER

The idea of the state of nature was a fundamental way for early modern thinkers to make sense of the emergence of the political.[1] With the help of this concept thinkers explained how complex political societies could arise from anarchic multitudes of human beings and how legal frameworks that regulated citizens' relationships between one another could emerge. Referring to a state of nature, the often conflict-laden relationship between natural law and civil laws was explored, and questions regarding the legitimisation of political power, political rule, and political sovereignty were answered.[2] Thomas Hobbes is often identified as, if not exactly having 'invented' the concept of the *status naturalis*, then at least having most influentially imagined it as a condition of war from which the commonwealth was established as a means of escape.[3] From Hobbes onwards, the historiographical narrative goes, the 'classical', broadly Aristotelian notion that polities were founded upon, and grew organically from, the natural sociability of human beings was replaced by the notion that the political was contracted. The state became an artificial body, defined by its contrast with nature. While it is thus emphasised that seventeenth-century thinkers operated with a new and different concept of how states came into being – which of course then had consequences for how these states were defined – historians of political thought still, tacitly perhaps, assume that one of the most important features of the classical conception of statehood had

---

[1] See, e.g., Benjamin Straumann, *Roman Law in the State of Nature: The Classical Foundations of Hugo Grotius' Natural Law* (Cambridge: Cambridge University Press, 2015).
[2] For a nuanced treatment of early modern understandings of nature, law, and the polity, see Annabel S. Brett, *Changes of State: Nature and the Limits of the City in Early Modern Natural Law* (Princeton: Princeton University Press, 2011) and Brett, *Liberty, Right and Nature: Individual Rights in Later Scholastic Thought* (Cambridge: Cambridge University Press, 1997).
[3] See, e.g., Harro Höpfl and Martyn P. Thompson, 'The History of Contracts as a Motif in Political Thought', *American Historical Review* 84 (1979), 919–44.

remained. Politics and the polity, whether organically grown or contracted from fear and necessity, seem to centre on male citizens and/or male subjects. The 'state' is seen as a male entity and politics as being constructed in opposition to the social, or the private.[4] Therefore, historical enquiries into seventeenth-century philosophy of the state have focused on the relationship among *male* citizens and the male citizens' relationships to a government, a sovereign entity, and political power itself. Male–female relationships have been seen as part of the apolitical, private sphere, just as broader questions pertaining to the social dimensions of human beings did not play any role in early modern narratives of the birth and the manifestation of the political.[5]

This chapter argues that early modern narratives of the emergence of politics had a gendered dimension at their core. The chapter focuses on Thomas Hobbes's famous account of the process of 'state-building' from a state of nature, and reads this in its broader context of early modern Roman law discourse. This shows that early modern thinkers did not conceive the polity as abstract and disembodied, as fleshless and sexless. Exploring this gendered dimension, and especially its relationship to 'biology' as that which is still (although often very subtly) thought to drive the differences between 'man' and 'woman' in politics, makes clear that topics like the equality of man and woman, natural and civil marriages, child-birth, and breastfeeding were no apolitical concerns. Rather, these 'private' matters were tightly enmeshed with the emergence and maintenance of the 'public' and the political, and so they defy any clear-cut categorisations. Focusing on these matters, then, helps us to understand early modern ideas of politics and the state's *raison d'être*, and leads us to re-examine inherent beliefs on the relationship of politics and gender, and the role of this relationship in our historical narrative.

Thomas Hobbes presents an apt starting point for the present enquiry since, with the exception perhaps of Machiavelli, no other early-modern author has attracted a comparably intense debate in feminist scholarship.[6] Feminist and

---

[4] See Hannah Arendt, *The Human Condition* (2nd ed.) (Chicago: Chicago University Press, 1998). For a different view, see Anna Becker, Gendering the Renaissance Commonwealth (Cambridge: Cambridge University Press, 2020) and 'Gender in the History of Early Modern Political Thought', *The Historical Journal* 60 (2017), 843–63.

[5] This historiographical narrative becomes even more complex when we take into account that our historical understanding and our historical categories are crucially shaped by nineteenth-century ideas of the emergence of the state, of civil society, of the public and the private.

[6] See the collected essays in Nancy J. Hirschmann and Joanne H. Wright (eds.), *Feminist Interpretations of Thomas Hobbes* (University Park, PA: Pennsylvania State University Press, 2012). This book has an illuminating interview with Quentin Skinner and Carole Pateman which makes apparent the differences between the approaches of political theorists and historians of political thought when it comes to the question of feminism and gender: at 18–43.

gender historians have identified as one of the most arresting features of Hobbes's theory that, in his works *De Cive* (1642) and *Leviathan* (1651), the author defended a radical equality of men and women in the state of nature, and denied that fathers had any natural dominion over children.

In *De Cive* Hobbes had written that 'in the state of nature every woman that bears children becomes both a *mother* and a *lord* [*domina*]'.[7] Mothers claimed this dominion, Hobbes wrote, since only mothers knew without any doubt that their offspring was theirs and, at least as importantly, mothers preserved their children's lives by (breast-) feeding them. Indeed, if a mother decided not to feed her child, she consequently lost her natural power over the infant, and this power went to anyone who took over the child's care. This was a most important point. While at first glance it seems that mothers are made lords over their children by the very act of giving birth, this seemingly natural and biological criterion was instantly qualified. A mother, Hobbes argued, could transfer her dominion in:

> divers wayes; first, if she quit and forsake her right by *exposing* the child. He therefore that shall bring up the childe thus exposed, shall have the same dominion over it, which the Mother had. For that life which the Mother had given it (not by *getting*, but *nourishing* it) she now by *exposing*, takes from it.[8]

Abandoning her children, Hobbes stated, was a mother's prerogative:

> by the right of nature; for as much as they who have the supreme power (*summum imperium*), are not tyed at all to the civill lawes. Adde also that in the state of nature it cannot be known who is the Father but by the testimony of the Mother; the child therefore is his whose the Mother will have it, and therefore hers; Wherefore originall Dominion over children belongs to the Mother, and among men no lesse than other creatures: The birth followes the belly (*Partus ventrum sequitur*).[9]

---

[7] Thomas Hobbes, *Man and Citizen: De Homine and De Cive*, ed. Bernard Gert (Hackett Publishing: Indianapolis, 1972), at 213. Thomas Hobbes, *Elementa philosophica de cive* (Basel, 1782), 155: 'Atque hoc modo, in statu naturae, omnis puerpera simul & *mater* sit & *domina*.'

[8] Hobbes, *De cive*, 156: 'A *matre* autem ad alios transit *dominium* diversis modis. Primo, si jus suum dereliquerit sive abjecerit, *filium exponendo*. Is igitur qui expositum educaverit, idem habebit dominium, quod habebat *mater* (non *generando*, sed *alendo*) dederat, *exponendo* tollit.'

[9] Ibid., 155–6: 'Neque de harum *liberis* statuunt *mariti*, sed *ipsae*; quod sanè *jure naturae* faciunt, siquidem qui summum habent imperium, legibus civilibus, ut supra ostensum est, non tenentur. Adde quod in statu naturae sciri non potest, cujus *patris filius* est, nisi indicio *matris*: ejus igitur est quem *mater* vult enim esse, & proinde *matris* est. Originale igitur in *liberos* dominium, *matris* est; & apud homines non minùs quam caetera animantia, partus ventrem sequitur.'

That Hobbes understood the natural rights of mothers as supreme power, *summum imperium*, and that he included in this supreme power a mother's right to abandon her child, has generated a great deal of attention in feminist scholarship. Many commentators find Hobbes's understanding of women in the state of nature both compelling and unconvincing. Authors who argue for a feminism of difference based on the appreciation of mothering think his theory quite unappealing and anti-feminist. But it can also be read as proto-feminist: Susanne Sreedhar, for example, has called Hobbes's argument a strikingly modern one, emphasising that Hobbes was an anti-essentialist, since for Hobbes, as we have seen above, 'there is nothing unnatural about a woman who chooses not to have children'.[10]

Situated in the background of this modern feminist debate – whether Hobbes was an anti-feminist or a proto-feminist – is Sreedhar's further statement that Hobbes's theory was 'a blatant rejection of the dominant claim, advanced by Hobbes's contemporaries, that child rearing is a woman's duty – or her fate'.[11] On this point most commentators on Hobbes's theory, whether gender historians or mainstream political scientists, agree: Hobbes's view on the power of women in the state of nature was innovative and very different from 'traditional' approaches to hierarchies in the family.[12] Rarely, however, are we informed in detail about what exactly these traditional ideas were, even if it is sometimes acknowledged that early modern notions of gender were complex.[13] Generally it appears that Sir Robert Filmer – whose political thought otherwise is often seen as a historical footnote – is taken at face-value in his approach to the parent–child relationship, and serves as the blueprint for the 'traditional' approach of the entire pre-modern era.

Filmer had argued in his *Observations on Mr Hobs Leviathan* that Hobbes was absolutely wrong to claim equality of human beings in the state of nature. Filmer also took issue with the idea of natural maternal *dominium* over children.

> It is said by Mr. Hobs ... *the Mother originally hath the government of her Children, and from her the Father derives his right, because she brings forth*

---

[10] Susanne Sreedhar, 'Hobbes on "The Woman Question"', *Philosophy Compass* 7 (2012), 772–81, at 775–6.
[11] Ibid., 776.
[12] See, e.g., Gordon J. Schochet, *The Authoritarian Family and Political Attitudes in 17th Century England: Patriarchalism in Political Thought* (Oxford: Basil Blackwell, 1975), 229; Wendy Gunther-Canada, 'Catherine Macaulay on the Paradox of Paternal Authority in Hobbesian Politics', *Hypatia* 21 (2006), 150–73, at 152.
[13] Sreedhar, 'Hobbes on "The Woman Question"', 781 n. 5.

and first nourisheth them. But we know that God at the Creation gave the Soveraignty to the man over the Woman, as being the mother and principle agent in generation.[14]

Regarding Hobbes's argument that only mothers knew without doubt the paternity of their children, he replied that it was 'not at the will of the mother to make whom she will the Father'.[15]

The *Observations* were completely in tune with the argument Filmer put forth in *Patriarcha* (written around 1630, first published in 1680), where he laid down his conviction that with creation God had instituted a natural and unquestionable inequality between the sexes. Filmer thought that Adam was the first monarch, and 'not only Adam but the succeeding patriarchs had, by right of fatherhood, royal authority over their children'.[16] Filmer's view, however, was heavily contested; most famously by John Locke in the first of his *Two Treatises of Government* (1684). The idea that paternal power was absolute, and that royal power directly derived from paternal power, was nothing less than ridiculous for Locke. 'There was never so much glib Nonsense put together in well sounding *English*', he remarked in the preface to the *Two Treatises*.[17]

Amazement about the fact that a seventeenth-century thinker could proclaim women's natural equality to men, and argue that mothers, not fathers, had *summum imperium* in their children, is a reaction of the twentieth and twenty-first rather than of the seventeenth century. We simply assume that all early modern thinkers must have put forward the argument that there was a natural absolute subordination of all kinds of women to all kinds of men. Similarly, the idea that a woman might abandon her child according to her own will, rather than having a natural and a biological urge to care for this child, and the idea that a parent–child relationship can be fostered by the simple act of feeding the child, which so resolves all notions of natural affinities, might not have been as shocking to the seventeenth-century reader as it appears to us. In what follows I would like to show that, if we read Hobbes in the context of early modern commentaries on Roman law (and one on Aristotle), Hobbes's understanding of the equality of the sexes in the state of

---

[14] Sir Robert Filmer, 'Observations on Mr Hobs Leviathan', in *Observations Concerning the Original of Government, Upon Mr Hobs Leviathan: Mr Milton against Salmasius: Hugo Grotius De Jure Belli* (London: R. Royston, 1652), 1–11, at 6.
[15] Ibid.
[16] Robert Filmer, *Patriarcha and other writings*, ed. Johann P. Sommerville (Cambridge: Cambridge University Press, 1991), 6.
[17] John Locke, *Two Treatises of Government* (1698 ed.), ed. Peter Laslett (Cambridge: Cambridge University Press, 2012 [1970]), 137.

nature, his idea of maternal power, and his anti-essentialist stance appear far less innovative than they are often perceived to be.

A first example for my claim is the outrage that was expressed when the French writer Jean Bodin, himself trained in the Roman law, proclaimed all-encompassing paternal power the pillar of his theory of absolute government. In his *Six livres de la Republique* (1576), still today considered to be the foundational work on the notion of sovereignty and absolutism, Bodin had stated that it was a universal natural and divine law that a father had *summum imperium ius* and even *patria potestas* over his wife and children, including the right to decide over his dependents' life and death.[18] In a scathing answer to Bodin, written in the context of his commentary on Aristotle's *Politics* from 1587, the Italian scholar and politician Antonio Montecatini accused Bodin of having confused in this matter legal categories. *Patria potestas*, the father's power over his children, Montecatini showed, was a matter of civil law, not of *ius naturale* or *ius gentium*. Montecatini paraphrased the *Institutiones* of Justinian, in which one could read that the *potestas* over children was 'a right peculiar to Roman citizens, since there are no other men who have such power over their children as the one we have'.[19] Indeed, Roman *patria potestas*, for Montecatini, was 'plain tyranny'. It had developed with and in Roman civilisation, but it had nothing to do with nature, and it certainly was 'not in use by any other peoples'.[20]

As part of his extensive attack against Bodin, Montecatini referred to the fifth book of Plato's *Republic* and repeated Socrates' analogy that in watch-dogs 'the females in the same way as the males (*foeminae aeque ac mares*)' care for the flock.[21] Plato had used this analogy to emphasise a foundational equality between men and women, and Montecatini here used this to the same effect. Montecatini also stressed that the *Decalogue* commanded the individual to honour father and mother, and from this he drew the conclusion that naturally both parents had *imperium* and *potestas* over their children.[22] These were 'natural laws' that were unchanging. On the other hand, the

---

[18] See Anna Becker, 'Jean Bodin on Oeconomics and Politics', *History of European Ideas* 40 (2014), 135–54.
[19] Justinian, *Institutiones*, 1.9. (*De patria potestate*) 2; see also Gaius, *Institutiones*, 1.55 (*De patria potestate*).
[20] Antonio Montecatini, *In politica, hoc est, in civiles libros Aristotelis progymnasmata* (Ferrara, 1587), 440: 'Iustinianus autem reprehenditur à Francisco Connano et à Ioanne Bodino, quasi perperam locum Caii interpretatus. Et tamen verissimum est quod ait Iustinianus: talem dominatum in filios, qualem Romani habuerint, quod erat planè tyrannicum, à nullo alio populo usurpatum fuisse.'
[21] Ibid., 441; referring to Plato, *The Republic*, 451d.
[22] Ibid., 440.

dissimilarities and disparities that were observable in the diverse customs and laws instituted amongst different peoples, 'change more than once'.[23] The way that Montecatini framed the issue of equality and the natural right of parents over their children as a matter of law resembled in its breadth sixteenth-century commentators on the Roman law. Indeed, one of the most famous of those, François Connan, Montecatini had quoted – unfavourably – in this passage. In the sixteenth century jurisconsults had commented on the Roman systematic division of private law into natural law, *ius gentium*, and civil law by drawing up immense meditations on the origins of justice, intricately interwoven with the development of humankind itself, from the most natural condition of human beings to that of civilised Romans in the sphere of the *res publica*. The commentators span together precepts from theology, arguments from ancient philosophy, and anthropological and historical narratives and so created a powerful story of origins that had dimensions that were both systematic and historical.

Since these were origin stories, the first title of the first book of Justinian's *Digest* – 'Concerning Justice and Law' – was carefully examined. This book begins with the division of law into public and private law and the threefold division of the latter *naturalibus praeceptis aut gentium aut civilibus*. Commentators enriched this systematic presentation of the law with a historical narrative of the development of human nature, from the origins to the creation of states. The *Digest* defined the natural law as:

> that which nature has taught to all animals, for this law was not peculiar to the human race, but applies to all creatures. Hence arises the union of the male and the female which we call marriage; and hence are derived the procreation and the education of children; for we see that other animals also act as though endowed with knowledge of this law.[24]

Matrimonium was also seen as an important part of the *ius gentium*, the 'law of nations'. This was the law observed by all of humankind, that regulated the space between states and the relationship of those human beings that did not fall into the realm of civil law.[25] *Ius gentium* could also be read as representing a stage in the development of humankind that catalysed the need for civil law and the political community. At the foundations of the legal system as well as at the imagined historical origins of justice and statehood stood marriage,

---

[23] Ibid: 'eas institutas non semel mutarunt'.
[24] *Digest*, 1.1.3.
[25] See Justininan, *Institutiones*, 1.2.1; Gaius, *Institutiones*, 1.1.

matrimonium, the development of which commentators, consequently, saw as intricately interwoven with the emergence of states.

Commentators brought the *Digest* together with the classical narratives of the beginning of political life. One of the most important of these, for the sixteenth-century theorists, was Cicero's *De inventione*, written very early in the Roman's career. In this text Cicero imagined a time 'when men wandered at random over the fields, after the fashion of beasts', in which 'no one had ever seen any legitimate marriages'.[26] Of course this seems to be at odds with the *Digest*, in which marriages were declared to be part of natural law, so commentators set out to resolve this inconsistency. In this they themselves were part of a long tradition. In the thirteenth century, in his commentaries to the *Sentences*, Thomas Aquinas (1225–74) had wondered 'whether matrimony was natural', and he had particularly paid attention to the idea that according to natural law human beings shared marriage and the act of procreation with animals. This Thomas solved by asserting that human marriage, while indeed natural, was nevertheless different from that of animals, since it involved virtue and adherence to the good of the children. It was in this context that he discussed *De inventione*, in which he held Cicero to have put forward that 'at the beginning men were savages and then no man knew his own children, nor was he bound by any marriage tie'. Thomas argued that:

> the assertion of Cicero may be true of some particular nation, provided we understand it as referring to the proximate beginning of that nation (*gens*) when it became a nation distinct from others; for that to which natural reason inclines is not realized in all things, and this (Cicero's) statement is not universally true, since Holy Writ states that there has been matrimony from the beginning of the human race.[27]

Thomas here did not deny outright the Ciceronian narrative, but he preferred to situate it at a very precise point in time and in a very precisely imagined place, in which such a situation of dispersed people without marriage-ties might have existed. Thus he portrayed this condition not as universal and natural, but rather as a 'cultural' matter. It was in this tradition that the lawyer François Connan, pupil of Andrea Alciato, managed to combine the

---

[26] Cicero, *De inventione*, I.2.ii. For the importance of *De inventione* in early modern ideas on the beginnings of 'the state', see Annabel Brett, '"The Matter, Forme, and Power of a Commonwealth": Thomas Hobbes and Late Renaissance Commentary on Aristotle's *Politics*', *Hobbes Studies* 23 (2010), 72–102.

[27] Thomas Aquinas, *In 4. Sententiarum*, Dist. 26. Q.1.a.1 (Utrum matrimonium sit naturale); also in *Summa Theologiae*, Supp., q. 41, a. 1, ad 2.

Ciceronian claim that human beings had originally lived isolated lives, with the Roman law precept that marriage was a fundamental part of human nature. He wrote in his commentary on 'What is the *ius gentium* according to Ulpian' that 'the *ius naturale* refers properly to the solitary man, leading his life in the fields with his wife and children'.[28] The 'solitary' man, therefore, was not doing his roaming on his own. In the legal tradition, he was already situated and envisaged within the framework of a family.

With this in mind, Hobbes's state of nature, in which human beings are dispersed, without government, yet randomly assembled into sorts of families, appears to be very close to sixteenth-century commentaries on the natural law and the law of nations. Regarding the state of nature, Hobbes famously wrote that:

> It may peradventure be thought, there was never such a time, nor condition of warre as this; and I believe it was never generally so, over all the world: but there are many places, where they live so now. For the savage people in many places of *America*, except the government of small Families, the concord whereof dependeth on naturall lust, have no government at all; and live at this day in that brutish manner ...[29]

This seemed to be an inconsistency, and on this Hobbes indeed was attacked by Filmer. While Hobbes declared human beings in the state of nature as leading completely independent lives (*fungorum more*), the example he gave was one of human beings organised into families.[30] This, however, was not inconsistent; it rather was completely in line with the logical reasoning of his forerunners.

Just as Hobbes would do later, sixteenth-century lawyers imagined that *matrimonium* existed under *ius naturale* and *ius gentium* only in a basic form. They termed these natural marriages, just as Cicero had in *De inventione*, 'unjust' or 'illegitimate' (*matrimonium injustum* or *illegitimum*). This did not mean that these marriages were morally wrong or not allowed; on the contrary the *ius gentium* existed partly to permit them, as we shall see. But they were not codified as civil law. Children from these relationships, accordingly, were *filii naturales*, natural sons or daughters, or indeed *illegitimi*, illegitimates. Nevertheless, illegitimate marriages held important points in common with civil marriages. Both were consensual and both had not only simple procreation as their end, but equally the care for and education of children, as reason

---

[28] François Connan, *Commentariorum Iuris Civilis Libri X* (Paris, 1558), fo. 19v: 'Ius itaque naturale proprium est hominis solitarii, vitam agentis in agro cum uxore et liberis'.
[29] Hobbes, *Leviathan*, ed. Richard Tuck (Cambridge: Cambridge University Press, 1991), 89.
[30] Filmer, 'Observations on Mr Hobs Leviathan', 1–2.

dictated it and to which nature impelled human beings.[31] Under *ius naturale* and *ius gentium* illegitimate marriages were held to establish kinship via the mother. As the famous lawyer Ulrich Zasius taught his students in the southern German university of Freiburg in the sixteenth century: 'the law of nature does not recognise *agnatio*'.[32] That is, it did not recognise relationships via the father. Through natural law children were legally related to their mother only. In his exposition to *De verborum significatione*, the lawyer Jean Brèche (1501–61) wrote that the legitimate, that is, the Roman civil family, indeed 'follows the father', but 'for all the rest, as far as origins are concerned, it is commonly established that children follow the mother. He who has no legitimate father derives his origin from his mother, which should be reckoned from the day on which he was born'.[33] Commenting on the same passage, Andrea Alciato (1492–1550) also specified that, while it was a general rule of Roman civil law that children 'followed the father', this did not mean that the civil law in general could not rule otherwise and establish 'a special grant' which made the mother have power over the children: such was the case with the people of Delphi, of Pontus, and of Troy, 'where it was proper ... that children born from a foreigner and his wife follow the mother' (that is, they were to become citizens of the mother's polity).[34]

That the *ius naturale* and the *ius gentium* provided that children were held to 'follow the mother' did not, however, necessarily establish the mother's *potestas* over her children. Claudius Cantiuncula (1490–1549), professor in Basel and Vienna (and the author of the first German translation of Thomas More's *Utopia*), when discussing *patria potestas* in his *Paraphrases Digesta*, acknowledged that *potestas* was part of the civil law only, and hence could derive only from *nuptiae iustae*. 'For neither mother nor father hold the natural and illegitimate children in *potestas*'.[35] This was only logical. The *ius gentium* was used in Roman law specifically to clarify the marriage

---

[31] Emile Stocquart, 'Marriage in Roman Law', trans. A. Bierkan, *Yale Law Journal*, 16 (1907), 303–27; Cesare Sanfilippo, *Istituzioni di diritto romano* (Soveria Manelli: Rubbettino Editore, 2002), 106–72.

[32] Ulrich Zasius, *In sequentes Digesti veteris titulos lecturae* (Basel, 1537), 10.

[33] Alciato et al., *Commentarii ad tit. digest. de verborum significatione, trium illustrium iuris interpretum, Alciati, Brechaei, Fornerii* (Lyon, 1589), 425 'Caeterùm, quatenus ad originem tantùm attinet, vulgò quaesitus matrem sequitur. Eius ... qui iustum patrem non habet, prima origo à matre, éxque eo die, quo editus est, numerari debet' (here quoting *Digest*, 50.1.9).

[34] Ibid., 425: 'Hoc regulariter proditum est, ut filii legitimi patris familiam sequantur, non matris, nisi specialiter aliud indultum sit, ... ut Iliensibus, Delphis, & Ponticis, quibus ex privilegio competit, ut ex alienigenis & eorum mulieribus nati, matris originem sequantur' (here following *Digest*, 1.5.24 and 50.1.2).

[35] Claudius Cantiuncula, *Paraphrases in Lib. I. Institutionum Iustiniani imperatoris* (Haguenau, 1533), no page numbers, *Titulus IX, De patria potestate*: 'Nam ut mater ... ita nec pater filios naturales tantum, aut illegitimos in sua tenet potestate.'

relations in cases of intermarriage between Romans and citizens of other nations or *gentes*. Only Romans possessed *connubium*, the right to just marriages. The *ius gentium* established that, if a Roman citizen married a non-Roman, the offspring was not considered a Roman citizen. Therefore *patria potestas* did not apply, and the children had to 'follow the mother'. What exactly her civil law state vis-à-vis the offspring was, was of no concern to the Romans, because it was of no concern to Roman civil law. In what sort of relationship she held her children was an issue of her *gens* and their civil law; this was the meaning behind Cantiuncula's affirmation that the *ius gentium* did not establish power-relationships. What mattered was that it was not *agnatio*, the relationship via the male line, that was established in both *ius gentium* and *ius naturale*, but *cognatio*, the relationship via the mother. The conclusions from this obviously had repercussions not only for children born in the Roman empire of late antiquity to parents who did not have *connubium* but for early modern European communities dealing with children born out of wedlock in general. When Zasius wrote the reformed *Stadtrecht* (the civil law) of the city of Freiburg, he followed the rule that *illegitimus partus semper matrem sequitur* and laid down the decree that all illegitimate children should have the right to inheritance from the mother.[36]

At this point we might draw a partial conclusion. Hobbes was not so very different from his contemporaries. Rather, he was part of a contemporary Roman law tradition, in that he only saw relationships via the mother established in the state of nature. That he granted mothers *summum imperium ius*, however, was indeed a turn from this tradition that affirmed that *potestas* could only derive from just marriages, not from natural ones. Aristotelians like Montecatini, on the other hand, half a century earlier than Hobbes, had defended something similar, when they argued that both mothers and fathers naturally shared *potestas* over their children (and the household as a whole). Seen in this context, Hobbes, defending male and female natural equality, was not so novel, after all. Certainly, the law precept that a natural child *matrem sequitur*, follows his or her mother, rather than the father, was indeed a cornerstone of the *ius naturale* and *ius gentium*.[37] It was almost impossible to deduce from the foundations of Roman law a right of life and death of the father over his children or his wife as a natural right. Jean Bodin, who had

---

[36] Hansjürgen Knoche, *Ulrich Zasius und das Freiburger Stadtrecht von 1520* (Karlsruhe: C.F. Müller, 1957), 141; see Ulrich Zasius, *Nüwe Stattrechten vnd Statuten der loblichen Statt Fryburg im Pryßgow gelegen* (Basel, 1520), 8.III, fol. 80r–82r.

[37] *Digest*, 1.5.24: 'Lex naturae haec est, ut qui nascitur sine legitimo matrimonio matrem sequatur, nisi lex specialis aliud inducit.'

argued that *patria potestas* was a natural and universal law, and who envisaged it as being pivotally deriving from the husband's *summum imperium* over his wife, was not defending a traditional or a standard view. Rather than being part of a tradition, he can be seen as its founder. Similarly, Filmer's attack on Hobbes was not so much a defence of the *status quo* against an innovator but rather the opposite: an 'invention of tradition' and a very powerful one at that. Taken together, these different strands of 'tradition', or 'context' show that Hobbes was part of a long-standing, nuanced, and complex debate, that not only raised a wide range of very different questions and problems, but also provided extremely diverse and divergent answers.

We will now turn to a further, seemingly very 'innovative' point regarding Hobbes's characterisation of the role of women in the state of nature, namely the issue of the rights of mothers to abandon their children. Hobbes had stated that it was a mother's prerogative in the state of nature to decide whether she wanted to raise a child or expose it, and that in the latter case the right over the child could be acquired by the person who fed it. Similar issues were also extensively discussed by early modern lawyers. In his lectures, Zasius had taught his students that the law of nature obliged parents to care for their children, but mothers and fathers were supposed to do so in different ways. Under natural law 'the father is not held to feed the offspring in the first three years, yet the mother nourishes it with milk'. Zasius quoted a massive array of law commentators, not least the famous medieval lawyer Baldus de Ubaldis, who had written in more detail about the issue of feeding children. Baldus's treatment included a closer look at the justification of the gendered parental division of labour involved in feeding ('in the first three years the child is fed with milk. And therefore the mother nurses him from her breasts, because a man does not have milk'), at the supposed obligations of aristocratic mothers to breast-feed their children (not obligatory), and at the supposed duty of poor women to do so (also not obligatory if they lacked the ability).[38] Zasius then wondered whether therefore under civil law the father could disinherit the child by simply choosing not to feed the child. It seemed that in that case a child would legally cease to be the father's offspring. 'If the father killed such a child, this would not be punished as patricide, but the punishment would be accounted as simple homicide.'[39] Zasius's treatment of the issue displayed

---

[38] 'Et hoc ideo, quia usque ad triennium puer alimentatur lacte. Et ideo mater ex uberibus suis lactat eum quia lac homo non habet, unde ad eam spectat.' I would like to thank Magnus Ryan who most generously provided me with a transcript of Baldus's commentary.

[39] Ulrich Zasius, *In sequentes Digesti veteris titulos lecturae* (Basel, 1537), fo. 10: 'Quod pater non teneatur primo triennio alere prolem, sed mater lacte nutriat. Noveris, quibus casibus filius exhaeredari potest. Eisdem etiam pater denegare potest alimenta, ... quia cessat esse filius quo

ambiguity. He was not entirely convinced that the father could volitionally under civil law cease any obligation towards the child. But we see here that the issue was extensively discussed and that it was at least legally plausible that the parent–child relationship should be dependent on the issue of providing, and being provided with, food. It is striking that in these legal debates kinship relations were understood purely as a matter of obligation, not as a matter of biology.

While of course abandonment was not allowed under canon law – and, from the third century on, not under Roman civil law either – it was still widely mentioned and discussed in medieval and early modern glosses and commentaries on the law. Thereby the kind of power that 'biological' parents had over their children was centrally debated. In the fourteenth century, Johannes Andreae, for example, made clear that the crime of abandonment destroyed all paternal power.[40] Earlier, in the thirteenth century, Accursius had stated that a father who did not provide food for his child lost all paternal power, including the right to reclaim the child.[41] Feeding and not feeding, especially nursing or not nursing, brought and took away obligations to and from a child. Roman parenthood, as depicted in the law, was not about biology. It was a legal and social institution, to be entered deliberately, as the normalcy of the concept of adoption shows, and which could also exited voluntarily. The avid discussion of these topics in medieval and early modern Europe shows that this was still – at least partly – relevant for its societies, in which the issue of the abandonment of children was of course a problem.[42] With the focus on this legal tradition, we can also conclude that Hobbes did not look so very different from the Roman law tradition and its early modern commentators. Hobbes was rather part of an early modern tradition that was able to ponder parent–child relations free from moral considerations or from the evocation of motherly sentiments.

---

ad mores civiles, licet non quo ad naturam, quia iura agnationes non tolluntur; quod adeo verum est, ut si pater talem filium occideret, non puniretur ut parricida ... sed poenam simplicis homicidii incidisset.'

[40] Johannes Andreae, *In quinque decretalium libros novella commentaria* x.5.11.1. v. liberatus, quoted in Charles J. Reid, *Power Over the Body, Equality in the Family: Rights and Domestic Relations in Medieval Canon Law* (Grand Rapids, MI: Wm. B. Eerdmans Publishing, 2004), at 86, 248 n. 165.

[41] Accursius, *Glossa in Codicem.* 8.46.9, v. consulta (Turin: Ex officina Erasmiana, 1968), 263va, quoted in Reid, *Power Over the Body*, at 86, 248 n. 169.

[42] See Colin Heywood, *A History of Childhood: Children and Childhood in the West from Medieval to Modern Times* (Cambridge: Polity Press, 2001); Catherine Panter-Brick and Malcolm T. Smith, *Abandoned Children* (Cambridge: Cambridge University Press, 2000).

In light of the early modern idea of the emergence of civil government and its relationship to marriage, then, we might now consider afresh an important point that Carol Pateman has made in the *Sexual Contract*. In this extremely influential work Pateman argued that Hobbes was not consistent when he proclaimed natural equality of the sexes while claiming that states were founded by fathers. The passage in *Leviathan* which attracted Pateman's scrutiny reads: 'In Commonwealths, this controversie [over children] is decided by the Civill Law, and for the most part, (but not alwayes) the sentence is in favour of the Father; because for the most part Commonwealths have been erected by the Fathers, not by the Mothers of families.'[43] For Pateman it simply did not make sense that women would contract themselves to a commonwealth, in which they are subordinated to men, and in which they lose this right over their children. Since Hobbes had described mothers as having *dominium*, and thus immense power over their children, and since mothers were the only kinds of people in the state of nature who were able to have natural allies with obligations to them, since their children were bound to their mothers in gratitude for having been kept alive, why should women enter a civil state in which all these powers were taken from them? Pateman's solution was that Hobbes must have envisioned a state of nature as a state of war of men against women, turning women into slaves before the state was being contracted, so that women were not part of the multitude of free persons that contracted the commonwealth.[44] However, looking at Hobbes in the context of early modern legal scholarship it becomes apparent that Hobbes did not leave a logical gap in his account of the emergence of civil life, and that he had not been as illogical as Pateman (and a cohort of scholars following her) made it seem. Neither had he been particularly brief or evasive in his account of the role of women in the emergence of civil government from a state of nature. As we have seen, Hobbes assumed a mother's right over her children in many ways more powerfully than his forerunners. Nevertheless, like the Roman law commentators, he understood this issue as pertaining to a pre-civic state, similar to how

---

[43] Hobbes, *Leviathan*, 139–40.
[44] Carole Pateman, *The Sexual Contract* (Stanford: Stanford University Press, 1988), 48–9; see also Pateman, '"God hath Ordained to Man a Helper": Hobbes, Patriarchy, and Conjugal Right', in Mary Lyndon Shanley and Carole Pateman (eds.), *Feminist Interpretations and Political Theory* (University Park, PA: Pennsylvania State University Press, 1991), 53–73, at 64–5. My analysis is not an attempt to fundamentally criticise Pateman's project. Her argument, insisting that we need to focus on the sexual and conjugal (rather than the paternal) dimensions in political thinking in order to grasp the consequences of the gendered state, is as valid today as it was thirty years ago.

early modern commentaries saw the *ius gentium*.⁴⁵ The *ius gentium*, according to the *Digest*, meant – besides the introduction of marriages – the introduction of wars, and thus fear, the passion that Hobbes most urgently identified as a reason to contract one's natural freedom away to a greater body. This immense right of mothers was thus only possible in a non-regulated sphere, before and between states, that was too insecure for anyone, even for mothers with potential allies in their children, to not try to escape it. From both the account of the origins of civil law and from his knowledge of history Hobbes also knew that it was a historical fact that men, and indeed 'fathers', had founded states. And he was able to ascertain historically that civil law had established *patria potestas* in the case of the Romans, a law that was later deemed tyrannical. It was thus a historical, but not a logical, let alone a natural, outcome that women were subordinated by the civil law. When Hobbes wrote that 'fathers *more* than mothers' were the founders of states, he indicated that state-building was not necessarily and systematically a biologically determined masculine or paternal endeavour. The Amazonian polity was a case in point and Hobbes, who mentioned female rulers very often, had no objections to a female monarch.

Hobbes was not as strikingly different to his contemporaries and forerunners as modern readers assume him to be. There had been a constant debate in Greek philosophy, in Roman jurisprudence and in medieval theology about what marriage was, and how it related to ideas of justice, and law, and in what way it was woven into what came to be 'the state'. Hobbes can be seen to have delivered a contribution to this debate which was shaped and re-shaped during the centuries. After all, marriage was, in the Roman tradition, what Cicero had called the *seminarium rei publicae*, and in the Roman law tradition it signalled the beginning of justice. Medieval theology did not put the focus predominantly on God's punishment after the Fall damning Eve to subordination. Rather medieval theologians thought marriage could be understood as consensual, as a union affected by mutual help and care. Indeed, in the writings of medieval lawyers, philosophers and theologians, we find a language that saw husband and wife as *aequales*.⁴⁶ This was brought together with the Roman law, which also understood marriage as a union in which the two partners 'share the same civil rights'.⁴⁷ In the Aristotelian tradition, the household was

---

⁴⁵ See Brett, '"The Matter, Forme, and Power of a Common-wealth".'
⁴⁶ See Gabriela Signori, *Von der Paradiesehe zur Gütergemeinschaft* (Frankfurt am Main: Campus, 2011).
⁴⁷ See *Digest*, 23.2.1. 'Nuptiae sunt coniunctio maris et feminae et consortium omnis vitae, divini et humani iuris communicatio.'

the space in which speech and reason first differentiated the *zoon politikon* from other animals, and commentators emphasised that the conjugal couple lived in friendship and relative equality.[48] This made for a medieval and early modern understanding of marriage that was very different from what is often assumed it must have been: one of absolute subordination of all women in all to all men. In the sixteenth century the reformation brought marriage completely in the realm of the temporal and it was further discussed extensively.[49] From our modern point of view, in which we assume that 'pre-modern' people did not even think about an equality of sexes, Hobbes indeed seems very 'innovative' when he assumed the natural equality of the sexes, but, seen in the tradition that I have sketched here, his point of view was more or less a standard stance. Essentialism, the idea that human beings are absolutely biologically determined to fulfil certain sex roles, is far more a tradition of a later natural law theory, that developed contemporaneously with Hobbes, admittedly, but that culminated with nineteenth-century ideas of evolutionist determinism. Today there is a rather worrying trend to view human behaviour through a lens of genetics that borders on a new predestinarianism. This, however, simply wasn't available to our early modern thinkers. Denying that political power had a gender was perhaps still possible for Hobbes, who said that 'though *Man* be *male* and *female*, *Authority* is not' and likewise 'authority does not take account of masculine and feminine'.[50] This is, however, certainly not possible for us now.

---

[48] See Becker, 'Gender in the History of Early Modern Political Thought'.
[49] See Anna Becker, 'Der Haushalt in der politischen Theorie der Frühen Neuzeit', in J. Eibach and I. Schmidt-Voges (eds.), *Haus im Kontext* (Munich: De Gruyter Oldenbourg, 2015), 667–85.
[50] Thomas Hobbes, *Considerations upon the reputation, loyalty, manners, & religion of Thomas Hobbes of Malmsbury written by himself, by way of letter to a learned person* (London, 1680), 49; Thomas Hobbes, *Leviathan, sive De Materia, Forma, & Potestate civitatis ecclesiasticae et civilis* (Amsterdam, 1670), 259.

14

Gender and the Lost Private Side of International Law

KAREN KNOP

Although new work on women's contributions is on the horizon, international lawyers have written relatively little history of their discipline from a gender perspective, whether on legal subjects or actors in international law, or on gender relations as a way of signifying or structuring legal power. Histories of women and diplomacy, studies of gender and empire, and feminist intellectual history might therefore seem like obvious sources with which to engage.

The impetus for this volume, however, is a warning by some international lawyers that the cost of interdisciplinarity with history is conservatism. The strongest caution is from Anne Orford, defending landmark post-colonial histories by international lawyers against the methodological criticisms of historians that this scholarship is marred by present-mindedness and inattentiveness to the ways in which legal forms are embedded in the particularities of context. Orford warns that respecting contextualism in the historian's sense has led some influential international lawyers to abandon the critical potential of earlier historical scholarship, and that studying the past simply as the past will make international lawyers more status quo.[1]

However well founded this concern,[2] there is reason to think it would apply differently to gender perspectives. Although methodological exchanges with historians are recent, feminist approaches to international law originated in the early 1990s, at a time when interdisciplinary research agendas for

---

[1] Anne Orford, 'International Law and the Limits of History', in Wouter Werner, Marieke de Hoon and Alexis Galán (eds.), *The Law of International Lawyers: Reading Martti Koskenniemi* (Cambridge: Cambridge University Press, 2017), 297–320.

[2] Responses to Orford include Lauren Benton, 'Beyond Anachronism: Histories of International Law and Global Legal Politics', *Journal of the History of International Law* 21 (2019), 7–40; Andrew Fitzmaurice, 'Context in the History of International Law', *Journal of the History of International Law* 20 (2018), 5–30; Kate Purcell, 'On the Uses and Advantages of Genealogy for International Law', *Leiden Journal of International Law* 33 (2020), 13–35.

international law and international relations theory were similarly suspect. Critics argued that, unlike such agendas, the goal of engagement with another discipline should be to unsettle, rather than solidify or subordinate, international law. Feminist approaches were among these 'counter-disciplinary' explorations of international law because they drew on feminist critiques in other disciplines, including international relations, political theory and postcolonial studies.[3] By the same token, gender as a category of analysis might identify directions for counter-disciplinary research between history and international law.[4] This chapter demonstrates the possibility, using the contextualist trend in the very scholarship that Orford criticizes: namely the growing historical focus on private law as the context of public international law's power, which she correlates with the marginalization of histories by Third World Approaches to International Law (TWAIL) scholars. Whether positively or negatively, international lawyers attribute such 'private-law contextualism', as I will call it, to the influence of the Cambridge intellectual historian Quentin Skinner. What precisely Skinnerian context means, however, can be bracketed for my purposes. What matters here is simply that, as received, it has made contemporaneous legal context – the legal 'surround' of public international law – central to historical inquiry by international lawyers.

I use the new private-law contextualism to illustrate how critiques of international law might profit from even further reconstruction of the private-law context and why that context, in turn, might profit from a gender analysis. Focusing on late-nineteenth-century European ideas of international law, the chapter begins by showing that private *international* law, or conflict of laws, is a missing legal context for the new private-law contextualism as well as for TWAIL histories (Section 14.1).

Private international law is the branch of a state's law that determines when its courts will take jurisdiction over a private-law case with a foreign element: for example, an inheritance that turns on the validity of a marriage celebrated

---

[3] Stepan Wood, 'Commentary: Toward a Counterdisciplinary Agenda for Research into International Law and International Relations', *Canadian Council on International Law Proceedings* 31 (2002), 260–73. See also, e.g., David Kennedy, 'When Renewal Repeats: Thinking against the Box', *New York University Journal of International Law and Politics* 32 (2000), 335–500, at 496; Jan Klabbers, 'Counter-Disciplinarity', *International Political Sociology* 4 (2010), 308–11; Martti Koskenniemi, 'Law, Teleology and International Relations: An Essay in Counterdisciplinarity', *International Relations* 26 (2012), 3–34.
[4] See Joan W. Scott, 'Gender: A Useful Category of Historical Analysis', *American Historical Review* 91 (1986), 1053–75.

14 Gender and the Lost Private Side of International Law

in another state (or another sub-unit in the case of a federal state). Further, if the court takes jurisdiction, does it apply its own law to determine the validity of the marriage? Or is the applicable law that of the state where the marriage was celebrated, the spouses' state of nationality, the state where they live, the state where the deceased lived or yet another state? In addition to issues of jurisdiction and choice of law, private international law also determines when a court will recognize and enforce the judgment of a foreign court. In the nineteenth century, international lawyers gave greater recognition to a conflict of laws between states belonging to the European 'family of nations' than to a conflict between one of these states and a state outside the European 'family'.[5] And between the metropolitan state and its colonies, the French conceived of *Droit international privé interne* or *le conflit de lois colonial*, which the Dutch termed *intergentiel recht*, while the English sometimes referred to intercommunal private law.[6] Some legal historians of the British empire use the term 'imperial conflict of laws', the law usually being some combination of imperial statutes and general common-law rules of private international law.[7]

This chapter argues that recuperating private international law as a lost side of international law can open up counter-disciplinary research on gender in the history of international law in at least three ways. First, international lawyers have yet to participate in the 'metropolitan turn' among historians of empire; that is, in studying empire's effects on the metropole as opposed to the colonies. In contrast, private international law has the potential to make visible the effects of colonial, as well as foreign, law on gender relations and national identity at home (Section 14.2). Second, feminists criticize international law as skewed by its development through grand episodes construed as international

---

[5] See, e.g., Norman Bentwich, 'The Adhesion of Non-Christian Countries to the Hague Conventions of Private International Law', *Journal of the Society of Comparative Legislation*, New Series 15 (1915), 76–82; Hisashi Harata, 'Civilized Universality of Private International Law Lost in the Last Decades of the 19th Century' (unpublished English draft of the author's 'Characteristics and Background of the Private International Law Understanding in the Last Decades of the 19th Century (1)', published in Japanese in *Hogaku-Kyokai Zassi* 133(1) (2016), 1–51); Karen Knop, 'Lorimer's Private Citizens of the World', *European Journal of International Law* 27 (2016), 447–75, at 457–9.

[6] R.D. Kollewijn, 'Conflicts of Western and Non-Western Law', *International Law Quarterly* 4 (1951), 307–25, at 311.

[7] See George Van Cleve, '"Somerset's Case" and Its Antecedents in Imperial Perspective', *Law and History Review* 24 (2006), 601–45, at 603; Daniel J. Hulsebosch, 'Nothing but Liberty: "Somerset's Case" and the British Empire', *Law and History Review* 24 (2006), 647–57 (commenting on Van Cleve). For a treatise of the period, see William Burge, *Commentaries on Colonial and Foreign Laws Generally, and in Their Conflict with Each Other, and the Law of England* (London: Saunders and Benning, 1838).

'crises'. Whereas critical scholars have responded by attending to the routine operation of international law on the ground in the contemporary developing world, the private side of international law offers historical terrain on which to examine transnational everyday life in the imperial centre, and the capacity of individuals' cross-border legal arrangements to cumulatively re-shape their state (Section 14.3). Third, feminist perspectives might illuminate our understanding of the private international law alternatives to core concepts of public international law and their contemporary resonance, specifically, its counterparts to nationality and to obligation between states (Section 14.4).

The sequencing of the chapter reflects successive phases of feminist legal scholarship.[8] In identifying new lines of historical research, the chapter begins by locating women in international law and then moves to gender and gender relations as analytics. Lastly, it brings in feminist legal theory, specifically ideas of gender discrimination and relational feminism. Whereas liberal feminism addresses discrimination by pursuing what has been called a de-gendering strategy, relational feminism values the feminine.[9] Critical of liberalism for its tendency to employ a pre-social conception of the individual, relational feminism derives an alternative conception from experiences and practices associated with the feminine. Relational feminism, in Marilyn Friedman's words, 'fundamentally acknowledges the role of social relationships and human community in constituting both self-identity and the nature and meaning of the particulars of individual lives', and it links this conception of the self to 'visions of the foundation of human society derived from nurturance, caring attachment, and mutual interestedness'.[10] The chapter draws on these varieties of feminist legal theory because they chime with its emphasis on a pluralist, quotidian international as neglected in the history of international law. A different picture would result from a focus, say, on those feminisms intertwined historically with transnational causes or those currently influential in international law. Indeed, in contemporary international law, particularly the international law governing armed conflict, there is debate about the consolidation and ascendancy of some types of feminism at the expense of anti-war feminism and anti-imperialist feminism, both long intertwined with transnational causes, as well as the marginalization of newer types

---

[8] See Nicola Lacey, 'Feminist Legal Theory and the Rights of Women', in Karen Knop (ed.), *Gender and Human Rights* (Oxford: Oxford University Press, 2004), 13–55, at 14–15.
[9] Kate Nash, 'Human Rights for Women: An Argument for "Deconstructive Equality"', *Economy and Society* 31 (2002), 414–33, at 419.
[10] Marilyn Friedman, 'Feminism and Modern Friendship: Dislocating the Community', *Ethics* 99 (1989), 275–90, at 275–6.

originating from domestic law such as sex-positive feminism and queer feminism.[11]

While the directions for research that I propose operate on the relationship between public and private international law and draw on feminist legal theory, I note at the outset that the public/private, male/female and other binaries at work here should not be assumed to be fixed and permanent in time – any more than they should be assumed to be universal across cultures, as post-colonial feminists have pointed out. Instead, feminist historian Joan Scott's prescription for the study of gender as an analytical category in political history might also apply to law:

> If we treat the opposition between male and female as problematic rather than known, as something contextually defined, repeatedly constructed, then we must constantly ask not only what is at stake in proclamations or debates that invoke gender to explain or justify their positions but also how implicit understandings of gender are being invoked and reinscribed.[12]

14.1 PRIVATE LAW AND PRIVATE INTERNATIONAL LAW: LOCATING WOMEN

International lawyers are increasingly attentive to the systemic impact of private economic power and to the historical role of private law in empire.[13] In his recent historiographical work, Martti Koskenniemi argues that histories of international law should expand from the law of sovereignty to include the law of property and their relationship with one other as the 'yin and yang of

---

[11] See Karen Engle, Vasuki Nesiah and Dianne Otto, 'Feminist Approaches to International Law', in Jeffrey L. Dunoff and Mark A. Pollack (eds.), *International Legal Theory: Foundations and Frontiers* (Cambridge: Cambridge University Press, forthcoming).

[12] Scott, 'Gender: A Useful Category', 1074. See also Denise Riley, *'Am I That Name?' Feminism and the Category of 'Women' in History* (Minneapolis: University of Minnesota, 1988).

[13] See, e.g., B.S. Chimni, 'Prolegomena to a Class Approach to International Law', *European Journal of International Law* 21 (2010), 57–82; James Thuo Gathii, *War, Commerce, and International Law* (New York: Oxford University Press, 2010); Martti Koskenniemi, 'Empire and International Law: The Real Spanish Contribution', *University of Toronto Law Journal* 61 (2011), 1–36; Doreen Lustig, *Veiled Power: International Law and the Private Corporation 1886–1891* (Oxford: Oxford University Press, 2020); Luigi Nuzzo, 'Territory, Sovereignty, and the Construction of the Colonial Space', in Martti Koskenniemi, Walter Rech and Manuel Jiménez Fonseca (eds.), *International Law and Empire: Historical Explorations* (Oxford: Oxford University Press, 2017), 263–92; Ileana M. Porras, 'Constructing International Law in the East Indian Seas: Property, Sovereignty, Commerce and War in Hugo Grotius, De Iure Praedae – The Law of Prize and Booty, or "On How to Distinguish Merchants from Pirates"', *Brooklyn Journal of International Law* 31 (2006), 741–804.

global power'.¹⁴ By approaching the history of international law in terms of states – war, diplomacy, treaties, institution-building – international lawyers cordon off the private-law relations that underlie and support those actions. Koskenniemi writes evocatively:

> Any international legal history would say something about the abolition of the slave trade but little if anything about the contractual form through which that trade was connected with Caribbean sugar production and the export of arms and manufactures to Africa. Its account of North American colonization would rarely include an analysis of the charters under which private companies and individual proprietors would rule the thirteen colonies.¹⁵

That is, by neglecting private law, historians of international law produce only a partial account of how power operates through international legal concepts and institutions.

Feminists would add that expanding to the private sphere of the market is not enough – we must also expand to the private sphere of the family. Before the nineteenth century, in fact, the public/private dichotomy was not, or not fully, in operation, and most of the leading international law treatises included questions of civil status, marriage, succession and family law, all of which were occasion to invoke the status of women.¹⁶ According to Martin Gallié and Maxine Visotsky-Charlebois, questions of women's rights disappear from the main treatises at the end of the eighteenth century.¹⁷ When they reappear at the start of the twentieth century, it is squarely in public international law: issues of diplomatic immunity for the household (the diplomat assumed to be male) and the nationality of married women.

This nineteenth-century silence brings us back to Koskenniemi's case for expanding histories of international law to take account of private law. The way he frames the case implies that the private is outside international law, or

---

¹⁴ Martti Koskenniemi, 'Expanding Histories of International Law', *American Journal of Legal History* 56 (2016), 104–12, at 112.
¹⁵ Ibid., 109. See also Martti Koskenniemi, 'Histories of International Law: Significance and Problems for a Critical View', *Temple International and Comparative Law Journal* 27 (2013), 215–40, at 235 (arguing that the law of contracts as well as the law of property should be included).
¹⁶ Martin Gallié and Maxine Visotsky-Charlebois, 'Le *droit des femmes* tel qu'il a été enseigné par les *Pères fondateurs* du droit international public et leurs héritiers. Notes de lecture sur les ouvrages et les manuels du XVIᵉ au XXIᵉ siècle', in Emmanuelle Tourme Jouannet, Laurence Burgorgue-Larsen, Horatia Muir Watt and Hélène Ruiz Fabri (eds.), *Féminisme(s) et droit international: Études du réseau Olympe* (Paris: Société de législation comparée, 2016), 189–224, at 195. Women also figured in matters of royal succession, the status of children born to enslaved women, and inclusion in political life: ibid.
¹⁷ Ibid., 198–200.

14 Gender and the Lost Private Side of International Law 363

perhaps blurs or doubles with it, as when the Dutch East India Company is both a private trading company and a representative of the sovereign.[18] But this does not hold for private *international* law. In an unpublished work, Koskenniemi actually mentions, without pursuing, that his 'men of 1873' – as he calls the founders of the *Institut de droit international* – understood private international law as part of international law. They treated public and private international law as united, although not all agreed on how.[19] Moreover, a number of them were also involved in efforts that led to the first meeting of the Hague Conference on Private International Law in 1893. Pasquale Mancini, the *Institut*'s first president, had spurred an earlier attempt, and the Conference was an initiative of *Institut* member Tobias Asser.[20] The goal was a series of treaties that would remove legal obstacles to transnational private relations and transactions such that, for example, a contract valid in the state where it was concluded would not be held invalid by a court in the state where it was performed due to differences in the contract law of the two jurisdictions. As opposed to harmonizing the substance of private law across states, the objective was to harmonize private international law rules, such that states were agreed on which state's private law regulated a given issue.

Since the unity of public and private international law has long ceased to figure in international law thought, the private side of international law has been lost, largely, to modern public international lawyers and requires historical context to reconstruct. '[P]ublic international lawyers frequently ignore private international law', notes private international lawyer Ralf Michaels, 'whereas historians of *private* international law are usually very aware of the relation'.[21] As Alex Mills, another private international law scholar, writes, this lack of context has implications for present-day international law as well:

> The standard history of international law is a story of public international law as an expanding, developing discipline, only recently engaging with the domain of the 'private'.... By leaving out the private history of international law, its rise and its decline, the history of international law, and also the

---

[18] Koskenniemi, 'Expanding Histories', 108.
[19] Martti Koskenniemi, 'Nationalism, Universalism, Empire: International Law in 1871 and 1919', paper delivered as part of the 'Whose International Community? Universalism and the Legacies of Empire' lecture series, Columbia University Department of History, April 2005, 15–20.
[20] Hans van Loon, 'The Hague Conference on Private International Law', *Hague Justice Journal* 2(2) (2007), 3–12, at 4.
[21] Ralf Michaels, 'Private Lawyer in Disguise? On the Absence of Private Law and Private International Law in Martti Koskenniemi's Work', *Temple International and Comparative Law Journal* 27 (2013), 499–521, at 512–13.

present development of international law, appear more natural, more progressive, more inevitable. The engagement of international law with the private domain appears to be a sign of maturity, not a return to the past.[22]

Moreover, if private international law was treated as part of international law, whether in theory or in practice, then transnational family law was part of it as well, rather than merely a backstory.[23] In other words, women and private-law gender relations did not disappear altogether from international law during the nineteenth century, contrary to what Gallié and Visotsky-Charlebois's survey of treatises indicates. Indeed, once public international lawyers think to look, this point is hiding in plain sight. Among the seven Hague conventions on private international law first concluded are conventions on marriage (1902), divorce (1902), guardianship (1902), the effects of marriage (1905) and the deprivation of civil rights (1905).[24]

I next suggest three ways in which recognizing private international law as part of the international law conversation in the late nineteenth century might open up new connections and inquiries between international lawyers and historians, particularly around women, gender and feminism.

14.2 EFFECTS OF EMPIRE AT THE CENTRE: GENDER AND NATION

To begin, note that private international law puts the focus in international legal history on the state at home as opposed to abroad, on the metropole as opposed to its colonies. In conflict-of-laws cases in the metropolitan courts, we have the legal raw material for a turn already taken by historians, literary

---

[22] Alex Mills, *The Confluence of Public and Private International Law: Justice, Pluralism and Subsidiarity in the International Constitutional Ordering of Private Law* (Cambridge: Cambridge University Press, 2009), 71. Private international lawyers interested in the present suggestiveness of this historical moment include Diego P. Fernández Arroyo, 'Réflexions autour du besoin réciproque entre le droit international privé et le droit international public', in *Le 90e anniversaire de Boutros Boutros-Ghali: Hommage du Curatorium à son Président* (London/Boston: Martinus Nijhoff, 2012), 113–35; Roxana Banu, *Nineteenth-Century Perspectives on Private International Law* (Oxford: Oxford University Press, 2018); Nikitas E. Hatzimihail, 'Reflections on the International Dimension of Private International Law', in Rafaël Jafferali, Vanessa Marquette and Arnaud Nuyts (eds.), *Liber Amicorum Nadine Watté* (Brussels: Bruylant, 2017), 287–301; Mills, *Confluence of Public and Private International Law*; Horatia Muir Watt, 'Private International Law beyond the Schism', *Transnational Legal Theory* 2 (2011), 347–428; Joel R. Paul, 'The Isolation of Private International Law'', *Wisconsin International Law Journal* 7 (1988), 149–78.
[23] While I will refer generally to 'family law,' in some systems this body of law was known as personal status law.
[24] Van Loon, 'The Hague Conference on Private International Law', 4–5.

theorists and others in the humanities,[25] but not yet taken by international lawyers doing history. This turn is to the effects of trade, or war, or empire, or other transnational relations on the centerre as opposed to the periphery. Also in keeping with this turn, private international law responds to and shapes the centre as heterogeneous. Its bread-and-butter issues come from the fact that home is not neatly separated from abroad: England, for instance, could include foreign merchants, enemy aliens, former colonial civil servants and their families, slaves brought by colonists, indigenous wives, and so on. When choice-of-law reasons therefore led an English court to apply a foreign or colonial law, that law was no longer just 'over there'. That law would decide the issue between the parties in England unless it violated the court's understanding of natural justice or the fundamental values of English society and thus fell within what is nowadays referred to as the 'public policy' exception in choice of law. In other words, the norm was respect for difference, and private international law regulated how heterogeneous English society became through property, contract, tort, marriage and other transnational legal relations entered into by individuals. This difference could be generated not only by foreign laws or laws indigenous to the colonies, but also by controversial settler laws such as those permitting slavery or acts of indemnity following the repression of a colonial uprising,[26] complicating a respect that might otherwise be equated positively with openness, tolerance or cosmopolitanism.

Private international law's potential to introduce colonial legal relations into the metropolitan state brings to the surface the other persistent 'anxiety of empire' (to use Anthony Pagden's term). Whereas public international lawyers have concentrated on anxiety over how to justify assertions of sovereignty abroad, private international law shifts attention to the 'fear that whatever occurred, in no matter how distant a corner of the globe, would inevitably have consequences for what took place in the metropolis'.[27] That the stakes differed from those of public international law can be seen from the fact that Turkey, Russia, China, Japan, Siam and other non-Christian powers were

---

[25] See, e.g., Antoinette Burton, *At the Heart of the Empire: Indians and the Colonial Encounter in Late-Victorian Britain* (Berkeley: University of California Press, 1998); Catherine Hall and Sonya O. Rose (eds.), *At Home with the Empire: Metropolitan Culture and the Imperial World* (Cambridge: Cambridge University Press, 2006); Edward W. Said, *Culture and Imperialism* (New York: Alfred A. Knopf, 1993), 80–97 (on empire in Jane Austen's fiction); Philip J. Stern, 'History and Historiography of the English East India Company: Past, Present, and Future!', *History Compass* 7 (2009), 1146–80, at 1152–5.
[26] See *Somerset v. Stewart* (1772) 98 ER 499 (KB); *Phillips v. Eyre* (1870) LR 6 QB 1.
[27] Anthony Pagden, 'Empire and Its Anxieties', *American Historical Review* 117 (2012), 141–8, at 141. While persistent, these anxieties also shift over time: ibid., 145.

included in the Hague Peace Conferences codifying public international law, but were not invited to the Hague Conferences of 1896, 1902 and 1905 aimed at agreement on principles of private international law.[28] The former 'apply to the whole of the civilised world, irrespective of race and religion', whereas the latter provided that they applied only to European territories of the state parties.[29]

The implications of imperial conflict-of-laws cases for the very nature of the metropole are at their starkest in *Somerset's Case*, the well-known 1772 judgment by Lord Mansfield, Chief Justice of the English Court of King's Bench.[30] James Somerset had been taken from Africa as a slave and sold to Charles Stewart in Virginia, a jurisdiction where slavery was legal. Stewart brought Somerset with him to England, where Somerset later escaped and was recaptured. After Stewart decided to sell him back into slavery in Jamaica, Somerset was bound in chains aboard ship awaiting departure when abolitionists successfully sought a writ of habeas corpus to obtain his freedom.[31] Legal historian Daniel Hulsebosch frames the anxiety of empire as follows:

> For almost two centuries, the English constitution had been constructed by contrasting English legal liberties to those available elsewhere, including in other jurisdictions in the empire. This legal alterity emerged from a political culture that was caught between wanting the gains and glory of imperial expansion and fearing that royal dominions abroad would be training grounds for arbitrary government that might travel back home. The tragic endpoint of this reverse migration was called 'slavery'.[32]

Among the arguments made by Somerset's counsel was that respecting Virginia's laws in England would corrupt English society: what would happen to their sense of liberty if the English became accustomed to seeing colonial masters whipping their slaves in the fields on the edge of London?[33] Lord Mansfield was clear that, however odious slavery was, a contract for the sale of a slave was recognized in England if it was from a jurisdiction where slavery was legal. But adopting the master–slave relation created under American law did not entail adopting all of its consequences and specifically not 'so high an

---

[28] Bentwich, 'The Adhesion of Non-Christian Countries', 76.
[29] Ibid. Although two of the private international law conventions provided that a party could extend the application to its territories, possessions or colonies outside Europe or to its consular jurisdictions in foreign states, none actually did so.
[30] *Somerset v. Stewart* (1772) 98 ER 499.
[31] See, e.g., Van Cleve, '"Somerset's Case" and its Antecedents'.
[32] Hulsebosch, 'Nothing but Liberty', 648.
[33] *Somerset v. Stewart* (1772) 98 ER 499, 503.

act of dominion' as keeping Somerset by force to be sold abroad.[34] In separating the recognition of the status of slave from recognition of the master's right to use force, the court instanced the choice-of-law distinction that a marriage entered into in one place 'was in all places the same, but the regulation of power over children from it, and other circumstances, very various'.[35]

Analyzing the incidents of slavery with reference to the incidents of marriage appears less jarring when we recall that gender relations were constructed as the paradigmatic case of national differences in private law. As noted earlier, most of the turn-of-the-century private international law conventions concerned family law, and differences simply between European states. Even between England and Scotland, the laws governing the constitution and dissolution of marriage were strikingly different.[36] As between the metropolitan state and its colonies, the notion that a uniform law of contracts, bankruptcy and so on was considered essential for the colonies left family law as almost the only area in which stark cases of conflict arose.[37] In addition to slavery cases, which lawyers have studied,[38] cases of polygamous marriage were among the textbook examples of the public policy exception to choice of law. With respect to family law, it was even argued that legal pluralism in the colonies restricted the availability of the public policy exception in the metropole. If a Christian country recognized Islamic marriage and divorce in its colonies, then, one 1914 International Law Association paper proposed, those relationships ought to be recognized in the mother country as well:

---

[34] Ibid., 509–10.
[35] Ibid., 504.
[36] Leah Leneman, 'English Marriages and Scottish Divorces in the Early Nineteenth Century', *Journal of Legal History* 17 (1996), 225–43, at 225.
[37] Kollewijn, 'Conflicts of Western and Non-Western Law', 311. See also, e.g., Lama Abu-Odeh, 'Modernizing Muslim Family Law: The Case of Egypt', *Vanderbilt Journal of Transnational Law* 37 (2004), 1043–146; Partha Chatterjee, *The Nation and Its Fragments: Colonial and Postcolonial Histories* (Princeton: Princeton University Press, 1993), chs. 6–7; Janet Halley and Kerry Rittich, 'Critical Directions in Comparative Family Law: Genealogies and Contemporary Studies of Family Law Exceptionalism', *American Journal of Comparative Law* 58 (2010), 753–75, at 771–5; Duncan Kennedy, 'Savigny's Family/Patrimony Distinction and Its Place in the Global Genealogy of Classical Legal Thought', *American Journal of Comparative Law* 58 (2010), 811–41; Philomila Tsoukala, 'Marrying Family Law to the Nation', *American Journal of Comparative Law* 58 (2010), 873–910.
[38] See, e.g., Robert M. Cover, *Justice Accused: Antislavery and the Judicial Process* (New Haven: Yale University Press, 1975), ch. 5; Paul Finkelman, *An Imperfect Union: Slavery, Federalism, and Comity* (Chapel Hill: University of North Carolina Press, 1981); Joel R. Paul, 'The Transformation of International Comity', *Law and Contemporary Problems* 71(3) (2008), 19–38, at 23–5.

> It is more repugnant to the public order that Mohammedans should have one law applied to them in the colony and another in the mother-country, than that there should be different laws as to marriage and divorce for different sections of the people in the same territory in Europe just as there is in North Africa.[39]

Conflicts cases in the metropolitan legal system thus forced an encounter between legal systems *inside* and *for* the metropole. They also potentially featured issues that not only involved women, but also involved gender relations as defining of the European state's moral core for its own society.

14.3 INTERNATIONAL CRISIS AND TRANSNATIONAL EVERYDAY: GENDER RELATIONS AS CHANGES OF STATE

Thus far I have sketched how the lost private side of international law invites international lawyers to participate in the metropolitan turn already taken by historians. This is also to share historians' interest in 'the formal and, more important, informal arrangements that royal subjects made in their legal arrangements as they traveled across the internal borders of the empire'.[40] I next suggest how this interest in mobile subjects might dovetail with feminist critiques of international law in a second direction for gendering histories of international law.

Feminist legal theorist Hilary Charlesworth has critically described (public) international law as a 'discipline of crisis'.[41] She argues that the tendency to construct situations like Kosovo in the late 1990s as 'crises' systematically skews the development of international law. Moreover, international lawyers' addiction to crises is bound up with gendered imaginaries. It plays to a sense of heroic mission, Charlesworth asserts, drawing on Anne Orford's analysis of the international discourse justifying military intervention in Kosovo.[42] Orford shows that a number of accounts 'justifying intervention relied on narratives ingrained in the popular imagination of the West to cast the international community as masculine action hero and the state targeted for intervention as helpless feminine victim'.[43] Charlesworth also parallels 'the international law attachment to crises and the way that traditional forms of history have

---

[39] Bentwich, 'The Adhesion of Non-Christian Countries', 79.
[40] Hulsebosch, 'Nothing but Liberty', 649.
[41] Hilary Charlesworth, 'International Law: A Discipline of Crisis', *Modern Law Review* 65 (2002), 377–92.
[42] Anne Orford, 'Muscular Humanitarianism: Reading the Narratives of the New Interventionism', *European Journal of International Law* 10 (1999), 679–711.
[43] Karen Knop, 'Introduction', in Karen Knop (ed.), *Gender and Human Rights* (Oxford: Oxford University Press, 2004), 1–12, at 9.

concentrated on "great men" and narrative representation of short-term political conflicts and crises',[44] arguing instead for a focus on everyday life and attention to longer-term trends and structural problems. Critical international lawyer Luis Eslava directs Charlesworth's challenge toward the traditional separation of international law from national and local affairs.[45] Arguing that international law should be understood as an ordinary component in the constitution of social relations, he focuses on places that have been subject to colonial rule and the target of development projects.[46]

In contrast to public international law, we do not have to go outside private international law to locate the everyday for women and gender relations. Moreover, to Charlesworth's structural point, individuals eloping to Gretna Green over the Scottish border (as Lydia in *Pride and Prejudice* plans to do) were not only everyday transnational actors. They were simultaneously actors changing the shape and composition of the English state by taking advantage of the fact that although a 1753 English law prevented couples aged under twenty-one from marrying in England without their parents' permission, English law recognized the 'border' marriages of English couples who travelled to Scotland to avoid these restrictions.[47] Divorce was another such example. From 1563 onward, Scotland resembled other Protestant countries in Europe in allowing both men and women a full divorce with the right to remarry, whereas England maintained the Roman Catholic doctrine that marriage was indissoluble, permitting only judicial separation. During the eighteenth century, divorce became possible in England by private act of parliament, but this was an option almost only for wealthy men.[48] Starting in the 1770s, increasing numbers of English spouses sued for divorce in Scotland.[49] Not only were the wife's chances of success better there, but the great majority of such divorces in the early nineteenth century were granted to couples of humble origin.[50] What eventually diminished this private international law modification of the English family and the English state was not

---

[44] Charlesworth, 'Discipline of Crisis', 388–9.
[45] Luis Eslava, *Local Space, Global Life: The Everyday Operation of International Law and Development* (Cambridge: Cambridge University Press, 2015), 30.
[46] Ibid., 33.
[47] See J.J. Fawcett, 'Evasion of Law and Mandatory Rules in Private International Law', *Cambridge Law Journal* 49 (1990), 44–62, at 46. On the phenomenon of Gretna Green marriages, see Lawrence Stone, *Road to Divorce: England 1530–1987* (Oxford: Oxford University Press 1990), 130–7. Stone gives a more varied historical picture of whether English courts recognized Gretna Green marriages as valid. Ibid., 133–4.
[48] Leneman, 'English Marriages and Scottish Divorces', 225, 232.
[49] Ibid., 225–6.
[50] Ibid., 241–2.

the Scottish courts' willingness to grant such a divorce, but the refusal of an English court to recognize it as a divorce in England.[51]

Cumulatively, then, the transnational legal arrangements that private individuals made to evade English marriage law could have systemic effects for the state. Some of these practices were de facto more egalitarian, as with Scottish divorces, while others were not. For most of the nineteenth century, there were strong debates in England about whether it should become legal for a man to marry his deceased wife's sister or whether it would be akin to legalizing marriage between siblings.[52] However, nothing points to this as an issue for feminists of the time concerned with the reform of marriage law; rather, their focus was on legal inequalities between husband and wife such as with regard to property rights and the guardianship of minor children.[53] A household scenario commonly cited as leading couples with means to marry abroad was that of an unmarried woman who lived with her late sister's family and helped to raise her children.[54] English courts, though, refused to recognize the marriages of English couples who wed in Denmark or Germany in order to evade the English law on the prohibited degrees of marriage. By differentiating the essential validity of a foreign marriage (at issue in these so-called Danish marriage cases) from the formal validity (including the parental consent issue in the Gretna Green marriage cases), English choice-of-law rules were able to recognize the latter and not the former.[55] But colonial laws allowing marriage to a deceased wife's sister could not as easily be kept at a distance, including because these unions were not evasive. They could be contracted in all of the Australian colonies and several other British possessions, and their status in England was a thorny question of imperial conflict of laws. For example, in his 1887 treatise on English and colonial marriage laws, James Hammick argued in favor of recognition, citing the possibility that otherwise a man who had legally married his deceased wife's sister in the colonies could return to England and remarry, leaving her and her offspring to

---

[51] Ibid., 233, 241–2.
[52] Nancy F. Anderson, 'The "Marriage with a Deceased Wife's Sister Bill" Controversy: Incest Anxiety and the Defence of Family Purity in Victorian England', *Journal of British Studies* 21 (1982), 67–86, at 67–8, 74–6.
[53] Cynthia Fansler Behrman, 'The Annual Blister: A Sidelight on Victorian Social and Parliamentary History', *Victorian Studies* 11 (1968), 483–502, at 494; Margaret Morganroth Gullette, 'The Puzzling Case of the Deceased Wife's Sister: Nineteenth-Century England Deals with a Second-Chance Plot', *Representations* 31 (1990), 142–66, at 146.
[54] Anderson, 'Incest Anxiety and the Defence of Family Purity', 73, 80–1; Behrman, 'The Annual Blister', 491–3.
[55] *Brook v. Brook* (1861) 9 HL Cas 193; A.V. Dicey, *The Law of Domicil as a Branch of the Law of England* (London: Stevens and Sons, 1879), 203–4; Fawcett, 'Evasion of Law', 45–6.

beg or starve.[56] As opponents of marriage to a deceased wife's sister feared, the 1906 Colonial Marriages Act, which granted full inheritance rights in England to children of these marriages entered into in the colonies, paved the way for legislation allowing sister-in-law marriages in England the following year.[57]

Returning to the parallel that Charlesworth draws between international law's development through crises and 'great men' histories and historical analyses of short-term political crises, we can thus add the potential parallel between private international law's development and other forms of history that aim to do justice to the everyday, including empire and the everyday. Beyond this potential parallel, the examples in this section highlight the ways in which rules on jurisdiction, choice of law and recognition of judgments furnished individuals with the means not only to order their own gender relations differently, but cumulatively to re-order the state.

To this direction for research into the gendered history of international law, it must be added that nineteenth-century private international law is often assumed to have been inhospitable to understanding individuals in their social contexts and to recognizing their transnational lives as lived. In recent historical work, however, Roxana Banu argues that modern conflicts scholars err by projecting onto nineteenth-century private international law thought the classical liberal ideas of the individual as isolated and autonomous, and of private matters as strongly separated from public.[58] Banu identifies and seeks to recover a lost alternative in the nineteenth-century scholarship that she interprets as theorizing 'various levels of relationships amongst individuals and with various communities in the transnational realm'. Distinct from individualism as well as state-centrism, this 'relational internationalist' alternative is characterized by efforts to draw out a growing range of factors as constitutive of the transnational context of a given interpersonal relationship.[59] For Banu, the underlying view of the self as social, rather than as atomistic, and the implications of this view resonate with contemporary relational feminism: the historical perspectives she reconstructs thus open up possibilities for developing a relational feminist account of current private international law.[60]

---

[56] James T. Hammick, *The Marriage Law of England* (2nd ed.) (London: Shaw & Sons, 1887), 249–53. See also Charlotte Frew, 'Sister-in-Law Marriage and the Empire: Religious Politics and Legislative Reform in the Australian Colonies 1850–1900', *Journal of Imperial and Commonwealth History* 41 (2013), 194–210.
[57] Anderson, 'Incest Anxiety and the Defence of Family Purity', 84.
[58] Banu, *Nineteenth-Century Perspectives on Private International Law*, 4–5.
[59] Ibid., 8–9.
[60] Roxana Banu, 'Nineteenth-Century Private International Law and Relational Feminism' (unpublished) (2016). For a summary, see Roxana Banu, '2016 PILIG Prize: A Relational

14.4 CITIZENSHIP AND INTERNATIONAL OBLIGATION: GENDER DISCRIMINATION AND RELATIONAL FEMINISM

The final direction for research I propose is what a gender perspective might bring to the historical understanding of membership in the state and of interstate obligation in international law. Not all international lawyers in the late nineteenth century subscribed to the unity of public and private international law. And even those who did differed on why and how the two should be integrated. What matters here is that public and private international law were seen relative to one another. With reference to common-law private international law, I take up the concepts of domicile and the 'comity of nations', which were debated as inferior to their respective public international law counterparts of nationality and binding obligation between states. I suggest both that gender may be relevant to the historical understanding of domicile and comity and that they may be useful for thinking about issues of gender discrimination and relational feminist approaches in present-day international law.

Domicile and Discrimination[61]

Following Mancini, the *Institut de droit international* endorsed nationality as the link for purposes of private, as well as public, international law.[62] Nonetheless, its members were divided over whether nationality should be the connecting factor that determined which state's laws governed an individual's status and capacity, family relations and corresponding rights and obligations. In particular, domicile was the connecting factor used by common-law systems of private international law and also advocated by Friedrich Carl von Savigny, who equalled Mancini as a giant in the field. Whereas nationality reflected a political bond, domicile was 'the fact of

---

Feminist Approach to Private International Law', *Commentaries on Private International Law* 3 (1) (2017), 21, available at www.asil.org/sites/default/files/documents/PIL_vol3_issue1_v2%20%281%29.pdf. See also Roxana Banu, 'A Relational Feminist Approach to Conflict of Laws', *Michigan Journal of International Law* 24 (2017), 1–52.

[61] This section draws on Knop, 'Lorimer's Private Citizens of the World' and Knop, 'Citizenship, Public and Private', *Law and Contemporary Problems* 71(3) (2008), 309–41.

[62] See 'Conclusions et Résolutions Proposées à l'Institut par M.M. Mancini et T.C. Asser', *Revue de droit international et de législation comparée*, 1st ser. 6 (1874), 582–4, at 583.

homeness, as the law gathers it'.⁶³ An 1869 House of Lords case defined domicile as:

> a residence freely chosen ... and it must be residence ... general and indefinite in its future contemplation. It is true that residence originally temporary, or intended for a limited period, may afterwards become general and unlimited, and in such a case so soon as the change of purpose ... can be inferred, the fact of domicil is established.⁶⁴

Thus an individual could change domicile sometimes even simply by changing his mind, whereas the acquisition and loss of nationality was a process involving the state.

On one hand, the common-law rules on domicile clearly reflected discriminatory European and imperial attitudes of the time. For instance, nineteenth-century jurists were divided over whether an Englishman could acquire domicile in a non-European nation such as China, India or Turkey, with the British courts dismissing the possibility by the end of the century. Among the underlying reasons were the notion of immiscibility and the incentives created for British nationals to incorporate foreign areas into the British empire.⁶⁵ On the other hand, domicile's history also shows its role as a more contextual and cosmopolitan form of private citizenship – perhaps even its suggestiveness for present-day citizenship.⁶⁶ Notably because nationality and domicile did not always align, in times of war an enemy national could be a British domiciliary, and vice versa. Whereas the public law relationship of enemy at the time involved the complete severing of ties between the citizens of the states at war, the private-law relationship was that of outlaw. Enemy domiciliaries could be sued in British courts, but not sue. But if the relationship of outlaw was more intimate than that of enemy, it also permitted an intimate, personalized form of harm because private individuals could wrong enemy domiciliaries without remedy during a war. Against this outlawing, British courts applied a shallower concept of 'commercial domicile' or 'trade domicile' and thereby expanded the category of enemy nationals who could belong to Britain, a state at war with their own, for private law purposes.⁶⁷ In

---

⁶³ James Lorimer, *The Institutes of the Law of Nations: A Treatise of the Jural Relations of Separate Political Communities* (Edinburgh: W. Blackwood & Sons, 1883), vol. 1, 423–4.
⁶⁴ *Udny v. Udny* (1869) LR 1 Sc & Div 441, 458.
⁶⁵ See David J. Bederman, 'Extraterritorial Domicile and the Constitution', *Virginia Journal of International Law* 28 (1988), 451–94, at 454–60.
⁶⁶ In the contemporary context, Theodora Kostakopoulou, for instance, argues that domicile is a better foundation altogether for citizenship: Kostakopoulou, *The Future Governance of Citizenship* (Cambridge: Cambridge University Press, 2008).
⁶⁷ See Knop, 'Citizenship, Public and Private', 321–8; Dicey, *The Law of Domicil*, 341–6.

his 1904 international law treatise, John Westlake hypothesized that the concept of commercial domicile as it originated in admiralty law may be 'in some degree referable to the fact that in England the admiralty judges have usually been also the judges in probate and matrimonial matters, accustomed in the latter capacity to apply domicile as a criterion'.[68] Again, here, we see how the private international law of the family might have been a prototype for other, seemingly unrelated areas.

There are also obvious historical relationships between domicile and gender discrimination. As with nationality, the domicile of a married woman depended on the domicile of her husband. Thus, for instance, a husband could desert his wife and move to another country, and the wife's domicile would follow his even if she had never set foot there. However, the campaign to abolish dependent nationality for married women was one of the early transnational feminist causes, along with suffrage, whereas dependent domicile was abolished only much later and still exists in some countries.[69]

While marked by a history of gender discrimination, domicile is potentially less discriminatory than nationality as a conception of belonging. Naturalization can privilege male immigrants because men more often work outside the home and therefore have greater opportunities to acculturate, learn the language and otherwise satisfy the publicly oriented requirements for citizenship. In contrast, domicile attaches individuals to a state in their own specific fashion. In developing a relational feminist approach to present-day private international law, as distinct from an anti-discrimination approach, however, Roxana Banu refers back to nineteenth-century private international lawyer Josephus Jitta for the view that no choice of connecting factor should be made broadly. While Jitta was against the adoption of nationality over domicile for all purposes, he also cautioned that a connecting factor ought not to be chosen as such, but as a way of structuring particular kinds of relationships.[70]

---

[68] John Westlake, *International Law: Peace* (Cambridge: University Press, 1904), vol. 1, 206.

[69] See, e.g., Annalise Acorn, 'Gender Discrimination in the Common Law of Domicile and the Application of the Canadian Charter of Rights and Freedoms', *Osgoode Hall Law Journal* 29 (1991), 419–56; Mary Keyes, 'Women in Private International Law', in Susan Harris Rimmer and Kate Ogg (eds.), *Research Handbook on Feminist Engagement with International Law* (Cheltenham: Edward Elgar, 2019), 103–17, at 106–7; Karen Knop and Christine Chinkin, 'Remembering Chrystal Macmillan: Women's Equality and Nationality in International Law', *Michigan Journal of International Law* 22 (2001), 523–85, at 524–7; Richard Frimpong Oppong, *Private International Law in Commonwealth Africa* (Cambridge: Cambridge University Press, 2013), 43.

[70] Banu, 'Nineteenth-Century Private International Law and Relational Feminism'.

Comity and Relationality

A second concept illuminated by seeing public international law together with private international law historically is the 'comity of nations'.[71] While comity is a notoriously indeterminate and multifaceted idea, the United States Supreme Court in *Hilton* v. *Guyot* provides a well-known late nineteenth-century formulation:

> 'Comity,' in the legal sense, is neither a matter of absolute obligation, on the one hand, nor of mere courtesy and goodwill, upon the other. But it is the recognition which one nation allows within its territory to the legislative, executive, or judicial acts of another nation, having due regard both to international duty and convenience, and to the rights of its own citizens or of other persons who are under the protection of its laws.[72]

In public international law, comity plays a relatively minor and interstitial role, whereas some schools of private international law see comity as the basic reason that one state would apply another state's law.[73] Contemporary public international lawyers tend to decry comity's softer nature as a poor second best to legal obligation, and a disdain for comity can also be found among those nineteenth-century international lawyers who subscribed to the unity of public and private international law. Arguing that states had a duty to recognize one another's private law, James Lorimer, for example, dismissed comity as '[t]he old woman's fable of a sort of international civility called the *comitas gentium*'.[74] Modern commentators are often skeptical that judges' references to comity accomplish anything, although recent scholarship in a number of

---

[71] Historical literature on comity, and on which schools of private international law subscribed to some conception of comity as foundational, includes G. Blaine Baker, 'Interstate Choice of Law and Early-American Constitutional Nationalism: An Essay on *Joseph Story and the Comity of Errors: A Case Study in Conflict of Laws*', *McGill Law Journal* 38 (1993), 454–516; Friedrich K. Juenger, 'A Page of History', *Mercer Law Review* 35 (1984), 419–60; Gerhard Kegel, 'Story and Savigny', *American Journal of Comparative Law* 37 (1989), 39–66; Joel R. Paul, 'Comity in International Law', *Harvard International Law Journal* 32 (1991), 1–79; Thomas Schultz and David Holloway, 'La *comity* dans l'histoire du droit international privé', *Journal du Droit International* [2012] 2, 571–95; Alan Watson, *Joseph Story and the Comity of Errors: A Case Study in Conflict of Laws* (Athens, GA: University of Georgia Press, 1992); Hessel E. Yntema, 'The Comity Doctrine', *Michigan Law Review* 65 (1966), 9–32.
[72] *Hilton* v. *Guyot* (1895) 159 US 113, 163–4.
[73] On comity and related concepts, including the public international law principle of good faith and the European doctrine of *Völkercourtoisie*, see Jörn Axel Kämmerer, 'Comity' (December 2006), *Max Planck Encyclopedia of Public International Law* online, Oxford University Press.
[74] Lorimer, *The Institutes of the Law of Nations*, vol. 1, 358.

common-law countries seeks to account for its prominence in judicial reasoning.[75]

A gender perspective has the potential to add historical context to the two concepts with which the US Supreme Court contrasts comity in *Hilton v. Guyot*: 'absolute obligation' and 'mere courtesy'. In this period, the legalists who predominated in US foreign policy circles saw obligation as underwritten by ideals of masculinity. Their proposals for international law combined an international court with the codification of legal rules. They made no provision for sanctions against lawbreakers other than public opinion, which they sought to educate.[76] '[T]he true basis of the peace and order in which we live is not fear of the policeman', wrote US Secretary of State Elihu Root, 'it is the self-restraint of the thousands of people who make up the community and their willingness to obey the law and regard the rights of others'.[77] Referencing Victorian-era definitions of manhood as 'restrained and upright behavior', historian Benjamin Coates argues that, in distinguishing themselves from pacifists, who were seen as effeminate, 'legalists highlighted their self-control and impartiality and, by extension, their manliness'.[78]

If codes of masculinity strengthened obligation, as Coates argues, then a gendered history of international law might pursue whether and how association with femininity weakened courtesy and, by extension, comity. The US Supreme Court in *Hilton v. Guyot* refers to 'mere courtesy'. Comity does not amount to an 'absolute obligation', but neither is it reducible to politeness or amiability. But was courtesy always 'mere'? More to the point, to what extent did jurists' impressions of comity as a source of behavioral expectations among states track ideas of courtesy as a class and gendered idea at the time? Historian Michael Curtin writes:

> From the Renaissance to the French Revolution manners were an essential aspect of the ideal of civilization and were thought worthy of the serious attention of intelligent men. The literary vehicle for the discussion of manners was the courtesy book, a genre that for almost three hundred years,

---

[75] See, e.g., Adrian Briggs, 'The Principle of Comity in Private International Law', *Recueil des cours* 354 (2011), 65–182; William S. Dodge, 'International Comity in American Law', *Columbia Law Review* 115 (2015), 2071–141; Thomas Schultz and Jason Mitchenson, 'Navigating Sovereignty and Transnational Commercial Law: The Use of Comity by Australian Courts', *Journal of Private International Law* 12 (2016), 344–78.

[76] Benjamin Allen Coates, *Legalist Empire: International Law and American Foreign Relations in the Early Twentieth Century* (Oxford: Oxford University Press, 2016), 71–2, 84.

[77] Elihu Root, 'The Need of Popular Understanding of International Law', *American Journal of International Law* 1 (1907), 1–3, at 2, quoted in Coates, *Legalist Empire*, 71–2.

[78] Coates, *Legalist Empire*, 60, 62–3, 74.

from Elyot to Chesterfield, remained a lively and important strand of English literature. While including discussions of the minor formulations of etiquette, courtesy literature was certainly not limited to these. A variety of different subjects might be examined, but typically the genre concerned itself with the advocacy of ideals of character, accomplishments, habits, manners, and morals – in short, the art of living in society.

It was, in fact, only when manners came to seem trivial and unworthy of association with serious moral thought that the courtesy book was doomed. ... Exiled from high culture, the discussion of manners was confined to the etiquette book, a genre that had existed for centuries under the shadow of courtesy.[79]

Courtesy literature, as Curtin traces, was almost entirely a masculine genre because its object was to teach readers how to get on 'in the world', a sphere populated mainly by men. Pleasing others was a matter of self-interest. In contrast, in the Victorian era, etiquette books became 'mere': they were addressed to women and stressed the importance of tact as a form of concern and kindliness toward others.[80] In this light, we could imagine expanding gender studies of the history of international law to include attention to contemporaneous understandings of manners and the ways in which they animated international law. Feminist international lawyers have already been critical of rape in wartime as an injury to honor, as opposed to an act of sexual violence,[81] and feminist historians have drawn connections between dueling and the regulation of diplomatic relations even into the twentieth century.[82] Because it deals with the nature of obligation, the relationship between comity and courtesy might be of even broader significance.

Finally, as *Hilton* v. *Guyot* also shows, judges may make assumptions about the shared priorities and cooperative behavior of states under the concept of comity. Thomas Schultz and David Holloway argue that Joseph Story, whose nineteenth-century conflict of laws treatise established private international law as a field in the United States, shifted the meaning of comity. Whereas

---

[79] Michael Curtin, 'A Question of Manners: Status and Gender in Etiquette and Courtesy', *Journal of Modern History* 57 (1985), 395–423, at 395–6. On the history of manners, see generally Anna Bryson, *From Courtesy to Civility: Changing Codes of Conduct in Early Modern England* (Oxford: Clarendon Press, 1998), chs. 1–2.
[80] Curtin, 'A Question of Manners', 418–23.
[81] See, e.g., Judith G. Gardam and Michelle J. Jarvis, *Women, Armed Conflict and International Law* (The Hague: Kluwer Law International, 2001), 107–12; Janet Halley, 'Rape at Rome: Feminist Interventions in the Criminalization of Sex-Related Violence in Positive International Law', *Michigan Journal of International Law* 30 (2008), 1–123, at 57–9.
[82] Amelia M. Kiddle, 'In Mexico's Defense: Dueling, Diplomacy, Gender and Honor, 1876–1940', *Mexican Studies/Estudios Mexicanos* 31 (2015), 22–47.

earlier understandings had been more communal, Story made the idea of friendship between peoples much less intrinsic. His approach saw comity instead as bilaterally shared and reciprocated.[83] Schultz and Holloway differentiate Story's idea of comity from the conception that accompanied the emergence and consolidation of the Westphalian system. From a private international law perspective, that international order could be conceived of as organized, albeit unequally, around sovereignty, territoriality and comity: 'from the existence of an international society flows the obligation that each of the member states not go as far as absolute territoriality'.[84] Some contemporary accounts, too, are adamant that 'comity is not, in any intelligent sense, a form of reciprocity'.[85]

In this respect, comity is worth investigating as a potential historical counterweight to feminist critiques that the state in international law replicates the image of the individual in classical liberalism as isolated, autonomous and/or self-interested.[86] In comity, we might find one litmus test for the state's social alter-ego, as Schultz and Holloway also seem to suggest. What would that alter-ego look like? 'Positive comity', for instance, is identified with international cooperation going beyond the requirements of international law.[87] One modern commentator argues that although the impact of comity in international affairs has been reduced largely to ceremonial issues and processes involving interstate information, its scope could also be expanding with the rise of international solidarity in forms such as disaster relief, remission of foreign debt and other assistance to states in need.[88] In a somewhat similar vein, there is emerging interest in reassessing the history of 'friendship' among nations as a concept in international relations, including in international law.[89]

* * *

[83] Schultz and Holloway, 'La *comity* dans l'histoire du droit international privé', 589.
[84] Ibid., 577 (quoting P. Lalive) (translation mine).
[85] Briggs, 'The Principle of Comity in Private International Law', 89.
[86] Pioneering feminist critiques in international law include Isabelle R. Gunning, 'Modernizing Customary International Law: The Challenge of Human Rights', *Virginia Journal of International Law* 31 (1991), 211–47; Moira L. McConnell, 'The Relationship between Theories about Women and Theories about International Law', *Canadian Council on International Law Proceedings* 21 (1992), 68–77. For contemporaneous developments in international relations, see V. Spike Peterson, *Gendered States: Feminist (Re)visions of International Relations Theory* (Boulder, CO: Lynne Rienner, 1992).
[87] See, e.g., *R v. Hape* [2007] 2 SCR 292, 322 (Supreme Court of Canada).
[88] Kämmerer, 'Comity'.
[89] See, e.g., Evgeny Roshchin, *Friendship Among Nations: History of a Concept* (Manchester: Manchester University Press, 2017); Heather Devere, 'Friendship in International Treaties', in Simon Koschut and Andrea Oelsner (eds.), *Friendship and International Relations* (New York: Palgrave Macmillan, 2014), 182–98.

This chapter has sought to identify dimensions of international law that have the potential to initiate counter-disciplinary conversations with historians about women as subjects of international law, transnational gender relations as a way of constructing the state through international law, and feminism as a lens on legal ideas of belonging to and cooperation between states that public international lawyers tend to overlook or dismiss. The proposed directions for research, it should be emphasized, are prompted by the particular debate about international lawyers doing history with which I began and are based on one particular private-law context in late-nineteenth-century European ideas of international law. Other contexts, and other feminisms, would undoubtedly suggest other directions for feminist histories of international law. Moreover, not only does context have many and different meanings in feminism, history and law, it is far from the only method in any of the three. In other words, this chapter is but one illustration of where new critical conversations might begin.

Index

academy, the, 1, 10, 66, 71–2, 79, 95, 111, 132, 149, 305, 317–18
action
 collective, 337
 economic models of, 311
 entrepreneurial, 13
 intentional, 330
 political, 33
 social, 110
actors(s), 76. *See also* agent
 civil society, 274
 corporate, 274
 everyday transnational, 369
 political, 38
 private and public, 94
 work of individual legal, 67
administration, colonial, 64, 107, 165
aesthetics, 110, 112
Africa, 10, 33, 84, 195, 201, 208, 210–11, 215–17, 219, 224, 226, 362, 366
 colonial partition of, 222
 decolonisation and independence of, 208
Agamben, Giorgio, 41, 143
agency, 7, 12, 14, 25, 31–2, 40, 312
 authorial, 330
 collective, 11
 corporate, 278
 creative, 312
 individual, 13
 linguistic, 38
 moral, 321
 political, 25
 social, 310
agent(s), 25, 324
 of the international community, lawyers as, 307

aggression, 106
Alexandrowicz, Charles, 104, 114–15
Allgemeine Staatslehre, 159
 limits of, 137
Althusser, Louis, 116
Álvarez, Alejandro, 51, 70, 85
America, *see* United States of America
American Declaration of Independence, 213
Americas, 213
Amerindians, 233–5, 237, 240, 250–1
 as barbarians (Vitoria), 241
 as enemies if hospitality denied (Vitoria), 242
 as *personae miserabiles*, 233
 original Spanish betrayal of the, 242
 property and expropriation of the, 305, 307
anachronism, 5, 73, 78, 100, 102, 105–6, 115, 118, 120, 125, 275
Anand, R.P., 85
Anghie, Antony, 62, 69, 77, 79, 81, 84, 89, 103, 118, 207
Ankersmit, Frank, 100, 111
Anschütz, Gerhard, 136–8
Anthropocene, the, 74
anthropology, 42, 85, 142–3, 149–50, 309, 347
 in dialogue with history, 38
antiquarianism, 45, 115
anti-slavery, 265
Aquinas, Thomas, 65, 348
arbitration, 103
archaeology, 20, 91
archival records, 305
Arendt, Hannah, 101, 106, 120–1, 144
Aristotle, 328, 341, 345–6, 351, 355
Armitage, David, 100, 194, 210, 213
Asia, 85–6, 201, 264
asylum, 73

381

Austin, John, 23
Australia, 257, 370
Austria, 331
authoritarianism, 92
authority, 1, 4, 9–10, 32, 35, 39, 49, 56, 58, 64, 74, 76, 81, 86, 88–9, 93, 106, 117, 134, 155, 169, 173, 179–80, 185, 195, 204, 248, 254, 261, 268, 271–2, 274, 277, 279–81
    as the basis of political community (Schmitt), 180
    as without gender, 356
    context as, 71
    creation of new forms of, 321
    current theories of, 275
    exercise of state, 168
    exercised by an occupier, 169
    institutional, 60
    international, 151
    law as a language of, 68
    of international lawyers, 72
    of the past over the present, 49
    public nature of state, 180
    social, cultural and intellectual, 25
    sovereign, 89, 91
    variety of co-existing sorts of, 213
author(s), 72, 78–9
authorship, 6
    as action, 4
    of history, 112
autonomy, 35

Badiou, Alain, 114–15
Baldus de Ubaldis, 107, 352
Balkans, 120
Bandung conference (1955), 52
Barkawi, Tarak, 207
Barthes, Roland, 330
Bassiouni, Cherif, 118
beggars, 246
Begriffsgeschichte, 67, see concepts, history of
behaviour
    animal, 320
    human, 65, 356, 360
Belgium, 61, 163, 167–8
Benjamin, Walter, 125, 143
Bentham, Jeremy, 196, 202–5
Benton, Lauren, 11, 48, 214, 232, 285
Berlin, 136, 144, 146, 158
Berlin Conference, 78
Berlin Final Act (1885), 58
Bhabha, Homi, 40

biology, 14, 356
Bloch, Marc, 102, 105, 116, 123
Bluntschli, Johann Kaspar, 177
Bodin, Jean, 49, 67, 149, 184, 346, 351
borders, 11, 73, 107, 152, 216
Braudel, Fernand, 19, 39, 47
breastfeeding, 14
Bretton Woods system, 83
Brierly, James Leslie, 260
Britain, 63, 196–7, 199, 202, 208, 263, 267, 270, 273
Burke, Edmund, 197, 202, 207
Burkina Faso, 59

Cambridge, 19, 358
Cameroon, 217, 223
Camus, Albert, 100
Canada, 257, 300
capital, 322
    legal construction of, 94
    transnational, 86
capitalism, 74, 78, 85, 91, 98, 123, 288, 305, 315, 326, 329, 335–6
Caribbean, 362
Carnegie Endowment for International Peace, 144
Cassin, René, 218
Castoriadis, Cornelius, 325
Catholicism, 132–3
change, 14, 211, 226
change, conceptual, 309
    'market-led' account of, 311
    as linguistic innovation (Skinner), 13
    economistic rendering of, 312
    'historicist' understandings of, 311
    models for, expressing ideological commitments, 310
    political, 43
    role of leadership in bringing about, 330
change, cultural, 19
    economic, 323, 327
    as revolutionary (Knight), 326
    historical, 13
    ideological, 314
    scientific, 317
    social, as creating new categories of people (Hacking), 322
    technical, 310
charity, 247, 249
Charles V, Holy Roman Emperor, 237
Charlesworth, Hilary, 87, 114–15, 368–9, 371

child-birth, 14, 342
children, 320, 322, 343, 362
Chile, 51, 70, 72, 85, 90
Chimni, B.S., 70
China, 12, 27–8, 90, 197, 199, 201, 272, 365, 373
Chitty, Joseph, 198–9, 204–5
Christianity, 85–7, 109, 134, 198, 240, 243, 367.
    See also Catholicism, Protestantism
Cicero, Marcus Tullius, 84
citizens, 14, 247, 341, 375
citizenship, 177, 372–4
city (*civitas*)
    as a trans-temporal legal category, 44
    generic, 98
    ocean-floating, 288
civil service, international, 263–4, 274
civilisation, 111
    as westernization, 215
    ideal of, 376
    meaning of and how to achieve it, 215
    through law, 104
coercion, 76, 151
Cold War, 87, 110, 118, 149, 156
colonialism, 69–70, 74–5, 78, 82–4, 89, 91, 93, 103, 109, 118, 160, 165, 203, 242, 251, 307
colonies, 35, 63, 198, 212, 359, 362, 364, 367, 370
    administration of former German, 256
    as catalysts of wars, 203
    as not possessing the requisite attributes of statehood, 209
    as opposed to the metropole, 359
    as the chief cause of war (Bentham), 203
colonisation, 63, 176
Columbus, Christopher, 232
comitas gentium, see comity
comity, 15, 372, 375, 377–8
commerce, 12, 105, 287, 315. See also trade
    as a norm of sociability between equal states, 12
    as underlying principle of seabed mining, 301
    defense of China's right to restrict, 199
    development and legitimation of international system of, 239
    equitable treatment of, 256
    right of every state to regulate, in best interest of its people (Vattel), 199
commissions
    international, 181, 256

common heritage of mankind principle, 300, 302
commons, 295–6, 308
communism, 218, 335
communities,
    administration of political, 67
    boundaries of legal, 252
    imagining of global, 252
    pan-African, 210
    religious, 210
community, 25
    international, 293, 301, 307
    universal human, 211
companies
    powers of colonial, 64
    private, 362
competition
    'natural' processes of, 333
concept(s), 8, 85, 107, 115, 157
    as self-evident, 157
    as subject to radical, unpredictable change, 309
    genealogies of, 2
    history of, 39, 67
    legal, 63, 67
    of the political (Schmitt), 139
conceptual change, 309, 314, 337
    in the human sciences, 325
    innovation model of, 323, 328
    self-referential nature of, 324
    unpredictability of, 327
conceptual frames, 3
confederations, 259, 276
conflict-of-laws cases, 364
Congress of Vienna, 102
conquest, 204
    legitimation of, 70
conquistadores, 233, 236, 242
conscience
    legal (la conscience juridique), 307
    of mankind, 110
constitution, 34
    ancient, 49
    English, 183, 366
constitutionalism, 91, 103, 139, 180
    global, 142
context(s), 2, 4–6, 8, 23, 27–9, 39, 41, 45, 57, 60, 66–7, 70–1, 76, 83, 87, 101–2, 106–7, 112, 114–16, 118, 122, 133, 304, 352, 363
    ability of international law to understand individuals in their social, 371

context(s) (cont.)
  a politics of, 337
  act in, 27
  as a certain time and place, 26
  as explanation, 29
  as interpretation, 29
  as power, 87
  as the imaginary frame for debates, 76
  choice of, 77
  concrete, 111
  consequences of making new, 72
  contest over, 45
  different meanings of, in feminism, history and law, 379
  European legal, 50
  global, 79, 244
  historical, 69
  intellectual or religious tradition as, 77
  international historical, 70
  legal, 107
  life choices and lived experiences as, 77
  linguistic, 97, 107
  meaning in, 3, 27–8, 30, 37, 40, 45
  nation as, 77
  private-law, 358
  profession as, 77
  re-narrating of, 75
  Skinnerian, 358
  transnational, of inter-personal relationships, 371
  uses of, 72
  Western, 39
contextualism, 3, 5, 24, 27–8, 36–7, 107, 275, 309, 311, 314, 357
  as both political decision and indeterminate method, 106
contextualization, 75
  historical, 88
  social, 79
contingency,
  false, 307
  historical, 43, 46
contract, 305, 363, 365–6
  freedom of, 333
  social, 227
contracts
  international, 64
  law of, 362
  transnational law of, 307
corporation(s), 11, 33, 93, 304, 326
  history of business, 68
  increased freedom for in seabed mining, 302
  transnational, 293
courtesy, 377
  feminine, 15
courts, 358
  British, 373
  English, 370
  French military, 173
  international, 53
  metropolitan, 364
  military, 174
  modern, 82
  recognition of judgments of foreign, 359
  Scottish, 370
creativity, 254, 317–18, 323, 328–9, 337
  as a property of 'community structure' (Kuhn), 330
  concept of (Kuhn), 317
  historiographical, 4, 47
  in science, 329
  reciprocal relationship between destruction and, 328
  scientific, 319
  theorists, 317, 330
credit
  legal construction of, 94
crisis, 115
  as a juridical moment of decision, 114
Cuba, 176
culture, 89, 98, 320
custom(s), 203, 347

decolonization, 10, 58–9, 69, 71, 73–4, 208–10, 212, 217, 225–7
  history of twentieth-century, 212
  in international history and thought, 218
  political thought of, 210
  role of international organisations in setting the terms of, 274
democracy, 88, 133, 141, 158, 206, 215, 262, 334
  European social, 89
  liberal parliamentary, 153
Derrida, Jacques, 26, 231–2, 247, 250
despotism, 26
  discourse of oriental, 200
determinism, 108, 314
  nineteenth-century, evolutionist, 356
development projects, 369
dictators, 304
dictatorship, 111, 161, 179, 182, 185–6
Diderot, Denis, 196, 203

diplomacy, 7, 50, 55, 61, 63, 67, 93, 107, 109, 111, 113, 120, 266, 269, 281, 362
  histories of women and, 357
  history of European, 60
  League of Nations as site of new, 262
  multilateral, 54
  of ancient Near East, 60
  open/public, 255
  secret, 253, 264, 267
diplomatic immunity, 105, 362
diplomat-lawyer, 49
diplomats, 2, 73, 287
discourse(s), 3, 8, 13, 31, 33, 39–40, 50
  economics as a, 311
  history of political, 30
  human rights, 53
  international legal, 259
  legal, 34, 43–4
  nineteenth-century colonial international legal, 88
  non-state-centric, 37
  non-Western, 37
  political, 25–6, 32, 38, 43–4
  politics of, 35
  pre-modern, 37
  Western totalizing, 79
discovery
  as a valid basis for title, 57
  process of as not subject to democratic control, 337
domicile, 15, 372–4
Dominican(s), 240
dominion (*dominium*), 239, 343–4
  natural, of mother over child, 343
droit des gens, 193
Droit public de l'Europe, 64
Dutch East India Company, 56, 83, 285
  as both private and sovereign, 363

econometrics, 323
economic development, 312
economics, 9, 12–13, 64, 86, 94
  as a discourse, 12, 311
  boundaries between politics and, 12
  dominance of in modern forms of political control, 180
  language of, 309
economists, 337
economy, 76
  capitalist political, 289
  global, 71
  of ocean regimes, 289
  political, 89
  post-feudal mercantile, 87
elite(s), 94, 304
  conceptions of the world by, 77
  post-colonial, 89, 212
  shared visions of, 76
  vocabularies of, 93
emancipation, 11, 85–6
  international law of, 70
  of colonies as precondition of international peace, 204
empire(s), 2, 9–10, 35, 48, 54, 77, 82–3, 90, 93, 104, 118, 124, 192–3, 243, 277, 366
  'anxiety' of, 365
  as danger to peaceful commerce, 203
  as incompatible with modern international law, 74
  critique of, 16
  crossing internal borders of the, 368
  discriminatory attitudes of, 373
  effects of on history of international law, 365
  historical context of, 125
  historical role of private law in, 361
  history of, 196
  informal, 11
  interpolity of, 48
  legacies of, 71
  'metropolitan turn' among historians of, 359
  modern history of, 35
  Spanish contribution to the practice of, 86
  studies of gender and, 357
Empire
  Anglo-American commercial and maritime, 134
  British, 257
  Chinese, 201
  European, 16, 36
  French, 199
  Moctezuma's Aztec, 237
  Ottoman, 105, 115
  Roman, 242
  Spanish, 248
enemies, 146
England, 365–7, 369–71, 374
  as both 'home' and 'abroad', 365
  early-modern, 315
Enlightenment, the, 85
enmity
  central place of, in politics, 146

enterprise, 310, 314, 319, 321–4, 326–7, 335
　as an adaptation to uncertainty in economic life, 333
　legitimation of capitalist, 315
　rhetorical, 315
　history, 68
　theory of, 14
　use of the language of in intellectual history, 314
entrepreneur(s), 13–14, 312
　as innovators, 312–13, 329
　creativity of, 326
　function of, 332
environment, natural
　exploitation of as structuring inequalities in Latin America, 240
　protection of marine, 297, 302
　transformed into natural resources available to commerce, 239
equality
　between men and women (Plato), 346
　international order based on, 215
　of men and women in the state of nature, 343
　sovereign, 74
ethics, 110, 321
　universal, 82
　writerly, 97
etiquette, 377
Eurocentrism, 46
　in the history of international law, 85
Europe, 1–2, 15, 27, 36, 39, 43–6, 50, 53–5, 58, 60–2, 67, 70, 74, 81, 84–90, 93–4, 104, 109, 118, 134, 141–2, 150, 152, 155, 158, 163, 166, 175, 179, 181, 193, 197–8, 200–3, 205, 207, 211, 234, 243, 246, 248, 251, 327, 351, 353, 358, 366–8, 373
　as a representative of the universal, 85
　mythology of, 179
　provincializing of, 85
　public law of, 201. See also Droit public de l'Europe
European imperial expansion, 196. See also empire
European Union, the, 74
everyday life
　as proper focus for international law, 369
　as transnational, 371
　forms of history that aim to do justice to, 371
evolution, 30

exception
　state of, 186
exile, 143
experts/expertise 79, 255

family, 2, 14–15, 86, 369, 372
　as a framework within the state of nature, 349
　gendered relations in, 14
　localization of, 89
　of nations, 104
　private international law of the, 374
　private sphere of the, 362
family law, 362, 367
fascism, 83
fathers
　as founders of states, 355
federation(s), 11, 16, 222
　failure of as political projects in Africa, 228
femininity, 376
feminism, 342, 379
fiction, 23, 97, 122. See also novels
Filmer, Robert, 344–5, 349, 352
force. See also violence
　master's right to use, 367
　use of, 25, 275
Ford, Lisa, 48, 214
foreigner(s), 93
　children born from male follow the mother, 350
　government by as violation of natural community (Schmitt), 182
　refusal to welcome as inherently evil (Vitoria), 242
Foucault, Michel, 39–40, 46, 65, 81, 281, 321, 330
France, 70, 72, 90, 103, 105, 109, 163, 176, 179, 196, 199, 202, 207–8, 263, 267, 299, 359
Franciscans, 241
free trade, 89, 93
freedom, 1, 159, 215, 221, 293
　as a delimited legal institution, 308
　natural, 355
　of commerce and trade, 86
　of communication and transit, 256
　of the seas, 13, 85, 285, 288, 293
　state, 65
　to beg, 248
friend-enemy concept, 147

friendship
  between nations, 15
frontiers
  intangibility of (uti possidetis principle), 59
functionalism, 62–3, 260

gender, 9, 14–16, 42, 87, 163, 247, 356–8, 360, 364, 376
  as a category of analysis, 358
  as relevant to the historical understanding of domicile and comity, 372
  in the history of international law, 359
  different approaches to, 82
  early modern understandings of, 8
  equality, 14
  relationship of politics and, 342
  studies of empire and, 357
gender relations, 359, 368
  as signifying or structuring legal power, 357
  as analytics, 360
  as the paradigmatic case of national differences in private law, 367
  private-law, 364
  re-ordering of through law and jurisdiction, 371
genealogy, 2, 46–7, 85, 88, 124, 149, 252, 329
  European, 206
  Foucauldian, 40
  Nietzschean, 40
Gentili, Alberico, 111, 113
Germany, 1, 10, 55, 58, 62, 108, 111–12, 114, 119, 131, 135, 142, 145–6, 148–9, 152, 160–4, 168, 172, 176–7, 179, 186, 196, 258, 267–8, 370
Ghana, 220–1
Gibbon, Edward, 41
Gierke, Otto von, 259
Ginzburg, Carlo, 113
global, 2, 4, 21, 28, 35, 37, 70, 91, 94
  relationship between local and, 70
global economic system, 86
global legal order, 73
global order
  non-hierarchical, 195
global, the, 47
  timing and spacing of, 21
globalisation, 52, 123
  discourses of, 252
governance, 72, 224, 279
  bureaucracy of international, 11
  contemporary technocratic or managerial, 75

  forms of suitable to Europeans and non-Europeans (Schmitt), 181
  global, 74
  of occupied territory, 171
  strengthening of in sixteenth-century Europe, 246
government, 11, 34, 342
  local, 93
  medieval forms of, 44
  post-colonial, 223
  theory of absolute (Bodin), 346
governors
  and governed, trans-historical reality of, 40
Great Britain, 109, 152, see Britain
Great Power(s), 109
Grewe, Wilhelm, 60, 62, 104, 108–11, 114–15, 158
Großraum (great space), 152
  as a concrete geographical space, 19, 21, 36, 45, 61, 65, 67, 77, 83–5, 90, 109, 111, 116–17, 152, 285, 291–2, 308. See also Schmitt, Carl
Grotius, Hugo, 19, 21, 36, 61, 65, 67, 77, 79, 83, 85–6, 90, 109, 111, 116–17, 285–6, 291–2, 308
Group of 77, 300
guest. See hospitality

Habermas, Jürgen, 135
Hacking, Ian, 13, 310, 314, 319–25, 327, 329–30
Hague Convention (1907), 166–9, 171
Hague Peace Conferences, 103, 366
Haiti, 202
Hammarskjöld, Dag, 274
Hegelianism, 146
Heidegger, Martin, 135
heroism, 7, 104, 108, 158, 368
Heyland, Carl, 164–71, 173–4
high seas, 289, 298
  law of, 293
historian(s), 1–3, 5, 8–9, 19, 26, 28–31, 33, 48, 72, 78, 88, 94–5, 101, 107, 181, 186, 212, 274, 277, 309, 311, 313–14, 329, 364
  academic, 99
  activist, 144
  contextual, 84, 92
  distinctive voice of, 20
  feminist, 377
  gender, 344
  historical and political commitments of, 30
  intellectual, 177

388　Index

historian(s) (cont.)
  international legal, 69, 72
  legal, 78, 109
  metropolitan turn taken by, 368
  objectivity of, 22
  of political thought, 34, 42, 45, 106
  relationship of with power, 40
  presentist concerns of current, 78
  revisionist, 85
historicism, 14, 160, 309–12
histories
  as acts of creation or ideological gestures, 119
  as having literary virtues, 100
  contextual, 69, 84, 90–1, 93
  conventional, 73
  corrective, 123
  of law, 105
  post-colonial, 357
  revisionist, 87, 91
  written and authorised by international tribunals, 113
historiography, 3, 6–7, 13, 29, 31, 33–4, 38–9, 41, 43–7, 56, 99, 123, 195, 276, 342, 361
  global, 48
  governing metaphors of, 46
  twenty-first century, 46
history, 3–8, 16, 19–20, 34, 36, 52, 66, 72, 75, 84, 97–9, 102–3, 108, 142, 149, 151, 208, 280, 355, 379
  anachronistic approach to, 106
  and international law, 70, 74, 105, 131
  arguments from, 50
  as authored, 112
  as classism, 113
  as a history of 'dead effects' (Benjamin), 125
  as a history of Great Men and their activities, 107
  as animated by natural law, 81
  as a tirade against the past, 123
  as endowed with a purpose, 102
  as framing action in time, 79
  as having fictive power, 100
  as History, 80
  as interpretation not fact, 80
  as linear chronicle, 103
  as method, 104
  as part of academic international law, 54
  as proof for the legality of international law, 73
  as source of precedents, 105
  as narrative art or story-telling, 30
  as 'usable' in legal projects, 106
  as what is seen by the historian, 7
  as what we remember, 6
  as writing, 21, 30, 116
  conceptual, 67, 280
  cultural, 23
  European imperial as central aspect of international law, 62
  feminist intellectual, 357
  global, 47
  in relation to philosophy, 21
  in relation to the present, 34, 41
  intellectual, 13, 21–2, 24, 28, 37, 40, 102
  international, 106
  international legal, 102, 107–9, 113, see law, international, history/histories of
  law as a practice of, 60
  law's uses of, 4
  legacies of imperial, 206
  legal, 8, 34
  misunderstanding of, 78
  natural laws of, 52
  of history (Pocock), 44
  of the church and its law, 43
  orality of, 6
  philosophy of, 115, 309, 334
  political, 19
  politics of, 6
  popular, 99
  progressive march of, 91
  realities of, 108
  search for a 'meaning' of, 313
  shared professional vision of, 72
  the turn to, 309
  translation and, 40
  use of to challenge authority of international law, 83
  Western, 41
  writing of to change the world, 71–2
  writing of as a response to crisis, 20, 24, 33, 109
Hobbes, Thomas, 1–2, 27–8, 30, 32, 36, 65, 149, 151, 271, 341–5, 349, 351–6
honour, 92
hospitality (*hospitium*), 11, 16, 233–5, 237, 241–4, 246–7, 250, 252
  right to, (*ius hospitii*), 232
hospitals, 11
host, 11–12

hostages
    both guests and hosts as, 232
    execution of, 111
household, 2
Huber, Max, 56–8
human kinds (Hacking), 319–20
human nature, 322
    historical narrative of the development of, 347
humanitarian crises, 206
humanitarianism, 120
    universal, 139
humanity, 1, 71, 85, 121, 141, 146, 156, 159, 171, 175, 194, 211, 215, 218, 222, 224, 227–8, 288
    crimes against, 105, 118, 121
Hunter, Ian, 37, 99, 111, 191

idealism, 67, 272, 305
ideas, history of, 23
ideology, 26, 33–6, 75–6, 87, 90, 300, 305, 309–10
    as a legitimating political language, 25
    as political illusion, 33
    concept of, 324
    legal, 289
    liberal capitalist, 307
    universalist, 123
imaginary/imaginaries, 368
imagination, 6, 76, 93, 101, 103, 117, 347–8, 368
    European Orientalizing, of 'others', 88
    Western historical, 20
imperialism, 71, 106, 109, 175, 181, 194, 209
    British, 152
    European, disclosure of, 193
    non-territorial, 86
    of the present (Tully), 193
    role of hospitals in Spanish, 234
imperium, 89
independence, 10, 59, 154, 175, 200–1, 204, 208–13, 219–24, 226–8, 257
    as absence of any state power, 220
    commercial, 200
    historical view of African, 209
    in eighteenth-century America, 213
    Indian, 194
    Kenyan, 224
    limits of mere 'flag', 209
    mid-twentieth-century arguments for, 213
    of African countries from colonial rule as imposition of western forms of political organisation, 208
    of states, 1
    of the League of Nations, 263
    redefined as a positive good (Vattel), 213
    shaping political imaginaries after, 224
    Tanganyikan, 224
    Ugandan, 224
    understood as the ability to create a new and better society, not as an end in itself, 220
India, 38, 63, 104, 194, 197, 202, 204, 257, 373
Indies, the, 86
indigenous inhabitants, 58
individual(s), 1, 11, 13, 32
    as simultaneously citizens of a state and members of a universal human community, 210
    classical liberal ideas of the 371
    emergence of as a state subject and a bearer of natural rights, 142
    legal status and capacity of, 372
    pre-social conception of the, 360
    right to free movement of, 252
individualism, 76, 135, 218, 335, 371
    liberal, 152
indoctrination, 25
Indonesia, 213
industrialisation, 145
inequality, 84, 89, 95, 235, 307, 345
    as continuous with colonialism, 75
    construction of, 234
    imperial relations of, 86
    legitimation of global, 252
inheritance, 358
    of children of colonial marriages, in England, 371
injury, 73
innovating ideologists (Skinner), 316
innovation, 9, 12–14, 38, 77, 310, 312–14, 316, 318–19, 322–3, 325–6, 330, 332–6
    as 'market-led', 14
    as a creative response to existing conditions, 314
    as a political concept, 310
    as a self-referential process, 325
    as a term with a distinctive history, 310
    as technical advancement, 310
    as the template for understanding conceptual change, 310
    benefits of, as a public good, 336
    concept of (Kuhn), 319
    conceptual, as the intentional repurposing of economics of, 310, 318

innovation (cont.)
  ideological (Skinner), 320
  in politics and moral life, 316
  and change, 14, 200, 317
  linguistic, 13
  politics of, 335
  scientific, 316
  theory of (Schumpeter), 322
  unpredictability of the products of conceptual, 315
Institut de droit international, 372
  founders of ('men of 1873'), 363
institutions, 9, 25, 53, 76, 82, 85, 94, 113
  collective, based on universal human values, 140
  international, 11, see also organisations, international
  intersecting, 11
  political, 32
  theorization of, 11
intentions
  recovery of authorial, 330
interdisciplinarity, 9, 80, 101–2, 116, 276–7, 357
interest
  collective, 305
  commercial, 13
  general, of mankind, 306
  national, 13
  state, 307
international, the, 15–16
  as a space of conceptual movement in history, politics and law, 9
  concept of, 8
  theorization of, 9
  whether and how the League might speak for, 12
  community, imagined as masculine action hero, 368
  legal community, restricted to Christian order, 204
  organisations, role of in shaping normative expectations of statehood, 274
  realm, 1
  relations, 64
  society, 51–2, 98, 213, 215, 227–8, 378
International Court of Justice, 49, 58, 195, 254
International Criminal Court (ICC), 84, 120
International Law Commission (ILC), 294
internationalism, 119, 255, 264, 277
internationalists, 268

interpretation
  as a creative act of making sense of an act, 29
intervention, 103
  humanitarian, 74
  legal right of, 175
investment
  international, 67
  law and practice of foreign, 64
Iran, 111
Iraq, 78
Islam, 367
ius communicandi, 239
ius gentium, 11, 14, 16, 67, 86, 346–7, 349, 351, 355, see law of nations
ius hospitii, 11–12, 15, see hospitality, right to
ius naturae et gentium, 1, see law, of nature and of nations
ius naturale 346, 349, 351, see law, natural
ius negotiandi, 12, see trade, right to
ius publicum Europaeum, 62, see law, European public

Jamaica, 366
Japan, 121, 199, 268, 294, 299, 365
Jellinek, Georg, 172, 258–9
judge(s), 275
  as law-makers, 138
  admiralty, 374
jurisdiction(s), 277
  border between national and international, 296
  local, 92
  over private-law cases with a foreign element, 358
  permanent international criminal, 120
  rules on, as giving means of re-ordering gender relations and the state, 371
  territorial, 12
jurisprudence, 8, 34, 49–50, 103, 108, 110, 145
  early-modern natural, 309
  natural, 36, 45
  political, 45
  positivist, 185
  Roman, 355
jurists, 54–5, 63, 73, 77–8, 81, 83, 94, 137, 180, 185, 257–8, 268
  eighteenth-century European, 213
  French, 260
  German, 136, 165, 184
  inadequacy of in institutional matters, 136
  international, 90

liberal, 142, 152
naturalist, 82
nineteenth-century, 373
of the 'New States', 194
positivist, 82
jus gentium, 155, see law of nations
jus publicum Europaeum, 178, see law, European public
justice, 66, 82, 183, 347, 355
  economic, 87
  gender, 87
  global system of criminal, 84
  imagined historical origins of, 347
  international, 51
  natural, 365
  particular instiutions canonized as, 94
  sixteenth-century narratives of the origins of, 347
  transitional, 73
  universal standard of, 34
Justinian, 346–7

Kant, Immanuel, 1–2, 65, 105, 150
Kelsen, Hans, 109, 113–14, 140, 258, 260, 263
Kenya, 219, 224
Kiribati, 302
knowledge, 79, 320
  expert, 76
  new forms of, 321
  objects of, 321
  scientific, 50
  varieties of prior, 75
Kojève, Alexandre, 133
Korea, 294
Koselleck, Reinhart, 67, 157, 334
Kosovo, 114, 368
Kuhn, Thomas, 13, 310, 314, 316–19, 323, 327, 329–30, 334

labour, 322
  division of, 312
  gendered parental, involved in feeding children, 352
  improvement in the conditions of, 256
  legal construction of, 94
language, 7, 13, 24–6, 29–31, 34, 38–41
  as like an ancient city (Wittgenstein), 41
  as structuring the international world, 7
  constitutive role of in politics, 26
  economic, 311
  international law as a virtuous, 303

legal, 36
legitimating, 33
  of innovation, development and enterprise (Schumpeter), 314
  political, 26, 33
  shared normative, 38
  political, 41–2
  political, history of, 38
Las Casas, 233, 236
Latin America, 85, 198, 202, 239, 264
Lauterpacht, Hersch, 83, 306
law, 1–4, 6–9, 13, 16, 19, 64, 379
  admiralty, 374
  as a professional ethics, 91
  as a language of authority, 68
  as a linguistic phenomenon, 66
  as a practice of history, 60
  as a social phenomenon, 14, 49
  as a story-maker, 45, 48
  as always political, 195
  as an act of sovereign power, 34
  as an institutional practice, 53
  as an instrument of policy, 35
  as constructing its own history, 44
  as distinctively concerned with making meaning move across time (Orford), 275
  as natural reason, 82
  as source of sovereign's authority, 81
  as struggle and disagreement, 66
  as the language used to dress up the self-interest of states, 305
  as the normative fabric authorizing and governing sovereigns, 73
  British imperial/colonial, 63
  colonial, 198
  common, 44, 64, 276, 279, 359, 372–3
  comparative, 71
  concept of, 280
  constitutional, 74, 91, 109, 132–3, 136, 139, 153, 168, 261, 276
  corporate, 90
  criminal, 90
  customary international, 290
  divine, 81
  domestic, 361
  domestic public, 153
  early-modern, 341
  English marriage, 370
  environmental, 54
  European public (*jus publicum Europaeum*), 134

law (cont.)
  feudal, 44
  global administrative, 142, 280
  interdisciplinary approaches to, 4
  interpretation of in political contexts, 10
  investment, 54
  liberal theories of, 141
  natural, 81
  nature of among sovereigns, 82
  non-state forms of, 47
  normative autonomy of, 73
  of international organisations, 254, 274
  of kings or commonwealths, 44
  of nature (*ius naturale*), 1 see also law, natural
  of occupation, 164
  of responsibility for international wrongs, 278
  of the sea, 86, 293
  of war crimes, 117
  plurality of bodies of, 14
  positivist, 13
  private, 12, 90, 93
  public, 67, 90, 93, 153
  Roman, 84, 86
  seen as providing a technical and apolitical vocabulary and set of institutions, 192
  trade, 54
  transnational, of contracts, 307
  vocabularies of, 65
  Weimar constitutional, 153
law of Christian nations, 175
law of nations (*ius gentium*), 174, 186, 193
  as catalyst for need for political communities, 347
  as universal, 196
  as emancipatory and egalitarian in relation to extra-European states., 195
  as not universal (Wheaton), 201
  Britain's violation of in India and the West Indies, 197
  dualistic approach to by jurists, 185
  European, 200
  history of (Schmitt), 182
  Muslim rulers depicted as violating provisions of (Vattel), 198
  rights to common property, trade, hospitality and citizenship under (Vitoria), 239
  shift in the history of at the turn of the nineteenth century, 194

law, canon, 233
law, civil, 14, 44, 346–7
  explanation of emergence of, 341
  origins of, 355
law, international, 7, 69, 94, 134
  'counter-disciplinary' explorations of, 358
  'imperial' and 'counter-imperial' dimensions of, 193
  a gendered history of, 376
  a politics of, 195
  account of the function and possibilities, 304
  and colonialism, 83
  and empire, 118
  and fascism, 83
  and political thought, dialogue between, 22
  Anglo-American, 259
  anxieties of, 134
  as involving multiple forms of discursive production, 42
  as offering a life of dignity for the poor and oppressed in the third world, 70
  as a 'discipline of crisis' (Charlesworth), 368
  as a European emancipatory project, 205
  as a global, egalitarian, universal family of nations, 104
  as a language and framework for political argument, 192
  as a late nineteenth-century European Protestant liberal professional cultural sensibility, 85
  as a medium for coordination, 303
  as a native or foreign language, 109
  as a practice of history, 56
  as a reflection of international society, 52
  as a tool and expression of colonial domination, 89
  as a tool for practical management, 82
  cerns cloaking pursuit of self-interest, 303
  as adapting to new circumstances (seabed mining), 301
  as an aspect of sovereign behaviour, 67
  as an expression of pan-European aspirations, 88
  as an expression of the dominant power's style of global leadership, 109
  as an ordinary component in the constitution of social relations, 369
  as an organising idea of international political life, 117
  as apology or as utopia, 52
  as colonial, 90

Index 393

as commercial, 90
as constituted in its encounter with colonialism, 109
as emphasising construction of institutions over inclinations of statespersons, 113
as epiphenomenal to the interests of states, 289, 303
as European, 84, 90
as expression of consolidated power, 82
as expression of universal reason, 82
as expressive of a normative continuity from origins to future, 84
as independent from states, 154
as independent of international society, 52
as made in the back and forth of political conflict/ within politics, 94
as natural jurisprudence, 36
as neither history nor political morality, 52
as not 'universal', 90
as not 'public', 86
as not shifting power or wealth from powerful to weak states, 304
as occupying a historyless present, 98
as outside and above ideology, 87
as private, 90
as professional activity, 103
as protecting impunity of states and corporations to exploit the ocean, 289
as ratifying inequality, 89
as reflecting the politico-economic interests of the capitalist class within and outside of powerful states, 304
as reinforcing unequal relations among nations, 86
as religious, 90
as rooted in conflict, 90
as simultaneously an instrument of domination and of emancipation, 193
as solely an emanation of underlying political configurations, 289
as speaking only to the interactions between European states, 205
as the expression of humanist wisdom, 82
as the only limitation on the exercise of the territorial jurisdiction of the occupying state, 169
as the product of European legal culture, 84
as what great men thought at different times, 113
aspirations of for universal justice, 207
attachment of to crises, 368

authority and legitimacy of, 71
Bentham's thought on, 202–5
binding force of based on the notion of the 'self-binding' will of states, 258
British Empire as a major site for the creation of, 196
changing character of the academy of, 55
Christian, 175
claims of to be universal, secular, progressive and fair, 88
claims of to universal wisdom and accepted power as undermined by use of history, 83
colonial and neo-colonial, resistance to, 86
colonial forms of, 178
coming to terms with the 'dark past' of, 86
complicity of in the world's injustices, 55
complicity of with imperial power, 195
conceptual change in, 67
consolidation of as an academic discipline, 192
constitutive power of, 307
construction of modern, 70
contextual history of, 28
contributions of Asian states to development of, 85
contributions of past jurists to, 83
conventional narratives of a progressive, 207
counter-disciplinary research between history and, 358
created through treaties entered into by sovereign states, 171
critiques of, 358
debates about around WW1, 178
decolonising of, 298
deconstruction of contemporary, 159
determining rules of, 306
discourse of, 70
discrediting of, 89
distributional outcomes of, 91
economic analysis of, 303
emancipatory role of, 195
epiphenomenality of, 307
Eurocentric orientation of, 50
Eurocentrism of, 104
exclusion of colonisation from history of, 63
experience of reading, 97
feminist approaches to, 16, 357
feminist critiques of, 359, 368
feminist histories of, 379
focus development of through crises instead of routine operation, 360

law, international (cont.)
  fragmentation of, 54
  function of codification of to reduce uncertainty about states' respective rights and duties (Bentham), 204
  German, 170
  global history of, 1, 85
  globalisation in, 51
  heroic vision of, 7
  heterogeneity of, 70
  historians of, 72
  historical context of, 63
  historical turn within, 22
  historicized, 104
  history as proof for the legality of, 73
  history/histories of, 8, 14–15, 21, 27–8, 31, 36–7, 47, 55, 64–5, 67, 69, 78, 98, 155, 359, 362, 364
  is made and applied in struggle, 83
  linked with universal reason, 88
  Literaturgeschichte of history of, 65
  long standing commitment to commerce of, 240
  loose sense of history in users of, 82
  lost private side of, 368
  machinery of, for distribution of power, wealth and prestige, 89
  maintaining a critical standpoint within, 60
  materialist history of, 304
  materials of as archaeological fragments, 91
  merits of political thought for, 131
  modern science of, 115
  nature of, 254
  neglecting of private law by historians of, 362
  nineteenth-century scholarship of, 88
  nineteenth-century, in the context of 'power', 81
  normative authority of, 82
  of nature and of nations (*ius naturae et gentium*), 1
  orientation to universality and coherence of, 90
  origin narratives of, 61
  origins of, 61
  papal encyclicals belonging to history of, 64
  past, present and future of, 70
  pluralism of, 72, 92
  political economy of, 307
  positive, 293
  practice in as a rhetorical skill, 53
  principles and practice of colonial administrators as origins of, 63
  private side of, 15
  professional competence in, 53
  professional period of, 55
  professionalisation of, 10, 103
  progressive development, 74
  progressive teleology of, 82
  public, 15, 362
  public European (*ius publicum Europaeum*) 88
  public/private distinction in, 87
  questioned as a concept, 154
  race as central to the definition of, 207
  reform of, 51, 86
  reformism in, 51
  relationship between public and private, 361
  relevance of political thought for, 135
  removed from economics, 89
  replacing divine law/Pope with natural law/ sovereign, 81
  role of in legitimising and sustaining colonialism, 86
  role of power and politics in history of, 64
  roots of, 104
  roots of in Christian European culture, 88
  sociology of, 8
  spatial order in, 140, 152
  Third World approaches to (TWAIL), 78
  treatises of, 362
  understood as a historically particular system, 202
  universalisation of, 104
  unselfconsciously anachronistic mode of, 105
  women as legal subjects or actors in, 357
  writing of, 109
law, international criminal, 106, 112
law, international economic, 74
law, intertemporal, 57
law, local, 44
law, marriage
  reform of, 370
law, natural, 14, 35, 65, 87, 142, 210, 239, 309, 341, 347
  as ideological, 36
  as legitimation of law, 35
  emergence of in colonial context, 81
  European school of, 84
  idiom of, 1

law, private, 67, 183, 347
    as the context of public international law's power, 358
    duty of states to recognise one another's, 375
    institutions of, 305
    law, private international, of domicile and 'comity of nations', 372, 375
law, private international, 358–9, 365–6, 375
    agreement on principles of, 366
    as a lost side of international law, 359
    as part of international law, 363
    common-law rules of, 359
    development of, 371
    established as a field in the United States, 377
    focus of as the state at home, not abroad, 364
    Hague conventions on, 364
    harmonising rules of, 363
    modification of the English family and the English state by, 369
law, Roman, 235, 346, 348–9, 351, 353–5
    commentaries on, 14
    division of law into public and private law under, 347
    division of private law into natural (ius gentium) and civil law in, 14
    early modern discourse, 342
    early-modern commentaries on, 345
    internal time of, 45
    right of foreigners to beg, 244
    sixteenth-century commentators on, 347
laws
    colonial marriage, 370
    conflict of, 358–9, 377
    contingency of, 52
    imperial conflict of, 359, 370
    indigenous to the colonies, 365
    Nazi racial, 131
    positive, 137
    validity of from reason alone, 141
laws, civil, 244, 341, 343
laws, foreign, 365
laws, settler, 365
laws, sixteenth-century poor, 248
lawyers, 1–5, 8–9, 13, 35, 42, 44, 49, 53, 60, 63, 67, 71, 101, 131, 162, 275, 277, 287, 308
    activist, 85
    Anglo-American, 261
    as people exercising authority, 68
    British in the 1950s, 306
    contemporary international, 103
    early seventeenth-century English 64
    environmental, 74
    feminist international, 377
    German, 160, 164, 168, 171, 174, 178
    intellectual and professional stance of, 277
    international, 2, 42, 50, 54, 70, 73–4, 91, 96, 99, 101, 171
    medieval, 355
    natural, 61
    professional role of, 12
    early-modern, 352
    tendency of to believe 'nothing happened' at different points of history, 117
    third world, 300
    US, 50
leadership, 77, 113, 139, 148, 153, 158, 330–1
    global, 109
    in the use of language, 316
League of Nations, 11–12, 58, 84, 90, 146, 152, 154, 163, 207, 214, 216, 253–81
    as a new agent and locus for the organisation of international life, 256
    as a new site of politics, 216
    as a nexus for interstate cooperation, 263
    as a scene of speech, 255
    as challenging to both juridical and historical analysis, 280
    Covenant of, 256–7
    effect of on United Nations, 273–4
legal positivism, 136–7
legalism, 111, 114
legislation, 34
    as political, 34
    imperial, ideology of, 35
legitimacy, 35, 65, 133
legitimation, 25, 32–3, 38
    discursive, 35
    of conceptual change through innovation, 315
    of killing, 147
    politics of, 26
    Skinnerian model of, 38
Leviathan, see Hobbes, Thomas
liberalism, 110, 133, 141, 143, 191–2, 371
    relational feminist critique of, 360
Liberia, 207
liberties, English legal, 366
liberty, 293
    as yielding obedience to magistrates (Vives), 249
    ruled by reason, 246

Libya, 114
Lieber, Francis, 177
Lin Zexu, 200
literature, 123
  in dialogue with history, 38
Locke, John, 345
  Foucauldian reading of, 39
longue durée, 47, 63, 66, 78
Lorimer, James, 15, 90, 107, 375

Machiavelli, Niccolo, 342
MacKinnon, Catherine, 115
Mali, 59
Malta, 296
mankind
  the conscience of, 121
manners, 376
  as part of gender studies of the history of international law, 377
Marcuse, Herbert, 143–4
Mare Liberum (Grotius), 286
market(s), 326
marriage(s) (*matrimonium*), 14–15, 117, 362, 365, 367
  and how it relates to ideas of law and justice, 355
  as natural under ius gentium, 349
  as not part of natural law (Cicero), 348
  as part of the law of nations (*ius gentium*), 347
  as interwoven with emergence of states (Roman law commentators), 347
  as the beginning of justice in the Roman law tradition, 355
  colonial laws on, 370
  determining validity of a, 358
  foreign, 370
  Hague Conventions on, 364
  illegitimate 349–50
  medieval and early-modern understanding of, 356
  natural and civil, 342
  relationship to of emergence of civil government, 354
Martens, Friedrich, 199
Marx, Karl, 51, 112
Marxist analysis, 13
masculinity, 376
master-slave relation, 366
matrimonium, 14, see marriage

meaning, 28, 39
  as interpretation by historian, 30
  formation of in law, 67
  historical, 30
  in context/ contextual, 30
  in history of international law, 28
  legal, 45–6, 48
  political, 30–1, 45, 48
memory, 73, 98
Menschheitswerte (human values), 141–2
mercantilism, 92–3
merchant companies
  acting like states, 181
merchants, 2, 239, 315, 365
metahistory, 7
metaphor, 147
  authorship as, 112
metaphysics, 314
method, 5, 7, 97, 100, *see* methodology
methodology, 3–6, 21, 24, 27–9, 60, 62, 71–2, 78, 80–1, 88, 92, 96–7, 99–100, 102, 105–12, 114–16, 118–20, 118, 122–3, 132, 306, 314–16, 357
  as choices, 115
  as informed by 'mood', 124
  contextualised historical, 99
  inter-disciplinary, 116
  limits of in history, 21
  macro-historical, 108
  micro-historical, 121
  of international legal contextualists, 80
metropole, the, 198, 359, 364, 366, 368
  public policy exception in, 367
Mexico, 242, 251
Michelet, Jules, 119
Middle East, 202
migration
  contemporary politics of, 252
Minerva
  owl of, 78
minorities, 265
modernisation, 103
modernism, 51, 78
modernity, 47, 49, 85, 135
  experience of our own, 334
  narrative of, 43
  political, 43
  the story of, 44
  Western, 44, 47
monarchy, 136

monasteries, 11
monasticism, Western, 240
money
  legal construction of, 94
Montesquieu, 200
More, Thomas, 350
Morgenthau, Hans, 143, 147
mothers, 343–5
moyenne durée
  European, 43, 45–6
  global, 48

Namibia, 59
Napoleon, 103, 112, 120, 196
narrative(s), 7, 10
  changing the, 74
  early encounter, 232
  historical, 72–3
  ingrained Western, 368
  large-scale, 90
  of foundation, 14
  sacred, 37
nation(s), 1, 9–10, 262
  as context, 77
  as moral communities of equal status, 10
  comity of, 372, 375
  European family of, 359
  family of, 104
  law of, 170, *see* law of nations
  principle of universality of, 105
  self-perfection of, 198
nation-state(s) 159
  African, formed and governed on European models, 208
  as aim of decolonisation, 212
  European, 176
nationalism, 82, 92, 163, 309
nationality, 359–60, 373–4
  acquisition and loss of as involving the state, 373
  as a political bond, 15
  as connecting factor governing an individual's legal status and capacity, 372
  campaign to abolish dependent, for married women, 374
  public international law concept of, 372
nationhood, 348
natural law 218, *see* law, natural
naturalism, 110, 117, 119
naturalization
  as privileging men, 374

nature, 46
  as context of eighteenth-century international law, 81
  early modern understandings of, 341
Nauru, 302
navigation, 181, 286, 304
Nazi Germany, 132, 141
Nazi party (NSDAP), 140, 148
Nehru, Jawaharlal, 112
neighbours, 240
neoclassical economic theory, 313
neoliberalism, 89, 300
  rise of, 52
Netherlands, 56, 61
New International Economic Order (NIEO), 300, 305–6
New World, 12, 66
  contribution of conquest of to economic growth of Europe, 207
New Zealand, 196, 257
Nicaragua, 206
Nietzsche, Friedrich, 40, 46, 100, 135
Nkrumah, Kwame, 220–1
North Africa, 368
North America, 46
North Atlantic, 43, 93
  interventions of in Africa, 84
novel(s), 20
Nuremberg, 106, 113, 117, 120–1, 131, 134
Nussbaum, Arthur, 61
Nyerere, Julius, 223–5
Nys, Ernest, 61

obedience, 151
  limits of, 180
obligation, 15, 378
  absolute, 15
  absolute, contrasted with comity and courtesy, 376
  as underwritten by ideals of masculinity, 376
  binding, between states, public international law concept of, 372
  international, 372
  religious, 11
occupation, 160–2, 174, 182
  effective, 57
  institution of within *ius publicum Europaeum*, 183
  military (*occupatio bellica*), 166, 170
  mixed (*Mischbesetzung*), 170
  of Belgium, 168

occupation (cont.)
  peaceful (*occupatio pacifica*), 166, 170
  sovereignty during, 167
  theories of, 182
  theory of (Schmitt), 184
  of the Rhineland, 9, 160–5, 172, 176, 178, 180–2, 186
occupier
  sovereign will of, 185
ocean. *see also* seas
  as a commons, 286
  as an intensely juridified space, 290
  as now entirely legally incorporated, 308
  as unoccupiable, inexhaustible, unalterable by human activity and irreducible to private ownership or state sovereignty (Grotius), 286
  constitution of the (LOSC), 287
  irreducible to territorial jurisdiction, 286
  legal lines delimiting, 292
  policing of, 286
  states claiming exclusive sovereign rights over parts of (post-1945), 287
  threat of depletion, 285
  utopian projects for building human habitats on, 288
Old World, 12
ontology, 321
opinion, public, 261
  use of the rhetoric of by League of Nations Secretariat staff, 265
Opium War, *see* War(s), Opium
Oppenheim, Lassa, 113, 259
orality, 6
order
  ideal global, 140
  international, 152
  global, 93
  legal, 1
  liberal global, 94
  liberal international, 92
  post-war liberal, 93
  universal international, 111
  absence of meaningful post-war (Schmitt), 134
  conceived of as organized unequally around sovereignty, territoriality and comity, 378
  precariousness of a law-based, 158
order, international legal,
  constitutional position of United Nations in, 274
  progressive universalization of, 75
order, political
  quest for the 'concrete' grounds of, 110
orders
  legal, 109
  national legal, 15
  transnational, 139
orders, legal
  personations of, 259
Orders, mendicant, 240, 243, 248
Orford, Anne, 2, 4, 60, 70, 77, 192, 274–5, 277, 357–8, 368
organisations
  as sites of social control, 11
  international, 11, 74, 140, 171, 254, 274–5, 278–80
  new forms of, 321
  non-government (NGOs), 265
origins
  narratives of, 4
  relativism of normative power of historica, 57
  search for, 105–6

pacifism, 140, 146, 150
  as effeminate, 376
pacta sunt servanda, 65
Pagden, Anthony, 239, 365
Pal, Justice Radhabinod, 121
palace, 26
  as institutional site of political discourse, 31
pan-Africanist thought, 215
Panama, 175
pan-Asian thought, 215
pan-Islamic thought, 215
Papacy, 107
paradiastolic redescription
  as political action, 315
paradigm, 319, 324, 327, 331
  concept of (Kuhn), 316, 318
paratext
  as a zone of transmission and transaction, 27
Pardo, Arvid, 298
parenthood
  as a legal and social institution under Roman law, 353
parents
  command to honour both (Decalogue), 346
parliament, 26, 136
  as institutional site of political discourse, 31
parliamentary representation, 133

past, the, 3, 5–7, 15, 19–20, 31, 41, 73, 107, 116,
    311, 357, 364
  ability to learn from, 78
  as stories, 6
  juridical and historical methods of critically
    engaging, 277
  meaning in, 40
  narratives of, 16
  popular accounts of, 112
  readings of as fundamental to critical
    perspectives on the present and the future,
    208
patria potestas, 346, 350, 352, 355
patriarchy, 91
patricide, 352
peace, 7, 51, 57, 65, 67, 74, 90, 93, 103, 112, 152,
    154, 159, 178, 202, 376
  debates on perpetual, 67
  enforced *(Diktatfrieden)*, 163
  offenses against international, 203
  progress towards global, 133
  realpolitik of, 146
  settlement, 256, 261
  through law, 257
  treaty, 152
  universalistic proposals for perpetual (Kant),
    150
Peace of Westphalia (1648), 56, 60, 115
peace-keeping, 203, 258, 275
peace-making, 50, 55
peoples
  indigenous, 84
  legal recognition of colonised, 58
  mandatory, 255
  movement of across the world, 214
  multiple allegiances of, transcending
    borders of states and empires, 214
  occluded, 104
  of the South, 84
  poor, 301
Permanent Court of International Justice, 146
personal status law, 364
personality, 257, 259
  artificial, 11
  group, 259
  international legal, 260
  legal, 254, 258–9, 262
  split, 322
personhood, 11–12, 321–2
person(s), 9, 11, 320, 329
  legal, 260

theorization of, 11
Peru, 72
Philippines, 56, 58
philology
  historical, 45
  political-philosophical, 45
philosopher(s), 55, 61, 275, 355
  and politics, 133
philosophy, 23, 34, 36, 41, 66, 103, 116, 141–2,
    309, 314
  ancient, 347
  as a politics of truth (Foucault), 40
  as creative of new meaning, 40
  dialogue with history, 40
  histories of, 41
  moral and religious, 35
  political, 33
piracy, 106, 115, 286
Plato, 243, 346
pluralism, 10, 14, 90, 92, 259
  as international not domestic, 154
  legal, 367
pluriverse, political world as a, 139
Pocock, John, 23, 25, 41, 330
poetic technique, 116
poetics, historical and legal, 6
poetry, 37, 47, 117
poiesis, 40
Poland, 104
political economy.
  history of, 66
political realism, 32
political scientists, 79
political theory, 106, 180, 191, 309, 311
political thought, 10
  European, 158
  global history of, 2
  historians of, 46, 191, 277, 314, 316, 341–2
  importance of sexual and conjugal
    dimensions in, 354
  limits of, 12
  medieval, 44
  realist, 9
  Secretariat of the League of Nations as a site
    for, 275
political thought, history of, 2, 3, 5, 7, 15, 21,
    26–9, 27, 34–6, 40, 42–3, 46, 65, 185, 191,
    210, 314
  'international turn' in the, 19, 208
  as an act of political thinking in the present,
    21

political thought, history of (cont.)
  Cambridge school of, 23, 27
  contextual, 23, 29–30, 32, 37
  dialogue with history of international law, 31
  evolution of as a discipline, 40
  global, 37
  history of itself as a stand-in for 'history', 22
  in the African present, 226
  Janus-face of, 47
  longue durée, 47
  new histories of, 16
  philosophical, 41
  realist 35
  temporality of, 22
  twentieth-century, 47
  view of law, 42
  writing of, 33
political, the, 14–15, 35
  as contracted, 341
  autonomy of, 35
  construction of as a construction of power, 40
  constructions of, 9, 41
  historicity of, 38
  history of, 38
  Indian, 38
  theorization of, 9
politicians, 78, 162
politics, 1–2, 8, 10, 16, 23–4, 28, 30–5, 46, 64, 76, 94, 115, 257
  absence of in Alexandrowicz's legal historical argument, 195
  agent-centred model of, 32
  and the political, distinction between, 35
  as being constructed in opposition to the social or the private, 342
  as outside expert rule, 94
  as political action to increase power, 7
  as within *Allgemeine Staatslehre*, 159
  boundaries between economics and, 12
  conflictual as driver of linguistic innovation, 38
  contemporary global, 71
  differences between 'man' and 'woman' in, 342
  different concepts of, 48
  domestic, 32
  early modern narratives of the emergence of, as gendered, 342
  role of international legal doctrines in, 69
  Hobbesian vision of, 36
  imperial, 35
  insistence on separation of law from, 307
  international, 32, 42
  legitimacy as defining characteristic of, 24
  modern global, 139
  of action, 41
  of legitimation, 26
  of the text, 41
  patriarchal, 14
  place of law in construction of, 31
  practitioners of real, 10
  real, 32
  realist vision of, 7
polity/polities, 1
  Amazonian, 355
  as centred on male citizens/subjects, 342
  Christian, 16
  early-modern understandings of, 341
  peripheral, 257
poor, the
  authority to coerce and imprison, 248
  care of in hospitals, 249
  debates about rights and freedoms of in sixteenth-century Europe, 243
  distinction between real and voluntary, 241
  freedom of movement of, 248
  global legal immobility of, 73
  having access to things of necessity via charity not as a right, 247
  natural rights of (Soto), 244
  seen as enemies rather than honoured guests, 234
pope, 81, 240
papal,
  encyclicals of as part of history of international law, 65
populism, 92–3, 95
Portugal, 198, 222
positivism, 65, 70, 87, 102–3, 105, 110, 117–18, 185, 279–80
  Eurocentric, 194, 198
  historical, 38
  legal, 171
possession
  right of, 239
postcolonialism,
  feminist critiques of, 358
postmodern, 40
postmodernism, 6

poverty, 11, 89, 206, 233
　as a sacred condtion within the Christian tradition, 243
　criminalisation of, 243
　of Christ as model for mendicant orders, 243
　valorised by mendicant orders, 243
power, 7, 11, 16, 31–3, 39, 70, 73, 83–4, 89, 92–3, 109, 321
　absolute paternal (Filmer), 345
　as context of nineteenth-century international law, 81
　as operating through international legal concepts and institutions., 362
　as without gender, 356
　balance of, 73, 109
　colonial, 88, 177
　construction of, 40
　context for exercise of, 76
　discursive, 39
　distribution of state, 303
　dynamics of movement and, 252
　gender relations as a way of signifying or structuring legal, 357
　hegemonic, 93
　historian's relationship with, 40
　human will to, 143
　international organisations as important sites of, 274
　law as challenge to and product of, 62
　legal construction of, 93
　legitimisation of political, 341
　location of in concept to hospitality, 244
　military exercise of as 'factual' validity of authority, 166
　moved from poor to rich in sixteenth-century Europe, 246
　new institutions for the exercise of, 322
　occupying, 181
　of master over slave, 25
　political, 25, 35
　private, 88–9, 93–4
　public as different from violence in a private capacity, 35
　realities of, 36
　relationship between law of sovereignty and law of property as 'yin and yang' of global (Koskenniemi), 362
　role of in history of international law, 65
　role of in the ascendancy of certain legal norms or institutions, 192
　sovereign, 34, 42, 170, 172
　supreme (*summum imperium*), of mothers over children in the state of nature, 343
　to command, 32
　transfer of in decolonisation, 212
　withdrawal of administering, 59
practice, 6
　international legal, 49
practices
　legal, 63
pragmatics, 27
pragmatism, 91, 103, 306
precedent, 73, 75
present, the
　requirements of, 106
presentism, 122
prestige, 89
principle of self-determination, 194
private, 2, 4, 89–90, 342, 363
　boundaries between public and, 12
　separation of, from public, 371
private ownership, 86
　ocean as irreducible to, 286
private property, 312, 333
processes, legal
　as themselves sites for creating or dismissing law, 307
profession
　as context, 77
professionalisation, 103
progress, 7, 51, 75, 156, 158, 215, 219
　modern concept of (Koselleck), 334
　technological, 146
　theory of, 329
progressivism, 51
　reformist, 52
property, 89, 305
　agriculturalist account of, used to defend settler colonialism (Vattel), 196
　as basis for order, 151
　as part of ius gentium, 67
　discourse of, 232
　division of (*divisio rerum*), 239
　in religious orders, 251
　law of, 361
　of the marine environment, 293
　private, 67
protection, 151, 175
　protection of, 155
　reform of colonial arrangements, 307
　right to common, under the law of nations, 239

protection (cont.)
    transmission of, 15
    protectionism, 74
protectorate, 175
Protestantism, 61, 65, 84, 329, 369
Prussia, 131, 149, 196
psychology, 33–4, 150
public, 2, 4, 14, 25, 342
    boundaries between private and, 12
public domain, 25
public good(s) 310
public opinion, 264, 272
    as sanction against lawbreakers, 376
public order, 175
public spaces, 31
public/private dichotomy, 362
Pufendorf, Samuel von, 105, 197

race, 366
raison d'état, 14, 65, 158, 309, 311
Rajagopal, Balakrishnan, 115
rape, 377
rational choice theory, 311
rationality, 141
readers/ audiences, 113
reading
    deconstructive techniques of, 27
realism, 3, 7, 32, 34, 37, 62, 67, 108–9, 143, 151, 158, 272, 306
    American, 110
    as a paradigm of history, politics and law, 7
    critical, 40
    legal, 50
    political, 33–4, 37–8, 42, 111
    structural, 106
realities, 108
Realpolitik, 79, 316
reason, 246
    expert and public, 76
    universal, 88
reason of state, 309
reason, professional and public, 71
Rechtsstaat, 163
redescription, critical, 71
    in legal thought, 71
reductionism, 314
Reformation, 330
reformism, 94
refugees, 73
relations
    between the 'natural' and the 'political', 15

interstate, 15
relations, international, 69, 152–3, 202, 232
    as an academic discipline, 7, 50, 64, 74, 101–2, 143, 206, 261, 276, 310, 358, 378
    hegemonic realities of, 153
relations, transnational private
    removing legal obstacles to, 363
relationship, parent–child
    as dependent on issue of providing food, 353
relativism, 327
religion, 82, 87–8, 90, 142, 203, 249, 366
    in dialogue with history, 38
Renaissance, 376
reparations, 162, 164, 168
representation, political, 180
res publica, 347
resistance, 77, 92
    legal and political, 45
    political, 45
    passive, 164
resources
    allocation of, 13
    allocation of, to invention, 318
    allocation of, to production, 335
    claims legal subjects have to, 67
    consumer-led allocation of, 312
    deep seabed petroleum, 299
    free movement of, 73
    hierarchy of distribution of (Augustinian Rule), 241
    ocean, 285, 289
    optimal allocation of, to research and development, 337
    rights to access, 11
    role of law in distribution of, 66
resources, linguistic and cultural
    unfamiliar deployment of, 316
resources, natural, 248, 289, 291, 303
    appropriation of, 240
    regimes for, 293
    right to, 239
Responsibility to Protect (R2P), 206
revisionism, 72
    third world historical, 89
revolution, 30, 319, 326–7
    moments of as vantage points to observe history at its most vivid, 114
    right of, 180
    transformative moments of, 114

revolution, scientific, 324
  theory of (Kuhn), 319
rhetoric, 28
Rhineland, 160, 162–3, 169, 172, 176, 178, 186
  occupation of the, 178, 180–1, 186
Ricoeur, Paul, 21
rights,
  civil, 365
  contractual, 68
  creation of as distinct from existence of, 57
  human, 65, 67, 74, 82, 85, 87–9
  in family relations, 68
  land, 68
  language of, 244
  natural, 142
  of nationals in foreign territory, 57
  private, 116
  reality of vested legal, 306
  sovereign, 82
  system of intervention, 178
  universal (to elect one's own government), 234
Rousseau, Jean-Jacques, 65, 67, 184
rule, emergency, 154
rulers
  as trained in the legal academy, 71
  female, 355
  Muslim, 198
rulership, 71–2, 76
  as elite articulation, 75
  colonial, 369
  expert, 75
  managerial, 75
  training for, 76
rules, legal, 50
Russia, 108, 115, 269, 365
Rwanda, 113, 120

Saint-Pierre, Charles-Irénée Castel, abbé de, 67
Salamanca, School of, 77
San Domingo, 175
sanctions, 295
satire, 26
savages
  as excluded from protections of the law of war, 83
Savigny, Friedrich Carl von, 49, 372
Scelle, Georges, 260
Schachter, Oscar, 55

Schelling, Friedrich Wilhelm Joseph von, 146
schematism, 314
Schmitt, Carl, 9–10, 12, 15, 44, 62, 104, 108, 110–12, 114–15, 132–7, 139–48, 151–6, 158, 160–1, 163, 174–82, 184–6, 259, 271
  anthropological assumptions of, 150
  anti-Semitism, 134
  as a German jurist, 136
  as a politician, 140
  as source for deconstruction of contemporary international law, 159
  construction of the state as one historically contingent political form, 139
  Großraum (great space), 152
  importance of innate human aggressiveness, 149
  importance of the exception/ extreme case, 138
  influence of work on law-makers in Germany, 142
  intellectual formation of, 135
  international thought of, 134
  polemical concept of the state, 149
scholars, 72, 212
  Asian, 86
  contemporary left-wing Schmittian, 187
  European, 246
  German, 258
  legal, 276
  modern conflicts, 371
  third world, 301
  Western, 86
scholarship, 3, 97, 112, 132, 196
  academic legal, used as propaganda in wartime, 133
  as marred by present-mindedness, 357
  contemporary international law, 91
  early modern legal, 354
  epoch-defining styles of, 108
  feminist, 342, 344
  feminist legal, 360
  French, 260
  German legal, 143
  in common-law countries, 376
  in context, 78
  international academic, 142
  international legal, 306
  late medieval and Renaissance Roman legal, 44
  legal, 35, 44–5, 137, 156
  Methodenlehre in German legal, 138

scholarship (cont.)
  nineteenth-century, 371
  public law, 155
  style of, 109
  traditions of, 43
scholasticism
  fifteenth-century, 77
Schumpeter, Joseph, 13, 310–14, 316, 319, 322–3, 325–8, 331–2, 335
Schwarzenberger, Georg, 111
science(s), 85, 94, 317
  creativity in (Kuhn), 319
  history of, 316
  human, 320
  legal, 91
  natural, 325
  philosophy of, 316
  social, 111
  tension between innovation and tradition in the history of (Kuhn), 310
  theory of (Kuhn), 317
scientists, 319, 322
  political, 344
Scotland, 367, 369
Scott, James Brown, 61
scripture, 20, 23, 47
sea(s), 110, 204
  law of, 296
  as an example of a tragic commons, 296
  ecological protection of, 308
  enduring political economy of the law of, 288
  freedom of the, 293–7
  idea of a free, 287
  imagined as an assemblage of jurisdictionally discrete sites of economic activity, 290
  multilateral treaties concerning uses of the, 290
  new law of the, 292, 303, 305, 308
  old law of the, 293
  political economy of the law of the, 293
  protection of rights to access and use, 293
  regulation of some uses of the, 287
  sovereign jurisdictions at (piracy, fishing), 286
  unconstrained use of, 293
  uneven distribution of rights to access and use, 308
  uses of the common areas of, 308
Searle, John, 23

secrecy, 148, 152, 263, 267
secularism, 133
self, the
  as social, 371
  conception of, 360
self-determination, 65, 69, 74, 215
self-government, 216, 219, 221, 311
  dependent on having achieved a standard of civilization defined in terms of the modern West, 215
self-identity, 360
self-preservation
  right of the political community to, 252
self-rule
  social contract of, 221
shame, 92, 163, 220, 248
shipping
  list of instruments relating to, 290
shipwreck
  as a case of exception for poor relief/hospitality, 246
Shotwell, James T., 144, 146
Siam, 365
siege, 161, 182, 185–6
  military state of as distinguished from dictatorship, 179
  'real' military vs political 'fictive' state of, 177
Skinner, Quentin, 13, 23–6, 28, 32, 36, 38, 43, 46, 78, 111, 113, 310, 314, 316, 319–21, 323–4, 327, 329–30, 342, 358
slavery, 248, 365–7
Smith, Adam, 67, 196, 203
social assistance, 234
social imaginary, 324
social imaginary significations (Castoriadis), 325
social interdependence, 76
social theory, 312
socialism, 335–6
society, 4, 325
sociology, 78–9, 92, 110, 150, 260, 268, 311, 327
Socrates, 346
solidarity, international
  rise of, 378
Somerset's Case (1772), 366
Soto, Domingo de, 244, 248
South Africa, 58–9, 222
South West Africa, 58–9
South, the
  emancipatory claims from, 85
sovereign(s), 81, 89, 91, 105, 342

Index   405

    as the origin and enforcer of law, 73
    as who decides on the exception (Schmitt), 139
    case for a unitary and supreme (Hobbes), 271
    constitutional limitations on, 168
    original claim of, 168
    territorial jurisdiction of, 168
sovereign state(s) 242, *see* state(s), sovereign,
sovereignty, 7, 12, 34, 56, 67, 70, 89, 103–4, 117, 124, 135, 141, 145, 164, 168, 171, 174, 185–6, 207, 209, 219, 222, 224, 257, 346, 378
    absolute, 142
    African, 209
    as a matter of military power, 81
    as consolidated power, 82
    as effective territorial jurisdiction, 183
    as part of collective life, 220
    as practices of government, 281
    as protection, 57
    as responsibility, 206
    as right to reject external interference, 221
    as source of law's authority, 81
    as the 'uninteresting leftovers of power' (Carl Schmitt), 174
    distinctions between formal claims to and actual territorial jurisdiction, 174
    during occupation, 167
    German over the Rhineland, 176
    illusion of, 103
    in formal juridical (and political) sense, 281
    juristic definition of (Schmitt), 139
    law of, 361
    legal, 167
    legal fiction of divided, mixed or suspended, 161
    mixed, 160
    nature of, 69
    of imperial state, 175
    of man over woman as God-given (Filmer), 345
    political, 160
    principle of, 152
    public, 67
    state, 62, 160, 184
    state territorial, 164
    state, as juristically fictive but historically and practically real, 172
    territorial, 57
    theorisation of, 255
    transformative potential of, 219

Soviet Union (USSR), 317
space
    theorisation of, 132
Spain, 11, 56, 61, 86, 109, 235, 238, 241–2, 244, 247–9, 251, 272
speech
    as animating principle of the League of Nations as a political actor, 269
speech act(s), 7, 26–7, 29–30, 33–4, 39–42
St Augustine, 240–1, 245, 271
St Gregory, 244
state, 2, 7, 9, 12, 33, 35, 57, 73, 89
    'natural', 14
    as a conceptual frame, 10
    as a legal institution, 184
    as international 'person', 11
    consequences of the gendered, 354
    creation of, 15
    duty of to protect its own people, 152
    federal, 359
    form of, 10
    formation of, 8
    interests of as exogenous to international law, 303
    model of the Westphalian, 212
    modern, 136
    modern, ideology of, 37
    nascent global, 84
    postcolonial, 11, 15
    right of to set own commercial policy, 12
    sovereign, 34, 174
    targeted for international intervention imagined as helpless feminine victim, 368
    totalitarian, 133
state interests
    as class interests, 304
state of nature, 343, 349, 351, 354
    as a state of war of men against women, 354
    early-modern concept of, 341
state sovereignty, 120
state, modern
    rise of, 309
state, sovereign, 34, 174
state, the, 15, 34, 42, 62, 139, 147, 319
    as a contingent form, 228
    as a historical phenomenon, 32
    as a male entity, 342
    as an artificial body, 341
    as most mature political form for the exercise of violence, 148
    as self-contained, 15

state, the (cont.)
  as the primary arena of politics, 32
  conceptualisation of, 254
  early modern ideas on the beginnings of, 348
  Hobbesian view of, 32
  international law and, 134
  limits and jurisdiction of, 211
  modern, 43
  modern, as focal meaning of politics, 44
  Nazi theory of, 132
  nineteenth-century ideas of the emergence of, 342
  power of, 50
  public law theory of, 260
  radical pan-African critiques of existing models of, 209
  re-ordering of through choice of law and rules on jurisdiction, 371
  seventeenth-century philosophy of, 342
  shift the conventional focus current theories of, 275
  space of as predetermined and limited, 42
  theorisation of, 255
  theorizations of, 14
  Weberian view of, 24
  Westphalian model of, 221
states, 9–10, 15–16, 254
  African post-colonial, 224
  as analogous to reasoning, liberal individuals (Wilson), 261
  as creatures in and of law, 276
  as founded by fathers (Hobbes), 354
  as legal equals but also global empires, 205
  as legal equals regardless of size or power (Vattel), 197
  Asian, 85–6, 200
  Barbary, 201
  collapsed, 88
  contingency of, 211
  creation of, 347
  emergence of contractual relations between, 142
  equality of in international realm, 203
  European, 134, 145, 200
  formation of, 10, 86
  imperial nature of modern liberal, 192
  inequalities of, 89
  international order made up of free and equal independent, 213
  jurisdiction of, 10
  Latin American, 85
  legal equality of newly decolonized, 197
  liberal, 205
  new post-colonial in Africa, 223
  non-European, 104
  obligation between, 360
  plurality of allows for diversity or identity, 151
  plurality of creates viability of, 151
  postcolonial, 16
  powerful, 93
  sovereign, 86
  sovereign will of, 258
  spatially alien, 152
  Third World, 86
  universal equality of, 204
states, colonial, 213
states, confederations of [*Staatenverbindungen*]
  legal nature of, 258
states, developed
  pioneer investor status of in seabed mining, 300
states, developing, 206, 294, 296–302, 307, 360
statebuilding, 355
state-centrism, 371
statecraft, 93
statehood, 7, 257
state-theory, liberal, 141
status naturalis, see nature, state of
status, civil, 362
stories/story-telling, 71, 73, 76
stranger(s),
  as both guest and enemy, 232
  as enemy (Schmitt), 151
  classical conception of hospitality as welcoming the, 241
  the poor as, 234
  welcoming of as a law of nature, 240
strategy, 77–8, 91
Strauss, Leo, 133, 150
Strauss-Kojève dialogue, 133
Strupp, Karl, 164, 170, 174, 178
style, 6, 97, 109
  as method, 110
  as persuasion, 97
Suárez, Francisco, 90
subjecthood
  interwar thinking on, 254
subjects
  acting on others, 321
  royal, 368
succession, 362

suicide, 322, 327
Switzerland, 196

Talleyrand, Charles Maurice de Talleyrand-Perigord, 183
Tanganyika, 213, 215–17, 220, 224
Tanzania, 209, 211, 221, 223
taxation, 285
  reframing of as a duty of citizenship in post-colonial states, 221
Taylor, Charles, 324–5
technology, 133, 145–6, 158, 292, 300, 303, 305, 317, 327, 334, 336
  investment in as a public good, 310
teleology, 5, 30, 43, 55, 105, 110, 114, 119, 314
temporality, 15, 22, 24, 39, 102, 311
  modern, 46
  of thought and of law, 21
terra nullius, 88
territoriality, 24–5, 73, 378
  absolute, 378
  non-self-governing, 58
territory/territories,
  administration of 'internationalised', 256
  administration of Ottoman, 256
  annexation of, 176
  colonial, 58
  gaining de facto control over, 178
  immediate change in sovereignty when occupied, 183
  no part of ocean can be counted in any people's, 286
  occupied, 166
terror
  war on, 106
terrorism, 111
text(s)
  and history of international law, 65
  as acts, 28
  fidelity to, 116
  making historical sense of, 41
  new editions of as new acts, 27
  nineteenth-century legal, 60
The Law of War and Peace, 48
theology/theologians, 55, 180, 355
  political, 44, 133
theorist(s),
  feminist legal, 368
  French post-Marxist, 324
  legal, 275

political, 275, 342
social, 309
theory,
  feminist critiques of political, 358
  feminist legal, 360–1
  history of international legal, 79
  normative claims of, 193
theory–practice distinction, 2
Third Reich, 111–12, 132
third world, 70, 89
Third World Approaches to International Law (TWAIL), 78, 86, 118
  marginalization of histories by, 358
Thirty-Years' War, 60
time, 101–3, 115
  immemorial, 106
  international law's preoccupations with, 114
  legal, 73
totalitarianism, 140, 143
trade, 63, 67, 88
  effects of in history of international law, 365
  right to (*ius negotiandi*) under the law of nations, 239
trading companies
  roles of in international law, 64
tradition(s), 288
  critical interpretive practice within, 79
  enlightenment, 135
  family, 86
  historical, 81
  intellectual or religious as context, 77
  'law and context', 79
  scholarly, 106
translation
  cultural, 40
travellers, 247
treaties, 74, 114, 124, 256, 278, 303, 305, 362–3
  as contested legal interpretations, 63
  as instruments of anachronism, 125
  as source of law, 279
  as sources for international law, 113
  bilateral, 290
  international, 34
  interpretation of, 53
  inter-sovereign, 286
  multilateral 290
  obligations of, 178
  of ancient Near East, 60
Treaty of Paris (1898), 56
Treaty of Utrecht, 109
Treaty of Versailles, 103

tribunal(s)
  war, 134
  human rights, 53
  international, 4
  international criminal (ICT), 84
  war crimes, 113
Trusteeship Territories of the United Nations,, 222
truth, 39, 321, 329
  historical, 186
Tully, James, 39, 193
Turkey, 58, 201, 365, 373
TWAIL 86, *see* Third World Approaches to International Law
tyranny, 180, 346, 355

Uganda, 224–5
uncertainty, 323, 326, 332, 337
  as a political choice (Dobb), 335, 337
  as an inevitable product of development driven by innovation, 325
  as one of the wages of capitalism, 335
  is the result of dynamic competition, 326
United Kingdom, 299
United Nations, 51, 53, 58–9, 73–4, 89, 105, 155, 214, 216–17, 222–3, 273–4, 277
United Nations General Assembly, 206, 296–8
  discredited use of resolutions of, 307
United Nations Secretary-General, 301
United Nations Trust Territory, 211
United Nations Trusteeship Council (1947), 216
United States of America, 50–1, 56, 61, 72, 84, 89–90, 92–3, 109–11, 131, 143, 152, 156, 161–2, 175–6, 178, 199, 205, 207, 268, 290, 294, 299–300, 317–18, 327, 335, 376
Universal Declaration of Human Rights (UDHR) 215
universalism, 109, 156, 194, 201–2, 204, 240
  as based on the law of nature, 194
  late-mediaeval, 109
  legal, 197
  moral, 191
universality
  claim to of international law, 71
universities, 90, 136
  as sites of socio-culturally authoritative discourse, 31
utilitarianism, 50
utopian, 52

Vattel, Emer de, 10, 65, 68, 90, 102, 113, 194–6, 198–9, 202–5, 207, 213
  as used by China, 200
  mixed legacy of to twentieth-century international thought, 202
  on commercial independence, 200
  reception of his *Droit des gens* (1758) in early nineteenth-century British debates, 193
  republican doctrine of, 198
Versailles, 120, 135, 141
  Peace Conference (1919), 112
  Treaty of, 161–3, 172, 176
Vienna Congress, 183
Vienna School, 258
violence, 32, 62, 141, 144–5, 148, 207
  a global system dominated by empires as doomed to incessant (Bentham), 203
  legitimate, 24
  normalisation of, 40
  literary, 122–3
Vitoria, Francisco de, 65–6, 77, 81, 84, 90, 111, 118, 233, 238–42, 244–7
  appeal to principle of hospitality, 238–40
  facilitation of appropriation of natural resources, 239
  right to hospitality as *ius communicandi*, 239
  use of *ius negotiandi*, 239
  normative, 315, 325
  of elite rule, 93
  of historicism, 309
  of law as vector for significance of past events in the present, 280
  of Protestant Christianity, 315
  social, 325
vocabulary(ies), 81, 257
  choice of, 50

war, 7, 50, 55, 57, 63, 67, 82, 90, 111–13, 139, 142, 144–5, 151, 156, 159, 161, 166, 170, 178, 311, 331, 362
  abolition of, 178
  against terrorism, 83
  as a case of exception for poor relief/hospitality, 246
  as lawful if hospitality denied, 242
  as neither the purpose nor content of politics (Schmitt), 150
  condition of, 349
  civil, 141
  criminalisation of, 145

effects of on history of international law, 365
enemy nationals as domiciliaries in time of, 373
English maritime (total), 183
Franco-Prussian, 177
humanisation of, 103
international laws of, 169
just (*bellum iustum*), 65
laws of, 118, 168
of aggression, intellectual preparation of, 132
on terror, 118
outlawing of, 145
perceiving the state through, 153
prevention of as part of the work of the League of Nations, 256
purely state character of (Talleyrand), 183
role for law in, 81
state of nature as a condition of, 341
the just, 65
use of academic legal scholarship as propaganda in times of, 133
wars, 73
  as a legitimate exercise of sovereignty, 145
  as not authored by Great Men, 112
  colonial, 207
  introduction of in *ius gentium*, 355
  just, 81
  of decolonization, 206
  trade, 89
War(s)
  Algerian, 207
  American Revolutionary, 197, 202
  Cold, 274
  Napoleonic, 183
  of Jenkins' Ear, 203
  Opium, 199–201, 207
  Seven Years', 202
  Vietnam, 207
war crimes, 118
  law of, 117
war crimes trials, 112
war criminals, 120
  German, 132
warfare, 86
  history of European, 60
wealth, 11, 16, 89, 92–4, 313
Weber, Max, 24, 32, 95, 149, 313, 315

Wehberg, Hans, 140, 258–9
Weimar, 114, 134, 141, 155
West Indies, 197
Westlake, John, 63, 374
Westphalia, 102, 104–5, 156
Wheaton, Henry, 115, 199, 201
Wilson, Thomas Woodrow, 163
Wittgenstein, Ludwig, 23, 41
Wolff, Christian, 113, 197
women, 364, 368–9
  and the social contract, 354–5
  as legal subjects or actors in international law, 357
  as slaves in a pre-contract state of war, 354
  as subjects of international law, 379
  as subordinated by the civil law, 355
  guatapera community as basis of hospitals especially for, 251
  historical subordination of, 14
  in international law, 360
  in matters of royal succession, 362
  in the state of nature (Hobbes), 344
  inclusion of in political life, 362
  nationality of married, 362
  position of, 2
  repression of the traffic in, 256
  rights of in international treatises, 362
  role of in the emergence of civil government, 354
  status of, 362
  status of children born to enslaved, 362
words, *see* language
World Bank, 78, 89
World War I, 117, 119, 135, 146, 155, 161, 255, 269
  consequences of, 144
World War II, 10, 74, 111, 117, 131, 150, 155–6, 159, 206, 266, 273
writing, 6
  conventions of historical, 41
  history of political thought, 26

Zasius, Ulrich, 350–2
Zilliacus, Konni, 268–74, 276, 279

www.ingramcontent.com/pod-product-compliance
Ingram Content Group UK Ltd.
Pitfield, Milton Keynes, MK11 3LW, UK
UKHW020504100325
455776UK00024BA/519